INSTITUTE OF HOME ECONOMICS
HOUSEHOLD ECONOMICS RESEARCH DIVISION

D1338270

SOCIAL CHARACTERISTICS OF URBAN AND RURAL COMMUNITIES, 1950

A VOLUME IN THE CENSUS MONOGRAPH SERIES

SOCIAL CHARACTERISTICS OF URBAN AND RURAL COMMUNITIES, 1950

by

OTIS DUDLEY DUNCAN

University of Chicago

and

ALBERT J. REISS, JR.

Vanderbilt University

for the

SOCIAL SCIENCE RESEARCH COUNCIL
in cooperation with the
U. S. DEPARTMENT OF COMMERCE
BUREAU OF THE CENSUS

JOHN WILEY & SONS, INC., NEW YORK
CHAPMAN & HALL, LIMITED, LONDON

This monograph is dedicated
by its authors

to
WILLIAM FIELDING OGBURN

FOREWORD

The statistical results compiled by the Bureau of the Census constitute a tremendous mass of detailed information about the population of the United States and its characteristics and economic activities. To meet the requirements of government agencies, business concerns, and investigators of social problems and to satisfy the needs of individual citizens, facts must be gathered and published, showing the distribution of the population in each large and small political unit with respect to age, sex, color, marital status, occupation, income, education, national origin, and other characteristics. This information provides the basis for apportionment of representatives in Congress, for answering many questions by direct reference, and for formulating many plans, at least in preliminary form.

It is the first business of the Bureau of the Census to put into print the census results that directly answer as many such questions as possible. Along with these results, similar data from one or two previous censuses are usually included. Limitations of time, space, and money prevent any extensive statement of the relations between particular results, the long-term trends of significant totals and subtotals, the shifting proportions of the people belonging to different categories, various interesting and important relations such as those between income, occupation, and age. It is not that the Bureau of the Census fails in any sense to appreciate the value and need for such analyses, but rather that it must concentrate on its basic concern with the summary statistics that constitute its unique contribution to knowledge.

When plans for the 1950 Census were made, the need for more extensive analysis was recognized and a series of census monographs similar to those issued after the 1920 Census was proposed. Because of the pressures caused by the depression in the early 1930's and by defense and war in the early 1940's, plans for monographs based on those censuses could not be carried out. Late in the 1940's interested persons from business, research, and government agencies expressed the need for a series that would provide analyses of the most significant results of the 1950 Census. The Social Science Research Council, with the assistance of Russell Sage Foundation, took the lead in stimulating the formulation of suitable plans and in June 1950 appointed a Committee on Census Monographs to cooperate with the Bureau in organizing this project. The members of the Committee are:

Ralph G. Hurlin, Russell Sage Foundation (Chairman)
Robert W. Burgess, formerly Western Electric Company, since February
    1953 Director of the Bureau of the Census
John D. Durand, United Nations
Ernest M. Fisher, Columbia University
F. F. Hill, Cornell University
Frederick F. Stephan, Princeton University
Conrad Taeuber, Bureau of the Census
Ralph J. Watkins, Dun & Bradstreet, Inc.
Paul Webbink, Social Science Research Council

J. Frederic Dewhurst, Twentieth Century Fund, and William F. Ogburn, University of Chicago, were members of the Committee during the first year and a half.

It is essential in any sound census monograph program to obtain the co-operation of authors with a broad understanding not only of the statistical information provided by the regular tabulations of the current census but also of the results of earlier censuses and other relevant knowledge and points of view from other sources and even from other countries. The preparation of a monograph should include broad exploration of new questions suggested by the new information, as well as narrowing the elements of doubt and controversy on old questions. The Social Science Research Council Committee early undertook, in consultation with leading figures in various professional fields, to develop a suggested list of monograph titles and authors and persuaded experts in the subject areas selected to undertake the preparation of memoranda outlining and discussing the topics proposed. Then, in 1951, arrangements were made for continuing cooperation between the Committee and the Bureau concerning the selection of topics, proposals of authors and consultants, and editorial supervision.

Throughout the conduct of the project there has been close collaboration with a number of interested Federal agencies and with universities and research organizations, which provided staff and facilities to help bring the project to completion. They and the Council, which also obtained necessary funds from the Rockefeller and Russell Sage Foundations, provided assistance without which the monographs could not have been prepared.

The task of preparing monographs is an essential part of the broad function of making the information secured by censuses fully available to satisfy the needs and interests of the community and to constitute a broad base for further studies in the social sciences. As Director of the Census and President of the Social Science Research Council, respectively, we wish to record our full approval of the monograph project. It is not implied, of course, that the views expressed in these reports are necessarily those of the Bureau of the Census, the Department of Commerce, or the

Social Science Research Council.   The views are those of the individual authors, each of whom has been given the freedom to interpret available materials in the light of his technical knowledge and competence.   This freedom of the individual authors is an essential element in making the most useful analyses and interpretations generally available to the community.

ROBERT W. BURGESS, DIRECTOR
BUREAU OF THE CENSUS

PENDLETON HERRING, PRESIDENT
SOCIAL SCIENCE RESEARCH COUNCIL

March 1955

PREFACE

In this monograph we explore some ways in which census statistics can be used to increase the fund of knowledge about the communities in which the people of the United States live. The approach is a comparative one, i.e., it is based on comparisons of communities of different sizes, types, and locations. The study deals with demographic data—characteristics of human populations. The analysis is in terms of concepts and hypotheses drawn from the discipline of human ecology or social morphology, as formulated, say, in Hawley's *Human Ecology* or Halbwachs' *Morphologie Sociale.*

The student of communities always has cause to be dissatisfied with census materials. The fundamental distinction between urban and rural territory did not become explicit in the procedures of the Bureau of the Census until 1890. The distinction between rural-farm and rural-nonfarm population was not introduced until 1920, and even yet it remains impossible to determine exactly what kinds of settlement patterns are represented by the rural-nonfarm category, and in what proportions. There has never been a complete census count of villages, nor a satisfactory compilation of statistics characterizing the entire village population.

On the other hand, there has been continual, if slow, progress in designing census procedures to reflect accurately the way in which the Nation's population is distributed by communities. In 1910 metropolitan districts were delineated around the larger cities, in recognition of the fact that the limits of the urban community usually did not correspond to the corporate boundaries of the central municipality. There were successive refinements and extensions of the metropolitan district concept in the Censuses of 1920 to 1940. At the same time, special rules were set up to classify as urban certain densely settled areas not included within municipal boundaries, and in 1940 a beginning was made in the delineation of unincorporated places. The 1950 Census introduced a number of procedures designed to improve the community units by which the population data were tabulated. These included the delineation of urbanized areas, standard metropolitan areas, and unincorporated places of 1,000 inhabitants or more.

A large part of this monograph consists of the exploitation of data resulting from the new census procedures. In fact, a major purpose of the monograph is to indicate the ways in which these procedures heighten the usefulness of census data for research on community structure. Needless to say, the monograph does not exhaust the possibilities of using census data to study the structure of communities. For example, we have not analyzed the materials available by census tracts for the larger cities, which are of great value in research on the differentiation of residential areas within the city. The study does consider the internal differentiation of the urban community in terms of comparisons among the central city, suburban, and rural-urban fringe populations. A logical extension of this approach would be to examine differences among "subcommunities" within the city limits. There is, conceptually, little difference between a "subcommunity" and a suburb, since both are differentiated parts of a more or less integrated whole.

The conceptual or theoretical contribution of the monograph is to indicate ways in which current concepts and hypotheses of community structure may be made specific and operational in research. The design of the study is basically a simple one. The dependent variables, which are studied in relation to a set of independent variables, include such population characteristics as age, sex, race-nativity, and family status composition; measures of socio-economic level and economic activities; and the distribution and movement of population in space. The independent variables comprise a selection of fundamental morphological characteristics and indexes: community size, location with respect to dominant centers, type of functional specialization, growth and stability, and regional context. The general hypothesis is that *differentiation among communities in one or another of these basic characteristics is associated with variation in other characteristics.* The underlying theoretical assumption is that population characteristics reflect the selective influences of different types of communities.

The important role assigned to the concept of urbanization is evident at various points in the monograph. The steady progress of urbanization is the cardinal fact about the evolution of community structure in the United States. The difference in level of urbanization is a major factor differentiating one community or region from another. In our view the concepts urban and rural can be defined only in relative terms. This means that the fruitful study of either type of community demands attention to the reciprocal role of the other. Among the most significant community problems are those arising from the increasing interpenetration of urban and rural types of settlement and ways of life, as was signalized by Galpin's proposed concept, the "rurban" community. Hence one should not misconstrue the emphasis on urbanization in the monograph as reflecting a failure to recognize the importance of rural communities in the national economy. Rather it represents an effort to provide a common perspective to the study of these polar types of community in cognizance of the realities of social change. The study does not go so far as to endorse fully some current conceptions concerning the so-called "rural-urban continuum." The issue of uni-dimensionality implicitly raised by this construct cannot be settled finally with the data and research design employed here. However, the evidence available is clear enough in its implication that there is no sharp dividing line between urban and rural communities, either in spatial terms or in terms of community size and functional specialization.

A further word may be said about the concept of "community" itself. This is not a term which has been operationally defined by the Bureau of the Census as has, for example, the term "central city." Probably this is a fortunate circumstance, for the present research and a voluminous body of other evidence show clearly that the delineation of areal limits for a given community cannot follow invariable rules. Rather, different conceptions of the areal scope of the community are appropriate for different research purposes. In general we mean to interpret the concept of community, as it has been formulated in human ecology, to denote the territorially oriented complex of human relationships through which a more or less localized population meets its sustenance and residence requirements. The concern throughout is with comparing classes and categories of communities, rather than with determining boundaries and characteristics of any particular community. A student with the latter type of interest may find the results of the monograph useful as a set of norms for comparison with the unique trait configuration of the community he is studying.

The preparation of this monograph involved a cooperative arrangement between two university research centers. The work reported in Chapters 2 to 13 was carried out at the University of Chicago, and that described in Chapters 14 to 20 at Vanderbilt University. The project is indebted to the Population Research and Training Center of the University of Chicago for providing facilities and services essential to its completion. A similar acknowledgment is due the Behavioral Sciences Division of the Ford Foundation and the Vanderbilt Institute of Research and Training in the Social Sciences for financial assistance supplementing the grant of the Social Science Research Council.

It is a pleasure to record our gratitude to the persons who capably assisted in the research: Beverly Duncan and Richard W. Redick at the University of Chicago, and Joseph R. Haas at Vanderbilt University. Clerical assistance at Vanderbilt University was ably provided by Virginia Grantham, Edith Kemp, Joyce Lovell, and Mary Lou Plunkett.

The initial planning of the monograph was facilitated by a memorandum prepared by Rupert B. Vance. For other constructive suggestions and criticism we wish to thank Donald J. Bogue, Otis Durant Duncan, Paul C. Glick, Wilson H. Grabill, Margaret J. Hagood, Philip M. Hauser, Amos H. Hawley, Evelyn M. Kitagawa, Henry S. Shryock, Jr., and Conrad Taeuber.

OTIS DUDLEY DUNCAN
ALBERT J. REISS, JR.

July 1956

CONTENTS

CHAPTER 1

INTRODUCTION

The urbanite and the countryman may no longer be as ignorant and suspicious of each other's way of life as they have been throughout most of history. But it is still easy to provoke a lively conversation on the relative merits of rural environment *versus* urban amenities. There is disagreement, too, on the comparative virtues of suburbs and metropolitan centers, small towns and large cities, and northern and southern, or eastern and western communities. People assign different values to one or another kind of community life. Some communities are popularly regarded as progressive, exciting, or friendly; others as dull, tradition-bound, or inhospitable. A common observation lies back of dissimilar evaluations. There is a great diversity in the kinds of communities in which men live.

The social scientist approaches the study of communities by accepting the common-sense observation of intercommunity variation. Without differentially evaluating the numerous varieties of community, he seeks to describe them systematically, and to discern the factors which produce variation. Like the taxonomist he develops classifications of the kinds and "species" of communities. Like the anatomist and physiologist he investigates the structural parts of communities and the arrangement and interrelations of these parts. Like the evolutionist he seeks an understanding of the emergence and development of different types of community structure.

This monograph contributes to the systematic study of communities. Its guiding assumption is that there are orderly—though doubtless complex—processes and relationships which produce the readily visible diversity in modes of community life. It focuses on a few factors, suspected to be of basic importance in shaping the character of communities, and relates to them a number of qualities differentiating communities—qualities which are concrete, observable, and at least roughly measurable. These characteristics, in turn, probably condition or determine still other qualities which cannot, as yet, be described with much precision.

The specific procedures of the study reflect this general approach, as well as the possibilities and limitations of the materials available for comparative analyses of a large number of communities. The most voluminous and reliable data for intercommunity comparisons are obtained by the modern census. Research workers have far from exhausted the potentialities of census materials for an improved understanding of community structure and processes. This monograph suggests some of these potentialities, but it requires concerted effort by a large number of specialists to advance our knowledge of communities as rapidly as is now technically possible.

The bulk of this volume consists of detailed analyses of the data relevant to the leading hypotheses. The details are, unfortunately, numerous. But there are summaries of the main results of the study in Chapter 2 and at the end of each chapter in Parts II, III, and IV of the monograph. These results are described in more general terms and placed in a broader perspective in the body of this chapter.

Variables studied

Four factors are studied as "independent variables" or "determinants of differences" among communities. These are (1) size of community, (2) spatial organization of communities, (3) community growth and decline, and (4) functional specialization of communities. A fifth factor, regional location, is regarded as a "control factor" whose effects sometimes need to be taken into account in the analysis. The findings of earlier studies—alluded to at various points in the monograph—suggest that these factors are among the basic morphological features of a community. The reader may test the plausibility of this hypothesis by considering, for example, what differences he would expect to find between a rapidly growing, large industrial suburb of a metropolitan center, and a small, stable college town located at a considerable distance from any metropolis.

The *1950 United States Census of Population* describes communities of different sizes and types in terms of the principal items on population composition. These include age, sex, race, nativity, marital status, mobility, education, income, and employment status of the population; family and household characteristics; and the occupational and industrial composition of the labor force. The analysis of these data in this study proceeds by raising such questions as the following: Do large or small communities have greater proportions of married persons? Is the rate of mobility higher in rapidly growing than in relatively stable cities? Does the proportion of farm workers in the rural population vary as between counties containing a large urban center and those lacking such a center? Are incomes higher or lower in manufacturing communities than in those which do not specialize in manufacturing? In short, the population characteristics are regarded as "dependent variables," and the problem is to find out how the "dependent variables" are related to the four "independent variables."

Community size

Marked differences between large and small communities may be expected. The metropolis generally provides a more extensive market for goods and services. Thus, it can more easily support a number of highly specialized activities, but it also requires a more or less diversified economic base. It tends to attract a greater variety of people than the small community, hence to serve as a forum for more heterogeneous interests. Its relations with a regional, national, or even international hinterland may be extensive. Because the problem of achieving efficient organization intensifies in some direct relationship with the scale of organization, the large community is apt to have structural complexities not found in the small community. These complexities are reflected in the specialization of occupational roles, adaptations of family and institutional life, and selectivity in the recruitment of population. The sheer physical contrast between the urbanized area of 2,500,000 inhabitants and the town of 2,500 is so striking that one would be amazed if there were not also important social contrasts. The aggregate population of a thousand separate towns, therefore, is expected to have characteristics quite different from those of an equally large population residing in a single urban agglomeration.

The data in Part I establish a number of significant relationships between demographic, economic, and socio-economic characteristics, and size of community. These relationships vary in degree and pattern, and are subject to various qualifications, making allowance for the influence of other variables. Nevertheless, one may claim that any investigation of differences among communities which overlooks the factor of community size is apt to neglect an important source of variation.

To work out a theoretically plausible "explanation" of the body of findings on correlates of community size is another matter. Only a limited beginning has been made in developing a theory of community structure with systematic attention to size of community, and such a development is not attempted here. The study suggests that the bulk of the specific research findings can be tentatively systematized in terms of three complexes of factors calculated to produce a pattern of variation in characteristics of communities according to size. These are (1) persistent currents of selective migration, (2) family organization and functions, and (3) economic structure and functions. These factors will be discussed briefly, in turn.

The present differences in race and nativity composition among American communities of different size were produced by historical movements of the several race and nativity groups within and to the United States. It is generally accepted that large cities tend to be more attractive to long-distance migrants than small places. The majority of the immigrants to this country originally entered the large cities, and many remained there. After a third of a century of drastically limited immigration, this tendency remains visible in the size of place differences in percentage foreign born. The Negro population, originally localized in the rural South, has become increasingly urban within the South and is migrating in large proportions to other regions. In these long-distance interregional movements, the destinations are typically the large cities. Thus, the selectivity of destina-

tion in long-distance migration is a factor of general significance in accounting for the relative ethnic diversity of large communities.   However, since
that factor alone fails to explain the findings completely, one must also consider the more specific historical movements of population in the United
States, such as those resulting in a concentration of American Indians in
the rural West.

The role of migration in producing rural-urban differences in the sex
ratio is fairly well understood.   In general, cities attract disproportionate
numbers of females, though this is not true of all types of cities.   How
selective migration affects community-size differences in age composition is
not equally clear, however.   The observed age distributions suggest a complex pattern of selective interchange of populations among different sized
places.   There seems to be a disproportionate drift of persons in the
younger productive ages toward large places and a counterdrift of older
males.   This formula is undoubtedly oversimplified, but more detailed
data on the streams of migration among places of different sizes are essential to clarify the matter.

Various indexes reflect the second complex, family organization and
functions.   Generally speaking, the larger the community the smaller is the
proportion married, and the larger are the indicators of family disruption.
In large places, the labor force participation of women is high, comparatively, and effective fertility low.   Several indicators of "normal," or generally preferred, family living arrangements vary inversely with community
size.   While homes are generally better equipped in large than in small
places, they carry a higher price, are more frequently in multiple-unit
structures, and are less frequently owned by the occupants.[1]   Numerous
writers have discerned an inverse correlation between urbanization and
familism of the traditional kind.   The explanation of this correlation involves sociological considerations about the evolution of family value systems.   Community size, the ecological factor in the situation, is associated
with conditions affecting the strength of familistic values.   As the size of
the community increases, more and more specialized agencies offer competition to the family in the performance of its traditional functions.   Urbanization reduces the economic return from children and increases the
cost of child rearing.   Housing facilities and living arrangements in large
communities are less suitable for large families.   Assuming that the foregoing factors are directly associated with community size, familism should
decrease with increasing size of community.   There is also some theoretical basis for expecting community-size variation in age distribution, insofar
as fertility is a function of familism.   Fertility is no doubt a more important factor than mortality in explaining such variation.

---

[1] Statements in this chapter concerning housing conditions in communities of different sizes are
based on data given in Otis Dudley Duncan, "Optimum Size of Cities," in *A Reader in Urban Sociology*, ed. by Paul K. Hatt and Albert J. Reiss, Jr., The Free Press, Glencoe, Ill., 1951.

The third major category of factors differentiating communities according to size is economic structure and functions. The study finds a direct correlation between community size and the proportion of the labor force engaged in white-collar occupations. This implies a tendency for urbanization to be accompanied by ever larger proportions of workers in tertiary pursuits, i.e., in service, administrative, and distributive activities, as opposed to extractive industries and physical production of goods. The extreme manifestations of this tendency are the pronounced, direct relationship between community size and the proportion of clerical workers, and the marked inverse correlation between size of community and the proportion engaged in farm occupations. One may surmise that the high proportion of clerical workers in large urban centers represents a tendency toward large scale organization of human activities, requiring a complement of technicians in record keeping and coordination. Perhaps the proportion of clerical workers is the best single occupational indicator of the complexity of the division of labor.

The marked, direct association between community size and income is not wholly a reflection of variations in the composition of the labor force by broad occupation groups. This suggests that generally comparable occupational activities are differentially rewarded in monetary terms in communities of different size. Whether a difference in real income exists is debatable, in view of a suspicion that the cost of living is also a direct function of community size. There are no cost-of-living data, however, that are directly comparable with the present size of place data on income. The median rent of dwelling units increases with increasing city size. Probably, in the larger places, services more often are purchased than exchanged in kind. Regardless of real income differences, the present data indicate a positive correlation between community size and socio-economic status, as measured by the average prestige level of occupations and by the formal educational attainment of the population. This cross-sectional relationship involving urbanization is consistent with the observation that the growth of cities has been accompanied by rising socio-economic levels and improving educational opportunities.

Spatial organization of communities

In a well-developed economy communities are highly interdependent. And while rural areas are no more dependent on urban areas than vice versa, there is much evidence that the units which mediate and control these dependency relationships tend to be localized in the large urban centers. The accumulation of this evidence has bolstered the hypothesis that an advancing industrial economy becomes a "metropolitan economy." In other words, one important level of organization of the economy is the system of metropolitan regions, territorially coextensive with the economy as a whole. A description of the economy in such terms means that one must recognize a set of nuclear "centers of dominance" and their tributary or hinterland areas as comprising the spatial plan of the economy. It is hypothesized that, within each metropolitan region, spatial relationships fall into a gradient pattern, with the organizing influence of the metropolitan center being most evident in its immediate vicinity and declining more or less regularly with increasing distance from the center.

The analyses in Part II deal with four aspects of the relationship between the metropolitan center and the outlying area. Chapter 11 investigates differences between central cities and the adjacent built-up area—the suburbs and urban fringe. Chapter 12 extends the comparisons, for one metropolitan area, to include not only the immediate built-up suburbs, but also the rural-urban fringe of the metropolitan center, i.e., that area in which the countryside is in process of transition from a rural to an urban mode of settlement. Chapter 13 contrasts that part of the rural population which is within the satellite zone of metropolitan centers (within standard metropolitan areas) and the rural population situated at greater distances from metropolitan centers. A similar analysis, in Chapter 14, concerns the differences between urban places, other than central cities, located within standard metropolitan areas and those enjoying a relatively "independent" status.

Two broad conclusions may be drawn from these analyses. First, the suburban population of the metropolitan area tends to differ systematically both from the central city population and from the population living in the nonmetropolitan cities. It is significant that not all differences between central cities and suburbs are explained by their difference in size, because many of them are in the opposite direction from that expected on a size basis. The size factor can also be ruled out as an explanation of differences between suburbs and independent cities.

Whether the comparison is with their own central cities or with independent cities, suburbs are distinctive in a series of interrelated traits. The suburban population is relatively homogeneous, ethnically; that is, a high proportion is native white. It enjoys a relatively high socio-economic status, as indicated by occupational composition, average educational attainment, or income. The suburban population shows evidences of a stronger familistic bent than the other urban population, in its comparatively high proportions married and levels of fertility, and its low rate of female labor force participation.

These findings on the differences between suburban and other urban populations are not inconsistent with the popular, perhaps romantic, stereotype of the suburb as an ideal place of residence, combining the best features of city and country, or metropolitan and small town life. But to maintain perspective it should be emphasized that the differences are not absolute. They are instead only a matter of degree—sometimes of rather small degree—and indicate only a general selective tendency, not a uniform pattern or difference in kind. There are many individual suburbs with few of the traits reflected in the aggregate figures, and there is a great deal of differentiation among suburbs. A number of writers have suggested, however, that suburbs tend to polarize into two major types, "dormitory" communities whose residents work elsewhere in the metropolitan area, and employing or industrial suburbs which have a sizable economic base.[2] The findings on the differences between suburban and other urban populations clearly suggest that the dormitory type is the modal one among the suburbs.

Another emphasis is needed in interpreting the distinctive characteristics of suburbs. The suburb is actually only one specialized part of a rather highly integrated whole—the metropolitan community. The only workable criterion yet discovered for identifying suburbs is their political separation from the central municipality. In fact, suburbs resemble those subareas of the central city which are located toward its periphery, although within its corporate limits. The suburb can specialize, say, in middle class residences, only because it is so closely dependent on the remainder of the community. Often a suburb developed as a desirable residential area is not the site of those activities by which its residents earn their livelihood. The suburb cannot be viewed, therefore, as an independent line of community evolution. The suburb is in almost all ways a political artifact, since the act of political incorporation often transfers it to the central political city. Many subareas of present day central cities were suburbs at one time. The process of annexing suburban areas to a central city is not a regular one, but nonetheless it occurs for almost every large city at some point in its history. Baton Rouge, La., Albuquerque, N. Mex., and Dallas, Texas, are examples of places which gained greatly in size during the 1940–50 decade by incorporation of suburban communities. Theoretically, then, the suburb is one of a relatively large number of subareas or communities of a metropolitan community, and its specific attributes are determined primarily by its relation to the center of dominance and other subareas.

The second broad conclusion from the analyses of spatial organization is that a large component of the population can no longer be characterized as strictly urban or rural, but has mixed characteristics in regard to residential patterns and social characteristics. No precise estimate of this "rural-urban fringe" population is available, but, in all likelihood, it numbered at least 10 to 15 million in 1950, i.e., perhaps as much as one-tenth of the total population. The fringe population is thought to be a rapidly growing one, though, of course, when fringe developments are consolidated and fringe areas are incorporated as cities, they tend to move into a more strictly "suburban" status.

---

[2] See, for example, Chauncy D. Harris, "Suburbs," *American Journal of Sociology,* 49 July 1943, pp. 1–13; and Grace M. Kneedler, "Economic Classification of Cities," *The Municipal Yearbook,* 1950, pp. 29–37 and 44–48.

The distinctive character of the fringe is apparent, whether viewed from the urban or the rural side. Fringe residents nominally classified as urban resemble central city residents in some respects and suburban residents in others, but there is relatively little difference between them and the fringe population classified as rural nonfarm under present Bureau of the Census definitions. On the other hand, both the rural-nonfarm and rural-farm fringe populations differ sharply from the nonfringe rural population. The interpenetration of urban and rural, most obvious in the case of the fringe somewhat narrowly defined, has also proceeded even at considerable distances from large urban centers. Only a little over a half of the employed males residing on farms within the entire satellite zone of the large metropolitan centers (within standard metropolitan areas) are actually employed in farm occupations, as compared with three-fourths of the rural-farm males in the country as a whole.

Although the fringe is described as an area of "mixed" rural and urban characteristics, the mixture is not entirely homogeneous. In other words, there is not always a smooth progression from urban to rural via the fringe. For example, the data for the Chicago metropolitan area show that the percentage of the population 65 years old and over declines as one proceeds from the central city through the suburbs to the urban and rural-nonfarm fringe, and then rises sharply for the remaining rural population in the satellite zone. These and other data in the monograph seriously call in question the current assumptions about a "rural-urban continuum."

The reader should be warned that in making detailed analyses of spatial organization it was necessary to define certain concepts in ways not wholly consistent with official Bureau of the Census usage, and even to vary the technical meaning of these concepts somewhat from chapter to chapter. These methodological difficulties merely reflect the complexities of the subject, and the fact that statistical categories must be developed at some lag behind the realities they seek to capture.

Community growth and decline

Community residents usually take it for granted that population growth exercises a beneficent influence on their welfare. Hence they often initiate action calculated to increase the growth rate of their community. Actually, scientific knowledge about community growth is insufficient either to indicate conclusively whether the optimistic attitude toward growth is justified, or to evaluate the efficacy of measures taken to increase growth.

At least three analytical problems about community growth may be distinguished. The first is to discover the conditions favoring growth.[3] The

---

[3] Important methodological work on this problem is reported in Donald J. Bogue and Dorothy L. Harris, *Comparative Population and Urban Analysis Via Multiple Regression and Covariance Analysis*, Scripps Foundation, Miami University, Oxford, Ohio, 1954.

second is to describe the growth process, i.e., the manner in which growth comes about. The third is to identify the consequences of growth or decline for community structure and processes. Only a very elaborate research design could adequately encompass all these problems. The simple design employed to study community growth in this monograph is most suggestive with respect to the third problem, but it enables some light to be shed on the other two.

Two groups of cities and standard metropolitan areas were studied: those manifesting high rates of growth over at least the last two decades, and those with very low growth rates or actual declines during the same period. The intermediate group of moderately growing communities was disregarded in the analysis, for sake of economy and greater contrast. Comparisons of the characteristics of rapidly growing and stable or declining communities were made as of a single point in time, 1950. This means that conclusions about the preconditions and processes of growth can have only inferential value, though some inferences seem to be strongly supported. Care was taken to arrange the comparisons in such a way that the present size and metropolitan status of the communities did not confound the results.

Attention will be directed first to the conclusions about conditions apparently favorable or unfavorable to growth. Despite the historical connection between urbanization and industrialization, the evidence is that the centers now experiencing rapid growth lack large concentrations of manufacturing activity. There is much less manufacturing in the communities of rapid growth than in those of relative stability or decline, whether measured by the proportion of the labor force engaged in manufacturing, or by the per capita value added by manufacture. This finding does not rule out the possibility that population growth accompanies expansion of manufacturing activity. It does indicate, however, that if manufacturing expansion is an important factor in growth, it is primarily in those communities not yet established as major manufacturing centers.

Government employment, on the other hand, may well have been an important factor in recent community growth. In the class-of-worker classification, the most rapidly expanding category in the Nation as a whole between 1940 and 1950 was government workers. Similarly, the most rapidly growing of the major industry groups was public administration. The comparisons between rapidly growing and stable or declining communities show clearly that the former have the higher proportions of government workers and of persons employed in public administration.

A high proportion of white-collar employment may also be a factor favoring community growth, since the white-collar occupations have been increasing more rapidly than the manual occupations. A community prepared to expand its white-collar employment probably has a better chance to grow than one whose economic base does not require much white-collar work.

At any rate, the rapidly growing communities presently have a larger proportion of white-collar workers than do the stable or declining communities.

It is usually supposed that population growth results from economic expansion, whatever the expanding industries or occupations may be. Consequently one expects a general indicator of employment opportunity to register higher in a growing community than in a stable one. There is some evidence, though inconclusive, that the percentage of males in the labor force is higher in rapidly growing communities than in those with little growth. The findings for females are mixed, partly, it is suspected, because the data for suburbs do not reflect local employment opportunities for women so much as they do certain selective factors operating against female labor force participation in residential suburbs. In any case, one can state that after at least two decades of rapid growth, the picture of employment opportunities in growing communities is at least as favorable, if not more so, as in stable or declining communities, where out-migration may have siphoned off an excess labor supply.

Considering next the question of the nature of the growth process, it should be noted that if territorial annexation is ruled out, a community can grow only by a net in-migration of population, an excess of births over deaths, or both. In a decade of high birth rates, it is likely that all urban and metropolitan communities would experience a positive natural increase. Hence this factor must be reckoned as more or less a constant. Probably the greater part of the variation in growth rates among communities is attributable to the direction and magnitude of migratory movements. The data studied favor this hypothesis, though they do not prove it. In all of the comparisons of rapidly growing with stable or declining communities, the former do have somewhat higher fertility ratios, but the magnitude of the difference is usually less than 25 percent of the fertility ratio of the nongrowing communities. By contrast, the rapidly growing communities experienced rates of in-migration from 1949 to 1950 running about double those of the stable or declining urban places and standard metropolitan areas. Perhaps the greater fertility of the high growth rate communities is explained in part by fertility differentials between migrants and nonmigrants. However this may be, it is evident that an explanation of community growth must be stated primarily in terms of factors related to migration.

The search for a general rubric under which to summarize the inferred effects of community growth tempts one to use the metaphorical term, "buoyancy." Casual observers have often noted a spirit of optimism and enterprise pervading the growing community. Certainly there are some characteristics of growing communities which suggest that such descriptions may be appropriate. The rapidly growing communities are more youthful than the nongrowing ones, partly because of their higher fertility, of course, but probably also because of an age selection in migration. The residents of rapidly growing places seem to be somewhat more "footloose and fancy free," to judge by the facts that a smaller proportion live in families, and that they apparently demand more entertainment and recreation services. On the other hand, larger numbers of their householders have assumed the responsibility of home ownership, though this may reflect merely a shortage of rental units.

The rapidly growing communities have a comparatively high socioeconomic status, as measured by occupational level and educational attainment. Their average income might show up higher as well, if allowances were made for differences in regional location and in the proportion of unrelated individuals (which affects median income figures based on families and unrelated individuals). The data suggest, too, that rapid growth encourages commercial ventures. The proportion of the labor force employed in both wholesale and retail trade is higher in rapidly growing places than in those growing only slightly or declining. Yet the per capita sales of the wholesale and retail establishments are no higher in the communities with high growth rates. This finding, if reliable, may mean that there is keener competition in the growing community among the suppliers of the effective consumer demand. Another possibility should be mentioned, though. It may be that the centers of rapid growth have not yet built up as much trade in their hinterlands as have the more stable centers. Whatever the reason, the more rapidly growing communities have a substantially higher proportion employed in the occupation group which includes the entrepreneurial class, i.e., managers, officials, and proprietors.

On the whole, therefore, communities with high growth rates present a relatively favorable picture in terms of economic indicators and characteristics closely related to them. The census data, unfortunately, do not permit one to assess the possible social costs and dislocations associated with rapid growth. Some measure of judicious interpretation, therefore, is in order in evaluating the research findings.

Functional specialization

Few communities are self-sufficient in the American economy. The extractive industries characteristic of rural areas generally are run on a commercial basis, since their labor force sustains itself primarily by exchanging its production for the goods and services of town and city dwellers. Correlatively, the size and density of settlement of cities prohibits the population from producing its own food and raw materials, and it therefore subsists in a symbiotic relationship with a hinterland or tributary rural area. The complexity of American society furthermore renders it uneconomic for any single place, no matter how large, to maintain itself by employment in all nonextractive industries. Every urban community thus becomes dependent upon some other urban communities for a part of the goods and services consumed locally. The relationships which each community develops with the others require, therefore, that it import and export goods and services.

Urban communities then perform a variety of functions both for their own populations and for those populations with which exchange relationships are established. The "residentiary employments" or "maintenance activities" performed for their own populations are more or less common to cities similar in size and in orientation to larger cities. The "economic base" or export function of a city is highly variable, however. Some places specialize in physical production to the virtual exclusion of all other basic employment. Other places have little or no manufacturing employment. Many cities have little wholesale trade, but some are wholesale centers for a network of smaller trade centers scattered over a wide service area. While all cities, save, perhaps, exclusively residential suburbs, have a variety of retail outlets to meet local needs, some have highly developed retail facilities to serve a sizable extralocal clientele.

Manufacturing and trade are the typical industries which bring income into a city for the sustenance of its population. Several other types of economic activity, nevertheless, figure significantly in the export function of some cities. College and university communities export educational services by attracting students from other communities, and they gain an appreciable part of their support from the expenditures of this "transient population," if the community is fairly small. Centers with highly developed entertainment and recreation facilities sustain themselves in part from the expenditures of vacationers, health seekers, retired persons, military personnel, and the like, sometimes to such a degree that they become known by the type of activity, such as "resort centers," "gambling towns," and the like. Sites of large State and Federal Government institutions are apt to profit considerably from the higher than average employment in public administration. In an era of extensive military mobilization, the primary functions of some places will include that of providing services to large military installations in their locality or hinterland. Some cities develop as transportation centers, particularly when they are located at strategic points on a transportation network, or when they are convenient collection points for raw materials or semiprocessed goods. Still other less important and relatively infrequent types of specialization could be mentioned. Religious shrines, mining towns, medical centers, financial centers, fishing communities, and "cultural centers" are some examples.

In theory, any goods or services which attract a nonlocal clientele may become the basis of an export function of a place and thus of "specialization." In practice, such special functions may be found in conjunction with one another. Most communities are not highly specialized, in the sense of having their export activity largely limited to one or two forms of economic activity. The export activity of the majority of cities will include the typical ones of manufacturing and trade together with some export in several of the services, e.g., professional and related services, business and repair services, public administration, and transportation. They are therefore more or less "diversified." Specialization, then, is a matter of degree, as well as of the type of function or functions. The economic activity of a community is made up of exporting and importing various kinds and amounts of goods and services. Consequently, any system of classifying communities by type of specialization reduces to a rationale for the criteria and categories of classification. The criteria for identifying export functions in this study are based on more or less arbitrary decisions about the variation in type and degree of economic activity.

Along with the variation in type of function, communities are subject to variation in the net returns from the performance of the specialized functions. At any rate, this appears to be part of the explanation for the considerable range in the average income level of communities of comparable size and metropolitan status. No doubt a number of factors are involved, such as natural and locational advantages or disadvantages, competition from centers performing similar economic functions, variation in the quality and quantity of labor, and the degree of organization in an industry. Whatever the explanation, the qualitative classification of urban economic functions should be supplemented with measurements of the over-all level of living achieved through the performance of such functions. Income data provide a starting point of these measurements.

This study makes two principal contributions to the analysis of functional differentiation of communities—limiting the problem to sizable urban places and metropolitan areas: (1) it proposes a set of techniques for functional classification, and applies them to the communities of the United States; (2) it investigates whether there are social and economic characteristics typically associated with one or another type of functional specialization. Disregarding the technical problems involved, the major functional classes used in the study will be indicated briefly.

The system of functional classification distinguishes between "manufacturing" and "nonmanufacturing" communities. The former are those for which there is evidence that manufacturing comprises a large part of the economic base, and the latter are those having well below average proportions employed in manufacturing. The residual, intermediate group of communities is disregarded in the analysis of socio-economic correlates of manufacturing specialization.

Recognizing that there is an intimate relationship between expenditures in retail and wholesale trade, and that the volume of trade reflects not only local and extralocal demand but also the purchasing power of the inhabitants, the classification of communities according to trade functions allows for a variety of possibilities. A given volume of trade is more apt to represent extralocal demand if the average local income is low than if it is high. Wholesale and retail specialization may occur jointly, or either may occur without the other in a political community. Many communities have about an average volume of trade, with retail and wholesale in approximate balance. Finally, some communities have so low a volume of trade that it can only be assumed that their trade function is very slightly developed. Recognition of all these possibilities leads to a ninefold classification, collapsed to five categories in analyzing the characteristics of places specializing in trade: wholesale trade centers, retail trade centers, trade centers, maintenance trade centers, and nontrade centers.

Five "minor types" of specialization are recognized. Each is indicative of a relatively high development of that particular function in a community. These types include centers of higher education ("college communities"), public administration centers, entertainment and recreation centers, transportation centers, and military centers. Income differences among communities are studied simply by classifying as "high" and "low" those communities in the extreme quintiles of the distribution of communities by median income of families and unrelated persons.

A novel feature of the classification system is that it permits a given community to have more than one type of specialization. It thus recognizes that many communities do not depend on only one outstanding specialty. Methodologically, this property of the classification permits investigation of the interrelationships among types of specialization—a problem that cannot be studied if each community is forced into one and only one functional category.

In studying the demographic, economic, and socio-economic correlates of functional specialization, the analysis was designed to hold constant the effects of community size and metropolitan status. Comparisons are made separately for metropolitan areas, central cities, suburbs, and independent cities, and by size levels within each of these groups. Scanning the many specific findings and ignoring qualifications of detail, one can discern certain general principles which seemingly underly the differences in demographic, economic, and socio-economic characteristics among communities of different functional types. It is, of course, difficult in many cases to specify the causal nexus involved in the observed relationships.

The several functions recognized are partly complementary to each other, and partly substitutes for each other. As instances of complementarity one may note that wholesale and transportation specialization frequently occur together, as do specialization in public administration and in servicing military establishments, and specialization in retail trade and entertainment and recreation. There is a positive correlation between wholesale and retail trade, such that about one-fourth of all places are trade centers specialized in both wholesale and retail trade. The relation between manufacturing and almost any other function tends to be substitutive. This is tantamount to saying that if a community has a large manufacturing base, it does not develop some other specialty. It is even the case that activities which are undoubtedly closely related, manufacturing and transportation, for example, are not usually joint bases of functional specialization. The foregoing must be qualified, nevertheless, by noting that manufacturing specialization is not absolutely incompatible with other types of specialization. Among manufacturing centers are found examples of each of the other categories of centers identified in the study, but only trade specialization occurs with manufacturing to any noticeable degree.

Functional specialization must be acknowledged as an important basis of demographic selection. Entertainment and recreation centers have disproportionate numbers of older persons, no doubt in part because they attract retired persons and those seeking health benefits. Manufacturing communities have a less mobile population than nonmanufacturing communities, and mobility is especially high in military, public administration, and entertainment and recreation centers. The proportion of married men in college communities is lower than in noncollege communities. The average household appears to be smaller in these places, and in places specialized in entertainment and recreation or in retail trade, than in all places, while it is somewhat larger than average in manufacturing places.

The level of economic activity of the population is influenced by the type of specialization. Manufacturing and wholesale specialization are favorable to high male labor force participation, and retail specialization to high female participation, while specialization in higher education depresses male labor force participation. Moreover, the level of living varies by type of specialization. High incomes are somewhat more characteristic of manufacturing than of nonmanufacturing communities. Yet, when the honorific or prestige values of economic roles are considered, manufacturing communities do not rank high. They are comparatively low in the proportion of white-collar workers, whereas retail and educational specialization seemingly heighten the proportion in the more esteemed occupation categories. They also rank comparatively low in the median level of educational attainment, whereas college communities, retail trade centers, and entertainment and recreation centers rank comparatively high.

Whatever its source—the type of specialization, or other conditions of community life—income variation produces significant differences in social and economic behavior. High income communities have a comparatively high per capita retail trade volume, high rates of labor force participation, and enjoy high levels of home ownership and educational attainment.

In sum, virtually every aspect of a community's structure is related to its basic functions. Reliable differences among the various types of communities are observed with respect to age and sex structure, mobility rates, labor force participation, industrial and occupational composition, educational attainment, income, and home ownership. This is not to state that each particular type of community has a distinctive pattern with respect to each of these characteristics, but rather, for each characteristic examined, at least one type of specialization was found to produce a considerable deviation from the average.   The results warrant the conclusion that type of functional specialization, in addition to the factors of community size, spatial orientation, and population growth, must be included among the principal determinants of morphological differences among communities. Put another way, understanding why a given community is unlike another one requires a knowledge of how the two compare on indicators of the type and degree of functional specialization.[4]

---

[4] To aid persons interested in particular communities to take account of the factor of specialization, appendix tables B–17 to B–20 indicate for each standard metropolitan area and urban place of 10,000 inhabitants or more in the United States the functional classification(s) assigned it in this study.

PART I

SIZE OF COMMUNITY

CHAPTER 2

COMMUNITY SIZE AND URBANIZATION

> It is a matter of common knowledge that as the size of the social aggregate increases the behavior of its members changes. . . . But we have little precise knowledge of the relation between size of population and organization. Apparently the relation has been so taken for granted that it has not been thought worthy of careful investigation. Yet size of population is doubtlessly one of the most important limiting factors in man's collective life. Amos H. Hawley, *Human Ecology* (Ronald Press, New York, copyright 1950), p. 122.

The comparative study of communities of different sizes is one approach to the study of urbanization. Urbanization has two aspects—the longitudinal and the cross-sectional. Longitudinally, it is a process involving an increase over time in the number and size of centers of population concentration.[1] The unitary nature of this process, at least for the United States since 1790, is demonstrated by Stewart's remarkable set of equations (which he calls the "fundamental structure of the United States population") interrelating the size of the total population, the number of cities, the size distribution of cities, and the proportion of the population living in cities.[2] Cross-sectionally, the concept of urbanization refers to variations at one point in time among areas in the degree of population concentration,[3] or to variations by size of community in the frequency of population characteristics or organizational traits.[4]

Cross-sectional and longitudinal studies of urbanization should not be regarded as antithetical, but as complementary approaches. A knowledge of the correlates of urbanization gained through cross-sectional analysis has presumptive value for understanding social changes in an economy undergoing urbanization. Thus, Thompson and Whelpton, having established a cross-sectional inverse relationship between urbanization and the birth rate, were able to demonstrate that changes in urban-rural distribution of the

---

[1] Hope Tisdale, "The Process of Urbanization," *Social Forces 20*, March 1942, pp. 311–316.

[2] John Q. Stewart, "Empirical Mathematical Rules Concerning the Distribution and Equilibrium of Population," *Geographical Review 37*, July 1947, pp. 461–485.

[3] See the "index of urbanism" used in Stuart A. Queen and David B. Carpenter, *The American City*, McGraw-Hill, New York, 1953; Otis Dudley Duncan, "Regional Comparisons Standardized for Urbanization," *Social Forces 26*, May 1948, pp. 430–433; and the comparison of regions in regard to urbanization, pp. 29–31.

[4] Otis Dudley Duncan, "Urbanization and Retail Specialization," *Social Forces 30*, March 1952, pp. 267–271; *see also* the comparison of race-nativity groups with respect to urbanization in Chapter 4.

population between 1920 and 1929 played a small but significant role in the decline of the birth rate over that period.[5]   The caution is required, however, that not all cross-sectional relationships afford a direct and immediate basis for projecting changes on the basis of expected increases in urbanization.

For the most part, cross-sectional studies of urbanization have been limited to gross comparisons between urban and rural communities, with the latter often being divided into nonfarm and farm components following the introduction of this distinction by the Bureau of the Census in 1920. A number of limitations on this procedure have become apparent.   The urban-rural classification lumps together in a single category the town of 5,000 inhabitants and the metropolis of 500,000.   But differences among urban centers of different sizes are frequently as significant as the difference between the rural and the urban population as a whole.   Further, in the threefold classification, villages—i.e., centers of less than 2,500 inhabitants—are not distinguished from other parts of the rural-nonfarm category. The rural-nonfarm population was at first assumed by some students to be substantially equivalent to the village population, but it is evident that this is no longer the case.   In fact, the rural-nonfarm population is now something of a hodgepodge of village, rural-urban fringe, and open country residents.   This remains true even under the 1950 Census procedures, which eliminated the densely settled urban fringe of metropolitan centers from the rural-nonfarm category, because the fringes of smaller urban centers and the "ribbon developments" along interurban highways are still classified as rural nonfarm for the most part.

Whether or not it is legitimate to posit the existence of a unidimensional "rural-urban continuum," as some writers suggest, it is clearly desirable to carry out cross-sectional research on urbanization with a fuller classification of community-size levels than the old trichotomy, urban, rural nonfarm, and rural farm.   The present study is one of a few which utilize a scale of size categories for urban communities.   It appears to be the first comprehensive study carrying the size classification below the urban level to include villages, as distinct from the other rural population.

Previous research

There have been only a few systematic studies of differentials in the composition and organization of communities according to size.   The most important of these is Ogburn's *Social Characteristics of Cities.*[6]   His monograph describes city-size differences in a large number of demographic, social, economic, and organizational characteristics.   The data were com-

[5] Warren S. Thompson and P. K. Whelpton, *Population Trends in the United States*, McGraw-Hill, New York, 1933, Chapter 8.

[6] William F. Ogburn, *Social Characteristics of Cities*, International City Managers' Association, Chicago, 1937.

piled by consolidating into size classes published statistics for a sample of cities. Many differences in organizational characteristics of different-sized cities are described in an unpublished study by Keyes.[7] Some research has also been devoted to the question of whether the social and economic differences between large and small cities shed any light on the planning concept of optimum city size.[8] For the most part general studies of population composition and trends have given inadequate attention to the community-size factor, a noteworthy exception being the *Recent Social Trends* monograph by Thompson and Whelpton.[9] Specialized inquiries of one kind or another have taken size of community as a major analytical variable.[10]

One reason for the scarcity of demographic studies comparing different-sized communities is that it is expensive to consolidate data for several thousand individual places into size-of-place categories. Then too, the data reported in the census for different sizes of place vary in scope and in detail according to size of place. Very little information is available in 1940 and earlier censuses for villages, and fewer characteristics have been tabulated for places under 100,000 or 50,000 inhabitants than for the larger places. Only a few official census tabulations by size of place have been published. The 1910 Census report included a number of tables showing population characteristics by city size. The last several censuses have regularly included a compilation of the number of places by size classes and their aggregate populations, and this series has been carried back to 1790. A city-size breakdown was given in the 1939 and 1948 Censuses of Business.[11] A rather comprehensive set of statistics by city size was prepared from the 1940 Census of Housing,[12] but the data on characteristics of population by size of place given in the 1940 Census reports were limited to a few characteristics, and the size-of-place classification varied from one subject to another.[13] A summary table of selected characteris-

---

[7] Fenton Keyes, "The Correlation of Social Phenomena with Community Size," unpublished Ph.D. dissertation, Yale University, 1942.

[8] Otis Dudley Duncan, "Optimum Size of Cities," in *Reader in Urban Sociology*, ed. by Paul K. Hatt and Albert J. Reiss, Jr., Free Press, Glencoe, Ill., 1951; and "An Examination of the Problem of Optimum City-Size," unpublished Ph.D. dissertation, University of Chicago, 1949.

[9] Thompson and Whelpton, *Population Trends in the United States, op. cit.*

[10] For example, Donald J. Bogue, *The Structure of the Metropolitan Community*, University of Michigan, Ann Arbor, 1949; Amos H. Hawley, "An Ecological Study of Urban Service Institutions," *American Sociological Review 6*, October 1941, pp. 629–639; Paul Marshall Rea, *The Museum and the Community*, The Science Press, Lancaster, 1932; Dwight Sanderson, *Relation of Size of Community to Marital Status*, Cornell University, Agricultural Experiment Station, Memoir 200, February, 1937.

[11] For one analysis of these data, see Duncan, "Urbanization and Retail Specialization," *op. cit.*

[12] U. S. Bureau of the Census, *Housing—Special Reports*, Series H–44, Nos. 1–7, 1944–45.

[13] See the special reports of the 1940 Census on *Employment and Family Characteristics of Women, Educational Attainment of Children by Rental Value of Home, Educational Attainment by Economic Characteristics and Marital Status, Women by Number of Children Under 5 Years Old*, and *Women by Number of Children Ever Born;* also "Age, Color, and Sex Composition of the Population in Urban Places Classified by Size and in Rural Areas, for the United States, By Regions: 1940," *Population*, Series P–10, No. 21, March 5, 1943.

tics of cities by city-size groups was given in the 1944 *Cities Supplement— Statistical Abstract of the United States.*

Study design

This study is based primarily on the statistics in the special report of the 1950 Census of Population entitled "Characteristics by Size of Place." The published data were supplemented with unpublished statistics giving regional breakdowns for all characteristics tabulated by size of place. The reader should be acquainted with the following features of these data.

The statistics on characteristics by size of place are based on a 3⅓-percent sample of the returns of the Seventeenth Decennial Census of Population. They are, therefore, subject to sampling variability, and are not expected to agree precisely with statistics derived from the complete count or from the 20-percent sample. In addition, minor tabulation errors in some instances cause the data to differ slightly from other data compiled for the 3⅓-percent sample. In the case of a few errors of major importance in the published figures, corrections were made by reference to photocopies of the original machine tabulation sheets of the regional tabulation.[14] The "Characteristics by Size of Place" report presents a statement on the expected sampling variability of the data. For the most part, however, the present study draws conclusions as to tendencies and relationships without employing exact probability tests. Even with the error tables given, such tests would be quite arduous to undertake for all the analyses of this study. It is believed that through careful inspection for consistency of relationship most errors of "overinterpretation" are avoided.

The present classification by size of place is one which has not appeared before in the Bureau of the Census reports. Three important innovations are involved, all of which appear to represent improvements over previous census classifications of communities by size. In the first place, the classification makes use of the new concept of "urbanized area."

> Each urbanized area contains at least one city with 50,000 inhabitants or more in 1940 or according to a special census taken since 1940. Each urbanized area also includes the surrounding closely settled incorporated places and unincorporated areas that comprise its urban fringe. The boundaries of these fringe areas were established to conform as nearly as possible to the actual boundaries of thickly settled territory, usually characterized by a closely spaced street pattern.[15]

Second, by regarding each urbanized area as a single "place," the classification groups together as one unit, the large central city (or cities) and

---

[14] Since this study was completed the Bureau of the Census has made available an errata sheet for the "Characteristics by Size of Place" report. The most important errors involve the female population of urbanized areas of 1 to 3 million inhabitants in the Northeast and North Central Regions, shown in tables 6 and 7 of the report.

[15] *1950 Census of Population,* Vol. IV, *Special Reports,* Part 5, Chapter A, "Characteristics by Size of Place," p. 6.

its suburban and urban fringe areas, rather than treating separately identifiable suburban municipalities as distinct from and coordinate with their central cities.   Thus, it follows that all the urban places under 50,000 inhabitants in this classification are actually independent cities, i.e., places outside the immediate sphere of influence of metropolitan centers.   Third, the size-of-place classification is carried below the urban level to include villages 1,000 to 2,500 and under 1,000 in population size.   In the former category are included both incorporated and unincorporated places, since the Bureau of the Census in advance of the 1950 enumeration delineated boundaries for the larger unincorporated places. The category of smaller villages, however, includes only the incorporated places.

The complete size-of-place classification is a complex one.   There are four size groups of urbanized areas, i.e., places of 3 million or more, 1 million to 3 million, 250,000 to 1 million, and below 250,000.   Each of these groups is subdivided into the population living in the central cities and the population living in what is called, in the 1950 Census reports, the "urban fringe."   Urban places outside urbanized areas are classified into three size groups, 25,000 and over, 10,000 to 25,000, and 2,500 to 10,000.   Actually, there is a slight overlap of sizes between the smallest urbanized areas and the largest urban places outside urbanized areas. There are 21 places above 50,000 inhabitants which were not designated as urbanized areas, since they did not attain that size until 1950, whereas the cities for which urbanized areas were delineated had to be selected before the 1950 counts became available.   For all practical purposes, however, the lower limit of the last category of urbanized areas may be taken as 50,000, which is in general also the upper limit of the first category of other urban places.   The rural population is classified into persons living in places of 1,000 to 2,500 (both incorporated and unincorporated), those in places of under 1,000 (incorporated places only), and those in "other rural" areas.   Each of these groups is subdivided into the population living on farms and the nonfarm population.

There are 17 categories in the complete size-of-place classification.   It seemed inadvisable to treat simultaneously all 17.   Hence in Part I of this monograph, the distinction between central cities and "fringes" of urbanized areas is disregarded, and a separate chapter in Part II is devoted to the analysis of differences between the central and suburban portions of urbanized areas.   The subclassification of the village categories by farm and nonfarm residence is neglected in the main analysis of Part I, with separate attention being given to the village-farm population in Chapter 10.   However, the distinction between the farm and nonfarm portions of the "other rural" category is maintained throughout.   The size-of-place classification actually used in Part I comprises but 11 categories, those indicated in table 2 (p. 30) and in subsequent tables.

The size-of-place tabulations were designed to provide cross-classifications of all characteristics by region, age, color, and sex.   The regional tabulation was not, however, published in complete detail.   Some use was made of the unpublished figures from the regional tabulation, but this was not done in all cases because of the expense involved in consolidating the figures from the machine tabulation sheets.   Hence, for the analysis of some characteristics regional differentiation is ignored.   Furthermore, analysis of age, color, and sex differentials was regarded as secondary to analysis by size of place.   Where, for example, the variation by size of place was similar in pattern for the two sexes, the sex breakdown was often dispensed with.   For analysis by color, only the tabulations for the total and the nonwhite populations were available, and it was necessary to secure figures for the white population by subtraction.   This was not done in cases where it appeared that the comparison of total and nonwhite data yielded an approximately accurate indication of white-nonwhite differentials.   Full use of the age data was not made, first in those cases where subdivision of the data by age appeared to make little difference in size-of-place comparisons, and second in those cases where the age detail was insufficient to control the influence of age on the characteristic being studied.   The age control in the tabulation involves but five intervals—under 14 years of age, 14 to 24, 25 to 44, 45 to 64, and 65 and over.   For certain characteristics, notably marital status and labor force status, the change in proportional frequency is very rapid around the ages of 14 to 24.   To control age in the analysis of such characteristics indirect standardization was used.   This could be carried out with the age intervals under 5, 5 to 13, 14 to 19, 20 to 24, 25 to 34, 35 to 44, 45 to 54, 55 to 64, 65 to 74, and 75 and over, since the age distribution of the population in each size-of-place group was available in terms of these intervals.   In summary, controls were used for size-of-place comparisons, not in all cases, but only in those cases where it seemed particularly critical to the interpretation to have such control.   Intensive research on size-of-place differentials would doubtless need to go further in this direction than this monograph does.

    There are some additional qualifications on the study, which arise from the nature of the available data and from the decisions made regarding their analysis and presentation.   The treatment of differentials by size of place disregards the variation among individual places within each of the size groups, although such variation is, in all cases, considerable.   Summarizing the data by size categories forestalls an appraisal of the relative influence of size of place in comparison with the numerous other influences accounting for differences among communities.

    The novelty of the size-of-place classification used here precludes making temporal comparisons to establish trends in population distribution or population characteristics by size of place.   At a few points reference is made to studies of data from earlier periods, to gain a general impression as to the stability over time of the size-of-place differences observed.

From a substantive standpoint this study overlaps with other projects in the Census Monograph Series which deal with such specific characteristics of the population as mobility or income.   In order to minimize the overlap of this monograph with the others, the analysis in each case proceeds only far enough to indicate the significant findings on differentials by size of place.   It has been necessary, therefore, to neglect certain interesting aspects of the data from the "Characteristics by Size of Place" report. Thus, for example, the subject of white-nonwhite differentials in marital status is not discussed, except insofar as such differentials appear to be related to size of place.

This study is conceived as an exploration of the research possibilities of a specific body of data, rather than as an effort to develop theory or to check specific experimental hypotheses.   Thus, the study seeks in only a limited way to "explain" the findings, or to relate them to other research.   It should prove useful to other research workers desiring to employ size of place as an independent, dependent, or control variable in their studies, especially when giving somewhat more detailed attention to the variation of particular population characteristics by size of place than has been done here.

The procedure of this study was to search for fairly clear-cut patterns or relationships by community size.   Where such a pattern did not emerge upon a somewhat elementary analysis of the data, the exploration was terminated.   It follows that the study probably errs in by-passing certain significant, but complex, relationships which more intensive analytical study might disclose.

Population distribution by size of place

Many students have noted that the number of communities of a given size found in a national economy is inversely related to the size of community.   Thus, there are nearly 10 times as many places of 2,500 to 5,000 inhabitants as there are places of 25,000 to 50,000.   Several efforts have been made to specify a more precise form for this relationship, notably Zipf's "rank-size rule." [16]   This rule states that the product of a community's population size times its rank in size is a constant.   Hence, if the largest community has a population of 12 million, the 10th ranking community is expected to have 1,200,000 inhabitants, and the 50th community, 240,000 inhabitants.   This rule has been shown to hold approximately for the United States city-size distributions of most of the census years, 1790 to 1940, and for the size distribution of metropolitan districts in 1940.

With the data available for this study, a more rigorous test of the rank-size rule can be made than has hitherto been possible.   The 1950 size-of-

---

[16] G. K. Zipf, *Human Behavior and the Principle of Least Effort*, Addison-Wesley Press, Cambridge, 1949, Part 2.

place data include unincorporated communities down to 1,000 inhabitants and give a more realistic indication of the sizes of larger places than was available before the introduction of the urbanized area concept.

Figure 1 enables one to check graphically the fit of the data to the rank-size rule. In this chart size of place has been plotted against rank, both variables being scaled in logarithms. Each place of 1 million or more is shown on the chart, but for smaller places only the lower limits of selected size intervals are shown. For the rank-size rule to hold precisely, all the points of the graph would have to lie on a straight line running at a 45-degree angle to the axes. It is clear from inspection that a 45-degree line could be fitted rather closely to the places of 100,000 or more, but it would then seriously overstate the number of smaller places.

The simple rank-size rule does not, thus, fit the distribution of 1950 size-of-place data. A better fit can be obtained by using the "generalized"

FIGURE 1.—RANK-SIZE RELATIONSHIP FOR URBANIZED AREAS AND OTHER PLACES OF 1,000 INHABITANTS OR MORE IN THE UNITED STATES: 1950

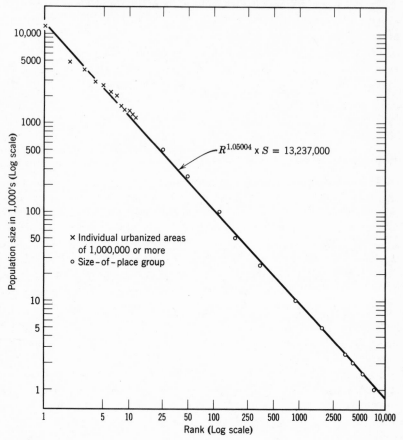

Note: Based on data in table 1.

rank-size rule,[17] which allows the rank to have an exponent other than unity. An approximate least squares solution yields the formula:

$$R^{1.05004} \times S = 13,237,000,$$

where R stands for rank and S for size. The graph of this equation is plotted in figure 1.

Since it is difficult to judge the fit of a curve on a double-log chart, table 1 compares the actual observations with the values calculated from this formula. The table presents the calculated and actual number of places in each size interval, and a similar comparison for the aggregate populations of places in the several intervals. The latter computation is somewhat rough, since the formulas involve the use of an integral as an approximation to the summation of discrete values.[18]

TABLE 1.—ACTUAL AND THEORETICAL DISTRIBUTION OF THE POPULATION, BY SIZE OF PLACE: 1950

Size of place	Number of places		Population (millions)		Error[1] (percent)
	Actual	Calculated	Actual	Calculated	
United States...................	7,568	8,421	102.9	103.9	0.9
1,000,000 or more....................	12	12	37.8	38.8	2.6
500,000 to 1,000,000................	13	11	8.8	7.4	-15.8
250,000 to 500,000..................	24	21	8.7	7.2	-16.9
100,000 to 250,000..................	70	56	10.9	9.3	-14.9
50,000 to 100,000..................	[2]59	103	4.3	6.8	57.2
25,000 to 50,000...................	172	190	5.9	6.6	10.8
10,000 to 25,000...................	547	547	8.2	8.4	1.7
5,000 to 10,000....................	908	879	6.2	6.1	-2.3
2,500 to 5,000.....................	1,605	1,700	5.6	5.9	5.4
2,000 to 2,500.....................	758	833	1.7	1.8	9.9
1,500 to 2,000.....................	1,272	1,372	2.2	2.3	8.0
1,000 to 1,500.....................	2,128	2,697	2.6	3.3	26.6

[1] Calculated minus actual population, divided by actual population (computed before rounding population figures to millions).

[2] Includes 38 urbanized areas and 21 other urban places.

Source: *1950 Census of Population*, Vol. I, *Number of Inhabitants*, U. S. Summary, table 5a.

The generalized rank-size rule applied to these data somewhat underestimates the number and aggregate population of places between 100,000 and 1 million. It overestimates seriously the number of villages of 1,000 to 1,500, but provides a tolerably good fit in the 1,500 to 25,000 range of sizes. The most serious error is for places of 50,000 to 100,000 inhabitants, where the formula requires more than two-thirds more places than are observed and overestimates the aggregate population by 57 percent. It is plausible to argue that this error represents, in part at least, a defect of the data. It will be recalled that 50,000 is the cutoff point for the delineation of urbanized areas. There are several places which, on the basis of the population within the incorporated limits of the central city, would fall into the 50,000 to 100,000 interval, but rise above 100,000 when the

---

[17] John Q. Stewart, *op. cit.*

[18] Carl Hammer, "Rank Correlation of Cities and Refinement," mimeographed report, Bureau of Applied Social Research, Columbia University, 1951.

suburban and fringe populations are added.   However, because of the cut-off, the 50,000 to 100,000 interval does not similarly gain numbers from the interval below.   It seems likely that if the urbanized area concept were applied to urban centers of all sizes, the generalized rank-size rule would fit better in the intermediate size range.   However, if this were done, some of the villages and small towns would be absorbed into urbanized areas, and their numbers and aggregate populations would be somewhat more seriously overestimated by the formula than they now are.

In summary, the new size-of-place data appear to require a generalization of the simple rank-size rule.   In generalized form, the rule provides a fairly good average fit, with the departures from a good fit partially reflecting a discontinuity in the application of the urbanized area concept.   The rule obviously does not fit well enough to permit close estimation for individual places.   But on the other hand, it concisely and conveniently summarizes the persistent inverse relationship between size of place and number of places.

The foregoing analysis makes no reference to places of less than 1,000 inhabitants, since the census data for these places pertain only to incorporated places, and many of these small villages are not incorporated.   The most recent systematic population estimates for places under 1,000 are for 1930.[19]   At that time, not quite half of the estimated 14,971 villages of 250 to 1,000 inhabitants, and less than one-twelfth of the estimated 37,203 places of less than 250 inhabitants were incorporated.   Between 1930 and 1950, the number of incorporated places of less than 1,000 reported by the census declined from 10,346 to 9,827; 9,649 of these villages were classified as being in rural territory under the new urban definition.   Moreover, the aggregate population of these 9,649 places was 8 percent smaller than that of the 10,346 villages in 1930, as compared to a difference of only 5 percent in the number of places.

It is possible to form a crude estimate of the total population of villages of less than 1,000 by making the assumptions (1) that the 9,649 incorporated rural places under 1,000 in 1950 were distributed in the size classes 250 to 1,000 and under 250 in the same proportion as in 1930; (2) that the proportions of villages incorporated in these size classes in 1950 were the same as the corresponding proportions (0.492 and 0.080, respectively) in 1930; (3) that the population per village in each size class in 1950 was the same as the corresponding ratio derived from Landis' 1930 estimates of number and aggregate population of villages.[20]   On these assumptions, the estimated population of all rural villages under 1,000 in 1950 was 2.25 times as large as the reported number of inhabitants of rural incorporated places of that size.

---

[19] Paul H. Landis, "The Number of Unincorporated Places in the United States and Their Estimated Populations," *Research Studies of the State College of Washington 6*, December 1938, pp. 160–188.
[20] *Ibid.*, tables 2 and 4.

If, in line with the trend observed for the period 1900 to 1930, the number of places under 1,000 has been decreasing, and if the proportion incorporated has increased, this estimate is too high. The estimate would also be too high if the average size of places of less than 1,000 actually decreased slightly. In any case, it seems reasonable to conclude that the 1950 population of all rural villages under 1,000 was something like twice as great as the population of rural incorporated places of that size, i.e., of the order of 8 million in place of around 4 million. (On any reasonable estimate of the total population in and number of places of 250 to 1,000, the rank-size rule established for larger places overestimates the magnitude of this population by something like 50 percent; and it would be even more seriously in error for the number of places below 250 inhabitants.)

This reasoning also leads to the conclusion that the "other rural-nonfarm" population includes something like 4 million inhabitants of small villages, since less than 6 percent of the small incorporated village population are farm residents. If this is the case, then an estimate of the non-village rural-nonfarm population would be of the order of 17 million instead of the nearly 21 million "other rural-nonfarm" population reported in the "Characteristics by Size of Place" tables.

Table 2 shows the distribution of population in 1950 by size of place for the United States and each of the four regions. The size-of-place classification given here is the one which will usually be used in Part I. Of the almost 151 million inhabitants of the United States enumerated in 1950, not quite one-half (46 percent) were living in urbanized areas, and another 18 percent were in other urban places. Hence, just under two-thirds of the population was classified as urban. The remaining 36 percent, the rural population, included 7 percent living in villages (if all unincorporated villages were included, this figure would be higher), 14 percent in "other rural-nonfarm" areas, and 15 percent in "other rural-farm" residences. The high degree of urbanization reached by 1950 is indicated not only by the urban proportion of two-thirds, but perhaps even more strikingly by the fact that the three largest urbanized areas together (New York, Chicago, and Los Angeles) contained a population almost as large as the entire "other rural-farm" population.

If the size-of-place distribution is taken as the criterion of relative urbanization, the ranking of the four regions is clear. The most highly urbanized region is the Northeast, followed by the West, the North Central, and the South, in that order. This ranking is invariant, whether the percent urban, or any other dividing line is used. For example, the Northeast has a total of 66.5 percent living in urbanized areas, compared with 49.8, 45.0, and 28.2 percent for the other three regions in the order already given. Conversely, the South has the largest proportion of "other rural-farm" residents (about one-fourth), followed by the North Central (one-sixth), the West (not quite one-tenth), and the Northeast (less than one-twentieth).

A more graphic impression of the differences among regions in degree of urbanization is given by figure 2, showing the distribution of urban and rural population in 1950. The Northeast contains an almost uninterrupted belt of urban settlement stretching from Boston to Philadelphia, as well as other major urban agglomerations in Pennsylvania and New York. A secondary belt of urban centers appears in those States of the North Central Region which border on the Great Lakes. The same States have a comparatively high density of rural population, while in the western part of the North Central Region rural density is lower and urban centers are smaller and less frequent. The comparatively high degree of urbanization of the West results primarily from the presence of several important urban agglomerations in the Pacific States, together with a generally low rural density. The South ranks low in urbanization, despite the presence of a number of sizable cities, because of the high density of its rural population.

TABLE 2.—PERCENT DISTRIBUTION OF THE POPULATION BY SIZE OF PLACE, BY REGIONS: 1950

Size of place	United States	Northeast	North Central	South	West
Total..........................	100.0	100.0	100.0	100.0	100.0
Urbanized areas:					
3,000,000 or more..............	14.0	31.2	11.1	...	20.3
1,000,000 to 3,000,000.........	11.1	17.0	12.3	5.2	10.6
250,000 to 1,000,000...........	11.6	8.3	13.1	13.2	10.6
Under 250,000..................	9.3	10.0	8.5	9.8	8.3
Places outside urbanized areas:					
25,000 or more.................	4.7	3.2	5.6	5.0	5.2
10,000 to 25,000..............	5.5	4.3	5.7	5.9	6.3
2,500 to 10,000...............	7.9	5.6	7.8	9.6	8.6
1,000 to 2,500................	4.3	3.1	4.8	4.9	4.1
Under 1,000 (incorporated).....	2.7	0.9	4.7	2.6	1.9
Other rural:					
Nonfarm.......................	13.9	12.0	10.0	18.9	14.6
Farm..........................	15.0	4.4	16.4	24.9	9.5

Source: *1950 Census of Population*, Vol. IV, *Special Reports*, Part 5, Chapter A, Characteristics by Size of Place, tables 1 and 6.

Incidentally, the use of "region" as a control factor introduces an ambiguity into the statement of relationships between dependent variables and size of place. Perhaps region may be thought of as a "contextual" rather than as an "analytical" variable. The four nominal regions differ widely as a result of many causes—geographic, historical, cultural, and economic. Therefore, in "controlling" region it is by no means clear just what factors are being controlled, since regional differences may reflect differences in climate, ethnic background, crops produced, traditional customs, and a host of other factors. Among other things the regions differ markedly in degree of urbanization and the rate at which they are becoming urbanized. Hence, region and urbanization are "confounded" variables, and it is impossible to determine by statistical analysis the influence of either variable independent of the other.

FIGURE **2.**—POPULATION DISTRIBUTION OF THE UNITED STATES, URBAN AND RURAL: 1950

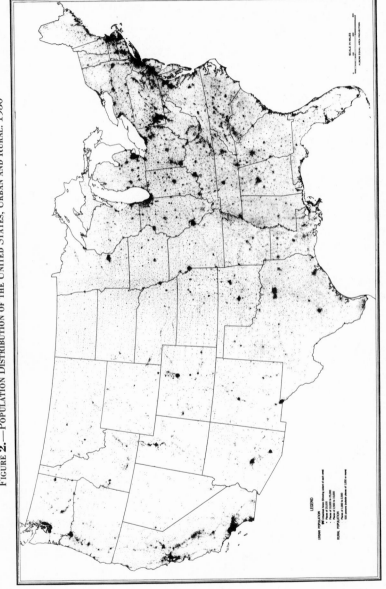

Source: U. S. Bureau of the Census.

The position taken in this monograph is that, since urbanization can be handled as an analytical variable whereas region cannot, most interpretations of relationships should hinge on the size-of-place factor. There is some reason to believe that as the analytical variables which differentiate regions are identified and incorporated in research designs it will appear less necessary and desirable to use region as a control factor. In the analyses of subsequent chapters, therefore, where a regional breakdown is involved, the major aim is to discover whether size-of-place differences have a similar pattern from one region to another. When they do, strong presumptive evidence is gained for the "causal" significance of size of place. When they do not, the situation remains equivocal, pending further research which controls additional analytical variables.

Quick summary of findings

So that the reader will not become lost in details in the succeeding chapters, it seems desirable to review quickly the major size-of-place differentials discovered in the study. This presentation, for the most part, disregards differences in size-of-place variation by region and neglects qualifications which should be stated to make the findings precisely applicable to particular age, color, and sex subgroups of the population.

The major findings are summarized graphically in figures 3 to 6. Most of the graphs are constructed on the principle of showing the index value for each size-of-place group as a deviation from the index value for the United States as a whole. The latter is shown on the chart as the base line, so that one can readily note in which size-of-place groups the index is higher than in the country as a whole, and in which ones it is lower. For example, the median age of the entire population is 30.2 years, and that for the population living in urbanized areas of 3 million or more is 33.7 years. Both these items of information are conveyed by the second graph in figure 3, as well as the fact that the median age in the largest urbanized areas exceeds that in the United States by 3.5 years. Since the size-of-place groups have unequal populations, it is well to remember that the United States figure is, in effect, a *weighted* average of the indexes for the 11 size-of-place groups.

One further explanation about figures 3 to 6 (which also applies to most of the figures in Part I of the monograph): The size-of-place groups are identified by code numbers, running from 1 to 11, with the largest urbanized areas shown as group 1, and the "other rural farm" as group 11. The complete code is as follows:

1. Urbanized areas of 3,000,000 or more
2. Urbanized areas of 1,000,000 to 3,000,000
3. Urbanized areas of 250,000 to 1,000,000
4. Urbanized areas of less than 250,000
5. Urban places outside urbanized areas of 25,000 or more
6. Urban places outside urbanized areas of 10,000 to 25,000

   7. Urban places outside urbanized areas of 2,500 to 10,000
   8. Villages (incorporated and unincorporated) of 1,000 to 2,500
   9. Villages (incorporated only) of less than 1,000
 10. Other rural, nonfarm
 11. Other rural, farm

Age and sex. (1) There is very little variation in the sex ratio of the total population by size of place, except for the high values observed for the "other rural" categories. (2) The median age of the total population is in general directly related to size of place; however, an exceptionally high figure is observed for the small villages. (3) The proportion of the population aged 65 and over varies inversely with size of place, over the urban-village range, despite the opposite gradient observed for median age. The lowest percentages of aged persons are in the "other rural" categories. (4) The fertility ratio (children under 5 per 1,000 women 20 to 44 years of age) bears a marked inverse relationship to size of place. (5) There is little significant variation in the pattern of sex ratios by age for native whites among the urban and village size groups, although the "other rural" population has a distinctive pattern. However, an exception to this generalization is that the sex ratio of the native white population aged 65 and over is inversely related to size of place.

Race and nativity. (1) The percentage of native whites decreases as size of place increases, over the urban-village range, while the percentages of foreign-born whites and Negroes are directly related to size of place. The gradient does not carry through to the "other rural" categories, because of the concentrations of Negroes in these groups in the South. (2) Compared with native whites, foreign-born whites are considerably urbanized in all four regions, and Negroes are even more urbanized, except in the South. Other nonwhites are less urbanized than native whites in all regions except the Northeast.

Marital status and family characteristics. (1) If allowance is made for age, the percentage married is inversely related to size of place, and the percentages single, widowed, and divorced are, on the whole, directly related to size of place. The "other rural" categories, because of their relatively high sex ratios, deviate from this pattern in the case of males. (2) In the nonwhite population the percentage of married persons reported as separated varies directly with size of place; a similar tendency, but less pronounced and regular, is observed for the white population. (3) The population living in quasi-households, expressed as a ratio to the population in households, varies directly with size of place. (4) The percentage of the population in households who are members of primary families tends to vary inversely, while the percentages classified as primary individuals and nonrelatives of the household head vary directly with size of place. (5) The average size of primary families varies only slightly by size of place among the urban and village groups, but is somewhat lower for these groups than for the "other rural" categories.

FIGURE 3.—INDEXES OF AGE, SEX, AND RACE-NATIVITY, BY SIZE OF PLACE: 1950

[See p. 32 for explanation of size-of-place code]

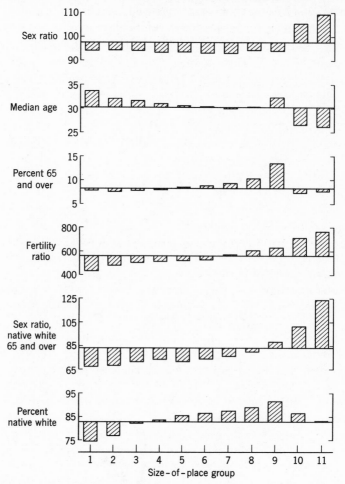

Note: Based on data in tables 3 to 6, 8, and 9.

Mobility. (1) Residential stability is greatest for the large urbanized areas and the "other rural-farm" population. Correlatively, the percentage of migrants from another county (on the basis of 1949 residence) or of movers from another house in the same county bears an inverted "U-shaped" relationship to size of place, the highest mobility rates being in urban places outside urbanized areas and the lowest rates in the largest urbanized areas and the "other rural-farm" areas. However, the highest residential mobility rates are observed for the "other rural-nonfarm" population. It is suggested that the 1949–50 mobility rate is positively related to the 1940–50 growth rate of different-sized communities. (2) The rate of in-movement from farms per 1,000 resident population is inversely related to size of place.

Education. (1) For the white population, there is little systematic variation by size among urban places in educational attainment. However, the median number of school years completed is higher in urbanized areas and other urban places than in villages, and higher, in turn, in the villages than in the "other rural" areas. (2) For the nonwhite population there is a pronounced direct relation between educational attainment and size of place. A regional breakdown reveals this to be the characteristic pattern of the South and the West, but it does not hold for nonwhites in the North Central and Northeast, where, except for the rural-urban differential, there is little systematic variation by size of place.

Labor force and occupation. (1) The labor force participation rate for males, when allowance is made for age distribution, shows little systematic

FIGURE 4.—INDEXES OF MARITAL STATUS AND FAMILY CHARACTERISTICS, BY SIZE OF PLACE: 1950

[See p. 32 for explanation of size-of-place code]

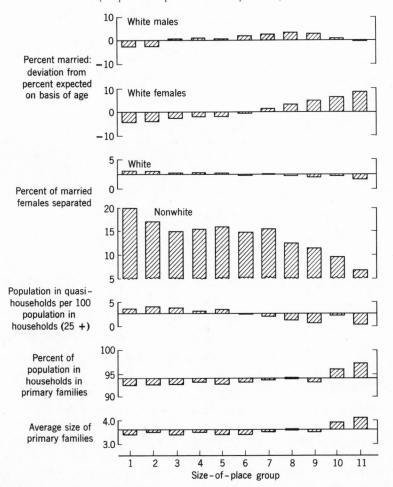

Note: Based on data in tables 15 to 19.

FIGURE 5.—INDEXES OF MOBILITY STATUS, EDUCATIONAL ATTAINMENT, AND INCOME, BY SIZE
OF PLACE: 1950

[See p. 32 for explanation of size-of-place code]

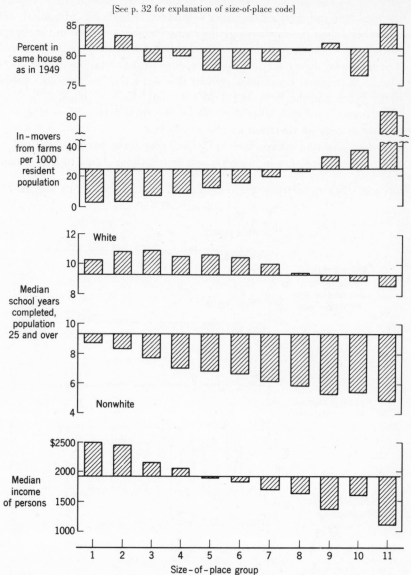

Source: Based on data in tables 21, 23, and 26; *1950 Census of Population*, Vol. IV, *Special Reports*, Part 5, Chapter A, Characteristics by Size of Place, table 4.

variation by size of place. However, there is a considerably higher rate for the "other rural-farm" category than for any other size group. (2) For females, both white and nonwhite, there is a general tendency for the rate of labor force participation to vary directly with size of place, though the progression is not entirely regular among the larger size groups. (3) The percentage unemployed, for nonwhites, tends to vary directly with size of place, but for whites it is relatively constant among size of place groups, except for the low rate in "other rural-farm" areas. (4) In general, the socio-economic status of the labor force, as indicated by the percentage in white-collar occupations, varies directly with size of place. (5) The percentage employed in farm occupations is related inversely to size of place. (6) Aside from farm occupations, the occupation group which varies most in relative size among different-sized places is clerical and kindred workers, the percentage being directly related to size of place. (7) The degree of dissimilarity between the male and female occupation distributions (i.e., the percentage of nonoverlapping of the two distributions) is inversely related to size of place, i.e., the larger the place, the more the female occupation distribution resembles the male. (8) The degree of dissimilarity between the white and nonwhite occupation distributions, for males, is comparatively low for the "other rural-farm" group and for the largest urbanized areas, with higher indexes of dissimilarity observed for the intermediate size groups. (9) For both whites and nonwhites the size-of-place gradients in some occupations for females are opposite to those for males. Hence, there is no simple generalization relating occupational composition to size of place which is valid for all labor force subgroups.

Income. (1) Median cash income of persons is directly related to size of place; this relationship is evident for the total population as well as for subgroupings by sex, age, color, and region. (2) Marked differences in median income among size-of-place groups persist when allowance is made for differences in occupation distribution (by major occupation groups) or in educational attainment. (3) There is some evidence to suggest that the degree of inequality of the income distribution is inversely related to size of place.

Village population. (1) In terms of population characteristics villages resemble small towns more than they do the "other rural" groups. (2) Though they have certain distinctive traits, in general, villages are intermediate between the smaller urban places and the "other rural" groups on indexes of demographic characteristics. (3) A small, but significant number of village residents live on farms. This population differs systematically both from the village-nonfarm and from the nonvillage-farm population.

Methodological implications of findings

The investigation of social correlates of community size falls within the research area traditionally designated "rural-urban differences." As noted above, most studies in this field have employed the census trichotomy of urban, rural-nonfarm, and rural-farm population. The question is here posed of the relative advantages of the size-of-place classification and the conventional classification. It may be accepted as a general principle that

FIGURE 6.—INDEXES OF LABOR FORCE AND OCCUPATION STATUS, BY SIZE OF PLACE: 1950

[See p. 32 for explanation of size-of-place code]

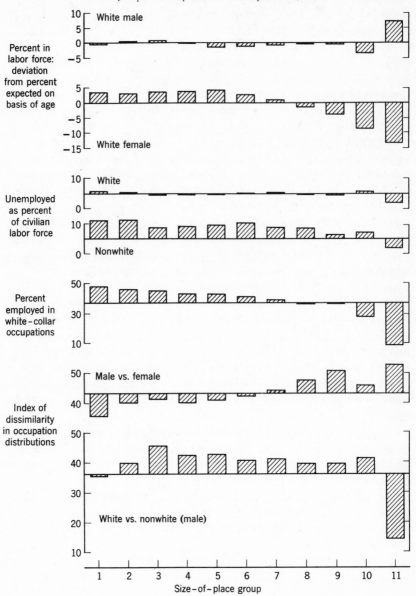

Note: Based on data in tables 30, 32, 33, 35, and 36.

any increase in the detail of a classification permits inferences which might otherwise be obscured, assuming not too high a price is paid in increased sampling variability. But there are additional advantages to the size-of-place classification.

Part II of the monograph offers comments on the difficulty of dealing with the heterogeneous "rural-nonfarm" category. In this respect, the size-of-place classification is superior to the trichotomy in that it permits a distinction between village residents and "other rural-nonfarm" population. The latter category, however, still includes an appreciable number of inhabitants of small unincorporated villages.

A second advantage is that the size-of-place classification does not commit the investigator to a fixed line of demarcation between "urban" and "rural" population. In this monograph, the census definition of "urban" is adhered to, and village residents are referred to as part of the "rural" population. But this is solely for convenience of exposition and to avoid unnecessary confusion. The data just reviewed certainly fail to support the 2,500 mark as a uniquely desirable dividing line between "urban" and "rural." Consider the indexes graphed in figures 3 to 6. The villages of 1,000 to 2,500 bear a closer resemblance to the small urban places of 2,500 to 10,000 than to the villages of less than 1,000 with respect to the median age, percent 65 years old and over, sex ratio of native whites aged 65 and over, percent native white, percent of white married females separated, percent of household residents in primary families, rate of in-movement from farms, median school years completed by nonwhites, median income, female labor force participation (adjusted for age), and percent of whites and nonwhites unemployed. There is greater resemblance between large and small villages than between large villages and small urban places with respect to a dozen other indexes shown on the graphs. It seems likely that large villages would resemble the smallest urban places more closely if the latter included only places of 2,500 to 5,000 inhabitants rather than 2,500 to 10,000. In any case, in terms of population characteristics, there is no uniform, sharp break between urban and rural on the size-of-place scale.

A meaningful comparison between the size-of-place classification and the urban, rural-nonfarm, and rural-farm classification is suggested by the question: Do differences by size of place follow the patterns suggested by gross rural-urban differences? One instance of a negative answer is the sex ratio of the total population. Despite the pronounced and long-standing difference between the urban and rural populations in the sex ratio, there is no gradient pattern of the sex ratio by size of place over the urban-village range. There are other cases where the "other rural" nonfarm and farm groups are out of line with fairly regular gradients observed over the entire range of places from the largest urbanized areas to the villages of less than 1,000. These characteristics include the percentage of the population 65 years old and over, the percentage native white, and the percentage of males married. For such characteristics as the ratio of quasi-household to household population, rate of mobility, median income, and male-female occupational dissimilarity, the "other rural-farm" index value falls into line with a size-of-place gradient or relationship observed over the urban-village range, while the "other rural-nonfarm" value is out of line. Evidently it is not safe to assume, *a priori*, that the pattern of size-of-place differences can be inferred from a study of gross rural-urban differences.

These observations bear on the proposals advanced by some students to substitute a construct of a "rural-urban continuum" for the conventional rural-urban dichotomy. One interpretation of such a proposal leads to the hypothesis that most indexes of population characteristics are monotonic (i.e., regularly increasing or regularly decreasing) functions of size of place. But the data of this study show that there are some important characteristics on which the largest urbanized areas resemble the "other rural-farm" category more closely than the smaller urban places. It is doubtful, therefore, that the "rural-urban continuum" can be regarded as unidimensional.

The results of the size-of-place study clearly indicate the desirability of supplementing census tabulations by the conventional rural-urban categories with tabulations by size of place, where possible, in order that investigators may test more exactly their hypotheses about rural-urban differences. There is, of course, the question of how much detail in the size-of-place classification is required. On this point, there is one interesting observation about the size-of-place differences. For many characteristics, e.g., the fertility ratio, percentage of females married (age-adjusted), median school years completed by the nonwhite population, median income, and percent employed in white-collar occupations, the difference between a community of 10,000 inhabitants and one of 100,000 is approximately equal to the difference between a community of 100,000 and one of 1 million. In other words, the regression of the characteristic on size of community is roughly linear in the logarithm of the independent variable, at least over a good part of its range. There is no characteristic examined for which the regression is even approximately linear in the absolute value of the size of community—i.e., no characteristic for which equal differences in the numerical sizes of two communities produce equal differences in the index of the characteristic. This observation confirms the wisdom of choosing a set of size intervals which are in approximate geometric progression, rather than equal size intervals, at any rate where the investigation is concerned with a wide range of community sizes.

CHAPTER 3

AGE AND SEX COMPOSITION

Population pyramid

A graphic portrayal of variations in age and sex structure by size of place is afforded by the population pyramid. Although this device permits only gross comparisons, differences among the size-of-place groups are readily apparent (see figure 7). It is evident, for example, that there is considerable differentiation between large and small urban places, and between the village and "other rural-nonfarm" populations. Such differences are lost when analyzing characteristics of communities with only the three conventional groupings, urban, rural nonfarm, and rural farm.

Inspection of the diagrams makes it plain that one must qualify carefully any general statement about urban-rural differences in age and sex structure. Generally, the urban pyramids do show a deficiency of persons between 5 and 20 years of age, with a great swelling of numbers between the ages of 20 and 55, particularly of females of these ages. The rural pyramids tend to be broader at the base and less full in the younger adult age groups. However, the small villages (under 1,000) have a distinctive pyramid: one which, with its large proportion of aged persons, approaches the outline of a stationary population more closely than does the pyramid of any other size-of-place group. The larger villages (1,000 to 2,500), on the other hand, have a pyramid which is intermediate between the small village and the urban ones. As compared with the urban pyramid, there are proportionately somewhat smaller numbers in the middle age brackets and larger numbers at the upper and lower ages. The "other rural-nonfarm" pyramid seems to resemble that of the villages of 1,000 to 2,500 rather more than it does those of the smaller villages and the "other rural-farm" populations. It is, however, somewhat broader at the base than is the pyramid for the larger villages. The "other rural-farm" pyramid is one whose deficits mirror the urban excesses, and vice versa. It is broad at the base and up to the age of 20, where there is a drastic "sculpturing" effect diminishing the breadth of the pyramid in the early adult years.

The following more detailed numerical analysis of age and sex composition can be checked for the most part by inspection of the population pyramids in figure 7.

41

FIGURE 7.—POPULATION PYRAMIDS

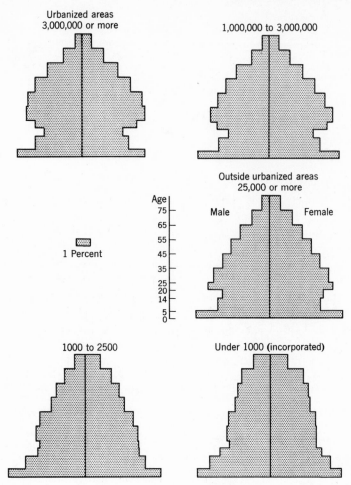

Source: *1950 Census of Population*, Vol. IV, *Special Reports*, Part 5, Chapter A, Characteristics by Size of Place, table 1.

Sex ratio

The term "sex ratio" refers to the number of males per 100 females in the total population, unless qualified as applying to particular subgroups of the population. There is a slight bias in the sex ratios calculated from the 3⅓-percent sample count, which somewhat exaggerates the amount of the excess of females over males. There is reason to believe, however, that this bias does not seriously affect comparisons among size-of-place groups. (See p. 56.)

Table 3 shows the sex ratios for the 11 size-of-place groups, for the United States and each of the four regions in 1950. There is remarkably little variation in the sex ratio from one size group to another in the United

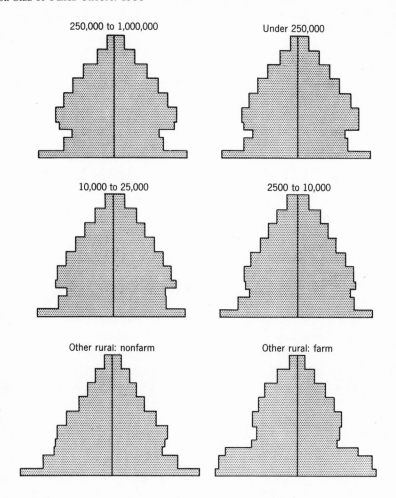

250,000 to 1,000,000

Under 250,000

10,000 to 25,000

2500 to 10,000

Other rural: nonfarm

Other rural: farm

States as a whole, except for the high masculinity of the "other rural" categories. In the remaining nine size groups the highest sex ratio is 94.3, this value appearing for urbanized areas of 1 million to 3 million and for places of 1,000 to 2,500; the lowest sex ratio, 93.0, is for urban places of 10,000 to 25,000. While there is somewhat more variation in the sex ratio among size-of-place groups within the four regions than in the country as a whole, there is little suggestion of a simple pattern or gradient of the sex ratio by size of place. The West may perhaps be regarded as an exception to this rule, for there is some tendency for an increasing sex ratio with decreasing size of place. In the West, all urbanized areas combined have a sex ratio of 95.1, as compared to 98.0 for all urban places outside

TABLE **3.**—SEX RATIO OF THE POPULATION BY SIZE OF PLACE, BY REGIONS: 1950

Size of place	United States	Northeast	North Central	South	West
Total..............................	97.6	95.0	98.3	97.7	101.1
Urbanized areas:					
3,000,000 or more........................	94.0	93.7	96.2	...	92.4
1,000,000 to 3,000,000..................	94.3	93.3	96.1	92.9	94.4
250,000 to 1,000,000....................	94.0	91.9	93.6	93.7	99.1
Under 250,000..........................	93.5	94.4	94.6	90.5	97.6
Places outside urbanized areas:					
25,000 or more.........................	93.7	93.7	93.9	93.6	93.6
10,000 to 25,000.......................	93.0	91.6	93.0	90.9	100.0
2,500 to 10,000........................	93.1	93.3	92.3	91.3	99.4
1,000 to 2,500.........................	94.3	93.3	93.1	93.1	102.9
Under 1,000 (incorporated).............	93.8	91.0	93.7	91.9	103.9
Other rural:					
Nonfarm:					
Total population......................	105.7	101.4	106.3	104.1	117.7
Civilian noninstitutional population..	99.3	97.4	101.2	97.3	106.6
Farm...................................	109.5	110.6	112.9	106.2	116.9

Source: *1950 Census of Population*, Vol. IV, *Special Reports*, Part 5, Chapter A, Characteristics by Size of Place, tables 1 and 6.

urbanized areas, 103.2 for the villages (places under 2,500), and 117.4 for the "other rural" areas.

The sex ratio of the village population is more similar to that of the urban population than it is to that of the "other rural" population, except in the West. (This is the only region in which any of the size groups, aside from the "other rural" categories, has a sex ratio exceeding 100.) In general, therefore, the urban pattern of an excess of females holds for villages as well as for all sizes of urban centers.

It is well to point out here that the distribution of the population in the Armed Forces (which are, of course, predominantly male) is a disturbing factor in certain size-of-place comparisons. While in the country as a whole about two-thirds of 1 percent of the population was in the Armed Forces in 1950, 2.1 percent of the "other rural-nonfarm" population was in the Armed Forces, as compared to 1 percent or less in each other size-of-place group. Especially large percentages in the Armed Forces occurred in the "other rural-nonfarm" areas of the South and West. Another disturbing factor is the location of institutions. About 1 percent of the entire population was classified in 1950 as institutional. Nearly half of the institutional population was located in "other rural-nonfarm" areas, while none of the rural-farm population was classified as institutional. The sex ratio was 152 in the total institutional population, but 181 in the "other rural-nonfarm" institutional population. An examination of the sex ratios of the civilian noninstitutional population for the size-of-place groups by region indicates that the principal comparisons affected are those between the "other rural nonfarm" and the other size-of-place groups, particularly in the South and the West.

Using the civilian noninstitutional figures for the "other rural-nonfarm" category, the farm portion of the "other rural" category had a sex ratio exceeding that of the nonfarm portion by 10 points for the United States as a whole, and by 13 points for the Northeast, 12 for the North Central, 9 for the South, and 10 for the West. It is perhaps significant that the difference between the farm and nonfarm parts of the "other rural" category is greatest in the Northeast, which is the most urban region, and least in the South, which is the least urban region. It is probable that in a highly urbanized region the rural-nonfarm population contains a substantial proportion of quasi-urban population: e.g., residents of the rural-urban fringe of cities under 50,000.

Interregional variations in the sex ratio appear to be partially explained by the sex ratios of the "other rural" categories and by variations in the proportions of the total population living in "other rural" areas. For the combined populations of all urban places and villages, interregional differences fall within the range of 92.2 for the South to 96.5 for the West, a difference of just over 4 points. However, as table 3 indicates, the South and the West differ by 9 points in their "other rural-nonfarm" civilian, noninstitutional sex ratios, and by 10 points in the sex ratios of their "other rural-farm" populations. Yet the difference in sex ratios for the total population of the two regions is less than 4 points. Further, the sex ratio for the Northeast as a whole (95.0) is below that of the South (97.7), despite higher sex ratios for all but two size-of-place groups in the Northeast.

Median age

A convenient summary index of age composition is the median age of the population. Table 4 shows the median age of the population in each size-of-place group for the United States and the four regions. Within the urban population of the entire country, median age is directly related to size of community. For the largest urbanized areas the median age is 33.7, while

TABLE 4.—MEDIAN AGE OF THE POPULATION BY SIZE OF PLACE, BY REGIONS (WITH COLOR FOR THE SOUTH): 1950

Size of place	United States	North-east	North Central	South		West
				White	Nonwhite	
Urbanized areas:						
3,000,000 or more	33.7	33.9	33.1	...	.	33.7
1,000,000 to 3,000,000	32.0	32.5	31.7	31.8	29.3	32.3
250,000 to 1,000,000	31.5	32.6	32.0	30.4	29.0	32.3
Under 250,000	30.9	32.9	31.0	29.9	27.9	30.7
Places outside urbanized areas:						
25,000 or more	30.4	32.5	31.2	28.8	27.9	30.3
10,000 to 25,000	30.3	32.3	31.0	29.0	27.4	30.1
2,500 to 10,000	29.9	32.1	31.6	28.5	26.5	28.8
1,000 to 2,500	30.2	31.6	32.3	28.5	25.8	28.9
Under 1,000 (incorporated)	32.3	32.2	34.3	31.1	25.0	28.8
Other rural:						
Nonfarm	26.5	29.6	27.8	24.4	22.7	26.9
Farm	26.1	29.7	28.9	25.8	18.4	28.1

Source: *1950 Census of Population*, Vol. IV, *Special Reports*, Part 5, Chapter A, Characteristics by Size of Place, table 1 and unpublished tabulations by region.

the median age for places of 2,500 to 10,000 is 29.9, a difference of 3.8 years.   This table reveals that there is a smooth gradation of the inter-mediate-sized places between these two extremes.   Villages of 1,000 to 2,500 have a median age very similar to that of the smaller urban places. However, the villages of less than 1,000 have a median age of 32.3, which is higher than that of any other size-of-place group except the urbanized areas over 3 million.   While all of the urban and village groups have median ages approximately as high as or exceeding that of the total United States population—30.2 years—the "other rural" groups are well below this average.   The medians are 26.5 and 26.1 years, respectively, for the nonfarm and farm portions of this category.

The foregoing generalizations require some qualification to be applicable to the situation within regions.   In each of the regions the highest median age is found for the size group of the largest urbanized areas, and the lowest medians occur for the "other rural" groups.   Although the relation-ship is somewhat irregular, there is also a clear tendency for the median age to vary directly with size of place, within the urban category.   The range of variation among the urban size groups differs considerably by region.   In the Northeast and North Central Regions there is a difference of only about two years between the highest and lowest medians for the urban size groups, while the difference is about three years in the South, and nearly five years in the West.   The regional breakdown reveals that it is primarily in the North Central Region and the white population of the South that the median age for the small villages is much greater than for the smaller urban places.   In the other two regions the village medians are about the same as those of the smallest urban places.   The variation from region to region in the median age for size-of-place groups is rather less among the urbanized areas than among the other groups.   Thus, large pop-ulation centers tend to be more similar in age composition from one region to another than do smaller places.   It might be worth-while to ex-plore the question of whether this holds for other characteristics as well.

The difference between the nonfarm and farm portions of the "other rural" population is clarified by examining the regional data, with a break-down by color in the South.   In the United States as a whole, the nonfarm population is slightly older than the farm population.   However, for the North Central Region, the West, and the white population of the South the nonfarm median age is lower than the farm median, by about a year, and the two medians are the same for the Northeast.   For the nonwhite pop-ulation of the South there is a large difference in the opposite direction with the "other rural-nonfarm" population having a median age more than four years greater than that of the "other rural-farm" population. Although the data are not shown in the table, it may be noted that a sim-ilar difference holds for the nonwhites in the Northeast and North Central Regions.

Sex differences in median age are not considered in the foregoing, since the relationship of median age to size of place tends to be very similar for males and females, although females are somewhat older than males in the total population.

Age distribution

While the analysis of median age has brought out the general tendency for the age of the population to increase with increasing community size, a study of the complete age distribution is necessary to understand how the differentials in median age come about. Actually, the higher median age in the larger communities results from their disproportionate numbers in the middle age groups, rather than from any excess of the aged.

Figure 8 shows the age distribution of the population in each of the 11 size-of-place groups. There is a very smooth gradation of the age distributions from the places of 3 million and over down to the villages of 1,000 to 2,500. There is a slight increase in the percentages of persons under 5 years of age (from 9.2 to 11.0 percent), of persons aged 5 to 19 (from 18.8 to 24.3), and of persons 65 years old and older (from 7.8 to 10.3). The other two age groups diminish regularly, going from the largest places to the villages of 1,000 to 2,500. The percent aged 20 to 44 decreases from 40.5 to 35.1, and the percent aged 45 to 64 decreases from 23.6 to 19.4.

FIGURE **8.**—PERCENT DISTRIBUTION OF THE TOTAL POPULATION, BY AGE: 1950

[See p. 32 for size-of-place code]

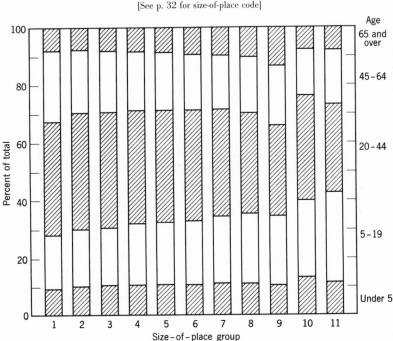

Note: See figure 7.

Some special features of the other three size groups require comment. The small villages (under 1,000 inhabitants) have the largest percentage over 65 of any of the size groups: 13.5 percent, as compared with the next largest figure, 10.3 percent. They have also a larger proportion over 45 than any of the other size groups, as well as a smaller proportion aged 20 to 44 than any except the "other rural-farm." The "other rural-nonfarm" population has the smallest proportion over 45, despite the disproportion- ate numbers of the institutional population, whose median age is about 44. The "other rural-farm" population differs from the "other rural-nonfarm" population in having a somewhat larger percentage under 20; a substan- tially smaller proportion aged 20 to 44: 30.6 percent as campared with 36.6 percent; and a somewhat larger proportion 45 to 64 years of age.

The foregoing description of size-of-place variations in age distribution requires only modification of details to be applicable to the situation within each of the regions (table 5). Perhaps the most striking exception to the generalizations made is that in the West the proportion aged 65 and over does not increase with decreasing size of place. Rather, the urbanized areas tend to have as high, or higher, percentages in this age group as do the other urban places. The tendency of the small villages to have a large percentage over 65 is most pronounced in the North Central Region and for the white population in the South. However, in all the regions the villages under 1,000 have a larger percentage over 65 than any other size-of-place group.

Fertility ratio

Of the three factors which account for size-of-place variations in age com- position, it is probable that differential fertility and migration are more important than is differential mortality. Fertility differentials can be in- dicated crudely, but no doubt reliably, by means of the fertility ratio, here defined as the number of children under the age of 5 per 1,000 women aged 20 to 44.[1]

Table 6 shows the fertility ratios of the size-of-place groups for the United States and the four regions. Fertility is clearly an inverse function of size of place. There are 433 children per 1,000 women in the largest urbanized areas, 570 in urban places of 2,500 to 10,000, and 766 in the "other rural-farm" areas, for the United States as a whole. There is a

---

[1] Among the possible sources of error in the comparisons are the following: differential mortality, differential completeness in enumeration of children, differences in age distribution of women between the ages of 20 and 44, and differences in marital status. Differential mortality probably affects the fertility ratio comparisons only very slightly. It is likely that underenumeration of children under 5 years old is more serious in rural than in urban areas; if so, the size-of-place differences tend to be somewhat understated. Some rough computations were made which indicate that standardization of fertility ratios for age and marital status would not materially alter the pattern of size-of-place differ- ences. A more refined analysis of fertility would, of course, permit a more precise measurement of the magnitude of the differences.

TABLE 5.—PERCENT DISTRIBUTION OF THE POPULATION BY AGE, BY SIZE OF PLACE, BY REGIONS (WITH COLOR FOR THE SOUTH): 1950

Region, size of place, and color	Total	Age (years)				
		Under 5	5 to 19	20 to 44	45 to 64	65 and over
NORTHEAST						
Urbanized areas:						
3,000,000 or more................	100.0	9.0	18.7	40.6	24.0	7.7
1,000,000 to 3,000,000.........	100.0	9.4	20.5	39.0	22.5	8.6
250,000 to 1,000,000...........	100.0	9.7	20.2	38.5	22.9	8.7
Under 250,000..................	100.0	9.5	20.4	38.2	22.6	9.3
Places outside urbanized areas:						
25,000 or more................	100.0	9.4	20.8	37.4	22.2	10.2
10,000 to 25,000..............	100.0	9.6	20.9	37.6	22.0	9.9
2,500 to 10,000...............	100.0	9.8	21.5	37.0	21.4	10.3
1,000 to 2,500................	100.0	10.4	22.6	35.9	20.6	10.5
Under 1,000 (incorporated).....	100.0	10.1	23.1	34.0	20.8	12.0
Other rural:						
Nonfarm......................	100.0	11.5	24.3	36.3	19.2	8.7
Farm.........................	100.0	10.3	27.4	31.2	21.3	9.8
NORTH CENTRAL						
Urbanized areas:						
3,000,000 or more.........	100.0	9.4	19.2	40.8	23.3	7.3
1,000,000 to 3,000,000.........	100.0	10.4	20.2	40.3	22.3	6.8
250,000 to 1,000,000...........	100.0	10.4	19.7	39.3	22.3	8.3
Under 250,000..................	100.0	10.6	21.2	38.6	21.1	8.5
Places outside urbanized areas:						
25,000 or more................	100.0	10.2	21.2	38.3	21.1	9.2
10,000 to 25,000..............	100.0	10.2	21.9	37.1	20.6	10.2
2,500 to 10,000...............	100.0	10.6	22.1	35.2	20.7	11.4
1,000 to 2,500................	100.0	10.6	23.0	32.9	20.6	12.9
Under 1,000 (incorporated).....	100.0	9.9	23.1	29.7	21.7	15.6
Other rural:						
Nonfarm......................	100.0	12.9	25.4	35.9	17.4	8.4
Farm.........................	100.0	10.9	28.4	31.3	21.5	7.9
SOUTH--WHITE						
Urbanized areas:						
3,000,000 or more.............	...	...	...	...	...	...
1,000,000 to 3,000,000.........	100.0	10.3	18.4	43.5	20.8	7.0
250,000 to 1,000,000...........	100.0	10.8	20.4	42.4	19.6	6.8
Under 250,000..................	100.0	10.9	21.3	41.8	19.1	6.9
Places outside urbanized areas:						
25,000 or more................	100.0	10.9	22.1	42.1	18.1	6.8
10,000 to 25,000..............	100.0	11.0	23.2	40.7	17.9	7.2
2,500 to 10,000...............	100.0	11.2	24.6	39.0	17.7	7.5
1,000 to 2,500................	100.0	11.3	25.4	37.1	17.8	8.4
Under 1,000 (incorporated).....	100.0	10.1	25.0	33.2	20.0	11.7
Other rural:						
Nonfarm......................	100.0	13.7	28.6	37.6	14.2	5.9
Farm.........................	100.0	10.9	32.2	30.6	18.8	7.5
SOUTH--NONWHITE						
Urbanized areas:						
3,000,000 or more.............	...	...	...	...	...	...
1,000,000 to 3,000,000.........	100.0	11.0	21.4	45.9	17.3	4.4
250,000 to 1,000,000...........	100.0	11.7	22.8	41.9	18.2	5.4
Under 250,000..................	100.0	12.2	24.2	41.1	17.0	5.5
Places outside urbanized areas:						
25,000 or more................	100.0	11.9	25.1	39.1	17.7	6.2
10,000 to 25,000..............	100.0	11.7	26.2	38.4	16.9	6.8
2,500 to 10,000...............	100.0	12.6	27.4	35.6	17.1	7.3
1,000 to 2,500................	100.0	12.9	28.7	34.0	16.6	7.8
Under 1,000 (incorporated).....	100.0	13.4	29.4	31.5	16.5	9.2
Other rural:						
Nonfarm......................	100.0	14.7	30.6	34.2	13.6	6.9
Farm.........................	100.0	15.1	38.5	27.2	13.4	5.8

TABLE 5.—PERCENT DISTRIBUTION OF THE POPULATION BY AGE, BY SIZE OF PLACE, BY REGIONS (WITH COLOR FOR THE SOUTH): 1950—Cont.

Region, size of place, and color	Total	Age (years)				
		Under 5	5 to 19	20 to 44	45 to 64	65 and over
WEST						
Urbanized areas:						
3,000,000 or more.............	100.0	9.7	18.5	40.1	22.5	9.2
1,000,000 to 3,000,000........	100.0	10.9	18.5	40.9	21.6	8.1
250,000 to 1,000,000..........	100.0	10.6	18.8	40.2	21.2	9.2
Under 250,000.................	100.0	11.2	21.6	39.1	19.7	8.4
Places outside urbanized areas:						
25,000 or more................	100.0	11.2	22.0	38.4	19.9	8.5
10,000 to 25,000..............	100.0	11.0	22.0	39.7	19.0	8.3
2,500 to 10,000...............	100.0	12.1	24.5	37.2	18.1	8.1
1,000 to 2,500................	100.0	11.4	25.6	35.5	18.9	8.6
Under 1,000 (incorporated).....	100.0	11.2	27.5	32.4	19.2	9.7
Other rural:						
Nonfarm.......................	100.0	12.4	26.4	37.7	16.9	6.6
Farm..........................	100.0	11.2	28.9	32.5	20.8	6.6

Source: *1950 Census of Population*, Vol. IV, *Special Reports*, Part 5, Chapter A, Characteristics by Size of Place, tables 1 and 6.

smooth gradation of the fertility ratios all along the size-of-place scale. With only minor irregularities the same sort of gradient appears for each of the regions. Especially marked variation by size of place occurs for the nonwhite population of the South. In the white population of the South the "other rural-nonfarm" fertility ratio is somewhat greater than the "other rural-farm" fertility ratio, while the difference in favor of the farm category is only slight in the North Central and the West. The fact that the farm exceeds the nonfarm ratio by about 50 children per 1,000 women in the United States as a whole is owing to a difference of about the same magnitude in the Northeast, and to the large excess—over 200 children

TABLE 6.—FERTILITY RATIO OF THE POPULATION BY SIZE OF PLACE, BY REGIONS (WITH COLOR FOR THE SOUTH): 1950

Size of place	United States	North-east	North central	South		West
				White	Nonwhite	
Urbanized areas:						
3,000,000 or more................	433	419	443	...	...	464
1,000,000 to 3,000,000...........	478	461	491	455	449	527
250,000 to 1,000,000.............	503	477	510	498	514	526
Under 250,000....................	510	481	531	494	526	563
Places outside urbanized areas:						
25,000 or more..................	522	482	519	519	550	567
10,000 to 25,000................	525	490	535	516	552	558
2,500 to 10,000.................	570	512	578	550	637	643
1,000 to 2,500..................	609	557	626	595	690	644
Under 1,000 (incorporated).......	629	575	640	582	747	692
Other rural:						
Nonfarm.........................	717	625	719	746	861	713
Farm............................	766	687	722	725	1,067	723

Source: *1950 Census of Population*, Vol. IV, *Special Reports*, Part 5, Chapter A, Characteristics by Size of Place, table 1 and unpublished tabulations by region.

per 1,000 women—of the farm over the nonfarm fertility ratio for the nonwhite population of the South.

The fertility ratios for the nonwhite population in the other regions show the same general tendency toward an inverse relationship with size of place, although, because of small numbers in some of the size-of-place groups, the gradients are somewhat irregular.

Dependency ratio

As a consequence of differences in effective fertility and in the proportion of aged, there is a striking differentiation of the size-of-place groups in the relative proportions of the age groups which comprise the bulk of the productive population and the age groups which contribute most heavily to the dependent population. Table 7 shows for the United States and the four regions the variation by size of place in the dependency ratio, here defined as the number of persons in the age intervals under 20 and 65 and over per 100 persons aged 20 to 64.

TABLE 7.—DEPENDENCY RATIO OF THE POPULATION BY SIZE OF PLACE, BY REGIONS (WITH COLOR FOR THE SOUTH): 1950

Size of place	United States	North-east	North Central	South		West
				White	Nonwhite	
Urbanized areas:						
3,000,000 or more.................	56	55	56	...	...	59
1,000,000 to 3,000,000...........	60	63	59	55	58	60
250,000 to 1,000,000.............	63	63	63	61	67	63
Under 250,000....................	66	64	67	64	72	70
Places outside urbanized areas:						
25,000 or more...................	69	68	68	66	76	71
10,000 to 25,000.................	71	68	73	71	81	70
2,500 to 10,000..................	78	71	79	76	89	80
1,000 to 2,500...................	84	77	87	83	98	84
Under 1,000 (incorporated).......	92	83	94	88	108	94
Other rural:						
Nonfarm..........................	89	80	88	93	109	83
Farm.............................	101	91	89	103	147	88

Source: See table 6.

The dependency ratio for the largest urbanized areas of the United States is 56 and rises regularly, proceeding down the size-of-place scale, to a value of 92 in the small villages. A similar gradient shows up for each of the regions, with the contrast between large and small places being even more marked for the nonwhite population of the South. The "other rural" category does not fit the gradient pattern perfectly, although the dependency ratios are higher for this category than for any of the urban size categories. In the United States as a whole, and in all the regions except the South, the "other rural-nonfarm" dependency ratio is slightly lower than that of the small villages.

In the Northeast and the South the "other rural-farm" dependency ratio is higher than that of any other size group, and it is second only to that of the small villages in the West and the North Central Region. For the United States as a whole the "other rural-farm" dependency ratio is 101, i.e., a third higher than that of the entire country (73), and nearly double the figure for the urbanized areas of 3 million inhabitants or more. Moreover, the burden of dependency in the farm population is increased by the fact that the income of persons in the productive ages is relatively low. (See chapter 9.)

Sex ratio by age

Differences in the sex ratio among residence groups are generally assumed to be due primarily to sex differentials in internal migration. If this is true, then it is advisable to study variations among residence groups in the sex ratios calculated for different age groups, since there is great variation in the rate of migration by age. There are two difficulties in the way of such a study. In the first place, the variation of the sex ratio by age in the foreign-born white and the Oriental population is greatly affected by change over time in the sex ratio of immigrants. This makes it difficult to interpret residence differentials in the pattern of sex ratios by age. Secondly, the pattern of sex ratios by age is very sensitive to errors in the enumeration of the population by age and sex, and there exist systematic errors of this kind in most census data.[2] The data for the native white population are least subject to these difficulties, and, apparently, have been improving in accuracy in recent censuses. Accordingly, the analysis here of sex ratios by age is restricted to the native white population.

Figure 9 shows the sex ratio of the native white population in urban, rural-nonfarm, and rural-farm areas, for each single year of age, through age 84. Analysis by single years of age is desirable, since the urban and rural sex ratios change very rapidly from one year of age to the next. The minor fluctuations in the ratios are not to be taken as significant, since they probably represent errors of reporting and other more or less random variations. However, the differences in the basic pattern of the sex ratios by age among the three residence groups emerge clearly. In the initial year of life the sex ratios of the three residence groups are practically identical. The rural-farm sex ratio rises gently to about age 13, and then very sharply to a peak value of 133 at age 19, while the urban sex ratio drops gently to age 14, and then sharply to a low of 84 at ages 19 and 20. The rural-nonfarm sex ratio is fairly steady to age 16, and then rises to a peak of 116 at age 19. After age 19, both the rural-farm and rural-nonfarm sex ratios drop sharply. The rural-farm sex ratio reaches a minimum

---

[2] J. Yerushalmy, "The Age-Sex Composition of the Population Resulting from Natality and Mortality Conditions," *Milbank Memorial Fund Quarterly 21*, January 1943, 37–63; Population Division, United Nations, "Accuracy Tests for Census Age Distributions Tabulated in Five-Year and Ten-Year Groups," *Population Bulletin 2*, October 1952, pp. 59–79.

FIGURE **9.**—SEX RATIO BY SINGLE YEARS OF AGE, FOR THE NATIVE WHITE POPULATION OF THE UNITED STATES, URBAN AND RURAL: 1950

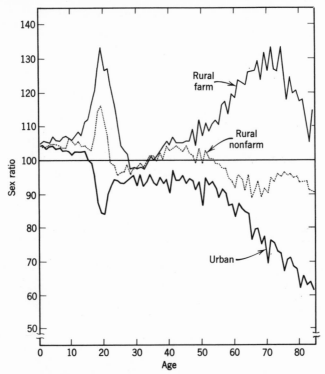

Source: *1950 Census of Population*, Vol. II, *Characteristics of the Population*, Part 1, U. S. Summary, table 94.

of about 98 for ages 28 to 32, and then rises to a second peak of about 130 for ages 69 to 74 before commencing a decline for the later years of life. The rural-nonfarm sex ratio drops from the peak at 19 to a low of about 96 for ages 24 to 26, then rises slightly to about 104 for ages 39 to 45 before beginning a decline for the later years. The urban sex ratio, after reaching a low value of 84 at ages 19 and 20, rises sharply to high values fluctuating around 94 for ages 23 to 53, and then begins a marked decline through the later years. The sex ratios for ages 85 and over are not shown on the graph, because of the pronounced year-to-year fluctuations at these ages. For the entire native white population aged 85 and over the sex ratio is 98.8 in rural-farm areas, 78.2 in rural-nonfarm areas, and 54.1 in urban areas, indicating that the pattern of declining sex ratios, for ages prior to 85, is continued beyond that point as well.

The rural-nonfarm sex ratio is considerably affected by the presence of disproportionate numbers of Armed Forces in rural-nonfarm areas. The civilian sex ratios for the total (native plus foreign-born) white rural-non-

farm population do not have a peak at age 19.   Rather, they decline from
a value of 103 at age 16 to a low of 82 at age 20, and then rise to around 90
for ages 23 and 24.   Their pattern is, therefore, similar to that of the urban
population, rather than to the rural-farm population, in the late teen and
early adult years.

To explain the variation in the pattern of sex ratios by age among the
residence groups in terms of migration differentials, one must hypothesize
several kinds of residential mobility.   The slight rise in the rural-farm sex
ratio and compensating decline in the urban sex ratio for the early years
of life may signify an excess movement of young females from farms to
cities, and/or possibly an excess movement of young males from cities to
farms.   The sharp rise in the rural-farm sex ratio from ages 13 to 19, and
correlative declines in the urban and civilian rural-nonfarm sex ratios,
must mean that there is a heavy excess of females in the urbanward movement of teenagers.   However, a compensation for this is an equally heavy
excess of males in the urbanward movement of young people in their
twenties, so that around the age of 30 the sex ratios of the three residence
groups are practically equal.   After the age of 30 the familiar female
excess in the urbanward movement reappears, although it may well be,
too, that the rising rural-farm sex ratio arises partly from an excess of
males in the movement from urban to rural areas.   The rapid decline in
the sex ratio for all residence groups in the later years is, of course, due
to the mortality rates highly favorable to females at these, as well as
earlier, ages.   Evidently, to account completely for the observed variations
in the sex ratio will require a more detailed age classification than is
ordinarily available for mobility statistics.

Unfortunately, the census data permit one to compute sex ratios of the
native white population for only broad age intervals by the detailed size-of-
place classification.   Table 8 shows the sex ratios for five age groups, by

TABLE **8.**—SEX RATIO OF THE NATIVE WHITE POPULATION BY AGE, BY SIZE OF PLACE: 1950

Size of place	Total	Age (years)				
		Under 14	14 to 24	25 to 44	45 to 64	65 and over
Urbanized areas:						
3,000,000 or more............	93.4	104.1	93.6	91.5	91.4	67.3
1,000,000 to 3,000,000..........	93.7	101.0	94.9	94.1	91.5	68.4
250,000 to 1,000,000..........	93.8	103.5	94.1	93.9	90.6	71.2
Under 250,000...................	93.7	103.4	90.5	94.2	91.5	73.1
Places outside urbanized areas:						
25,000 or more.................	93.8	101.6	95.3	96.1	88.9	71.9
10,000 to 25,000...............	92.9	102.8	90.7	94.3	88.7	74.2
2,500 to 10,000...............	93.1	103.0	89.2	95.3	88.3	76.7
1,000 to 2,500................	94.3	103.2	90.2	96.7	89.3	80.3
Under 1,000 (incorporated).....	93.6	101.2	94.6	93.9	86.5	88.5
Other rural:						
Nonfarm........................	105.4	105.7	112.0	102.3	105.2	101.5
Farm...........................	110.1	106.7	119.5	102.3	113.2	124.5

Source: *1950 Census of Population*, Vol. IV, *Special Reports*, Part 5, Chapter A, Characteristics by Size
of Place, table 1.

size of place. This material indicates that there is relatively little significant variation among different-sized urban places in the pattern of sex ratios by age, and that the village patterns much more closely resemble those of the urban areas than those of the "other rural" areas. The "other rural" nonfarm and farm sex ratios have distinctive patterns, as indicated in the description of figure 9. Significantly, there is a strong and regular upward gradient in the sex ratio of the population aged 65 and over, going from a low of 67 males per 100 females, for the urbanized areas of 3 million or more, to a high figure of 124 for the "other rural-farm" areas. Though variations in the mortality differential of the sexes possibly account for this tendency, it more probably indicates a movement of females of advanced age toward large cities and of males aged 65 and over toward small towns and rural areas.

Historical note

There is a well-known difference between urban and rural areas in the sex ratio. For example, in 1950 the sex ratio of the total urban population was 94.6, as compared to 103.6 for the total rural-nonfarm population, and 110.1 for the total rural-farm population. This long standing difference has suggested the hypothesis that the sex ratio is inversely related to size of place, within the urban category. However, several earlier investigations of the subject have failed to reveal such a relationship. The 1940 data, classified by size of city, show that the highest sex ratios were found in the largest cities: 97.7 for the cities of 1 million or more, and 96.4 for cities of 500,000 to 1 million. The next highest sex ratios occurred for the smallest cities: 95.8 and 95.5, respectively, for cities of 2,500 to 10,000 and 10,000 to 25,000. For the four intermediate city-size groups, the sex ratios varied between 93.3 and 95.4.[3]

Differentials in median age by city size similar to those noted in this study have been observed at earlier dates. In 1910 the median age was 25.9 for cities of 500,000 or more; 27.0 for cities of 100,000 to 500,000; 26.4 for cities of 25,000 to 100,000; and 26.1 for cities of 2,500 to 25,000. In 1930 the medians were 29.0, 29.0, 28.5, and 27.8 for the same size groups.[4] In 1940 the median age was 31.8 for cities of 100,000 or more; 30.5 for urban places of 10,000 to 100,000; and 29.5 for urban places of 2,500 to 10,000. The same sort of differential held consistently for both males and females, in the white and nonwhite population, classified by regions, although the magnitude of the differences by city size

---

[3] U. S. Bureau of the Census, *Cities Supplement—Statistical Abstract of the United States*, September 1944, table 4. For a more detailed treatment, see Joseph H. Greenberg, *Numerical Sex Disproportion*, University of Colorado Press, Boulder, 1950, Chapter 2. For data for earlier years, see William F. Ogburn, *Social Characteristics of Cities*, International City Managers' Association, Chicago, 1937, Chapter 1; and Warren S. Thompson and P. K. Whelpton, *Population Trends in the United States*, McGraw-Hill, New York, 1933, table 52.

[4] Computed from age distributions given by Thompson and Whelpton, *op. cit.*, table 34.

varied from one group to another.[5]   It appears, therefore, that the differences among city-size groups have become more marked in recent decades and more clearly related to city size.

The present gradient of fertility ratios by size of place represents the persistence of a long-standing tendency for inhabitants of large population centers to have lower fertility than those of small centers.   In 1940 cities of 1 million or more had a crude birth rate of 14.8 as compared to the rate of 19.0 births per 1,000 population in urban places under 25,000, with a steady gradient between these extremes for the places of intermediate sizes.[6]   Ogburn's data for 1930 show an increase in the birth rate from 18 to 25 per 1,000 going from places over 1 million to those between 10,000 and 25,000.[7]   Fertility ratios computed by Thompson and Whelpton show a city-size gradient appearing definitely in 1930, though somewhat obscured in earlier years by the presence of disproportionate numbers of foreign born in the largest cities.[8]   A marked urban-rural differential in fertility has, of course, been observed in every period for which the data are available.

Note on sampling variation and bias of the sex ratio

It seems unlikely that sampling variation distorts appreciably the comparisons of the sex ratios of the size-of-place groups for the United States, since each computed sex ratio has a base of 4 million persons or more. With a base of 5 million persons and a true sex ratio of 100.0, according to sampling theory two out of three 3⅓-percent samples would have sex ratios between 99.6 and 100.4, and 95 out of 100 samples would have sex ratios varying only between 99.2 and 100.8.

However, the 3⅓-percent sample tabulation is known to be biased toward the inclusion of somewhat too many females and too few males. It should be noted that the sex ratio tends to be sensitive to the sample bias, since the numerator is underestimated and the denominator overestimated.   The sex ratio for the entire United States from the sample count is 97.6 as compared with 98.6 from the complete count.   This is too large a difference to be accounted for readily by sampling variability.   In each of the regions the sex ratio from the sample count is approximately one point below that from the complete count, the error varying from −0.8 in the sex ratio for the South to −1.2 in the sex ratio for the North Central Region.   By area of residence, the greatest error is for the rural-nonfarm population.   The errors are −0.8 for the urban, −2.0 for the rural-nonfarm, and −0.7 for the rural-farm population.   The absolute errors in the

---

[5] U. S. Bureau of the Census, "Age, Color, and Sex Composition of the Population in Urban Places Classified by Size and in Rural Areas, for the United States by Regions: 1940," *Population*, Series P–10, No. 21, March 5, 1943, table 1.

[6] *Cities Supplement—Statistical Abstract of the United States, op. cit.*, table 4.

[7] Ogburn, *Social Characteristics of Cities, op. cit.*, p. 2.

[8] *Population Trends in the United States, op. cit.*, table 78.

sex ratios computed from the 3⅓-percent sample, by region and area of residence, are as follows:

	All areas	Urban	Rural nonfarm	Rural farm
Northeast	−1.1	−0.7	−3.0	−1.7
North Central.	−1.2	−0.9	−2.4	−1.2
South.	−0.8	−0.8	−1.4	−0.2
West	−1.0	−1.2	−0.4	−0.8

Unfortunately it requires too laborious a computation to determine whether the error in the sex ratio for the rural-nonfarm population occurs differentially for the village and "other rural" parts. However, some allowance for the bias in the sex ratio of one or both these groups should be made in interpreting the size-of-place data.

For breakdowns of the population by other characteristics such as age or race-nativity (except for native white) it seems likely on the whole that sampling variability is a more important source of error in the comparisons of size-of-place groups (particularly, within-region comparisons) than is the bias of the sample toward females. There is a slight age bias in the sample, in that persons under 14 years old are overrepresented; but the bias is in the same direction for the two sexes.

CHAPTER 4

RACE AND NATIVITY COMPOSITION

The historical tendencies which have led to a differentiation among size-of-place groups in race-nativity composition are well known and need be reviewed only briefly. The immigrants to this country, particularly the later waves, have settled and remained predominantly in the larger cities. The Negro population has historically been concentrated in the rural South, but in recent decades has rapidly become more urban, both in the South itself, and by movement to the urban centers of the North and West. The Indian population has always been a predominantly rural group, while some groups of Oriental extraction have tended to live in urban areas.

Race-nativity distribution

Table 9 shows the percentage distribution of the population in each size-of-place group by four race-nativity categories. The native white population, of course, constitutes a large majority in each size of place. However, in the largest urbanized areas only three-quarters of the population is native white, as compared with nine-tenths in the small villages (under 1,000), which have the highest proportion of native white population. The proportion of the population classified as foreign-born white is directly related to size of place, ranging from over 16 percent in the largest urbanized areas to about 2 percent in the "other rural-farm" population. The next to largest proportion of Negro population, 12 percent, is in urbanized areas of 1 to 3 million inhabitants, and diminishes to about 5 percent going down the size scale to the small villages. The largest proportion of Negroes is 13.8 percent, for the "other rural-farm" population.

Since there is considerable diversity among the four regions in race-nativity composition, size-of-place differences are somewhat clarified by examining them within each region. (See table 10.) The high proportion of Negroes in the "other rural-farm" population is entirely due to the situation in the South, since in each of the other three regions Negroes comprise less than 1 percent of the population in this size category. The largest urbanized areas in the country as a whole have a smaller proportion of Negroes than do the next five size-of-place categories, primarily because there is no urbanized area of over 3 million inhabitants in the South. In the other three regions the urbanized areas of 3 million or more have larger percentages of Negroes than any size-of-place group except urbanized areas

TABLE **9.**—PERCENT DISTRIBUTION OF THE POPULATION BY RACE AND NATIVITY, BY SIZE OF PLACE: 1950

Size of place	All classes	White		Negro	Other races
		Native	Foreign born		
Urbanized areas:					
3,000,000 or more.................	100.0	74.7	16.4	8.4	0.5
1,000,000 to 3,000,000...........	100.0	76.9	10.7	12.0	0.4
250,000 to 1,000,000.............	100.0	82.4	6.3	11.1	0.2
Under 250,000....................	100.0	83.5	6.6	9.7	0.2
Places outside urbanized areas:					
25,000 or more..................	100.0	85.7	5.1	9.0	0.2
10,000 to 25,000.................	100.0	86.7	4.5	8.6	0.2
2,500 to 10,000.................	100.0	87.5	3.9	8.3	0.3
1,000 to 2,500..................	100.0	88.9	3.8	7.0	0.3
Under 1,000 (incorporated).......	100.0	91.6	3.0	5.2	0.2
Other rural:					
Nonfarm.........................	100.0	86.6	3.6	8.9	0.9
Farm............................	100.0	83.1	2.3	13.8	0.8

Source: *1950 Census of Population*, Vol. IV, *Special Reports*, Part 5, Chapter A, Characteristics by Size of Place, table 1.

of 1 to 3 million. In each of the regions there is a general tendency for the proportion native white to be inversely related and both the proportion foreign-born white and the proportion Negro to be directly related to size of place. The principal exception is the high percentage of Negroes in the "other rural-farm" population of the South. The small villages have the largest percentage native white, except in the North Central Region, where the figure for the "other rural-farm" population is slightly higher. In the South the population of these villages is 83 percent native white, and it is 95 percent native white in each of the other regions.

Only in the West does any size-of-place group have an "other races" population exceeding 1 percent of the total. There, the urbanized areas and the "other rural" categories exhibit this feature. Doubtless the main components are the population of Oriental extraction in the large centers, and the Indian population in the "other rural" areas.

Urbanization of race-nativity groups

Table 11 presents, for summary purposes, an index of urbanization for each of the three race-nativity groups other than native white, whose distribution is taken as a standard against which the urbanization of the other groups is measured. The procedure followed in calculating the urbanization index may be indicated by reference to figure 10. To construct the curves shown in this figure the cumulative percentage of the foreign-born white population is plotted against the corresponding cumulative percentage of the native white population, the cumulation being from the largest to the smallest size-of-place groups, through the "other rural" nonfarm and farm categories. A similar plot is made for the Negro and other nonwhite groups. The disproportionate share of the foreign-born white population held by large urban centers is indicated by the bowing of the curve

TABLE **10.**—PERCENT DISTRIBUTION OF THE POPULATION BY RACE AND NATIVITY, BY SIZE OF PLACE AND REGIONS: 1950

Region and size of place	All classes	White		Negro	Other races
		Native	Foreign born		
NORTHEAST					
Urbanized areas:					
3,000,000 or more................	100.0	72.0	19.7	8.0	0.3
1,000,000 to 3,000,000............	100.0	78.7	12.2	9.0	0.1
250,000 to 1,000,000.............	100.0	84.5	12.6	2.8	0.1
Under 250,000....................	100.0	84.8	12.3	2.9	...
Places outside urbanized areas:					
25,000 or more...................	100.0	87.0	11.0	2.0	...
10,000 to 25,000.................	100.0	88.0	9.5	2.5	...
2,500 to 10,000..................	100.0	90.0	8.4	1.6	...
1,000 to 2,500...................	100.0	90.9	7.6	1.4	0.1
Under 1,000 (incorporated).......	100.0	94.7	4.6	0.7	...
Other rural:					
Nonfarm..........................	100.0	90.9	7.1	1.8	0.2
Farm.............................	100.0	92.5	6.7	0.7	0.1
NORTH CENTRAL					
Urbanized areas:					
3,000,000 or more................	100.0	74.5	13.3	11.8	0.4
1,000,000 to 3,000,000............	100.0	75.7	11.3	12.9	0.1
250,000 to 1,000,000.............	100.0	86.2	5.9	7.8	0.1
Under 250,000....................	100.0	90.6	5.1	4.2	0.1
Places outside urbanized areas:					
25,000 or more...................	100.0	92.0	4.5	3.4	0.1
10,000 to 25,000.................	100.0	93.9	3.4	2.6	0.1
2,500 to 10,000..................	100.0	94.9	3.7	1.3	0.1
1,000 to 2,500...................	100.0	95.1	3.9	0.8	0.2
Under 1,000 (incorporated).......	100.0	95.5	3.9	0.4	0.2
Other rural:					
Nonfarm..........................	100.0	93.6	3.9	1.6	0.9
Farm.............................	100.0	96.2	3.0	0.5	0.3
SOUTH					
Urbanized areas:					
3,000,000 or more................	...	...	...	...	...
1,000,000 to 3,000,000............	100.0	72.8	4.8	22.2	0.2
250,000 to 1,000,000.............	100.0	75.8	2.7	21.4	0.1
Under 250,000....................	100.0	74.8	2.5	22.6	0.1
Places outside urbanized areas:					
25,000 or more...................	100.0	76.3	2.0	21.6	0.1
10,000 to 25,000.................	100.0	77.4	1.6	20.8	0.2
2,500 to 10,000..................	100.0	78.9	1.3	19.6	0.2
1,000 to 2,500...................	100.0	80.9	1.0	18.0	0.1
Under 1,000 (incorporated).......	100.0	82.9	0.6	16.2	0.3
Other rural:					
Nonfarm..........................	100.0	80.1	1.0	18.6	0.3
Farm.............................	100.0	72.8	0.6	26.1	0.5
WEST					
Urbanized areas:					
3,000,000 or more................	100.0	83.0	10.3	5.4	1.3
1,000,000 to 3,000,000............	100.0	79.2	11.1	6.8	2.9
250,000 to 1,000,000.............	100.0	88.3	7.8	2.8	1.1
Under 250,000....................	100.0	88.1	7.7	2.7	1.5
Places outside urbanized areas:					
25,000 or more...................	100.0	90.9	6.2	2.2	0.7
10,000 to 25,000.................	100.0	91.6	6.2	1.5	0.7
2,500 to 10,000..................	100.0	92.7	5.6	0.8	0.9
1,000 to 2,500...................	100.0	92.3	6.0	0.5	1.2
Under 1,000 (incorporated).......	100.0	95.0	4.1	0.5	0.4
Other rural:					
Nonfarm..........................	100.0	89.3	5.4	1.4	3.9
Farm.............................	100.0	87.7	6.5	0.5	5.3

Source: *1950 Census of Population*, Vol. IV, *Special Reports*, Part 5, Chapter A, Characteristics by Size of Place, table 6.

FIGURE 10.—URBANIZATION CURVES FOR FOREIGN-BORN WHITE, NEGRO, AND OTHER RACES,
IN COMPARISON WITH NATIVE WHITE: 1950

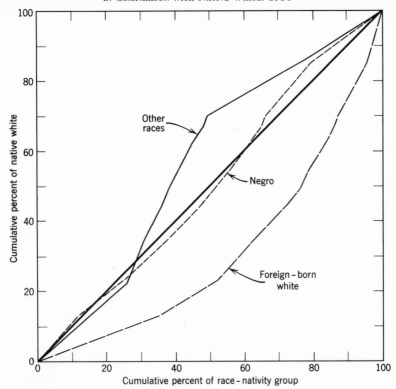

Note: See table 9.

below the diagonal of the figure. The other nonwhite population is shown
to be less urbanized than the native white by the rising of its curve above
the diagonal. The summary index of urbanization is the area contained
on the graph between the curve and the diagonal, as a proportion of the
entire area below the diagonal, under the convention that the area above
the diagonal is negative in algebraic sign. The computation is made
according to the formula,

$$\text{Index of Urbanization} = \sum_{1}^{11} X_{i-1} Y_i - \sum_{1}^{11} X_i Y_{i-1},$$

where there are 11 size-of-place groups; X_i is the cumulative proportion,
through the ith size-of-place group, of the race-nativity group whose urbanization is being measured; and Y_i is the corresponding proportion of the
native white population.[1] The index theoretically can vary from -1.00
(least possible urbanization) to $+1.00$ (greatest possible urbanization).

---

[1] This type of urbanization index is discussed in Otis Dudley Duncan, "Urbanization and Retail
Specialization," *Social Forces 30*, March 1952, 267–271; and Leo A. Goodman, "On Urbanization
Indices," *ibid. 31*, May 1953, 360–362.

TABLE 11.—INDEX OF URBANIZATION OF THE FOREIGN-BORN WHITE, NEGRO, AND OTHER NON-
WHITE POPULATION, RELATIVE TO THE NATIVE WHITE POPULATION, BY REGIONS: 1950

[See text for method of computing index]

Region	Foreign-born white	Negro	Other races
United States...............	[1]0.38	-0.01	-0.14
Northeast.......................	0.25	0.37	0.23
North Central...................	0.34	0.54	-0.12
South..........................	0.34	-0.03	-0.28
West...........................	0.16	0.40	-0.22

[1] This figure is higher than for any region because the South, which has the lowest proportion of foreign-born white population, has no urbanized area of 3,000,000 or more, whereas the foreign-born white population is concentrated in centers of this size in the other regions.

Source: *1950 Census of Population*, Vol. IV, *Special Reports*, Part 5, Chapter A, Characteristics by Size of Place, tables 1 and 6.

In the United States as a whole the foreign-born white population is considerably urbanized, compared with the native white population, while the Negro population is very slightly, and the other nonwhite population considerably less urbanized than native whites.   There are important variations by region.   Whereas foreign-born whites are urbanized in all regions they are rather more so in the North Central and the South than in the Northeast and the West, relative to the native white population in each of the respective regions.   The Negro population is rather highly urbanized in each of the regions, except the South, where it has an urbanization index which is negative, but nearly zero.   The other nonwhite population is more highly urbanized than the native white only in the Northeast, where it is comprised of Orientals primarily.   This population has moderately large negative urbanization indexes in each of the other regions, where it includes a substantial proportion of American Indians.

Age distribution of race-nativity groups

Table 12 shows a percentage distribution by five age intervals for each of the race-nativity groups, in each of the 11 size-of-place categories.   The size-of-place differentials for the native white population are somewhat similar to those already noted in Chapter 3 for the total population and need not be described again.   The foreign-born white population is, of course, much older than the native white population, the respective median ages being about 56 and 29 years for the country as a whole in 1950.   However, the size-of-place variation in the proportion aged 65 and over for the foreign-born resembles that for the native white population.   There is a striking increase in the percentage aged 65 and over, in going from the largest urbanized areas to the small villages.   Whereas less than a quarter of the foreign-born white population in the former size group is as old as 65, nearly half of the foreign-born whites in small villages are 65 or older. There is an opposite size-of-place gradient in the proportion aged 45 to 64, from 51.5 percent in the urbanized areas of 3 million or more to 35.6 percent in the villages of less than 1,000.   The "other rural" groups, non-

TABLE **12.**—PERCENT DISTRIBUTION OF THE POPULATION BY AGE, BY RACE AND NATIVITY,
BY SIZE OF PLACE: 1950

Size of place, race, and nativity	Total	Age (years)				
		Under 14	14 to 24	25 to 44	45 to 64	65 and over
NATIVE WHITE						
Urbanized areas:						
3,000,000 or more..............	100.0	25.3	16.3	35.2	18.1	5.1
1,000,000 to 3,000,000.........	100.0	25.4	16.4	33.9	18.5	5.8
250,000 to 1,000,000...........	100.0	24.6	16.4	32.9	19.5	6.6
Under 250,000.................	100.0	25.3	16.9	32.4	18.7	6.7
Places outside urbanized areas:						
25,000 or more................	100.0	24.6	18.3	30.8	18.9	7.4
10,000 to 25,000..............	100.0	25.1	17.7	30.7	18.6	7.9
2,500 to 10,000...............	100.0	26.4	17.1	29.7	18.4	8.4
1,000 to 2,500................	100.0	27.3	16.2	28.6	18.6	9.3
Under 1,000 (incorporated).....	100.0	26.3	15.1	25.7	20.4	12.5
Other rural:						
Nonfarm.......................	100.0	31.2	17.5	29.5	15.4	6.4
Farm..........................	100.0	30.6	17.3	25.4	19.6	7.1
FOREIGN-BORN WHITE						
Urbanized areas:						
3,000,000 or more..............	100.0	1.4	2.9	21.6	51.5	22.6
1,000,000 to 3,000,000.........	100.0	1.3	2.8	19.9	51.3	24.7
250,000 to 1,000,000...........	100.0	1.5	2.9	18.7	48.6	28.3
Under 250,000.................	100.0	1.6	2.7	17.9	49.1	28.7
Places outside urbanized areas:						
25,000 or more................	100.0	1.9	3.7	18.7	45.3	30.4
10,000 to 25,000..............	100.0	1.9	4.0	18.9	45.4	29.8
2,500 to 10,000...............	100.0	2.2	3.4	19.1	42.6	32.7
1,000 to 2,500................	100.0	1.7	3.1	16.3	41.9	37.0
Under 1,000 (incorporated).....	100.0	1.7	2.1	10.8	35.6	49.8
Other rural:						
Nonfarm.......................	100.0	3.1	4.1	20.3	43.5	29.0
Farm..........................	100.0	3.3	4.3	17.3	44.7	30.4
NEGRO						
Urbanized areas:						
3,000,000 or more..............	100.0	23.4	16.4	38.3	17.8	4.1
1,000,000 to 3,000,000.........	100.0	25.5	16.3	35.8	18.2	4.2
250,000 to 1,000,000...........	100.0	25.8	16.7	33.6	18.5	5.4
Under 250,000.................	100.0	27.4	17.4	32.5	17.3	5.4
Places outside urbanized areas:						
25,000 or more................	100.0	27.3	17.8	31.0	17.8	6.1
10,000 to 25,000..............	100.0	28.0	17.6	30.1	17.4	6.9
2,500 to 10,000...............	100.0	29.6	17.8	27.8	17.4	7.4
1,000 to 2,500................	100.0	30.9	17.7	26.7	16.8	7.9
Under 1,000 (incorporated).....	100.0	32.0	17.6	24.1	16.9	9.4
Other rural:						
Nonfarm.......................	100.0	33.2	19.6	26.2	14.1	6.9
Farm..........................	100.0	39.7	20.4	20.5	13.5	5.9
OTHER RACES						
Urbanized areas:						
3,000,000 or more..............	100.0	20.9	17.1	35.1	22.2	4.7
1,000,000 to 3,000,000.........	100.0	22.0	18.7	34.2	20.5	4.6
250,000 to 1,000,000...........	100.0	23.1	19.8	34.5	17.2	5.4
Under 250,000.................	100.0	27.8	18.4	32.6	16.5	4.7
Places outside urbanized areas:						
25,000 or more................	100.0	25.2	28.1	29.8	12.9	4.0
10,000 to 25,000..............	100.0	28.5	21.9	29.8	15.9	3.9
2,500 to 10,000...............	100.0	35.5	19.5	27.0	12.7	5.3
1,000 to 2,500................	100.0	34.8	18.5	26.3	15.0	5.4
Under 1,000 (incorporated).....	100.0	37.0	19.4	21.7	15.2	6.7
Other rural:						
Nonfarm.......................	100.0	39.0	20.7	22.4	12.0	5.9
Farm..........................	100.0	36.3	20.2	23.5	14.4	5.6

Source: *1950 Census of Population*, Vol. IV, *Special Reports*, Part 5, Chapter A, Characteristics by Size of Place, table 1.

farm and farm, have proportions in these two age intervals intermediate between the extremes represented by the large urban centers and the villages.

The Negro population, which is 2½ years younger than the native white in terms of medians for the country as a whole, has a somewhat similar pattern of size-of-place differentials. However, the rise in the proportion of young Negro people, from the large urban places to the rural areas, is much more marked and steady than for the native white population. In the urbanized areas of 3 million or more only two-fifths of the Negroes are under 25, while three-fifths are under 25 in the "other rural-farm" population, with a regular gradient between these extremes. As is the case for the native white population, the proportion of Negroes over 65 in the small villages is more than twice as great as in the large urbanized areas, and substantially greater than the proportion of aged persons in the "other rural" areas.

The age distributions for the nonwhite population other than Negroes vary somewhat erratically from one size of place to the next, but nevertheless exhibit gradients of the kind already mentioned: an increase in both the proportions under 25 and 65 and over between the largest urban centers and the rural areas.

One may conclude that the forces producing a differentiation of size-of-place groups in terms of age structure operate in somewhat the same way for all race-nativity groups, despite the marked differences among these groups in average age and regional and size-of-place distribution.

Sex ratios of race-nativity groups

Table 13 presents sex ratios by size of place and region for the four race-nativity groups. The size-of-place classification is condensed in order to minimize fluctuations in the sex ratio due to small numbers of cases.

For the native white, as for the total population, a size-of-place gradient within the urban and village categories appears only in the West, where the sex ratio is inversely related to size of place. The foreign-born white population of the West also shows an increasing sex ratio with decreasing size of place, but this pattern is not evident in the other regions, if the high sex ratios of the "other rural" nonfarm and farm groups are disregarded.

In the South, which contains over two-thirds of the Negro population, there is no indication of a size-of-place gradient in the Negro sex ratio, except that the "other rural" sex ratios considerably exceed those of all the urban and village groups. However, in each of the other three regions the urbanized areas have distinctly lower sex ratios than the other urban places and villages. The opposite tendency appears for the other nonwhite races. In their case, the greatest excesses of males appear in urbanized areas, where males outnumber females by nearly 3 to 2 in the country as a whole. In each of the regions the sex ratio of the other nonwhite

TABLE **13.**—SEX RATIO OF THE POPULATION BY RACE AND NATIVITY, BY SIZE OF PLACE
(CONDENSED CLASSIFICATION) AND REGIONS: 1950

Region, race, and nativity	All places	Urbanized areas	Other urban places	Villages	Other rural	
					Nonfarm	Farm
United States.........	97.6	94.0	93.2	94.1	105.7	109.5
Native white................	97.6	93.6	93.2	94.0	105.4	110.1
Foreign-born white...........	102.2	99.1	100.4	103.7	115.2	136.1
Negro......................	93.8	89.8	88.9	89.7	104.2	101.8
Other races................	127.7	148.8	129.2	117.6	112.9	117.9
Northeast................	95.0	93.5	92.9	92.8	101.4	110.6
Native white................	94.9	93.3	92.2	92.8	101.0	110.4
Foreign-born white...........	96.5	96.1	96.3	89.7	99.7	113.0
Negro......................	90.5	87.8	104.3	108.6	131.5	124.9
Other races................	176.6	202.7	163.9	110.7	114.2	129.2
North Central............	98.3	95.1	93.0	93.4	106.3	112.9
Native white................	97.7	94.0	92.4	92.9	105.0	112.3
Foreign-born white...........	109.2	106.8	102.7	105.3	125.0	132.7
Negro......................	95.9	93.4	100.6	98.0	154.5	110.3
Other races................	120.2	144.2	131.6	120.8	102.9	111.1
South....................	97.7	92.4	91.7	92.7	104.1	106.2
Native white................	98.8	93.5	93.0	93.5	104.8	107.7
Foreign-born white...........	104.0	97.7	94.9	104.7	121.7	144.0
Negro......................	93.6	88.0	86.7	88.7	100.0	101.5
Other races................	110.3	136.3	104.0	92.0	117.4	103.3
West.....................	101.1	95.1	98.0	103.2	117.7	116.9
Native white................	99.8	93.9	96.9	101.6	115.9	113.3
Foreign-born white...........	109.5	98.7	109.7	128.4	139.8	165.5
Negro......................	101.7	95.6	103.2	112.1	177.5	128.8
Other races................	128.6	139.5	139.5	131.7	115.1	128.0

Source: *1950 Census of Population*, Vol. IV, *Special Reports*, Part 5, Chapter A, Characteristics by Size of Place, tables 1 and 6.

races varies directly with size of place in the urban-village range, and this race group furnishes an exception to the general rule that the "other rural" nonfarm and farm sex ratios exceed those of any urban or village group. This relationship doubtless reflects the urbanization of the nonwhites of Oriental extraction, with their heavy excess of males, and the concentration in rural areas of the American Indians, with their more normal sex ratio. An examination of sex ratios by age (not shown here) makes it clear that the pattern described for the other nonwhite population is largely due to the imbalance in the sex composition at the higher ages.

Historical note

Thompson and Whelpton [2] give race-nativity distributions by city-size groups and for the rural-nonfarm and rural-farm population in 1920 and 1930 which permit the computation of urbanization indexes for each of four race-nativity groups, relative to the native white population of native parentage. The indexes for 1920 and 1930, respectively, are 0.27 and 0.26 for the native white population of mixed parentage; 0.41 and 0.40

---

[2] Warren S. Thompson and P. K. Whelpton, *Population Trends in the United States*, McGraw-Hill, New York, 1933, Chapter 2.

for native whites of foreign parentage; 0.47 and 0.47 for foreign-born whites; and −0.12 and −0.05 for Negroes.   These data indicate that the relative urbanization of the race-nativity groups 20 and 30 years ago formed a pattern similar to the present one, and reveal the increasing urbanization of the Negro population.   It is interesting that the native white groups of foreign and of mixed parentage were intermediate between foreign-born whites and native whites of native parentage in degree of urbanization.

C H A P T E R   5

MARITAL STATUS AND FAMILY
CHARACTERISTICS

Age at marriage

There are no data available to measure directly differentials in age at
marriage among the size-of-place groups. An approximation to the median
age at first marriage can be made from census data giving the distribution
of the population by marital status, by single years of age. However, the
necessary age data are available only for the urban, rural-nonfarm, and
rural-farm population, and not for the detailed size-of-place groups. Table
14 shows estimated median ages at first marriage by color, sex, and area
of residence, for 1950. The method of computing these medians was to
find the age at which the percentage of the population ever married was
exactly one-half of the corresponding percentage for the population aged
45 to 64. The assumption of this method is that a cross section of the
population by age and marital status at a given point in time may be taken
to represent the experience of an age cohort over a period of time.

The differences among urban, rural-nonfarm, and rural-farm areas in
median age at first marriage are insignificant for the nonwhite population.
For white males, the rural-nonfarm median is lower than the urban median
by eight-tenths of a year and lower than the rural-farm median by a full
year. For white females, the rural-nonfarm median is lower than the
rural-farm median by only three-tenths of a year, but falls below the urban
median by 1.3 years. Thus, while for males the urban and rural-farm medians differ only slightly, there is nearly a year's difference in the median
age at first marriage of urban and rural-farm females. This pattern of
residence differences is rather similar to that holding in 1940, although
for all groups in the white population there was a considerable decline in
median age at first marriage between 1940 and 1950.[1] In both years the
urban and rural-farm medians for males were substantially higher than the
rural-nonfarm median; and the urban median was substantially higher than
the rural medians for females.

---

[1] U. S. Bureau of the Census, "Age at First Marriage," Wilson H. Grabill, *Population—Special Reports*, Series P–45, No. 7, May 28, 1945.

TABLE **14.**—ESTIMATED MEDIAN AGE AT FIRST MARRIAGE BY COLOR AND SEX, URBAN AND
RURAL: 1950

Area	Male			Female		
	Total	White	Nonwhite	Total	White	Nonwhite
United States..........	22.9	22.9	22.6	20.2	20.2	19.8
Urban......................	23.1	23.1	22.5	20.6	20.6	19.9
Rural nonfarm..............	22.4	22.3	22.8	19.3	19.3	19.5
Rural farm.................	23.2	23.3	22.5	19.7	19.6	19.8

Source: *1950 Census of Population,* Vol. II, *Characteristics of the Population,* Part 1, U. S. Summary,
table 104.

Marital status

Figure 11 shows the percentage distribution by marital status of the
males and females aged 14 and over for each size-of-place group. For
males the percentage of the population classified as married fluctuates between 67 and 70 for the first nine size-of-place groups, with little indication of a regular pattern; it then drops to 65 and 64 for the "other rural"
nonfarm and farm groups, respectively. The percentage single varies
irregularly between 24 and 26 for the urban and village groups. The
"other rural-nonfarm" and "other rural-farm" groups have somewhat
higher percentages, 29 and 31 respectively, classified as single. The percentage widowed is greatest in the small villages (under 1,000), with 5.5
percent, and least in the "other rural-farm" areas with 3.8 percent; the
remaining groups vary from 4.0 to 4.5, with little apparent relation to size
of place. The percentage classified as divorced is slightly higher in all of
the urban groups than in any of the rural groups; the largest value is 2.6
percent for the urbanized areas of 250,000 to 1 million. It is well to remember, of course, that the classifications, widowed and divorced, refer
only to current marital status, and do not include those who have been
widowed or divorced but are married again.

For females the relationship of the percentage married to size of place
is somewhat clearer than for males. The first six groups have percentages
of 63 to 64. The percentage rises to 65 for the smallest urban places, to
66 for the large villages and 67 for the small villages, and to 71 for both
the "other rural" nonfarm and farm groups. The percentage single is
somewhat higher for the urban places, with figures varying between 19
and 22, than for the villages and "other rural-nonfarm" groups, with percentages around 17 and 18. However, the "other rural-farm" females,
with 20.5 percent single, resemble the urban groups more closely in the
relative frequency of single persons than they do the remaining rural groups.
The percentage of females classified as widowed increases from around 12
and 13 for the urban groups to 14 for the large villages and 15 for the
small villages. The "other rural" percentages of widowed are much lower,
10 percent for the nonfarm and 8 percent for the farm population. The
percentage of females in the category of divorced persons is highest in the

size group 1 to 3 million, where the percentage is 3.5; thereafter it declines regularly with decreasing size of place, to less than 1 percent for "other rural-farm" females.

The variation in marital status composition for the nonwhite population by size of place differs in some respects from the pattern for the total population. However, it seems best to discuss these differences in connection with the treatment of marital status standardized for age.

FIGURE 11.—PERCENT DISTRIBUTION OF PERSONS 14 YEARS OLD AND OVER BY MARITAL STATUS, BY SEX AND SIZE OF PLACE: 1950

[See p. 32 for size-of-place code]

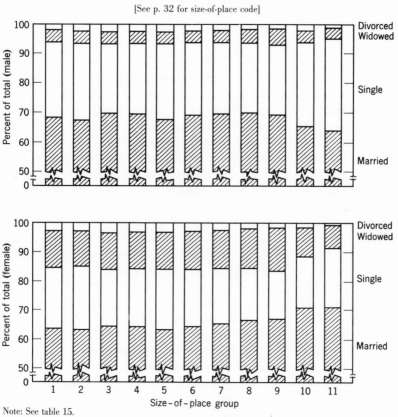

Note: See table 15.

Age-standardized comparisons of marital status

The interpretation of differences among size-of-place groups in marital status composition is somewhat equivocal, owing to the variation among them in age composition. For instance, the large urban centers would be expected to have a smaller proportion of their population classified as widowed than would the villages, simply because a smaller proportion falls in the age groups where widowhood is most frequent. A natural way to overcome this problem would be to examine the marital status distributions for different age groups.   However, the age control for the size-of-place tabulations involves only four broad age intervals: 14 to 24, 25 to 44, 45 to 64, and 65 and over.   This is an insufficient amount of detail for the purpose, because in the early adult years both the distribution by marital status and the rate of migration from rural to urban areas are changing very rapidly from one year of age to the next.   It is desirable, therefore, to use the most detailed age data available in order to hold constant variations in marital status due to age distribution in making size-of-place comparisons.

The method used to hold constant age is as follows.   For the United States as a whole there is available a classification of the population by detailed age groups and marital status.[2]   From these data the percentages single, married, widowed, and divorced were computed for each of the age intervals 14 to 19, 20 to 24, 25 to 34, 35 to 44, 45 to 54, 55 to 64, 65 to 74, and 75 and over, the computations being carried out separately for males and females.   Then, for each size-of-place group an "expected" number of persons in each marital status category was computed by applying the percentage distribution for a given age interval in the total population of the United States to the number of persons in that age interval in the specified size-of-place group, and summing the result over the eight age intervals.   The expected distribution was then converted to percentages by marital status in order to compare it with the actual distribution. For example, for white males in the urbanized areas of 3 million or more, the actual classification of the population aged 14 and over is 25.6 percent single, 68.3 percent married, 4.2 percent widowed, and 1.9 percent divorced; the corresponding percentages for the expected distribution are 23.0, 70.8, 4.1, and 2.1.   Hence, in this size-of-place group, there is an excess in the number of males classified as single, amounting to 2.6 percent of the total white males aged 14 and over (25.6 percent minus 23.0 percent), as compared with the number expected on the basis of the age-specific marital status distribution for the total male population 14 and over of the United States, and the age distribution of this size-of-place group.   Similarly, there is a deficit in the number of married persons of 2.5 percent of the total, an excess of 0.1 percent in the number of widowed, and a deficit of 0.2 percent in the number of divorced persons.

Table 15 shows the differences between the actual and "expected" marital status distributions, by color and sex, for each size-of-place group. In the white population, for both males and females, the general tendencies are for the departures of the actual from the expected distributions to be in the direction of excesses of single, widowed, and divorced persons, and deficits of married persons in the larger places, with the opposite holding for the smaller places.   There are some exceptions to these tendencies:

---

[2] *1950 Census of Population*, Vol. IV, *Special Reports*, Part 2, Chapter D, Marital Status, table 1.

"Other rural-farm" males have a 2-percent excess of single persons and the "other rural-nonfarm" males a less than 1-percent deficit of single persons, as compared with a 2-percent deficit for small urban places and large villages. The "other rural-nonfarm" males also have about the expected proportions of widowed and divorced persons, as compared with the deficits in these classifications of the adjacent size groups. Significantly, the size-of-place variation in the degree of departure of the actual from the expected distributions is greater for females than for males, although similar gradients hold for the two sexes, aside from the "other rural" categories. It is noteworthy, too, that the villages have deficits in the number of widowed persons as compared with the number of widowed expected on the basis of their age distribution.

For the nonwhites a fairly clear size-of-place gradient, of the type observed for whites, appears for the proportions married and divorced. The variation is irregular for the widowed. For males the first two size-of-place groups and the "other rural-nonfarm" group have excesses of single persons,

TABLE 15.—Percent Distribution of the Population by Marital Status, Color, and Sex, Expressed as Deviations from the Distribution Expected on the Basis of Their Age Composition, by Size of Place: 1950

[Persons 14 years old and over]

Size of place and color	Male				Female			
	Single	Married	Widowed	Divorced	Single	Married	Widowed	Divorced
WHITE								
Urbanized areas:								
3,000,000 or more................	2.6	-2.5	0.1	-0.2	3.8	-4.2	0.3	0.1
1,000,000 to 3,000,000..........	2.0	-2.4	0.2	0.2	4.0	-4.1	-0.2	0.3
250,000 to 1,000,000............	-1.0	0.5	-0.1	0.6	1.4	-2.6	0.3	0.9
Under 250,000....................	-1.3	1.0	-0.1	0.4	1.0	-1.8	0.1	0.7
Places outside urbanized areas:								
25,000 or more..................	-1.0	0.7	-0.2	0.5	1.2	-1.8	-0.1	0.7
10,000 to 25,000................	-1.6	1.9	-0.4	0.1	...	-0.7	0.3	0.4
2,500 to 10,000.................	-2.2	2.6	-0.4	...	-1.4	1.3	0.1	...
1,000 to 2,500.................	-2.2	3.1	-0.6	-0.3	-2.3	3.2	-0.5	-0.4
Under 1,000 (incorporated).......	-1.3	2.7	-1.0	-0.4	-2.8	4.9	-1.4	-0.7
Other rural:								
Nonfarm........................	-0.7	0.5	0.1	0.1	-4.0	6.2	-1.4	-0.8
Farm...........................	1.8	-0.2	-0.8	-0.8	-2.7	8.4	-4.0	-1.7
NONWHITE								
Urbanized areas:								
3,000,000 or more................	1.0	-3.3	2.1	0.2	1.0	-8.3	6.1	1.2
1,000,000 to 3,000,000..........	0.5	-2.8	2.2	0.1	-0.4	-6.1	5.6	0.9
250,000 to 1,000,000............	-2.7	-0.8	2.5	1.0	-3.5	-5.2	6.9	1.8
Under 250,000....................	-1.9	-1.0	2.7	0.2	-2.6	-6.4	8.2	0.8
Places outside urbanized areas:								
25,000 or more..................	-1.9	-0.6	2.3	0.2	-2.9	-5.1	7.2	0.8
10,000 to 25,000................	-1.7	-0.4	2.0	0.1	-2.9	-5.0	7.3	0.6
2,500 to 10,000.................	-1.8	-0.5	2.4	-0.1	-2.3	-5.7	7.8	0.2
1,000 to 2,500.................	-1.9	0.2	1.8	-0.1	-2.9	-3.6	7.0	-0.5
Under 1,000 (incorporated).......	-1.6	1.0	1.8	-1.2	-4.1	-2.3	6.6	-0.2
Other rural:								
Nonfarm........................	2.3	-3.9	2.1	-0.5	-2.2	-1.8	4.8	-0.8
Farm...........................	-2.2	3.0	0.3	-1.1	-2.7	3.2	1.0	-1.5

Source: *1950 Census of Population*, Vol. II, *Characteristics of the Population*, Part 1, U. S. Summary, table 104; Vol. IV, *Special Reports*, Part 5, Chapter A, Characteristics by Size of Place, tables 3 and 3a.

while the other size-of-place groups all have considerable deficits of single persons. As is the case for whites, the departures of the actual from the expected distributions are greater for females than for males. In other words, size-of-place variation in marital status composition is more pronounced for females than for males.

The excess of single persons among white males in "other rural-farm" areas is no doubt related to the high sex ratio of those areas, since there is no similar excess for females. However, in general, variation in marital status composition among size-of-place groups is not attributable to the sex ratio. The data suggest the possibility that first marriages take place at a later age in the larger urban places than in the smaller ones. They suggest also the possibility of higher rates of marital dissolution in the large urban centers. However, the marital status of the population is affected both by remarriage and by internal migration, and the frequency of widowed and divorced persons reflects only indirectly and imperfectly the rate of marital dissolution.

Separated persons

Table 16 shows for each size-of-place group, by color and sex, the percentage of married persons classified as separated, i.e., those living apart from their spouses with intentions of obtaining a divorce as well as those permanently or temporarily estranged from their spouses because of marital discord. This classification is subject to considerable response error, as is evident from the fact that the number of females reported as separated exceeds the number of males by over one-quarter in the white population and is more than 50 percent greater in the nonwhite population. Unfortunately there is no way to determine whether this error varies by size of place. However, the pattern of variation by size of place in the percentage separated is rather similar for males and females.

TABLE **16.**—SEPARATED PERSONS AS PERCENT OF MARRIED PERSONS BY COLOR AND SEX, BY SIZE OF PLACE: 1950

Size of place	Total		White		Nonwhite	
	Male	Female	Male	Female	Male	Female
Urbanized areas:						
3,000,000 or more..............	2.7	4.1	1.9	2.7	11.9	19.8
1,000,000 to 3,000,000.........	3.1	4.3	1.9	2.6	11.8	17.1
250,000 to 1,000,000...........	2.6	3.7	1.7	2.3	10.2	15.1
Under 250,000.................	2.5	3.6	1.7	2.4	10.7	15.4
Places outside urbanized areas:						
25,000 or more................	2.3	3.5	1.5	2.3	10.5	15.9
10,000 to 25,000..............	2.1	2.9	1.4	1.8	10.4	14.9
2,500 to 10,000...............	2.1	3.0	1.6	2.0	9.0	15.5
1,000 to 2,500................	2.0	2.4	1.6	1.7	8.3	12.4
Under 1,000 (incorporated).....	1.4	1.7	1.2	1.3	9.2	11.4
Other rural:						
Nonfarm.......................	2.2	2.2	1.7	1.6	8.0	9.6
Farm..........................	1.5	1.5	1.1	0.8	5.0	6.7

Source: *1950 Census of Population,* Vol. IV, *Special Reports,* Part 5, Chapter A, Characteristics by Size of Place, tables 3 and 3a.

In the white population, for both males and females, the percentage separated is somewhat greater in the urbanized areas than in the smaller urban places and rural areas. In the nonwhite population there is a strong size-of-place gradient. The percentage of married males reported as separated varies from 12 in the largest urbanized areas to 5 in the "other rural-farm" areas, with the corresponding variation for females being from 20 to 7 percent. Thus, the gradient for the total population is primarily a function of that for the nonwhite population.

Family characteristics

The classification of the population by family status in the size-of-place tabulations is the following:

```
Living in quasi-households
    Institutional population
    Other quasi-household member
Living in households
    In primary families
        Head of household
        Wife of household head
        Child of household head
        Other relative of household head
    Primary individual
    Nonrelative of household head
```

The term "institutions" denotes such places as homes and schools for dependent or delinquent children, the mentally or physically handicapped, and the aged; places providing specialized medical care; and prisons and jails. The category other quasi-household member includes such persons as those living in houses with at least five lodgers, hotels, labor camps, and military barracks. A primary family includes the head of a household and all persons living in the household who are related to him. A primary individual is a head of a household who lives alone or with other persons, all of whom are unrelated to him. The category nonrelative of household head includes all persons living in households who are not related to the head. Approximately three-fourths of these persons in the United States as a whole are lodgers in households; the remainder are members of secondary families (not related to the head) or are resident employees of the household.[3] In making size-of-place comparisons the category of institutional population should be dealt with separately from the others. Size-of-place variation in the proportion of the population classified as inmates of institutions reflects primarily the administrative policies which govern the location of institutions, rather than the residential characteristics of different sizes of place. The four groups of urbanized areas, listed in order of size, have 0.5, 0.7, 0.7, and 0.9 percent, respectively, of their

---

[3] For further discussion of these definitions and detailed family status statistics for the United States, see Vol. IV, *Special Reports, op. cit.*

population in this category; and in the three size groups of other urban places, 1.2, 1.2, and 0.9 percent of the population is classified as institutional.   In the large villages only 0.4 percent, and in the small villages only 0.2 percent, of the population lives in institutions, while none of the "other rural-farm" population is institutional, by definition.   In marked contrast to all the other size-of-place groups, 3.6 percent of the "other rural-nonfarm" residents are classified as institutional inmates.   It was pointed out that this disproportionate distribution of the institutional population complicates certain types of comparisons between the "other rural-nonfarm" and the remaining size-of-place categories.   In the remainder of the discussion of family characteristics, only the noninstitutional population will be considered.

Turning to the category of other quasi-household members, table 17 presents, for the population 25 and older, the ratio of the number of persons in this category to the number of persons living in households, for each size-of-place group.   This computation omits persons aged 14 to 24 in order to eliminate the bulk of the population living in military barracks and college dormitories.   There are, of course, members of the Armed Forces aged 25 and over living in quasi-households.   However, only about a third of the Armed Forces aged 25 and over live in quasi-households, as compared with nearly nine-tenths of those aged 14 to 24.   Hence, their inclusion should not greatly affect size-of-place comparisons, except for the "other rural-nonfarm" category.   Table 17 reveals that residence in quasi-households is much more common in large urban centers than in the smaller places.   In the first three size groups there are about 4 persons in other quasi-households per 100 persons in households, with the ratio dropping to about 2 per 100 in the smallest urban places, and 0.3 per 100 in the "other rural-farm" areas.   The gradient by size of place is especially marked for the nonwhite population, with ratios running from 9.4 per 100 in the largest urbanized areas, down to 0.8 in the small villages and 0.7 in the "other rural-farm" areas.   The difference between whites and non-whites gains significance when noting that in the United States as a whole, of the population over 25 living in quasi-households, only one-fifth of the whites (21.3 percent) are members of secondary families (the remainder being classified as secondary individuals), while nearly one-half (46.8 percent) of the nonwhites are members of secondary families.   Some of these nonwhite families are perhaps employees of hotels, lodginghouses, and the like.   Probably, however, a substantial proportion simply reside in crowded quarters lacking the facilities required for classification as distinct dwelling units.

In table 18 the population of all ages living in households is classified by family status.   The bulk of the population, in all sizes of place, are members of primary families.   However, the percentage in primary families is somewhat less in large places than in small, running from 92

TABLE **17.**—POPULATION 25 YEARS OLD AND OVER IN QUASI-HOUSEHOLDS (EXCEPT INSTITU-
TIONS) PER 100 POPULATION IN HOUSEHOLDS, BY COLOR, BY SIZE OF PLACE: 1950

Size of place	Total	White	Nonwhite
Urbanized areas:			
3,000,000 or more.....................	3.7	3.3	9.4
1,000,000 to 3,000,000..............	4.0	3.4	8.7
250,000 to 1,000,000...............	3.8	3.6	5.4
Under 250,000......................	3.1	2.9	4.9
Places outside urbanized areas:			
25,000 or more......................	3.4	3.4	3.7
10,000 to 25,000....................	2.6	2.6	2.3
2,500 to 10,000.....................	1.9	1.9	1.7
1,000 to 2,500......................	1.2	1.2	1.3
Under 1,000 (incorporated).........	0.6	0.6	0.8
Other rural:			
Nonfarm.............................	2.3	2.3	3.1
Farm................................	0.3	0.3	0.7

Source: *1950 Census of Population*, Vol. IV, *Special Reports*, Part 5, Chapter A, Characteristics by Size of Place, tables 3 and 3a.

and 93 in urbanized areas, and 93 and 94 in other urban places and villages, to 96 and 97 in "other rural" areas. The same tendency is more
pronounced for the nonwhite population, for which the percentage in primary families varies from 82 in the largest urbanized areas to 97 for the
"other rural-farm" category. For the total population (though not for
nonwhites) the highest percentage of persons living as primary individuals
is found in the small villages, where 4.7 percent of the population is so
classified. For the large villages and urban size groups the percentages
fluctuate between 3.5 and 4.1 with no apparent relationship to size of
place, while in "other rural" nonfarm and farm areas, respectively, only
2.6 and 1.4 percent of the population in households are primary individuals. Except in the "other rural" areas, there is a great predominance of
females among primary individuals. For the villages and urban groups
the sex ratios of primary individuals vary between 42 and 59 males per
100 females, while in the "other rural-nonfarm" population their sex ratio
is 122, and in the "other rural-farm," 205. The category nonrelative of
household head accounts for 3 to 4 percent of the population in households in the urban size groups, about 2 percent in the village groups, and
about 1.5 percent in "other rural" areas. For the nonwhite population
there is a pronounced gradient in the percentage so classified. In the largest urbanized areas over 12 percent are nonrelatives of the head, and the
percentage declines steadily with decreasing size of place to only 1.5 percent in "other rural-farm" areas. In both the white and the nonwhite population the great majority of the nonrelatives of household head are lodgers
in the household, the minority being resident employees of households and
their families.

Some characteristics of primary families, by size of place, are given in
table 19. The average size of family does not vary greatly in the urban-
village range, where the number of persons per family fluctuates between

TABLE **18.**—PERCENT DISTRIBUTION OF POPULATION IN HOUSEHOLDS BY FAMILY STATUS AND
COLOR, BY SIZE OF PLACE: 1950

Size of place and color	Total	Member of primary family	Primary individual	Nonrelative of household head
TOTAL				
Urbanized areas:				
3,000,000 or more...................	100.0	92.4	4.1	3.5
1,000,000 to 3,000,000..............	100.0	92.5	3.5	4.0
250,000 to 1,000,000................	100.0	92.7	3.8	3.5
Under 250,000.......................	100.0	93.1	3.6	3.3
Places outside urbanized areas:				
25,000 or more......................	100.0	92.7	3.9	3.4
10,000 to 25,000....................	100.0	93.0	3.9	3.1
2,500 to 10,000.....................	100.0	93.6	3.7	2.7
1,000 to 2,500.....................	100.0	93.9	3.8	2.3
Under 1,000 (incorporated)..........	100.0	93.1	4.7	2.2
Other rural:				
Nonfarm.............................	100.0	95.8	2.6	1.6
Farm................................	100.0	97.1	1.4	1.5
NONWHITE				
Urbanized areas:				
3,000,000 or more...................	100.0	82.1	5.6	12.3
1,000,000 to 3,000,000..............	100.0	84.7	4.3	11.0
250,000 to 1,000,000................	100.0	87.4	4.8	7.8
Under 250,000.......................	100.0	87.8	4.7	7.5
Places outside urbanized areas:				
25,000 or more......................	100.0	88.2	5.1	6.7
10,000 to 25,000....................	100.0	89.2	5.1	5.7
2,500 to 10,000.....................	100.0	90.2	5.3	4.5
1,000 to 2,500.....................	100.0	91.1	4.9	4.0
Under 1,000 (incorporated)..........	100.0	92.0	4.9	3.1
Other rural:				
Nonfarm.............................	100.0	93.5	3.7	2.8
Farm................................	100.0	97.2	1.3	1.5

Source: See table 17.

3.4 and 3.6.   Primary families in "other rural" territory are substantially
larger: 3.9 persons per family in the nonfarm part and 4.1 in the farm
part.   The size-of-place variation is somewhat greater for nonwhite primary families, which have an average of 3.6 persons in the largest urbanized
areas, 3.8 persons in each of the other urban size groups, 4.1 and 4.2 persons in the village groups, and 4.6 and 5.2 persons in the nonfarm and
farm parts of the "other rural" category, respectively.   There is a clear
size-of-place gradient in number of children per family, somewhat more
pronounced in the nonwhite than in the total population.   For the total
population the range is from 1.2 children per family in the largest urbanized areas to 1.9 in the "other rural-farm" group. For nonwhites the number of children per family varies between 1.3 and 2.6 for the extreme size
groups.   It should be remembered that the status child of household head
includes persons of all ages with a filial relationship to the head of the
household.   In the total population, the number of other relatives of the
household head per family is somewhat greater in the urbanized areas,
where the ratio is 0.3 or higher, than in the remaining size groups with
ratios slightly under 0.3, except for the "other rural-farm" group, which
has the highest ratio, 0.36 other relatives per family.   However, in the

nonwhite population, the lowest ratio, 0.58 other relatives per family, is found in the largest urbanized areas. In the next seven size groups it fluctuates between 0.62 and 0.64, increasing to 0.71 for small villages, 0.72 for the "other rural-nonfarm" group, and to 0.78 for the "other rural-farm" group.

A final characteristic covered in table 19 is the proportion of heads of primary families who are females. As far as the total population is concerned, urban primary families are somewhat more frequently headed by females than are rural families. In the seven urban size groups the percentage of female heads varies between 10.2 and 10.7, with no apparent relation to size of city, while in the two village groups it is slightly under 10, dropping to 6.9 and 4.8 in the nonfarm and farm parts, respectively, of the "other rural" category. In the nonwhite population primary families with female heads are about twice as frequent, in each size-of-place group, as in the total population. Variation in the percentage of female heads is somewhat erratic for the urban and village groups, between the limits of 18.2 and 22.3; for the "other rural-nonfarm" the percentage is 17.2, and in "other rural-farm" areas only 8.7 percent of nonwhite primary families have female heads.

An analysis of the family status of children under 14 years of age, as it varies by size of place, is made possible by the data given in table 20. The percentage of children living in institutions is 0.3 or 0.4 in the urban size groups, 0.2 and 0.1 in the village groups, with the high figure of 0.7 appearing for the "other rural-nonfarm" group. As previously noted, the proportion classified as inmates of institutions should be understood to indicate primarily the location of institutions, and not the incidence of factors leading to institutionalization. There is a size-of-place gradient in the ratio of children living in quasi-households (other than institutions) to

TABLE 19.—CHARACTERISTICS OF PRIMARY FAMILIES BY COLOR, BY SIZE OF PLACE: 1950

Size of place	Persons per family		Children of household head per family		Other relatives of household head per family		Female heads as percent of total heads	
	Total	Non-white	Total	Non-white	Total	Non-white	Total	Non-white
Urbanized areas:								
3,000,000 or more..............	3.4	3.6	1.2	1.3	0.31	0.58	10.4	20.7
1,000,000 to 3,000,000.........	3.5	3.8	1.3	1.4	0.34	0.63	10.6	18.4
250,000 to 1,000,000...........	3.4	3.8	1.2	1.4	0.31	0.63	10.2	18.2
Under 250,000..................	3.5	3.8	1.3	1.4	0.30	0.64	10.5	20.8
Places outside urbanized areas:								
25,000 or more................	3.4	3.8	1.3	1.4	0.28	0.62	10.7	21.4
10,000 to 25,000..............	3.4	3.8	1.3	1.4	0.28	0.62	10.4	21.4
2,500 to 10,000...............	3.5	3.8	1.4	1.5	0.28	0.63	10.4	22.3
1,000 to 2,500................	3.6	4.1	1.4	1.7	0.28	0.64	9.6	19.9
Under 1,000 (incorporated).....	3.5	4.2	1.4	1.7	0.26	0.71	9.7	19.5
Other rural:								
Nonfarm........................	3.9	4.6	1.7	2.0	0.28	0.72	6.9	17.2
Farm...........................	4.1	5.2	1.9	2.6	0.36	0.78	4.8	8.7

Source: See table 17.

TABLE 20.—FAMILY STATUS OF CHILDREN UNDER 14 YEARS OLD BY COLOR, BY SIZE OF PLACE:
1950

Size of place and color	Inmates of institution as percent of total children	Children in other quasi-households per 100 children in households	Members of primary families as percent of total children	Nonrelatives of household head as percent of total children in households	Other relatives of household head as percent of total children in primary families
TOTAL					
Urbanized areas:					
3,000,000 or more............	0.3	1.1	97.6	1.0	7.8
1,000,000 to 3,000,000.......	0.4	1.2	97.3	1.2	8.7
250,000 to 1,000,000.........	0.4	0.9	97.8	0.9	8.4
Under 250,000................	0.4	0.8	98.0	0.9	8.6
Places outside urbanized areas:					
25,000 or more...............	0.3	0.7	98.3	0.7	8.5
10,000 to 25,000.............	0.4	0.5	98.4	0.7	8.3
2,500 to 10,000..............	0.3	0.4	98.7	0.6	8.4
1,000 to 2,500...............	0.2	0.4	98.9	0.6	7.9
Under 1,000 (incorporated)...	0.1	0.3	98.9	0.6	8.0
Other rural:					
Nonfarm......................	0.7	0.4	98.3	0.7	7.2
Farm.........................	...	0.2	99.2	0.6	9.2
NONWHITE					
Urbanized areas:					
3,000,000 or more............	0.2	6.9	89.0	4.7	18.5
1,000,000 to 3,000,000.......	0.2	5.9	90.7	3.8	19.6
250,000 to 1,000,000.........	0.2	3.3	94.1	2.6	21.9
Under 250,000................	0.2	3.3	94.0	2.6	21.5
Places outside urbanized areas:					
25,000 or more...............	0.2	1.9	95.9	2.1	23.1
10,000 to 25,000.............	0.3	1.2	96.8	1.8	24.0
2,500 to 10,000..............	0.2	1.1	97.2	1.5	23.6
1,000 to 2,500...............	0.1	0.7	97.6	1.5	21.9
Under 1,000 (incorporated)...	0.3	0.7	97.6	1.5	25.2
Other rural:					
Nonfarm......................	0.6	1.0	97.3	1.1	20.4
Farm.........................	...	0.3	99.2	0.5	19.5

Source: See table 17.

children living in households. However, this gradient for the total population is primarily due to the pronounced difference between large and small places for the nonwhite population. In the largest urbanized areas there are nearly 7 nonwhite children living in quasi-households (other than institutions) for every hundred living in households. This ratio drops regularly to 1 per 100 in the smallest urban places, and 0.3 per 100 in the "other rural-farm" areas. The percentage of all children living in primary families varies only slightly by size of place in the total population, from 97.6 in the largest urbanized areas to 99.2 in "other rural-farm" territory. In the nonwhite population, where there is a noticeable size-of-place gradient, the largest urbanized areas have only 89 per cent of their nonwhite children living in primary families, as compared to 99 percent in "other rural-farm" areas. The size-of-place gradient for the total population in the percentage of children living in households as nonrelatives of the household head is likewise greatly influenced by the situation for nonwhites. In the urbanized areas of 3 million or more, nearly 5 percent of the nonwhite children in households are nonrelatives of the head, and the percentage declines to 1.5 in the small urban places and villages, and to only 0.5 in the "other rural-farm" areas. In neither the total nor the non-white population is there any clear relationship between the percentage of children in primary families classed as other relatives of the household head and size of place.

None of the foregoing discussion of family characteristics makes allowance for size-of-place variations in age and marital status composition. It would be highly desirable to have the comparisons standardized for these two factors. The proportion of primary individuals, for example, is much higher among widowed and divorced persons than among married and single persons. Hence, size-of-place variation in the proportion of primary individuals is at least partly accounted for by variation in marital status. The computation of standardized comparisons of family characteristics, which could only be carried out by the indirect method, was too time-consuming to be feasible in this study.

Historical note

The principal source on community size as a factor in marital status is Sanderson's study of 1930 data. Using a city-size classification, together with statistics for the rural-nonfarm and rural-farm population and for a sample of villages, and standardizing for age, sex, race, and nativity, Sanderson concluded:[4]

> This study has shown that the proportion of persons 15 years of age or over who are married, tends to decrease with the size of the community, and that the proportion of such persons who have ever been married—that is, who are either married, widowed, or divorced—has the same trend. Conversely, the proportion of persons who are single or who have never married, increases with the size of the community.

It appears, therefore, that the relationship of marital status to community size found in the present study reflects the influence of persistent factors.

---

[4] Dwight Sanderson, *Relation of Size of Community to Marital Status*, Cornell University Agricultural Experiment Station, Memoir 200, February 1937, p. 36.

CHAPTER 6

MOBILITY

The mobility status of the population, in the 1950 Census, is determined by comparing the 1949 residence with the 1950 residence of all persons one year of age and older. For the size-of-place tabulations the population is classified as nonmovers (those living in the same house in both years), and movers. The movers are subclassified into nonmigrants (those living in a different house in 1950 but in the same county), and migrants. The migrants are further broken down into those coming from a different county within the same state and those coming from a different state. The final, residual, category includes those abroad in 1949 and those whose 1949 residence was not reported. In addition, movers were classified according to whether the 1949 residence was on a farm or not. For the country as a whole only 0.3 percent of the population was abroad in 1949, while 1.7 percent did not report on mobility status. Hence, variations in the percentage "abroad and not reporting" reflect primarily variations in non-response to the mobility question.

Mobility status of the population

Table 21 shows the distribution of the total population one year of age and over by mobility status for each size-of-place group. Disregarding the "other rural-nonfarm" population, there is a "U-shaped" relationship of mobility status to size of place. The percentage reported as living in the same house in 1949 and 1950 is highest at the extremes of the size-of-place range. Both the urbanized areas of 3 million or more and the "other rural-farm" group have 85 percent of their population classed as non-movers, while the percentage so classified drops to a minimum of about 78 or 79 percent for the intermediate size groups, i.e., the urban places outside urbanized areas.

The "other rural-nonfarm" group does not conform to this U-shaped relationship, since its proportion of nonmovers, 76.5 percent, is lower than that of any other size group. There may be some question as to whether this is due in part to the disproportionate number of persons in the Armed Forces in the "other rural-nonfarm" population. There is some evidence on this point from the Bureau of the Census surveys of the mobility of the civilian population during the 1940–50 decade.[1] These have

---

[1] U. S. Bureau of the Census, *Current Population Reports*, Series P–20, Nos. 14, 22, 28, and 36.

TABLE **21.**—PERCENT DISTRIBUTION OF THE POPULATION 1 YEAR OLD AND OVER BY MOBILITY STATUS, BY SIZE OF PLACE: 1950

Size of place	Total	Same house	Different house, same county	Different county, same State	Different State	Abroad and not reported
Urbanized areas:						
3,000,000 or more.............	100.0	85.1	9.0	1.6	1.8	2.5
1,000,000 to 3,000,000.........	100.0	83.4	9.8	1.9	2.5	2.4
250,000 to 1,000,000...........	100.0	78.9	13.1	2.4	3.4	2.2
Under 250,000..................	100.0	79.9.	12.7	2.6	3.2	1.6
Places outside urbanized areas:						
25,000 or more................	100.0	77.5	13.1	3.5	4.0	1.9
10,000 to 25,000..............	100.0	77.8	12.9	4.1	3.5	1.7
2,500 to 10,000...............	100.0	79.0	12.3	4.1	3.2	1.4
1,000 to 2,500................	100.0	81.0	11.0	4.0	2.7	1.3
Under 1,000 (incorporated).....	100.0	82.1	10.2	4.0	2.5	1.2
Other rural:						
Nonfarm.......................	100.0	76.5	12.7	4.6	3.7	2.5
Farm..........................	100.0	85.2	9.1	3.0	1.6	1.1

Source: *1950 Census of Population*, Vol. IV, *Special Reports*, Part 5, Chapter A, Characteristics by Size of Place, table 2.

uniformly shown the civilian rural-nonfarm population to have a smaller proportion of nonmovers than either the urban or the rural-farm population. For the period March 1949 to March 1950 the estimated percentages of nonmovers in the civilian population were: urban, 81.1 percent; rural nonfarm, 78.2 percent; rural farm, 83.8 percent.

The category "different house, same county" accounts for about 9 percent of the population in the extreme size groups, with the percentage increasing to a maximum of about 13 percent for the intermediate size groups. The "other rural-nonfarm" group is out of line with the adjacent size groups, with 12.7 percent in this category, as compared with only 10.2 percent for the small villages and 9.1 percent for the "other rural-farm" group.

The proportion of migrants—combining intrastate and interstate migrants—bears a similar relationship to size of place. It is at a minimum of 3.4 percent in the urbanized areas of 3 million or more, increases to around 7.5 percent in the urban size groups outside urbanized areas, then decreases to 4.6 percent in the "other rural-farm" areas. The "other rural-nonfarm" group is again out of line, with a higher proportion of migrants—8.3 percent—than any other size group.

The four regions differ considerably in the mobility of their populations. The percentages classified as nonmovers are about 87, 83, 77, and 73, respectively, for the Northeast, North Central, South, and West. Furthermore this ranking of the four regions by the percentage of nonmovers is reproduced for each size-of-place group (table 22). However, within each region the relationship of the mobility status distribution to size of place is very much like that already described for the United States as a whole. The most outstanding exception is that in the West the only urbanized area over 3 million—Los Angeles—has a markedly higher proportion of intracounty movers than any other size-of-place group.

TABLE **22.**—PERCENT DISTRIBUTION OF THE POPULATION 1 YEAR OLD AND OVER BY MOBILITY STATUS, BY SIZE OF PLACE, BY REGIONS: 1950

Size of place	Total[1]	Same house	Different house, same county	Different county	Total[1]	Same house	Different house, same county	Different county
		Northeast				North Central		
Urbanized areas:								
3,000,000 or more............	100.0	88.8	5.1	3.3	100.0	84.8	10.2	2.8
1,000,000 to 3,000,000........	100.0	87.2	7.8	2.9	100.0	83.5	11.0	3.6
250,000 to 1,000,000..........	100.0	87.5	8.3	2.6	100.0	81.4	12.0	4.7
Under 250,000.................	100.0	88.2	7.9	2.6	100.0	79.6	13.2	5.7
Places outside urbanized areas:								
25,000 or more................	100.0	85.5	9.3	3.4	100.0	80.4	12.2	6.0
10,000 to 25,000..............	100.0	85.3	8.9	3.6	100.0	79.8	12.0	6.8
2,500 to 10,000...............	100.0	86.2	8.4	3.9	100.0	81.0	11.2	6.5
1,000 to 2,500................	100.0	87.0	7.9	3.8	100.0	82.6	10.1	6.1
Under 1,000 (incorporated)....	100.0	86.9	7.5	4.3	100.0	83.8	9.2	5.8
Other rural:								
Nonfarm.......................	100.0	83.3	8.6	5.3	100.0	78.6	11.3	7.8
Farm..........................	100.0	90.0	5.5	3.2	100.0	88.8	6.0	4.2
		South				West		
Urbanized areas:								
3,000,000 or more............	...	...	...	...	100.0	73.7	19.4	4.9
1,000,000 to 3,000,000........	100.0	78.9	10.4	7.4	100.0	75.8	12.7	7.7
250,000 to 1,000,000..........	100.0	74.4	15.8	7.5	100.0	72.2	16.0	8.8
Under 250,000.................	100.0	75.2	15.3	7.7	100.0	73.3	16.1	8.6
Places outside urbanized areas:								
25,000 or more................	100.0	73.2	14.9	9.7	100.0	71.0	15.8	10.8
10,000 to 25,000..............	100.0	74.8	14.7	9.1	100.0	70.5	16.2	11.2
2,500 to 10,000...............	100.0	76.5	14.0	8.1	100.0	72.2	15.4	10.8
1,000 to 2,500................	100.0	78.7	12.6	7.5	100.0	74.0	13.8	10.3
Under 1,000 (incorporated)....	100.0	79.5	12.2	7.2	100.0	76.8	11.7	10.2
Other rural:								
Nonfarm.......................	100.0	74.7	14.6	8.6	100.0	67.5	15.9	13.3
Farm..........................	100.0	82.8	11.4	4.6	100.0	81.8	9.4	7.2

[1] Includes persons abroad in 1949 and mobility status not reported.

Source: *1950 Census of Population*, Vol. IV, *Special Reports*, Part 5, Chapter A, Characteristics by Size of Place, table 7.

The mobility status classification pertains to the point of destination of movement. Hence, an area losing population by a net outward movement is more likely to have a high proportion of its population classified as nonmovers at any given time than one gaining population through in-movement. It appears, in fact, that the percentage of nonmovers in an area in 1950 is negatively associated with its rate of population increase over the entire 1940–50 decade. The ranking of the four regions according to the decennial percentage increase in population is precisely the reverse of that already given for the percentage of nonmovers. Furthermore, computation of the correlation between percent in the same house, 1949 and 1950, with the decennial percentage change in population, for the 151 standard metropolitan areas having a population of 100,000 or more in 1950,[2] shows that there is a strong inverse relationship between these two variables. The correlation coefficient is −0.8, and according to the regression equation a difference of 10 in the percentage of nonmovers produces a difference of

---

[2] These data are conveniently tabulated in *1950 Census of Population*, Vol. II, *Characteristics of the Population*, Part 1, table 86, p. 138.

27 in the decennial percentage change in population. For example, on the average, an SMA with 85 percent nonmovers experienced a population increase of only about 19 percent, while an SMA with 75 percent nonmovers gained about 46 percent in population over the decade. Although the numerical constants of this regression relationship cannot be assumed to hold for size-of-place groups, it is probable that size-of-place variation in the mobility status distribution reflects differentials in population growth over the 1940–50 decade.

Rates of in-migration, by age

The proportion of migrants in a population may be interpreted as an approximate rate of in-migration, since it relates the number of migrants entering and remaining in an area over the period of one year to the population of that area.[3] The material already presented indicates that, generally speaking, the rate of in-migration has an inverted U-shaped relationship to size of place.

Figure 12 shows in-migration rates per 1,000 population by age for each of 6 groups in a condensed size-of-place classification. For purposes of graphic presentation it was desirable to use fewer than 11 size groups; hence categories were combined whose age patterns of in-migration rates were closely similar. The figures pertain to total migrants, intra- and interstate combined.

While the six size-of-place groups generally have similar age patterns of in-migration rates, the variation among them in rates is greater at the younger ages than at the older ages. However, the ranking of the groups by rate of in-migration is rather similar from one age group to another. The lowest rates of in-migration are for the urbanized areas of 1 million or more and the "other rural-farm" group. The highest rates are for the "other rural-nonfarm" group and the urban places outside urbanized areas, and rates of intermediate magnitudes are found for the smaller urbanized areas and the villages. That is, disregarding the "other rural-nonfarm" group, the form of the relationship between in-migration rates and size of place is similar for each age interval to that described for the population of all ages. For each size group the peak rate of in-migration is at ages 14 to 24.

For nonwhites the in-migration rates generally are lower than for whites. Although the relationship of in-migration rates to size of place is not quite

---

[3] This is strictly true only for a place contained within a county, because the migration data relate to movements across county lines. Inasmuch as the larger urbanized areas frequently lie in two or more counties, some movement within urbanized areas is reported as intercounty migration. It may be assumed, therefore, that the "in-migration rates" for urbanized areas—especially those of 1 million and over—are exaggerated. It seems unlikely, though, that this error vitiates the conclusion that the in-migration rate bears an inverted-U relationship to size of place. In fact, the actual in-migration rates would differentiate the urbanized areas from the other urban places even more than the rates shown here.

FIGURE **12.**—RATE OF IN-MIGRATION, BY AGE, COLOR, AND SIZE OF PLACE (CONDENSED CLASSI-FICATION): 1949 to 1950

[*A*—Urbanized areas of 1,000,000 or more; *B*—Urbanized areas under 1,000,000; *C*—Other urban places; *D*—Villages under 2,500; *E*—Other rural nonfarm; *F*—Other rural farm]

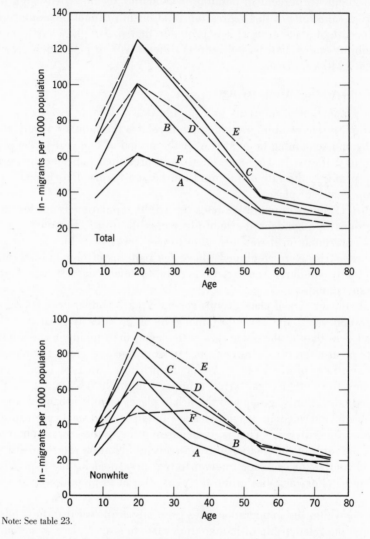

Note: See table 23.

as consistent as for the total population, the data for nonwhites exhibit most of the features already described. The age interval 14 to 24 has the peak rate for all groups except the "other rural farm," and at this age the inverted-U relationship of the rate of in-migration to size of place is clearly evident.

Movement from farms

Between 1949 and 1950 about 3,650,000 persons moved from a farm to a nonfarm residence, and about 2,950,000 from a nonfarm to a farm residence.   There was, therefore, a net gain from the movement of about 700,000 persons for nonfarm areas, or about one-half of 1 percent of their 1950 resident population.   Correspondingly, the net loss of 700,000 from the farm population amounted to about 3 percent of its 1950 level.

The size-of-place groups did not share proportionately in the gain from movement from farms.   As table 23 shows, the largest urbanized areas received only 2.5 movers from farms per 1,000 of their 1950 resident population.   The rate of in-movement from farms is an inverse function of size of place, increasing from the figure just cited to 12.2 for the urban places 25,000 or more outside urbanized areas, 19.6 for the smallest urban places, 33.1 for small villages, and 37.4 for "other rural-nonfarm" areas. The same relationship holds for the nonwhite population, whose rates of in-movement from farms are consistently higher than are those for the total population.

Unfortunately, it is not possible to break down the movement from non-farm to farm areas by size of place, nor to trace movement between communities of different sizes.   As far as they go, however, the data are consistent with Ravenstein's hypothesis that urbanward movement largely progresses by short distance moves from rural areas to the larger urban centers.

TABLE 23.—MOVERS FROM FARMS, 1949 TO 1950, PER 1,000 RESIDENT POPULATION 1 YEAR
OLD AND OVER, BY COLOR, BY SIZE OF PLACE: 1950

Size of place	Total	Non-white	Size of place	Total	Non-white
Urbanized areas:			Places outside urbanized areas—		
3,000,000 or more..............	2.5	3.7	Cont.		
1,000,000 to 3,000,000.........	3.3	4.0	2,500 to 10,000.................	19.6	27.5
250,000 to 1,000,000...........	7.1	7.4	1,000 to 2,500.................	23.3	30.8
Under 250,000..................	8.5	10.3	Under 1,000 (incorporated)......	33.1	55.0
Places outside urbanized areas:			Other rural:		
25,000 or more................	12.2	17.5	Nonfarm.......................	37.4	58.5
10,000 to 25,000..............	15.4	23.5	Farm..........................	82.5	136.5

Source: *1950 Census of Population*, Vol. IV, *Special Reports*, Part 5, Chapter A, Characteristics by Size of Place, tables 2 and 2a.

Characteristics of movers

Table 24 presents sex ratios of movers classified by farm residence in 1949 and by distance moved, for each size-of-place group.   There is a slight excess of females among all movers in the urban and village groups, except one.   These size groups have sex ratios between 97 and 101. Movers to the "other rural" areas, on the other hand, have a substantial excess of males, with sex ratios of 113 and 111 for the nonfarm and farm portions, respectively.   It is curious that the relatively small stream of movers from farms to large urbanized areas contains a large excess of males. For the first three size groups the sex ratios of movers from farms are 128, 122, and 116, respectively.   For the remaining urban and village size groups the sex ratio for movers of farm origin varies only between 96 and 102 and is not uniformly higher than the sex ratio of movers of non-

TABLE **24.**—SEX RATIO OF MOVERS BY FARM RESIDENCE IN 1949 AND BY DISTANCE MOVED, BY COLOR, BY SIZE OF PLACE: 1950

Size of place and color	Total movers	Residence in 1949		Distance moved		
		Farm	Nonfarm	Different house, same county	Different county, same State	Different State
TOTAL						
Urbanized areas:						
3,000,000 or more..............	98	128	97	97	98	101
1,000,000 to 3,000,000.........	98	122	98	96	95	106
250,000 to 1,000,000...........	98	116	98	95	99	111
Under 250,000..................	97	96	98	95	97	106
Places outside urbanized areas:						
25,000 or more.................	101	102	101	97	101	116
10,000 to 25,000...............	99	99	99	98	98	105
2,500 to 10,000................	98	97	98	96	98	106
1,000 to 2,500.................	99	96	99	97	98	108
Under 1,000 (incorporated).....	100	102	100	99	98	104
Other rural:						
Nonfarm........................	113	110	113	106	114	142
Farm...........................	111	111	110	109	109	123
NONWHITE						
Urbanized areas:						
3,000,000 or more..............	94	121	94	96	96	85
1,000,000 to 3,000,000.........	95	121	94	94	100	96
250,000 to 1,000,000...........	94	116	92	91	103	109
Under 250,000..................	89	81	90	89	76	103
Places outside urbanized areas:						
25,000 or more.................	98	92	98	93	105	117
10,000 to 25,000...............	99	90	100	97	113	96
2,500 to 10,000................	90	87	92	87	95	104
1,000 to 2,500.................	91	100	89	90	89	96
Under 1,000 (incorporated).....	97	94	95	95	99	107
Other rural:						
Nonfarm........................	114	97	123	101	137	164
Farm...........................	103	102	106	102	103	111

Source: See table 23.

farm origin. Movers to "other rural" areas, whether of farm or nonfarm origin, have the high sex ratios characteristic of the resident population of those areas.

The sex ratio tends to vary directly by distance moved. For all size groups but one the sex ratio of intracounty movers is as low as or lower than that of movers between counties within the same state, although the differences are generally very small. Interstate migrants to all sizes of place have substantially higher sex ratios than intrastate movers. For none of the distance categories, however, is there any indication of a clear relationship of the sex ratio of movers to size of place, except for the markedly higher sex ratios found for movers in "other rural" areas.

The sex ratios of movers in the nonwhite population vary more erratically than those of the total population. It is again notable, however, that movers from farms to the large urbanized areas have exceptionally high sex ratios. For the most part the nonwhite sex ratio tends to vary directly with distance moved, though not so regularly as in the total population. An exception is that nonwhite interstate migrants to the largest urbanized areas have the very low sex ratio of 85.

Table 25 shows the median age of movers by category of movement for each size-of-place group.   The computation of these medians was necessarily somewhat rough, because it was necessary to interpolate over an 11-year interval when the median was in the 14 to 24 range, and over a 20-year interval when it was between 25 and 44.   In both the total and the nonwhite population the movers from nonfarm residences and the intracounty movers have a gradient of age by size of place which is similar to that found for the total population.   One may presume that both these categories of movers are heavily weighted with persons whose movements were within one community.   Movers from farm residences tend to be considerably younger than those from nonfarm residences, but do not show as distinct a gradient by size of place.   Movers from farms to the urbanized areas of 1 million or more are substantially older than those moving to communities of any other size.   The next highest median is for movers from farms to the small villages, although this does not differ greatly from the medians for the other village and urban size groups.   For both intercounty and interstate migrants the most striking size-of-place differences again pertain to the selectivity of the first two size groups for older migrants.   Other differences among size groups in the urban-village range are minor and irregular.

TABLE **25.**—MEDIAN AGE OF MOVERS BY RESIDENCE IN 1949 AND BY DISTANCE MOVED, BY COLOR, BY SIZE OF PLACE: 1950

Size of place and color	Total movers	Residence in 1949		Distance moved		
		Farm	Nonfarm	Different house, same county	Different county, same State	Different State
TOTAL						
Urbanized areas:						
3,000,000 or more.................	30.5	28.5	30.5	31.0	29.7	28.7
1,000,000 to 3,000,000...........	29.0	26.1	29.0	29.7	28.1	27.2
250,000 to 1,000,000.............	28.0	23.5	28.1	28.8	25.4	26.4
Under 250,000....................	27.0	23.5	27.2	27.6	24.9	26.7
Places outside urbanized areas:						
25,000 or more...................	25.8	22.7	25.9	26.7	24.1	25.0
10,000 to 25,000.................	25.3	23.0	25.6	26.0	24.0	25.1
2,500 to 10,000..................	25.1	23.1	25.5	25.4	24.8	24.8
1,000 to 2,500...................	25.4	23.8	25.5	25.4	25.4	25.1
Under 1,000 (incorporated).......	25.2	24.3	25.5	25.7	24.5	25.1
Other rural:						
Nonfarm..........................	23.7	21.5	24.1	23.6	24.7	23.0
Farm.............................	22.0	21.1	23.3	21.7	22.3	23.1
NONWHITE						
Urbanized areas:						
3,000,000 or more.................	28.9	24.9	29.0	29.4	29.0	25.5
1,000,000 to 3,000,000...........	28.7	22.4	28.8	29.3	26.9	24.9
250,000 to 1,000,000.............	27.6	22.3	27.8	28.3	25.5	24.2
Under 250,000....................	26.1	22.4	26.2	27.0	23.0	24.3
Places outside urbanized areas:						
25,000 or more...................	25.8	22.6	26.0	26.3	24.3	25.1
10,000 to 25,000.................	25.1	22.7	25.7	25.8	23.9	24.0
2,500 to 10,000..................	24.0	22.0	24.5	24.2	24.6	22.7
1,000 to 2,500...................	23.8	22.8	23.7	23.4	24.6	24.4
Under 1,000 (incorporated).......	22.6	20.4	24.1	21.9	23.6	25.9
Other rural:						
Nonfarm..........................	22.6	20.9	23.3	21.9	24.2	23.3
Farm.............................	19.8	19.3	21.8	19.6	19.8	21.2

Source: See table 23.

C H A P T E R 7

EDUCATION

The measure of educational status used in this chapter is the median number of school years completed by the population. It is desirable to consider the white and nonwhite population separately, since the pattern of variation in educational attainment by size of place is quite different for the two categories.

Figure 5 (p. 36) shows the median school year completed for the white and nonwhite population aged 25 and over, for each size-of-place group. For the white population, all the urban groups have a substantially larger median than any of the rural groups, although the median school year completed does not vary monotonically by size of place within the urban range. The largest urbanized areas have a median of 10.3 school years; their comparatively low figure is probably due to the disproportionate number of foreign-born persons. The median rises to 10.9 for the urbanized areas of 250,000 to 1 million, then declines to 10.0 for the smallest urban places, 9.4 for the larger villages, 8.9 for the small villages and "other rural-nonfarm," and to 8.5 for the "other rural-farm." For the nonwhite population the relationship of educational attainment to size of place is more regular and pronounced. From a high of 8.7 school years in the largest urbanized areas it declines regularly with decreasing size of place to 4.8 school years for the "other rural-farm" group. Thus, while the difference between the white and nonwhite medians amounts to only about 1½, 2½, and 3 years for the first three size-of-place groups, it rises to around 3½ to 4 years for the remaining size groups.

Further variations in the relationship of educational attainment to size of place are noted with a subdivision of the data by age and sex (table 26). For the nonwhite population, the size-of-place gradient for each of the three age groups 25 to 44, 45 to 64, and 65 and over is similar to that noted for all persons over 25. However, for the white population the major portion of the variation by size of place is contributed by the age group 25 to 44. The other two groups vary only slightly by size of place. For white females aged 25 to 44 the median number of school years completed remains virtually constant at 12.0 to 12.2 throughout the urban-village range, then drops abruptly to 10.7 and 9.7 for the nonfarm and farm parts of the "other rural" group, respectively. For white males aged 25 to 44 the median is similarly constant for the first six size groups,

TABLE **26.**—MEDIAN YEARS OF SCHOOL COMPLETED BY PERSONS 25 YEARS OLD AND OVER, BY AGE, COLOR, AND SEX, BY SIZE OF PLACE: 1950

Size of place and color	Total, 25 years old and over	25 to 44 years old		45 to 64 years old		65 years old and over	
		Male	Female	Male	Female	Male	Female
WHITE							
Urbanized areas:							
3,000,000 or more...............	10.3	12.1	12.1	8.8	8.8	8.3	8.4
1,000,000 to 3,000,000.........	10.8	12.1	12.1	8.9	8.9	8.3	8.5
250,000 to 1,000,000............	10.9	12.1	12.2	8.9	9.2	8.3	8.5
Under 250,000...................	10.5	12.0	12.1	8.8	9.0	8.2	8.5
Places outside urbanized areas:							
25,000 or more..................	10.6	12.1	12.1	8.8	9.1	8.3	8.5
10,000 to 25,000................	10.4	12.0	12.1	8.8	9.1	8.3	8.6
2,500 to 10,000.................	10.0	11.5	12.1	8.7	8.9	8.2	8.5
1,000 to 2,500..................	9.4	11.1	12.0	8.6	8.9	8.2	8.4
Under 1,000 (incorporated)......	8.9	11.0	12.0	8.6	8.8	8.2	8.4
Other rural:							
Nonfarm.........................	8.9	9.9	10.7	8.4	8.6	7.7	8.2
Farm............................	8.5	8.7	9.7	8.2	8.5	7.5	8.1
NONWHITE							
Urbanized areas:							
3,000,000 or more...............	8.7	9.3	9.6	7.9	7.8	6.1	6.1
1,000,000 to 3,000,000.........	8.3	8.8	9.4	6.9	7.3	5.1	5.5
250,000 to 1,000,000............	7.7	8.3	8.7	6.3	6.7	4.6	4.8
Under 250,000...................	7.0	7.6	8.2	5.6	6.3	4.2	4.4
Places outside urbanized areas:							
25,000 or more..................	6.8	7.4	8.1	5.6	6.1	4.1	4.2
10,000 to 25,000................	6.6	7.2	7.8	5.3	6.2	3.8	4.2
2,500 to 10,000.................	6.1	6.5	7.4	4.9	5.6	3.7	4.0
1,000 to 2,500..................	5.8	6.4	7.3	4.8	5.4	3.5	3.7
Under 1,000 (incorporated)......	5.3	5.9	6.7	4.0	5.3	3.4	4.0
Other rural:							
Nonfarm.........................	5.4	6.1	6.8	4.2	4.9	3.3	3.4
Farm............................	4.8	4.9	6.2	3.8	4.9	3.4	3.5

Source: *1950 Census of Population,* Vol. IV, *Special Reports,* Part 5, Chapter A, Characteristics by Size of Place, tables 2 and 2a.

dropping to 11.5 for the smallest urban places, 11.1 and 11.0 for the village groups, and 9.9 and 8.7 for the nonfarm and farm parts of the "other rural" group. For both whites and nonwhites in all three age groups there is a general, though by no means invariable, tendency for the difference between females and males to increase with decreasing size of place. Only in the larger size groups are there instances where the male median equals or exceeds the female median.

The marked size-of-place gradient in educational attainment for the non-white population is partly a regional phenomenon. Table 27, which shows the median school year completed for nonwhite males and females aged 25 to 44 by region, reveals that in the Northeast and North Central Regions there is only a slight gradient, if any, over the entire urban range, whereas the gradient is pronounced in the South and the West.

Table 28 shows the median school year completed for the population aged 14 to 24, by region. The size-of-place gradient appears most clearly for the South, particularly for its nonwhite population. In the other three regions differences by size of place within the urban range are small and erratic, although urban places have somewhat higher medians than villages,

TABLE **27.**—MEDIAN YEARS OF SCHOOL COMPLETED BY NONWHITE PERSONS 25 TO 44 YEARS OLD BY SEX, BY SIZE OF PLACE, BY REGIONS: 1950

[Median not shown for fewer than 100 sample cases]

Size of place	Northeast		North Central		South		West	
	Male	Female	Male	Female	Male	Female	Male	Female
Urbanized areas:								
3,000,000 or more...............	8.9	9.1	9.2	9.7	...	...	10.8	11.3
1,000,000 to 3,000,000..........	8.8	9.3	8.8	9.3	8.5	9.2	9.7	10.5
250,000 to 1,000,000............	8.4	8.9	9.0	9.8	7.7	8.3	10.2	11.1
Under 250,000...................	8.7	9.3	8.9	9.4	7.0	7.7	9.6	10.0
Places outside urbanized areas:								
25,000 or more.................	8.7	8.8	9.0	9.4	6.8	7.6	9.5	9.7
10,000 to 25,000...............	8.8	9.2	9.0	10.0	6.7	7.5	8.7	8.7
2,500 to 10,000................	8.8	9.1	8.5	9.0	6.2	7.3	8.6	9.3
1,000 to 2,500.................	...	...	...	...	6.1	7.0	...	...
Under 1,000 (incorporated)......	...	...	...	...	5.7	6.5	...	...
Other rural:								
Nonfarm........................	8.4	8.6	8.6	8.6	5.5	6.5	8.4	8.4
Farm...........................	...	...	8.2	8.2	4.6	6.1	8.2	8.4

Source: Unpublished tabulations by the Bureau of the Census.

whose medians, in turn, are higher than those for the "other rural" categories. It must be remembered that the population of this age interval includes a substantial proportion still in school, whose education is not yet completed.

Size-of-place differences in educational attainment are produced by differences in age of entering and leaving school and in rate of advancement in school. At the age of 13, 96.4 percent of the population in urbanized areas, 96.3 percent in other urban places, 95.5 percent of the rural-non-farm population, and 94.8 percent of the rural-farm population is enrolled in school. For the 13-year-olds enrolled in school, the median year in

TABLE **28.**—MEDIAN YEARS OF SCHOOL COMPLETED BY PERSONS 14 TO 24 YEARS OLD BY SEX, BY SIZE OF PLACE, BY REGIONS (WITH COLOR FOR THE SOUTH): 1950

Size of place	Northeast		North Central		South				West	
					White		Nonwhite			
	Male	Fe-male	Male	Fe-male	Male	Fe-male	Male	Fe-male	Male	Fe-male
Urbanized areas:										
3,000,000 or more...............	11.1	11.6	11.2	11.7	...	...	...	...	11.5	11.9
1,000,000 to 3,000,000..........	11.2	11.7	10.9	11.4	11.2	11.8	9.2	10.2	11.6	12.1
250,000 to 1,000,000............	10.9	11.6	11.3	11.8	11.0	11.4	8.7	9.7	11.4	12.0
Under 250,000...................	10.8	11.3	11.3	11.8	10.9	11.4	8.5	9.5	11.1	11.7
Places outside urbanized areas:										
25,000 or more.................	11.0	11.3	11.6	12.1	11.6	11.5	8.2	9.2	11.4	11.8
10,000 to 25,000...............	11.0	11.5	11.5	12.0	10.5	11.2	7.9	8.9	11.6	11.7
2,500 to 10,000................	11.0	11.6	11.0	11.6	10.0	10.7	7.6	8.8	10.5	11.1
1,000 to 2,500.................	10.6	11.4	10.7	11.3	9.6	10.3	7.4	8.6	10.4	10.8
Under 1,000 (incorporated)......	10.4	11.2	10.6	11.1	9.8	10.6	6.8	7.8	10.4	10.9
Other rural:										
Nonfarm........................	10.1	10.8	10.1	10.7	9.0	9.5	7.0	7.9	10.1	10.4
Farm...........................	9.5	10.4	9.8	10.5	8.4	9.1	6.2	7.4	9.9	10.3

Source: Unpublished tabulations by the Bureau of the Census.

school for the same four residence groups is 8.1, 7.8, 7.6, and 7.5.[1] Thus, even by the age of 13 a substantial difference in educational attainment among size-of-place groups has appeared. At each single year of age from 6 through 29, the percentage enrolled in school is highest in the urban population and lowest in the rural-farm population, with the rural-nonfarm population in an intermediate position. The differences are slight at ages 6 to 13 but become substantial thereafter. Based on interpolations from these single-year-of-age data, the estimated median ages at leaving school are 18.6 for urban males, 18.0 for rural-nonfarm males, and 17.9 for rural-farm males, the corresponding figures for females being 18.2, 18.0, and 18.1.[2]

---

[1] Based on data in *1950 Census of Population*, Vol. IV, *Special Reports*, Part 5, Chapter B, Education, table 1.

[2] Based on data in *1950 Census of Population*, Vol. II, *Characteristics of the Population*, Part 1, table 111.

C H A P T E R 8

LABOR FORCE AND OCCUPATION

Labor force participation

Size-of-place variation in the percentage of the population 14 years old and over in the labor force (table 29) is to be expected, because the larger places have disproportionate numbers of their population in the ages of high labor force participation. However, not all size-of-place differences in labor force participation rates can be explained in terms of age. Table 30 shows labor force participation rates, by color and sex, for the size-of-place groups as deviations from the rates for all males and females in the United States, and the deviations of the actual rates from the rates expected if each age interval in each size-of-place group had the same rate as the corresponding interval in the total population of the United States.[1]

TABLE 29.—PERCENT OF PERSONS IN THE LABOR FORCE BY SEX, BY SIZE OF PLACE: 1950

Size of place	Male	Female	Size of place	Male	Female
Urbanized areas:			Places outside urbanized areas—		
3,000,000 or more...............	80.5	34.0	Cont.		
1,000,000 to 3,000,000.........	80.5	33.0	2,500 to 10,000.................	77.0	30.4
250,000 to 1,000,000...........	80.9	33.9	1,000 to 2,500.................	76.7	27.2
Under 250,000...................	79.5	34.1	Under 1,000 (incorporated)......	73.9	23.4
Places outside urbanized areas:			Other rural:		
25,000 or more..................	77.6	33.9	Nonfarm.........................	73.4	21.1
10,000 to 25,000................	77.4	32.6	Farm............................	˙83.0	16.0

Source: *1950 Census of Population*, Vol. IV, *Special Reports*, Part 5, Chapter A, Characteristics by Size of Place, table 4.

Disregarding the influence of age distribution, the general tendency is for labor force participation rates to be directly related to size of place. For all males, the percentage in the labor force declines from about 80 or 81 in the urbanized areas, to 77 in the smallest urban places and large villages, and 73 in the "other rural-nonfarm" category. However, the highest rate—83 percent—is observed for "other rural-farm" males. The gradient for all females is much more pronounced. In the urbanized areas

---

[1] Standard rates, by sex, for the total population by the appropriate age intervals were computed from *1950 Census of Population*, Vol. II, *Characteristics of the Population*, Part 1, table 118. It should be noted that standardization for age does not eliminate possible differentials in completeness of reporting of labor force participation; nor does it yield an adjustment for seasonal effects due to the taking of the census in the month of April.

and larger places outside urbanized areas, around 33 to 34 percent of females aged 14 and over are in the labor force, compared with 30 percent in the smallest urban places, 27 and 23 percent in the two classes of villages, and 21 and 16 percent in the nonfarm and farm parts, respectively, of the "other rural" category.

When age is held constant, the size-of-place gradient in labor force participation rates for males virtually disappears, and even tends to reverse itself in the case of the nonwhite population, as is shown by the pattern of

TABLE **30.**—PERCENT OF PERSONS IN THE LABOR FORCE, EXPRESSED AS DEVIATION FROM UNITED STATES TOTAL AND FROM PERCENT EXPECTED ON THE BASIS OF THEIR AGE DISTRIBUTION, BY COLOR AND SEX, BY SIZE OF PLACE: 1950

Size of place	Male				Female			
	White		Nonwhite		White		Nonwhite	
	Deviation from--		Deviation from--		Deviation from--		Deviation from--	
	Total[1]	Ex-pected	Total[1]	Ex-pected	Total[2]	Ex-pected	Total[2]	Ex-pected
Urbanized areas:								
3,000,000 or more.............	1.8	-0.3	-0.5	-5.0	3.8	3.6	16.5	14.2
1,000,000 to 3,000,000.........	2.0	0.1	-1.7	-5.4	3.2	3.1	10.3	8.2
250,000 to 1,000,000...........	2.2	0.7	-0.3	-2.9	4.0	3.8	12.4	10.8
Under 250,000..................	0.9	-0.1	-2.1	-4.1	4.0	3.9	15.6	14.1
Places outside urbanized areas:								
25,000 or more................	-1.1	-1.5	-3.5	-4.4	3.9	4.1	15.9	14.9
10,000 to 25,000..............	-1.3	-1.3	-4.3	-4.4	2.6	2.8	14.7	13.9
25,000 to 10,000..............	-1.6	-1.0	-5.5	-4.3	0.3	0.8	14.1	13.6
1,000 to 2,500................	-1.9	-0.3	-6.3	-4.3	-2.6	-1.5	8.6	8.4
Under 1,000 (incorporated)......	-5.0	-0.6	-5.9	-1.5	-6.1	-3.9	4.2	4.7
Other rural:								
Nonfarm.......................	-4.7	-3.7	-12.6	-7.4	-8.5	-8.8	-2.2	-2.4
Farm..........................	4.1	7.0	4.4	10.3	-13.9	-13.5	-7.0	-7.1

[1] Percent of total males in labor force is 78.9.

[2] Percent of total females in labor force is 29.0.

Source: *1950 Census of Population,* Vol. II, *Characteristics of the Population,* Part 1, U. S. Summary, table 118; Vol. IV, *Special Reports,* Part 5, Chapter A, Characteristics by Size of Place, tables 4 and 4a.

deviations of actual rates from rates expected on the basis of age. However, the greatest deviation below the expected rate, for both white and nonwhite males, occurs for the "other rural-nonfarm" group. This may be partly, but probably not entirely, accounted for by the disproportionate size of the institutional population in this group. Unlike the situation for males, adjustment for age does not affect the pattern of variation by size of place in female labor force participation. For white females the gradient already described for all females continues to hold, with labor force participation rates in urbanized areas exceeding expected rates by 3 to 4 points, and falling short of the expected rate by 13.5 points in the "other rural-farm" group. The pattern by size of place for nonwhite females is likewise little affected by the age adjustment. However, in the case of nonwhite females, rather than a fairly regular size-of-place gradient, an "S-shaped" pattern is found. High rates prevail for the largest urbanized areas, but the rates for the two succeeding size groups are lower than those of the remaining urban groups. From a peak for the urban places of 25,000 or more, the rate declines steadily and markedly with decreasing size of place.

With or without the age adjustment, labor force participation rates of nonwhite females exceed those of white females in all size-of-place groups. The reverse is true for males, i.e., the nonwhite rates are lower in every size-of-place group except the "other rural-farm" group.

In sum, size of place appears to have a marked effect on labor force participation rates of females, but to be rather insignificant for males, when age is taken into account, except for the high percentage of male farm residents in the labor force.

More detailed age breakdowns of the labor force than are available in the size-of-place tabulations permit the estimation of median age of males at entry into, and departure from, the labor force, for a condensed size-of-place classification. (See table 31.) The procedure was to interpolate for the lower and upper age at which the percentage in the labor force equals exactly half the percentage for the age interval 35 to 44.[2] Entry into the labor force takes place at a slightly higher age in the urbanized areas than in other urban places and villages, where, in turn, the median is somewhat higher than in rural-farm areas. The range of the median age of entry is from 18.3 for the white rural-farm males to 18.9 for white males in urbanized areas, with a similar but somewhat larger difference for nonwhite males. Departure from the labor force is postponed in rural-farm areas well beyond the age of departure in other size-of-place groups. Disregarding the rural-farm population, age of departure for white males varies directly with size of place, the median age being about 66 in urbanized areas and the larger urban places, dropping to less than 63 in rural-nonfarm areas outside large villages. However, no such gradient is observed for the nonwhite males. It is perfectly possible, of course, that

TABLE 31.—ESTIMATED MEDIAN AGE OF MALES AT ENTRY INTO AND DEPARTURE FROM THE LABOR FORCE, BY COLOR, BY SIZE OF PLACE: 1950

Size of place	Total		White		Nonwhite	
	Entry	Departure	Entry	Departure	Entry	Departure
Urbanized areas...............	18.9	65.7	18.9	65.7	18.9	64.8
Other places:						
25,000 or more..............	18.7	65.8	18.8	65.8	18.6	64.3
2,500 to 25,000.............	18.7	65.2	18.8	65.2	18.6	65.3
1,000 to 2,500..............	18.8	64.6	18.8	64.5	18.6	65.9
Other rural:						
Nonfarm.....................	18.6	62.8	18.6	62.6	18.3	64.8
Farm........................	18.3	71.5	18.3	71.4	(1)	72.7

[1] Under 18.

Source: *1950 Census of Population*, Vol. IV, *Special Reports*, Part 1, Chapter A, Employment and Personal Characteristics, table 4.

---

[2] Data in *1950 Census of Population*, Vol. IV, *Special Reports*, Part 1, Chapter A, Employment and Personal Characteristics, table 4.

these results reflect differential migration, as well as the labor force dynamics of different sizes of place.

Unemployment

Table 32 shows the percentage of the civilian labor force reported as unemployed for each size-of-place group, by color. The nonwhite unemployment rate is higher than the white for each size-of-place group except the "other rural-farm," but the pattern of variation by size of place is similar for the two color categories. However, the nonwhite rates vary somewhat more by size of place than the white rates. For both whites and nonwhites the highest rates of unemployment are observed for the two largest size groups. Yet, the lowest rates in the urban-village range are for areas of 250,000 to 1 million, from which point they rise to a secondary peak at 2,500 to 10,000 for whites and 10,000 to 25,000 for nonwhites, and then decline regularly to the lowest value for the "other rural-farm" population.

It is unknown how accounting for "underemployment," e.g., the ability to find only part-time employment, would modify the above-described pattern.

TABLE 32.—PERCENT OF THE CIVILIAN LABOR FORCE UNEMPLOYED BY COLOR, BY SIZE OF PLACE: 1950

Size of place	Percent unemployed			Ratio of nonwhite percentage to white percentage
	Total	White	Nonwhite	
Urbanized areas:				
3,000,000 or more.............	6.1	5.6	11.0	2.0
1,000,000 to 3,000,000.........	5.8	5.1	11.0	2.2
250,000 to 1,000,000...........	4.8	4.4	8.3	1.9
Under 250,000..................	5.1	4.7	8.8	1.9
Places outside urbanized areas:				
25,000 or more.................	5.1	4.6	9.2	2.0
10,000 to 25,000...............	5.3	4.8	9.8	2.0
2,500 to 10,000................	5.2	4.9	8.4	1.7
1,000 to 2,500.................	4.9	4.7	8.1	1.7
Under 1,000 (incorporated).....	4.3	4.2	5.9	1.4
Other rural:				
Nonfarm........................	5.4	5.2	6.7	1.3
Farm...........................	1.7	1.7	1.6	0.9

Source: *1950 Census of Population*, Vol. IV, *Special Reports*, Part 5, Chapter A, Characteristics by Size of Place, tables 4 and 4a.

Occupation

The distribution of the employed labor force by major occupation groups is shown in table 33 for each size-of-place group. There are fairly substantial differences among the size groups. For example, the index of dissimilarity between the largest urbanized areas and the smallest urban places is 9.5 percent. This means that nearly a tenth of the employed persons in the places of 2,500 to 10,000 would have to change their occupation classification to make the distribution for this size group identical with the one for urbanized areas of 3 million or more.

The most general way to summarize the pattern of size-of-place differences is to state that there is a declining gradient in the socio-economic status of the labor force, from the largest urbanized areas to the rural groups.

TABLE 33.—PERCENT DISTRIBUTION OF EMPLOYED PERSONS BY MAJOR OCCUPATION GROUP AND SEX, BY SIZE OF PLACE: 1950

Size of place and sex	Total[1]	Profess'l, techn'l, and kindred workers	Managers, officials, & propr's, exc. farm	Clerical and kindred workers	Sales workers	Craftsmen, foremen, and kindred workers	Operatives and kindred workers	Private household workers	Service workers, exc. private hshld.	Laborers, except farm and mine	Farm occupations[2]
TOTAL											
Urbanized areas:											
3,000,000 or more	100.0	11.0	11.1	17.8	7.9	14.4	20.9	2.2	8.8	4.6	0.4
1,000,000 to 3,000,000	100.0	10.9	9.1	17.8	8.1	15.5	20.0	2.4	8.9	5.9	0.3
250,000 to 1,000,000	100.0	10.1	9.9	16.7	8.6	15.3	19.8	2.8	9.5	5.9	0.3
Under 250,000	100.0	9.8	9.7	14.6	8.6	15.2	22.3	3.1	9.1	6.0	0.6
Places outside urbanized areas:											
25,000 or more	100.0	10.4	10.0	13.6	8.8	14.6	21.3	3.3	9.9	6.0	0.9
10,000 to 25,000	100.0	10.1	10.2	12.0	8.7	14.8	22.2	3.3	9.3	6.5	1.7
2,500 to 10,000	100.0	9.6	10.2	10.6	8.2	15.0	22.7	3.6	8.9	6.9	3.0
1,000 to 2,500	100.0	9.3	10.7	9.1	7.4	15.5	23.2	3.2	7.7	7.5	4.9
Under 1,000 (incorporated)	100.0	9.6	11.8	8.2	6.9	14.7	18.1	2.9	7.7	8.5	9.8
Other rural:											
Nonfarm	100.0	6.9	8.1	7.1	5.4	17.3	25.3	2.5	6.3	10.0	9.5
Farm	100.0	2.4	1.8	2.3	1.6	4.7	8.6	1.1	1.5	3.5	70.9
MALE											
Urbanized areas:											
3,000,000 or more	100.0	10.7	14.2	10.0	8.3	20.2	20.0	0.2	8.6	6.5	0.5
1,000,000 to 3,000,000	100.0	10.3	11.5	9.6	7.9	21.9	21.4	0.2	7.7	8.2	0.3
250,000 to 1,000,000	100.0	9.1	12.6	9.1	8.5	21.8	21.3	0.2	7.6	8.3	0.5
Under 250,000	100.0	8.5	12.4	8.0	8.4	21.8	23.3	0.2	7.2	8.5	0.8
Places outside urbanized areas:											
25,000 or more	100.0	8.6	13.0	7.4	8.4	21.2	22.4	0.2	7.9	8.6	1.3
10,000 to 25,000	100.0	8.4	12.9	6.4	8.1	21.1	23.4	0.2	7.0	9.2	2.3
2,500 to 10,000	100.0	7.8	12.9	5.6	7.5	21.2	23.8	0.2	6.3	9.7	3.9
1,000 to 2,500	100.0	7.3	12.8	4.9	6.2	21.4	24.9	0.1	4.9	10.1	6.2
Under 1,000 (incorporated)	100.0	6.9	13.5	5.0	5.5	19.4	19.7	0.2	4.8	11.1	12.4
Other rural:											
Nonfarm	100.0	5.4	8.9	4.0	4.5	22.0	26.0	0.2	4.1	12.6	11.1
Farm	100.0	1.1	1.8	1.0	1.1	5.3	7.8	0.1	0.8	4.0	76.0
FEMALE											
Urbanized areas:											
3,000,000 or more	100.0	11.8	4.5	34.5	6.9	1.8	22.7	6.6	9.2	0.6	0.2
1,000,000 to 3,000,000	100.0	12.4	3.8	35.7	8.4	1.8	16.8	7.3	11.6	0.8	0.1
250,000 to 1,000,000	100.0	12.0	4.2	32.6	8.8	1.8	16.7	8.3	13.5	0.7	0.1
Under 250,000	100.0	12.5	4.0	28.4	8.8	1.5	20.4	9.0	13.0	0.8	0.2
Places outside urbanized areas:											
25,000 or more	100.0	13.9	4.1	25.9	9.4	1.3	19.3	9.6	14.0	0.7	0.4
10,000 to 25,000	100.0	13.5	4.5	23.8	10.0	1.4	19.6	9.9	14.2	0.8	0.6
2,500 to 10,000	100.0	13.6	4.4	21.6	10.0	1.2	20.1	11.2	14.6	0.8	1.0
1,000 to 2,500	100.0	14.4	5.3	19.5	10.3	1.2	19.3	10.9	14.8	0.9	1.3
Under 1,000 (incorporated)	100.0	17.4	7.1	17.3	10.8	1.2	13.8	10.6	15.7	1.2	2.2
Other rural:											
Nonfarm	100.0	12.0	5.4	17.7	8.5	1.4	22.7	10.4	14.0	1.1	4.2
Farm	100.0	9.8	1.9	10.0	4.4	0.7	13.4	7.2	5.7	0.7	41.3

[1] Includes persons with occupation not reported.

[2] Includes "Farmers and farm managers" and "Farm laborers and foremen."

Source: *1950 Census of Population*, Vol. IV, *Special Reports*, Part 5, Chapter A, Characteristics by Size of Place, table 5.

The percentage employed in white-collar occupations,[3] graphed in figure 13, declines from about 48 in the urbanized areas of 3 million or over, to 43 in the smallest urbanized areas, 39 in the smallest urban places, 36.5 in the villages, and 27.5 and 8 in the nonfarm and farm parts, respectively, of the "other rural" category. Another general feature of the gradient pattern is the regularly rising percentage of workers in farm occupations, going from the largest to the smallest size groups. Even within the urban range there is an increase from less than ½ of 1 percent to 3 percent of employed persons engaged in farm occupations, as between the largest urbanized areas and the smallest urban places. Similarly, the gradient in the percentage of manual[4] workers is generally upward, from

FIGURE **13.**—PERCENT DISTRIBUTION OF THE EMPLOYED LABOR FORCE, BY BROAD OCCUPATION GROUP AND SIZE OF PLACE: 1950

[See p. 32 for size-of-place code]

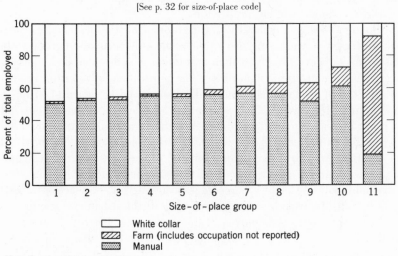

Note: Based on data in table 33.

about 51 percent in the largest urbanized areas, to 57 percent in the smallest urban places and large villages, and 61 percent in the "other rural-nonfarm" category. The gradient is interrupted, however, by the low figure of 52 percent for small villages, as well as the figure of only 19 percent for the "other rural-farm" category, in which about seven-tenths of all employed persons are engaged in farm occupations.

Considering the major occupation groups individually, the most pronounced gradient occurs for the percentage of workers employed in clerical and kindred occupations. In the two largest size groups nearly 18 percent are clerical workers, and the percentage decreases regularly to less than 11 for the smallest urban places, 8 for small villages, and about 2 for

---

[3] These include professional, technical, and kindred workers; managers, officials, and proprietors, except farm; clerical and kindred workers; and sales workers.

[4] This group includes all except white-collar occupations, farmers and farm managers, and farm laborers and foremen.

the "other rural-farm" category. There is also a slight and irregular declining gradient in the percentage employed as professional, technical, and kindred workers. The other two white-collar occupation groups deviate from this pattern. The percentage of nonfarm managers, officials, and proprietors drops from 11 to 9 percent, going from the first to the second size group, and then grades upward to a high of 12 percent in the small villages. The percentage of sales workers rises from 7.9 percent in the largest urbanized areas to 8.8 percent in urban places 25,000 or more outside urbanized areas, and then declines to 6.9 percent in the small villages, and 5.4 and 1.6, respectively, in the nonfarm and farm parts of the "other rural" category. Thus the over-all downward gradient in the percentage of white-collar workers reflects primarily the gradient for clerical workers and secondarily that of professional and related occupations; it is only partly characteristic of sales workers and is generally opposite to the gradient for managers, officials, and proprietors.

Although there is a general upward gradient for the percentage of manual workers with decreasing size of place, the only occupation group within this broad category for which such a gradient is substantial and consistent over most size groups is laborers. The percentage of laborers in small villages (10.0) is more than double the corresponding figure (4.6) for the largest urbanized areas. The percentage employed as private household workers increases regularly from 2.2 in the largest urbanized areas to a high of 3.6 in places of 2,500 to 10,000, then declines to 2.5 and 1.1 in the nonfarm and farm parts, respectively, of the "other rural" category. A somewhat similar pattern appears for the service workers, except private household, with the highest percentage occurring for the places of 25,000 or more outside urbanized areas, and with all the urban size groups having higher percentages employed in this occupation group than any of the rural size groups. There is some tendency for the percentage employed as operatives and kindred workers to increase with decreasing size of place, although the gradient is rather irregular. In the first three size groups the percentage of operatives is around 20 to 21, rising to 21 to 22 in the next three groups, with the smallest urban places and large villages having 23 percent employed as operatives. The highest percentage of operatives, 25, occurs in "other rural-nonfarm" areas, doubtlessly owing, in part, to concentrations of miners there, while the low figures of 18 and 9 percent, respectively, are noted for small villages and the "other rural-farm" category. As is the case for operatives, the percentage employed as craftsmen, foremen, and kindred workers varies only relatively slightly by size of place. Disregarding the "other rural" category the largest percentage for any size group is 15.5, and the smallest 14.4, while the "other rural-nonfarm" areas have 17.3 percent employed as craftsmen, foremen, and kindred workers, and the "other rural-farm" 4.7 percent. Within the urban-village range there is little to suggest a regular pattern of variation in the percentage in this occupation group by size of place.

Another way of looking at the variations in occupation structure concerns the relative numerical importance of the several occupations groups in different sizes of place. Farm occupations are, of course, greatly predominant in the "other rural-farm" areas. However, in the case of all the other size groups the largest occupation group is operatives and kindred workers. Second place goes to clerical and kindred workers in only the first three size groups, and to craftsmen, foremen, and kindred workers in the remaining nonfarm groups. Clerical and kindred workers remain the third largest occupation group in all the urban groups below 250,000 inhabitants, but drop as low as fifth to seventh place in the rural size groups. Other such shifts can be observed in the data given in table 33.

Although the foregoing materials depict in general outline the variations in over-all occupation structure by size of community, patterns of variation in the occupational composition of labor force subgroups also are important. Tables 33 and 34 give the occupation distribution for each size-of-place group with a color and sex breakdown.

In reference to sex differences in occupational composition, each size-of-place group reproduces the general pattern of differences between the male and female occupational distributions. In the United States as a whole there are five major occupation groups in which females are disproportionately represented: private household workers; clerical and kindred workers; service workers except private household; professional, technical, and kindred workers; and sales workers. In each size-of-place group the percentage of females employed as private household workers exceeds the corresponding percentage for males; and a similar statement holds for each of the other four "female occupations" listed, with the single exception that in the largest urbanized areas the percentage of males employed as sales workers exceeds that of females. Similarly, with only three minor exceptions, in every size-of-place group the percentage of males employed in each of the "male occupations" is greater than the corresponding percentage of females.

Despite the consistency in the general pattern of sex differences in occupation composition by size of place, the extent of such differences is clearly a function of size of place. Table 35 shows the index of dissimilarity between the male and female occupation distributions for each size-of-place group.[5] The lowest value of the index, about 36, is observed for

---

[5] The index of dissimilarity is the percentage of nonoverlapping of two distributions. Its computation may be illustrated as follows:

Occupation	Male	Female	Overlap
Total	100%	100%	55%
A	10	30	10
B	15	25	15
C	55	10	10
D	20	35	20

Index of dissimilarity = 100% − 55% = 45%.

TABLE **34.**—PERCENT DISTRIBUTION OF NONWHITE EMPLOYED PERSONS BY MAJOR OCCUPATION GROUP AND SEX, BY SIZE OF PLACE: 1950

Size of place and sex	Total[1]	Profess'l, techn'l, and kindred workers	Managers, officials, & propr's, exc. farm	Clerical and kindred workers	Sales workers	Craftsmen, foremen, and kindred workers	Operatives and kindred workers	Private household workers	Service workers, exc. private hshld.	Laborers, except farm and mine	Farm occupations[2]
MALE											
Urbanized areas:											
3,000,000 or more............	100.0	3.4	4.6	8.8	2.6	11.3	26.7	1.5	21.3	17.8	0.6
1,000,000 to 3,000,000.......	100.0	2.8	3.1	7.2	2.0	10.6	26.1	1.2	18.7	26.1	0.4
250,000 to 1,000,000.........	100.0	2.6	2.9	3.7	1.4	9.7	24.9	1.3	21.6	30.2	0.5
Under 250,000................	100.0	2.8	3.2	2.4	1.6	10.4	25.2	1.3	20.0	30.4	1.4
Places outside urbanized areas:											
25,000 or more...............	100.0	3.4	3.2	1.6	1.2	10.0	23.5	1.7	22.4	29.5	2.1
10,000 to 25,000.............	100.0	3.7	2.8	1.4	1.5	10.0	27.0	1.7	16.4	29.6	4.3
2,500 to 10,000..............	100.0	3.3	2.0	1.1	1.3	9.2	25.5	1.7	14.4	30.8	9.5
1,000 to 2,500...............	100.0	2.8	2.1	1.0	0.7	8.8	29.8	0.9	8.9	30.0	13.7
Under 1,000 (incorporated)...	100.0	2.5	2.0	1.0	1.1	6.1	20.7	1.0	4.5	31.7	27.8
Other rural:											
Nonfarm......................	100.0	2.1	1.3	0.9	0.6	6.4	21.5	1.0	5.9	30.7	27.9
Farm.........................	100.0	0.4	0.2	0.1	0.1	1.2	5.0	0.2	0.6	6.1	85.2
FEMALE											
Urbanized areas:											
3,000,000 or more............	100.0	4.7	1.5	9.1	1.8	1.3	31.5	31.9	14.9	1.7	0.3
1,000,000 to 3,000,000.......	100.0	5.5	1.2	10.2	1.9	1.0	18.6	34.9	23.1	2.0	0.2
250,000 to 1,000,000.........	100.0	5.2	1.7	3.7	1.7	0.7	13.6	42.7	27.6	1.7	0.2
Under 250,000................	100.0	5.6	1.5	2.9	1.2	0.4	13.2	47.4	24.2	1.6	0.5
Places outside urbanized areas:											
25,000 or more...............	100.0	6.0	1.6	2.3	1.1	0.6	10.8	50.4	24.3	1.2	0.8
10,000 to 25,000.............	100.0	7.1	1.5	1.7	1.7	0.4	10.8	52.7	19.2	1.2	2.4
2,500 to 10,000..............	100.0	7.9	1.6	1.2	1.2	0.3	9.0	55.7	16.9	0.9	4.0
1,000 to 2,500...............	100.0	8.0	2.0	1.1	0.8	0.1	6.8	57.0	16.3	1.0	5.3
Under 1,000 (incorporated)...	100.0	6.0	2.0	0.8	1.0	0.2	5.3	57.9	11.7	1.7	11.5
Other rural:											
Nonfarm......................	100.0	5.3	1.5	1.1	1.3	0.2	9.1	47.1	13.2	1.6	17.2
Farm.........................	100.0	4.2	0.4	0.3	0.4	...	2.7	17.9	3.6	0.5	66.7

[1] Includes persons with occupation not reported.
[2] Includes "Farmers and farm managers" and "Farm laborers and foremen."

Source: *1950 Census of Population*, Vol. IV, *Special Reports*, Part 5, Chapter A, Characteristics by Size of Place, table 5a.

TABLE **35.**—INDEX OF DISSIMILARITY FOR MALE VERSUS FEMALE OCCUPATION DISTRIBUTIONS, BY COLOR, BY SIZE OF PLACE: 1950

[In computing the index, "Farmers and farm managers" was treated as a distinct occupation group from "Farm laborers and foremen"]

Size of place	Total	Non-white	Size of place	Total	Non-white
Urbanized areas:			Places outside urbanized areas— Cont.		
3,000,000 or more..............	35.7	36.8	2,500 to 10,000..................	44.0	61.3
1,000,000 to 3,000,000.........	40.0	43.8	1,000 to 2,500...................	47.4	69.2
250,000 to 1,000,000...........	41.0	50.3	Under 1,000 (incorporated)......	50.6	67.9
Under 250,000..................	39.9	53.8			
Places outside urbanized areas:			Other rural:		
25,000 or more.................	40.7	53.9	Nonfarm..........................	45.8	58.4
10,000 to 25,000...............	42.0	57.7	Farm.............................	52.6	49.0

* Source: *1950 Census of Population*, Vol. IV, *Special Reports*, Part 5, Chapter A, Characteristics by Size of Place, tables 5 and 5a.

the largest urbanized areas, with values of 40 to 41 for the next four size groups, 42 and 44 for the two smallest urban groups in order, 47 and 51 for large and small villages, respectively, and 53 for "other rural-farm" employed persons. The only major interruption of the increasing gradient of the index is the value of about 46 for the "other rural-nonfarm" category. Hence, it is generally true that the larger the community, the more similar are the occupation distributions of males and females. A similar gradient appears for nonwhites, among whom sex differences in occupation composition are generally greater than in the total employed labor force.

Among the specific differences in the pattern of variation by size of place of the male and female occupation distributions, the following are salient. The percentage of males employed in professional, technical, and kindred occupations declines regularly and markedly with decreasing size of place, whereas a gradient in the opposite direction holds for females until the "other rural" categories are reached. Throughout the urban-village range, there is a distinct upward gradient, with decreasing size of place, in the percentage of females employed as sales workers, but an irregular tendency toward a downward gradient for males. The gradients run also in opposite directions for the two sexes in the case of the percentage employed as service workers, except private household, with the male percentages decreasing generally with decreasing size of place and the female percentages increasing throughout the urban-village range. The rising gradient, with decreasing size of place, in the percentage of females employed as private household workers has no counterpart in the male occupation distributions.

In the case of nonwhite employed persons, there are two significant contrasts between the sexes. There is a pronounced increase in the percentage of females employed as private household workers, from 32 to 58, going from the largest urbanized areas to the small villages, but this gradient is not in evidence for nonwhite males. The gradient in the opposite direction for the percentage of females employed as operatives and kindred workers likewise is not reproduced for males. Evidently, employment opportunities for nonwhite females, in other than domestic service work, are more favorable in large than in small places.

Differences in the occupational composition of the total and the nonwhite employed labor force show up clearly in the data in tables 33 and 34. The percentage of total males employed in each of the white-collar occupations and in the craftsmen, foremen, and kindred group exceeds the corresponding percentage for nonwhite males in every size-of-place group. With only four minor exceptions in the rural groups, the reverse is true for each of the other manual occupations and for farm occupations, taken as a single group. At the same time, the degree of white-nonwhite occupational differentiation for males varies somewhat by size of place as is indicated by the data in table 36. The index of dissimilarity between the

TABLE **36.**—INDEX OF DISSIMILARITY FOR WHITE VERSUS NONWHITE OCCUPATION DISTRIBU-
TIONS, BY SEX, BY SIZE OF PLACE, FOR THE UNITED STATES AND THE SOUTH: 1950

[In computing the index, "Farmers and farm managers" was treated as a distinct occupation group from
"Farm laborers and foremen"]

Size of place	United States		South	
	Male	Female	Male	Female
Urbanized areas:				
3,000,000 or more................	35.5	46.3	...	...
1,000,000 to 3,000,000.........	39.9	48.9	48.6	52.6
250,000 to 1,000,000............	45.5	57.1	52.7	58.3
Under 250,000...................	42.5	57.9	52.0	57.4
Places outside urbanized areas:				
25,000 or more..................	42.7	58.7	49.5	57.0
10,000 to 25,000................	40.6	56.2	46.9	56.2
2,500 to 10,000.................	41.1	56.2	45.1	56.1
1,000 to 2,500..................	39.7	57.3	42.1	58.8
Under 1,000 (incorporated).....	39.8	63.2	43.1	63.1
Other rural:				
Nonfarm........................	41.5	56.8	42.3	56.5
Farm...........................	14.7	44.2	15.7	45.9

Source: *1950 Census of Population*, Vol. IV, *Special Reports*, Part 5, Chapter A, Characteristics by Size of
Place, tables 5, 5a, and 7; and unpublished tabulations by region.

white and nonwhite occupation distributions for males is lowest in the
"other rural-farm" category, since the great majority of both whites and
nonwhites are employed in farm occupations. The pattern for the other
size-of-place groups is for the least dissimilarity to occur in the largest urbanized areas with the index rising to a peak value for urbanized areas of
250,000 to 1 million, and declining fairly regularly thereafter. The South
exhibits a similar pattern, but with a sharper decline from the peak and
generally higher values of the index of dissimilarity. Thus in both the
South and the United States as a whole the general tendency is for the
occupation distributions of white and nonwhite males to be more dissimilar, the larger the size of the community, up to a size of 1 million.

The comparison of the data for total and nonwhite females in tables 33
and 34 indicates that in all size-of-place groups higher percentages of total
females than of nonwhite females are engaged in each of the white-collar
occupations. Further, the percentage of total females employed as craftsmen, foremen, and kindred workers is higher than the corresponding nonwhite percentage, in every size group, as is also the case for operatives
and kindred workers in all but the first two size groups. With but four
exceptions the nonwhite percentage is the higher in each size-of-place
group for all of the remaining manual occupations. Hence, the general
pattern of differences between total and nonwhite females is reasonably
consistent from one size-of-place group to another. There is, further, no
clear gradient in the index of dissimilarity between the white and nonwhite
occupation distributions for females, either in the United States as a whole,
or in the South. Relatively low indexes are observed for the two largest
size groups and for the "other rural-farm" category, and an exceptionally
high index value for small villages. There are only small differences among
the remaining size groups.

C H A P T E R   9

INCOME

Of all the differences among communities of different size revealed in this study, perhaps the most striking is the pronounced direct relationship between size of place and income. Figure 14 shows the median income in 1949 for all persons 14 years old and over with income, for each size-of-place group. For both males and females there is a regular gradient from the peak income in the largest urbanized areas to the lowest income in "other rural-farm" territory. The gradient is interrupted only by the figure for the "other rural-nonfarm" population, which is higher than that for small villages, but below the median for the large villages. On the average, the median income for males of a given size-of-place group is nearly $150 greater than that of the next smaller size group, and the average differential is over $100 for females.

Furthermore, the gradient pattern clearly persists when the data are subclassified by age, color, and region, as may be seen from tables 37 and 38. There is variation in the rate of change by size of place among subgroups, and minor irregularities appear here and there. However, the proposition that median income increases with increasing size of place is a generally valid one, regardless of the region or population subgroup referred to.

It is true also that color and sex differences in income are highly consistent by size of place; i.e., in every size group the male median considerably exceeds the female median, and the median for whites is much greater than that for nonwhites. Since there is a distinct size-of-place gradient for each age group, size-of-place differences in income for the total population cannot be attributed to differences in age composition.

Regional differences in income are not highly consistent by size of place. The size-of-place gradient for white males is steeper in the South than in the other regions, and their median income is lower than for any other region, in places outside of urbanized areas; but for white females in the South median income is higher in most size-of-place groups than in the North Central and West. In all but one size-of-place group white females in the Northeast have a higher median than in any other region. Nonwhite income is consistently lower in the South for both males and females than in the other regions. The size-of-place gradient appears to be somewhat less steep in the Northeast than in other regions, for both sexes and color cate-

FIGURE 14.—MEDIAN INCOME IN 1949 OF PERSONS 14 YEARS OLD AND OVER WITH INCOME, BY SEX

[See p. 32 for size-of-place code]

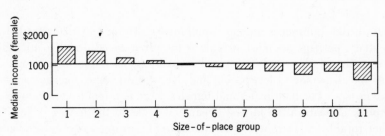

Size-of-place group

Note: Based on data in table 37.

TABLE 37.—MEDIAN INCOME IN 1949 OF PERSONS 14 YEARS OLD AND OVER WITH INCOME, BY AGE, COLOR, AND SEX, BY SIZE OF PLACE: 1950

[In dollars]

Size of place and color	Total, 14 years and over		14 to 24 years		25 to 44 years		45 to 64 years		65 years and over	
	Male	Female	Male	Female	Male	Female	Male	Female	Male	Female
TOTAL										
Urbanized areas:										
3,000,000 or more............	3,078	1,603	1,621	1,440	3,348	1,853	3,399	1,692	1,847	808
1,000,000 to 3,000,000........	3,026	1,471	1,587	1,257	3,300	1,713	3,371	1,611	1,831	782
250,000 to 1,000,000..........	2,779	1,215	1,461	1,039	3,144	1,451	3,149	1,381	1,579	671
Under 250,000................	2,692	1,121	1,335	925	3,061	1,356	3,083	1,295	1,460	676
Places outside urbanized areas:										
25,000 or more...............	2,554	1,003	1,147	799	2,984	1,283	3,004	1,202	1,463	645
10,000 to 25,000.............	2,484	926	1,156	693	2,916	1,217	2,872	1,112	1.280	609
2,500 to 10,000..............	2,354	839	1,077	647	2,811	1,081	2,669	955	1,082	566
1,000 to 2,500...............	2,268	749	1,126	579	2,745	990	2,535	838	940	520
Under 1,000 (incorporated)....	1,935	626	924	476	2,565	859	2,207	722	832	475
Other rural:										
Nonfarm......................	2,029	718	1,106	553	2,565	932	2,301	818	777	431
Farm.........................	1,379	459	623	400	1,791	544	1,589	508	784	394
NONWHITE										
Urbanized areas:										
3,000,000 or more............	2,213	1,278	1,525	1,064	2,342	1,408	2,312	1,229	1,299	752
1,000,000 to 3,000,000........	2,226	1,072	1,453	840	2,374	1,252	2,313	1,002	1,144	693
250,000 to 1,000,000..........	1,695	723	1,200	571	1,878	809	1,803	728	857	480
Under 250,000................	1,543	633	986	457	1,722	719	1,656	659	771	424
Places outside urbanized areas:										
25,000 or more...............	1,407	569	896	443	1,607	666	1,511	561	682	393
10,000 to 25,000.............	1,275	469	770	372	1,495	565	1,425	484	577	383
2,500 to 10,000..............	1,134	415	730	345	1,411	487	1,229	408	539	350
1,000 to 2,500...............	1,092	377	664	327	1,413	417	1,198	388	499	331
Under 1,000 (incorporated)....	807	333	551	283	1,134	365	821	353	433	308
Other rural:										
Nonfarm......................	974	376	744	331	1,296	421	1,016	378	437	337
Farm.........................	569	312	402	284	765	331	631	328	402	302

Source: *1950 Census of Population*, Vol. IV, *Special Reports*, Part 5, Chapter A. Characteristics by Size of Place, tables 4 and 4a.

gories, so that, for example, white males in urbanized areas generally have lower incomes in the Northeast than in any of the other regions, whereas the Northeast ranks first or second in the rural size groups. More important than the regional differences revealed by the data in table 38 is the fact that there is a marked size-of-place gradient in income within each region.

The data in earlier chapters show that educational attainment is generally greater in large than in small places, and that the socio-economic status of the labor force, as measured by occupation, is generally higher. Hence,

TABLE **38.**—MEDIAN INCOME IN 1949 OF PERSONS 14 YEARS OLD AND OVER WITH INCOME BY COLOR AND SEX, BY SIZE OF PLACE, BY REGIONS: 1950

[In dollars]

Size of place and color	Northeast		North Central		South		West	
	Male	Female	Male	Female	Male	Female	Male	Female
WHITE								
Urbanized areas:								
3,000,000 or more.............	3,121	1,768	3,377	1,699	...	...	3,106	1,304
1,000,000 to 3,000,000.........	2,935	1,454	3,335	1,523	3,262	1,846	3,291	1,628
250,000 to 1,000,000...........	2,781	1,380	3,125	1,350	2,834	1,312	2,984	1,218
Under 250,000..................	2,686	1,345	3,037	1,185	2,757	1,219	2,925	1,060
Places outside urbanized areas:								
25,000 or more.................	2,587	1,232	2,832	1,126	2,441	1,099	2,927	996
10,000 to 25,000...............	2,558	1,187	2,653	973	2,479	1,005	2,888	930
2,500 to 10,000................	2,540	1,072	2,538	868	2,249	930	2,771	846
1,000 to 2,500.................	2,498	944	2,402	769	2,138	818	2,546	741
Under 1,000 (incorporated).....	2,380	837	2,061	647	1,690	692	2,248	636
Other rural:								
Nonfarm........................	2,408	976	2,384	786	1,819	732	2,319	743
Farm...........................	1,821	769	1,827	620	1,142	468	1,974	562
NONWHITE								
Urbanized areas:								
3,000,000 or more.............	2,098	1,319	2,380	1,271	...	...	2,205	1,089
1,000,000 to 3,000,000.........	2,122	1,060	2,395	974	2,088	1,186	2,324	1,095
250,000 to 1,000,000...........	2,135	966	2,130	899	1,555	665	2,021	957
Under 250,000..................	1,951	923	2,244	768	1,423	599	1,926	745
Places outside urbanized areas:								
25,000 or more.................	1,858	980	2,040	689	1,303	541	1,799	724
10,000 to 25,000...............	2,000	910	1,461	534	1,209	449	1,732	763
2,500 to 10,000................	1,840	759	1,394	566	1,094	404	1,524	642
1,000 to 2,500.................	1,917	750	1,065	468	1,046	368	1,565	515
Under 1,000 (incorporated).....	1,550	875	961	542	780	324	1,813	417
Other rural:								
Nonfarm........................	1,535	698	1,022	412	947	364	1,212	474
Farm...........................	1,340	731	756	354	546	308	952	427

Source: Unpublished tabulations by the Bureau of the Census.

the question arises as to whether either of these factors accounts for the size-of-place gradient in income. There is indirect evidence that even with educational or broad occupational differences eliminated, substantial variation in income by size of place remains.

Table 39 shows for males aged 25 to 44 the deviation of the median income in each size of place from the median for males of this age in the entire United States. This series is compared with the deviations from what would be the medians if in each size-of-place group males 25 to 44 in each category of educational status had the same income distribution as

TABLE 39.—MEDIAN INCOME IN 1949 OF MALES 25 TO 44 YEARS OLD BY SIZE OF PLACE, EXPRESSED AS DEVIATION FROM UNITED STATES MEDIAN INCOME, AND AS DEVIATION FROM MEDIAN EXPECTED ON THE BASIS OF THEIR DISTRIBUTION BY EDUCATIONAL STATUS: 1950

[In dollars]

Size of place	Deviation from—		Size of place	Deviation from—	
	United States median	Ex-pected median		United States median	Ex-. pected median
Urbanized areas:			Places outside urbanized areas —Cont.		
3,000,000 or more..............	461	314	2,500 to 10,000..............	-76	-86
1,000,000 to 3,000,000........	413	291	1,000 to 2,500..............	-142	-131
250,000 to 1,000,000..........	257	150	Under 1,000 (incorporated)...	-322	-325
Under 250,000.................	174	99	Other rural:		
Places outside urbanized areas:			Nonfarm......................	-322	-166
25,000 or more................	97	16	Farm.........................	-1,096	-785
10,000 to 25,000..............	29	-28			

Source: *1950 Census of Population,* Vol. IV, *Special Reports,* Part 5, Chapter A, Characteristics by Size of Place, table 4; and Part 5, Chapter B, Education, table 12.

all males of this age in the United States.[1] The reason for confining the analysis to this particular age group is that at this age a substantial direct relationship between education and income becomes apparent. As the comparison in table 39 makes clear, although size-of-place variation in income is somewhat reduced when allowance is made for educational differences, there still remains a very pronounced size-of-place gradient in income.

A similar analysis, holding constant occupation, is summarized in table 40.[2] There is some uncertainty in the results, since not all males with income are in the experienced labor force. A rough adjustment for the difference was made by subtracting from the expected medians the difference, $216, between the median income of all males 14 years old and over in the experienced labor force and the median income of all males 14 and over with income (as determined from the 3⅓-percent sample statistics). Holding constant the distribution by major occupation groups has a large effect on the income of "other rural-farm" males; but as far as the other size-of-place groups are concerned, a pronounced size-of-place gradient remains after the influence of broad occupation differences is eliminated.

A final point in the analysis of income differences by size of place concerns the inequality of the income distribution. To determine the degree of income inequality it was necessary to estimate the aggregate income received by income recipients in each class interval of income. To make this estimate it was assumed that the mean income of persons with less than $500 income was $250, that the mean income of persons with incomes of $6,000 and over was $10,000, and that the mean income in each

---

[1] The requisite distributions of income by educational status were obtained from *1950 Census of Population,* Vol. IV, *Special Reports,* Part 5, Chapter B, Education, table 12.

[2] The income distribution by occupation of the male experienced labor force was obtained from *1950 Census of Population,* Vol. II, *Characteristics of the Population,* Part 1, table 129.

TABLE **40.**—MEDIAN INCOME IN 1949 OF MALES 14 YEARS OLD AND OVER BY SIZE OF PLACE, EXPRESSED AS DEVIATION FROM UNITED STATES MEDIAN INCOME, AND AS DEVIATION FROM MEDIAN INCOME EXPECTED ON THE BASIS OF THEIR OCCUPATION DISTRIBUTION: 1950

[In dollars]

Size of place	Deviation from--		Size of place	Deviation from--	
	United States median	Ex-pected median[1]		United States median	Ex-pected median[1]
Urbanized areas:			Places outside urbanized areas --Cont.		
3,000,000 or more.............	626	354	2,500 to 10,000...............	-98	-240
1,000,000 to 3,000,000........	574	347	1,000 to 2,500................	-184	-290
250,000 to 1,000,000..........	327	104	Under 1,000 (incorporated)...	-517	-524
Under 250,000..................	240	36			
Places outside urbanized areas:			Other rural:		
25,000 or more.................	102	-96	Nonfarm......................	-423	-353
10,000 to 25,000..............	32	-143	Farm........................	-1,073	36

[1] Adjusted for difference between total males with income and male experienced labor force.

Source: *1950 Census of Population*, Vol. II, *Characteristics of the Population*, Part 1, U. S. Summary, table 129; Vol. IV, *Special Reports*, Part 5, Chapter A, Characteristics by Size of Place, table 4.

other class interval was the midpoint of the interval.[3] From the estimates of aggregate income, Lorenz curves were constructed to compare the cumulative percentages of total aggregate income received with the percentages of income recipients, by amount of income.

Table 41 shows, for each size-of-place group, the Gini index of income inequality (concentration ratio) derived from the Lorenz curves. With the exception of the "other rural-nonfarm" group, the indexes increase regularly with decreasing size of place. In other words, income inequality is least in the largest places, which also have the highest median income. This result must be considered tentative, in view of the crudeness of the data and of the estimation procedure. In particular, it is possible that the assumption of a uniform mean income for the open-end interval, $6,000 and over, biases the indexes in the direction of the obtained relationship, and that, if this is the case, the relationship is spurious. Nevertheless, a very similar result is obtained using data from the 1953 sample survey of

TABLE **41.**—GINI INDEX OF INCOME INEQUALITY FOR ALL PERSONS WITH INCOME IN 1949, BY SIZE OF PLACE: 1950

Size of place	Index	Size of place	Index
Urbanized areas:		Places outside urbanized areas--Cont.	
3,000,000 or more..................	0.402	2,500 to 10,000.....................	0.458
1,000,000 to 3,000,000.............	0.402	1,000 to 2,500......................	0.461
250,000 to 1,000,000...............	0.423	Under 1,000 (incorporated).........	0.478
Under 250,000......................	0.430		
Places outside urbanized areas:		Other rural:	
25,000 or more.....................	0.444	Nonfarm.............................	0.453
10,000 to 25,000...................	0.449	Farm................................	0.512

Source: *1950 Census of Population*, Vol. IV, *Special Reports*, Part 5, Chapter A, Characteristics by Size of Place, table 4.

---

[3] Compare the procedures used to estimate aggregate income described in U. S. Bureau of the Census, *Current Population Reports* Series P–60, No. 14, December 31, 1953.

income,[4] which are presented in considerably greater detail, with an open-end interval of $25,000 or more. The inequality indexes calculated from these data are 0.41 for urbanized areas of 1 million or more, 0.42 for areas of 250,000 to 1 million, 0.43 for urbanized areas under 250,000, 0.46 for all other urban places, 0.44 for rural-nonfarm, and 0.55 for rural-farm areas. Accordingly, there is some justification for suggesting that the rising average level of income associated with increasing size of community is accompanied by a slight decrease in the degree of inequality of the income distribution.

---

[4] *Ibid.*

CHAPTER 10

VILLAGE POPULATION

The foregoing chapters present numerous comparisons involving villages. It is desirable to review these materials to gain perspective on what has undoubtedly been one of the most neglected areas in American demography. Prior to the 1950 Census there were no data available for a comprehensive analysis of village population characteristics, although the available fragmentary data had been studied in an exploratory way.[1]

The size of the village population in relation to the other rural categories is shown in table 42. The figure for villages of 1,000 to 2,500 is taken directly from the census reports, while the one for the smaller villages involves an estimate which may be subject to considerable error (Chapter 2). Apparently, the village population amounts to more than one-quarter of the rural population, and not quite one-tenth of the total population of the United States.

TABLE 42.—ESTIMATED DISTRIBUTION OF THE RURAL POPULATION BY FARM RESIDENCE AND SIZE OF PLACE: 1950

[Population in millions]

Size of place	Total	Nonfarm	Farm
Total..............................	54.2	31.2	23.0
1,000 to 2,500..........................	6.5	6.4	0.1
Under 1,000[1]..........................	8.0	7.6	0.4
Other rural[1]..........................	39.7	17.2	22.5

[1] Distribution based in part on estimates. Estimates assume that the population of unincorporated places under 1,000 equals the enumerated population in incorporated places of that size.

Source: *1950 Census of Population*, Vol. II, *Characteristics of the Population*, Part 1, U. S. Summary, tables 5a and 34; Vol. IV, *Special Reports*, Part 5, Chapter A, Characteristics by Size of Place, table 1; estimates described in the text.

In reviewing the size-of-place comparisons one is struck by the large number of instances in which the village population characteristics are more similar to those of small urban places than to the "other rural" categories. For example, the villages, like the urban size groups, have a sex

[1] See, for example, C. Luther Fry, *A Census Analysis of American Villages*, Institute of Social and Religious Research, New York, 1925; Irving Lorge, *American Agricultural Villages: 1930*, American Statistical Association, New York, 1933; T. Lynn Smith, "Some Aspects of Village Demography," *Social Forces 20*, October 1941, pp. 15–25.

ratio well below 100, whereas there is a considerable excess of males in both the nonfarm and farm parts of the "other rural" category.

Table 43 aids in comparing the resemblance between small town and village population characteristics with the resemblance between village and "other rural" characteristics. This table shows the index of dissimilarity between the distributions of certain population characteristics for each pair of size-of-place groups in the set including the small towns, the two village groups, and the two "other rural" groups. The index of dissimilarity is the percentage of nonoverlapping of two distributions. For example, the index of dissimilarity between small towns and large villages with respect to the percentage distribution by age and sex is 2.3—i.e., 2.3 percent of the large village population would have to be shifted to other age-sex categories to make the two distributions identical. The index of dissimilarity between the large village and "other rural-farm" age-sex distributions is more than four times as large. Hence, with respect to age and sex composition, it is concluded that large villages resemble small towns much more than they resemble "other rural-farm" areas. A systematic study of the comparisons of this kind which can be made from the information in table 43 leads to the following conclusions:

1. On the whole the two size-of-place groups, out of the five, which bear the greatest resemblance to each other are the small towns and the large villages. For 8 of the 12 distributions the index of dissimilarity for this pair is smaller than for any other pair.

2. In general, the next closest resemblance is between the large villages and the small villages.

3. The small villages resemble the towns more closely than they do either of the "other rural" groups.

4. Both village groups resemble the "other rural-nonfarm" category more than they do the "other rural-farm" category.

The above conclusions do not hold uniformly for all the distributions of characteristics, but each holds in a large majority of the cases. As far as the data in table 43 go, they support the proposition that the village groups tend to "belong" with the group of small urban places rather than with the "other rural" groups. It may be assumed that such a conclusion would be even more pointed if it were possible to consider separately the urban places of 2,500 to 5,000 and the "other rural-nonfarm" group exclusive of the unincorporated village population which it includes.

In general the villages have population characteristics intermediate between those of the smaller urban places and the "other rural" groups. However, there are certain characteristics for which this statement does not hold (figures 3 to 6, pp. 34 to 38). For example, the villages have a higher proportion aged 65 and over, a higher proportion of native white population, and a higher proportion of married males (holding age constant) than any other size-of-place group. That villages have these distinctive characteristics does not, however, gainsay the proposition that in most respects the villages fall in line with a gradient pattern of population characteristics observed for urban places arranged by size classes.

TABLE **43.**—INDEXES OF DISSIMILARITY BETWEEN DISTRIBUTIONS OF POPULATION CHARACTERISTICS FOR SMALL TOWNS AND RURAL AREAS, BY SIZE OF PLACE: 1950

Distribution and size-of-place group	1,000 to 2,500	Under 1,000 (incorp.)	Other rural Non-farm	Other rural Farm	Distribution and size-of-place group	1,000 to 2,500	Under 1,000 (incorp.)	Other rural Non-farm	Other rural Farm
AGE AND SEX					**MOBILITY STATUS**				
2,500 to 10,000	2.3	6.7	6.5	9.5	2,500 to 10,000	2.0	3.1	2.5	6.2
1,000 to 2,500	...	4.6	6.8	8.4	1,000 to 2,500	...	1.1	4.5	4.2
Under 1,000 (incorp.)	...	...	10.0	9.6	Under 1,000 (incorp.)	...	...	5.6	3.1
Other rural, nonfarm	...	...	...	7.6	Other rural, nonfarm	...	...	...	8.7
RACE AND NATIVITY					**EDUCATIONAL STATUS**				
2,500 to 10,000	1.4	4.1	1.2	6.0	2,500 to 10,000	2.9	7.7	9.0	19.9
1,000 to 2,500	...	2.7	2.5	7.3	1,000 to 2,500	...	5.0	7.5	17.2
Under 1,000 (incorp.)	...	...	5.0	9.2	Under 1,000 (incorp.)	...	...	9.2	13.9
Other rural, nonfarm	...	...	...	4.9	Other rural, nonfarm	...	...	...	12.6
MARITAL STATUS					**LABOR FORCE STATUS**				
Male					_Male_				
2,500 to 10,000	0.6	1.2	4.5	7.1	2,500 to 10,000	0.5	3.1	8.6	9.6
1,000 to 2,500	...	1.1	5.0	7.5	1,000 to 2,500	...	2.8	8.5	9.4
Under 1,000 (incorp.)	...	...	5.2	7.4	Under 1,000 (incorp.)	...	...	6.3	11.4
Other rural, nonfarm	...	...	...	2.6	Other rural, nonfarm	...	...	...	17.7
Female					_Female_				
2,500 to 10,000	1.5	3.3	5.6	7.1	2,500 to 10,000	3.2	7.0	9.4	14.5
1,000 to 2,500	...	1.8	4.4	6.9	1,000 to 2,500	...	3.8	6.2	11.3
Under 1,000 (incorp.)	...	...	5.0	8.0	Under 1,000 (incorp.)	...	...	2.7	7.5
Other rural, nonfarm	...	...	...	3.0	Other rural, nonfarm	...	...	...	5.1
FAMILY STATUS					**OCCUPATION**				
Male									
2,500 to 10,000	2.2	3.4	8.0	10.0	2,500 to 10,000	4.2	10.5	14.8	68.2
1,000 to 2,500	...	1.7	8.0	8.3	1,000 to 2,500	...	7.6	11.1	66.1
Under 1,000 (incorp.)	...	...	9.5	8.9	Under 1,000 (incorp.)	...	...	13.9	61.1
Other rural, nonfarm	...	...	...	9.8	Other rural, nonfarm	...	...	...	61.4
Female					**INCOME**				
2,500 to 10,000	2.0	3.0	6.8	10.5	2,500 to 10,000	1.7	7.3	2.7	14.5
1,000 to 2,500	...	2.3	6.1	9.3	1,000 to 2,500	...	5.8	1.8	13.1
Under 1,000 (incorp.)	...	...	7.7	10.9	Under 1,000 (incorp.)	...	...	6.0	7.8
Other rural, nonfarm	...	...	...	6.3	Other rural, nonfarm	...	...	...	12.2

Source: *1950 Census of Population,* Vol. IV, *Special Reports,* Part 5, Chapter A, Characteristics by Size of Place, tables 1 to 5.

Village farm population

In the preceding chapters the classification of the rural population into nonfarm and farm residents was carried through only for the "other rural" category, and was disregarded for the two size groups of villages. Actually, this procedure has little effect on the data for characteristics of the village or of the farm population, since the village-farm population is not a large proportion of either group. Despite its small size, there is a theoretical interest in ascertaining how the village-farm population's characteristics compare with those of other farm residents and of nonfarm village residents. Also, a word should be said about the urban-farm population, which amounts to a little over a quarter of a million of the total of 23⅓ million persons living on farms.

There are no data available on characteristics of the urban-farm population except color and sex.[2] The urban-farm population has 122 males per 100 females, compared with 110 for the rural-farm population, while in the total urban population females outnumber males. Nonwhites comprise 8.2 percent of the urban-farm population, compared with 10.1 percent of the total urban population, and 14.5 percent of the rural-farm population. In the United States as a whole, 1.2 percent of the total farm population is urban. The ratio of urban-farm to total farm population is 4.1 percent in the Northeast, 3.8 percent in the West, 0.9 percent in the North Central Region, and 0.5 percent in the South. This is the same ranking of the regions as that based on the urbanization of their total population (Chapter 2).

Tables 44 and 45 summarize certain characteristics of the village-farm population by size of village, with comparative figures for the remaining rural categories. It should be kept in mind that such comparisons involve a relatively large sampling error, because of the small numbers in the village-farm categories.

Rather than attempting a verbal summary of all the comparisons in tables 44 and 45, attention centers on the pattern and consistency of dif-

TABLE 44.—GENERAL CHARACTERISTICS OF THE RURAL POPULATION BY FARM RESIDENCE, BY SIZE OF PLACE: 1950

Population characteristic and residence	1,000 to 2,500	Under 1,000 (incorp.)	Other rural	Population characteristic and residence	1,000 to 2,500	Under 1,000 (incorp.)	Other rural
Sex ratio:				Percent married--Cont.			
Nonfarm	94.1	93.1	105.4	Female:			
Farm	106.8	103.2	110.1	Nonfarm	66.4	66.6	70.8
Median age:				Farm	67.8	69.9	70.9
Nonfarm	30.1	32.4	26.5	Percent of married females separated:			
Farm	32.5	31.2	26.1	Nonfarm	2.4	1.8	2.2
Fertility ratio:				Farm	1.7	1.4	1.5
Nonfarm	610	627	717	Percent in same house, 1950 and 1949:[1]			
Farm	592	672	766	Nonfarm	80.8	81.9	76.5
Percent 65 and over:				Farm	87.4	87.5	85.2
Nonfarm	10.3	13.6	7.3	Percent of movers with farm residence in 1949:			
Farm	11.0	11.1	7.5	Nonfarm	12.8	18.8	17.8
Percent native white:				Farm	38.4	49.1	60.4
Nonfarm	88.9	91.8	86.6	Median school years completed:[2]			
Farm	85.6	87.9	83.1	Nonfarm	9.1	8.9	8.7
Percent married:				Farm	8.8	8.7	8.4
Male:							
Nonfarm	69.9	69.4	65.2				
Farm	68.6	64.9	63.9				

[1] Persons 1 year old and over.

[2] Persons 25 years old and over.

Source: *1950 Census of Population*, Vol. IV, *Special Reports*, Part 5, Chapter A, Characteristics by Size of Place, tables 1, 2, and 3.

---

[2] *1950 Census of Population*, Vol. II, *Characteristics of the Population*, Part 1, table 34.

TABLE **45.**—Economic Characteristics of the Rural Population by Farm Residence, by Size of Place: 1950

Characteristic and residence	1,000 to 2,500	Under 1,000 (incorp.)	Other rural
PERCENT IN LABOR FORCE			
Male:			
Nonfarm......................	76.7	73.5	73.4
Farm.........................	78.4	80.2	83.0
Female:			
Nonfarm......................	27.3	23.6	21.1
Farm.........................	22.3	19.5	16.0
PERCENT IN FARM OCCUPATIONS[1]			
Male:			
Nonfarm......................	5.2	9.2	11.1
Farm.........................	47.5	60.6	76.0
Female:			
Nonfarm......................	1.1	1.6	4.2
Farm.........................	20.7	16.3	41.3
MEDIAN INCOME IN 1949 OF PERSONS WITH INCOME			
Male:			
Nonfarm..............dollars..	2,276	1,961	2,029
Farm................dollars..	1,864	1,478	1,379
Female:			
Nonfarm..............dollars..	752	632	718
Farm................dollars..	579	482	459

[1] Employed persons 14 years old and over.

Source: *1950 Census of Population*, Vol. IV, *Special Reports*, Part 5, Chapter A, Characteristics by Size of Place, tables 4 and 5.

ferences between the village-farm and the remaining categories. The two tables together contain information on 17 characteristics. In all but three cases, the difference between the nonfarm and farm categories for the villages is in the same direction as the difference between the "other rural-nonfarm" and "other rural-farm" categories. Hence, the conclusion is that farm residence has a generally selective effect, irrespective of village *versus* open country residence.

Secondly, the characteristics of the farm population of villages of 1,000 to 2,500 and the villages of under 1,000 in all cases differ in the same direction from those of the "other farm" population—e.g., in the farm population of both the large and small villages the sex ratio is lower than that of the "other rural-farm" population. For most of the characteristics, the difference between the village-farm and "other farm" population is in the same direction as the difference between the nonfarm village and "other nonfarm" population. For all characteristics except the indexes of age, fertility, and mobility, the two village-farm groups are intermediate between the two nonfarm village groups, on the one hand, and the "other rural-farm" group, on the other. Hence, village residence is a general selective factor, to some extent independent of farm *versus* nonfarm residence.

PART II

SPATIAL ORGANIZATION OF COMMUNITIES

CHAPTER 11

SUBURBS AND URBAN FRINGE

The concept of "suburb" has not been completely standardized in the research literature. Possibly one reason for this is that the Bureau of the Census has not provided an official definition of the concept, as it has for such concepts as "urban" and "rural." In the usage of most writers the term "suburb" appears to denote an urban place (usually an incorporated place) outside the corporate limits of a large city, but either adjacent thereto or near enough to be closely integrated into the economic life of the central city and within commuting distance of it. The criterion distinguishing a suburb from other territory on the city's periphery but within its corporate limits is, therefore, not economic or ecological, but political. There are even "suburbs," like Hamtramck and Highland Park in the Detroit (Mich.) Urbanized Area, which are completely enclosed by the central city.

In accordance with the conception of the suburb as a distinct political entity which is actually part of the economic city, many research workers have considered as suburbs those urban places which are within the limits of the metropolitan district but outside the central city or cities.[1] An analogous definition, more appropriate for use with the 1950 Census statistics, would classify as suburbs all places of 2,500 inhabitants or more within the urbanized area, but outside the central city or cities.[2]

The 1950 Census uses the term "urban fringe" to denote all territory within urbanized areas but outside their central cities. This terminology is poorly chosen, because the term "fringe" has been applied heretofore to areas of mixed urban and rural types of settlement on the periphery of the well built-up urban area. But the "urban fringe" as defined in 1950 contains incorporated places as large as 250,000, and nearly half of the "urban-fringe" population (48.7 percent) resides in incorporated places of 10,000 or more, i.e., places generally designated as suburbs in previous research. Table 46 gives a breakdown by size of place of the population inside urbanized areas but outside central cities, i.e., the "urban-fringe"

---

[1] Chauncy D. Harris, "Suburbs," *American Journal of Sociology 49*, July 1943, 1–13; Grace M. Kneedler, "Functional Types of Cities," *Public Management 27*, July 1945, 197–203; William F. Ogburn, *Social Characteristics of Cities*, International City Managers' Association, Chicago, 1937.

[2] In Chapters 14 to 20 the standard metropolitan area is taken as the unit within which suburbs are distinguished, while in this chapter the urbanized area is the unit.

TABLE 46.—DISTRIBUTION OF THE POPULATION INSIDE URBANIZED AREAS OUTSIDE CENTRAL
CITIES, BY SIZE OF PLACE: 1950

Size of place	Number of places		Population (thousands)		Percent of total	
	Incorporated	Unincorporated[1]	Incorporated	Unincorporated[1]	Incorporated	Unincorporated[1]
Total.....................	1,316	86	13,528	7,344	64.8	35.2
250,000 or more.................	1	...	251	...	1.2	...
100,000 to 250,000.............	10	1	1,234	135	5.9	0.6
50,000 to 100,000.............	37	2	2,562	142	12.3	0.7
25,000 to 50,000.............	71	21	2,495	718	11.9	3.4
10,000 to 25,000.............	231	36	3,629	577	17.4	2.8
5,000 to 10,000.............	268	13	1,893	89	9.1	0.4
2,500 to 5,000.............	241	13	886	57	4.2	0.3
Under 2,500.................	457	(2)	578	5,626	2.8	27.0

[1] Unincorporated places of 2,500 or more are those places designated as urban under special rules in 1940, and which remained unincorporated in 1950; the population given for these places is on the basis of the new urban definition.

[2] Places not separately identified.

Source: *1950 Census of Population*, Vol. II, *Characteristics of the Population*, Part 1, U. S. Summary, tables 3 and 5a.

category of the 1950 Census reports.   Over three-fifths of this population (62.0 percent) is in incorporated places of 2,500 or more.   An additional 8.2 percent is in unincorporated places of 2,500 or more which were designated as urban places under the special rules of the 1940 Census.   Altogether at least seven-tenths of the census "urban-fringe" population lives in suburbs, rather than the "fringe," in any strict sense of the latter term. Actually, to include among "suburbs" the unincorporated places of 2,500 or more, which are not now separately identified, and incorporated places of 1,000 to 2,500 would raise the suburban proportion even higher.   With some justification one might regard these places as small suburbs rather than as part of the fringe.

The term "urban fringe" will be used in this monograph to denote the nonsuburban population of the territory in urbanized areas outside central cities.   Thus the urbanized area is conceived as having three components, central city or cities, suburbs, and urban fringe.[3]   These three components

[3] This is the only instance in this monograph in which a term is used deliberately with a different meaning from that given it in the census reports.   The justifications for violating this rule are, first, that the Bureau of the Census terminology is inconsistent with an already established usage; second, that it was necessary to make a distinction (between suburbs and fringe) not explicitly recognized in census categories; and third that no suitable alternative term is available.   Actually, the usage here is, in part, suggested by the Bureau's discussion of the components of urbanized areas on p. 4 of the "Characteristics by Size of Place" report: "The census definition of a place as a concentration of population, which may be independent of legal limits, implies the possibility that a place or city may be defined in terms of the entire area of continuous concentrated settlement rather than the area defined by corporate limits.   Under this definition a place or physical city includes not only the principal incorporated area or areas but also adjacent *suburban and satellite areas.* . . . To isolate the suburban and satellite areas, an urbanized area is divided into its central city or cities and urban fringe as indicated in the formal definitions" (italics added).   The terminology used in this monograph involves substituting the term "suburbs and urban fringe" for the phrase "suburban and satellite areas," on the grounds already indicated.   In this chapter, where the data do not permit a separation of suburbs and urban fringe, the combined category is referred to, for convenience, simply as "suburbs."   In the following chapter the distinction between suburbs and the urban part of the rural-urban fringe is maintained throughout.

account for 69.8, 21.2, and 9.0 percent respectively, of the total population in urbanized areas in 1950.   Table 47 shows the composition of
urbanized areas, by size of area.   The central city component is substantially higher in the smaller than in the larger urbanized areas.   Also, the
relative magnitudes of the suburban and urban-fringe components vary by
size of urbanized area.   In the urbanized areas of 1 million or more about
four-fifths of the noncentral city population live in suburbs, compared with
about three-fifths in the areas with under 250,000 inhabitants.

The analyses of this chapter compare population characteristics of central cities of urbanized areas with those of the portions of urbanized areas
outside central cities.   The data are derived from the 3⅓-percent sample
statistics of the "Characteristics by Size of Place" report used in Part I.
Unfortunately, these statistics do not include a breakdown into suburban
and urban-fringe components of the noncentral parts of urbanized areas.
Hence these two categories are treated as a single group, referred to, for
convenience, as "suburbs"; but it must be borne in mind that it includes a
substantial population living outside suburbs, as that term is more con-
ventionally used.

TABLE 47.—CENTRAL, SUBURBAN, AND URBAN-FRINGE COMPONENTS OF URBANIZED AREAS,
BY SIZE OF AREA: 1950

| Size of area | Population | Percent of total | | | |
		Total area	Central cities	Suburbs[1]	Urban fringe[2]
All urbanized areas.............	69,249,148	100.0	69.8	21.2	9.0
3,000,000 or more.....................	21,213,879	100.0	67.1	26.1	6.8
1,000,000 to 3,000,000...............	16,603,189	100.0	60.7	31.9	7.4
250,000 to 1,000,000................	17,427,511	100.0	74.8	15.4	9.8
Under 250,000.......................	14,004,569	100.0	78.9	8.2	12.9

[1] Includes unincorporated places classified as urban under special rules in 1940 and all incorporated
places of 2,500 inhabitants or more.
[2] Incorporated places of less than 2,500 and unincorporated territory except that classified as urban under
special rules in 1940.
Source: Donald J. Bogue, *Population Growth in Standard Metropolitan Areas, 1900–1950, With an
Explanatory Analysis of Urbanized Areas*, Government Printing Office, Washington, 1953, table 24.

Age and sex composition

In all urbanized areas combined the sex ratio is 94.0, indicating a substantial excess of females in their population.   As a whole, central cities
have relatively more females than do suburbs; the respective sex ratios are
93.5 and 95.1.   This difference reflects only slightly the disproportionate
numbers of Armed Forces personnel in suburban areas.   The sex ratios of
the civilian population are 92.9 for all urbanized areas, 92.6 for central
cities, and 93.8 for suburbs.

The sex ratio is lower in the central than in the suburban areas of each size
group of urbanized areas, except the class of urbanized areas with more
than 3 million inhabitants (table 48).   The exception here is attributable
entirely to the situation in the New York Urbanized Area, since both the

Chicago and Los Angeles areas have slightly higher sex ratios in their suburbs than in the central cities.

On the average, the suburban population of urbanized areas is somewhat younger than the central city population. The median age in the central cities of all urbanized areas combined is 32.7 as compared with 30.9 for suburbs, a difference of 1.8 years. Such a difference appears for each of the size groups of urbanized areas (table 49). In fact, the smaller the urbanized area, the greater is the difference in median age between central city and suburbs.

Figure 15 shows population pyramids for the central city and suburban population of all urbanized areas combined. Although both graphs reveal the age-sex structure typical of the United States urban population in 1950, there are significant differences between them. As compared with the central city population, the suburban population has a substantial excess of persons aged 0 to 4 and 5 to 13, a slight excess of persons in the age intervals 14 to 19, 25 to 34, and 35 to 44, and relative deficiencies of persons in the interval 20 to 24, as well as in all age intervals above 45.

The age differences just noted are reflected as well in the higher fertility ratio of suburbs. In all central cities combined there are 452 children under 5 years of age per 1,000 women aged 20 to 44, as compared with 534 children per 1,000 women in the combined suburban population. The central and suburban parts of each of the four size groups of urbanized areas differ by about the same amount (table 50).

Dependency ratios are likewise higher in suburbs than in central cities. However, the differences are not great, since the suburban excess of young persons is nearly balanced by the central city excess of persons over 65. In the combined central cities there are 59 persons under 20 and over 65 per 100 persons aged 20 to 64. The corresponding ratio for suburbs is 65, a difference of only 6 points. As shown in table 51, there is a difference in the same direction of 7 or 8 points for each of the four size groups of urbanized areas.

TABLE **48.**—SEX RATIO OF THE POPULATION, FOR CENTRAL CITIES AND SUBURBS OF URBANIZED AREAS, BY SIZE OF AREA: 1950

Size of area	Total area	Central cities	Suburbs and urban fringe
All urbanized areas...	94.0	93.5	95.1
3,000,000 or more.......	94.0	94.2	93.5
1,000,000 to 3,000,000..	94.3	93.8	95.0
250,000 to 1,000,000....	94.0	93.3	96.0
Under 250,000..........	93.5	92.5	97.4

Source: *1950 Census of Population*, Vol. IV, *Special Reports*, Part 5, Chapter A, Characteristics by Size of Place, table 1.

TABLE **49.**—MEDIAN AGE OF THE POPULATION, FOR CENTRAL CITIES AND SUBURBS OF URBANIZED AREAS, BY SIZE OF AREA: 1950

Size of area	Total area	Central cities	Suburbs and urban fringe
All urbanized areas...	32.2	32.7	30.9
3,000,000 or more.......	33.7	34.2	32.7
1,000,000 to 3,000,000..	32.0	32.8	30.9
250,000 to 1,000,000....	31.5	32.0	29.8
Under 250,000..........	30.9	31.5	28.9

Source: See table 48.

TABLE **50.**—FERTILITY RATIO OF THE POP-
ULATION, FOR CENTRAL CITIES AND SUB-
URBS OF URBANIZED AREAS, BY SIZE OF
AREA: 1950

Size of area	Total area	Central cities	Suburbs and urban fringe
All urbanized areas...	476	452	534
3,000,000 or more.......	433	404	495
1,000,000 to 3,000,000..	478	444	531
250,000 to 1,000,000....	503	480	569
Under 250,000...........	510	490	586

Source: See table 48.

TABLE **51.**—DEPENDENCY RATIO OF THE
POPULATION, FOR CENTRAL CITIES AND
SUBURBS OF URBANIZED AREAS, BY SIZE
OF AREA: 1950

Size of area	Total area	Central cities	Suburbs and urban fringe
All urbanized areas...	61	59	65
3,000,000 or more.......	56	54	61
1,000,000 to 3,000,000..	60	57	65
250,000 to 1,000,000....	63	61	68
Under 250,000...........	66	65	72

Source: See table 48.

FIGURE **15.**—POPULATION PYRAMIDS FOR CENTRAL CITIES AND SUBURBS AND URBAN FRINGE
OF ALL URBANIZED AREAS COMBINED: 1950

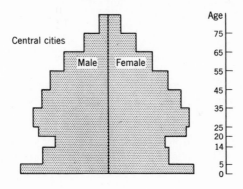

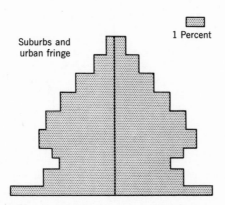

Source: *1950 Census of Population*, Vol. IV, *Special Reports*, Part 5, Chapter A, Characteristics by Size
of Place, table 1.

Race and nativity composition

Table 52 shows the race-nativity distribution of the central city and suburban populations of all urbanized areas combined. The suburbs have a considerably higher proportion of native whites, and corresponding smaller proportions of the other three race-nativity groups than the central cities. It is especially striking that the proportion of Negroes in central cities is nearly 3 times that in the suburbs—12.6 as compared with 4.5 percent. This difference doubtlessly reflects a typical pattern of migration of nonwhites to the central portions of urbanized areas, the residential segregation of nonwhites, and socio-economic differences between central cities and suburbs.

The index of dissimilarity in race-nativity distribution of central cities *versus* suburbs is 10.3 percent. For the urbanized areas of 3 million or more, and those of 1 to 3 million, the indexes are 14.0 and 14.2, respectively, compared with only 8.0 and 6.9 for the two smaller size groups. This variation by size of community is due to the increasing predominance of native whites with decreasing size of place, which leaves little room for central-suburban variation in race-nativity composition.

Central-suburban differences in the sex ratio follow the pattern already noted for the total population, i.e., proportionately more females in the central cities, in the case of native whites and Negroes. However, for foreign-born whites and other nonwhites, the higher sex ratios are observed in the central cities (table 53). For all groups except foreign-born whites the sexes are more nearly equal in numbers in the suburbs than in the central cities.

TABLE **52.**—PERCENT DISTRIBUTION OF THE POPULATION BY RACE AND NATIVITY, FOR CENTRAL CITIES AND SUBURBS OF URBANIZED AREAS: 1950

Race and nativity	Total area	Central cities	Suburbs and urban fringe
All classes.......	100.0	100.0	100.0
Native white..........	78.9	75.9	86.2
Foreign-born white....	10.5	11.1	9.1
Negro..................	10.2	12.6	4.5
Other races...........	0.4	0.4	0.2

Source: See table 48.

TABLE **53.**—SEX RATIO OF THE POPULATION BY RACE AND NATIVITY, FOR CENTRAL CITIES AND SUBURBS OF URBANIZED AREAS: 1950

Race and nativity	Total area	Central cities	Suburbs and urban fringe
All classes.......	94.0	93.5	95.1
Native white..........	93.6	92.9	95.1
Foreign-born white....	99.1	100.2	96.0
Negro..................	89.8	89.6	91.4
Other races...........	148.8	151.7	135.5

Source: See table 48.

Marital status and family characteristics

Table 54 shows the distribution of the central city and suburban population aged 14 and over by marital status, for all urbanized areas combined. For whites of both sexes the percentage married is greater in the suburbs, and the percentage in each of the remaining marital status categories is smaller. In the case of nonwhites, central cities have somewhat

TABLE **54.**—PERCENT DISTRIBUTION OF THE POPULATION BY MARITAL STATUS, BY COLOR AND
SEX, FOR CENTRAL CITIES AND SUBURBS OF URBANIZED AREAS: 1950

[Persons 14 years old and over]

Color and marital status	Total area		Central cities		Suburbs and urban fringe	
	Male	Female	Male	Female	Male	Female
White....................	100.0	100.0	100.0	100.0	100.0	100.0
Single...................	25.0	20.9	25.8	21.6	23.2	19.2
Married..................	68.7	63.9	67.4	62.3	71.6	67.8
Widowed..................	4.1	12.2	4.3	12.9	3.5	10.7
Divorced.................	2.2	3.0	2.5	3.2	1.7	2.3
Nonwhite.................	100.0	100.0	100.0	100.0	100.0	100.0
Single...................	25.2	18.9	25.0	18.8	26.4	20.0
Married..................	67.1	62.6	67.2	62.3	66.9	63.6
Widowed..................	5.3	14.8	5.3	15.1	4.7	13.2
Divorced.................	2.4	3.7	2.5	3.8	2.0	3.2

Source: *1950 Census of Population*, Vol. IV, *Special Reports*, Part 5, Chapter A, Characteristics by Size of
Place, tables 3 and 3a.

higher percentages widowed and divorced, for both males and females.
However, unlike whites, the percentage of males married is greater in central cities, while the percentage single for both males and females is
greater in the suburbs.

When age is taken into account, central-suburban differences for whites
and nonwhites fall into the same pattern. Table 55 shows the deviation of
the actual marital status distributions from those which would be observed
if age-specific marital status distributions by sex were the same in central
cities and suburbs as those of the total population of the United States.
A comparison of these deviations for central cities and suburbs discloses
that, relative to central cities, suburbs have an excess of married persons
and a deficiency of single, widowed, and divorced persons, for each color

TABLE **55.**—DEVIATION OF ACTUAL PERCENT DISTRIBUTION BY MARITAL STATUS FROM THE
DISTRIBUTION EXPECTED ON THE BASIS OF AGE, BY COLOR AND SEX, FOR CENTRAL CITIES AND
SUBURBS OF URBANIZED AREAS: 1950

Color and marital status	Central cities		Suburbs and urban fringe	
	Male	Female	Male	Female
WHITE				
Single.......................	1.8	3.5	-1.4	0.7
Married......................	-2.3	-4.7	1.9	0.2
Widowed......................	0.1	0.5	-0.2	-0.7
Divorced.....................	0.4	0.7	-0.5	-0.2
NONWHITE				
Single.......................	-0.6	-0.2	-1.4	-1.8
Married......................	-2.3	-6.9	-0.3	-4.0
Widowed......................	2.4	6.8	1.7	5.1
Divorced.....................	0.5	1.3	...	0.7

Source: *1950 Census of Population*, Vol. II, *Characteristics of the Population*, Part 1, U. S. Summary,
table 104; Vol. IV, *Special Reports*, Part 5, Chapter A, Characteristics by Size of Place, tables 3 and 3a.

and sex group. Thus a standardization for age composition enables one to show that suburbs are more selective of married persons than are central cities.

Table 56 shows the percentage of married persons reported as separated for central cities and suburbs of all urbanized areas combined. Although in the statistics on separated persons there is a discrepancy between the figures for males and females (Chapter 5), the data are consistent in showing a substantially larger percentage of separated persons in central cities than in suburbs. This holds for both whites and nonwhites, as well as for the total population.

Turning to an analysis of family and household characteristics, one sees first that there is little difference between central cities and suburbs of all urbanized areas combined in the percentage of the population classified as inmates of institutions. Only 0.7 percent of the total central city population and 0.6 percent of the suburban population live in institutions. The same percentages are observed for whites, but the corresponding figures for nonwhites are 0.8 and 1.0 percent, respectively.

Residence in quasi-households other than institutions is somewhat more common in central cities than in suburbs. There are 4.3 persons in quasi-households per 100 persons residing in households in central cities, compared with a ratio of only 2.1 in suburbs. The corresponding ratios for the white population are 3.9 and 2.0, and for the nonwhite, 7.4 and 4.1.

The central city and suburban population residing in households is classified by family status in table 57. It is apparent that a somewhat larger percentage of suburban persons, in the case of both whites and nonwhites, lives in primary families, while there is a greater relative frequency of primary individuals and nonrelatives of the household head in central cities.

Table 58 shows selected summary statistics characterizing primary families in central cities and suburbs. Although the difference is not great,

TABLE **56.**—SEPARATED PERSONS AS PERCENT OF MARRIED PERSONS BY COLOR AND SEX, FOR CENTRAL CITIES AND SUBURBS OF URBANIZED AREAS: 1950

Color and sex	Total area	Central cities	Suburbs and urban fringe
TOTAL			
Male	2.7	3.2	1.6
Female	4.0	4.7	2.3
WHITE			
Male	1.8	2.1	1.3
Female	2.5	2.8	1.8
NONWHITE			
Male	11.2	11.5	8.8
Female	16.9	17.5	13.4

Source: *1950 Census of Population*, Vol. IV, *Special Reports*, Part 5, Chapter A, Characteristics by Size of Place, tables 3 and 3a.

TABLE 57.—PERCENT DISTRIBUTION OF POPULATION IN HOUSEHOLDS BY FAMILY STATUS AND COLOR, FOR CENTRAL CITIES AND SUBURBS OF URBANIZED AREAS: 1950

Color and family status	Total area	Central cities	Suburbs and urban fringe
Total........................	100.0	100.0	100.0
In primary families................	92.6	91.5	95.0
Primary individuals................	3.8	4.4	2.5
Nonrelative of head................	3.6	4.1	2.5
White.........................	100.0	100.0	100.0
In primary families................	93.4	92.6	95.4
Primary individuals................	3.7	4.2	2.4
Nonrelative of head................	2.9	3.2	2.2
Nonwhite......................	100.0	100.0	100.0
In primary families................	85.3	84.9	88.1
Primary individuals................	4.9	5.1	3.5
Nonrelative of head................	9.8	10.0	8.4

Source: See table 56.

suburban families are somewhat larger on the average (3.6 persons) than those in central cities (3.4). Suburban families have 1.4 children of the household head per family, as compared to 1.2 in central city primary families. Both these differences are somewhat more pronounced for nonwhite than for white families. On the other hand, there are slightly fewer "other relatives" of the household head in proportion to the number of families in suburbs than in central cities for the white population, though not for the nonwhite. A somewhat larger proportion of central city than of suburban primary families are headed by females.

TABLE 58.—CHARACTERISTICS OF PRIMARY FAMILIES BY COLOR, FOR CENTRAL CITIES AND SUBURBS OF URBANIZED AREAS: 1950

Area and color	Persons per family	Children of household head per family	Other relatives of household head per family	Female heads as percent of total heads
TOTAL				
Total area...............	3.5	1.3	0.32	10.4
Central cities................	3.4	1.2	0.33	11.5
Suburbs and urban fringe.......	3.6	1.4	0.28	8.0
WHITE				
Total area...............	3.4	1.3	0.29	9.6
Central cities................	3.4	1.2	0.30	10.5
Suburbs and urban fringe.......	3.5	1.3	0.27	7.7
NONWHITE				
Total area...............	3.8	1.4	0.62	19.4
Central cities...............	3.7	1.3	0.62	20.0
Suburbs and urban fringe.......	4.1	1.6	0.63	15.3

Source: See table 56.

Mobility

As table 59 indicates, the suburban population is somewhat more mobile than the central city population. Of the total population one year of age and over, 81.6 percent in the suburbs and 82.3 percent in the central cities

TABLE **59.**—PERCENT DISTRIBUTION OF THE POPULATION 1 YEAR OLD AND OVER BY MOBILITY STATUS AND COLOR, FOR CENTRAL CITIES AND SUBURBS OF URBANIZED AREAS: 1950

Color and residence in 1949	Total area	Central cities	Suburbs and urban fringe
Total..........................	100.0	100.0	100.0
Same house as 1950....................	82.0	82.3	81.6
Different house, same county..........	11.0	11.1	10.7
Different county, same State..........	2.1	1.7	2.8
Different State.......................	2.7	2.4	3.2
Abroad and not reported...............	2.2	2.5	1.7
White..........................	100.0	100.0	100.0
Same house as 1950....................	82.1	82.4	81.5
Different house, same county..........	10.8	10.8	10.7
Different county, same State..........	2.2	1.8	2.9
Different State.......................	2.7	2.5	3.2
Abroad and not reported...............	2.2	2.5	1.7
Nonwhite..........................	100.0	100.0	100.0
Same house as 1950....................	81.8	81.6	81.9
Different house, same county..........	12.6	12.8	11.7
Different county, same State..........	1.2	1.1	1.8
Different State.......................	2.0	2.0	2.6
Abroad and not reported...............	2.4	2.5	2.0

Source: *1950 Census of Population,* Vol. IV, *Special Reports,* Part 5, Chapter A, Characteristics by Size of Place, tables 2 and 2a.

lived in the same house in 1950 as in 1949. The proportion of migrants from a different county is higher in the suburbs than in central cities; but the proportion of intracounty movers is slightly lower. The higher proportion of intracounty movers in central cities is largely accounted for by the difference in this direction for nonwhites, as there is scarcely any difference for whites.

Table 60 shows the rate of in-migration from other counties to central cities and suburbs. The suburbs have an in-migration rate nearly 50 percent higher than that of the central cities. Furthermore, for each

TABLE **60.**—IN-MIGRANTS PER 1,000 RESIDENT POPULATION BY AGE, COLOR, AND SEX, FOR CENTRAL CITIES AND SUBURBS OF URBANIZED AREAS: 1950

[Includes persons residing in different county, same State, and different county, different State, in 1950 as compared with 1949]

Age and color	Total area, both sexes	Central cities		Suburbs and urban fringe	
		Male	Female	Male	Female
Total population 1 year old and over.............................	48	44	40	62	58
White.....................................	49	46	41	62	59
1 to 13 years........................	48	39	42	61	62
14 to 24 years.......................	83	80	77	93	90
25 to 44 years.......................	58	57	45	78	67
45 to 64 years.......................	25	23	21	31	32
65 years and over....................	24	18	22	31	35
Nonwhite..................................	32	31	30	46	42
1 to 13 years........................	20	24	11	34	30
14 to 24 years.......................	60	58	59	75	62
25 to 44 years.......................	33	35	28	55	46
45 to 64 years.......................	18	16	17	29	30
65 years and over....................	17	15	18	12	30

Source: See table 59.

subgroup of the population, by age, color and sex (except for nonwhite males 65 and over), the suburban in-migration rate is higher than the corresponding rate for central cities.   However, the central city and suburban migration rates have a similar pattern by age, with the highest rate observed for persons 14 to 24 years old.   The in-migration rate for males, among both whites and nonwhites, is slightly higher than for females in both central cities and suburbs.   The white in-migration rate exceeds the nonwhite rate for all age and sex groups in both central cities and suburbs. Hence, despite the higher in-migration rate to suburbs, there seems to be no outstanding pattern of selection of migrants—in terms of age, color, or sex—which distinguishes migration to suburbs from migration to central cities.

Persons whose 1949 residence was on a farm constitute a slightly larger percentage of all movers (intra- and intercounty combined) in central cities than in suburbs—the respective percentages being 3.3 and 3.0.   When the number of movers from farms is related to the resident population, the in-migration rates for central cities and suburbs are practically identical: 5.0 and 4.9 per 1,000, respectively.

Education

Table 61 shows the median school years completed by the adult population in central cities and suburbs.   For whites there is a difference of a full year in educational attainment, the median for central cities being 10.3 years and for suburbs, 11.3 years.   However, for nonwhites the difference is in the opposite direction, the central city median exceeding that for the suburbs by 0.2 of a year.   Differences between whites and nonwhites are, therefore, somewhat more pronounced in the suburbs than in the central cities.   Central-suburban differences in educational attainment no doubt reflect differences in occupational composition.

When urbanized areas are classified by size, it is found that the greatest central-suburban differences in educational attainment occur for the larger areas.   In the areas of 3 million or more and 1 to 3 million, the median

TABLE **61.**—MEDIAN YEARS OF SCHOOL COMPLETED BY PERSONS 25 YEARS OLD AND OVER BY COLOR AND SEX, FOR CENTRAL CITIES AND SUBURBS OF URBANIZED AREAS: 1950

Color and sex	Total area	Central cities	Suburbs and urban fringe
Total......................	10.3	9.9	11.1
Male............................	10.1	9.8	11.0
Female.........................	10.4	10.0	11.2
White.......................	10.6	10.3	11.3
Male............................	10.5	10.2	11.2
Female.........................	10.7	10.4	11.4
Nonwhite....................	8.1	8.1	7.9
Male............................	7.9	7.9	7.6
Female.........................	8.3	8.3	8.1

Source: See table 59.

for the total population in suburbs exceeds that of the central city population by 1.6 and 1.9 years, respectively; whereas in the smaller areas the differences, though in the same direction, amount to only 0.4 and 0.2 years. For nonwhites there is a slight difference in favor of central cities in each size category.

Labor force and occupation

Differences in labor force participation rates for males between central cities and suburbs are slight, as revealed by the data in table 62. In central cities 80.2 percent of white males are in the labor force, compared with 81.6 percent in the suburbs. For nonwhite males there is no difference between central and suburban labor force rates. In the case of females, both white and nonwhite, the rate of labor force participation is somewhat higher in central cities than in suburbs. The difference amounts to more than 5 percent for white females and nearly 3 percent for nonwhite females.

There is a somewhat higher proportion of unemployed persons in central cities than in suburbs for white persons in the civilian labor force, but there is scarcely any difference for nonwhites. In central cities 5.3 percent of whites are unemployed as compared to 4.2 percent in the suburbs. The corresponding figures for nonwhites are 9.9 and 10.1.

The distributions by major occupation groups of employed persons in central cities and suburbs are shown in table 63. For total employed persons the index of dissimilarity between the central city and suburban occupation distributions is 7.0 percent. By and large this difference represents the higher level of socio-economic status of the suburban as compared with the central city labor force. The suburbs have somewhat higher proportions employed in the white-collar occupations, except clerical and kindred, and in the craftsmen, foremen, and kindred group than do the central cities, and smaller proportions in the clerical and other manual occupations.

TABLE **62.**—PERCENT OF THE POPULATION IN THE LABOR FORCE BY COLOR AND SEX, FOR CENTRAL CITIES AND SUBURBS OF URBANIZED AREAS: 1950

Color and sex	Total area	Central cities	Suburbs and urban fringe
Total....................	56.0	56.7	54.4
Male.........................	80.4	79.9	81.5
Female.....................	33.8	35.5	29.5
White......................	55.7	56.3	54.2
Male.........................	80.7	80.2	81.6
Female.....................	32.7	34.4	29.0
Nonwhite.................	59.1	59.3	58.0
Male.........................	77.8	77.8	77.8
Female.....................	42.5	42.9	40.0

Source: *1950 Census of Population*, Vol. IV, *Special Reports*, Part 5, Chapter A, Characteristics by Size of Place, tables 4 and 4a.

TABLE **63.**—PERCENT DISTRIBUTION OF EMPLOYED PERSONS BY MAJOR OCCUPATION GROUP, BY COLOR AND SEX, FOR CENTRAL CITIES AND SUBURBS OF URBANIZED AREAS: 1950

Area, color, and sex	Total[1]	Profess'l, techn'l, and kindred workers	Managers, officials, & propr's, exc. farm	Clerical and kindred workers	Sales workers	Craftsmen, foremen, and kindred workers	Operatives and kindred workers	Private household workers	Service workers, exc. private hshld.	Laborers, except farm and mine	Farm occupations[2]
TOTAL											
Both sexes..................	100.0	10.5	10.0	16.9	8.2	15.0	20.8	2.6	9.1	5.5	0.4
Central cities.............	100.0	9.9	9.7	17.4	8.2	14.2	20.8	2.8	10.1	5.6	0.3
Suburbs and urban fringe...	100.0	12.0	11.0	15.5	8.4	17.2	20.3	2.1	6.6	5.2	0.7
WHITE											
Male:											
Central cities.............	100.0	9.8	13.6	10.2	9.1	21.8	21.0	0.1	7.3	5.9	0.3
Suburbs and urban fringe...	100.0	11.9	14.1	8.4	8.5	24.0	20.6	0.1	5.0	5.9	0.7
Female:											
Central cities.............	100.0	12.8	4.5	37.4	9.0	1.9	19.3	2.9	10.4	0 5	0.1
Suburbs and urban fringe...	100.0	13.8	4.6	35.5	9.3	1.8	19.2	4.3	9.3	0.6	0.2
NONWHITE											
Male:											
Central cities.............	100.0	3.0	3.5	6.1	2.0	10.4	25.6	1.2	21.4	24.8	0.5
Suburbs and urban fringe...	100.0	2.3	2.9	3.6	1.2	11.0	27.2	2.4	13.5	32.9	1.6
Female:											
Central cities.............	100.0	5.5	1.5	7.0	1.7	1.0	20.4	36.9	22.8	1.8	0.2
Suburbs and urban fringe...	100.0	3.3	1.2	4.7	1.7	0.4	15.7	50.7	17.8	1.7	0.7

[1] Includes persons with occupation not reported.
[2] Includes "Farmers and farm managers" and "Farm laborers and foremen."

Source: *1950 Census of Population*, Vol. IV, *Special Reports*, Part 5, Chapter A, Characteristics by Size of Place, tables 5 and 5a.

Both the pattern and the degree of central-suburban occupational differentiation vary by color and sex. The indexes of dissimilarity between suburbs and central cities are 5.2 and 3.2 for white males and females, respectively, and 12.6 and 15.2 for nonwhite males and females. Thus, the least difference between suburbs and central cities occurs for white females, and the greatest difference for nonwhite females. Furthermore, while for whites, particularly males, the occupation groups of high socio-economic levels tend to be disproportionately represented in suburbs, the contrary is the case for nonwhites. As a consequence, the dissimilarity between the white and nonwhite occupation distributions is considerably greater in suburban areas than in central cities. The indexes of dissimilarity for whites *versus* nonwhites are 39.5 and 48.9 for males and females, respectively, in central cities, and 45.9 and 57.2 for males and females in suburbs.

Income

The median incomes of central city and suburban residents of all urbanized areas combined are shown in table 64. For all classes of income recipients, the median in the suburbs is $250 greater than the median in

TABLE **64.**—MEDIAN INCOME IN 1949 OF PERSONS 14 YEARS OLD AND OVER WITH INCOME BY
COLOR AND SEX, FOR CENTRAL CITIES AND SUBURBS OF URBANIZED AREAS: 1950

[In dollars]

Color and sex	Total area	Central cities	Suburbs and urban fringe
Total...................	2,315	2,249	2,499
Male.......................	2,912	2,808	3,166
Female.....................	1,372	1,393	1,310
White....................	2,433	2,385	2,557
Male.......................	3,053	2,970	3,227
Female.....................	1,455	1,496	1,346
Nonwhite.................	1,470	1,467	1,499
Male.......................	1,937	1,925	2,023
Female.....................	889	896	831

Source: *1950 Census of Population*, Vol. IV, *Special Reports*, Part 5, Chapter A, Characteristics by Size of Place, tables 4 and 4a.

central cities. However, central-suburban differences are more pronounced
for whites than for nonwhites, and the difference for females is in the opposite direction from that for males. Thus, for white males, the suburban
median exceeds the central city median by over $350, while for nonwhite
males the difference is not quite $100. For white females the suburban
median is $150 less than the central city median, and a difference in the
same direction of $65 is observed for nonwhite females.

The index of income inequality for all income recipients is somewhat
higher in the suburbs than in central cities, the respective index values
being 0.423 and 0.408. The same qualifications must be placed on this
computation as on those described in Chapter 9, owing to the crudeness
of the estimates of aggregate income. In the central-suburban comparison
the difference in inequality is in the same direction as the difference in
median income level, whereas in the size-of-place comparisons, the differences are in opposite directions.

Summary and conclusions

This study takes the point of view that the suburb is a specialized area
within the larger economic city. The implications of this position sometimes have been overlooked in those urban research studies which have
compared suburbs and cities of similar size but of independent status,
without regard to the factors differentiating suburban and nonsuburban
places. The implicit assumption of such comparisons is that characteristics distinguishing central cities and suburbs are functions of the differences in size between them. A test of this assumption can be made utilizing
the materials presented in this chapter and in the earlier chapters dealing
with community size.[4]

---

[4] Additional materials relevant to this point are presented in Chapters 12 and 14.

If central-suburban differences are simply functions of differences in size of place, then suburbs would be expected to differ systematically from central cities in the same ways that small places differ from large. Generally speaking, this expectation is confirmed with regard to those characteristics related to family organization and functions. It is not confirmed with regard to economic characteristics; and the picture is mixed for the remaining characteristics. Thus, as compared with central cities, suburbs have higher fertility ratios, higher percentages married, lower percentages separated, higher percentages in primary families, lower ratios of quasi-household residents to population in households, and lower percentages of women in the labor force. Essentially the same comparisons are obtained for urban places outside urbanized areas *versus* urbanized areas. With regard to economic characteristics, the suburban labor force has a higher socio-economic status, with a higher median income than that of central cities, whereas the smaller urban places differ from the urbanized areas in having lower median incomes and a labor force of a generally lower socio-economic level. Furthermore, no consistency exists between the central-suburban and size-of-place comparisons with respect to labor force participation of males or unemployment (when color is taken into account).

Suburbs have a lower median age than central cities, and small urban places a lower median than urbanized areas. However, this consistency reflects, at least in part, the fertility differentials already referred to. Whereas suburbs have a lower percentage of the population aged 65 and over than central cities, small urban places have a higher proportion than urbanized areas. The difference between suburbs and central cities in the sex ratio is not paralleled by a similar difference by size of place. Suburbs resemble small urban places in having a comparatively high proportion of their population classified as native white. There is also a resemblance in that both have a relatively low percentage classified as nonmovers; however, there is no counterpart in the central-suburban comparison to the marked difference between urbanized areas and smaller urban places in the rate of in-movement from farms. Finally, although the central-suburban and urbanized area-small city differences in educational attainment for nonwhites are somewhat similar, the same cannot be said for differences in median school years completed by the white population.

In sum, the types of intracommunity specialization and selection reflected in the differences between central cities and suburbs resemble only in part the differentiations associated with size of community. (It should be kept in mind that the data on "suburbs" in this chapter include with the suburbs the urban-fringe component of urbanized areas.)

Most of the foregoing analyses involve comparisons for all central cities of the United States with all suburbs, with little attention to the factors of size of urbanized area and regional location as possible influences on central-suburban differences.   If the differences noted between central cities and suburban areas represent general tendencies of intracommunity specialization, then one may expect them to persist in comparisons within regions and size-of-place groups.   To reach a summary judgment on the validity of this expectation, certain characteristics were selected for such a consistency check.   Fifteen comparisons are involved—four size-of-place groups by four regions, with the South not being represented in the size group 3 million or more.   (Limitations of space preclude the presentation of tables from which these comparisons are taken.)

The sex ratios of central cities are lower in 12 of the 15 comparisons, with all 3 of the exceptions being in the Northeast.   The median age for central cities is higher than for suburbs in all 15 comparisons, as is the percentage of the population aged 65 and over.   The suburbs have consistently higher fertility ratios.   In each of the 15 comparisons the suburbs have a higher percentage classified as native white than the corresponding central cities.

A regional breakdown for marital status is lacking, but for both males and females in all four size-of-place groups the percentage married in the suburbs exceeds the percentage married in central cities.   The percentage separated is consistently higher in central cities than in suburbs.

As regards mobility, suburbs have a higher percentage of movers than central cities in 10 of the 15 comparisons for males and 11 for females.   The exceptions are in the smaller urbanized areas of the Northeast and North Central Regions.   It was noted that central-suburban differences in educational attainment, in favor of the suburbs, are consistent as to direction by size of place; a regional breakdown is not available.

The pattern of differences in occupation composition between central cities and suburbs is not highly consistent under the test being used here. The percentage of all employed males in the two major occupation groups— professional, technical, and kindred workers, and managers, proprietors, and officials—is higher in suburbs in 10 of the 15 comparisons.   The same is true for females.   Four of the five exceptions for both sexes are accounted for by the urbanized areas of less than 250,000 in the North Central and the South and by those of less than 1 million in the West.

As noted above, the largest difference in median income between central cities and suburbs occurred for white males.   In 14 of the 15 comparisons the median income for white males in the suburbs exceeds that in the central cities.   The same is true in only 7 of the 15 comparisons for nonwhite males.   The reverse difference—central city median income exceeding the suburban—is noted in all 15 comparisons for white females and in 14 of the 15 comparisons for nonwhite females.

In conclusion, it appears that rather persistent tendencies are involved in suburban-central city differentiation.   This summary has, of course, neglected the magnitudes of the differences, which might well be a func-

tion of community size, type, and location.   In any intensive research on
the subject it would probably be necessary to subclassify suburbs according to their functional relationship to the central city, distinguishing, for
instance, between industrial and dormitory suburbs.[5]   Such distinctions
would involve analysis of data for individual places, rather than the summary tabulations of the "Characteristics by Size of Place" report used here.

---

[5] Cf. Harris, "Suburbs," *op. cit.*; Kneedler, "Functional Types of Cities," *op. cit.*   The data in Chapter 17 on manufacturing and nonmanufacturing suburbs are relevant to this point.   As is pointed out
below (pp. 256, 257), differences between central cities and suburbs may arise from residential specialization of the two parts of the extended urban area, without necessarily reflecting differences in economic function.   This is because population data pertain to place of residence, rather than place of work.

C H A P T E R 1 2

RURAL-URBAN FRINGE

There has been a marked growth of interest in the characteristics and problems of the rural-urban fringe during the last two decades.[1] Even longer ago the introduction of the concept "rurban community" had warned students that in many areas there is no longer a sharp demarcation of urban from rural territory. The rural-urban fringe is usually conceived as an area of mixed urban and rural land uses on the periphery of a city. Other characteristics of the fringe may or may not be included in its definition, according to the preferences of different authors, which vary considerably.

Despite the considerable interest in fringe problems, demographic analysis of fringe areas has not been highly developed. The obvious reason for that is the difficulty—in fact the virtual impossibility—of isolating fringe from other areas in published census statistics for 1940 and earlier years. One striking characteristic of the fringe is that its limits seldom, if ever, coincide closely with political boundaries. Recent research seems to imply that any reasonably precise delimitation of a fringe area requires meticulous field observation.[2] Furthermore, since the fringe is probably the most dynamic component of the total community area, the boundary of the fringe delineated at any given point in time is apt to become rapidly obsolete.

These observations suggest that census analyses can provide at best only a suggestive rather than a definitive characterization of the fringe. However, with the 1950 Census definition of "urban," one can focus such a characterization much more sharply than was heretofore possible. The procedures described below hinge on a concept of the rural-urban fringe involving urban, rural-nonfarm, and rural-farm components, according to current census definitions. The analysis suggests that the urban and rural-nonfarm components are practically indistinguishable in terms of demographic characteristics. The rural-farm component, though differing in many respects from the other two, has characteristics which set it apart from the farm population residing beyond the limits of the fringe.

---

[1] For recent critical discussions and bibliography, see Samuel W. Blizzard and William F. Anderson II, *Problems in Rural-Urban Fringe Research: Conceptualization and Delineation*, Pa. Agricultural Experiment Station Progress Report No. 89, November 1952; and the symposium by Charles E. Lively, *et al.*, "The Sociological Significance of the Rural-Urban Fringe," *Rural Sociology 18*, June 1953, pp. 101–120.

[2] Blizzard and Anderson, *op. cit.*

In the previous chapter exception was taken to the 1950 Census concept "urban fringe." For purposes of research on the rural-urban fringe, as it is generally described in the literature, the census concept is both too broad and too narrow. On the one hand, the census "urban fringe" includes long-established and well built-up urban places which, logically, are suburbs. On the other hand, it fails to include the areas just beyond the densely settled urban core where urban types of occupancy extend into rural territory, but where the urban pattern of settlement is not yet fully dominant. However, the field delineation procedures used to establish urbanized areas for 1950 make it possible to identify separately those areas which are urban by virtue of their settlement pattern and proximity to a large center rather than incorporation as a political entity of 2,500 persons or more. Such areas on the periphery of a city probably represent either (1) areas of relatively recent urban expansion and habitation, or (2) former rural centers—hamlets and villages—relatively recently enveloped by the radial growth of the city.

Accordingly, it is here proposed to designate as the urban component of the rural-urban fringe that portion of the urbanized area outside places of 2,500 or more.[3] Perhaps one should also exclude from the "urban fringe" both incorporated and unincorporated places with a population of 1,000 to 2,500. However, since unincorporated places are not separately identified within the limits of urbanized areas, it is impossible to exclude them. To exclude the smaller incorporated places from the urban fringe is possible, but only at the cost of sacrificing data on the characteristics of the urban fringe population. In all the urban-fringe areas of the United States, with just over 6 million total population, 7.7 percent of the population lives in incorporated places of 1,000 to 2,500, 1.6 percent in incorporated places of less than 1,000, and 90.7 percent in unincorporated territory.

The delineation of the rural portion of the rural-urban fringe is a somewhat problematical matter, if reliance is placed wholly on census area units. The approximation suggested here is to define as rural-fringe population rural residents inside the metropolitan district, as delineated on the basis of minor civil divisions in 1940. No published data are available for this

---

[3] The total of 7,922,018 inhabitants of urbanized areas living outside central cities and other *incorporated* places of 2,500 or more within urbanized areas includes 577,992 residents of incorporated places of less than 2,500 and 7,344,026 persons living in unincorporated territory. In the latter category are 1,718,422 inhabitants of separately identifiable places which were classified as urban under the special rules of the 1940 Census. The definition in the text thus regards the urban component of the rural-urban fringe population as the 6,203,596 inhabitants of territory classified as urban, not in its own right, but by virtue of its inclusion in urbanized areas. Unfortunately, it is sometimes impossible to use this definition for studying fringe population characteristics, since data on characteristics of places urban under 1940 special rules are not given separately. (This is a matter which could be remedied in future census tabulations.) The problem does not arise in connection with the Chicago data described below, since the Chicago Urbanized Area does not include any places formerly urban under special rules.

population.   However, for those census tract cities for which the area adjacent to the city also is tracted, the census tract summary cards enable investigators to identify and tabulate characteristics of urban residents of places 2,500 or more, other urban residents, rural-nonfarm, and rural-farm residents.   A study of the available materials for Chicago, described below, illustrates the possibilities of this procedure.   It provides comparisons among the urban, rural-nonfarm, and rural-farm fringe components, as well as comparisons between fringe and nonfringe components of the Chicago metropolitan area.

The Chicago fringe: a case study

This study was unable to assemble national data on characteristics of the fringe population.   However, since so little is known about this population, exploratory research involving only one metropolitan area should be of value, from both a substantive and a methodological standpoint.   The Chicago area was selected for such a study, partly for reasons of convenience.   An important consideration was that the layout of census tracts in the Chicago area makes it possible to obtain not only data on the characteristics of the urban component of the fringe, but also comparable material on the rural-nonfarm and rural-farm portions of the rural-urban fringe.

The area for which 1950 census tract data are available is identical with the Chicago Metropolitan District delineated in 1940.   It happens that there is a close similarity between this area and the Chicago Urbanized Area.   All but two of the townships included in the metropolitan district contain some portion of the urbanized area.   In a few places the urbanized area extends slightly beyond the metropolitan district, but these extensions contain fewer than 12,000 inhabitants.   In general, the metropolitan district is somewhat more inclusive than the urbanized area, containing some 60,000 persons in urban localities (suburbs) and a little over 100,000 rural population not in the urbanized area.

For immediate purposes, this study defines the urban component of the fringe to include that portion of the urbanized area within the metropolitan district, but outside of incorporated places of 2,500 or more.   Thus defined, Chicago's urban fringe includes some 46,000 residents of incorporated places under 2,500 and about 77,000 inhabitants of unincorporated urban territory.   The rural component of the fringe includes all persons residing in the metropolitan district outside of urban territory.   It contains nearly 92,000 rural-nonfarm and about 11,000 rural-farm fringe population.   The separation of the rural-urban fringe into urban, rural-nonfarm, and rural-farm components was made possible by the fact that the Bureau of the Census prepared a separate summary card for each of these parts of each census tract in the metropolitan district.

For comparative purposes the study also included the population of the Chicago Standard Metropolitan Area living outside the metropolitan district. This is designated "satellite" territory. It was also considered desirable to distinguish the Chicago suburbs from the city proper, and to maintain a size classification of the suburbs.

Table 65 gives a complete breakdown of the population of the Chicago Standard Metropolitan Area, according to the several principles of classification just described. Manifestly the urbanized area appears neither as an entity nor as any combination of categories in this classification scheme. Rather, the boundaries of the urbanized area serve only to delimit the urban-fringe category. A very minor portion of the urbanized area, with a population of only 881, does not lie within the standard metropolitan area. Moreover, since the urbanized area extends beyond the metropolitan district at certain points, there is a population of 6,681 which belongs, strictly, to the urban fringe, but which had to be combined with the satellite towns under 10,000 in the tabulations of population characteristics.

TABLE 65.—POPULATION OF THE CHICAGO STANDARD METROPOLITAN AREA AND CENTRAL, SUBURBAN, FRINGE, AND SATELLITE COMPONENTS: 1950

Component	Population	Component	Population
Standard metropolitan area, total.....	5,495,364	Outside metropolitan district............	422,963
Inside metropolitan district..............	5,072,401	Satellite urban........................	250,171
Chicago city...........................	3,620,962	Cities, 10,000 or more...............	146,400
Large suburban cities, 50,000 or more...	531,762	Towns, 2,500 to 10,000..............	97,090
Small suburban cities, 10,000 to 50,000.	389,582	Other urban.........................	6,681
Suburban towns, 2,500 to 10,000........	303,564	In incorporated places under 2,500.	[1]3,854
Fringe.................................	226,531	In unincorporated territory........	[2]2,827
Urban...............................	123,479	Satellite rural.........................	172,792
In incorporated places under 2,500..	46,366	Nonfarm..........................	130,996
In unincorporated territory.........	77,113	Farm..............................	41,796
Rural nonfarm........................	91,731		
Rural farm...........................	11,321		

[1] Excludes 429 inhabitants of urbanized area outside standard metropolitan area.
[2] Excludes 452 inhabitants of urbanized area outside standard metropolitan area.

Source: *1950 Census of Population*, Vol. I, *Number of Inhabitants*, tables 7 and 9 for Illinois and Indiana; census tract summary cards for the Chicago Metropolitan District.

The Chicago SMA (Standard Metropolitan Area) includes six counties, Cook, Du Page, Kane, Lake, and Will in Illinois, and Lake County, Indiana (see figure 16). It is approximately coextensive with the area within a 50-mile radius of the central business district of Chicago. The metropolitan district, composed of minor civil divisions of five of these counties, is approximately the area within a 25-mile radius of the center of the city, although it extends somewhat farther along the north shore of Lake Michigan and to the south and southeast. The bulk of the city proper rests within a 10-mile radius, with the city limits being somewhat closer than this on the west, and extending somewhat farther south. Hence, by and large, the suburban and fringe populations occupy a belt 10 to 25 miles distant from the city center, and the satellite population spreads to distances of 25 to 50 miles. On the whole, the rural fringe extends to greater distances from

FIGURE 16.—CHICAGO STANDARD METROPOLITAN AREA: 1950

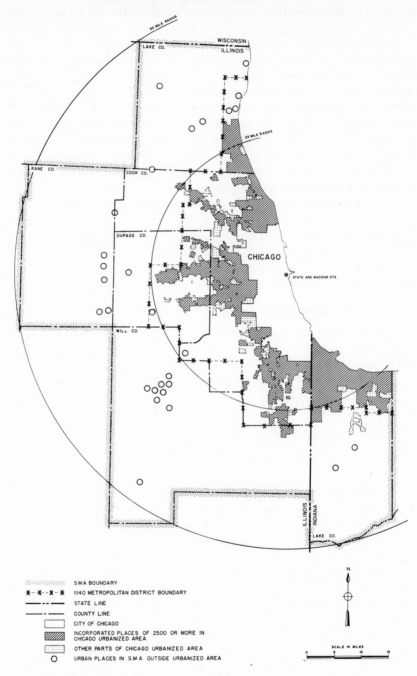

Source: U. S. Bureau of the Census.

the city center than do the suburbs and the urban fringe. However, there
are some rural-nonfarm and rural-farm residents within 12 miles, and the
suburbs and urban fringe protrude in some places to the outer limits of
the metropolitan district.

Many of the following tables exclude four census tracts from the data.
These are tracts containing large institutions and/or Armed Forces installations. To have retained them in the tabulations would have distorted
significantly certain comparisons for the civilian noninstitutional population of the urban and rural-nonfarm fringe. It was, however, not possible
similarly to exclude the significantly large institutional populations of the
satellite rural-nonfarm areas and the satellite cities of 10,000 and over.
For statistics affected by the relative size of the institutional population,
comparisons involving these two components need qualification.

The following paragraphs describe selected characteristics of the fringe
population in comparison with that of the central city, suburbs, and satellite areas of the Chicago SMA. Certain comparisons are also possible between the rural fringe in the Chicago SMA and the rural population of all
counties in the East North Central Division located in SMA's containing
urbanized areas of 250,000 or more, since Chapter 13 contains these data.

Age and sex composition

Table 66 shows selected indexes of age and sex distribution, and figure
17 presents the population pyramid for each of the component parts of the
SMA. Within the metropolitan district there is generally an upward gradient of the sex ratio from the central city outward to the rural-farm fringe.
In fact, the urban fringe, in marked contrast to all the other urban com-

TABLE **66.**—Sex Ratio, Median Age, Fertility Ratio, and Percent Aged 65 and Over,
for the Chicago Standard Metropolitan Area, by Components: 1950

Component	Sex ratio	Median age	Fertility ratio	Percent 65 and over
Standard metropolitan area, total.....	97.8	32.9	458	7.4
Inside metropolitan district:				
Chicago city...........................	96.4	33.6	424	7.6
Suburbs:				
50,000 or more.......................	97.9	32.8	458	7.2
10,000 to 50,000.....................	95.7	32.6	493	7.0
2,500 to 10,000......................	98.6	30.4	579	5.5
Fringe:				
Urban[1].............................	106.8	27.4	672	4.2
Rural nonfarm[1].....................	106.3	27.9	647	5.2
Rural farm...........................	113.2	31.9	550	8.0
Outside metropolitan district:				
Satellite urban:				
10,000 or more.......................	92.3	35.6	452	10.4
Under 10,000.........................	99.7	30.6	584	7.8
Satellite rural:				
Nonfarm..............................	109.8	30.3	633	7.7
Farm.................................	114.4	30.9	669	7.3

[1] Excludes census tracts CC–7, CC–21, LC–2, and LC–4.

Source: *1950 Census of Population*, Vol. II, *Characteristics of the Population*, Part 13, Illinois, and Part
14, Indiana, tables 33, 48, and 49; census tract summary cards for the Chicago Metropolitan District.

FIGURE 17.—POPULATION PYRAMIDS FOR CENTRAL, SUBURBAN, FRINGE, AND SATELLITE

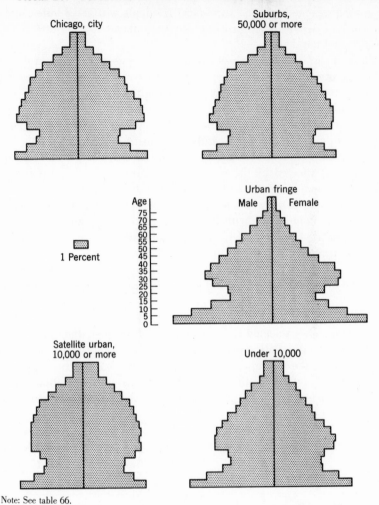

Note: See table 66.

ponents of the SMA, has a sex ratio as high as that of the rural-nonfarm fringe.   From the population pyramids it may be seen that the urban fringe population is heavily masculine at ages 35 and over, relative to the other urban components.

Going from the central city out to the fringe areas, the population becomes younger.   The urban fringe has the lowest median age, 27.4, this figure being more than 6 years below that for the central city.   In general, although the rural-nonfarm fringe population is slightly older than that of the urban fringe, both components differ from the suburbs and the central city in having higher proportions under 20 years of age and smaller proportions 45 and over.   Hence, in these two fringe components there are

COMPONENTS OF THE CHICAGO STANDARD METROPOLITAN AREA: 1950

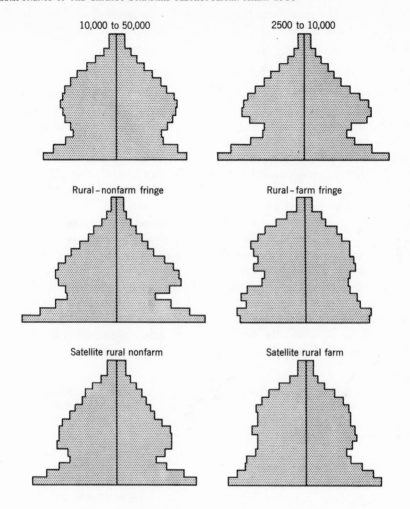

about 3 persons in the age intervals of greatest dependency for every 4 persons in the productive ages, while the ratio is 2 to 3, or less, in the suburbs, and almost as low as 1 to 2 in the central city. In contrast to the other two fringe components, the rural-farm fringe has a population more advanced in years, with the highest proportion over 65 of any component within the metropolitan district.

The age and sex distributions indicate marked differences among the components in effective fertility. The peak fertility ratio—672 children under 5 years old per 1,000 women aged 20 to 44—observed for the urban fringe is more than half again as large as that of the central city. The fertility ratio of the rural-nonfarm fringe is only slightly lower than that of the urban fringe and is substantially higher than any of the suburban ratios. The rural-farm fringe, however, has a relatively low fertility ratio—one which is decidedly lower than that of the satellite rural-farm areas.

Marital status and family characteristics

The percentage distributions by marital status of the population in the several components of the SMA are shown in table 67. Both the urban and rural-nonfarm fringe components, as well as all groups of suburbs, differ from the central city in having relative excesses of married persons and deficiencies of single and widowed or divorced persons. For females the difference is most pronounced in the urban fringe, where 75 percent of the females are married, as compared with only 63 percent in the central city. The highest percentage of males married occurs in the small suburbs, but the proportion in the urban fringe is nearly as high. The rural-farm fringe is notable for its high percentage of single persons, especially males, which is at least in part attributable to its high sex ratio.

To take account of differences in age composition, as they affect comparisons of marital status, the expected distribution by marital status was calculated for each component of the SMA on the supposition that its marital status distribution in each interval of age was the same as that in the entire SMA. Table 68 shows the deviation of the actual distribution by marital status from that expected on the basis of age. The pattern of differences

TABLE 67.—PERCENT DISTRIBUTION OF THE POPULATION BY MARITAL STATUS AND SEX, FOR THE CHICAGO STANDARD METROPOLITAN AREA, BY COMPONENTS: 1950

[Persons 14 years old and over]

Component	Male				Female			
	Total	Single	Married	Widowed or divorced	Total	Single	Married	Widowed or divorced
Standard metropolitan area, total......................	100.0	26.0	67.4	6.6	100.0	20.4	64.8	14.8
Inside metropolitan district:								
Chicago city....................	100.0	26.4	66.5	7.1	100.0	20.9	63.2	15.9
Suburbs:								
50,000 or more...............	100.0	24.9	68.8	6.3	100.0	20.3	65.7	14.0
10,000 to 50,000..............	100.0	22.8	72.3	4.9	100.0	19.9	67.4	12.7
2,500 to 10,000..............	100.0	21.3	74.4	4.3	100.0	18.0	71.5	10.5
Fringe:								
Urban[1]....................	100.0	22.1	73.4	4.5	100.0	16.6	75.0	8.4
Rural nonfarm[1].................	100.0	25.2	70.0	4.8	100.0	16.9	74.6	8.5
Rural farm....................	100.0	34.9	59.9	5.2	100.0	24.5	67.6	7.9
Outside metropolitan district:								
Satellite urban:								
10,000 or more...............	100.0	25.0	67.8	7.2	100.0	22.3	61.8	15.9
Under 10,000.................								
Satellite rural:	100.0	25.2	68.8	6.0	100.0	17.6	71.3	11.1
Nonfarm......................								
Farm........................								

[1] Excludes census tracts CC-7, CC-21, LC-2, and LC-4.

Source: *1950 Census of Population*, Vol. II, *Characteristics of the Population*, Part 13, Illinois, and Part 14, Indiana, table 34; census tract summary cards for the Chicago Metropolitan District.

TABLE **68.**—DEVIATION OF ACTUAL PERCENT DISTRIBUTION BY MARITAL STATUS FROM DISTRI-
BUTION EXPECTED ON THE BASIS OF AGE, BY SEX, FOR THE CHICAGO STANDARD METROPOLI-
TAN AREA, BY COMPONENTS: 1950

Component	Male			Female		
	Single	Married	Widowed or divorced	Single	Married	Widowed or divorced
Inside metropolitan district:						
Chicago city.....................	1.2	-1.5	0.3	0.9	-1.9	1.0
Suburbs:						
50,000 or more................	-1.0	1.3	-0.3	-0.4	1.1	-0.7
10,000 to 50,000..............	-3.3	5.0	-1.7	-0.8	3.0	-2.2
2,500 to 10,000..............	-4.8	6.5	-1.7	-3.0	5.8	-2.8
Fringe:						
Urban[1].......................	-5.4	6.4	-1.0	-6.2	9.1	-2.9
Rural nonfarm[1].................	-3.6	4.6	-1.0	-5.0	9.2	-4.2
Rural farm....................	6.0	-3.8	-2.2	1.7	5.5	-7.2
Outside metropolitan district:						
Satellite urban:						
10,000 or more...............	0.8	-0.3	-0.5	3.0	-1.1	-1.9
Under 10,000................						
Satellite rural:	-1.6	2.6	-1.0	-3.9	7.8	-3.9
Nonfarm.....................						
Farm........................						

[1] Excludes census tracts CC-7, CC-21, LC-2, and LC-4.

Source: *1950 Census of Population*, Vol. II, *Characteristics of the Population*, Part 13, Illinois, tables 34
and 57, and Part 14, Indiana, table 34; census tract summary cards for the Chicago Metropolitan District.

among components remains generally like that already described. However, holding constant age diminishes somewhat the apparent excess of
single persons in the rural-farm fringe. The smaller suburbs and the
urban fringe have the greatest excesses of married males, relative to age-
expectancy, while the urban and rural-nonfarm fringe have the largest
excesses of married females.

Table 69 shows the average household size and the percentage of married couples without households of their own in each component of the

TABLE **69.**—POPULATION PER HOUSEHOLD AND PERCENT OF MARRIED COUPLES WITHOUT OWN
HOUSEHOLD, FOR THE CHICAGO STANDARD METROPOLITAN AREA, BY COMPONENTS: 1950

Component	Population per household[1]	Percent of married couples without own household	Component	Population per household[1]	Percent of married couples without own household
Standard metropolitan area, total............	3.3	8.6	Outside metropolitan district:		
Inside metropolitan district:			Satellite urban:		
Chicago city...............	3.2	9.4	10,000 or more.........	3.2	6.6
Suburbs:			Under 10,000...........		
50,000 or more..........	3.3	8.5	Satellite rural:	3.5	5.4
10,000 to 50,000.........	3.5	7.5	Nonfarm................		
2,500 to 10,000..........	3.6	6.5	Farm..................		
Fringe:					
Urban....................	3.7	5.8			
Rural nonfarm............	3.6	4.7			
Rural farm...............	3.9	8.4			

[1] Excludes institutional population and residents of quasi-households.

Source: *1950 Census of Population*, Vol. II, *Characteristics of the Population*, Part 13, Illinois, and Part
14, Indiana, table 34; census tract summary cards for the Chicago Metropolitan District.

SMA.   Although the extent of doubling up diminishes in going out from
the central city to the urban and rural-nonfarm fringe areas, the average
size of household increases somewhat.   The percentage of couples without
own household is twice as great in the central city as in the rural-nonfarm
fringe.   However, in the rural-farm fringe the extent of doubling up, as
this measure reveals, is larger than in any but the central and large suburb
components.

Mobility

The distribution of the population by mobility status is shown for each
component of the SMA in table 70.   The small suburbs and the urban and
rural-nonfarm fringe have the highest percentage of mobility, whereas the
least mobile component is the rural-farm fringe.   Unfortunately, the mobility data do not permit the direct study of population movements within
the SMA.   Furthermore, in some cases, a move from the central city to a
suburb or fringe area was reported only as a change of house within a
county, whereas similar moves sometimes involved crossing county lines.
It seems probable that a considerable proportion of the migrants from different counties found in the fringe actually lived within the SMA in 1949.
In that part of the fringe lying in Cook County—the county containing the
city of Chicago—intracounty movers comprised 12.6 percent of the population, and intercounty movers made up 4.1 percent; whereas in the fringe
areas outside Cook County only 8.5 percent were intracounty movers, and
9.2 percent were migrants from another county.   It seems reasonable to
conclude that the fringe areas both inside and outside Cook County absorbed a heavy movement from the central city.

TABLE 70.—PERCENT DISTRIBUTION OF THE POPULATION 1 YEAR OLD AND OVER BY MOBILITY
STATUS, FOR THE CHICAGO STANDARD METROPOLITAN AREA, BY COMPONENTS: 1950

Component	Total	Residence in 1949			
		Same house as in 1950	Different house, same county	Different county or abroad	Not reported
Standard metropolitan area, total...	100.0	84.4	10.1	3.6	1.9
Inside metropolitan district:					
Chicago city............................	100.0	85.2	10.0	2.6	2.2
Suburbs:					
50,000 or more........................	100.0	84.2	10.4	4.1	1.3
10,000 to 50,000......................	100.0	83.8	10.1	5.1	1.0
2,500 to 10,000.......................	100.0	80.6	12.1	6.4	0.9
Fringe:					
Urban[1]................................	100.0	82.3	11.5	5.0	1.2
Rural nonfarm[1].......................	100.0	79.2	11.7	7.5	1.6
Rural farm.............................	100.0	88.8	5.4	4.4	1.4
Outside metropolitan district:					
Satellite urban:					
10,000 or more........................	100.0	85.7	8.3	5.0	1.0
Under 10,000..........................					
Satellite rural:	100.0	83.2	8.6	7.1	1.1
Nonfarm...............................					
Farm..................................					

[1] Excludes census tracts CC–7, CC–21, LC–2, and LC–4.

Source: See table 69.

Education

The educational attainment of the population 25 years of age and over in each component of the SMA is indicated in table 71 by the median number of school years completed. The rural-farm fringe has the lowest median. The urban and rural-nonfarm fringe population, while having slightly higher medians than the central city, fall below each group of suburbs in educational attainment. There is, in fact, a sharp difference between the suburbs of 2,500 to 10,000 and the urban fringe, the former's population having completed nearly 12 years of school on the average as compared with only 10 years for the latter.

TABLE 71.—MEDIAN YEARS OF SCHOOL COMPLETED FOR THE POPULATION 25 YEARS OLD AND OVER BY SEX, FOR THE CHICAGO STANDARD METROPOLITAN AREA, BY COMPONENTS: 1950

Component	Total	Male	Female
Standard metropolitan area, total..	9.9	9.9	9.9
Inside metropolitan district:			
Chicago city...........................	9.5	9.6	9.5
Suburbs:			
50,000 or more......................	10.5	10.5	10.5
10,000 to 50,000....................	11.8	11.9	11.7
2,500 to 10,000....................	11.9	12.0	11.7
Fringe:			
Urban[1]............................	10.0	9.9	10.1
Rural nonfarm[1].....................	9.8	9.7	10.0
Rural farm..........................	8.6	8.5	8.7
Outside metropolitan district:			
Satellite urban:			
10,000 or more......................	10.1	9.9	10.3
Under 10,000.......................	10.3		
Satellite rural:		9.3	10.2
Nonfarm.............................	9.7		
Farm...............................	8.9		

[1] Excludes census tracts CC–7, CC–21, LC–2, LC–4.

Source: See table 69.

The percentage of the population enrolled in school in the younger age groups is shown in table 72 for the several components of the SMA. In general, the rural-farm fringe has the lowest percentages of persons enrolled. The urban and rural-nonfarm fringe have a low enrollment rate for children aged 5 and 6, indicating more than likely a scarcity of kindergarten facilities. However, at ages 7 to 13 their enrollment rate is slightly above those of the central city and the suburbs. Above the age of 15 the proportions enrolled in school in the urban and rural-nonfarm fringe tend to be below the proportions for the central city, while except for the age group 25 to 29, the suburban proportions are higher than those of the central city.

Labor force and occupation

Labor force participation rates of the population aged 14 and over are shown in table 73 for each component of the SMA, together with the deviations of these rates from those expected on the basis of the age-specific

TABLE 72.—PERCENT OF THE POPULATION 5 TO 29 YEARS OLD ENROLLED IN SCHOOL BY AGE, AND PERCENT OF THE POPULATION 5 AND 6 YEARS OLD ENROLLED IN KINDERGARTEN, FOR THE CHICAGO STANDARD METROPOLITAN AREA, BY COMPONENTS: 1950

Component	Enrolled in kinder-garten — 5 and 6 years old	Enrolled in school, by age (years)						
		5 and 6	7 to 13	14 and 15	16 and 17	18 and 19	20 to 24	25 to 29
Standard metropolitan area, total......................	29.8	43.5	96.8	96.4	82.1	33.4	13.9	7.1
Inside metropolitan district:								
Chicago city....................	29.7	46.9	96.4	96.0	82.0	31.7	14.1	7.9
Suburbs:								
50,000 or more...............	38.0	38.6	97.3	97.2	86.1	43.9	16.9	6.8
10,000 to 50,000.............	35.8	37.5	97.7	97.6	89.1	42.0	16.0	6.1
2,500 to 10,000.............	33.3	36.2	97.9	97.6	85.7	40.5	14.5	5.3
Fringe:								
Urban[1]........................	16.4	39.1	98.2	97.6	78.3	29.7	6.8	5.0
Rural nonfarm[1]...............	14.7	37.1	98.1	97.1	77.7	36.8	11.1	3.4
Rural farm....................	8.3	40.3	95.8	88.2	75.0	35.1	6.4	2.7
Outside metropolitan district:								
Satellite urban:								
10,000 or more...............	33.3	40.8	96.4	96.8	82.9	34.9	9.8	4.5
Under 10,000..................								
Satellite rural:	18.0	38.8	96.6	95.2	78.9	26.5	7.1	3.8
Nonfarm......................								
Farm.........................								

[1] Excludes census tracts CC-7, CC-21, LC-2, and LC-4 for persons 16 years and over.

Source: See table 69.

TABLE 73.—PERCENT OF PERSONS IN THE LABOR FORCE AND DEVIATION FROM THE PERCENT EXPECTED ON THE BASIS OF THEIR AGE DISTRIBUTION, BY SEX, FOR THE CHICAGO STANDARD METROPOLITAN AREA, BY COMPONENTS: 1950

Component	Percent in labor force		Deviation from expected percent	
	Male	Female	Male	Female
Standard metropolitan area, total..........................	82.0	34.8	...	...
Inside metropolitan district:				
Chicago city......................	81.8	37.7	-0.7	2.9
Suburbs:				
50,000 or more....................	83.9	31.0	1.4	-3.9
10,000 to 50,000..................	84.1	30.4	2.1	-4.3
2,500 to 10,000..................	85.0	27.4	2.1	-8.0
Fringe:				
Urban[1]...........................	84.1	25.1	1.1	-11.2
Rural nonfarm[1]..................	81.9	25.7	0.2	-10.2
Rural farm........................	83.8	19.9	5.3	-14.4
Outside metropolitan district:				
Satellite urban:				
10,000 or more....................	78.8	32.6	-2.3	-0.6
Under 10,000......................	81.4	28.4	0.3	-5.9
Satellite rural:				
Nonfarm...........................	73.1	24.1	-7.5	-10.4
Farm..............................	86.3	16.5	7.1	-17.8

[1] Excludes census tracts CC-7, CC-21, LC-2, and LC-4.

Source: *1950 Census of Population*, Vol. II, *Characteristics of the Population*, Part 13, Illinois, and Part 14, Indiana, tables 35, 48, and 49; census tract summary cards for the Chicago Metropolitan District.

rates for the SMA as a whole and the age distributions of the components. The rate of labor force participation of females declines markedly in going from the central city out to the fringe areas, the gradient being interrupted only by a slightly higher figure for the rural-nonfarm than for the urban fringe. However, for males, when age is taken into account, the urban and rural-nonfarm fringes do not fall into such a gradient pattern. There are, in fact, only slight differences among the components of the metropolitan district in labor force participation rates, except for the high figure for the rural-farm fringe. Such differences as there are incline in the direction of high rates for the suburban groups, intermediate rates for the urban and rural-nonfarm fringes and low rates for the central city. (The data in table 73 for the satellite components, particularly the rural-nonfarm and larger urban areas, must be interpreted with caution, since they are affected by the large institutional populations in these areas.)

There is a suggestion of a gradient in unemployment, going from the central city to the fringe areas. The percentages of the civilian labor force reported as unemployed were 4.8 for the city of Chicago; 3.5, 2.7, and 2.3 for the three groups of suburbs in order of size; 2.7 for both the urban and rural-nonfarm fringe; and 1.9 for the rural-farm fringe.

The occupation distribution of males and females for each component of the SMA is given in table 74. The high percentage engaged in farm occupations necessarily dominates the rural-farm fringe distribution. It is striking, however, that the proportion employed in nonfarm occupations in the rural-farm fringe amounts to nearly half the employed males. By contrast, less than a third of the males in the satellite rural-farm component are engaged in nonfarm occupations.

As for the other two components of the fringe—the urban and the rural nonfarm—their occupation distributions resemble each other in the pattern of differences observed in comparisons with the central city on the one hand, and the suburbs on the other. For example, whereas the suburbs tend to have higher proportions of white-collar workers than the central city, those of the urban and rural-nonfarm fringes are lower than that of the central city. These two fringe components have a distinctly higher proportion among males of craftsmen, foremen, and kindred workers, than either the suburbs or the central city, as well as higher proportions of operatives and kindred workers and of laborers (excepting the high figure for the largest suburbs, which is attributable to the concentration of heavy industry in the suburb of Gary). In general, therefore, the socio-economic level of the labor force is highest in the suburbs, lowest in the fringe, and intermediate in the central city, although this formulation neglects some details of the occupation distributions. It is pertinent, for example, that the percentage of female service workers, except private household, is considerably higher for the two fringe components than for any of the suburban groups or the central city.

TABLE **74.**—PERCENT DISTRIBUTION OF EMPLOYED PERSONS BY MAJOR OCCUPATION GROUP AND SEX, FOR THE CHICAGO STANDARD METROPOLITAN AREA, BY COMPONENTS: 1950

Component and sex	Total[1]	Profess'l, techn'l, and kindred workers	Managers, officials, & propr's, exc. farm	Clerical and kindred workers	Sales workers	Craftsmen, foremen, and kindred workers	Operatives and kindred workers	Private household workers	Service workers, exc. private hshld.	Laborers, except farm and mine	Farm occupations[2]
MALE											
Standard metropolitan area, total..............	100.0	9.3	11.6	10.0	7.1	22.2	21.9	0.2	7.9	8.0	0.9
Inside metropolitan district:											
Chicago city.................	100.0	8.5	10.9	10.9	7.2	21.4	22.9	0.1	9.3	7.8	0.1
Suburbs:											
50,000 or more.............	100.0	10.6	11.2	8.4	6.5	24.6	21.4	0.2	5.4	10.7	0.1
10,000 to 50,000...........	100.0	14.0	17.0	9.3	8.3	21.9	16.8	0.3	5.0	6.3	0.4
2,500 to 10,000............	100.0	14.1	15.4	8.4	7.7	23.7	17.9	0.3	4.3	6.6	0.9
Fringe:											
Urban......................	100.0	8.8	10.9	6.9	4.8	29.5	23.2	0.2	5.3	8.7	1.0
Rural nonfarm..............	100.0	8.4	9.8	6.4	4.1	29.5	23.4	0.1	5.9	8.6	2.8
Rural farm.................	100.0	4.1	5.3	2.7	1.9	11.2	11.9	0.2	1.8	5.7	53.8
Outside metropolitan district:											
Satellite urban:											
10,000 or more.............	100.0	8.9	12.4	8.6	7.4	23.8	23.4	0.1	6.6	7.2	0.6
Under 10,000...............	100.0	8.9	11.1	7.4	5.8	26.7	23.6	0.1	5.4	8.8	1.2
Satellite rural:											
Nonfarm....................	100.0	7.6	11.3	6.3	5.2	26.9	23.2	0.3	5.6	9.0	3.7
Farm.......................	100.0	2.5	4.0	1.8	1.6	7.9	8.3	0.3	1.1	3.7	67.8
FEMALE											
Standard metropolitan area, total..............	100.0	10.6	4.0	36.8	7.5	2.1	21.5	4.5	10.5	1.0	0.2
Inside metropolitan district:											
Chicago city.................	100.0	9.6	3.9	37.4	7.0	2.3	23.4	3.8	10.4	1.1	...
Suburbs:											
50,000 or more.............	100.0	14.2	4.7	36.8	9.4	2.0	15.0	5.1	10.6	1.0	...
10,000 to 50,000...........	100.0	13.7	4.3	37.8	9.1	1.6	13.5	8.3	9.6	0.7	0.1
2,500 to 10,000............	100.0	12.4	4.2	36.8	8.5	1.7	15.8	8.5	9.6	0.9	0.3
Fringe:											
Urban......................	100.0	13.0	4.3	30.5	6.8	2.0	22.7	4.5	12.5	1.5	0.5
Rural nonfarm..............	100.0	12.6	3.6	29.5	6.7	2.0	20.4	4.5	15.8	1.0	0.9
Rural farm.................	100.0	9.7	2.1	31.8	6.7	0.4	15.3	8.9	7.7	0.4	15.0
Outside metropolitan district:											
Satellite urban:											
10,000 or more.............	100.0	14.4	3.5	30.7	9.3	1.8	21.8	3.5	11.6	0.7	0.1
Under 10,000...............	100.0	11.8	4.0	33.0	9.8	2.0	20.2	4.7	11.4	1.1	0.2
Satellite rural:											
Nonfarm....................	100.0	12.3	5.1	27.1	8.5	2.0	20.8	5.8	15.4	1.0	0.6
Farm.......................	100.0	11.3	3.0	25.7	5.9	1.9	12.6	9.7	7.6	0.7	17.7

[1] Includes persons with occupation not reported.

[2] Includes "Farmers and farm managers" and "Farm laborers and foremen."

Source: See table 73.

Income

The income data available for the fringe study differ from those used in earlier chapters in that they are reported for families or families and unrelated individuals, rather than for persons. Table 75 shows the median income of families and of families and unrelated individuals for the several components of the SMA. The relative positions of the components differ somewhat in the two series. However, in both, the three groups of suburbs have medians which are higher than any of the fringe groups, as well as the central city. The rural-farm fringe has by far the lowest median of any of the components within the metropolitan district. Family units in the urban and rural-nonfarm fringe have median incomes very close to the median for the central city. However, the median for families and unrelated individuals is nearly $450 higher in the urban fringe than in the central city, and the median in the rural-nonfarm fringe exceeds that in the central city by $280. The difference is probably attributable to a higher ratio of unrelated individuals to families in the central city than in the fringe.

TABLE 75.—MEDIAN INCOME IN 1949 OF FAMILIES, AND FAMILIES AND UNRELATED INDIVIDUALS, FOR THE CHICAGO STANDARD METROPOLITAN AREA, BY COMPONENTS: 1950

[In dollars]

Component	Families	Families and unrelated individuals	Component	Families	Families and unrelated individuals
Standard metropolitan area, total...........	4,063	3,485	Outside metropolitan district:		
Inside metropolitan district:			Satellite urban:		
Chicago city..............	3,956	3,360	10,000 or more..........	3,952	3,478
Suburbs:			Under 10,000............		
50,000 or more..........	4,259	3,753	Satellite rural:	3,752	3,512
10,000 to 50,000........	4,686	4,177	Nonfarm.................		
2,500 to 10,000..........	4,651	4,316	Farm....................		2,956
Fringe:					
Urban....................	4,054	[1]3,807			
Rural nonfarm...........	3,936	[1]3,640			
Rural farm..............	3,521	3,017			

[1] Excludes census tracts LC-2 and LC-4.

Source: *1950 Census of Population*, Vol. II, *Characteristics of the Population*, Part 13, Illinois, and Part 14, Indiana, tables 37, 45, and 46; census tract summary cards for the Chicago Metropolitan District.

Summary and conclusions

The results of the Chicago case study strongly indicate the advisability of distinguishing between the rural-urban fringe population and other components of the urban and rural populations. Whether the Chicago findings would prove to be typical of other urban and metropolitan areas is not known. However, Chicago's suburban and urban-fringe area as a whole exhibits characteristic differences from the central city similar to those observed between all suburbs and central cities of the United States (Chapter 11).

The study clearly shows that in some respects the fringe experiences a type of residential selection distinct from that of the suburbs, though in many characteristics the two resemble each other in their differences from the central city. Omitting the rural-farm fringe, there are several population characteristics on which the central city has a low value, the suburbs generally intermediate values, and the urban and rural-nonfarm fringes high values. Such a gradient holds for the sex ratio, fertility ratio, percentage married, population per household, and the percentage of movers. A gradient in the opposite direction occurs for the median age, the percentage aged 65 and over, the percentage of married couples without own household, and the labor force participation rate of females. However, economic characteristics, generally, move along no such regular rising or declining gradient. Rather, in regard to such characteristics as the male labor force participation rate, the socio-economic level of the labor force, and income, the suburbs have high values compared with both the fringe and the central city. This observation suffices to show that the suburbs and the fringe do not fit neatly into a "rural-urban continuum," if such a continuum is to be construed in terms of distance from a dominant urban center.

The residential characteristics of the rural-farm fringe reflect its interstitial location pattern, in that they reveal the mixture of urban and rural selective influences. The rural-farm fringe has the characteristic high sex ratio of the farm population, but its fertility ratio is comparatively low. The percentage of the labor force of the rural-farm fringe employed in farm occupations is very low compared with the figure for the rural-farm labor force in areas not under the immediate influence of a large city.

The above findings prompt one other comment on the nature of the fringe. On most characteristics of the resident population there is a close similarity between the urban and rural-nonfarm fringe. This becomes particularly evident when the differences between urban and rural-nonfarm fringe and the remaining components of the metropolitan area are noted. Such a finding strongly suggests that the rural-nonfarm population in the vicinity of a large city consists primarily of urban-oriented residents. Many of these no doubt live in so-called "ribbon developments," which do not qualify as urban under the procedures used for delineating urbanized areas, but which might well be regarded as urban under a somewhat more flexible definition. Unfortunately, one cannot determine from census statistics where fringe residents earn their livelihoods. For fringe studies, particularly, it might be desirable to determine rural-urban status on the basis of workplace rather than residence.

Although in the case of Chicago the lack of certain data and the distorting influence of institutional population diminish the value of comparing satellite with other metropolitan components, a review of the data indicates that it is theoretically worthwhile to distinguish this component from the suburbs and fringe.[4] In other words, discrimination is gained if the boundaries of the fringe are drawn relatively close to the central city. It is hoped that the experiment along these lines reported here will stimulate other efforts to obtain a close approximation to the fringe population from census sources, and possibly lead to revision of census procedures for handling this increasingly important element of the Nation's population.

---

[4] The contribution by Stuart A. Queen and David B. Carpenter to the *Rural Sociology* symposium cited above defines the rural-urban fringe as the entire area within the standard metropolitan area which is outside the urbanized area.

C H A P T E R   1 3

URBAN INFLUENCES ON RURAL POPULATION
CHARACTERISTICS

There is a considerable body of evidence which indicates that the rural population which lives within ready access of large urban centers differs in its characteristics from the rural population located at more remote distances from such centers.[1] The research findings have generally indicated that both the size of the urban center and the distance away from the center are important factors in producing differentials in rural characteristics. The most thorough and comprehensive study of metropolitan dominance is Bogue's *Structure of the Metropolitan Community*. However, Bogue's research, insofar as it dealt with the rural population, was limited to an analysis of population density. Other studies, dealing with the characteristics of the rural population, have usually concerned a selected group of metropolitan centers whose influence was examined. An ideal, but formidably laborious, research design would call for an analysis of population characteristics cross-classified by size of metropolitan center, zonal distance from center, proximity to subdominant centers, and transportation access to centers. The design employed here is much less ambitious, but aims at comprehensiveness in covering all counties of the United States.

The procedure followed was suggested by previous research employing classifications of counties according to metropolitan and nonmetropolitan location and size of largest city in the county.[2] Counties were classified as metropolitan if they were inside standard metropolitan areas as delineated in 1950. In the case of New England counties, the metropolitan category was assigned to a county any portion of which was inside an SMA (the New England SMA's having been delineated on a minor civil division,

---

[1] Donald J. Bogue, *The Structure of the Metropolitan Community*, University of Michigan, Ann Arbor, 1949; Edmund de S. Brunner and J. H. Kolb, "Rural and Urban Relationships," *Rural Social Trends*, McGraw-Hill, New York, 1933, Chapter 5; E. T. Hiller, "Extension of Urban Characteristics into Rural Areas," *Rural Sociology 6*, September 1941, pp. 242–257; Warren S. Thompson and Nelle E. Jackson, "Fertility in Rural Areas in Relation to their Distance from Cities, 1930," *Rural Sociology 5*, June 1940, pp. 143–162.

[2] Margaret Jarman Hagood, "Rural Population Characteristics," in Carl C. Taylor, *et al.*, *Rural Life in the United States*, Knopf, New York, 1949, Chapter 12; Otis Dudley Duncan, "Fertility of the Village Population in Pennsylvania, 1940," *Social Forces 28*, March 1950, pp. 304–309; Vincent Heath Whitney, "Rural-Urban People," *American Journal of Sociology 54*, July 1948, pp. 48–54.

rather than county, basis).[3]   Metropolitan counties were subclassified according to the size of the central urbanized area of the SMA, with one
group comprising those SMA's containing an urbanized area of 250,000
inhabitants or more, and the other group all remaining metropolitan counties (some of which did not actually contain an urbanized area, but all of
which had a central city of at least 50,000 inhabitants).   Nonmetropolitan
counties were subclassified by size of largest city in the county, into those
containing an urban place of 25,000 or more, and those with no place as
large as 25,000.

The hypothesis was that the greatest urban influence would be manifest
for the rural population in metropolitan counties of SMA's having a center
of 250,000 or more, and that the apparent degree of urban influence for
the remaining groups of counties would diminish in the order in which
they have just been listed.   Statistics on age, sex, race and nativity, educational status, labor force status, and occupation, for the rural-nonfarm and
rural-farm population were tabulated for each group of counties.[4]   It was
actually necessary to consolidate the statistics only for the first three groups
of counties, the figures for the last group being obtained by subtraction.
As a test of the generality of the observed relationship between the degree
of urbanization of the county of residence and demographic characteristics,
the analysis was carried out separately for each of the nine geographic
divisions of the United States.

Population distribution by type of county

Figure 18 shows, on an outline map of the United States, the location
of standard metropolitan areas.   It serves, *ipso facto*, to identify the metropolitan counties, except in New England, where the county units are, of
course, somewhat more extensive than the SMA's.   Comparing figure 18
with figure 2 (p. 31) discloses that the metropolitan counties frequently
contain concentrations of rural, as well as urban, population.   There is,
however, a marked difference between the rural-nonfarm and rural-farm
populations in their type-of-county distributions.   Nonmetropolitan counties whose largest population center is under 25,000 contain about four-
fifths of the rural-farm population, while only three-fifths of the rural-nonfarm population lives in these counties.   At the other extreme, one-sixth
of the rural-nonfarm population is in metropolitan counties near large
centers (250,000 or more), as compared to only one-twentieth of the rural-
farm population.   In each geographic division, the percentage of the rural-

---

[3] An alternative procedure was to fall back on the State economic area classification of counties as
metropolitan and nonmetropolitan.   However, this would have involved classifying as nonmetropolitan
one county which contained a standard metropolitan area in 1950.   There are two other counties containing portions of SMA's but not belonging to metropolitan State economic areas.   All three of these
counties contain cities of 25,000 inhabitants or more.

[4] These data were taken from *1950 Census of Population*, Vol. II, *Characteristics of the Population*,
Parts 2–50.

FIGURE 18.—STANDARD METROPOLITAN AREAS OF THE UNITED STATES: 1950

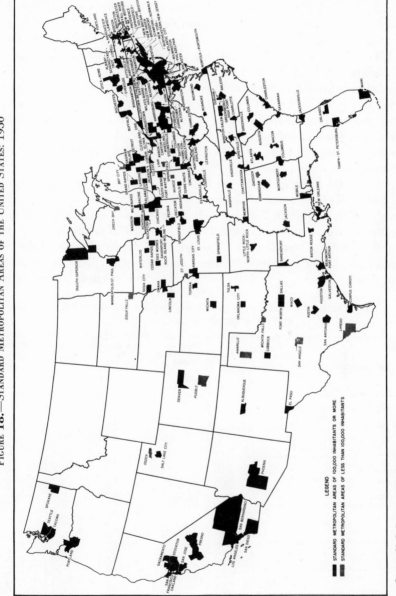

LEGEND

STANDARD METROPOLITAN AREAS OF 100,000 INHABITANTS OR MORE
STANDARD METROPOLITAN AREAS OF LESS THAN 100,000 INHABITANTS

Source: U. S. Bureau of the Census.

farm population located in the least urban counties exceeds the corresponding percentage of the rural-nonfarm population.

Comparing figures 2 and 18 suggests, also, that there are wide variations
among the geographic divisions in the distribution of rural population by
type of county.   This is confirmed by data in tables 76 and B–2.   In the
Middle Atlantic Division the least urban counties have just over one-half
the rural-farm population, whereas in the West North Central, and East
and West South Central Divisions the proportion is around nine-tenths.
In the New England Division only about one-third of the rural-nonfarm
population is located in the least urban counties, compared with over four-
fifths in the West North Central Division.   Table 77 shows for each
geographic division the percentages of the total rural population which the
nonfarm and farm residence categories comprise.   A comparison of these
figures with those in table 76 makes it evident that the divisions in which
the rural-nonfarm category accounts for a large percentage of the rural
population are those in which the latter is most heavily concentrated in
the metropolitan counties.   Conversely, in the divisions where the percentage of the rural population residing on farms is relatively high, the
rural population tends to be heavily concentrated in counties where the
largest center is under 25,000.   The conclusion appears justified that an
appreciable part of the rural-nonfarm population, particularly in the more
urbanized divisions, is actually tributary to and oriented toward large

TABLE **76.**—PERCENT DISTRIBUTION OF THE RURAL-NONFARM AND RURAL-FARM POPULATION
BY TYPE OF COUNTY, BY DIVISIONS: 1950

Division and residence	All counties	Metropolitan, by size of largest place in standard metropolitan area		Nonmetropolitan, by size of largest place in county	
		250,000 or more	Under 250,000	25,000 or more	Under 25,000
RURAL NONFARM					
United States................	100.0	16.7	12.5	9.6	61.2
New England.....................	100.0	41.2	15.3	8.9	34.6
Middle Atlantic....................	100.0	36.3	16.0	8.6	39.1
East North Central..................	100.0	17.8	14.8	11.2	56.2
West North Central.................	100.0	8.1	5.2	5.4	81.3
South Atlantic.....................	100.0	8.3	14.3	11.1	66.3
East South Central.................	100.0	8.8	8.5	5.5	77.2
West South Central.................	100.0	7.4	8.3	8.2	76.1
Mountain.........................	100.0	2.5	10.3	11.7	75.5
Pacific...........................	100.0	21.9	15.0	15.0	48.1
RURAL FARM					
United States................	100.0	4.9	6.7	6.9	81.5
New England.....................	100.0	22.1	10.9	10.6	56.4
Middle Atlantic....................	100.0	21.2	17.9	9.8	51.1
East North Central..................	100.0	6.3	9.5	10.3	73.9
West North Central.................	100.0	2.5	3.4	5.0	89.1
South Atlantic.....................	100.0	2.2	6.2	6.6	85.0
East South Central.................	100.0	1.9	3.5	4.0	90.6
West South Central.................	100.0	1.7	3.6	5.1	89.6
Mountain.........................	100.0	1.9	6.1	7.1	84.9
Pacific...........................	100.0	15.5	15.8	14.9	53.8

Source: *1950 Census of Population*, Vol. II, *Characteristics of the Population*, Parts 2 to 50, tables 48
and 49.

TABLE **77.**—PERCENT DISTRIBUTION OF THE RURAL POPULATION BY FARM AND NONFARM RESIDENCE, BY DIVISIONS: 1950

Division	Total	Non-farm	Farm	Division	Total	Non-farm	Farm
United States......	100.0	57.5	42.5	South Atlantic..........	100.0	57.1	42.9
New England............	100.0	81.8	18.2	East South Central......	100.0	42.1	57.9
Middle Atlantic........	100.0	76.4	23.6	West South Central......	100.0	50.2	49.8
East North Central.....	100.0	59.8	40.2	Mountain................	100.0	62.5	37.5
West North Central.....	100.0	44.8	55.2	Pacific.................	100.0	70.5	29.5

Source: *1950 Census of Population,* Vol. II, *Characteristics of the Population,* Part 1, U. S. Summary, table 58.

urban centers rather than being a strictly rural group. If, in each geographic division, the ratio of rural-nonfarm to rural-farm population were the same in all four types of counties as in the nonmetropolitan counties with no place larger than 25,000, then the total rural-nonfarm population of the United States would be some 6 million less than it actually is, i.e., around 25 million in place of about 31 million. While this computation does not yield a precise estimate of the rural-nonfarm fringe population, it does suggest that fringe residents constitute a substantial proportion of the rural-nonfarm population.

Age and sex composition

Population pyramids for the rural-nonfarm and rural-farm populations, by type of county, are shown in figure 19. It is evident that proximity to large centers affects both categories of the rural population. Most apparent to the eye are the widening of the base of the rural farm pyramid, proceeding from the metropolitan to the nonmetropolitan counties, and the constricting of the midportion of the rural-nonfarm pyramid. The nonfarm and farm pyramids are clearly distinguished from each other in all types of counties. However, there is a greater dissimilarity between them in the metropolitan counties with large centers than in any other type of county, and least dissimilarity in the counties with the smallest centers. In the metropolitan counties the rural-nonfarm pyramid appears to resemble that of suburbs (Chapter 11), while in the least urban counties the resemblance to the village pyramids (Chapter 3) is greater.

Tables 78 and B–3 (Appendix B) present sex ratios of the nonfarm and farm populations by type of county. The figures for the rural-nonfarm population are based on the civilian population, to avoid the distortion of comparisons resulting from the irregularly distributed concentrations of population in the Armed Forces. For the United States as a whole, there is a discernable downward progression of the sex ratio from a high value in metropolitan counties with large centers to a low figure for the least urban counties. This relationship holds for both the nonfarm and farm populations. However, the differences by type of county are not pronounced, amounting to only about 2 points between the extremes. Only

FIGURE 19.—POPULATION PYRAMIDS FOR THE RURAL-NONFARM AND RURAL-FARM POPULATION,
BY TYPE OF COUNTY: 1950

[A—Metropolitan counties with center 250,000 or more; B—Metropolitan counties with center under
250,000; C—Nonmetropolitan counties with center 25,000 or more; D—Nonmetropolitan counties with
center under 25,000]

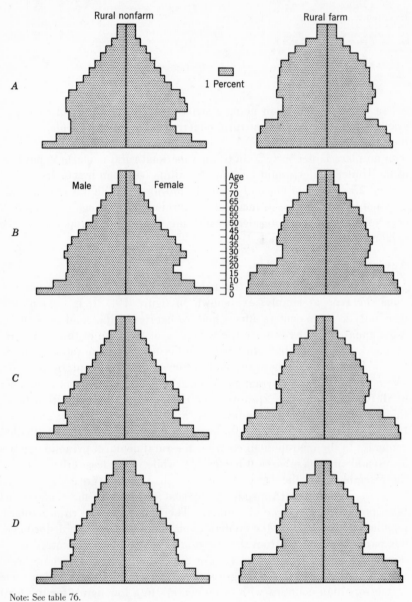

Note: See table 76.

two of the nine geographic divisions exhibit a regular downward progression in the sex ratio of the rural-nonfarm population, the East North Central and South Atlantic, while for the rural-farm population only the South Atlantic and West South Central Divisions have this gradient. In three of the nine divisions the least urban counties have the highest rural-nonfarm sex ratios, rather than the lowest, as in the United States as a whole. The same is true for four divisions in the case of the rural-farm population. In sum, the classification by type of county used here appears to be a rather insignificant factor in producing variations in rural-nonfarm and rural-farm sex ratios. (Moreover, the sex ratio—the number of males divided by the number of females—gives a somewhat exaggerated impression of the disproportion of the sexes; small differences between sex ratios are usually of little importance.)

The median ages of the nonfarm and farm populations by county type are shown in tables 78 and B-4. In the United States as a whole both categories have a downward gradient in median age, going from the metropolitan counties with large centers to the nonmetropolitan counties with no place larger than 25,000. The gradient is much more pronounced for the farm, where the difference between the extremes amounts to over 6 years, than for the nonfarm category, where this difference is only 1.3 years. Thus, in metropolitan counties, the rural-farm median age exceeds that of the rural-nonfarm population—by nearly 3 years in the case of metropolitan counties with large centers. In nonmetropolitan counties the reverse is true, particularly in those counties whose largest center is under 25,000, where the rural-nonfarm median is 2 years greater than the rural-farm median.

TABLE 78.—SEX RATIO, MEDIAN AGE, FERTILITY RATIO, AND PERCENT AGED 65 AND OVER, FOR THE RURAL-NONFARM AND RURAL-FARM POPULATION, BY TYPE OF COUNTY: 1950

Residence and characteristic	All counties	Metropolitan, by size of largest place in standard metropolitan area		Nonmetropolitan, by size of largest place in county	
		250,000 or more	Under 250,000	25,000 or more	Under 25,000
Sex ratio:					
Rural nonfarm[1]	100.7	102.0	101.9	101.1	100.0
Rural farm	110.1	111.7	110.9	110.8	109.9
Median age:					
Rural nonfarm	27.9	29.1	27.3	27.4	27.8
Rural farm	26.3	31.9	28.0	27.0	25.7
Fertility ratio:[2]					
Rural nonfarm	681	618	670	671	704
Rural farm	762	613	700	741	778
Percent aged 65 and over:					
Rural nonfarm	8.6	7.3	7.0	7.8	9.5
Rural farm	7.6	9.2	7.9	7.6	7.5

[1] Civilian population only.
[2] Children under 5 years old per 1,000 women aged 20 to 44.

Source: See table 76.

The median age gradient is not reproduced regularly within geographic divisions. For the rural-farm population, there are only two divisions where the gradient is entirely regular, the South Atlantic and the East South Central. However, in all divisions but one, metropolitan counties with large centers have the highest median, and in all divisions the figure for this group of counties substantially exceeds that for the least urbanized counties. In the case of the rural-nonfarm population, not one of the divisions has a perfectly regular downward gradient of median age. In four divisions the median age for the least urban counties actually exceeds that for the metropolitan counties with large centers. Regardless of direction, the differences among the groups of counties are fairly small in most divisions. In short, it appears that there is a fairly strong tendency for the median age of the rural-farm population to reflect the degree of urbanization of the county in which it is located, but this tendency is not at all pronounced for the rural-nonfarm population.

Tables 78 and B–5 show the fertility ratios of the nonfarm and farm populations according to county type. In the United States as a whole, the fertility ratio is inversely related to the degree of urbanization of the county in which the rural population is located. The tendency is somewhat more pronounced for the rural-farm population than for the rural-nonfarm, and also more consistent within geographic divisions. The rural-farm population has a regular upward gradient in the fertility ratio in six divisions, as well as the United States as a whole. Such a gradient appears for only two divisions and the United States total in the case of the rural-nonfarm population. However, in virtually every division, in the case of both residence categories, there is a discernable inverse relation between fertility and the degree of urbanization of the county of residence.

It should be noted that the fertility ratios shown here were not standardized for age. Hence, small differences between the rural-nonfarm and rural-farm fertility ratios must be interpreted with caution. For the United States as a whole, the age distribution of rural-nonfarm females 20 to 44 years old is somewhat more favorable to high fertility than is that of the rural-farm females. It is quite unlikely, though, that the type-of-county gradient in fertility for either the rural-nonfarm or the rural-farm population is attributable to age composition.

Opposite tendencies appear for the rural-nonfarm and rural-farm categories as to the variation by type of county in the percentage of the population 65 years old and over (tables 78 and B–6). The rural-nonfarm population has a much higher percentage of aged persons in the least urban group of counties than in any of the other three groups in the United States as a whole. Furthermore, in all but one geographic division this group of counties has a higher proportion of aged than any other group. This is consistent with the supposition that the rural-nonfarm population is heavily weighted with rural-urban fringe residents in the more urban counties, and with country village residents in the least urban counties. In the case of the rural-farm population, the metropolitan counties with large centers have a somewhat higher percentage aged 65 and over than any other group of counties in the United States as a whole. In all geographic divisions, except two, this group of counties has the highest percentage of old persons. Thus the age selectivity of residence near large urban centers runs in different directions for the rural-farm and the rural-nonfarm population. In the United States as a whole the percentage of old people is greater for the nonfarm population than for the farm population in the least urban counties; and the same is true of all divisions except one. The difference between the rural-nonfarm and rural-farm population is in the opposite direction for the metropolitan counties with large centers.

Race and nativity composition

It is difficult to find any simple relationship between race-nativity composition and type of county for the rural population. Clearly, the analysis must take into account regional variations, since foreign-born whites comprise a substantial proportion of the rural population only in the North and the West, while Negroes are a large element in the rural population of the South and not in any of the other regions. Tables 79, B-7, and B-8 show the race-nativity distributions for the rural-nonfarm and rural-farm population for the United States and each geographic division. Attention will be directed to the race-nativity groups other than native white.

In general, the foreign-born white group comprises a larger proportion of the rural population in those counties which are most highly urbanized in terms of the type-of-county classification. For the United States as a

TABLE 79.—PERCENT DISTRIBUTION OF THE RURAL-NONFARM AND RURAL-FARM POPULATION BY RACE AND NATIVITY, BY TYPE OF COUNTY: 1950

Residence, race, and nativity	All counties	Metropolitan, by size of largest place in standard metropolitan area		Nonmetropolitan, by size of largest place in county	
		250,000 or more	Under 250,000	25,000 or more	Under 25,000
RURAL NONFARM					
All classes....................	100.0	100.0	100.0	100.0	100.0
Native white.....................	87.7	88.5	89.8	89.0	86.9
Foreign-born white..................	3.6	6.5	3.8	3.8	2.7
Negro............................	8.0	4.8	6.0	6.7	9.5
Other races......................	0.7	0.2	0.4	0.5	0.9
RURAL FARM					
All classes....................	100.0	100.0	100.0	100.0	100.0
Native white.....................	83.1	87.8	85.7	84.3	82.6
Foreign-born white..................	2.4	7.0	4.4	3.2	1.9
Negro............................	13.7	4.4	8.7	11.8	14.8
Other races......................	0.8	0.8	1.2	0.7	0.7

Source: See table 76.

whole, foreign-born whites amount to 6.5 percent of the rural-nonfarm and 7.0 percent of the rural-farm population in metropolitan counties with large centers, but only 2.7 and 1.9 percent, respectively, of the nonfarm and farm population in counties with no center above 25,000. There are four geographic divisions in which the percentage of foreign-born whites in the rural-nonfarm population is higher in both the metropolitan county groups than in either group of nonmetropolitan counties. The reverse is true only in the Mountain Division, while the relationship of the percentage foreign-born to type of county is unclear in the Middle Atlantic, West North Central, South Atlantic, and West South Central Divisions. There are six divisions in which the rural-farm percentages of foreign born in both groups of metropolitan counties exceed the percentage for either nonmetropolitan group, while in the Middle Atlantic, East South Central and West South Central Divisions, the relationship is unclear.

In the United States as a whole, for both the rural-nonfarm and rural-farm population, the percentage of Negroes moves upward, going from the metropolitan counties with large centers to the least urban counties. However, the same regular gradient is observed only for the West South Central Division in the case of the rural-nonfarm population, and only for the South Atlantic in the case of the rural-farm. There is a general tendency for the proportion of Negroes to be highest in the metropolitan counties of the northern divisions and in the least urban counties of the southern divisions, for both the rural-nonfarm and rural-farm population. However, there are numerous exceptions to this tendency.

The "other races" category (nonwhites other than Negroes) is a substantial element of the rural population in only two divisions. Other races comprise a larger percentage of the rural-farm population in metropolitan than in nonmetropolitan counties of the Pacific Division, but the reverse is true in the Mountain Division. They have a relatively high percentage in the rural-nonfarm population of the least urban counties of the Mountain Division, but there is little relationship of the percentage of other races to type of county in the rural-nonfarm population of the Pacific Division.

Another type of comparison affords a somewhat clearer picture. In the three divisions of the South the percentage of Negroes is greater in the rural-farm than in the rural-nonfarm population, for each type of county, except the metropolitan counties with large centers in the South Atlantic and West South Central Divisions. By contrast, in all the six divisions of the North and West the percentage of Negroes is greater in the rural-nonfarm than in the rural-farm population. This holds for every type-of-county group in these divisions.

The percentage of foreign-born whites in the rural-farm population exceeds that of the rural-nonfarm population in all groups of counties in the New England and Middle Atlantic Divisions. This is true likewise in the metropolitan counties of the South Atlantic, West South Central, East North

Central, and Mountain Divisions.   The reverse holds in the remaining groups of counties.   Although there are a few exceptions to this generalization, it appears that the rural-farm population has a comparatively high proportion of foreign-born population primarily in the highly urbanized divisions of the Northeast and in certain groups of urbanized counties elsewhere in the country.

Education

Tables 80 and B–9 show by type of county the median year of school completed by the rural-nonfarm and farm populations.   The educational attainment of the rural population generally reflects directly the degree of urbanization of the county of residence.   The relationship is somewhat

TABLE **80.**—MEDIAN YEARS OF SCHOOL COMPLETED, PERCENT IN THE LABOR FORCE BY SEX, AND PERCENT OF THE CIVILIAN LABOR FORCE UNEMPLOYED, FOR THE RURAL-NONFARM AND RURAL-FARM POPULATION, BY TYPE OF COUNTY: 1950

Residence and characteristic	All counties	Metropolitan, by size of largest place in standard metropolitan area		Nonmetropolitan, by size of largest place in county	
		250,000 or more	Under 250,000	25,000 or more	Under 25,000
Median school years completed:[1]					
Rural nonfarm....................	8.8	10.0	9.0	8.9	8.7
Rural farm.......................	8.4	8.8	8.6	8.5	8.3
Percent in labor force:					
Male:					
Rural nonfarm[2].................	73.0	74.2	74.1	72.3	72.6
Rural farm......................	82.7	82.1	82.1	82.9	82.8
Female:					
Rural nonfarm...................	22.7	23.5	23.3	23.9	22.2
Rural farm......................	15.7	20.0	18.8	17.6	15.0
Percent of civilian labor force unemployed:					
Rural nonfarm...................	5.1	4.3	4.7	5.6	5.3
Rural farm......................	1.7	2.4	2.4	2.2	1.6

[1] Persons 25 years old and over.
[2] Civilian population only.

Source: See table 76.

more pronounced for the rural-nonfarm than for the rural-farm population, but it is evident, though by no means entirely regular, for both residence categories in the United States as a whole and in most geographic divisions.

In the rural-nonfarm population the median school year completed drops from 10.0 to 8.7, going from the metropolitan counties with large centers to the nonmetropolitan counties with no center above 25,000.   In all divisions but one, these metropolitan counties have medians as large as, or larger than, that of any other group of counties.   Similarly, in all divisions but two the least urban counties have the lowest medians.

The relationship of educational attainment to degree of urbanization for the rural-farm is similar to that in the rural-nonfarm population, and about as consistent.   However, there are three divisions, the Middle Atlantic and the two North Central Divisions, where there is very little differentiation of the county groups in terms of median school years completed. In all 36 of the comparisons between the rural-nonfarm and rural-farm population (using the 4-way county classification and the breakdown into nine geographic divisions) the rural-nonfarm median exceeds the rural-farm. In general, the amount of the difference is less in the group of nonmetropolitan counties with centers under 25,000 than in the nonmetropolitan counties with larger urban centers and in the metropolitan counties.

Labor force and occupation

Tables 80, B–10, and B–11 show for males and females, respectively, the rates of labor force participation of the population 14 years old and over for the rural-nonfarm and rural-farm residence categories by type of county. In computing the rates for the rural-nonfarm population, persons in the Armed Forces were excluded from both the members of the labor force and the base population.

For males, it is difficult to discern any pronounced general tendency for labor force participation to vary systematically by type of county. For rural-nonfarm males, the percentages of persons in the labor force are slightly higher in the metropolitan than in the nonmetropolitan counties. The same sort of difference occurs for six of the nine geographic divisions. For rural-farm males, nonmetropolitan counties have higher rates of labor force participation than metropolitan, but the difference amounts to less than 1 percentage point and occurs in only four of the nine divisions as well as the United States as a whole. The labor force participation rate is substantially greater for rural-farm than for rural-nonfarm males in every group of counties in each division.

For rural-nonfarm females (table B–11) there is very little relation between labor force participation and type of county. Although in the United States as a whole the least urban counties have a slightly lower percentage in the labor force than any other group of counties, these differences occur in only two geographic divisions.

Labor force participation rates of rural-farm females differ fairly substantially among the type-of-county groups. There is a regular gradient between the figure of 20 percent characterizing the metropolitan counties with large centers and the 15 percent for the least urban counties. The same sort of gradient appears for five of the divisions, and in each of the remaining four divisions the lowest rate of labor force participation occurs for the least urban counties. Thus, there is a relatively clear-cut finding for the rural-farm females, although not for males and rural-nonfarm females.

Differences between nonfarm and farm labor force participation rates for females are in the opposite direction from those for males. In each of the 36 comparisons in table B–11 the rural-nonfarm rate is higher than the rural-farm rate. The largest differences are generally found for the least urban group of counties.

The percentage of unemployment for each group of counties is shown in tables 80 and B–12. For the rural-nonfarm labor force the unemployment rate is somewhat higher in nonmetropolitan counties than in metropolitan counties, although there is not a regular gradient by type of county. This relationship holds for the United States as a whole, and for five of the divisions, four of which are in the North. In the remaining four divisions unemployment is clearly lower in the metropolitan counties with large centers than in any of the other groups of counties. It appears, therefore, that location near large centers is generally favorable to low percentages of unemployment for the rural-nonfarm population.

The relation of unemployment to type of county tends, if anything, to be reverse for the rural-farm labor force. Slightly higher percentages of unemployed persons occur for the metropolitan counties in the United States as a whole and in four of the divisions. The picture is mixed, however, since there is no such demonstrable tendency for the remaining five divisions, in one of which the metropolitan counties have clearly lower unemployment rates than the nonmetropolitan counties. In general the variation in unemployment by type of county is greater for the rural-nonfarm than for the rural-farm labor force. The rural nonfarm has, uniformly, the higher proportions unemployed. It seems likely that the low unemployment rate of the rural-farm labor force masks a significant proportion of underemployment, particularly in the least urban counties.

The occupational composition of the rural-nonfarm labor force, with a breakdown by sex, is shown for the United States as a whole by type of county in table 81. In general there is a downward gradient in the socio-economic status of the male labor force, going from the metropolitan counties with large centers to the counties with no center larger than 25,000. Such a gradient is observed for each of the white-collar groups, except nonfarm managers, proprietors, and officials, and also for craftsmen, foremen, and kindred workers. A gradient in the opposite direction appears for nonfarm laborers, and for the three groups of farm occupations. An examination of occupation distributions for the several geographic divisions (not shown here) uncovers similar tendencies, although there is less regularity within divisions than for the United States as a whole. Most divisions have clear downward gradients for clerical and kindred workers and craftsmen, foremen, and kindred workers, and upward gradients for the farm occupation groups. Where irregularities occur they are generally minor.

The most striking feature of the occupation distributions for rural-nonfarm females is the marked downward gradient in the proportion employed in clerical and kindred occupations. In the metropolitan counties with large centers over 26 percent are in this group, as compared with only 16

TABLE 81.—PERCENT DISTRIBUTION OF THE RURAL-NONFARM EMPLOYED LABOR FORCE BY MAJOR OCCUPATION GROUP AND SEX, BY TYPE OF COUNTY: 1950

Major occupation group[1] and sex	All counties	Metropolitan, by size of largest place in standard metropolitan area		Nonmetropolitan, by size of largest place in county	
		250,000 or more	Under 250,000	25,000 or more	Under 25,000
Male..	100.0	100.0	100.0	100.0	100.0
Professional, technical, and kindred workers........	6.1	8.1	5.9	6.0	5.5
Managers, officials, and proprietors, except farm...	10.7	10.9	9.7	10.1	10.9
Clerical and kindred workers.........................	4.3	5.7	4.9	4.4	3.8
Sales workers..	5.1	5.7	5.3	5.2	4.9
Craftsmen, foremen, and kindred workers..............	21.6	26.1	24.3	23.0	19.6
Operatives and kindred workers.......................	25.0	23.6	27.3	25.4	24.9
Private household workers............................	0.2	0.3	0.2	0.2	0.2
Service workers, except private household...........	4.3	4.6	4.1	4.8	4.2
Laborers, except farm and mine......................	11.8	9.4	10.3	11.1	12.9
Farmers and farm managers............................	3.0	1.4	1.8	2.3	3.9
Farm laborers, unpaid family workers................	0.5	0.1	0.2	0.3	0.6
Farm laborers, except unpaid, and farm foremen......	6.0	3.0	4.8	5.9	7.1
Occupation not reported.............................	1.4	1.1	1.2	1.3	1.5
Female..	100.0	100.0	100.0	100.0	100.0
Professional, technical, and kindred workers........	13.3	12.9	11.4	12.3	13.9
Managers, officials, and proprietors, except farm...	5.7	4.8	5.0	5.3	6.2
Clerical and kindred workers.........................	18.6	26.3	20.5	18.4	16.0
Sales workers..	9.4	8.0	8.8	9.1	10.0
Craftsmen, foremen, and kindred workers..............	1.3	1.6	1.5	1.3	1.1
Operatives and kindred workers.......................	20.4	20.3	25.0	23.3	19.1
Private household workers............................	10.3	8.7	9.0	9.1	11.2
Service workers, except private household...........	14.4	13.1	12.9	14.6	15.1
Laborers, except farm and mine......................	1.1	0.9	1.2	1.2	1.1
Farmers and farm managers............................	0.5	0.3	0.3	0.4	0.5
Farm laborers, unpaid family workers................	0.5	0.2	0.3	0.4	0.7
Farm laborers, except unpaid, and farm foremen......	2.0	0.9	1.6	2.2	2.4
Occupation not reported.............................	2.5	2.0	2.5	2.4	2.7

[1] The order in which the occupation groups are given is not necessarily their rank order by socio-economic status.

Source: *1950 Census of Population*, Vol. II, *Characteristics of the Population*, Parts 2 to 50, table 48.

percent in the least urban counties. Partially compensating for this are slight upward gradients in the proportions employed as sales workers and as nonfarm managers, proprietors, and officials. The percentage of females employed in all white-collar occupations is 52 in the metropolitan counties with large centers, and 45 to 46 in each of the other three groups of counties. As for males, there is a distinct upward gradient in the percentage in each of the farm occupation groups, and also in the percentage of private household workers. Within divisions there is a high degree of consistency with the relationship for clerical and kindred workers and craftsmen, foremen, and kindred workers. There is less consistency for the other occupational gradients, but there are, nevertheless, general tendencies in the directions noted.

Occupation distributions for rural-farm males and females, by type of county, are given in table 82. Examining first the data for males, it is clear that the major variation is in the proportion in farm occupations. In the metropolitan counties with large centers just over half (52.9 percent) of the male labor force is in farm occupations. The percentage rises to 62.1 for the remaining metropolitan counties, and to 70.7 percent for the nonmetropolitan counties with centers over 25,000. In the least urban counties well over three-fourths (78.3 percent) of the employed persons are in farm occupations. There is, as well, a marked differentiation within the group of farm occupations. In the counties with no center over 25,000 there are 32 farm laborers and foremen (including unpaid family workers) per 100 farmers and farm managers, as compared with ratios of 39 to 42 in the other three groups of counties. Furthermore, while farm laborers employed as unpaid family workers are only one-fourth as numerous as other farm laborers and foremen in the metropolitan counties with large centers, there are nearly 5 unpaid family workers for every 6 paid farm laborers in the least urban counties.

As a consequence of the pronounced upward gradient for farm occupations, there is a downward gradient in the proportion of rural-farm males in each other occupation group, going from the metropolitan counties with large centers to the nonmetropolitan counties with no places above 25,000. There is a particularly marked drop in the proportion of white-collar workers between the two groups of metropolitan counties. In those with centers over 250,000, manual workers outnumber white-collar workers by 2½ to 1, whereas the ratio is from 3⅓ to 3½ in the remaining groups of counties.

TABLE 82.—PERCENT DISTRIBUTION OF THE RURAL-FARM EMPLOYED LABOR FORCE BY MAJOR OCCUPATION GROUP AND SEX, BY TYPE OF COUNTY: 1950

Major occupation group[1] and sex	All counties	Metropolitan, by size of largest place in standard metropolitan area		Nonmetropolitan, by size of largest place in county	
		250,000 or more	Under 250,000	25,000 or more	Under 25,000
Male......................................	100.0	100.0	100.0	100.0	100.0
Professional, technical, and kindred workers.........	1.2	3.4	1.8	1.4	1.0
Managers, officials, and proprietors, except farm...	2.0	4.8	3.0	2.2	1.7
Clerical and kindred workers......................	1.0	2.6	1.9	1.3	0.9
Sales workers....................................	1.1	2.3	1.7	1.3	1.0
Craftsmen, foremen, and kindred workers...........	5.5	12.4	9.6	7.1	4.5
Operatives and kindred workers....................	7.8	12.8	12.3	9.4	7.0
Private household workers.........................	0.1	0.2	0.1	0.1	...
Service workers, except private household..........	0.8	1.7	1.3	1.1	0.6
Laborers, except farm and mine....................	4.0	5.8	5.1	4.3	3.8
Farmers and farm managers........................	56.3	37.8	43.8	50.8	59.1
Farm laborers, unpaid family workers..............	8.1	3.0	5.0	6.9	8.7
Farm laborers, except unpaid, and farm foremen.....	11.0	12.1	13.3	13.0	10.5
Occupation not reported..........................	1.1	1.1	1.1	1.1	1.2
Female....................................	100.0	100.0	100.0	100.0	100.0
Professional, technical, and kindred workers........	10.0	11.1	9.4	9.2	10.1
Managers, officials, and proprietors, except farm...	2.0	2.9	2.3	2.0	1.9
Clerical and kindred workers......................	10.2	22.4	15.2	12.0	8.4
Sales workers....................................	4.6	5.6	5.4	5.1	4.3
Craftsmen, foremen, and kindred workers...........	0.7	1.4	1.0	0.8	0.6
Operatives and kindred workers....................	13.2	15.6	18.3	14.8	12.4
Private household workers.........................	7.1	9.6	7.6	7.7	6.7
Service workers, except private household..........	5.9	7.4	6.6	6.7	5.6
Laborers, except farm and mine....................	0.7	0.9	0.9	0.7	0.6
Farmers and farm managers........................	8.5	6.6	6.9	7.6	8.9
Farm laborers, unpaid family workers..............	26.5	9.4	17.7	22.6	29.4
Farm laborers, except unpaid, and farm foremen.....	5.5	3.9	5.2	6.2	5.6
Occupation not reported..........................	5.1	3.2	3.5	4.6	5.5

[1] The order in which the occupation groups are given is not necessarily their rank order by socio-economic status.

Source: 1950 Census of Population, Vol. II, Characteristics of the Population, Parts 2 to 50, table 49.

Although the proportion of rural-farm females employed in farm occupations is much less than the proportion of males, females have a similar type-of-county gradient. In the metropolitan counties with centers of 250,000 or more, 19.9 percent of employed females are in farm occupations. The percentages increase to 29.8 in the metropolitan counties with smaller centers, 36.4 in the nonmetropolitan counties with centers of 25,000 or more, and 43.9 in the least urban counties. The gradient is especially marked for the farm laborers employed as unpaid family workers. There is a compensating downward gradient for most of the other occupation groups. In the metropolitan counties with large centers rural-farm females employed as white-collar workers outnumber the manual workers, whereas the reverse is true in each of the other groups of counties.

Table 83 shows for each geographic division the percentages of rural-farm males and females employed in farm occupations, by type of county. For the most part the gradient described for the United States is reproduced in each of the divisions, with most of the irregularities being minor. Significantly, type-of-county differentiation is less pronounced in the highly urbanized divisions of the Northeast than in the North Central divisions and those of the South.

Tables 84 and 85 provide other measures of nonfarm economic activities in relation to type of county. These figures are based on statistics

TABLE **83.**—PERCENT OF THE RURAL-FARM EMPLOYED LABOR FORCE IN FARM OCCUPATIONS BY SEX, BY TYPE OF COUNTY AND DIVISION: 1950

Division and sex	All counties	Metropolitan, by size of largest place in standard metropolitan area		Nonmetropolitan, by size of largest place in county	
		250,000 or more	Under 250,000	25,000 or more	Under 25,000
MALE					
United States..................	75.4	52.9	62.1	70.7	78.3
New England.........................	58.6	50.2	54.9	58.7	62.9
Middle Atlantic.....................	59.7	50.0	59.1	63.7	63.6
East North Central.................	71.0	50.5	59.2	70.6	74.2
West North Central.................	88.4	66.6	75.0	84.4	89.7
South Atlantic.....................	70.0	46.9	55.9	65.5	72.0
East South Central.................	77.7	51.5	58.5	68.7	79.4
West South Central.................	78.5	52.5	70.7	74.9	79.7
Mountain...........................	81.9	62.0	63.1	74.3	84.1
Pacific............................	68.1	57.7	70.2	67.6	70.5
FEMALE					
United States..................	40.5	19.9	29.8	36.4	43.9
New England.........................	17.0	12.7	16.1	22.3	18.5
Middle Atlantic.....................	24.0	16.3	25.6	24.9	27.0
East North Central.................	35.9	18.0	24.1	38.9	39.0
West North Central.................	53.5	27.0	50.7	46.4	55.1
South Atlantic.....................	40.4	12.5	24.1	33.7	43.3
East South Central.................	42.5	18.1	40.0	37.2	43.7
West South Central.................	46.6	19.6	40.5	42.4	48.0
Mountain...........................	39.6	37.7	23.7	29.5	41.8
Pacific............................	36.4	34.6	34.9	39.3	36.8

Source: See table 82.

TABLE **84.**—PERCENT OF FARM OPERATORS WORKING OFF THEIR FARM 100 DAYS OR MORE IN 1949, BY TYPE OF COUNTY AND DIVISION: 1950

Division	All counties[1]	Metropolitan, by size of largest place in standard metropolitan area		Nonmetropolitan, by size of largest place in county	
		250,000 or more	Under 250,000	25,000 or more	Under 25,000
United States..................	23.3	39.7	34.5	28.0	21.0
New England.........................	37.6	39.0	38.9	39.3	36.4
Middle Atlantic.....................	33.3	38.5	33.5	31.4	31.5
East North Central..................	24.9	39.7	33.7	25.3	22.5
West North Central..................	12.8	31.0	26.0	16.3	11.5
South Atlantic......................	26.3	43.6	37.8	30.5	24.6
East South Central..................	21.1	41.6	37.8	28.7	19.7
West South Central..................	23.6	47.2	33.4	27.4	22.5
Mountain...........................	23.8	36.0	42.8	31.6	21.6
Pacific............................	35.8	41.0	34.7	37.1	33.7

[1] Figures vary slightly from published percentages, since they are based on total farms rather than operators reporting.

Source: *1950 Census of Agriculture,* Vol. I, *Counties and State Economic Areas,* Parts 1 to 33, county table 1 for each State.

from the Census of Agriculture and pertain to farm operators rather than to rural-farm residents. Table 84 shows that for the United States as a whole nearly two-fifths (39.7 percent) of the farm operators in the metropolitan counties with large centers worked off their farms 100 days or more during 1949.[5] This compares with 34.5 percent for the other metropolitan counties, 28.0 percent for the nonmetropolitan counties with centers over 25,000, and only one-fifth (21.0 percent) of farm operators in the remaining nonmetropolitan counties who worked 100 days or more off their farms during that year. In most of the geographic divisions the same sort of gradient is observed. The differentiation by type of county is especially marked in the North Central divisions and those in the South.

Table 85 shows the percentage of farm operators with other income of the family exceeding the value of agricultural products sold in 1949, by

TABLE **85.**—PERCENT OF FARM OPERATORS WITH OTHER INCOME OF FAMILY EXCEEDING VALUE OF AGRICULTURAL PRODUCTS SOLD IN 1949, BY TYPE OF COUNTY AND DIVISION: 1950

Division	All counties	Metropolitan, by size of largest place in standard metropolitan area		Nonmetropolitan, by size of largest place in county	
		250,000 or more	Under 250,000	25,000 or more	Under 25,000
United States..................	29.1	41.9	37.9	31.9	27.3
New England.........................	41.5	39.5	44.5	44.7	41.0
Middle Atlantic.....................	35.0	38.4	34.2	32.4	34.4
East North Central..................	25.6	38.4	32.4	23.8	23.8
West North Central..................	14.6	31.6	27.1	17.6	13.4
South Atlantic......................	35.0	49.1	47.2	39.1	33.4
East South Central..................	32.4	46.8	48.4	38.3	31.2
West South Central..................	33.2	53.0	37.3	33.9	32.5
Mountain...........................	26.1	40.2	46.1	33.2	23.9
Pacific............................	40.9	48.0	37.6	43.4	38.5

Source: See table 84.

type of county.[5]   Again, the data indicate that nonfarm economic activity is more prevalent in the more highly urbanized counties, although there is somewhat less regularity in the type-of-county gradients within divisions and less differentiation by type of county.

Summary and conclusions

Significant patterns of differences by degree of urbanization of county are the main concern of this chapter.   The gradient of urban influence is especially marked for fertility (particularly for the rural-farm population), educational attainment (particularly for the rural-nonfarm population), labor force participation of rural-farm females, occupation composition, and economic activities of farm operators.   These results make it clear that blanket characterizations of the rural population tend to be less accurate to the degree that the rural population falls into the area of dominance of urban centers.   Probably no part of the rural population in the United States is completely free from urban influence.   But the degree of such influence varies greatly, at least partly as a function of proximity to urban centers and the size of those centers.

Some of the data treated above manifest a tendency for the gradient of urban influence to appear stronger in those geographic divisions which are on the whole less urbanized.   It is possible that the type-of-county classification used is simply not as sensitive an indicator of urban influence in a highly urbanized region as in a less urbanized region.   However, there is an alternative interpretation which is also plausible, i.e., that in a highly urbanized region all sectors of the rural population have to a considerable degree come under urban influences, while in a less urbanized region the rural population not in close proximity to large urban centers has not yet experienced urban influences to so marked an extent.   Thus, for example, the percentage of rural-farm males employed in farm occupations is lower in the least urban counties of New England than in the most urban counties of the West North Central Division.   The percentage of farm operators reporting 100 days or more of off-farm work is higher in all groups of counties in the Middle Atlantic Division than in any group of counties in the West North Central Division.   There is by no means a one-to-one correspondence between the level of urbanization of a geographic division and the magnitude of the gradient of urban influence within the division. But relationships like those just noted are observed frequently enough to make such an hypothesis of some value in explaining intercounty variations in rural population characteristics.

There is, of course, another interpretation which can be placed on the findings.   Some students prefer to think of urbanization in terms of occupation and economic activities, rather than size of place.   Under a defini-

---

[5] Data compiled from *1950 Census of Agriculture*, Vol. I, *Counties and State Economic Areas*, Parts 1–33, county table 1.

tion of urban and rural population derived from such an approach the results of this chapter would indicate a tendency for "urban" population to be a large component of the areas adjacent to large cities, and for relatively homogeneous "rural" areas to be found only in places at substantial distances from sizable population centers. There are probably few counties in the United States where "rural" types of activities are not intermixed with "urban" to a considerable extent.

C H A P T E R   1 4

METROPOLITAN SUBURBS AND INDEPENDENT CITIES

The preceding chapter compared rural areas within standard metropolitan areas (SMA's) with those outside SMA's. This chapter carries out a somewhat similar analysis for urban places. The general hypothesis is that urban places located near large metropolitan centers differ systematically in their demographic and socio-economic characteristics from places of comparable size located at greater distances from these centers of dominance. The data introduced here may be viewed also as supplementing those in Chapter 11, which compared suburbs and central cities of urbanized areas. Here suburbs (defined somewhat differently) are compared with places outside the immediate sphere of influence of central cities.

The universe of study comprises all urban places having in 1950 10,000 inhabitants or more, except those classified as central cities of SMA's. These places are classified into metropolitan suburbs and independent cities. Metropolitan suburbs include all urban places, other than central cities, inside SMA's.[1] Independent cities include all urban places outside SMA's.[2] Each of these two groups is subclassified according to size. This is to eliminate the size factor as a possible explanation of the differences, particularly since some suburbs exceed 50,000 inhabitants, whereas by definition no independent city can be larger than 50,000.

The tables in this chapter were prepared by consolidating data published for individual urban places into the categories used here.[3] In view of the considerable clerical work involved, the data had to be limited for the most part to selected indicators of demographic and socio-economic characteristics. Hence the analysis does not go into as much detail with

---

[1] Hence, the term "suburb," as used in this chapter, is more inclusive than the category of "suburbs" employed in Chapter 11. It includes both "suburbs" and "satellites," as those terms were defined for the purposes of Chapter 12. The usage of the term "suburb" established in the present chapter will be adhered to throughout Parts III and IV of the monograph; the qualifying adjective "metropolitan" is used only in this chapter to emphasize the distinction between "suburbs" as here defined and as defined in Chapter 11.

[2] The term "independent cities" as used in this monograph is not to be confused with the same term used in census reports to denote cities which are independent of any county organization and thus constitute primary political divisions of their States.

[3] Data for individual places were obtained from the following U. S. Bureau of the Census publications: *Census of Business: 1948*, Vols. III and V; *Census of Population: 1950*, Vols. I and II; and *Census of Housing: 1950*, Vol. I.

respect to distributions of population characteristics as have the foregoing chapters.

Table 86 shows the population of metropolitan suburbs and independent cities by size groups, together with the regional distributions of these places. There are 410 metropolitan suburbs (of 10,000 inhabitants or more), with an aggregate population of about 11.5 million. The 659 independent cities have a slightly larger population, 13.0 million. The average metropolitan suburb is, therefore, considerably larger than the average independent city. This size difference is controlled by showing data separately for metropolitan suburbs of 50,000 or more, for which there is no corresponding class of independent cities.

TABLE 86.—NUMBER, REGIONAL DISTRIBUTION, AND POPULATION OF URBAN PLACES OF 10,000 INHABITANTS OR MORE CLASSIFIED AS METROPOLITAN SUBURBS AND INDEPENDENT CITIES, BY SIZE: 1950

Type and size of place	Population (thousands)	Number of places	Percent of places, by region				
			United States	North-east	North Central	South	West
Metropolitan suburbs..........	11,477	410	100	42	29	10	19
50,000 or more.....................	4,364	53	100	49	28	4	19
25,000 to 50,000....................	2,837	81	100	42	36	5	17
10,000 to 25,000....................	4,276	276	100	41	28	12	19
Independent cities.............	13,027	659	100	17	33	35	15
25,000 to 50,000....................	5,436	157	100	17	32	37	14
10,000 to 25,000....................	7,591	502	100	17	33	35	15

Source: Appendix tables B–19 and B–20; *1950 Census of Population*, Vol. II, *Characteristics of the Population*, Parts 2 to 50, table 10.

A comparison of the maps showing location of urban places (figure 2, p. 31) and SMA's (figure 18, p. 153) suggests, and the statistics in table 86 demonstrate, a marked concentration of metropolitan suburbs in the Northeast, corresponding to the concentration of metropolitan population in general. The independent cities, on the other hand, are located disproportionately in the South. The two classes of cities differ only slightly in the proportions in the North Central States and in the West. A correct interpretation of differences between metropolitan suburbs and independent cities depends on recalling the difference between their regional distributions.

Demographic characteristics

Table 87 shows selected indexes of age, color, sex, marital status, household size, and mobility. This table, like others in this chapter, permits gross comparisons between metropolitan suburbs and independent cities, as well as comparisons within size groups. The latter are useful as an indication of the generality of the differences observed on a gross basis.

There is only a slight difference in the sex ratio between metropolitan suburbs and independent cities. Furthermore, the difference is not consistent within size groups. Both categories of cities exhibit the prevailing

TABLE 87.—SELECTED DEMOGRAPHIC CHARACTERISTICS OF THE POPULATION, FOR METROPOLITAN
SUBURBS AND INDEPENDENT CITIES OF 10,000 INHABITANTS OR MORE, BY SIZE: 1950

Type and size of place	Sex ratio	Percent 21 years old and over	Percent non-white	Percent married, male	Persons per house-hold[1]	Percent living in same house, 1949 and 1950[2]
Metropolitan suburbs........	94.7	68.5	5.3	72.7	3.40	82.6
50,000 or more.....................	93.9	69.9	6.7	74.6	3.28	83.6
25,000 to 50,000..................	94.4	68.7	4.3	70.2	3.34	82.6
10,000 to 25,000..................	95.8	66.9	4.5	72.5	3.40	81.7
Independent cities..........	93.9	66.0	9.5	68.5	3.19	77.5
25,000 to 50,000..................	94.1	66.6	10.1	67.6	3.19	77.3
10,000 to 25,000..................	93.8	65.6	9.0	69.2	3.20	77.7

[1] The figure shown is the one for the median place in each group.
[2] Persons 1 year old and over.

Source: *1950 Census of Population*, Vol, II, *Characteristics of the Population*, Parts 2 to 50, tables 33 and 34.

urban pattern of an excess of females, but they evidently differ little in the degree of selectivity for females.

The population of metropolitan suburbs is somewhat older than that of independent cities. In metropolitan suburbs as a group, 68.5 percent of the population is 21 years old or over, compared with but 66.0 percent of the population in all independent cities. The comparisons within size groups reveal similar differences. The inference is that the median ages of the two classes of cities differ in the same direction, but the data do not indicate anything about the relative proportions of very young or very old people.

The nonwhite proportion of the population is nearly twice as great in independent cities as in metropolitan suburbs—9.5 as compared to 5.3 percent. Disregarding the largest suburbs, as not strictly comparable with respect to size, accentuates the difference. This difference is doubtless due in part to the relative concentration of independent cities in the South. However, other data in the monograph, where regional differences are not involved, indicate that metropolitan suburbs generally have comparatively low percentages of nonwhites.

There is a substantially higher proportion of males married in metropolitan suburbs than in independent cities. The difference amounts to 4.2 percentage points for the gross comparison, and to 2.6 and 3.3 percentage points for comparisons within size groups. The difference is evidently not attributable to differences in sex ratio, and probably not to differences in age. The tentative conclusion is; therefore, that suburbs are more selective of married persons than are independent cities.

Although the difference is slight, average household size in metropolitan suburbs exceeds that in independent cities, with the comparison being consistent by size groups. There are about 3.3 or 3.4 persons per household in metropolitan suburbs, and 3.2 in independent cities.

The independent cities have a more mobile population than do metropolitan suburbs. On a gross basis the percentage living in the same house in 1949 and 1950 is about 5 points less in independent cities than in suburbs, and differences of similar magnitude appear within size groups. This may reflect a regional difference in urban growth rates, because the independent cities are found disproportionately in the South, where 1940–50 urban growth rates were comparatively high. Data in other chapters demonstrate that the in-migration rate for the last year of the decade is highly correlated with the growth rate for the entire decade.

Economic characteristics

Table 88 compares metropolitan suburbs and independent cities with respect to the proportions of males and females in the labor force. For males, the suburbs have the greater labor force participation, but the opposite difference occurs for females. Nearly 81 percent of the males 14 years old and over are in the labor force in metropolitan suburbs, as compared with only 77 percent in independent cities. The difference between the two classes of cities is 4.9 percentage points for places of 25,000 to 50,000, and 2.4 points in the same direction for the smaller places. The difference in the opposite direction for females is of about equal importance in relative terms. Exactly one-third of the females in independent cities are in the labor force, but only 31.4 percent in the metropolitan suburbs—a difference of 1.9 percentage points. The difference is consistent by size groups: 2.4 points for places of 25,000 to 50,000, and 3.5 points for places of 10,000 to 25,000. Obviously, there is a clear differentiation of labor force patterns as between suburbs and independent cities. A cogent explanation of the variation in pattern is not, however, available from other data in this chapter.

The economic indexes shown in table 89 pertain to government employment, employment of males in manufacturing, and volume of trade. The classification of places as metropolitan suburbs and independent cities produces substantial differences with respect to each of these characteristics.

The proportion of employed persons working for government agencies, irrespective of type of industry, is larger in independent cities than in metropolitan suburbs. Government workers comprise 11.6 percent of the working

TABLE **88.**—Percent of Persons in the Labor Force, by Sex, for Metropolitan Suburbs and Independent Cities of 10,000 Inhabitants or More, by Size: 1950

Type and size of place	Male	Female	Type and size of place	Male	Female
Metropolitan suburbs.......	80.7	31.4	Independent cities..........	76.8	33.3
50,000 or more..................	80.6	33.2	25,000 to 50,000..................	76.5	34.1
25,000 to 50,000.................	81.4	31.7	10,000 to 25,000..................	77.1	32.7
10,000 to 25,000.................	80.5	29.2			

Source: *1950 Census of Population,* Vol. II, *Characteristics of the Population,* Parts 2 to 50, table 35.

force in all independent cities combined, but only 9.1 percent in all suburbs. This difference is consistent by size of place. In interpreting this
finding reference should be made to the fact, noted in later chapters, that
cities in the South (where independent cities are relatively concentrated)
are more likely to have large military establishments than those in the
North. Military personnel are not included in the foregoing comparison,
but military establishments give rise to considerable government employment of civilians.

The metropolitan suburbs, as a class, have a much larger proportion of
males employed in manufacturing than do independent cities. The difference is about 11 percentage points—39.6 as compared with 28.4
percent—on a gross basis, and 13 and 10 points for the comparisons of

TABLE **89.**—SELECTED INDUSTRIAL CHARACTERISTICS OF THE POPULATION, FOR METROPOLITAN
SUBURBS AND INDEPENDENT CITIES OF 10,000 INHABITANTS OR MORE, BY SIZE: 1950
AND 1948

Type and size of place	Government workers as percent of all employed persons, 1950[1]	Percent of employed males in manufactur- ing, 1950	Per capita sales, 1948[2] (dollars)	
			Retail trade	Wholesale trade
Metropolitan suburbs..........	9.1	39.6	1,013	513
50,000 or more......................	8.7	39.3	1,043	625
25,000 to 50,000....................	9.0	41.8	1,137	524
10,000 to 25,000....................	9.5	38.5	900	391
Independent cities............	11.6	28.4	1,322	850
25,000 to 50,000....................	11.7	28.8	1,340	1,023
10,000 to 25,000....................	11.5	28.2	1,309	726

[1] Based on class-of-worker statistics; includes persons employed by a government unit (Federal, State, or
local), regardless of the activity engaged in.
[2] Sales according to location of establishment; base populations are for 1950. Excludes places for which
sales data were not available.

Source: *1950 Census of Population*, Vol. II, *Characteristics of the Population*, Parts 2 to 50, table 35;
1948 Census of Business, Vol. III, *Retail Trade—Area Statistics*, table 102 for each State; and Vol. V, *Wholesale Trade—Area Statistics*, table 103 for each State.

places 25,000 to 50,000 and 10,000 to 25,000, respectively. The results
are no doubt weighted by the concentration of industrial suburbs in the
Northeast and the concentration of nonmanufacturing independent cities in
the South—despite recent trends toward industrialization in the latter
region.

Independent cities have a larger volume of trade, both wholesale and
retail, in relation to population than do metropolitan suburbs. Although
the per capita figures are only approximate, owing to the difference in
census dates for business and population, the differences are undoubtedly reliable as to direction. The volume of retail trade in 1948, per
capita, was about $1,300 in all independent cities but only $1,000 in all
suburbs. An even larger difference, $400, is noted when the comparison
is made for places of 10,000 to 25,000. The contrast in per capita volume

of wholesale trade is equally striking.   Independent cities of 25,000 to 50,000 have a per capita trade $500 greater than that of metropolitan suburbs comparable in size; and the difference is over $300 in the size group 10,000 to 25,000.   To some extent, the higher trade volume of independent cities may be simply the inverse of their lesser activity in manufacturing.   However, a variety of evidence suggests that independent cities are more likely to be self-sufficient with respect to retail facilities than are metropolitan suburbs, whose population may depend heavily on the nearby central city for certain types of retail services.   Similarly, whereas the independent city may be a wholesale center for a local trade territory, this function is more apt to fall to the central city than to the suburb of a metropolitan area.

TABLE **90.**—PERCENT DISTRIBUTION OF EMPLOYED MALES BY MAJOR OCCUPATION GROUP, FOR METROPOLITAN SUBURBS AND INDEPENDENT CITIES OF 10,000 INHABITANTS OR MORE, BY SIZE: 1950

Major occupation group	Metropolitan suburbs				Independent cities		
	Total	50,000 or more	25,000 to 50,000	10,000 to 25,000	Total	25,000 to 50,000	10,000 to 25,000
All occupations......................	100.0	100.0	100.0	100.0	100.0	100.0	100.0
Professional, technical, and kindred wkrs...	10.9	10.6	10.5	11.6	8.6	8.7	8.6
Managers, officials, and proprietors........	13.4	12.7	13.0	14.5	13.6	13.7	13.5
Clerical and kindred workers................	8.3	8.6	8.2	8.0	6.6	7.1	6.3
Sales workers...............................	7.9	7.7	7.8	8.2	8.4	8.6	8.3
Craftsmen, foremen, and kindred workers.....	22.4	22.3	22.9	22.3	20.7	20.6	20.8
Operatives and kindred workers..............	21.5	21.9	22.7.	20.3	22.7	22.3	22.9
Private household and service workers.......	6.3	6.9	6.5	5.5	7.8	8.3	7.4
Laborers, except farm.......................	7.6	8.1	6.9	7.6	8.7	8.5	8.8
Other and occupation not reported[1].........	1.6	1.3	1.5	2.0	2.9	2.3	3.3

[1] Includes "Farmers and farm managers" and "Farm laborers."

Source: *1950 Census of Population*, Vol. II, *Characteristics of the Population*, Parts 2 to 50, table 35.

Table 90 shows the distribution of the male employed labor force by major occupation groups, for metropolitan suburbs and independent cities.   There is a significant differentiation of occupational structure in terms of this classification of cities.   The index of dissimilarity between the two occupation distributions is 5.6 percent for places of 25,000 to 50,000, and 7.1 percent for places of 10,000 to 25,000.   To summarize the bearing of occupation on comparative socio-economic status, the metropolitan suburbs have a somewhat higher proportion of white-collar workers. The professional, managerial, clerical, and sales occupations account for 40.6 percent of the employed males in suburbs, as compared to 37.3 percent in independent cities.   The difference is somewhat more pronounced for the smaller places than for the larger ones.   The proportion of male white-collar workers in metropolitan suburbs of 25,000 to 50,000 is 39.5 percent, as against 38.1 percent in independent cities of the same size; the corresponding figures for places 10,000 to 25,000 are 42.3 and 36.7 percent.   Although these differences are only moderate in size, they gain significance by recognizing that metropolitan suburbs have more manufacturing workers than do independent cities, and that manufacturing employment is primarily in manual occupations. Thus, the suburbs' socio-economic level, as measured by occupation, is higher than would be inferred from their industrial composition alone.

Examination of the individual occupation group comparisons in table 90 reveals that the principal difference, on the white-collar level, between metropolitan suburbs and independent cities is in regard to the percentage of professional, technical, and kindred workers. The difference, in favor of the suburbs, amounts to 2 percentage points for places of 25,000 to 50,000, and to 3 percentage points for places of 10,000 to 25,000. As to the other white-collar occupations, the difference between suburbs and independent cities in the percentage of managers, proprietors, and officials is slight, and not consistent by size of place. The metropolitan suburbs have a somewhat higher proportion of clerical and kindred workers, but a slightly lower proportion of sales workers, than do independent cities.

The difference in socio-economic status, in favor of metropolitan suburbs, is apparent even on the manual occupational level. The suburbs have a slightly higher percentage of males employed as craftsmen, foremen, and kindred workers than do the independent cities, but somewhat lower percentages of each of the other manual occupation groups. In comparisons within size groups these differences generally amount to about 1 or 2 percentage points. The only exception to this pattern is that independent cities of 25,000 to 50,000 have a very slightly smaller percentage of operatives and kindred workers than do metropolitan suburbs of the same size.

Table 91 presents selected occupational comparisons for females, which disclose differences much larger than those for males. In metropolitan suburbs 41.6 percent of the employed females are sales or clerical and kindred workers, as compared with only 34.3 in independent cities; a similar difference occurs within each size group. The comparatively high proportion of female sales and clerical workers in metropolitan suburbs apparently does not result from the suburban industrial structure, since

TABLE 91.—PERCENT OF EMPLOYED FEMALES IN SELECTED MAJOR OCCUPATION GROUPS, FOR METROPOLITAN SUBURBS AND INDEPENDENT CITIES OF 10,000 INHABITANTS OR MORE, BY SIZE: 1950

Type and size of place	Sales, clerical, and kindred workers	Operatives and kindred workers	Private household and service workers	Type and size of place	Sales, clerical, and kindred workers	Operatives and kindred workers	Private household and service workers
Metropolitan suburbs..	41.6	19.7	16.7	Independent cities....	34.3	19.2	24.4
50,000 or more.........	41.5	20.8	15.9	25,000 to 50,000........	34.8	18.8	24.5
25,000 to 50,000.......	41.6	20.4	16.9	10,000 to 25,000........	33.9	19.5	24.3
10,000 to 25,000.......	41.8	18.0	17.5				

Source: See table 90.

suburbs have a relatively high proportion of residents employed in manufacturing and a relatively low level of trade volume.   One infers that the
factor involved is a specialization of suburbs in residential patterns selective of female sales and clerical workers.   There is little difference between
metropolitan suburbs and independent cities in the proportion of female
operatives and kindred workers, despite the higher proportions of manufacturing workers living in suburbs.   This reinforces the conclusion that
one must explain the differential occupational characteristics of suburbs in
terms of residential selection within metropolitan areas, rather than the
industrial structure of suburbs.   Independent cities have a considerably
higher proportion of female private household and service workers than do
metropolitan suburbs.   Regional patterns explain at least a part of the
difference.   The independent cities are relatively concentrated in the
South, where domestic employment is more important than in other regions.

Socio-economic status

Other indicators of socio-economic status support the inferences drawn
from the occupation data.   Table 92 presents comparisons with regard to
education, income, and home ownership.

The median number of school years completed by the population aged
25 and over is 10.8 in metropolitan suburbs and 10.1 in independent
cities.   Essentially the same difference occurs within size groups.   In addition, a somewhat higher proportion of the college-age population is
enrolled in school in the metropolitan suburbs than is the case for independent cities.   The percentage enrolled, for persons 20 to 24 years old,
is 11.6 for all suburbs and 7.8 for all independent cities, a difference of
3.8 percentage points.   The difference is likewise 3.8 points for places
of 10,000 to 25,000, but only 1.9 points for places of 25,000 to 50,000.
Apparently suburban residents have somewhat more opportunity for
higher education.   Their advantage doubtless comes in part from the
possibility for students to commute to college between suburban and central parts of the metropolitan area or between suburbs.

The median income of families and unrelated individuals is around
$3,400 for all size groups of suburbs, but only $2,600 to $2,700 for in-
dependent cities.   Regional variations in income account for a large share
of this difference.   However, in view of the central city-suburb comparisons
in previous chapters, it is a reasonable hypothesis that the difference would
persist even with standardization for region.   Incidentally, this income
difference lends significance to the difference in trade noted earlier, since
the volume of retail trade, in particular, is related to income.   The higher
volume of retail sales in independent cities occurs despite the unfavorable
income level.

The contrast in percentage of home ownership between metropolitan
suburbs and independent cities is not marked in terms of the gross com-

TABLE **92.**—SELECTED SOCIO-ECONOMIC CHARACTERISTICS OF THE POPULATION, FOR METRO-
POLITAN SUBURBS AND INDEPENDENT CITIES OF 10,000 INHABITANTS OR MORE, BY SIZE: 1950

Type and size of place	Median school years completed[1] — Persons 25 years old and over	Percent enrolled in school — Persons 20 to 24 years old	Median 1949 income of families and unrelated individuals[1] (dollars)	Percent of occupied dwelling units owner-occupied
Metropolitan suburbs..........	10.8	11.6	3,424	55.6
50,000 or more.....................	10.8	12.5	3,360	47.8
25,000 to 50,000..................	10.8	11.8	3,389	56.3
10,000 to 25,000..................	10.9	11.0	3,458	63.5
Independent cities............	10.1	7.8	2,602	54.9
25,000 to 50,000..................	10.1	10.0	2,682	53.8
10,000 to 25,000..................	10.0	7.1	2,593	55.7

[1] The figure shown is the one for the median place in each group.

Source: *1950 Census of Population*, Vol. II, *Characteristics of the Population*, Parts 2 to 50, tables 11 and 37; *1950 Census of Housing*, Vol. I, *General Characteristics*, Parts 2 to 6, table 1.

parison. But disregarding suburbs of 50,000 or more, and making comparisons within size groups clearly gives the suburbs the higher proportions of home ownership. In the metropolitan suburbs of 25,000 to 50,000, owners occupy 56.3 percent of the occupied dwelling units, as compared with 53.8 percent in the independent cities of the same size; the corresponding figures for places of 10,000 to 25,000 are 63.5 and 55.7 percent—an even greater difference.

Summary

The comparison of metropolitan suburbs and independent cities was designed to reveal differences between urban places within the immediate sphere of influence of metropolitan centers and places of comparable size at greater distances from metropolitan centers. For the most part there are clear and substantial differences between metropolitan suburbs and independent cities. These differences can be accounted for only partly by the concentration of suburbs in the Northeast and independent cities in the South. The more generic ground of interpretation is the hypothesis that because of their proximity to, and close functional interdependence with, large central cities, suburbs are apt to be economically and residentially specialized in ways not generally open to independent cities.

Specifically, the data of this chapter show that metropolitan suburbs have smaller proportions of nonwhite population, higher proportions of married males, slightly larger households, and smaller proportions of mobile persons than do independent cities. In the metropolitan suburbs the proportion of males in the labor force is higher than in independent cities, but the proportion of females in the labor force is smaller. Suburbs have relatively fewer government workers, but more employed in manufacturing than do independent cities. Independent cities, however, have much the higher volume of retail and wholesale trade. All indicators of socio-economic status examined here favor the metropolitan suburbs over the independent cities. The suburbs are higher in the percentage of white-collar workers; the percentage of craftsmen, foremen, and kindred workers; the median level of educational attainment; the percentage of college-age persons enrolled in school; the median income of families and unrelated individuals; and the percentage of home ownership.

Virtually all the differences observed hold not only for the aggregate of all metropolitan suburbs *versus* all independent cities, but also within size-of-place groups.

PART III
COMMUNITY GROWTH AND DECLINE

CHAPTER 15

GROWING AND DECLINING STANDARD
METROPOLITAN AREAS AND URBAN PLACES

A central problem in the study of communities is to determine what characteristics are related to their growth and decline. Not too much is known about the differences between cities which are increasing and those which are decreasing in size of population. This is so for a number of reasons. Only a few empirical studies have been made which compare the social characteristics of the population in cities with high and low rates of growth.[1] In these studies little attempt has been made to control both size and type of urban place.[2] This means that previous comparisons of growing and declining cities do not distinguish among central cities, suburbs, and independent cities and/or large and small urban places. The paucity of data which are of theoretical relevance to an understanding of the growth and decline of cities also has hindered such comparisons.

Ogburn concludes his analysis of cities increasing and decreasing in population from 1920 to 1930 with the observation: "Characteristics that are peculiar to increasing and decreasing cities seem to be related to the two factors of increased opportunity for income and migration."[3] This conclusion is based on a study of over 30 characteristics, such as occupational and industrial structure, family composition, and socio-economic level of the population. The comparison of growing with declining urban places in this chapter is a retest of Ogburn's hypothesis. Both metropolitan status and size of place are controlled in the comparisons.

Scope and technique of analysis

The 1940–50 rate of growth of urban places with 10,000 inhabitants or more in 1950 was examined for each of six urban place-size groups: central cities with fewer than, and more than, 100,000 inhabitants; suburbs with 10,000 to 25,000, and 25,000 inhabitants or more; independent cities

---

[1] William F. Ogburn has a brief chapter on "Increasing and Decreasing Cities" in his study, *Social Characteristics of Cities*, International City Managers' Association, Chicago, 1937. See also, Pek Si Wu, "The Social Characteristics of Increasing, Stable and Decreasing Cities," unpublished Ph. D. dissertation, University of Chicago, 1945.

[2] Throughout this chapter, type of urban place refers to the classes "central city," "independent city," and "suburb."

[3] William F. Ogburn, *op. cit.*, p. 65.

with 10,000 to 25,000, and 25,000 to 50,000 inhabitants. The rate of growth during the 1940–50 decade for SMA's with fewer than 250,000, and 250,000 inhabitants or more, also was examined. A high growth rate and a low growth rate category was then established for each of these groups of places.

The procedure for classifying growth rates as "high" or "low" was as follows. All urban places which showed a sizable increase or decrease in population during the 1940–50 decade first were selected. The rate of growth of each of the urban places during the 1930–40 decade also was obtained. Urban places with a high rate of growth then were defined as places having a sizable increase during both the 1930–40 and 1940–50 decades. All places were excluded where the simple fact of annexation accounted for the place falling within the high rate-of-growth group. The procedure for doing this was as follows: the size of the 1940 and 1950 population both within the 1940 boundaries, and outside the 1940 but within the 1950 boundaries, was calculated or estimated from existing tabulations to yield separate rates of growth for the original 1940 and annexed parts of the urban place.[4] When the rate of growth for either the 1940 area and/or the annexed area, as well as that for the total 1950 area, was "high," it was classified as a high rate-of-growth place. Thus, while it is not always the case that the population within the 1940 boundaries showed a "high" growth rate, the area included within the 1950 boundaries did experience rapid population growth during the decade, over and above the growth achieved simply by annexation of the 1940 population to the original area.[5] This procedure seems justified on the grounds that the objective of the chapter is to measure characteristics at the close of the 1940–50 decade. It seemed more reasonable, therefore, to adjust the growth rate to the 1950 rather than the 1940 boundaries. Similarly, urban places with a low rate of growth were defined as places with a small gain or an actual decrease in population during each of the two decades. The upper and lower limits of increase or decrease in population size during the 1930–40 and 1940–50 decades for inclusion in the high and low rate-of-growth urban place size groups are given in table 93. The exact number

---

[4] The data used were taken from *1950 Census of Population*, Vol. I, *Number of Inhabitants*, Parts 2–50, table 6. Comparable data for 1940 and 1950 are not available for all minor civil divisions, and the estimation procedure is somewhat rough even when they are. This means that there is some doubt as to the correct classification of one or two cities whose growth rates are near the minimum value for the "high growth rate" category. Even in these cases, however, there is unmistakable evidence of substantial growth.

[5] If 1940 boundaries rather than 1950 boundaries are taken, the 1940–50 adjusted rate of growth for the places with annexation in appendix table B–14 is as follows: Albuquerque, N. Mex., 90.8; Baton Rouge, La., 44.7; Columbia, S. C., 18.9; Dallas, Texas, 2.4; Denver, Colo., 23.8; Greenville, S. C., −0.7; Jackson, Miss., 22.4; Lubbock, Texas, 27.6; and Phoenix, Ariz., 11.7. Only Albuquerque, N. Mex., and Baton Rouge, La., then would qualify for inclusion in the high rate-of-growth cities. In the remainder of these places, then, high rate of growth is estimated to have occurred in the annexed areas as well as for the total area through annexation.

of places included in the high and low rate-of-growth classes was determined somewhat arbitrarily.   The procedure followed in selecting the
number of places to be included in a class was first to select a number of
urban places which could reasonably be described as having a relatively
low rate of growth or an actual decrease during both the 1930–40 and
1940–50 decades.   The number of urban places with a high rate of growth
then was made equal to the number of places with a low rate of growth.
This procedure results in having as many places in the high growth rate
category as in the low growth rate category, for each of the groups of places
classified by metropolitan status and size of place.

The growth rate categories for SMA's depended primarily on the 1940–
50 growth rates, since there is a high correlation between growth rates in
the two decades.   In the size group 50,000 to 250,000, the 13 SMA's

TABLE **93.**—LIMITS USED TO SELECT CITIES WITH HIGH OR LOW GROWTH RATES, BY METRO-
POLITAN STATUS AND SIZE: 1930 TO 1950

[Minus sign (−) denotes decrease]

| Metropolitan status and size of place | High growth rate | | | Low growth rate | | |
| | Number of cities | Minimum percent increase | | Number of cities | Maximum percent increase | |
		1940 to 1950	1930 to 1940		1940 to 1950	1930 to 1940
Central cities:						
Under 100,000.................	18	30.0	[1]10.0	18	5.0	4.0
100,000 or more...............	19	29.0	[2]10.0	19	4.0	5.0
Suburbs:						
10,000 to 25,000..............	21	150.0	45.0	21	-1.0	-0.1
25,000 or more................	19	50.0	[3]15.0	19	2.0	2.0
Independent cities:						
10,000 to 25,000..............	18	70.0	25.0	18	-1.0	-1.0
25,000 to 50,000..............	21	65.0	14.0	21	3.0	5.0

[1] Includes Ogden, Utah (8.5) and Waco, Texas (5.9).
[2] Includes Fort Worth, Texas (8.7) and Spokane, Wash. (5.6).
[3] Includes Independence, Mo. (5.0) and Royal Oak, Mich. (9.5).

Source: Appendix tables B–14, B–15, and B–16.

which grew least rapidly from 1940 to 1950 were matched with the 14
SMA's which grew most rapidly, except that the El Paso, Texas, SMA was
not included in the "high" group, because it actually declined slightly in
population between 1930 and 1940.   Similarly, the 12 SMA's, among
those with 250,000 inhabitants or more, which grew the least over the
1940–50 decade were matched with the 11 most rapidly growing SMA's
in this size group.

Tables B–13 to B–16 in the appendix identify the cities and SMA's
selected for study, and show the 1940–50 and 1930–40 growth rates for
each place selected.

Over 25 characteristics of the population of SMA's and urban places
were selected to test the hypothesis that differences between growing and

declining communities [6] are a function of increased opportunity for income and migration.   The question naturally arises: Are the observed differences between extreme groups of high and low rate-of-growth places true differences, in the sense that they are consistent for most comparisons of individual places as well as for the comparison of group averages?   In order to obtain a reliable answer to this question it seemed best to rely on a formal test of statistical significance.   The median test was used to test the significance of differences between the "high" and "low" groups of places.   This is a significance test which requires no assumptions about the form of the distribution. [7]   The null hypothesis was rejected when the probability level was less than 0.05.   When n_1 and n_2 for the two samples exceeded 10 places, exact probabilities were not computed, since the chi-squared distribution with one degree of freedom provides approximate probabilities.

The use of the median test as a test of statistical significance reduces the possibility of assuming that there are differences between groups, when, in fact, no real differences exist.   This criterion of significance, however, makes the study subject to statistical errors of the second kind.   That is, the analysis is relatively unlikely to detect real, but small, differences given the small sample sizes.   To some extent this limitation can be overcome by inspecting for the consistency of differences among the eight metropolitan status-size groups of places.

A special problem arises in inferring causality from the differences observed.   Significant differences in the characteristics of places with high and low rates of growth may not be due to differences in the rate of growth *per se*, since the growing communities also seem to have more economic opportunity than the declining ones.   The present study is not designed to determine the separate causal effects of these factors.   There also are marked differences in regional location and age of urban places with high and low rates of growth which complicate the problem of analysis.   The growing cities are found in large part in the South and the West—regions which had sizable gains in urban population during the past two decades.   Urban places with a low rate of growth are found disproportionately in the Northeast and North Central Regions, which experienced less rapid growth (table 94).   Over 23 percent of the fastest growing urban places were in California and 16 percent were in Texas, while 28 percent of the declining urban places were in Pennsylvania and 17 percent in New England.   It seems quite likely that a decline in textile manufacturing in New England and of mining in Pennsylvania and West Virginia accounts for the popula-

---

[6] The terms "declining community," "decreasing urban place," and "low rate of growth" are treated as equivalent terms in this chapter.   The reader should keep in mind the fact that not all urban places classified as "declining" showed a decrease in population during one or both decades.   Some of the places actually showed a small increase in population.

[7] For a detailed description of the median test, see A. M. Mood, *Introduction to the Theory of Statistics*, McGraw-Hill, New York, 1950, pp. 394–398.

TABLE **94.**—STANDARD METROPOLITAN AREAS AND URBAN PLACES BY HIGH OR LOW GROWTH RATE, BY DIVISIONS: 1950

Division	Standard metropolitan areas		Urban places									
			Total				Central cities		Suburbs		Independent cities	
	High	Low	High		Low		High	Low	High	Low	High	Low
			Number	Percent	Number	Percent						
United States...	25	25	116	100.0	116	100.0	37	37	39	39	40	40
New England.........	...	11	...	...	22	18.9	...	9	...	7	...	6
Middle Atlantic.....	...	8	3	2.6	63	54.3	...	18	2	26	1	19
East North Central..	...	2	9	7.8	18	15.5	1	4	7	6	1	8
West North Central..	1	3	5	4.3	6	5.2	...	3	3	...	2	3
South Atlantic......	4	1	19	16.3	5	4.3	9	3	3	...	7	2
East South Central..	1	...	9	7.8	1	0.9	5	...	...	...	4	1
West South Central..	9	...	28	24.1	...	...	10	...	3	...	15	...
Mountain............	3	...	10	8.6	1	0.9	4	...	1	...	5	1
Pacific.............	7	...	33	28.5	...	...	8	...	20	...	5	...

Source: Appendix tables B–13 to B–16.

tion decline in a sizable proportion cf the declining independent cities, central cities, and suburbs. The age of declining places is on the average greater than that of growing urban places. But the pattern is by no means a clear one, because many of the urban places of the South are old in point of settlement yet show sizable rates of growth.

Another problem of interpretation is created by the 1950 Census procedure of enumerating college students living away from home as residents of the communities in which they were residing while attending college, rather than as persons temporarily absent from their parental homes, as was the practice in earlier censuses. This procedure has two implications for the analysis of data here. First, it created some "artificial growth" and "artificial decline" in the size of urban places between 1940 and 1950. The amount of decline is doubtless negligible for places of 10,000 inhabitants or more, which are the urban places used in this chapter. But the rate of growth is inflated noticeably for the smaller independent cities and suburbs with a college(s). However, since the criterion for classification into the group of rapidly growing places required that an urban place show sizable growth during the 1930–40 as well as the 1940–50 decade, this artifact of statistical growth during the 1940–50 decade does not materially affect the composition of groups of places selected for analysis in this chapter. The second way in which the change in reporting procedures for college students affects the analysis is that it often reduces the per capita or percentage statistics based on a resident population which includes the college age group. Thus, the per capita economic and labor force statistics for college communities are somewhat artificially reduced in size for comparative purposes in this chapter. Similarly, since the female college population is included in the age group 18 to 44, fertility statistics are considerably lower than one would expect for the full-time resident population of the college community. The inclusion of urban places with a large college population, therefore, renders comparisons with noncollege communities somewhat equivocal. In this chapter, comparisons are made only for those urban places having less than 25 percent of the population aged 20 to 24 enrolled in school, where the particular statistics being compared are "artifically reduced" by the inclusion of college students.[8]

The difficulties encountered in analyzing data for places with a sizable proportion of students in the 20-to-24 age group suggest that the method of reporting characteristics of the population for these places might be modified in later censuses. There are strong arguments for enumerating the college population at the place of college attendance, since the inclusion of this group more nearly represents the "true population" resident in the area at a given moment. But at the same time, this college population is sufficiently different in social and economic characteristics from the noncollege population that their inclusion does not result in a profile of the community structure or of its processes which will be directly comparable with that of other places. To achieve both objectives in reporting, in future censuses, the population attending college in a given community might be reported separately. Perhaps the age, sex, and labor force status of this population might be given, as well. These totals then could be added to those of the resident population of the community. It would also be desirable to have a similar reporting procedure for population in institutions and Armed Forces installations, whose effects on comparability are analogous.

There is, finally, a special problem of interpretation arising from the lack of homogeneity in social and economic characteristics within a high or low rate-of-growth group of places. There seems to be a fairly high degree of homogeneity in these respects for all but the small SMA and central city size groups with low growth rates. The small declining SMA's and central cities include places such as Atlantic City, N. J., Sioux City, Iowa, and St. Joseph, Mo., which do not seem to fit the more general hypotheses about low population growth which apply to the other places in this group. It seems reasonable to assume, however, that in each size group a set of local conditions may explain the very low rate of growth of some of the places. The analysis in this chapter simply is not directed toward this level of explanation.

Population composition

There are two major ways in which a place may increase in population. One is natural increase, i.e., excess of births over deaths. The other is net in-migration, which occurs when more people move into an area than

---

[8] A procedure for estimating the number of students attending college from the rural and urban areas of each county in a State, based upon census data, is presented by Burton L. French, "Procedure for Adjusting 1940 Census Data for College Students to be Comparable with 1950 Data," *Agricultural Economics Research 6*, April 1954, pp. 54–62. It was not feasible to follow this procedure in the present research because of the laborious computation procedure involved in making the estimates.

move out.   Conversely, an urban place may decrease in population when deaths exceed births or through net out-migration.

Urban places which increased markedly in size during the 1930–40 and 1940–50 decades appear to have grown to a great extent through net in-migration, though the evidence for this is indirect.   There are no data on the number of persons entering and leaving each urban place annually during the two decades.   Data on the mobility status of the population during the last year of the 1940–50 decade provide some indirect evidence on the source of population for growing cities.   The mobility status of the 1950 population is determined by comparing the 1949 residence with the 1950 residence of all persons one year of age and over. [9]   Since the figures are for the point of destination of movers, an area of net out-movement should have a higher proportion of nonmovers at a given time than an area gaining in population through net in-movement.

Table 95 shows that declining SMA's, central cities, suburbs, and independent cities, regardless of size, had lower rates of residential mobility than rapidly growing places.   Over 85 percent of the residents in declining urban places of each size and type of urban place were nonmovers while less than three-fourths of the residents in growing places of each size and type were in the same house in 1949 and 1950.   The proportion of the population classified as migrants can be viewed as an approximate rate of in-migration, since it relates the number of migrants who enter and remain in an area over the period of one year to the population of that area at the end of the year.   The measure, however, seems clearly valid only for single county SMA's.   For multicounty standard metropolitan areas the approximation *may* be fairly poor, as there can be extensive movement between counties of the SMA without any in-migration into the SMA from the outside.   The measure also may be fairly poor for cities, as the movement into the county in which a city is located may largely be to areas outside the city, rather than to the city itself.   It seems reasonable to assume, however, that a consistency in the observation of differences between groups of places minimizes errors of this kind, unless of course the bias itself is systematic. [10]   The rate of in-migration was found to be considerably greater to rapidly growing than to declining urban places, regardless of size of place.   The rate of in-migration to rapidly growing independent cities and suburbs was about four times as great as that to declining independent cities and suburbs of each size group.   The rapidly growing SMA's and central cities had a rate of in-migration about three

---

[9] The population is classified into movers and nonmovers, that is, those living in the same house in both 1949 and 1950.   The movers are subclassified into nonmigrants, that is, those living in a different house in 1950 but in the same county, and migrants.

[10] The discussion about the validity of the rate of in-migration for multicounty SMA's and cities applies also to the measure of residential movement, since the data are for "different house, same county."   The discussion of validity does not refer to a general dichotomy of "residentially stable" and "residentially mobile," however, as the data for residential stability refer to "same house."

times as great as that of the corresponding declining SMA's and central
cities (table 95 and figure 20).   Since almost all of the rapidly growing,
small and large, SMA's are single county SMA's, while over one-half of
the declining large SMA's are multicounty SMA's, this conclusion cannot
be due to invalidity in the measure of in-migration.   This relationship between growth and mobility is to be expected, since the fertility differentials
among the cities are generally too small to take any large role in explaining growth differentials.   Rapidly growing urban places also show a much
higher rate of residential movement among nonmigrants than do declining
urban places.   Roughly twice as many residents moved at least once within
the county in rapidly growing as in declining places, regardless of size and
type of place.

TABLE **95.**—MOBILITY STATUS OF THE POPULATION 1 YEAR OLD AND OVER, FOR SELECTED
STANDARD METROPOLITAN AREAS AND URBAN PLACES, BY METROPOLITAN STATUS, SIZE, AND
GROWTH RATE: 1950

[Asterisk (*) denotes difference between high and low groups significant at 0.05 level of probability]

Metropolitan status and size of place	Growth rate	Percent by mobility status[1]		
		Same house, 1949 and 1950	Different house, same county	Different county
Standard metropolitan areas:				
50,000 to 250,000	High	*72.1	*16.3	*10.1
	Low	86.0	8.9	3.7
250,000 or more	High	*71.2	*15.8	*10.1
	Low	87.6	7.7	3.1
Central cities:				
Under 100,000	High	*72.3	*15.3	*10.3
	Low	85.8	9.3	3.5
100,000 or more	High	*72.3	*17.8	*7.7
	Low	87.4	8.5	2.6
Suburbs:				
10,000 to 25,000	High	*71.7	*17.4	*10.8
	Low	91.3	6.0	1.8
25,000 or more	High	*73.2	*17.9	*9.8
	Low	89.0	7.2	2.7
Independent cities:				
10,000 to 25,000	High	*64.2	*16.6	*17.6
	Low	87.0	8.0	3.2
25,000 to 50,000	High	*66.3	*16.9	*15.1
	Low	85.6	10.8	3.9

[1] Percentages do not total 100 because of the omission of persons abroad in 1949 and those whose 1949
residence was not reported.

Source: *1950 Census of Population,* Vol. II, *Characteristics of the Population,* Parts 2 to 50, table 34.

The differences in the distribution of the population by mobility status
produced by the growth rate classification seem more important than the
differences associated with size and type of place.   Differences among size
groups in the rate of in-migration are generally no larger than 1 or 2 percentage points.   The differences between groups of central cities and suburbs comparable with respect to growth rates are less than the differences
between rapidly and slowly growing places within either type of place.
   There is a larger proportion of persons over 21 years of age in the declining places than in the rapidly growing places of each size and metropolitan status group.   The differences, however, are small (table 96).
Much of the difference in the proportion under 21 years between the rapidly

FIGURE **20.**—MOBILITY STATUS OF THE POPULATION 1 YEAR OLD AND OVER IN SELECTED STANDARD METROPOLITAN AREAS AND URBAN PLACES, BY METROPOLITAN STATUS AND GROWTH RATE: 1950

[Base line: Mobility status of all urban persons in the United States]

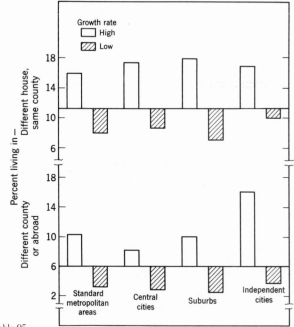

Note: See table 95.

growing and declining places is accounted for by a somewhat larger proportion of children under 5 years of age in the rapidly growing places. This fact suggests a somewhat higher fertility for the population in rapidly growing as compared with declining urban places. The fertility ratio was employed as a measure of fertility. It is defined here as the number of children under 5 years of age per 1,000 women 18 to 44 years old. In 7 of the 8 comparisons the group of rapidly growing places has a significantly higher fertility ratio than the group of places with low growth rates.[11] The differences are particularly marked for the independent cities and suburbs, as may be observed in figure 21.

The sex ratio is significantly higher in rapidly growing than in declining places in the case of independent cities and the smaller central cities and SMA's. The differences between the other groups of rapidly growing and declining places are not significant. These somewhat greater sex ratios in rapidly growing as compared with declining urban places do not seem consistent with economic differentials between these groups. It will be seen

---

[11] In these comparisons, the urban places with a relatively large female college population 18 to 24 were excluded. The enumeration of all women in college at the place of college attendance distorts the fertility ratio since it "artificially increases" the number of women of childbearing age for that particular place.

TABLE **96.**—AGE AND SEX COMPOSITION, FERTILITY RATIO, AND PERCENT NONWHITE, FOR
SELECTED STANDARD METROPOLITAN AREAS AND URBAN PLACES, BY METROPOLITAN STATUS,
SIZE, AND GROWTH RATE: 1950

[Asterisk (*) denotes difference between high and low groups significant at 0.05 level of probability]

Metropolitan status and size of place	Growth rate	Percent by age			Sex ratio	Fertility ratio[1]	Percent nonwhite
		Under 5 years	5 to 21 years	21 years and over			
Standard metropolitan areas:							
50,000 to 250,000............	High........	*12.3	25.5	*62.2	*99.0	*549	*15.5
	Low.........	9.9	23.9	66.2	93.9	490	2.8
250,000 or more..............	High........	*10.8	21.7	*67.5	102.0	*489	*10.1
	Low.........	9.6	22.8	67.6	96.0	452	3.0
Central cities:							
Under 100,000................	High........	*10.5	22.9	*66.6	*96.8	458	*16.2
	Low.........	9.3	21.0	69.7	91.5	446	4.1
100,000 or more..............	High........	*10.1	20.5	*69.4	94.2	*436	*15.6
	Low.........	9.1	20.9	70.0	94.5	414	8.9
Suburbs:							
10,000 to 25,000.............	High........	*13.8	22.4	*63.8	98.6	*593	*1.5
	Low.........	9.3	22.6	68.1	98.2	425	5.2
25,000 or more...............	High........	*11.2	21.1	*67.7	94.9	*503	3.4
	Low.........	9.1	20.5	70.4	96.2	417	3.7
Independent cities:							
10,000 to 25,000.............	High........	*12.0	25.8	*62.2	*105.6	*552	*9.6
	Low.........	9.3	21.9	68.8	93.9	455	2.6
25,000 to 50,000.............	High........	*11.3	25.4	*63.3	*102.0	*535	*15.0
	Low.........	9.2	21.3	69.5	91.7	444	3.4

[1] Excludes from comparisons all places with 25 percent or more of the population 20 to 24 years old enrolled in school.

Source: *1950 Census of Population*, Vol. II, *Characteristics of the Population*, Parts 2 to 50, table 33.

below that rapidly growing independent and central cities have proportionately fewer workers in manufacturing, and that there are no significant
differences in the proportion of men and women in the labor force between
rapidly growing and declining independent and central cities and SMA's.

Rapidly growing SMA's, central cities, and independent cities of each
size group show a much higher proportion of nonwhite residents than do
declining SMA's, central cities, and independent cities (table 96). The
difference in all cases is considerable. This difference between the rapidly
growing and declining SMA's and urban places seems in large part a function of their regional location. Two-thirds of the declining central and
independent cities are in the New England and Middle Atlantic Divisions,
where the nonwhite populations are small, while two-thirds of the rapidly
growing central and independent cities are in the South Atlantic and East
and West South Central Divisions, where historically the proportion of
nonwhites is comparatively large. The pattern for suburbs is quite different. The proportion of nonwhites in suburbs is very small for both rapidly
growing and declining suburbs. But rapidly growing suburbs with 10,000
to 25,000 inhabitants had significantly fewer nonwhites on the average
than did declining suburbs. The direction of the difference is the same
for suburbs with 25,000 inhabitants or more. Since slightly more than
one-half of the rapidly growing suburbs are in the Pacific Division where
the nonwhite population is small, and two-thirds of the declining suburbs
are in the Middle Atlantic Division, where the nonwhite population is

FIGURE **21.**—FERTILITY RATIOS FOR SELECTED STANDARD METROPOLITAN AREAS AND URBAN
PLACES, BY METROPOLITAN STATUS AND GROWTH RATE: 1950

[Base line: Fertility ratio for the total urban population of the United States]

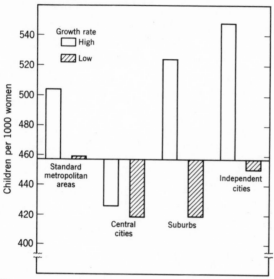

Note: See table 96.

somewhat larger, these differences also may reflect regional location. They suggest, however, real differences in patterns of residential segregation in the two types of suburbs.

Table 97 shows the percentage of the population 14 years old and over living in families and the percentage classified as unrelated individuals. A family is defined in the 1950 Census as a group of two or more persons related by blood, marriage, or adoption and living together. Unrelated individuals are persons (other than inmates of institutions) who are not living with any relatives. All statistics on unrelated individuals in this chapter are limited to persons 14 years of age and older. One would expect the proportion of persons in families to be smaller for rapidly growing than for declining places. Correlatively, the proportion of unrelated individuals among persons 14 years of age and over should be greater in rapidly growing than in declining places. This follows from the assumption that the proportion of single individuals generally is greater among migrant populations, and in-migrants form a larger proportion of the population in growing than in declining places. The data for all types and size groups of places generally support this view.[12]   However, only the SMA's and the central cities with 100,000 inhabitants or more show a signifi-

---

[12] All comparisons for families and unrelated individuals exclude places with 25 percent or more of the population aged 20 to 24 in school in 1950.   These places are excluded since the proportion of unrelated individuals in these places, in 1950, always is high, given the 1950 Census procedure of enumerating students at the place of school attendance.

TABLE **97.**—FAMILY STATUS, MARITAL STATUS, AND HOUSEHOLD SIZE OF THE POPULATION, FOR
SELECTED STANDARD METROPOLITAN AREAS AND URBAN PLACES, BY METROPOLITAN STATUS,
SIZE, AND GROWTH RATE: 1950

[Asterisk (*) denotes difference between high and low groups significant at 0.05 level of probability]

Metropolitan status and size of place	Growth rate	Percent by family status[1]		Percent married, male[1]	Persons per house- hold[2]
		In families	Unrelated individuals		
Standard metropolitan areas:					
50,000 to 250,000...............	High.........	*87.5	*12.5	*69.6	3.33
	Low..........	91.4	8.6	67.3	3.30
250,000 or more..................	High.........	*84.8	*15.2	*67.9	*3.19
	Low..........	91.4	8.6	64.0	3.44
Central cities:					
Under 100,000...................	High.........	87.0	13.0	*71.9	3.18
	Low..........	86.9	13.1	66.3	3.21
100,000 or more.................	High.........	*84.7	*15.3	*69.3	3.20
	Low..........	88.7	11.3	64.5	3.35
Suburbs:					
10,000 to 25,000...............	High.........	94.2	5.8	*80.1	*3.37
	Low..........	93.5	6.5	63.3	3.50
25,000 or more.................	High.........	89.7	10.3	*75.1	3.18
	Low..........	91.4	8.6	65.7	3.40
Independent cities:					
10,000 to 25,000...............	High.........	90.6	9.4	*74.3	3.29
	Low..........	91.4	8.6	66.5	3.29
25,000 to 50,000...............	High.........	87.3	12.7	*70.1	3.20
	Low..........	89.2	10.8	68.2	3.15

[1] Persons 14 years old and over. Excludes from comparisons all places with 25 percent or more of the
population 20 to 24 years old enrolled in school.

[2] The figure shown is the one for the median place in each group.

Source: *1950 Census of Population*, Vol. II, *Characteristics of the Population*, Parts 2 to 50, table 34.

cantly greater percentage of unrelated individuals in rapidly growing than
in declining communities. Standard metropolitan areas with 250,000 inhabitants or more which grow rapidly had about 6 percent more unrelated
individuals than did the SMA's in this size group which declined in population. The large and rapidly growing central cities, suburbs, and independent cities all seem to have somewhat higher proportions of unrelated
individuals than do the large and declining central cities, independent
cities, and suburbs. Only small and nonsignificant differences are observed
in the proportion of unrelated individuals between the rapidly growing and
the declining cities of smaller size.

The percentage of men married (table 97) is somewhat higher in rapidly
growing than in declining places, regardless of metropolitan status or size of
place. The percentage of males 14 years of age and over who were married was significantly greater for all groups of rapidly growing places than
for comparable groups of declining places.[13] The percentage married, of
course, varies somewhat by size of place, being greater in the small than
in the large places.

The variation in household size (table 97) with the rate of growth is not
pronounced or consistent as to direction among all the 8 comparisons of

---

[13] Places with 25 percent or more of the population aged 20 to 24 in school are excluded from the
analysis. This quasi-residential population artificially lowers the percentage married for a given urban
place.

growing with declining places. There is perhaps some tendency for rapidly growing places to have smaller households than places growing slowly or declining. Two of the comparisons on the number of persons per household yield a significant difference in this direction (the small suburbs and the larger SMA's).

Economic characteristics

Economic growth is viewed as both a cause and an effect of population growth. Migrants presumably are attracted to urban places with opportunities for employment or a higher standard of living, and they often are forced to leave places where jobs are not available. Economic opportunity and economic growth therefore stimulate population growth, while the absence of opportunity leads to population loss. In the long run, however, an increase in population may stimulate economic growth, since it increases the demand for consumer goods and usually provides an abundant labor supply in an employer's market. With the data available, these cause and effect relationships cannot be separated. The findings can only be stated as relationships between economic factors and growth and decline of cities and SMA's.

Economic differences between growing and declining communities are first measured in terms of the percentages of males and females in the labor force. It is postulated, for purposes of this analysis, that a high rate of labor force participation represents a situation of comparatively great economic opportunity.[14] Table 98 shows that in each of the 8 comparisons the high growth rate communities have larger percentages of males in the labor force than do the low growth rate communities. However, in

TABLE **98.**—LABOR FORCE PARTICIPATION BY SEX, FOR SELECTED STANDARD METROPOLITAN AREAS AND URBAN PLACES, BY METROPOLITAN STATUS, SIZE, AND GROWTH RATE: 1950

[Asterisk (*) denotes difference between high and low groups significant at 0.05 level of probability. All places with 25 percent or more of the population 20 to 24 years old enrolled in school are excluded from comparisons]

Metropolitan status and size of place	Growth rate	Male	Female	Metropolitan status and size of place	Growth rate	Male	Female
Standard metropolitan areas:				Suburbs:			
50,000 to 250,000...	High......	79.4	30.9	10,000 to 25,000....	High.....	*84.8	*25.4
	Low.......	75.0	32.6		Low......	78.2	29.7
250,000 or more.....	High......	79.8	32.2	25,000 or more......	High.....	81.9	*30.4
	Low.......	76.9	29.3		Low......	81.7	35.0
Central cities:				Independent cities:			
Under 100,000.......	High......	78.2	34.6	10,000 to 25,000...	High.....	*83.6	32.6
	Low.......	77.2	34.5		Low......	76.6	28.5
100,000 or more.....	High......	80.0	35.8	25,000 to 50,000...	High.....	82.3	*28.9
	Low.......	79.1	35.4		Low......	79.0	34.0

Source: *1950 Census of Population*, Vol. II, *Characteristics of the Population*, Parts 2 to 50, table 35.

---

[14] Places with 25 percent or more of the population aged 20 to 24 enrolled in school are excluded from the analysis. Inclusion of the college population would tend to diminish "artificially" the rates of labor force participation.

only 2 of the comparisons is the difference as large as 5 percentage points, and these are the only 2 which also meet the criterion of statistical significance accepted here. The results for female labor force participation are inconclusive. The 3 statistically significant comparisons run in the opposite direction to the finding for males. For both size groups of suburbs and for the larger independent cities, the rapidly growing places have the smaller percentages of females in the labor force. A difference in the opposite direction, though nonsignificant, is observed in 4 other comparisons, however.

The main finding which runs counter to the hypothesis that growing places have greater economic opportunities than stable or declining places is the one for female labor force participation in suburbs. This finding, however, may merely indicate a type of population selection experienced by rapidly developing residential suburbs, rather than any relation between economic opportunity and population growth. It may be that the comparatively low rate of female labor force participation in all suburbs, noted in earlier chapters, is in fact characteristic mainly of those suburbs specializing in residence, rather than of suburbs *per se*.

The labor force participation rates of men in rapidly growing places are not particularly substantial when compared with the rates for all places of comparable size and metropolitan status in Chapter 19. Only the rate for rapidly growing small central cities is somewhat greater than that for all small central cities. The rates for rapidly growing large and small SMA's and large central cities are roughly equal to that of all comparable groups of places, while the rates for rapidly growing suburbs and independent cities are substantially below the average for comparable metropolitan status size groups. For 5 of the 8 comparisons for declining urban places, the labor force participation rate is below that of comparable groups of all places. These comparisons suggest that rapidly growing places provide roughly the same or less opportunity for entrance into the labor force than does the average place, even though declining places generally do present somewhat less opportunity than rapidly growing ones. Chapters 17 and 19 present data which show that the male labor force participation rate is substantially greater in manufacturing places than in nonmanufacturing places, or in all places. The average manufacturing place, therefore, provides more economic opportunity than does the average rapidly growing place. It is shown below that declining places have far more employment in manufacturing, however, than do rapidly growing places, so that the absence of substantial proportions of manufacturing employment is not a reasonable explanation for the "average economic opportunities" presented by rapidly growing places.

In sum, the data provide only mild support for the proposition that growing places evidence greater economic opportunity than nongrowing ones. It is true that the growing communities must have experienced an expansion of job opportunities over the decade in order for their position at the end of the decade to be at least as favorable as that of the average place, or that of declining communities. But, it likewise is true that a substantial number of places had greater economic opportunity, as measured by high labor force participation rates, than did either rapidly growing or declining places.

The volume of manufacturing is much greater in declining than in rapidly growing urban places, regardless of size. Two indicators were employed to compare growing and declining places with respect to manufacturing activity—the per capita value added by manufacture and the percentage of all workers employed in manufacturing. (See table 99.) The statistics on value added by manufacture are reported for the place in which the manufacturing establishment is located. The data on employment in manufacturing industries reported here pertain to the place of residence of the worker.

Both the per capita value added by manufacture and the percentage employed in manufacturing are considerably lower in growing than in declining SMA's and urban places, regardless of size. The per capita value added by manufacture is at least twice as great in declining as in rapidly growing SMA's, central cities, suburbs, and independent cities. About twice as many workers are employed in manufacturing in declining as in growing urban places, regardless of size (table 99 and figure 22).

TABLE 99.—EMPLOYMENT IN MANUFACTURING, 1950, AND PER CAPITA VALUE ADDED BY MANUFACTURE, 1947, FOR SELECTED STANDARD METROPOLITAN AREAS AND URBAN PLACES, BY METROPOLITAN STATUS, SIZE, AND GROWTH RATE

[Asterisk (*) denotes difference between high and low groups significant at 0.05 level of probability]

Metropolitan status and size of place	Growth rate	Workers in manufacturing as percent of all employed persons[1]	Per capita value added by manufacture[2] (dollars)
Standard metropolitan areas:			
50,000 to 250,000	High	*15.2	303
	Low	35.8	[3]
250,000 or more	High	*16.8	*317
	Low	34.6	581
Central cities:			
Under 100,000	High	*15.2	*289
	Low	34.6	725
100,000 or more	High	*18.5	*387
	Low	35.8	952
Suburbs:			
10,000 to 25,000	High	*27.6	[3]
	Low	47.8	804
25,000 or more	High	*27.5	*388
	Low	46.6	1,403
Independent cities:			
10,000 to 25,000	High	*13.6	[3]
	Low	31.6	414
25,000 to 50,000	High	*11.8	*96
	Low	34.4	776

[1] 1950 resident employed labor force.
[2] 1947 value added by establishments located in the standard metropolitan area or urban place.
[3] Insufficient data reported because of disclosure rule.

Source: *1950 Census of Population*, Vol. II, *Characteristics of the Population*, Parts 2 to 50, table 35; *1947 Census of Manufactures*, Vol. III, *Statistics by States*, table 2.

FIGURE **22.**—PERCENT OF EMPLOYED PERSONS IN MANUFACTURING, WHOLESALE AND RETAIL TRADE, AND GOVERNMENT, IN SELECTED STANDARD METROPOLITAN AREAS AND URBAN PLACES, BY METROPOLITAN STATUS AND GROWTH RATE: 1950

[Base line: All urban employed persons in the United States]

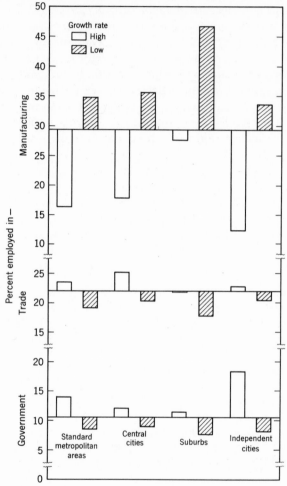

Note: See tables 99, 100, 101.

It would seem that a changing technology and patterns of production in certain manufacturing and related industries account in large part for the population decrease in independent cities with a large percentage in manufacturing. The declining independent cities not infrequently are those where textile industries have been large sources of employment and revenue. In fact, some decline in textiles occurred for somewhat less than one-half of the 40 declining independent cities selected for the study. These textile cities are localized in New England. Textiles are generally not a major part of the economic base in the rapidly growing independent cities selected for this study, so that textiles do not explain rapid growth.

A decline in textiles and related industries also seems to account in large part for the pattern of decline in central cities and suburbs. An additional factor is suggested, however. Certain of the central cities appear to be losing population to adjacent centers or to suburbs, and certain suburbs appear to be losing population to other parts of the standard metropolitan area. The highly industrialized suburbs of SMA's which actually continue to industrialize are examples of this form of development. Industry both makes these places less desirable for residence and reduces the land available for residential purposes. Specific cases which illustrate this pattern of decline are the suburbs of Kearny, Passaic, Perth Amboy, and Paterson, N. J.; East Cleveland and Lakewood, Ohio; and the central cities of New Haven, Conn., and Rochester and Buffalo, N. Y.

The much greater incidence of employment in manufacturing and the greater productive capacity of manufacturing establishments in declining than in growing urban places [15] raises the interesting question of the conditions under which an increase in manufacturing activity is a factor in rapid urban growth. It is commonly assumed that manufacturing was a major cause of the rapid growth of cities during the nineteenth century. The present data cannot answer this question, since they pertain to only a single point in time. Yet it remains true that for the urban places which showed a sizable gain in *residential* population, the proportion engaged in manufacturing is quite low. While 31.9 percent of all urban males were employed in manufacturing in 1950,[16] the rapidly growing independent and central cities had a far smaller proportion, 21 percent or less, in manufacturing. Only rapidly growing suburbs had proportions of males in manufacturing comparable to the United States average. By contrast, declining urban places had proportions of males in manufacturing equal to or greater than the average for all urban territory.

This is not to suggest, however, that an increase in manufacturing is not a factor in the rapid growth of urban places. Two of the most rapidly growing urban places during the 1940–50 decade were the "artificially created" manufacturing cities of Oak Ridge, Tenn., and Richland, Wash. Oak Ridge, Tenn., for example, has 53 percent of all men employed in manufacturing, and manufacturing employs 74 percent of all males in Richland, Wash. It is likely that the inclusion of manufacturing industries in a local economy is a factor in some, if not most, urban growth. But it may generally give rise to a slower rate of growth than is characteristic of the rapidly growing urban places in the present sample. It may also be true that past manufacturing growth may lower present population growth, given

---

[15] Ogburn observed that declining urban places had only a slightly smaller percentage in manufacturing than did cities which grew rapidly over the 1910–30 decades—43 as compared to 46 percent. The difference, though small, is in the same direction as that discovered in the present study. (See Ogburn, *op. cit.*, p. 63.)

[16] All United States figures on the percent of urban employed persons in industry groups cited in this chapter are based on data in *1950 Census of Population*, Vol. II, *Characteristics of the Population*, Part I, table 55, p. 103.

substantial employment in manufacturing. There is also the likelihood that after a given level of manufacturing activity is reached in an economy, manufacturing expansion is no longer the major factor in the growth of cities.

Places growing rapidly during the past two decades have a somewhat larger proportion of workers employed by Federal, State, and local governments than do declining places.[17] Somewhat less than twice as many workers are government employees in rapidly growing SMA's, central cities, and independent cities, regardless of size of place, as in the corresponding groups with low growth rates. The differences are in the same direction for suburbs, although not statistically significant (table 100 and figure 22). The proportion of all employed urban workers in the United States at work for governments was 10.6 percent in 1950. At least 14 percent of all employed workers in rapidly growing SMA's, central cities, and independent cities, except central cities with 100,000 inhabitants or more, were employed by governments in 1950, while 9 percent or less of all workers in declining SMA's, central cities, independent cities, and suburbs had government employers in 1950. The percentage of male workers in public administration[18] is somewhat greater in rapidly growing than in declining places for all groups. The differences are statistically significant, however, only for SMA's. Just what part government employment had in increasing the size of places over the past two decades is not known from these statistics. The opportunity for employment in government certainly is greater in the rapidly growing than in the declining urban places.[19] Whether relative differences in expenditures by local governments or the location of extralocal governmental activities in local urban places accounts for this greater opportunity in rapidly growing places is not known. Certainly the difference is not accounted for by a sizable number of State capital or government centers. Only five State capital cities showed rapid growth during the past two decades.

There is little significant variation, by rate of growth, in the proportions of all workers employed in transportation, in mining, and in hotels and lodging places. Declining SMA's with 250,000 inhabitants or more do have a significantly larger proportion of workers employed in mining (5.2 percent) than do rapidly growing SMA's in this size group (0.3 percent). Central cities and independent cities with a rapid rate of growth would appear to have a somewhat higher proportion of workers in transportation

---

[17] Government workers are defined here as a subclass of class-of-worker statistics. They are persons who worked for any governmental unit (Federal, State, or local) regardless of the activity which the particular agency carried on.

[18] Public administration includes postal service, and Federal, State, and local public administration.

[19] The few obvious examples of urban places entirely created by the Federal Government during the 1940–50 decade are not included among the most rapidly growing urban places in the sample. Since the interest is in sustained growth or decline over two decades, cities of recent rapid growth such as Oak Ridge, Tenn., and Richland, Wash., are excluded in this study.

TABLE 100.—EMPLOYMENT IN SELECTED NONMANUFACTURING INDUSTRIES, FOR SELECTED STANDARD METROPOLITAN AREAS AND URBAN PLACES, BY METROPOLITAN STATUS, SIZE, AND GROWTH RATE: 1950

[Asterisk (*) denotes difference between high and low groups significant at 0.05 level of probability]

Metropolitan status and size of place	Growth rate	Government workers as percent of all employed persons[1]	Percent of all employed persons in—		Percent of all employed males in—		
			Mining	Transportation	Public administration	Hotels and lodging places	Entertainment and recreation services
Standard metropolitan areas:							
50,000 to 250,000........	High.....	*14.2	0.7	6.3	*8.0	0.9	*1.2
	Low......	7.8	0.8	7.2	4.4	1.2	1.1
250,000 or more..........	High.....	*14.0	*0.4	6.5	*8.3	*1.3	*1.4
	Low......	8.8	5.2	5.6	4.5	0.6	0.9
Central cities:							
Under 100,000............	High.....	*15.4	0.3	5.7	7.4	1.2	*1.3
	Low......	8.8	1.4	6.8	5.2	1.5	1.2
100,000 or more..........	High.....	*11.4	0.6	5.1	6.7	1.2	2.5
	Low......	9.1	0.2	6.7	5.5	1.2	1.0
Suburbs:							
10,000 to 25,000..........	High.....	9.6	0.6	6.2	4.8	0.4	*1.7
	Low......	8.2	5.4	5.8	4.1	0.3	0.7
25,000 or more...........	High.....	12.0	0.8	5.4	6.5	0.8	*1.9
	Low......	7.6	0.1	5.1	4.5	0.4	0.8
Independent cities:							
10,000 to 25,000..........	High.....	15.9	6.8	4.6	4.8	*2.2	2.9
	Low......	7.9	10.7	6.4	3.4	0.5	1.4
25,000 to 50,000..........	High.....	*19.8	2.5	*4.2	6.0	*1.6	*1.6
	Low......	8.3	1.7	6.8	4.4	0.7	1.2

[1] Based on class-of-worker statistics; includes persons who worked for any governmental unit (Federal, State, or local), regardless of the activity which the particular agency carried on.

Source: *1950 Census of Population*, Vol. II, *Characteristics of the Population*, Parts 2 to 50, table 35.

than declining ones. But the differences are small and significant only for independent cities with 25,000 to 50,000 inhabitants. The rapidly growing independent cities, regardless of size, and SMA's with 250,000 inhabitants or more have a somewhat larger proportion of men employed in hotels and lodging places. But there are no significant differences among the central cities. This suggests that central cities, regardless of their rate of growth, require about the same proportion of workers to deal with the transient population, but rapidly growing independent cities have somewhat greater relative requirements for a transient population.

The 1940–50 decade in the United States was one in which the number and size of permanent military establishments were increased considerably. It is well known that in some cases the location of a military establishment at a place contributed to the rapid growth of the place, particularly during the wartime period. It also is known that some of these places experienced some population loss during the decade due to the closing of a military establishment or a decrease in the number of personnel at the installation. Data were available on the number of military personnel in SMA's and urban places, and these were used to define specialized military places in the next chapter. No data were available on places which lost a military installation. It therefore is possible only to learn whether places which showed rapid population growth during the decade may have experienced some of the growth because they also are the site of a relatively large military installation. The number of specialized military centers, of course, is small. There were 12 of the 50 SMA's and 31 of the 230 urban places with a relatively large military installation for the combined growing and declining places in this chapter. For all metropolitan status and size groups, however, more of the high than of the low rate-of-growth places also are military installations. The results are particularly striking for the small places, which are most likely to be affected by the location of a military installation. There was no declining urban place with a relatively large military installation, but 6 of the 14 small rapidly growing SMA's and 14 of the 43 small rapidly growing urban places were specialized in military national defense. The results also are clear for the large places, particularly for the urban places, as only 4 of the low rate-of-growth compared with 14 of the high rate-of-growth places had relatively large military installations. Although not all the data necessary to the inference are available, it appears that part of the reason for rapid population growth in some of the high rate-of-growth places in this chapter is the fact that they are the site of a relatively large military installation.

There usually is both local and extralocal demand for entertainment and recreation services in an urban community. The local demand for entertainment and recreation services probably is highly variable, since commercial entertainment and recreation services are among the least "necessary," and most readily dispensed with, of the maintenance requirements of an urban population, particularly of families. Therefore, it would be expected that workers in entertainment and recreation services would comprise a smaller proportion of employed persons in declining than in rapidly growing places. The relatively larger proportions of unrelated individuals in rapidly growing places, however, should increase the demand for entertainment and recreation services in all rapidly growing places. The general increase in time for leisure activity in the United States has led to increased demand for places specialized in entertainment and recreation services, and hence to the rapid growth of some specialized places. It may be true that declining urban places have relatively more employment in the public and private institutions devoted to "the arts," and even in municipal recreation programs, than do rapidly growing ones. But these forms of entertainment and recreation comprise only a small proportion of the total employment in entertainment and recreation, since the commercial forms of entertainment and amusement are the major sources of employment. The differences in the percentage of employed males in entertainment and recreation services between rapidly growing and declining places are consistent with these postulates. The differences, however, are very small in actual percentages, since men employed in entertainment and recreation services constitute but a very small proportion of the total employed. Suburbs, regardless of size, show the greatest relative difference between growing and declining places in the proportion employed in entertainment and recreation services.   Since the data on employment in entertainment and recreation services are for places of residence rather than places of work, the higher incidence of these workers in rapidly growing suburbs may reflect only differences in occupational composition of the resident population in the two classes of suburbs.   There is a likelihood that some of the difference in the proportion of employed males in entertainment and recreation services between rapidly growing and declining urban places is a function of the nature of the economic base in the two types of places, and is not directly related to the rate of growth.   It is known, for example, that manufacturing places (Chapter 17) employ smaller proportions of men in entertainment and recreation services than do nonmanufacturing places, and, of course, more of the declining than of the rapidly growing places have large proportions employed in manufacturing.   It is not altogether clear, then, that rapidly growing places attract larger numbers of unattached individuals who stimulate employment in entertainment and recreation services than do declining places.   Rapidly growing places on the average, however, have a larger proportion of employed males than do all comparable groups of places (Chapter 19), while the proportion in declining places generally is well below that of all comparable groups of places.

Rapidly growing places show a somewhat larger proportion of workers in trade than do declining places, regardless of size (table 101 and figure 22).   The differences are not large: roughly 4 percent more of the employed workers are in wholesale or retail jobs in growing than in declining places, except for small independent cities.   The difference is significant for each type of place and size group when the retail and wholesale categories are combined.   For rapidly growing SMA's and urban places, wholesale and retail trade provide a somewhat greater opportunity for employment than is the case for comparable places with low growth rates.

Where statistics for the volume of wholesale and retail trade are available, the per capita volume of wholesale and retail trade in dollars is no greater in rapidly growing than in declining urban places.   In fact, per capita wholesale sales are significantly greater in declining suburbs, regardless of size, and in independent cities with 25,000 inhabitants or more than in comparable places gaining rapidly in population.   It should be noted that, since the sales data are for 1948 and the population data for 1950, there is a downward bias in the per capita sales figures for growing places (which, presumably, had smaller populations in 1948 than in 1950).   However, it seems doubtful that an adjustment for this bias would essentially change the conclusion that rapidly growing places have no greater per capita trade volume than declining places.   The conclusion is perhaps more uncertain for retail than for wholesale trade.

The findings, then, are that employment in wholesale and retail trade is greater in rapidly growing than in declining SMA's and cities.   But the per capita volume of retail and wholesale trade is no greater for growing

TABLE **101.**—EMPLOYMENT, 1950, AND PER CAPITA SALES IN WHOLESALE AND RETAIL TRADE, 1948, FOR SELECTED STANDARD METROPOLITAN AREAS AND URBAN PLACES, BY METROPOLITAN STATUS, SIZE, AND GROWTH RATE

[Asterisk (*) denotes difference between high and low groups significant at 0.05 level of probability]

Metropolitan status and size of place	Growth rate	Percent of employed workers in wholesale and retail trade[1]			Per capita sales[2] (dollars)	
		Total	Wholesale trade	Retail trade	Wholesale trade	Retail trade
Standard metropolitan areas:						
50,000 to 250,000................	High........	*23.0	*4.6	*18.4	1,027	924
	Low.........	19.5	3.6	15.9	1,211	921
250,000 or more..................	High........	*23.8	*5.1	*18.7	1,650	1,026
	Low.........	19.2	3.5	15.7	1,420	901
Central cities:						
Under 100,000....................	High........	*25.7	*5.3	*20.4	1,273	1,347
	Low.........	20.9	3.7	17.2	1,520	1,320
100,000 or more..................	High........	*25.2	*5.5	*19.7	2,519	1,235
	Low.........	20.3	4.0	16.3	3,004	1,249
Suburbs:						
10,000 to 25,000.................	High........	*21.8	*5.4	*16.4	*61	597
	Low.........	15.8	1.7	14.1	380	905
25,000 or more...................	High........	*21.8	*4.0	*17.8	*220	1,042
	Low.........	18.4	3.3	15.1	906	1,047
Independent cities:						
10,000 to 25,000.................	High........	*21.9	3.2	18.7	525	1,155
	Low.........	19.7	2.6	17.1	466	1,101
25,000 to 50,000.................	High........	*24.8	4.1	*20.7	*870	1,215
	Low.........	21.0	3.4	17.6	970	1,370

[1] 1950 resident employed labor force.

[2] 1948 sales by establishments located in the standard metropolitan area or urban place.

Source: *1950 Census of Population*, Vol. II, *Characteristics of the Population*, Parts 2 to 50, table 35; *1948 Census of Business*, Vol. III, *Retail Trade—Area Statistics*, tables 102 and 103; and Vol. V, *Wholesale Trade—Area Statistics*, tables 102 and 103.

than for declining SMA's and central cities. Among suburbs, regardless of size, the rapidly growing places show a somewhat greater proportion of employed persons in wholesale and retail trade when compared with declining suburbs, and a somewhat smaller per capita value of wholesale trade, but no significant differences in per capita retail sales. Finally, rapidly growing independent cities with 10,000 to 25,000 inhabitants do not differ significantly from declining independent cities in this size group in per capita expenditures or percentage of employed persons in wholesale or in retail trade. The independent cities with 25,000 to 50,000 inhabitants which are growing rapidly seem, however, to be more like the suburbs in that they have a somewhat lower per capita expenditure for wholesale trade than do declining independent cities of this size, but a somewhat greater percentage of men employed in retail trade.

Problems of interpretation arise when the proportion of employment in wholesale and retail trade for a place is compared with its per capita volume of wholesale or retail trade. First, the statistics measure different things. The dollar volume for wholesale or retail trade is the amount of business actually transacted in the given urban place. The percentage of employed persons in wholesale and retail trade for an urban place reflects the industrial pursuits of the residents of, rather than the persons employed in, the place. Furthermore, both dollar volume and percent em-

ployed are affected by the volume of commercial activity by non-residents
as well as residents of the place. Finally, the level of income of a population in a community affects the rate of expenditures for retail trade in
that community. With these qualifications in view, it would seem nonetheless that there is a somewhat greater proportion of the working force in
wholesale and retail trade in the SMA's and the metropolitan urban places
which are growing rapidly. This suggests that there is a somewhat greater
specialization in commerce in these rapidly growing places. For independent cities, however, the older and declining cities of 25,000 to 50,000
may have a somewhat greater volume of wholesale trade than do the rapidly
growing ones since they function as wholesale trade centers for a hinterland. The existence of such a hinterland for independent cities, whether
growing or declining, probably accounts somewhat for the greater similarity of the proportions of employed persons in trade in growing and
declining independent cities.

Socio-economic status

The occupational structure of rapidly growing places, when compared
with declining places, shows a somewhat higher percentage of male and
female workers employed in white-collar occupations, regardless of size of
place (tables 102 and 103 and figure 23). Conversely, of course, declining places have a somewhat greater percentage of men and women employed in manual occupations than do rapidly growing places. This finding is consistent with the statistics showing a greater percentage of persons
employed in manufacturing in declining urban places.

The large proportion of male white-collar workers in growing places in
large part is accounted for by significantly greater proportions of men employed as professional, technical, and kindred workers, and as managers,
officials, and proprietors. The results also suggest that the percentage of
men employed in sales work is generally greater in rapidly growing than
in declining places, regardless of size or type of place (table 102). Statistically significant differences between the high and low growth rate
groups are observed for all but SMA's with 50,000 to 250,000 inhabitants
and independent cities in the percentage of men employed in sales occupations. Somewhat higher proportions of female clerical and sales workers
are found in rapidly growing than in declining places, though the differences are sizable only for SMA's with 50,000 to 250,000 inhabitants, independent cities with 10,000 to 25,000 inhabitants, and suburbs.

The significantly larger percentage of manual workers in declining than
in rapidly growing places in large part is accounted for by much larger
proportions of persons engaged as operatives and kindred workers. There
is at least a 10-point difference in the percentage of men employed as operatives and kindred workers between declining places and rapidly growing
ones. For employed women, the difference in the percentage employed as

Table 102.—Percent Distribution of Employed Males by Major Occupation Group, for Selected Standard Metropolitan Areas and Urban Places, by Metropolitan Status, Size, and Growth Rate: 1950

[Asterisk (*) denotes difference between high and low groups significant at 0.05 level of probability]

Metropolitan status and size of place	Growth rate	White-collar occupations					Manual occupations				
		Total[1]	Profess'l, techn'l, and kindred workers	Managers, officials, & propr's, exc. farm	Clerical and kindred workers	Sales workers	Total[1]	Craftsmen, foremen, and kindred workers	Operatives and kindred workers	Private household and service workers	Laborers, except farm
Standard metropolitan areas:											
50,000 to 250,000...	High....	*35.2	*8.2	12.0	7.4	7.6	*54.7	20.0	*17.4	7.3	10.0
	Low.....	30.4	6.1	11.0	6.2	7.1	64.1	21.1	27.1	7.3	8.6
250,000 or more.....	High....	*39.7	*9.4	*13.5	8.1	*8.7	*53.2	21.3	*15.3	8.2	8.4
	Low.....	33.2	8.1	10.5	7.7	6.9	63.7	21.5	25.7	7.0	9.5
Central cities:											
Under 100,000.......	High....	*42.6	*9.5	*15.4	7.4	*10.3	*54.6	20.1	*16.6	8.5	9.4
	Low.....	34.3	7.5	11.5	7.5	7.8	64.5	20.7	26.3	8.9	8.6
100,000 or more.....	High....	*43.8	*10.7	*14.8	8.5	*9.8	*54.4	20.2	*16.8	9.0	8.4
	Low.....	33.4	7.4	10.0	9.1	6.9	65.5	21.8	25.0	9.0	9.7
Suburbs:											
10,000 to 25,000....	High....	*50.7	*14.6	*17.8	7.6	*10.7	*47.8	24.6	*14.8	*4.0	*4.4
	Low.....	23.2	4.8	7.1	7.2	4.1	72.8	23.0	29.3	6.6	13.9
25,000 or more......	High....	*42.8	*11.3	*14.6	8.0	*8.9	*55.6	*24.9	*18.7	*6.0	6.0
	Low.....	31.8	7.3	10.0	8.5	6.0	67.2	21.7	28.8	7.3	9.4
Independent cities:											
10,000 to 25,000....	High....	*38.0	*12.0	13.3	5.7	7.0	*57.3	19.3	*19.9	10.0	8.1
	Low.....	30.7	6.3	11.2	6.4	6.8	67.6	20.3	31.9	6.7	8.7
25,000 to 50,000....	High....	*42.1	*11.6	*14.9	*6.3	9.3	*55.2	*19.7	*16.3	9.6	*9.6
	Low.....	34.7	7.1	12.6	7.2	7.8	64.3	20.9	27.9	7.9	7.6

[1] Sum of white-collar and manual occupations does not equal 100, because farm occupations and persons whose occupations were not reported are omitted.

Source: *1950 Census of Population*, Vol. II, *Characteristics of the Population*, Parts 2 to 50, table 35.

Figure 23.—Percent of Employed Males in White-Collar Occupations in Selected Standard Metropolitan Areas and Urban Places, by Metropolitan Status and Growth Rate: 1950

[Base line: All urban employed males in the United States]

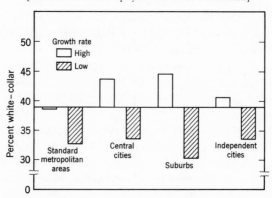

Note: See table 102.

operatives and kindred workers between rapidly growing and declining places is even greater. About 15 percent more of the women in declining places are employed as operatives and kindred workers. Since operatives and kindred workers are, in large part, employed in establishments classified as manufacturing industry, these striking differences are consistent with the differences observed for employment in manufacturing.

The proportion of men in private household and service work is lower in rapidly growing than in declining suburbs, regardless of the size of the suburb. By contrast, the rapidly growing places have significantly larger proportions of the employed women in private household and service work than do the declining urban places, regardless of size and type of place.

TABLE **103.**—PERCENT OF EMPLOYED FEMALES IN SELECTED MAJOR OCCUPATION GROUPS, FOR SELECTED STANDARD METROPOLITAN AREAS AND URBAN PLACES, BY METROPOLITAN STATUS, SIZE, AND GROWTH RATE: 1950

[Asterisk (*) denotes difference between high and low groups significant at 0.05 level of probability]

Metropolitan status and size of place	Growth rate	Sales, clerical, and kindred workers	Operatives and kindred workers	Private household and service workers
Standard metropolitan areas:				
50,000 to 250,000...............	High..........	*37.3	*9.3	*28.9
	Low...........	27.2	36.6	15.2
250,000 or more..................	High..........	42.9	*11.3	*22.2
	Low...........	39.2	24.2	15.8
Central cities:				
Under 100,000...................	High..........	37.1	*12.4	*27.3
	Low...........	34.1	27.8	18.0
100,000 or more.................	High..........	40.4	*12.6	*25.2
	Low...........	38.8	25.3	16.7
Suburbs:				
10,000 to 25,000................	High..........	*46.7	*9.9	17.1
	Low...........	36.5	33.7	13.2
25,000 or more..................	High..........	*46.3	*11.3	*18.7
	Low...........	38.7	32.7	11.5
Independent cities:				
10,000 to 25,000................	High..........	*36.0	*12.9	*30.0
	Low...........	34.0	26.3	18.0
25,000 to 50,000................	High..........	37.0	*8.1	*31.3
	Low...........	33.4	29.5	17.0

Source: See table 102.

These data refer to the resident population, rather than the working population, in suburbs. It, therefore, is somewhat difficult to interpret this difference for men and women without further data on the characteristics of male and female private household and service workers in suburbs.

The educational level (table 104) of the residents in growing places of each size group is much higher than that of residents in declining places, regardless of size and metropolitan status. The median number of years of school completed for all persons 25 years of age and over is approximately two years higher for residents of rapidly growing places. Residents of declining SMA's, central cities, suburbs, and independent cities had a median education level of about ninth grade, while for residents of the corresponding groups of growing places the median was about an eleventh grade educational level. This considerably higher median educational level of residents in rapidly growing cities cannot be attributed to the somewhat higher proportion of students attending college in these places, since the data for median school years completed are only for persons 25 years old and over. There are, furthermore, no statistically significant differences among urban place size groups in the percentage of persons aged 20 to 24 and 25 to 29 attending school in 1950. It seems, in fact, that the differences in educational level among growing and declining places are a function of the differences in occupational and industrial composition of these places described above.

If economic opportunity is greater in rapidly growing than in declining places, one might expect the median level of income for families and unrelated individuals to be greater in rapidly growing places. This is not necessarily the case, since there are marked differentials in urban income by region, race, and family status of the individual, and type of economic base, which can affect differences in the median income of the population of places which are compared. Differences in the regional, racial, and family status composition of the inhabitants between the rapidly growing and the declining places do affect the present comparisons. Since many of the rapidly growing places are in the South, where the median level of

TABLE 104.—SELECTED POPULATION AND HOUSING CHARACTERISTICS, FOR SELECTED STANDARD METROPOLITAN AREAS AND URBAN PLACES, BY METROPOLITAN STATUS, SIZE, AND GROWTH RATE: 1950

[Asterisk (*) denotes difference between high and low groups significant at 0.05 level of probability]

Metropolitan status and size of place	Growth rate	Median school years completed[1] Persons 25 years old and over	Percent enrolled in school[1] Persons 20 to 24 years old	Median income of families and unrelated individuals[2] (dollars)	Percent of occupied dwelling units owner-occupied
Standard metropolitan areas:					
50,000 to 250,000.............	High.........	*10.6	12.2	2,692	58.7
	Low..........	9.0	10.4	2,654	50.7
250,000 or more...............	High.........	*11.0	*11.2	2,778	53.8
	Low..........	9.1	12.0	2,828	51.3
Central cities:					
Under 100,000.................	High.........	*11.2	12.0	2,555	*53.4
	Low..........	9.5	11.3	2,693	47.2
100,000 or more...............	High.........	*10.8	11.6	2,783	48.8
	Low..........	9.1	12.3	2,864	38.7
Suburbs:					
10,000 to 25,000.............	High.........	*12.3	13.7	*4,034	*75.3
	Low..........	8.7	9.1	3,026	43.5
25,000 or more...............	High.........	*12.0	12.5	*3,779	*57.5
	Low..........	8.8	11.3	3,232	36.6
Independent cities:					
10,000 to 25,000.............	High.........	*10.6	6.1	*2,979	*51.7
	Low..........	9.0	7.5	2,514	58.2
25,000 to 50,000.............	High.........	*11.3	20.0	*1,347	54.8
	Low..........	9.4	8.6	2,874	50.2

[1] The figure shown is the one for the median place in each group.

[2] Excludes from comparisons all places with 25 percent or more of the population 20 to 24 years old enrolled in school. The figure shown is the one for the median place in each group.

Source: *1950 Census of Population*, Vol. II, *Characteristics of the Population*, Parts 2 to 50, tables 10, 34, and 37; *1950 Census of Housing*, Vol. I, *General Characteristics*, Part 1, U. S. Summary, table 22, and Parts 2 to 6, table 1.

urban income is lower than in the Northeast and North Central, the areas of the declining urban places, comparisons of the income level of rapidly growing and declining urban places may simply reflect these differences. In addition, the proportions of unrelated individuals and of nonwhites are higher in rapidly growing than in declining places.

As is indicated in table 104, there are no significant differences in the median income for families and unrelated individuals between rapidly growing and declining SMA's or central cities. Rapidly growing suburbs and independent cities with 10,000 to 25,000 inhabitants have significantly higher median incomes than do comparable declining places. Independent cities with 25,000 to 50,000 inhabitants show the reverse pattern; the median income level of declining independent cities in this size group is significantly greater than that for rapidly growing ones. Excluding independent cities in this size group which had a large percentage of persons 20 to 24 years old in school, the difference between rapidly growing and declining places remains as great. The rapidly growing independent cities with 25,000 to 50,000 inhabitants include a fairly large proportion of places where other factors appear to affect the median income level. There are, for example, the resort and/or "military" cities of Fort Lauderdale and Panama City, Fla.; Biloxi, Miss.; and Rapid City, S. D., with below average income.

The data on median income of families and unrelated individuals in rapidly growing as compared with declining urban places do not present a uniform set of findings on the relationship of rate of growth to income of residents. Taking into account the differences in income level which are a function of differences in regional location, it would seem that rapidly growing places generally have a somewhat greater median income level than do declining ones (table 104). The differences, however, are very small except for the smaller independent cities and suburbs. No doubt the suburbs which are rapidly growing are more selective of higher income groups than declining ones. This is particularly evident in the significantly greater percentage of home owners in rapidly growing as compared with declining suburbs. Large independent cities which are rapidly growing have a much lower median income than those which are declining. This difference seems due to two facts: More of the growing cities are in the South, and most of the growing cities in this group also have large military establishments. The income level is low for populations of this type.

The percentage of home ownership (table 104) is somewhat greater in rapidly growing than in declining urban places, except in the case of independent cities of 10,000 to 25,000 inhabitants. The difference is greatest for the suburbs with 10,000 to 25,000 inhabitants. Three-fourths of all residents of these growing suburbs owned their own home while only roughly two-fifths of the residents in these declining suburbs owned their own home. The percentage of home ownership also was considerably greater in growing suburbs than in declining ones with 25,000 inhabitants or more. The greater difficulty in securing housing in growing central and independent cities generally may increase the percentage of home owner-ship. The much greater percentage of home ownership for growing than declining suburbs, however, seems due to other factors. The rapidly grow-ing suburbs generally were developed for home owners in United States communities during the 1940–50 decade.

Summary

This chapter has explored the relationship of economic opportunity to the growth rate of cities. The most rapidly growing urban places, when compared with the declining ones, do not show significantly greater eco-nomic opportunities as measured by participation of men and women in the labor force. The rapidly growing cities, however, have a higher socio-economic level, and the general character of their economic base is such as to foster relatively greater opportunities in white-collar occupations. This can be seen in the higher percentage of men and women in white-collar occupations, the higher median level of school completed, and the greater incidence of workers in commerce, government, and entertainment in rapidly growing as contrasted with declining urban places, regardless of size of place. In contrast, declining urban places have a higher percent-age of men and women employed in manual jobs, particularly as opera-tives and kindred workers. Manufacturing is the industrial affiliation of at least one-third of all employed persons in declining urban places, regard-less of size.

The more rapidly growing places appear to tend toward greater natural increase than do declining urban places. This can be seen in the higher fertility ratios and the percentage of married men 14 years of age and over. They also have a more mobile population. The percentage of the popula-tion who are migrants or who were residentially mobile in the year 1949 to 1950 is greater in the rapidly growing places.

Historical note

The present study follows Ogburn's and Wu's studies in comparing rapidly growing with declining urban places.[20] There are differences in the design of the three studies, however, which make exact comparison difficult. This study compares rapidly growing with declining SMA's, cen-tral cities, independent cities, and suburbs, by size group. At times income, enrollment in higher education, and region are controlled for par-ticular comparisons. Ogburn did not distinguish among types of urban places, although he excluded the very large central cities from the study, and he did not control any other salient factors in comparisons. Wu com-pares growing and declining cities. He does not control metropolitan status and size in all his comparisons, but region, city size, distance from a metropolitan district, and income are controlled for selected comparisons.

---

[20] See William F. Ogburn, *op. cit.*, Chapter 13, and Pek Si Wu, *op. cit.*

Ogburn's cities showed sizable rates of growth or decline for the 1910–20 and 1920–30 decades. Wu's cities showed substantial rates of growth or decline for the 1920–30 and 1930–40 decades. The urban places selected for this analysis showed a sizable increase or decrease in population for the 1930–40 and 1940–50 decades. Despite the differences in study design, an attempt is made below to summarize the evidence for findings where there are roughly comparable statistics in the three studies in the three time periods.

The replications among the three studies show substantial agreement in findings. Ogburn, Wu, and the foregoing data show that rapidly growing when contrasted with declining places in the United States have a high proportion of the following: (1) employment in trade, (2) employment as private household and service workers (for women, only, in the present study) and (3) home owners, and a low proportion of (4) employment in manufacturing. Ogburn found that a greater percentage of the working population were employed in hotels and restaurants in the increasing cities; Wu found a greater proportion of employed persons in hotels and lodging places, regardless of size of place, but no consistent difference was found by proximity to metropolitan district; the present study finds a greater proportion of employed persons in hotels and lodging places, regardless of size. Ogburn and the current study have comparable data which show that the proportion of (1) professional workers, (2) married persons, and (3) unrelated individuals is greater in growing than in declining places. Wu and the current study have comparable data which show that rapidly growing urban places have a greater proportion of (1) nonwhite persons (due to regional location of places); (2) children under 5 years of age; (3) employment in government; and (4) employment in entertainment and recreation, than do declining urban places. The two studies also agree in that, (5) the median number of school years completed is greater in rapidly growing than in declining places. They likewise show that (6) the percentage of persons 14 years old and over in the labor force and (7) the proportion employed in transportation are about the same in rapidly growing as in declining urban places.

There is some apparent disagreement for a few findings where the data are comparable. Ogburn and Wu found that the percentage of persons 21 years of age and over is greater in rapidly growing than in declining urban places; the reverse finding holds, regardless of metropolitan status and size of place, in the present study. The fertility ratio was greater in the declining than in the rapidly growing urban places in Ogburn's study, while Wu's study and the present investigation show substantially higher fertility ratios in rapidly growing than declining urban places, regardless of type and size of place. Wu found that the per capita retail sales were greater in rapidly growing than declining urban places regardless of size and distance from a metropolitan district. The data in this chapter show no substantial differences in per capita retail sales for high and low growth rate places when metropolitan status and size of place are controlled.

PART IV

FUNCTIONAL SPECIALIZATION
OF COMMUNITIES

C H A P T E R   16

TYPES OF FUNCTIONAL SPECIALIZATION

The pattern of economic production varies in modern urban communities. Some places are thought of as specializing in a form (or forms) of economic production while other places are thought to be balanced or diversified in their economic production. This chapter attempts to define types of functional specialization which characterize specialized urban communities in terms of forms of economic activity. To classify communities according to functions, however, requires some statement of the concept of "function" and a set of standardized procedures for assigning communities to one or another functional specialization. The chapter considers these matters as a preliminary to the use of the functional types in later chapters. These later chapters show that differences in functional specialization, i.e., in economic production, are related to other morphological differences in communities—demographic, economic, and socio-economic.

Nature of functional specialization

Rural communities are principally characterized by agricultural or extractive economic activities. There are, of course, other economic functions performed which are incidental to these principal activities, i.e., some services are rendered locally to the rural population. Occasionally, too, industries other than extractive ones are important to the economy of a rural community. In this part of the monograph, no attention is given to rural communities, since the data required for delineating open country-village communities and for classifying their functions are not available on a mass basis. The problem, therefore, is limited to the functional classification of cities (urban places of 10,000 inhabitants or more) and standard metropolitan areas.

The place of a city's economic activity in a larger economy and its basis of support are discussed by Harris and Ullman:

> The support of a city depends on the services it performs not for itself but for a tributary area. Many activities serve merely the population of the city itself. . . . The service by which the city earns its livelihood depends on the nature of the economy and of the hinterland. . . . Modern mechanization, transport, and a complex interdependent economy enable much of the economic activity of mankind to be centered in cities. . . . The support of cities as suppliers of urban services for the earth can be summarized in three categories . . . 1. Cities as central places performing comprehensive services for a surrounding area . . . 2. Transport cities performing break-of-

bulk and allied services along transport routes, supported by areas which may be remote in distance but close in connection because of the city's strategic location on transport channels. . . . 3. Specialized-function cities performing one service such as mining, manufacturing, or recreation for large areas, including the general tributary areas of hosts of other cities. . . . Most cities represent a combination of the three factors, the relative importance of each varying from city to city.[1]

Central-place cities are typically commercial centers, but in some instances political or cultural functions may provide an important part of their support. Cities situated at strategic breaks in transportation may be characterized by highly developed wholesale trade functions, and they may attract, as well, those manufacturing establishments whose transport costs can be minimized by locating at a point of transshipment.[2] The most important category of "specialized-function" cities is manufacturing centers. Mining, educational, and resort cities also fall into this category, as do those cities whose major source of support is servicing nearby military establishments.

The position taken in this chapter is that the problem of functional classification is best undertaken by considering functional specialization in terms of the kinds of *export activity* of a community which creates an inflow of money to the community. Urban land economists and planners refer to this as the "economic base" of communities. Richard Andrews, for example, defines the economic base as "the export activities of a community that bring in its *net* earnings and enable it to continue as an independent economic entity."[3] They are, then, the activities of a community which involve the export of goods, services, or capital to places of *extra-local demand*, and the source of payment is beyond the limits of the economic community satisfying the demand. The remaining economic activity in a community goes to satisfy *local demand* and may be said to constitute the *maintenance activity* of a community. There are three major kinds of maintenance activity in any city: that required for maintenance of the physical city such as construction and transportation; the services, including trade, necessary to maintain the population at a level of living; and the manufacturing activity for local consumption. Export and maintenance activities, then, comprise the *total* economic activity of a community. Generally, for any urban place, the percentage of employment in maintenance activities is greater than that in export activities. Jaffe estimated that in 1940 about four-fifths of all urban employment was accounted for by maintenance activities. The total of 81 percent of the working force engaged in maintenance activities was divided among the three categories—main-

[1] Chauncy D. Harris and Edward L. Ullman, "The Nature of Cities," *Annals of the American Academy of Political and Social Science 242*, November 1945, pp. 7–17 (quotation from pp. 7–9).

[2] See Edgar M. Hoover, *The Location of Economic Activity*, McGraw-Hill Book Co., New York, 1948, Chapter 3.

[3] Richard B. Andrews, "Mechanics of the Urban Economic Base: The Problem of Terminology," *Land Economics 29*, August 1953, pp. 263–268 (quotation from p. 263).

tenance of the physical city (11.8 percent); services, including trade (47.7 percent); and manufacture for local consumption (21.5 percent).[4]

It rarely occurs that the export activity of a sizable community includes only one type of industrial activity.[5]   Perhaps the closest approximation to this situation is found in small manufacturing, college, resort, and mining towns.   Most cities export a number of goods and services, and therefore have a more or less "diversified" economic base.   The contrast between "diversified" and "specialized" cities is, therefore, only a matter of degree of specialization.   An urban or metropolitan community might be said to be diversified if its export activity was about the same as that of the "average" community.   In devising an appropriate "average," one would have to take account of community size and location with respect to larger communities, since these factors influence the export functions of a community.   Similarly, a functionally "specialized" community would be one where the export activity is quite different from that of the average community.

The Bureau of the Census does not provide statistics for the exports of communities.   (A community can export a product, either by shipping it out or by temporarily drawing in persons from other areas to purchase the goods or services where they are produced; radio and television broadcasts are "exported" by wire and wireless transmission, as are news services, while persons are drawn to retail trade establishments as customers.)   Hence the export function cannot be measured directly or precisely with census data.   When a community has a high proportion employed or a high per capita output in a given industry, relative to other communities in the economy, however, it probably exports the products of that industry.   At any rate, it must import them to a lesser extent.   Statistics on the industrial composition of the labor force or on per capita volume of activity, analyzed comparatively, therefore, permit rough inferences as to export functions.   For example, when a given community has a much larger proportion of its labor force engaged in manufacturing than the average of an appropriate group of communities, there is a presumption that it exports manufactured goods and, therefore, specializes in manufacturing.

Two other considerations enter into the formulation of criteria of specialization: the size and metropolitan status of a place.   There is a division of labor among communities of different sizes and between different parts of the metropolitan region.   For example, wholesale trade establishments tend to be relatively concentrated in large cities and toward the centers of metropolitan regions.   This division of labor, of course, should be studied for its own sake.   But the problems here are different.   They are (1) to

---

[4] A. J. Jaffe, "Production-Maintenance Functions of the Working Force," mimeographed report, Columbia University, Bureau of Applied Social Research, 1952.

[5] The number of industrial activities in a community, of course, is a function of the total number of categories of industry which are defined.

classify communities comparable as to size and location in the metropolitan region, according to functional criteria, and (2) to determine whether other aspects of community structure are related to functional differentiation, independently of metropolitan status and size. Accordingly, the study does not apply a uniform criterion of specialization to all places.

Some explanation of the metropolitan status and size categories is needed. The analysis employs two types of area units (see Appendix A): standard metropolitan areas and urban places. An urban place may lie within or outside an SMA. Urban places outside SMA's in 1950 are classified as *independent cities* in this study. Urban places within SMA's are either *central cities* or *suburbs*. An urban place is defined as a central city by the Bureau of the Census when it is the largest city of an SMA. Any other city in the SMA with 25,000 inhabitants or more, having a population amounting to one-third or more of that of the largest city, is also a central city, except that no SMA has more than three central cities. All urban places other than central cities within SMA's are referred to as suburbs in this part of the monograph.[6]

Metropolitan status is partly based on size. Hence, it was necessary to use only two size categories within each metropolitan status group to obtain fairly close control of size. All urban places of 10,000 inhabitants or more are, therefore, classified into six groups. Group 1 consists of the 95 central cities with 100,000 inhabitants or more, and group 2 of the 98 central cities with fewer than 100,000 inhabitants. Group 3 includes the 134 urban places classified as suburbs with 25,000 inhabitants or more, and group 4 includes the 276 suburbs with 10,000 to 25,000 inhabitants. The 157 urban places classified as independent cities with 25,000 to 50,000 inhabitants make up group 5, and the 502 independent cities with 10,000 to 25,000 inhabitants make up group 6. These six groups are mutually exclusive, and account for all of the 1,262 urban places with 10,000 inhabitants or more listed in the 1950 Census of Population. In addition, the 168 standard metropolitan areas were divided into 77 SMA's with 250,000 inhabitants or more and 91 with 50,000 to 250,000 inhabitants. An SMA is a county or group of contiguous counties which contains at least one city of 50,000 inhabitants or more. Standard metropolitan areas therefore include, in addition to residents of the central cities and suburbs of 10,000 and over, some population living in urban territory outside places of 10,000 and over, and some rural population.

---

[6] This means that the term "suburb," as used here, is inclusive of both suburban and satellite places, as defined in Chapter 12 (though limited to those of 10,000 inhabitants or more). The conceptual difference between a suburb and a satellite city is that the former is assumed to be more closely integrated with the central city than the latter. While it would be expected that such a difference would produce differences in functional specialization, this problem is not investigated here. Aside from the considerable labor involved in distinguishing between suburbs and satellites for all the SMA's in the United States, it is not known whether the procedure of Chapter 12 would be suitable for all SMA's. It should be noted that neither concept, suburb or satellite, is currently recognized in official census tabulations.

In identifying communities as specialized in manufacturing, higher education, public administration, and transportation, the criteria of specialization actually do not vary a great deal by size and metropolitan status. Nevertheless, it is desirable to maintain these as control classifications in investigating the effects of functional specialization, independent of size and metropolitan status. The case is different for specialization in trade, as may be seen by comparing the criteria of trade specialization for suburbs and independent cities (figure 28, p. 234). By the procedures described below, a suburb may be classified as a "trade center," even though its per capita trade volume in some cases is less than that of an independent city of the same size classified as a "nontrade center." This can happen because suburbs, in general, supply less of their own trade services than do independent cities, since they depend more upon either other suburban, or (more likely) central city trade outlets. It cannot be assumed that there is an absence of trade specialization in suburbs. Given the same criteria for defining trade specialization in suburbs as in independent cities, however, a suburb with higher than average (for suburbs) trade volume does not necessarily export any significant volume of trade services, whereas the independent city probably does. Yet if the suburb approaches self-sufficiency in trade, it may still be said to "specialize" in trade, as compared with other suburbs, since trade volume in the "average" suburb is below that required for self-sufficiency. Some suburbs, however, may be more highly "specialized" than any central or independent city, since they become "suburban shopping centers," for surrounding areas.

The procedures of this study for classifying communities according to function differ from those of previous studies [7] in two principal respects: (1) The criteria of functional specialization are varied according to community size and metropolitan location. (2) It is possible for a given community to appear in more than one functional class—for example, to be both a trade center and a center of higher education. These properties of the classification system are desirable in view of the ultimate purpose of the study. This purpose is to determine the effects on other aspects of community structure of having a particular type of export activity. The activities considered are manufacturing, trade, higher education, public administration, transportation, entertainment and recreation, and services rendered to military establishments. The succeeding sections of this chapter are concerned with the details of classifying communities as to specialization in each of these activities.

Manufacturing specialization

Manufacturing may affect the demographic growth and cultural development of an urban community both directly, through the location of an

---

[7] Grace M. Kneedler, "Functional Types of Cities," *Public Management 27*, July 1945, pp. 197–203; Victor Jones, "Economic Classification of Cities and Metropolitan Areas," *The Municipal Yearbook*, 1953, pp. 49–57; Chauncy D. Harris, "A Functional Classification of Cities in the United States," *Geographical Review 33*, January 1943, pp. 86–99.

employing manufacturing establishment in the community, and, indirectly, by providing employment opportunities to residents of nearby places. The area over which a manufacturing establishment conditions population and resource aggregation, regardless of political boundaries, theoretically is the area separating the producing community from its export market. Unfortunately, the census tabulations are not easily adapted to this theoretical delimitation of production areas. Data from the Census of Population on industry attachment are tabulated for the workers *resident* in a particular urban place (a city) or census area (e.g., an SMA). Data from the Census of Manufactures are tabulated for the *establishment,* located in a particular urban place or census area. Specifically, data on value added by manufacture and production workers in the 1948 Census of Manufactures are for urban places or census tabulation areas in which the *establishments are located.* Data on employment in specific industries in the 1950 Census of Population are for urban places or census tabulation areas in which the *employed person lives.* There is a positive relationship between place of urban residence and work, but the relationship is affected to a great extent by the size and metropolitan status of the urban place. For example, some suburbs rank low in value added by manufacture or production workers when compared with their central city, but they may have a fairly large resident population of persons employed in manufacturing establishments which are located elsewhere. By way of illustration, Lincoln Park, Michigan, ranks in the upper quintile of all suburbs with 25,000 inhabitants or more on the percentage employed in manufacturing, but it ranks in the lower quintile of these suburbs in number of production workers per 1,000 inhabitants and in per capita value added by manufacturing. This discrepancy is accounted for by the relative absence of manufacturing establishments in the incorporated suburb of Lincoln Park.

Figure 24 depicts the frequency distribution of each of the eight metropolitan status-size groups of places by the per capita value added by manufacture. Figure 25 similarly represents the distributions with respect to the percentage of the resident working force employed in manufacturing. On both measures, within each metropolitan status group, the smaller places have somewhat higher proportions at the upper and lower extremes of the distributions. The difference between the value added distribution (which is on an establishment basis) and the employment distribution (residence basis) is very striking for suburbs. On the basis of the percentage employed in manufacturing, the distributions for suburbs are similar to those of SMA's and central cities, being uni-modal with a concentration of the distribution around the central tendency. But on the basis of per capita value added, the suburban distributions are asymmetrically U-shaped. The largest classes are those with less than $200 per capita value added, and the next largest are those with $1,400 or more. Suburbs, then—particularly small suburbs—tend to be rather sharply divided

FIGURE **24.**—PERCENT DISTRIBUTION OF PLACES BY PER CAPITA VALUE ADDED BY MANUFAC-
TURE, FOR STANDARD METROPOLITAN AREAS AND URBAN PLACES, BY METROPOLITAN STATUS
AND SIZE: 1947

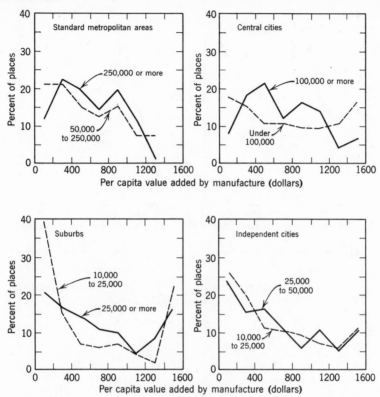

Note: See table 105.

into those with very little manufacturing activity and those with a great
deal of manufacturing. There is considerable similarity, however, between
the value added and the employment in manufacturing distributions for
each group of places, when suburbs are excluded. The curves for SMA's
and central cities resemble each other closely, but independent cities are
distinctive in having comparatively large numbers of places at the lower
extreme of very little manufacturing activity or employment.

The characteristics just noted lead to some variation in the quintile
values of the distributions for per capita value added by manufacture and
the percentage employed in manufacturing among the metropolitan status
and size groups. The quintile values are shown in table 105. The difference between the extreme quintiles is greater for small places, within a
metropolitan status group, than for large places, since the only exception
is for independent cities on per capita value added. There also is considerable variation in quintile values by metropolitan status. On the per-

FIGURE 25.—PERCENT DISTRIBUTION OF PLACES BY PROPORTION OF THE EMPLOYED LABOR FORCE IN MANUFACTURING, FOR STANDARD METROPOLITAN AREAS AND URBAN PLACES, BY METROPOLITAN STATUS AND SIZE: 1950

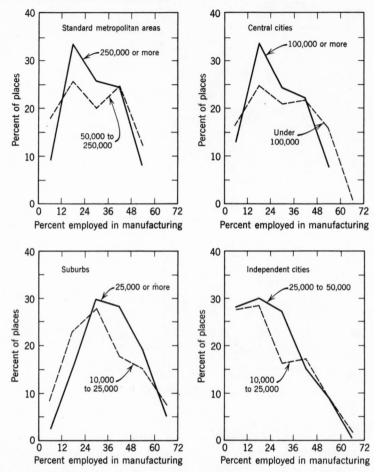

Note: See table 105.

centage employed in manufacturing, the upper quintiles range from 39 percent for large independent cities to 50 percent for suburbs, and the lower quintiles from 9 percent for small independent cities to 24.5 percent for large suburbs.   On per capita value added the range of upper quintiles is from about $900 for SMA's to nearly $1,600 for small suburbs; and the range of lower quintiles is from about $70 for small suburbs to nearly $300 for large central cities.   There is, nevertheless, a substantial difference between the extreme quintiles in every comparison.   On the percentage employed in manufacturing, suburbs have higher quintile values than the other metropolitan status groups; but, on per capita value added, small suburbs have both the highest upper quintile value and the lowest lower quintile value.

Table **105.**—Upper and Lower Quintiles of the Distributions of Places by per Capita Value Added by Manufacture, 1947, and by Percent of the Resident Employed Labor Force in Manufacturing, 1950, for Standard Metropolitan Areas and Urban Places, by Metropolitan Status and Size

Metropolitan status and size of place	Per capita value added by manufacture, 1947[1] (dollars)		Percent employed in manufacturing, 1950	
	Upper quintile	Lower quintile	Upper quintile	Lower quintile
Standard metropolitan areas:				
50,000 to 250,000..............	907	188	43.6	12.9
250,000 or more................	909	247	40.4	16.6
Urban places of 10,000 or more[2]....	1,172	153	44.7	12.4
Central cities:				
Under 100,000..................	1,383	218	46.2	13.0
100,000 or more................	1,060	297	41.4	15.4
Suburbs:				
10,000 to 25,000..............	1,573	69	49.5	20.4
25,000 or more................	1,289	185	49.7	24.5
Independent cities:				
10,000 to 25,000..............	1,090	148	41.3	9.0
25,000 to 50,000..............	1,143	147	39.4	9.5

[1] Excludes places for which value added was not disclosed.
[2] Does not include standard metropolitan areas.

Source: *1950 Census of Population*, Vol. II, *Characteristics of the Population*, Parts 2 to 50, table 10; *1947 Census of Manufactures*, Vol. III, *Statistics by States*, table 2.

It is evident that the two indicators of manufacturing activity—percent employed in manufacturing, and per capita value added by manufacture—will not lead to identical classifications of communities by degree of manufacturing specialization. Yet for most metropolitan status groups there is a fair degree of agreement, and a relatively high probability that a community ranking high on one measure will also rank high on the other. Table 106 shows the amount of agreement between the quintile classifications of the two measures. It was necessary to exclude a fairly large number of places, since the per capita value added by manufacture data were not available for comparisons, particularly for small suburbs and independent cities. The percentage agreement between the quintile classifications of the two measures is quite high for SMA's and central cities. The lower quintiles of suburbs are the only groups where there is less than 50 percent agreement. In almost all other comparisons, it is roughly three-fifths or more of all places.

Given a fairly close agreement between the classifications of manufacturing specialization produced by the two measures, the choice between them rests primarily on practical considerations. In this case the major factor is that, while the labor force data are available for all SMA's and urban places, the establishment data are lacking for some places because of the Census of Manufactures disclosure rule. In the treatment of manufacturing specialization in Chapter 17, the criteria for classifying places as high or low in manufacturing specialization, therefore, are the quintile limits for percentage employed in manufacturing (shown in table 105). The choice of the quintile as the cutting point, of course, is somewhat arbitrary.

TABLE **106.**—PERCENT OF AGREEMENT BETWEEN QUINTILE CLASSIFICATIONS OF STANDARD
METROPOLITAN AREAS AND URBAN PLACES BY PERCENT EMPLOYED IN MANUFACTURING AND
PER CAPITA VALUE ADDED BY MANUFACTURE, BY METROPOLITAN STATUS AND SIZE OF PLACE

Metropolitan status and size of place	Number of places in quintile groups on percent employed in manufacturing[1]		Places classified the same on percent employed in manufacturing and per capita value added by manufacture			
	Upper quintile	Lower quintile	Upper quintile		Lower quintile	
			Number	Percent[2]	Number	Percent[2]
Standard metropolitan areas:						
50,000 to 250,000..............	18 (12)	18 (18)	9	75	13	72
250,000 or more.................	16 (15)	16 (16)	12	80	14	88
Central cities:						
Under 100,000....................	20 (20)	19 (16)	11	55	12	75
100,000 or more.................	18 (18)	19 (18)	12	67	16	89
Suburbs:						
10,000 to 25,000................	55 (30)	56 (19)	19	63	9	47
25,000 or more..................	27 (22)	27 (24)	13	59	9	38
Independent cities:						
10,000 to 25,000................	97 (72)	100 (33)	45	63	27	83
25,000 to 50,000................	31 (30)	31 (24)	19	63	15	63

[1] Numbers in parentheses are the numbers of places for which data were available on value added by manufacture.

[2] Percentages are based on the number of places for which data were available on value added by manufacture.

Source: See table 105.

Specialization in trade

A community broadens its sustenance base by trade, i.e., by exchange
with other areas or communities. This may lead to specialization in trade,
if the community possesses certain locational or other advantages, such as
size.[8] A community may specialize in wholesale trade, or in retail trade,
or in both. The average urban community has a smaller volume of wholesale trade than of retail trade, since wholesale is concentrated in fewer
centers of wholesaling. For the same reason, many communities have
little or no wholesale trade, while the greater decentralization of retailing
means that most cities have some retail trade.

Previous studies of functional specialization have placed retail centers
and wholesale centers in mutually exclusive classes.[9] This procedure neglects the fact that a community may export both wholesale and retail trade
to other areas, i.e., it may specialize in both types of trade. The fact suggests the advisability of developing a joint set of criteria for trade specialization. In order to present the rationale for this set of criteria, it is necessary to consider, first, the nature of the available trade data and some
characteristics of wholesale and retail trade.

Retail trade, as defined in the 1948 Census of Business, includes establishments which are primarily engaged in selling merchandise for personal,
household, or farm consumption. The count includes all establishments

[8] For a discussion of trade and its relation to the sustenance base, see Amos H. Hawley, *Human Ecology*, Ronald Press, New York, 1951, pp. 353–355.

[9] See Kneedler, *op. cit.*; Jones, *op. cit.*; Harris, *op. cit.*

in business at the close of 1948. The per capita retail sales was computed for each urban place with 10,000 inhabitants or more. Data on retail sales in thousands of dollars were obtained from the 1948 Census of Business.[10] Data on population counts were obtained from the 1950 Census of Population.[11] Sales were defined in the 1948 Census of Business as total receipts from customers during 1948, after deduction of refunds or allowances for merchandise returned by customers. Income from investments, etc., and the amount of sales or excise taxes paid directly to the taxing agency are excluded from the total sales reported. The data were lacking for a number of the places with 10,000 to 25,000 inhabitants in 1950, either because the place was not of this size in 1940 or because the data were withheld to avoid disclosure for individual establishments. Data were available for 1,214 urban places out of the 1,262 reported in the 1950 Census of Population.

In some cases the per capita retail sales, calculated as described, may be somewhat too low. There are two reasons for this. Both the size of population and the volume of retail sales probably increased for most urban places between 1948 and 1950. The per capita figure is a ratio of 1948 dollar volume in retail sales to 1950 population. The discrepancy between the base years for population and for retail sales tends to decrease the per capita values. The distribution of places by per capita retail sales is also affected by the reporting system used in the Census of Business. Federal law does not permit the publication of figures which will lead to disclosure for individual businesses. Almost invariably, urban places for which data are withheld are those which are small and have only a few retail establishments. The mean per capita retail sales for all small places probably is raised somewhat by this bias in reporting. This may also account, in part, for the fact that the distribution of all places by per capita retail sales is positively skewed.

Wholesale trade, in the 1948 Census of Business, includes establishments primarily engaged in selling merchandise to retailers and industrial, commercial, professional, or institutional users; or to other wholesalers; or acting as agents in selling merchandise to (or buying merchandise for) such persons or companies. The per capita sales for wholesale trade during 1948 was computed for each urban place with 10,000 inhabitants or more. Data for sales in wholesale trade establishments in each urban place were obtained from the 1948 Census of Business,[12] while population counts were obtained from the 1950 Census of Population. Sales for wholesale trade in the 1948 Census were defined as receipts from merchandise sold during 1948 together with all receipts from repairs or other services to customers, after returns, allowances, and trade discounts were

---

[10] *1948 Census of Business*, Vol. III, *Retail Trade—Area Statistics*, table 103, column 3.

[11] *1950 Census of Population*, Vol. I, *Number of Inhabitants*, Parts 2–50, table 7.

[12] See *1948 Census of Business*, Vol. V, *Wholesale Trade—Area Statistics*, table 103, column 3.

deducted. Sales of merchandise for others on a commission basis were included, as well as sales for the account of the reporting establishment. Data are missing for certain of the places with 10,000 inhabitants or more in 1950, because the place was not of this size in 1940 or because the data were not reported to avoid disclosures for individual establishments. Data were available for 1,109 of the 1,262 urban places with 10,000 inhabitants or more in 1950. The per capita wholesale trade figures are subject to errors similar to those noted for retail, owing to the difference in the dates of the Censuses of Business and Population and to the bias produced by the disclosure rule.

A problem was encountered in compiling data on wholesale and retail trade for SMA's with respect to those New England SMA's not designated as such before 1950. New England SMA's are built up from minor civil divisions. County data from the 1948 Census of Business therefore could not always be consolidated to obtain an SMA figure. Altogether, data were obtained for 166 of the 168 SMA's.

Figure 26 shows the distributions of urban places with 10,000 inhabitants or more by per capita sales in retail and in wholesale trade. The frequency polygon for per capita retail sales is fairly symmetrical around the mean of $1,237, though there is some positive skewness in that 15 places have per capita sales of more than $2,500. By contrast, the frequency polygon for per capita wholesale trade is much flatter, and is markedly skewed in

FIGURE 26.—PERCENT DISTRIBUTION OF PLACES BY PER CAPITA RETAIL SALES AND PER CAPITA WHOLESALE SALES IN 1948, FOR URBAN PLACES WITH 10,000 INHABITANTS OR MORE IN 1950

[Retail data exclude 48 places for which data were not available and 1 place with per capita sales of $4,400; wholesale data exclude 153 places for which data were not available and 26 places with per capita sales over $3,600]

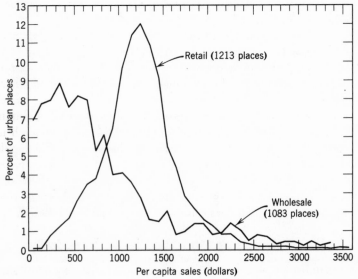

Note: See table 107.

the positive direction. The bulk of the places lie below the mean of $918, but some have per capita values of several thousand dollars—as high as $7,022 and $8,777 for the independent cities of Salina, Kansas, and Sioux City, Iowa, respectively, and $30,962 for suburban South St. Paul, Minnesota.

The striking differences between the wholesale and retail distributions can be related to differences in the way that the two branches of trade operate. The volume of retail sales in an urban area tends to be directly related to the number of people in a local area, since the bulk of the sales are made to customers who can readily gain access to the establishment. To specialize in retail trade a city must ordinarily draw consumers from a relatively restricted area in its immediate hinterland. There are some cases where specialization may arise from mail-order retail business, or by drawing customers from greater distances for certain types of highly specialized luxury goods.

The volume of wholesale trade, on the other hand, is comparatively independent of the size of the population in the immediate vicinity of the establishment, even though the volume of wholesale trade is positively correlated with the volume of retail trade, which, in turn, is closely dependent on the size of the local population. The main consideration in determining the volume of wholesale trade in an area is that the path of goods between wholesaler and consumer almost always is intersected by a retailer. The time-cost distance affecting the location of wholesalers, therefore, primarily is measured for retailers to wholesalers, not from consumers to wholesalers. Theoretically, then, it is possible for a city to have no wholesale trade or a very high volume of wholesale trade, regardless of its metropolitan status or size. The size of the population in the wider hinterland and the number of urban centers competing for wholesale trade, of course, operate as major factors determining the volume of wholesale trade. The relatively greater independence of the volume of wholesale than of retail trade from the population of the city in which the establishment is located results in a greater range of per capita wholesale trade than of per capita retail trade. The fact that wholesaling is relatively independent of the population aggregate in which the establishment is located also produces the flatness of the per capita wholesale distribution and its positive skewness. Apparently, the majority of places must rely upon a much smaller number of places specialized to a high degree in the wholesale export of goods.

Wholesale and retail trade also differ in the way they are related to size of place. Figure 27 shows the "urbanization curves" of wholesale and retail sales for places of 10,000 inhabitants or more, ordered by size of place.[13] The curve for wholesale trade reveals a marked concentration of sales by establishments located in large cities; the urbanization index is

---

[13] For an explanation of the urbanization curve, see Duncan, "Urbanization and Retail Specialization," *op. cit.*, and Chapter 4 of the present monograph.

FIGURE **27.**—URBANIZATION CURVES FOR 1948 WHOLESALE AND RETAIL TRADE FOR ALL URBAN PLACES OF 10,000 INHABITANTS OR MORE IN 1950

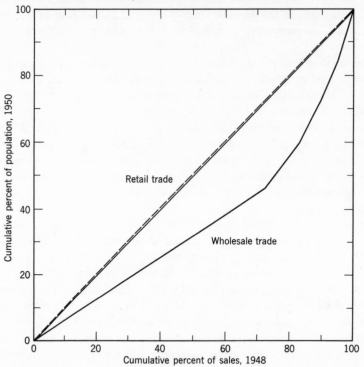

Note: See table 107.

0.30.   No such tendency is in evidence for retail trade.   Its urbanization curve is practically indistinguishable from the diagonal of the graph, and the urbanization index is only −0.008.

Table 107 shows the mean and standard deviation of per capita retail and wholesale trade for SMA's and urban places grouped by size.   The mean per capita retail sales for all urban places is $1,237, with a standard deviation of $441.   There is little variation in the mean by size of place, except that for places of 500,000 or more there is a somewhat lower value of $1,187.   The standard deviation is inversely related to size of place, however, varying from $492 for urban places with 10,000 to 25,000 inhabitants to $128 for places of 500,000 or more.   The distributions of places by per capita retail sales for the several size groups all resemble the one for all urban places in figure 26, in that there is some positive skewness and the frequency polygon is rather peaked.   The data for SMA's in table 107 show relatively little variation by size of SMA in the mean and standard deviation of per capita retail sales.   The means for SMA's are lower than for urban places, and the frequency curves show somewhat less skewness.

The mean per capita wholesale trade for all urban places is $918, with a standard deviation of $945. The means for size groups vary directly with size of place, rising from $667 for places of 10,000 to 25,000 inhabitants to $3,450 for places of 500,000 or more. The standard deviation varies directly with size of place, except that it is greater in the size group 250,000 to 500,000 than in the group 500,000 or more. The distribution of places by per capita wholesale trade for each size group tends to resemble the distribution for all places (figure 26) in being flat and markedly skewed in the positive direction. However, there is less skewness for the larger places, and their distributions tend to be almost rectangular in form. The data for SMA's likewise show a tendency for mean per capita sales to vary directly with size, except that the lowest mean occurs for SMA's with 100,000 to 250,000 inhabitants. There is little regularity in the relation of the standard deviation to size of SMA. The means for SMA's are lower than those of central cities in comparable size groups. While the distributions of SMA's by per capita wholesale trade are rather irregular owing to the small numbers of SMA's in the size groups, there is a general tendency for them to be roughly rectangular in form.

The per capita volume of trade varies with the metropolitan status as well as the size of a place. The median per capita retail sales of all central cities is $1,239, as compared to only $952 for all suburbs. The median for all SMA's of $956 is close to that for suburbs. The SMA figure is more like that of suburbs than central cities, since it includes not only residents of suburbs but also those of places under 10,000, and some

TABLE 107.—MEAN AND STANDARD DEVIATION OF PER CAPITA RETAIL AND WHOLESALE SALES, FOR STANDARD METROPOLITAN AREAS AND URBAN PLACES, BY SIZE: 1948

Area and size of place	Per capita retail sales			Per capita wholesale sales		
	Number of places	Mean (dollars)	Standard deviation (dollars)	Number of places	Mean (dollars)	Standard deviation (dollars)
Standard metropolitan areas.....	167	950	130	166	1,304	989
1,000,000 or more....................	14	995	70	14	2,006	717
500,000 to 1,000,000................	19	991	121	19	1,949	957
250,000 to 500,000..................	45	942	110	45	1,197	798
100,000 to 250,000..................	72	932	137	72	1,057	984
50,000 to 100,000...................	17	966	168	16	1,342	1,089
Urban places.....................	1,215	1,237	441	1,110	918	945
500,000 or more....................	17	1,187	128	17	3,450	1,152
250,000 to 500,000.................	23	1,263	195	23	2,836	1,699
100,000 to 250,000.................	65	1,230	232	64	1,692	1,041
50,000 to 100,000..................	126	1,221	294	123	1,132	1,059
25,000 to 50,000...................	249	1,240	415	237	914	893
10,000 to 25,000[1].................	735	1,239	492	646	667	593

[1] Excludes South St. Paul with a per capita wholesale sales of $30,962, since it is an extreme value.

Source: *1950 Census of Population*, Vol. II, *Characteristics of the Population*, Parts 2 to 50, table 10; *1948 Census of Business*, Vol. III, *Retail Trade—Area Statistics*, tables 102 and 103; and Vol. V, *Wholesale Trade—Area Statistics*, tables 102 and 103.

rural population.   The median for all independent cities is $1,243, almost the same as that for central cities.   The difference between central cities and suburbs is much more pronounced for wholesale trade than for retail trade.   The median per capita wholesale sales for all central cities is $1,529, but only $367 for suburbs.   The figure for SMA's, $992, is intermediate between these two.   The median per capita wholesale sales for independent cities, $701, is well below that of central cities, or even SMA's, but substantially above the figure for suburbs.   As is shown below, these relationships are modified when allowance is made for differences in income and size of place within metropolitan status groups.

The main significance of the relation of trade volume to metropolitan status seems clear.   There is a differentiation of functional areas within the metropolitan community, such that the central areas provide some retail services for the entire community.   This shows up in the comparatively low per capita figures for suburbs, despite recent trends toward "suburbanization" of retail trade.   The higher per capita wholesale figures for SMA's as compared to independent cities reflect the tendency, already noted, for wholesaling to be concentrated in large centers.   The wholesale differentiation within SMA's, between central and suburban cities, reflects the well-known tendency for wholesale establishments to seek fairly central locations within the metropolitan community.

The income level of a population affects its per capita expenditures for trade.   Both wholesale and retail trade are related to the income level of SMA's and urban places, but the relationship is not the same.   To study these relationships, places in each of the eight groups (two size groups, each, of SMA's, central cities, suburbs, and independent cities) were classified as high or low income according to whether their median income (of families and unrelated individuals) was above or below that of the median place in the group.   Figure 28 (p. 234) shows the quartile values of per capita wholesale and retail trade for high and low income places, by metropolitan status and size of place.

Retail sales per capita vary considerably with the income level of a population.   The higher the median income of a population, the greater the per capita retail sales expected.   Figure 28 shows that retail sales per capita are greater for high median than low median income SMA's, central cities, and independent cities.   Retail sales per capita, however, are lower in high median income than in low median income suburbs.   This suburban deviation from the pattern for other types of places probably is explained by the fact that higher income suburbs are more likely to zone against the location of business establishments within the suburb, and that the central city is more likely to serve the consumer tastes of the upper than the lower income suburbanite.

Wholesale sales per capita likewise vary with the income level of the population of an urban place, but generally in the opposite direction to that noted for retail.   The higher the median income of a population, the lower the per capita sales for wholesale trade.   Figure 28 indicates that sales in wholesale trade are greater in low income than in high income central cities, suburbs, and independent cities, regardless of size, and in SMA's with fewer than 250,000 inhabitants.   The SMA's with 250,000 inhabitants or more are exceptions, in showing somewhat greater per capita expenditures in wholesale trade for the high income SMA.

The difference in the patterns of variation for wholesale and retail sales per capita with median income of a community undoubtedly is due to the nature of the wholesaler-retailer-customer nexus.   The location of many types of retail establishments is more closely connected with the immediate location of the consumer's residence (source of demand) than is that of wholesale establishments; hence, greater volume of sales per capita in retail trade is related to greater income of the resident population.   The location of wholesalers is more determined by access to retailers and the means by which they are supplied than it is by the residence of customers; hence, wholesalers are somewhat freer to locate according to considerations of the cost of space than are retailers.   The locations for wholesale trade typically are adjacent to, or within, the lower income residential areas of large cities.   It appears, too, that specialization in wholesale trade occurs more often in the low income than in the high income independent city. The finding on retail trade for suburbs confirms the general causal explanation given above.   Suburbs with a low median income have a higher per capita retail sales than do suburbs with a high median income.   This is related to the fact that business establishments of all kinds are found less often in the high than in the low income suburb, and that high income persons are more likely to patronize the specialty stores found only in the central city.[14]

The relationship between the volume of wholesale and of retail trade needs to be taken into account, if places are to be classified with respect to wholesale and retail specialization simultaneously.   There is a substantial positive relationship between per capita wholesale trade and per capita retail trade, as is indicated by a regression analysis summarized in table 108.   Except for urban places of 10,000 to 25,000, there is a correlation of about 0.4 to 0.5 between the two variables, for each size-of-place group. However, the regression equation varies markedly by size of place. Its slope is very low for small cities and increases directly with size of place.   In the scatter diagrams there is some indication of curvilinearity, particularly for the large cities and SMA's.

The foregoing discussion demonstrates that a number of factors must be considered in framing a wholesale-retail trade classification.   It also has

---

[14] This is suggested by the data in Amos H. Hawley, "An Ecological Study of Urban Service Institutions," *American Sociological Review 6*, October 1941, p. 636ff.

TABLE **108.**—SUMMARY OF ANALYSIS OF REGRESSION OF PER CAPITA WHOLESALE TRADE ON PER CAPITA RETAIL TRADE, FOR URBAN PLACES OF 10,000 INHABITANTS OR MORE, BY SIZE OF PLACE: 1948

[Asterisk (*) denotes significance at 0.05 level of probability]

Size of place	Regression constants[1]		Standard error of estimate[2] (dollars)	Correlation coefficient
	Intercept	Slope		
250,000 or more...............	-2,382	4.452	1,311	*0.51
100,000 to 250,000............	-248	1.572	975	*0.35
50,000 to 100,000.............	-771	1.559	953	*0.44
25,000 to 50,000.............	-351	1.009	789	*0.47
10,000 to 25,000.............	+450	0.201	1,326	0.08

[1] For the regression line, $Y = a + bX$, where Y is per capita wholesale trade in dollars, X is per capita retail trade in dollars, a is the intercept, and b the slope.

[2] Per capita wholesale trade.

Source: See table 107.

some implications for the procedures appropriate for devising such a classification. Some account must be taken of the relationship of the volume of trade to the metropolitan status, size, and income level of the community, and of the relationship between the volume of wholesale and of retail trade. The difference between the frequency distributions of per capita retail trade and per capita wholesale trade and the extreme skewness of the latter suggest that it would be difficult to work with deviations from the means in standard deviation units. The same characteristics, plus the evidence of curvilinearity of the regression of wholesale on retail trade, indicate the inadvisability of working with deviations from the regression line. The procedure outlined below, however, rests on the same logical basis as these two procedures.

From the point of view adopted in this chapter, specialization in trade is to be identified with a volume of trade in excess of that required to maintain a local population. Yet there are no data to measure the amount of trade necessary to maintain the local population, or that available for export either by sending goods outside the community, or by "importing" customers. The problem of classification, therefore, has to be approached somewhat deductively. It is assumed in this study that a community with a very low volume of trade in relation to its income and in comparison with the volume of trade in communities of comparable size and metropolitan status is importing trade from other communities. Correlatively, a community with a disproportionately high volume of trade is, *prima facie,* an exporter of trade. Theoretically, then, a community may have a high retail volume and a low wholesale volume, or vice versa, even though the two are positively related, in general. It may also be relatively low in both, high in both, or have intermediate levels of both wholesale and retail trade.

In summary, the following criteria are proposed for a classification of functional specialization in wholesale and retail trade based on the relative amount of trade which is exported: (1) The correlation between income and wholesale and retail trade must be controlled. (2) Differences in wholesale and retail trade sales by metropolitan status and size of place must be controlled. (3) The maintenance requirements of a community for wholesale and retail trade do not give rise to specialization; rather there must be evidence of an "export" function. (4) The deviation from a measure of central tendency should be taken account of in the interest of statistical logic. (5) The number of places classified as functionally specialized in wholesale or retail trade must be sufficiently large to permit comparisons among the groups. The procedure developed to meet these requirements is described below.

First, all urban places of 10,000 or more for which data on per capita sales in wholesale and retail trade were available were classified by metropolitan status and size of place (six groups). There were 1,102 of the total 1,262 urban places with 10,000 inhabitants or more in 1950 for which data were available. Classification into six metropolitan status-size groups provides a rough control of variation in per capita volume of wholesale and retail sales by size and metropolitan status of urban places. Each of the six metropolitan status-size groups was further subdivided into income categories, with the "high" income category comprising places above the median of the median incomes of all places in the group, and the "low" income category the remaining places. The correlation between income and wholesale and retail trade was roughly controlled in this way.

Analogous operations yielded four groupings, by size and income, for the 166 SMA's for which data were available.

The next step was to determine the quartiles for retail sales per capita and for wholesale sales per capita for each of the 12 metropolitan status-size-income groups and the 4 SMA size-income groups. Then each urban place and SMA was classified by its quartile position on both wholesale and retail trade. This yielded 16 classes: 4 wholesale times 4 retail quartiles. By combining certain of these, a 9-class system of wholesale-retail trade was arrived at. This is depicted graphically in figure 28. The 9 classes, identified by the numbered cells of the schematic diagram, are as follows:

1. *Wholesale trade center* (cells 1, 2, and 5), a high per capita value of sales in wholesale trade but a low per capita value of retail sales.

2. *Retail trade center* (cells 12, 15, and 16), a high per capita value of retail sales with a low per capita value of sales in wholesale.

3. *Trade center* (cell 4), a high per capita value of sales in both wholesale and retail trade.

4. *Trade center, wholesale* (cell 3), a trade center, with some dominance of wholesale over retail trade.

5. *Trade center, retail* (cell 8), a trade center, with some dominance of retail over wholesale trade.

6. *Nontrade center* (cell 13), a low per capita value of sales in both wholesale and retail trade.

FIGURE **28.**—SCHEMATIC REPRESENTATION OF WHOLESALE-RETAIL TRADE CLASSIFICATION, AND DISTRIBUTION OF STANDARD METROPOLITAN AREAS AND URBAN PLACES ACCORDING TO THE CLASSIFICATION, BY METROPOLITAN STATUS, SIZE, AND INCOME LEVEL: 1950

Note: See table 107.

The chart depicts a nine-category system of wholesale-retail trade classification, based on quartiles of the distributions of per capita sales.

On the opposite page are eight similar diagrams, one for each metropolitan status and size-of-place group.

The numbers within each section of the diagrams refer to the number of places in each category of the classification. The first figure of each pair is the number of high income places, and the second is the number of low income places.

The dollar values on the vertical scales refer to the quartile limits of per capita wholesale sales. The left-hand scale shows the limits for the high income subgroup, and the right-hand scale the limits for the low income subgroup.

The dollar values on the horizontal scales refer to the quartile limits of per capita retail sales. The upper scale shows the limits for the high income subgroup, and the lower scale the limits for the low income subgroup.

The diagram for SMA's of 50,000 to 250,000 inhabitants shows, for example, that there are 7 high income SMA's of this size classified as trade centers (TC), with per capita wholesale sales of $1,306 or more and per capita retail sales of $1,064 or more. There are 3 low income SMA's in the same size group classified as trade centers, with per capita wholesale sales of $1,367 or more and per capita retail sales of $958 or more.

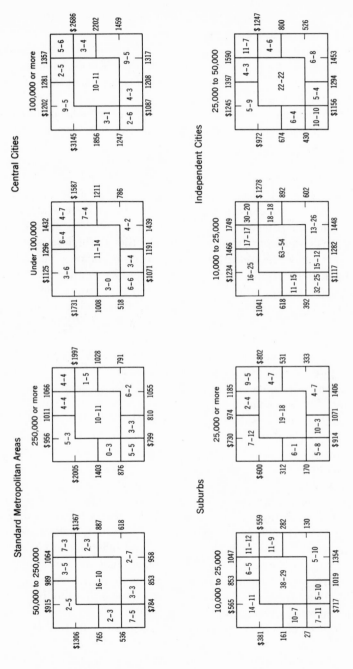

Note: See table 107.

7. *Nontrade center, wholesale* (cell 9), a nontrade center, with somewhat more wholesale than retail trade.

8. *Nontrade center, retail* (cell 14), a nontrade center, with somewhat more retail than wholesale trade.

9. *Maintenance trade center* (cells 6, 7, 10, and 11), the per capita value of wholesale trade and retail sales is about average for that of all cities, and it is therefore roughly considered to be a level of trade necessary to maintain the local population.

Figure 28 also shows the distribution of places by metropolitan status, size, income level, and wholesale-retail classification, together with the quartile limits of per capita wholesale and retail trade defining the latter. Each of the smaller diagrams stands for one metropolitan status-size group. The left-hand vertical scale shows the quartile limits for per capita whole-sale trade for the high income subgroup, and the right-hand vertical scale the quartile limits for per capita wholesale trade for the low income sub-groups.   The quartiles for per capita retail trade are shown on the horizontal scale, the upper row being the quartiles for high income places, and the lower row the quartiles for low income places.   The numbers within the diagram are the frequencies of places in the nine classes of the wholesale-retail classification; the first figure of each pair is the number of high income places, and the second figure is the number of low income places.   Thus, there are seven high income SMA's of 50,000 to 250,000 inhabitants classified as trade centers (TC); these have per capita wholesale sales of $1,306 or more and per capita retail sales of $1,064 or more. There are three low income SMA's of the same size group classed as trade centers, having per capita wholesale sales of $1,367 or more and per capita retail sales of $958 or more.

Table 109 summarizes the distribution of places by the wholesale-retail classification.   The distributions for SMA's and all urban places are quite similar, with about one-tenth of the places classed as wholesale trade cen-- ters, one-tenth as retail trade centers, one-fourth as nontrade centers, and a little over one-quarter, each, as trade centers and maintenance trade centers.   By metropolitan status, central cities have a somewhat higher proportion of retail trade centers and of trade centers than do suburbs or independent cities; suburbs have a higher proportion of maintenance trade centers than either of the other two groups; and independent cities have a somewhat larger percentage of nontrade centers than do central cities and suburbs.   However, most of these differences are small.   Indeed it virtually follows from the classification procedures that the distributions by wholesale-retail classes will be rather similar.

The purpose of the wholesale-retail classification in this study is to classify a community according to the extent to which it either exports or imports wholesale and/or retail trade.   It was postulated, therefore, that some places will import both wholesale and retail trade, i.e., they are non-

TABLE **109.**—PERCENT DISTRIBUTION OF STANDARD METROPOLITAN AREAS AND URBAN PLACES BY 1948 WHOLESALE-RETAIL CLASSIFICATION, BY METROPOLITAN STATUS

Metropolitan status	Number of places	Percent of all places, by wholesale-retail classification					
		Total places	Ww	Rr	TC, TCw, and TCr	NT, NTw, and NTr	MTC
Standard metropolitan areas........	166	100.0	9.0	10.3	27.1	25.3	28.3
Urban places[1].....................	1,102	100.0	10.9	9.0	27.0	24.8	28.3
Central cities.................	187	100.0	12.3	10.7	30.5	21.9	24.6
Suburbs......................	342	100.0	12.3	7.6	24.8	24.3	31.0
Independent cities...........	573	100.0	9.6	9.3	27.2	26.0	27.9

[1] Places of 10,000 inhabitants or more, excluding those for which sales data are not available.

Source: Appendix tables B–17 to B–20.

trading communities; others will export wholesale and/or retail trade, i.e., they are centers of trade; and, still others will have just enough trade to meet the requirements of the local population, i.e., they are maintenance trading centers. The within-group regression of wholesale on retail trade provides the operational definition of these functional classes of wholesale-retail centers in this study. The validity of this operational definition is open to question, since the economy of most urban communities probably includes the export of some retail trade, while most communities probably export very little, if any, wholesale trade (figure 26, p. 226).

The problem of validity of classification perhaps is most serious for the operational definitions of nontrade centers and maintenance trade centers. It is postulated that places which rank in the lower quartile of wholesale and of retail trade are nontrade centers in the sense that they import both wholesale and retail trade. This postulate seems reasonable for wholesale, but perhaps not for retail trade in all cases. The residents of suburbs which rank low on both wholesale and retail sales very likely import most of their trade by going to other urban places for retail expenditures. It seems less likely, however, that SMA's, central, or independent cities classified as nontrade centers, under this operational procedure, actually are large importers of retail trade. The trading areas of these latter places probably are so sparsely populated or restricted in scope, or the population has such a low average income, that the volume of retail sales is low as compared with that of the other SMA's, central, or independent cities. It is true, of course, that these nontrading centers have the least export trade, if any. It also seems reasonable to assume that such "nontrading" places may "import" a rather large volume of specialty and related types of goods so that they can validly be classified as relatively the largest "importers" of retail goods.

Places which have a volume of wholesale and of retail sales which is roughly the average for that of all places in a particular metropolitan status, size, and income class are said to neither import nor export trade. They are, rather, considered places which carry on just enough trade to maintain the local population, i.e., to meet its daily requirements. This postulate seems reasonable for the case of retail trade.   There may be exceptions for wholesale trade, however.   The median per capita wholesale sales is only $367 for suburbs, while it is $1,529 for all central cities.   Most suburbs classified as maintenance trade centers, therefore, probably import a rather large wholesale volume for their retail operations.   Correlatively, most central cities classified as maintenance trade centers, therefore, probably export some wholesale.

The relative invalidity of the operational procedure used to define the degree to which trade is exported or imported into a community should be kept in mind in the comparisons of types of wholesale-retail trade communities in the following chapters.   The reader who is concerned with this general problem may keep in mind the following facts of the operational procedure: Wholesale trade, retail trade and trade centers are simply places which have more trade than the average for their size, metropolitan status, and income class; maintenance trade centers are those with about average for the class; and nontrade centers are below the average for the class.   This means that a relative procedure of classification is used where some places have more or less of wholesale and/or retail trade than other places, and the comparisons are for these classes of places, only.

Specialization in higher education

What is meant by "specialization in higher education"?   The implication is that the social structure and the economic base of the community are conditioned to some extent by a college, university, or professional educational institution.   These effects generally are thought to include such things as the size and composition of the student body and faculty, its general "excellence," and its contributions to the reputation of the community as an "educational center."   The community specialized in higher education, however, generally exports a service, education, by importing relatively large numbers of students.   The college or professional school student who is "imported" then becomes a purchaser of a rather large number of other goods and services such as food, clothing, housing, entertainment and recreation, and personal services, since his purchases generally are over a fairly extended period.   Specialization in higher education, therefore, may have important consequences for the social morphology of a community.   The goods and services purchased by students in fact are, theoretically, export activities of the community from the viewpoint of this chapter.[15]   What then constitutes "industry specialization" in higher education?   In the United States in 1950, only 3.8 percent of all urban employed persons were in educational services.[16]

---

[15] This point of view is given a more detailed treatment in Richard B. Andrews, "Mechanics of the Urban Economic Base: Special Problems of Base Identification," *Land Economics 30*, August 1954, pp. 262, 263.

[16] *1950 Census of Population*, Vol. II, *Characteristics of the Population*, Part I, table 55.

Employment in higher education comprises an unknown but undoubtedly only a small fraction of all persons employed in educational services. The majority of such persons are employed in preschool, primary, and secondary education. Thus, unless a place is very small, employment in higher education comprises only a small proportion of its total employment. Specialization in higher education cannot be approached in quite the same way, therefore, as specialization in, say, manufacturing. Even in the very large central cities, workers in manufacturing comprise a relatively large part of the total employed labor force.

This study uses an operational definition of specialization in higher education which is based on the percentage of persons enrolled in school. In the reports of the 1950 Census, the term "school enrollment" refers to attendance of persons 5 to 29 years old at a regular school between February 1, 1950, and the date of enumeration. A "regular school" is one where enrollment leads to an elementary or high school diploma, or to a college, university or professional school degree. Persons in vocational, trade, or business schools were excluded from the enrollment figures, unless such schools were graded and considered part of a regular school system. Enrollment figures include both full and part time students.

There are no separate figures reported for urban places on enrollment in higher education. College students were enumerated in 1950 at their college residence. The percentage of persons of "college age" enrolled in school, therefore, provides an indirect measure of enrollment in higher education. The census age intervals are 18 to 19 years, 20 to 24 years, and 25 to 29 years. The age interval 18 to 19 years was disregarded, because a substantial proportion of 18-year-olds are in secondary schools. There is, furthermore, no differentiation between local and nonlocal students. It is assumed for purposes of this study that places defined as specialized in higher education have substantial proportions of nonlocal students, so that the community exports higher education.

Table 110 presents the distributions of places, classified into metropolitan status and size groups, by the percentage of persons 20 to 24 years old enrolled in school and by the percentage of persons 25 to 29 years old enrolled in school.[17] Both distributions are positively skewed. The distribution for persons aged 25 to 29 is somewhat more leptokurtic than is the distribution of persons aged 20 to 24; the latter distribution is some-

---

[17] The statistics on number of persons enrolled in school for both the 20-to-24 and 25-to-29-year age groups appear to contain some, but an unknown, amount of error in that almost no independent cities or suburbs were found with less than 0.1 percent of the persons in these age groups enrolled in school. This, literally, would mean that almost all of the 1,262 urban places with 10,000 inhabitants or more in 1950 have a college, university, or professional school. This is not the case, as is clear from the lists of institutions of higher education of the U. S. Office of Education. It seems likely that in some cases a person enrolled in a college, university, or professional school was enumerated as living at his home residence, rather than at the place where he was attending school. Actually, since some students commute to college, it is not paradoxical for a suburb to have persons enrolled in college even though no college is located there.

what more normal in appearance.   The age group 20 to 24 enrolled in school seems to approximate closely the undergraduate college and first year graduate school population.   The age group 25 to 29 enrolled in school closely approximates the graduate and professional school population.   As table 111 shows, places which rank high on the percentage of persons aged 20 to 24 enrolled in school also are likely to rank high on the percentage of persons aged 25 to 29 enrolled in school.   This is particularly true for SMA's, central cities, and suburbs.   The percentage agreement is somewhat less for independent cities.   This is not surprising since the liberal arts college with only four years of work more often is found in the independent city, while the four-year college with graduate and professional schools more often is found in SMA's or suburbs.   Lacking the educational facilities of more specialized institutions of learning, some independent cities which rank in the upper quintile on the percentage of persons 20 to 24 years old enrolled in school, in fact, rank in a lower quintile on the percentage of persons aged 25 to 29 enrolled in school. The upper quintile of the distribution for persons aged 20 to 24 enrolled in school was chosen to classify places as having a high degree of specialization in higher education.   This provides an indicator of specialization in higher education for the college community without graduate or profes-

TABLE 110.—PERCENT DISTRIBUTION OF PLACES BY PERCENT OF PERSONS 20 TO 24 YEARS OLD AND OF PERSONS 25 TO 29 YEARS OLD ENROLLED IN SCHOOL, FOR STANDARD METROPOLITAN AREAS AND URBAN PLACES, BY METROPOLITAN STATUS AND SIZE: 1950

Age, metropolitan status, and size of place	Number of places	Percent of all places, by percent enrolled in school							
		Total places	0–3.9	4–7.9	8–11.9	12–15.9	16–19.9	20–23.9	24 and over
PERSONS 20 TO 24 YEARS OLD									
Standard metropolitan areas:									
Under 250,000	91	100.0	1.1	21.1	31.2	17.8	12.2	7.7	8.0
250,000 or more	77	100.0	...	7.5	33.3	34.8	14.1	6.4	3.9
Central cities:									
Under 100,000	98	100.0	3.1	23.7	29.6	14.3	8.2	5.2	15.9
100,000 or more	95	100.0	...	5.4	30.3	35.6	11.7	9.6	7.4
Suburbs:									
10,000 to 25,000	276	100.0	5.9	19.8	30.3	14.5	10.5	4.4	14.6
25,000 or more	134	100.0	0.7	17.8	29.3	23.6	12.5	5.0	11.1
Independent cities:									
10,000 to 25,000	502	100.0	19.3	37.1	14.7	5.0	4.9	3.0	16.0
25,000 to 50,000	157	100.0	3.9	31.2	22.3	9.5	7.6	5.7	19.8
PERSONS 25 TO 29 YEARS OLD									
Standard metropolitan areas:									
Under 250,000	91	100.0	24.4	55.6	13.4	2.2	2.2	2.2	...
250,000 or more	77	100.0	7.7	69.2	20.5	2.6	...	...	...
Central cities:									
Under 100,000	98	100.0	26.0	49.1	15.7	6.5	1.8	...	0.9
100,000 or more	95	100.0	4.1	62.2	23.1	9.5	...	1.1	...
Suburbs:									
10,000 to 25,000	276	100.0	24.2	43.8	22.1	6.2	1.1	0.4	2.2
25,000 or more	134	100.0	8.2	60.8	23.7	4.5	1.4	0.7	0.7
Independent cities:									
10,000 to 25,000	502	100.0	47.6	32.0	9.4	3.0	2.0	0.6	5.4
25,000 to 50,000	157	100.0	33.2	40.2	12.6	2.6	1.9	1.9	7.6

Source: *1950 Census of Population*, Vol. II, *Characteristics of the Population*, Parts 2 to 50, table 34.

TABLE **111.**—UPPER QUINTILE OF THE DISTRIBUTION OF STANDARD METROPOLITAN AREAS AND URBAN PLACES BY PERCENT OF PERSONS 20 TO 24 YEARS OLD ENROLLED IN SCHOOL, AND PERCENT OF AGREEMENT BETWEEN QUINTILE CLASSIFICATIONS FOR TWO AGE GROUPS, BY METROPOLITAN STATUS AND SIZE: 1950

Metropolitan status and size of place	Upper quintile on percent of persons 20 to 24 enrolled in school		Places in upper quintile classified the same on percent of persons 20 to 24 enrolled and percent of persons 25 to 29 enrolled in school	
	Number of places	Percent enrolled	Number	Percent
Standard metropolitan areas:				
50,000 to 250,000.................	18	18.8	12	67
250,000 or more....................	15	18.8	14	93
Central cities:				
Under 100,000....................	20	20.3	14	70
100,000 or more....................	20	19.2	17	85
Suburbs:				
10,000 to 25,000.................	52	19.8	39	75
25,000 or more....................	27	18.0	20	71
Independent cities:				
10,000 to 25,000.................	95	19.5	55	58
25,000 to 50,000.................	34	23.8	23	66

Source: See table 110.

sional school specialization, and includes, as well, a large number of places with institutions offering post-graduate work.

Table 111 also shows the upper quintile values for each of the eight groups of places. For example, of the 91 SMA's with 50,000 to 250,000 inhabitants, 18 have 18.8 percent or more of their population aged 20 to 24 enrolled in school. In general, according to this criterion, an urban place or an SMA is regarded as having "high" specialization in higher education if about 19 to 20 percent or more of the population of college age (20 to 24) is enrolled in school.

Public administration specialization

Government employs rather large numbers of persons, since historically in the United States a large number of communal functions are carried on by government agencies. Employment in government occurs in a variety of industrial activities. The Federal Government and most State governments, in fact, usually employ workers in all major industry groups, including, in a few instances, manufacturing. Local governments do not employ persons in such a large range of industries. Large numbers of persons are employed by local government in only four of the major industry groups: transportation, public utilities, professional and related services (particularly educational services and medical and other health services), and public administration.

Some government employment is necessary in every urban place in the United States to maintain the local population. This employer function most usually is shared by the local urban place or "municipality" and non-local governing units such as the township or county. An exception occurs for the unincorporated urban place where all government employment necessary to maintain the population in these places arises from nonlocal governing units.   In addition to the government employment necessary to maintain the local population, some communities may be said to export government.   The reason for this is that any governing unit which functions for a wider area than a particular locality must generally locate in an urban place.   These centers which specialize in government often are referred to by particular names such as "county seat," State capital, or by the name of some government institution which is localized in the community such as a prison, mental hospital, or a military installation.

The functional classification employed in this section excludes all classes of industry in which government is an employer, other than public administration.   The reason for this is twofold.   There is the fact that the classification system employed in this study is for the most part based on major types of economic activity rather than on employer status.   For example, some urban places with a large percentage of persons employed by government are places with a large State university.   Under the functional classification system employed here, these places are classed as specialized in higher education rather than as specialized in government.   There is also the problem that the major employment in government activities other than public administration, e.g., transportation, public utilities, and professional and related services, is more closely tied to maintenance of the local population than it is to export activity.   Public administration, as the industry group is defined by the Bureau of the Census, includes only those activities which are uniquely governmental functions in the sense of legislative and judicial activities and most executive agency activities allied with these functions.   The industry group classification places all other persons employed by a government employer in the appropriate industry category.   For example, persons employed as faculty members of a State university are classified under "professional and related services."   It is assumed in this study that urban places which rank high in the percentage of persons employed in public administration are exporting this service to other places.   They are, therefore, functionally specialized as centers of government.

The distributions of SMA's and urban places by the percentage of employed males 14 years old and over at work in public administration are shown in table 112.   The distribution is positively skewed and somewhat leptokurtic in form for each size class of SMA and type of urban place.   Most urban places have a small percentage of employed males in public administration, and only a few urban places have a large percentage.

On the basis of the data shown in table 112 the upper decile of the distribution for each metropolitan status and size group was calculated.   The decile values also are shown in table 112.   It was necessary to use deciles, rather than quintiles, in order to obtain groups of places deviating greatly

TABLE **112.**—PERCENT DISTRIBUTION OF PLACES BY PERCENT OF EMPLOYED MALES IN PUBLIC ADMINISTRATION, AND UPPER DECILE OF THE DISTRIBUTION, FOR STANDARD METROPOLITAN AREAS AND URBAN PLACES, BY METROPOLITAN STATUS AND SIZE: 1950

Metropolitan status and size of place	Number of places	Percent of all places, by percent of employed males in public administration											Upper decile	
		Total places	1-1.9	2-2.9	3-3.9	4-4.9	5-5.9	6-6.9	7-7.9	8-8.9	9-9.9	10 and over	Number of places	Percent in public administration
Standard metropolitan areas:														
50,000 to 250,000.	91	100.0	...	23.1	20.8	14.3	23.1	1.1	8.8	2.2	3.3	3.3	10	7.9
250,000 or more...	77	100.0	1.3	14.3	14.3	26.0	15.5	9.1	3.9	3.9	1.3	10.4	9	9.8
Central cities:														
Under 100,000.....	98	100.0	14.4	25.8	14.4	13.4	11.4	4.1	6.2	3.1	3.1	4.1	10	9.2
100,000 or more...	95	100.0	1.0	7.4	11.6	22.1	20.0	10.5	8.4	4.2	5.3	9.5	11	9.8
Suburbs:														
10,000 to 25,000..	276	100.0	4.7	22.5	22.1	19.2	12.7	6.5	1.8	1.8	...	8.7	28	8.3
25,000 or more....	134	100.0	2.2	16.3	15.6	25.9	15.6	15.6	3.7	2.2	0.7	2.2	14	6.9
Independent cities:														
10,000 to 25,000..	502	100.0	1.4	14.9	35.8	22.5	10.0	4.2	3.0	1.6	1.2	5.4	51	7.6
25,000 to 50,000..	157	100.0	1.3	8.3	31.8	24.8	7.7	7.0	3.8	3.8	3.8	7.7	15	9.6

Source: *1950 Census of Population*, Vol. II, *Characteristics of the Population*, Parts 2 to 50, table 35.

from the average percentage of males employed in public administration. This follows from the fact that the distributions in table 112 are heavily concentrated around the central tendency, with extreme percentages being relatively rare. Using the results in table 112, a place may be designated as a "government center" if it has from 7 to 10 percent of its male working force employed in public administration, depending on its size and metropolitan status.

Specialization in transportation

Every city with 10,000 inhabitants or more requires some employment in transportation to facilitate the local movement of persons and goods. At the same time, some urban places are centers of transportation in the sense that they provide the place of employment and/or residence for workers who move goods and persons to and from a hinterland. Generally, the transportation of people and goods by auto, rail, air, or water transport becomes a specialized function of a city when it is a collection center for distribution to a large number of places, or when it is located at the point of breaks in transportation systems.[18] From an operational point of view, it is difficult to separate the proportion of the work force required for the local movement of people and goods from that required for extralocal movement. By functional specialization in transportation, however, this section refers only to the "export" function of transportation—that required for extralocal movement of people and goods.

[18] See James A. Quinn, *Human Ecology*, Prentice-Hall, Inc., New York, 1950, pp. 173–176, for a discussion of the "median location" and "break-in-transportation" theories of urban location.

There has been no census of transportation, corresponding to the Censuses of Manufactures and Business.   Hence, the only data on employment in transportation are those in the 1950 Census of Population, based on place of residence rather than place of work.   It is true, of course, that some persons employed in transportation, such as drivers, pilots, trainmen, and ships' crews, have no fixed place of work but travel between transport centers.   A large proportion of transportation workers, however, are in administrative, clerical, maintenance, and service occupations at the terminal and intermediate points of transportation routes.   It seems safe to assume, therefore, that the residence data are adequate for identifying transportation centers.   Errors arising from their use are perhaps most likely to involve central cities and suburbs, because the place of residence is not necessarily in the same part of the metropolitan area as the place of work.

The definition of transportation center used in this section is based on the distribution of employed persons in transportation in 1950.   Six percent of all employed persons in the urban United States in 1950 were employed in transportation.[19]   But the percentage of persons employed in transportation varies both with metropolitan status and with size of place (table 113).   For SMA's, central cities, and independent cities, the larger the place, the greater the percentage of places having more than 6 percent of the working force employed in transportation.   For example, about 63 percent of all central cities with 100,000 inhabitants or more, as compared with only 30 percent of all central cities with fewer than 100,000 inhabitants, have 6 percent or more of the employed persons in transportation.   The size-of-place difference may reflect the fact that large communities have greater maintenance needs for local transportation than small communities, aside from any tendency to specialize to a greater extent in the export of transportation services.[20]   For suburbs, the reverse pattern exists.   Only 20 percent of all suburbs with 25,000 inhabitants or more, as compared with 28 percent of all suburbs with 10,000 to 25,000 inhabitants, have 6 percent or more of all employed persons in transportation.

Transportation centers, as this class of communities is operationally defined here, comprise those SMA's and urban places having a comparatively high percentage of all employed persons working in transportation.   In accordance with the findings just noted, the classification was carried out separately for each metropolitan status and size group of places.   Since the distributions of places by the percentage of persons employed in transportation are quite leptokurtic, although positively skewed, the upper decile was taken as the criterion.

Table 113 also shows the decile values for each of the eight groups of places.   In each case the upper decile exceeds the percentage of trans-

---

[19] 1950 Census of Population, Vol. II, Characteristics of the Population, Part 1, table 55, p. 103.

[20] See Duncan, "Optimum Size of Cities," cited in Chapter 1, footnote 1.

TABLE **113.**—Percent Distribution of Places by Percent of All Employed Persons in Transportation, and Upper Decile of the Distribution, for Standard Metropolitan Areas and Urban Places, by Metropolitan Status and Size: 1950

Metropolitan status and size of place	Number of places	Percent of all places, by percent employed in transportation								Upper decile	
		Total places	0– 1.9	2– 3.9	4– 5.9	6– 7.9	8– 9.9	10– 11.9	12 and over	Number of places	Percent in transportation
Standard metropolitan areas:											
50,000 to 250,000...	91	100.0	1.1	34.5	35.5	11.2	7.7	4.4	5.6	9	10.3
250,000 or more.....	77	100.0	...	14.1	34.6	34.6	11.5	2.6	2.6	7	8.4
Central cities:											
Under 100,000.......	98	100.0	4.1	28.9	37.1	8.2	7.2	5.2	9.3	9	12.0
100,000 or more.....	95	100.0	...	16.9	22.1	33.6	16.8	9.5	1.1	10	10.9
Suburbs:											
10,000 to 25,000....	276	100.0	6.5	40.9	25.0	16.0	4.3	4.0	3.3	27	8.9
25,000 or more......	134	100.0	3.7	41.5	34.9	9.6	5.9	0.7	3.7	14	8.2
Independent cities:											
10,000 to 25,000....	502	100.0	8.0	43.6	20.7	9.8	5.8	2.2	9.9	50	12.0
25,000 to 50,000....	157	100.0	3.8	36.9	17.9	19.8	10.8	4.4	6.4	16	10.3

Source: See table 112.

portation workers in the entire urban United States (6 percent). However, the deviation from the average in terms of absolute percentage points is not large. Transportation accounts for an extremely high percentage of all employed persons in very few urban places. Conneaut, Ohio, with 23,696 inhabitants in 1950, had the highest percentage (40.1) of employed persons in transportation of any city with 10,000 inhabitants or more. It is closely followed by Altoona, Pa., with 77,177 inhabitants in 1950 and 39.1 percent of the employed persons in transportation. Only eight other urban places with 10,000 inhabitants or more have 25 percent or more of all employed persons in transportation. It is not surprising, therefore, that an urban place is said to be highly specialized in transportation when only 8 to 12 percent of the employed persons are in transportation, depending upon the type and size of urban place.

Military specialization

Military centers represent a somewhat different sort of functional specialization from the other types considered in this chapter. The medieval period in Europe and, to some extent, the frontier period in the United States provide examples of true "fortress towns." But the typical military center in the contemporary United States is simply a city or town which serves as a host community to a nearby military establishment. Inasmuch as the location of military establishments is determined by Federal executive and legislative authority, there are fewer purely local considerations in determining whether a particular city becomes a military center. That is, this type of specialization is less likely, than are the other types, to be determined by local natural advantages and the relationship of a community to its hinterland. Furthermore, the size and number of military establishments fluctuates in accordance with national defense policies. Hence, many communities which experienced a "boom" with the influx of military personnel during World War II have since returned to more normal levels of population and economic activity. Nevertheless, there are towns and cities whose growth over a period of years is largely attributable to their proximity to a permanent military establishment. Moreover, any community which acquires a military establishment also acquires an increment to its economy. Military personnel and establishments draw their income from outside the community, but spend a portion of it in the community. The community may be said, therefore, to "export" certain services to the military establishment.

At the time of the 1950 Census, there were approximately 1 million members of the Armed Forces stationed in the United States. Over half of them (52 percent) were enumerated as residents of urban territory, and one-third (33 percent) as rural residents (almost entirely rural nonfarm) of metropolitan counties and nonmetropolitan counties containing urban centers of 25,000 inhabitants or more. Thus, the great bulk of the Armed Forces were either in urban places and urbanized areas, or else stationed relatively near to them. It may be assumed that a substantial proportion of the Armed Forces enumerated in urban territory were actually stationed in military posts near cities, but were residing off their military establishments. It is clear, in any case, that on the basis of their numbers alone, the military population must have a considerable influence on the social and economic life of those urban communities serving as hosts to military establishments. Furthermore, about a third of the military personnel were reported as "married, spouse present," [21] and no doubt many of them had one or more children.

In this study a community (SMA or urban place of 10,000 inhabitants or more) is designated a "military center," given evidence that there is a sizable military establishment near it, or within its boundaries. The relevant evidence is comprised by the employment status statistics. These include, for each SMA and urban place, the total labor force (including Armed Forces) and the civilian labor force. The military population is readily obtained by subtraction. These statistics almost necessarily understate the size of the military establishment, particularly for urban places, since only a fraction of the military personnel may be enumerated as residents of the community. The remainder are counted at the site of the establishment, which often is outside the community boundaries. A closer approximation to the size of the establishment could be obtained by taking in the entire county in which a city is located, but this procedure would be a misleading basis for classifying urban places in counties containing more than one urban place. It is clear that these data permit only a rough

---

[21] *1950 Census of Population*, Vol. IV, *Special Reports*, Part 1, Chapter A, Employment and Personal Characteristics, table 10, p. 100.

and arbitrary procedure for classifying communities as military centers. Nonetheless, it seems possible to identify the more important military centers with reasonable accuracy.

Table 114 indicates the criteria for designating military centers, and the incidence of these centers in each class of place by size and metropolitan status. Central cities and SMA's with more than 100,000 inhabitants were classed as military centers if they contained 2,000 members or more of the Armed Forces in 1950. All other SMA's and all urban places of 50,000 to 100,000 inhabitants were required to have at least 500 military persons, and all urban places with less than 50,000 inhabitants were classified as military centers if they had 200 or more military persons residing within their boundaries. As table 114 indicates, these criteria classify from 6.8 percent of the independent cities with 10,000 to 25,000 inhabitants to 26.0 percent of the SMA's with 250,000 inhabitants or more of the several size and metropolitan status groups as military centers.

TABLE 114.—CRITERIA FOR CLASSIFYING MILITARY CENTERS, AND NUMBER AND PERCENT OF MILITARY CENTERS, FOR STANDARD METROPOLITAN AREAS AND URBAN PLACES, BY METROPOLITAN STATUS AND SIZE: 1950

Metropolitan status and size of place	Minimum number of military persons	Total places	Military centers	
			Number	Percent
Standard metropolitan areas:				
50,000 to 100,000	500	91	15	16.5
100,000 to 250,000	2,000			
250,000 or more	2,000	77	20	26.0
Central cities:				
Under 50,000	200	98	11	11.2
50,000 to 100,000	500			
100,000 or more	2,000	95	18	18.9
Suburbs:				
10,000 to 25,000	200	276	30	10.9
25,000 to 50,000	200			
50,000 to 100,000	500	134	15	11.2
100,000 or more	2,000			
Independent cities:				
10,000 to 25,000	200	502	34	6.8
25,000 to 50,000	200	157	18	11.5

Source: See table 112.

Specialization in entertainment and recreation

The reduction of time spent at work in American society now makes it possible for people to spend a considerable part of their daily living cycle in leisure activity. Most urban places, therefore, generally provide commercial and public leisure facilities. The increased demand for leisure in the form of vacations or holidays seems, also, to have led to an increase in leisure time facilities, and to a specialization of some urban places in providing these facilities. There are other reasons for both an increase in the relative importance of leisure activities in American society and the development of functionally specialized centers of leisure, but these need not be developed here.

Community specialization in leisure activities is based on the extralocal demand for the activity, together with certain local advantages for some forms of leisure. Variations in demand may be produced by such diverse factors as an unusually high sex ratio (as that induced by a nearby military installation, a mining or a lumbering camp), or a high rate of transiency (as that induced by commerce and shipping). The local advantages leading to specialization in leisure may include such diverse factors as legalization of gambling, natural scenic endowment, geographical location, natural resources, such as live game, and the existence of special cultural institutions such as motion picture production, religious attractions, or "Latin quarters." These diverse facts can be seen as producing three major types of leisure centers, however: those based primarily on (1) recreation and natural advantages, generally called "resort places"; (2) commercial forms of entertainment or amusement, often characterized in terms of a particular commercial form, such as a "gambling town" or a "race track town"; (3) "cultural centers" in the sense of aesthetic institutions devoted to the arts and science, e.g., museums, art galleries, and botanical and zoological gardens. Generally speaking, a country such as the United States has only a relatively few "cultural centers" and large numbers of resort centers and commercial entertainment or recreation centers. The place specialized in leisure need not involve availability of hotels and lodging places, as is sometimes assumed. A resort place usually must provide hotels and lodging places as well, but other entertainment and recreation centers do not necessarily need to provide these facilities.

The nonresident who enters a community because it is specialized in entertainment and recreation has somewhat the same relationship to the economy of that community as does the nonresident college student. He brings in capital from the outside to consume goods and services which the community has available. The shorter average stay of the consumer of entertainment and recreation services as compared with that of the student may restrict the range of goods and services bought by the former. But, the total contribution of consumers of entertainment and recreation services to the export activity of a community may, in fact, be greater than that for students to college communities.

Ideally, specialization in entertainment and recreation should be measured by the extralocal demand for it, since almost all urban places provide some leisure facilities for the local population. No statistical source provides a convenient operational measure in this form. Certain rough indicators are available, however, such as the per capita expenditures for amusement services (from the Census of Business) and the percentage of employed persons in entertainment and recreation services (from the Census of Population). The Census of Business data are withheld for some urban places to avoid disclosure for individual firms. The definition of an entertainment and recreation center used in this section, therefore, is based on the distribution of employed males in entertainment and recreation in 1950, as the data are available for all urban places. In the urban United States, 1.3 percent of all employed men were at work in entertainment and recreation services in 1950.[22] Table 115 shows that the percentage of men employed in entertainment and recreation varies somewhat by metropolitan status and size of place, but the variation is small. Moreover, the variation in the percentage of males employed in entertainment is small within any metropolitan status–size-of-place group. Less than 5 percent of all places in any metropolitan status-size group of places have 3 percent or more of the employed males in entertainment and recreation. In fact, among SMA's the highest percentage of employed males in entertainment and recreation observed was 3.3 percent for Los Angeles, while among central cities it was 4.7 percent for Los Angeles. Among suburbs, Culver City, Calif., with 11.6 percent, and Beverly Hills, Calif., with 11.3 percent, had the highest percentages. Both of these places are associated with the production and distribution of motion pictures, as is metropolitan Los Angeles. Las Vegas, Nev., with 19.2 percent, and Sarasota, Fla., with 9.2 percent of employed males in entertainment and recreation, provide the highest percentages for independent cities. Clearly, no urban place with 10,000 inhabitants or more in the United States provides more than one-fifth of the employed males with employment in entertainment and recreation.

Entertainment and recreation centers, as this class of communities is operationally defined here, comprise those SMA's and urban places in the

TABLE **115.**—PERCENT DISTRIBUTION OF PLACES BY PERCENT OF ALL EMPLOYED MALES IN ENTERTAINMENT AND RECREATION, AND UPPER DECILE OF THE DISTRIBUTION, FOR STANDARD METROPOLITAN AREAS AND URBAN PLACES, BY METROPOLITAN STATUS AND SIZE: 1950

Metropolitan status and size of place	Number of places	Percent of all places, by percent of employed in entertainment and recreation								Upper decile	
		Total places	0– 0.4	0.5– 0.9	1.0– 1.4	1.5– 1.9	2.0– 2.4	2.5– 2.9	3.0 and over	Number of places	Percent in entertainment and recreation
Standard metropolitan areas:											
50,000 to 250,000...	91	100.0	...	38.5	56.0	3.3	1.1	...	1.1	9	1.5
250,000 or more.....	77	100.0	...	36.4	53.2	6.5	1.3	1.3	1.3	8	1.4
Central cities:											
Under 100,000.......	98	100.0	...	23.5	59.2	14.3	1.0	1.0	1.0	12	1.6
100,000 or more.....	95	100.0	...	17.9	65.3	13.7	...	2.1	1.0	10	1.6
Suburbs:											
10,000 to 25,000....	276	100.0	4.7	37.7	35.9	9.8	4.7	2.9	4.3	29	2.2
25,000 or more......	134	100.0	0.8	50.8	32.1	8.2	3.7	1.5	3.0	15	1.7
Independent cities:											
10,000 to 25,000....	502	100.0	1.2	17.7	48.4	23.3	5.8	1.4	2.2	50	2.0
25,000 to 50,000....	157	100.0	...	15.9	54.8	21.7	3.2	...	4.4	15	1.9

Source: See table 112.

[22] *1950 Census of Population*, Vol. II, *Characteristics of the Population*, Part 1, table 55, p. 103.

upper decile of the distribution of places by the percentage of employed males in entertainment and recreation. As table 115 shows, the skewness of the distributions places the upper decile for each metropolitan status–size-of-place group quite close to the national average of 1.3 percent for all urban places.

High and low income communities

In addition to the materials comparing different functional types of communities, this part of the monograph includes a chapter on high and low income communities. Variation among communities in income level is, of course, related to the type of functional specialization, both as cause and consequence. It may also reflect a different dimension of specialization, i.e., specialization with regard to residential characteristics, as instanced by the "exclusive" suburb, for example.

The procedures for classifying communities by income level are discussed in Chapter 20.

Correlates of functional specialization

The morphology of a community is presumably conditioned by the functions performed by its population. Differences in functional type should, therefore, be reflected in differences in morphological traits. These differences may not be pronounced, however, since cities are basically alike in having common maintenance functions and a characteristic division of labor. Yet a highly specialized city is apt to have a distinctive social structure. For example, government centers employ large numbers of white-collar workers. Given the patterns of employment prevailing in the United States it is understandable, therefore, that Washington, D. C., has a low sex ratio, a high ratio of white-collar to manual workers, and a lower average age than most cities in the United States. The question naturally arises, however, *whether relatively large numbers of communities which achieve a relatively high degree of functional specialization are significantly different in their demographic, economic, and socio-economic characteristics from communities which lack this functional specialization.* This is the problem explored in the following chapters.

The relationship between functional specialization in a particular type of economic activity in a community and its social morphology can be examined in at least three different ways. The average of any social characteristic for a group of functionally specialized places can be compared with the average of the characteristic for all places, the characteristics of places with high and low degrees of functional specialization can be compared, or types of functionally specialized urban places can be compared on a particular set of social characteristics. If one makes such comparisons, at least four major problems must be taken into account which affect the comparisons.   The first problem is that functional specialization is related to size of place.   The second problem is that functional specialization is associated with the metropolitan status of an urban place.   The third problem is that some places may specialize in more than one form of economic activity, thus complicating the problem of causal analysis.   The fourth problem is that specialization in industrial activities which comprise a relatively small part of the total industrial activity of the country can have, on the average, relatively less effect on the social morphology of large than small communities, thus complicating the problem of causal analysis.   The first two problems are dealt with in this study by classifying the urban places into the six metropolitan status–size-of-place groups.   It must be recognized, however, that this meets the problems only in part, since the criterion of functional specialization was varied somewhat for different metropolitan status–size-of-place groups.   The third problem is generally ignored in that comparisons are made for functional groupings of urban places, rather than for specific urban places.   Therefore, it seems likely that for specific urban places which specialize in more than one form of industrial activity, the problem of causal analysis is more complex than it is for others in a functional class.   The fourth problem is met in part by the criterion that observed differences should be consistent and significant for a number of the metropolitan status–size-of-place groups to be treated in either the causal or descriptive analysis.   It is recognized, however, that this may lead to a rather stringent criterion of significance, a matter discussed in Chapter 15.

The relationship between degree of functional specialization in a particular economic activity and the social morphology of communities is examined in the succeeding chapters.   Functional specialization in manufacturing is examined by observing differences in characteristics between communities with a high and with a low degree of specialization in manufacturing.   Comparisons for community differences in income levels also are made in this way.   The case of trade specialization is treated in a different way.   Places in each of the five major types of trade specialization are compared with the other types to discover differences in social morphology.   The effects of minor types of functional specialization on community morphology are investigated either by comparing the average on any characteristic with the average for all places of comparable size and metropolitan status, or by comparing the functionally specialized types of places with one another.   The question naturally arises whether the observed differences between groups of places are true differences, in the sense that they are consistent for most comparisons of individual places, as well as for the comparison of group averages.   This problem is dealt with separately in each chapter, depending upon the particular type of comparison employed.

Summary

Urban communities differ in the form and degree of specialization in economic activities.   Functional specialization is defined in this monograph as specialization in an economic activity for which there is a non-local market, i.e., there is an export function.   Functional classes of SMA's and urban places were defined for manufacturing, wholesale and retail trade, higher education, public administration, transportation, military national defense, and entertainment and recreation.[23]   The purpose of this functional classification of places is to determine whether a high degree of functional specialization of a community significantly affects its demographic, economic, and socio-economic characteristics.   This problem is explored for each of the types of functional specialization in the following chapters.   Communities differing in income level also are compared in the final chapter.

---

[23] The five minor types of functional specialization considered in this chapter were selected from among a larger number of theoretical types.   An effort should be made in further research to compare them with at least the following types of specialization: finance, extractive industries, professional services, and business and repair services.   Since it is difficult to think of construction as an export function of a single urban place, it is excluded from consideration.   It might also be fruitful to establish subcategories for some of the classes defined above, e.g., by classifying manufacturing communities according to the type of manufacturing, or by distinguishing among the several kinds of entertainment and recreation centers.

CHAPTER 17

FUNCTIONAL SPECIALIZATION IN MANUFACTURING

The rise of the modern city was concomitant with the Industrial Revolution, and the historical connection between industrialization and urbanization has been generally recognized. There are, however, many sizable urban and metropolitan centers whose economic base includes little manufacturing industry. This chapter investigates some differences between communities which are highly specialized in manufacturing and those whose economic activities are predominantly in industries other than manufacturing.

In this chapter a standard metropolitan area or urban place is considered to be functionally specialized in manufacturing if it falls in the upper quintile on the distribution of places by the percentage of all employed persons working in manufacturing. As explained in Chapter 16, quintiles were calculated separately for each subgroup of SMA's and urban places classified by metropolitan status and size. For convenience, places in the upper quintile are said to rank "high" in manufacturing specialization, while those in the lower quintile are said to rank "low."

Places ranking high in manufacturing are compared with those ranking low for some 30 social characteristics of the population. The median test was employed as in Chapter 15, to test the significance of differences between places with a high and low degree of specialization in manufacturing. The null hypothesis was rejected when the probability of an observed difference was less than 0.05.

Problems of analysis

The practice of enumerating college students in the place where they were attending college in 1950 creates difficulties of interpretation for such statistics as the proportion in the labor force, the proportion married, and the median income of families and unrelated individuals. Since more of the nonmanufacturing than of the manufacturing communities are also college communities, college communities are eliminated from the comparisons for these statistics.

There is marked variation in the regional location of SMA's or urban places associated with the percentage of persons employed in manufacturing. The differences are so clear that one can predict with considerable accuracy that a city specializing in manufacturing will be in the Northeast or North Central Regions, while those with little manufacturing will be in the South or West. Table 116 shows that 51.4 percent of all places which rank high in manufacturing are in the Northeast, and 37.3 percent are in the North Central Region. For cities ranking low in manufacturing specialization, 37.0 percent are in the West, and 39.7 percent are in the South. Analysis of regional location by metropolitan status and size-of-place groups shows that places specializing in manufacturing are in the Northeast or North Central, while places with little manufacturing are in the South or West, irrespective of type and size of place. Generally speaking, a central city or suburb specializing in manufacturing, when located outside the North, is more likely to be in the South than in the West; while a central city or suburb ranking low in manufacturing, when located outside the South or West, is more likely to be in the Northeast than in the North Central Region. For independent cities the situation is reversed. Independent cities specializing in manufacturing, when located outside the

TABLE 116.—PERCENT DISTRIBUTION OF CENTRAL CITIES, SUBURBS, AND INDEPENDENT CITIES, BY REGIONS, BY LEVEL OF SPECIALIZATION IN MANUFACTURING: 1950

Region	Specialization level	
	High	Low
United States, number of places......	249	254
Percent.........................	100.0	100.0
Northeast...............................	51.4	8.3
North Central...........................	37.3	15.0
South...................................	8.9	39.7
West....................................	2.4	37.0

Source: Appendix tables B–18, B–19, and B–20.

North, are more usually in the South; while independent cities ranking low in manufacturing are more often in the North Central Region, if located outside the South or West. Standard metropolitan areas follow the general pattern for independent cities. All large SMA's which specialize in manufacturing are in the Northeast (50 percent) or North Central (50 percent) Regions; the few small SMA's specializing in manufacturing located outside the North (5.6 percent) all are in the South. All small SMA's ranking low in manufacturing are in the West (10.5 percent) or the South (89.5 percent); the few large SMA's ranking low in manufacturing and located outside the West or South (6.2 percent) all are in the North Central Region.

In summary the regional patterns are as follows: For central cities, regardless of size, at least nine-tenths of those specializing in manufacturing are in the Northeast or North Central, while at least three-fourths of those ranking low in manufacturing are in the South. Roughly, the same pattern holds for independent cities and SMA's regardless of size. The pattern is different for suburbs. At least nine-tenths of all suburbs specializing in manufacturing are in the Northeast or North Central Regions, but more of the suburbs ranking low in manufacturing employment are in the West than in the South, regardless of size of suburb. In the subsequent analysis it must be remembered that the effects of manufacturing specialization cannot always be distinguished from other influences related to regional location.

Population composition

Table 117 presents selected demographic comparisons between places ranking high and low in manufacturing specialization. There are proportionately more persons 21 years of age and over in the high ranking

TABLE 117.—AGE, SEX, COLOR, AND MOBILITY OF THE POPULATION, FOR SELECTED STANDARD METROPOLITAN AREAS AND URBAN PLACES, BY METROPOLITAN STATUS, SIZE, AND LEVEL OF SPECIALIZATION IN MANUFACTURING: 1950

[Asterisk (*) denotes difference between high and low groups significant at 0.05 level of probability]

Metropolitan status and size of place	Specialization level	Percent 21 years old and over	Sex ratio	Percent nonwhite	Percent living in same house, 1949 and 1950[1]
Standard metropolitan areas:					
50,000 to 250,000	High	*66.6	*97.1	*2.5	*85.7
	Low	61.8	99.9	17.5	71.6
250,000 or more	High	*67.7	*97.8	6.8	*86.6
	Low	66.0	98.7	14.1	72.9
Central cities:					
Under 100,000	High	68.6	95.0	*3.4	*86.0
	Low	66.9	95.6	12.7	73.9
100,000 or more	High	*69.5	96.8	*10.5	*84.5
	Low	67.6	93.7	20.7	73.7
Suburbs:					
10,000 to 25,000	High	66.3	*99.4	5.5	*87.3
	Low	67.8	94.4	4.3	74.0
25,000 or more	High	*67.7	*100.1	6.3	*85.7
	Low	71.7	89.1	6.0	76.5
Independent cities:					
10,000 to 25,000	High	*66.0	*93.9	*4.2	*83.6
	Low	64.6	99.0	8.0	70.6
25,000 to 50,000	High	*67.8	*93.9	*3.5	*84.4
	Low	66.1	98.0	11.1	69.1

[1] Persons 1 year old and over.

Source: *1950 Census of Population*, Vol. II, *Characteristics of the Population*, Parts 2 to 50, tables 33 and 34.

SMA's, central cities, and independent cities than in the corresponding places ranking low. This difference cannot be accounted for by the fact that more of the nonmanufacturing than of the manufacturing communities also are college communities. The elimination of the college communities does not substantially alter the percentage differences. Some of the difference is accounted for by the fact that the nonmanufacturing community is more likely to have a sizable military population. The differences in military composition are not sufficiently large, however, to account for very much of these differences in population composition, except in the very large places. The somewhat greater average age of the population in manufacturing than in nonmanufacturing communities probably is due to the fact that the rate of migration into manufacturing cities is below that for nonmanufacturing cities. Since the average age of migrants is quite low, one would expect the population in manufacturing cities to be somewhat older. The pattern of age distribution is not the same for suburbs, where the proportion of persons 21 years and older is greater in the nonmanufacturing suburbs.

The sex ratio of the population is lower in SMA's and independent cities which specialize in manufacturing than in those which do not. Manufacturing suburbs, however, have a higher sex ratio than nonmanufacturing suburbs. Since the nonmanufacturing suburb is often only a residential area, the low sex ratio is understandable. There are no significant differences between the sex ratios of central cities with a high and those with a low degree of specialization in manufacturing.

There is a considerably larger proportion of nonwhite persons in nonmanufacturing than in manufacturing SMA's, central cities, and independent cities, but no significant differences are observed for suburbs. These differences in percentage nonwhite clearly reflect the regional pattern of location of places by degree of specialization in manufacturing. Nonmanufacturing SMA's, central, and independent cities are disproportionately located in the South, where the nonwhite population is relatively large. However, the proportion of nonmanufacturing suburbs in the South is below that in the West; hence, there is no clear difference in the percentage nonwhite between manufacturing suburbs and nonmanufacturing suburbs. By contrast, most of the manufacturing cities and SMA's are in the Northeast and North Central Regions, where nonwhite persons comprise a smaller part of the total population.

The stability of residence is considerably greater in manufacturing than in nonmanufacturing communities. At least 10 percent more of the residents over one year of age in cities and SMA's specializing in manufacturing, regardless of size, were classified as nonmovers (percent resident in the same house, 1949 and 1950) than in places lacking specialization in manufacturing. The difference is greater for SMA's and independent cities than it is for central cities and suburbs. The rate of migration and residential mobility combined, therefore, is greater for nonmanufacturing than manufacturing communities. These rather large differences in the stability of residents between manufacturing and nonmanufacturing communities can be accounted for in part by the fact that nonmanufacturing communities more often are communities with colleges and/or large military establishments, where the proportion of nonmovers is somewhat lower, particularly for central and independent cities. In addition, the regional pattern must be kept in mind. The typical manufacturing community is a relatively slowly growing place in the North, while the typical nonmanufacturing community is in the South or West—regions experiencing rapid

urban growth.   It is shown elsewhere in the monograph that the proportion of nonmovers is inversely related to the 1940–50 growth rate.   The
differences between manufacturing and nonmanufacturing communities in
degree of residential stability therefore appear to be linked with regional
differences in urban growth patterns.

Family composition

Table 118 shows the percentage married for males in places ranking
high and low in manufacturing employment.   The differences are very
small and nonsignificant for SMA's, and central and independent cities,
and this finding is not materially altered by the inclusion or exclusion of
college communities in the comparisons.   By contrast, the proportion married is greater in nonmanufacturing than in manufacturing suburbs, regardless of size.   Perhaps the sex ratios favorable to male marriages in nonmanufacturing suburbs account in small part for the somewhat higher
percentages of married men.   Whatever the explanation, it is evident that
nonmanufacturing suburbs—which are often what are called "dormitory
suburbs"—experience a strong selection in favor of married persons.

A household includes all persons who occupy a single dwelling unit.
A dwelling unit, in general, is defined as a group of rooms or a single room
occupied, or intended for occupancy, as separate living quarters by a group
of persons living together or by a person living alone.   The number of

TABLE 118.—MARITAL STATUS OF THE POPULATION AND PERSONS PER HOUSEHOLD, FOR
SELECTED STANDARD METROPOLITAN AREAS AND URBAN PLACES, BY METROPOLITAN STATUS,
SIZE, AND LEVEL OF SPECIALIZATION IN MANUFACTURING: 1950

[Asterisk (*) denotes difference between high and low groups significant at 0.05 level of probability]

Metropolitan status and size of place	Special- ization level	Percent married, male[1]	Persons per household[2]
Standard metropolitan areas:			
50,000 to 250,000	High	68.9	3.38
	Low	67.8	3.42
250,000 or more	High	68.7	*3.37
	Low	68.2	3.27
Central cities:			
Under 100,000	High	68.4	*3.31
	Low	67.9	3.14
100,000 or more	High	67.8	*3.31
	Low	67.9	3.23
Suburbs:			
10,000 to 25,000	High	*68.5	*3.55
	Low	74.1	3.24
25,000 or more	High	*68.4	*3.40
	Low	72.4	3.16
Independent cities:			
10,000 to 25,000	High	70.3	*3.29
	Low	70.1	3.12
25,000 to 50,000	High	69.2	3.23
	Low	69.1	3.13

[1] Excludes from comparisons all places with 25 percent or more of the population 20 to 24 years old
enrolled in school.

[2] The figure shown is the one for the median place in each group.

Source: 1950 Census of Population, Vol. II, Characteristics of the Population, Parts 2 to 50, table 34.

households and the number of occupied dwelling units in the 1950 Census are identical by definition. The average population per household is obtained by dividing the population in households by the number of households, excluding all quasi-households. Table 118 presents the data for the number of persons per household. With the exception of small SMA's, the number of persons per household is greater in manufacturing than in nonmanufacturing places. These differences are small, but in conformity with the observation that industrial workers have larger families than other urban groups.

Economic characteristics

Manufacturing can account for a very large proportion of the economic activity in a community, even when the urban agglomeration is very large. The Detroit, Mich., SMA, with 3,016,197 inhabitants in 1950 had 46.9 percent of all employed persons in manufacturing. For small independent cities, the percentage of persons in manufacturing can be as great as that for Southbridge, Mass., with 16,748 inhabitants in 1950 and 68 percent of all employed persons in manufacturing. By contrast, manufacturing may comprise only a very small proportion of the total economic activity of a community, regardless of the size of the urban agglomeration. The Washington, D. C., SMA, with 1,464,089 residents in 1950, had but 7.3 percent of all employed persons in manufacturing. In some small independent cities, such as the college town of State College, Pa., with 17,227 inhabitants and only 2.7 percent of employed persons in manufacturing, or the mining town of Snyder, Texas, with 12,010 inhabitants and but 2.3 percent of all employed persons in manufacturing, there is almost no reliance on manufacturing for local employment. It seems clear, however, that whenever the employment in manufacturing is very small, some other form of economic specialization, generally, will characterize the community.

The economic characteristics of a community may be affected not only by the presence of manufacturing in general, but also by the specific type of manufacturing, e.g., whether in durable or nondurable goods. For example, women are not employed in large numbers in certain kinds of durable goods manufacture such as primary metal industries, while they are very heavily employed in certain kinds of nondurable goods manufacture, such as food and kindred products or apparel and other fabricated textile products. Statistics, by urban place, are available for employment in these manufacturing industry groups. The systematic examination of these data, though not undertaken here, might be of value in refining the conclusions of this chapter.

Table 119 presents male and female labor force participation rates. The data in table 119 exclude all urban places with 25 percent or more of the persons aged 20 to 24 enrolled in school, since more of the nonmanufacturing than of the manufacturing communities are college communities.

Labor force participation rates also are affected by the ratio of the civilian to the military population. Since there are more nonmanufacturing than manufacturing communities with sizable military establishments, the effect of the military population on these rates also was examined. The elimination of all urban places with large military establishments decreases the rates of participation in the labor force, since the military population is included in the total population 14 years old and over and in the labor force. However, differences in labor force participation between manufacturing and nonmanufacturing communities are not eliminated when all places with substantial military populations are omitted from the comparisons.

The percentages of males in the labor force are greater in central cities, suburbs, and independent cities which specialize in manufacturing than in those which do not, regardless of city size. The same differences exist for

TABLE 119.—PERCENT OF PERSONS IN THE LABOR FORCE BY SEX, FOR SELECTED STANDARD METROPOLITAN AREAS AND URBAN PLACES, BY METROPOLITAN STATUS, SIZE, AND LEVEL OF SPECIALIZATION IN MANUFACTURING: 1950

[Asterisk (*) denotes difference between high and low groups significant at 0.05 level of probability. All places with 25 percent or more of the population 20 to 24 years old enrolled in school are excluded]

Metropolitan status and size of place	Specialization level	Male	Female	Metropolitan status and size of place	Specialization level	Male	Female
Standard metropolitan areas:				Suburbs:			
50,000 to 250,000...	High......	81.7	33.6	10,000 to 25,000....	High......	*83.1	29.7
	Low......	79.7	31.1		Low......	78.4	26.6
250,000 or more.....	High......	81.7	30.9	25,000 or more......	High......	*86.0	32.6
	Low......	79.5	32.8		Low......	79.7	31.9
Central cities:				Independent cities:			
Under 100,000.......	High......	*82.2	35.8	10,000 to 25,000....	High......	*82.3	*35.6
	Low......	76.4	31.3		Low......	75.5	30.7
100,000 or more.....	High......	*82.2	33.7	25,000 to 50,000....	High......	*80.4	34.9
	Low......	79.9	39.5		Low......	78.1	32.6

Source: *1950 Census of Population*, Vol. II, *Characteristics of the Population*, Parts 2 to 50, table 35.

SMA's, although they are not significant. It appears that manufacturing is more conducive to a high rate of male participation in the labor force than are the economic activities, other than mining, which characterize the nonmanufacturing community.

There are no significant differences in labor force participation for women in each type and size of urban place, other than for independent cities with 10,000 to 25,000 inhabitants. In these small independent cities the percentages of females in the labor force are greater in the manufacturing community. The fact that the finding is more clear-cut for males than for females is in accordance with the sex differences in industry of employment observed in the entire urban United States. A somewhat higher proportion of males than of females is employed in manufacturing, while females are found disproportionately in such nonmanufacturing industries as professional services; personal services; finance, insurance, and real estate; and wholesale and retail trade.[1]   The presence of manufacturing in a community is, therefore, likely to stimulate male employment.   The same might hold true for female employment, in the case of certain types of non-durable goods manufactures; however, this possibility is not investigated here.

There is considerable evidence that specialization in manufacturing precludes specialization, or substantial development of employment, in non-manufacturing industries.   Table 120 presents data for employment in certain nonmanufacturing industries: government, mining, transportation, public administration, hotels and lodging places, and entertainment and recreation services.

Places with little employment in manufacturing are much more likely to be centers of public administration as well as centers where government is a major employer than are places with little employment in manufacturing.   The fact that government more often is an employer in nonmanufacturing than in manufacturing centers is not surprising, given the fact that more of the nonmanufacturing centers are also educational centers and military centers, as well as centers of public administration.   Government employs many persons in the public educational system, and, of course, military establishments provide civilian as well as military employment by

TABLE 120.—EMPLOYMENT IN SELECTED NONMANUFACTURING INDUSTRIES, FOR SELECTED STANDARD METROPOLITAN AREAS AND URBAN PLACES, BY METROPOLITAN STATUS, SIZE, AND LEVEL OF SPECIALIZATION IN MANUFACTURING: 1950

[Asterisk (*) denotes difference between high and low groups significant at 0.05 level of probability]

Metropolitan status and size of place	Specialization level	Government workers as percent of all employed persons[1]	Percent of all employed persons in—		Percent of all employed males in—		
			Mining	Transportation	Public administration	Hotels and lodging places	Entertainment and recreation services
Standard metropolitan areas:							
50,000 to 250,000........	High.....	*6.4	0.2	*3.1	*3.1	*0.3	*0.8
	Low......	13.8	1.0	5.7	7.4	1.0	1.2
250,000 or more..........	High.....	*7.7	0.1	*4.3	*3.9	*0.5	*0.9
	Low......	20.2	1.0	6.8	13.0	1.4	1.4
Central cities:							
Under 100,000............	High.....	*6.9	0.1	*2.8	*3.8	*0.4	*0.9
	Low......	14.0	0.8	9.3	7.2	2.1	1.5
100,000 or more..........	High.....	*7.6	*0.1	*4.4	*4.0	*0.5	*1.0
	Low......	21.0	0.6	7.1	13.7	1.5	1.6
Suburbs:							
10,000 to 25,000........	High.....	*6.5	0.2	3.7	*2.8	*0.2	*0.8
	Low......	14.8	1.8	4.7	7.6	0.8	1.7
25,000 or more..........	High.....	*6.3	0.1	4.0	*3.4	*0.2	*0.8
	Low......	13.1	0.5	4.9	7.4	1.0	2.0
Independent cities:							
10,000 to 25,000........	High.....	*6.9	*0.1	*3.0	*3.1	*0.4	*1.0
	Low......	16.4	4.5	6.6	6.1	1.6	1.9
25,000 to 50,000........	High.....	*7.6	0.2	3.7	*3.4	*0.4	*1.0
	Low......	18.3	2.8	5.9	7.8	2.0	2.0

[1] Based on class-of-worker statistics; includes persons who worked for any governmental unit (Federal, State, or local), regardless of the activity which the particular agency carried on.

Source: See table 119.

[1] 1950 Census of Population, Vol. II, Characteristics of the Population, Part 1, table 55, p. 103.

government employers. Table 120 shows that the percentage of persons employed by a government employer is roughly twice as great in nonmanufacturing as in manufacturing communities, regardless of metropolitan status and size of place. The same ratio exists for employment of men in public administration, as for the employment of persons by a government employer, regardless of type and size of place, except that in the large central cities and the large SMA's, about three times as many of the employed males in nonmanufacturing communities as in manufacturing centers are at work in public administration. Of all urban males in the United States, 5.6 percent are employed in public administration.[2] Figure 29 shows that manufacturing centers as a group have a lower proportion in public administration than does the urban United States as a whole, while the reverse is the case for nonmanufacturing communities. It is noted later that urban places which specialize in public administration rank low in manufacturing.

Nonmanufacturing communities are somewhat more likely to be transportation centers than are manufacturing centers. This is somewhat surprising, given the fact that manufacturing requires a rather large volume of transportation of raw materials and manufactured products. Table 121 shows that a significantly smaller proportion of the employed persons in manufacturing centers than in nonmanufacturing centers are employed in transportation, for SMA's, central cities, and small independent cities; and the direction of the difference is the same for all other groups of places. These data do not gainsay the idea that manufacturing centers have a relatively large volume of transportation, but they do indicate that manufacturing centers are not very likely to develop specialization in transportation as well.

FIGURE **29.**—PERCENT OF EMPLOYED MALES IN PUBLIC ADMINISTRATION IN SELECTED STANDARD METROPOLITAN AREAS AND URBAN PLACES, BY METROPOLITAN STATUS AND LEVEL OF SPECIALIZATION IN MANUFACTURING: 1950

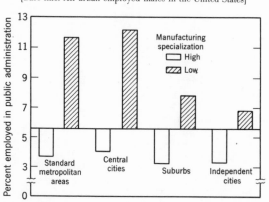

[Base line: All urban employed males in the United States]

Note: See table 119.

[2] *Ibid.*

A sizable proportion of employment in mining also is not very general for urban places of any size, since the conditions which give rise to extractive activities are determined by natural factors which are not distributed geographically in the same way as are all urban places. There appears to be a larger number of places with substantial employment in mining among nonmanufacturing than among manufacturing communities, regardless of type and size of place. However, the differences are statistically significant only for small independent cities.

Figure 30 shows that manufacturing centers provide proportionately fewer opportunities for male employment in hotels and lodging places or in entertainment and recreation services than do nonmanufacturing centers. Since the proportions employed in these industries are small, the differences are not large. Excluding small SMA's, however, the proportion of males employed in entertainment and recreation services in all manufacturing communities is below 1.3 percent (the figure for all urban males in the United States), while that in nonmanufacturing communities is above the United States proportion, regardless of type and size of place. The proportion of males employed in hotels and lodging places is roughly 1 percent greater in communities ranking low in manufacturing than in communities ranking high in manufacturing employment. The number of hotel rooms per 1,000 inhabitants also is much greater in places ranking low than in those ranking high in manufacturing employment, for each group of places (table 121).

TABLE 121.—SCHOOL ENROLLMENT, 1950, AND HOTEL ROOMS AND WHOLESALE AND RETAIL TRADE CHARACTERISTICS, 1948, FOR SELECTED STANDARD METROPOLITAN AREAS AND URBAN PLACES, BY METROPOLITAN STATUS, SIZE, AND LEVEL OF SPECIALIZATION IN MANUFACTURING

[Asterisk (*) denotes difference between high and low groups significant at 0.05 level of probability]

Metropolitan status and size of place	Specialization level	Number of hotel rooms, 1948, per 1,000 inhabitants	Percent enrolled in school, 1950[1]	Per capita sales, 1948 (dollars)	
				Wholesale trade	Retail trade
Standard metropolitan areas:					
50,000 to 250,000	High	...	*10.2	*504	901
	Low	...	4.2	1,184	836
250,000 or more	High	...	13.4	1,335	981
	Low	...	12.2	1,231	949
Central cities:					
Under 100,000	High	*5.9	8.6	*634	1,163
	Low	38.5	14.3	1,389	1,383
100,000 or more	High	*11.4	10.9	*2,051	1,209
	Low	37.3	13.1	1,413	944
Suburbs:					
10,000 to 25,000	High	1.3	*8.4	220	805
	Low	6.9	14.5	293	947
25,000 or more	High	1.2	*8.3	609	1,046
	Low	22.9	18.0	570	1,311
Independent cities:					
10,000 to 25,000	High	*4.5	*5.2	*443	1,137
	Low	17.7	8.2	824	1,351
25,000 to 50,000	High	*7.3	*8.5	613	1,216
	Low	24.6	13.5	988	1,407

[1] Persons 20 to 24 years old; the figure shown is the one for the median place in each group.

Source: *1950 Census of Population*, Vol. II, *Characteristics of the Population*, Parts 2 to 50, table 34; *1948 Census of Business*, Vol. III, *Retail Trade—Areas Statistics*, tables 102 and 103; Vol. V, *Wholesale Trade—Area Statistics*, tables 102 and 103; Vol. VII, *Service Trade—Area Statistics*, table 103C.

FIGURE **30.**—PERCENT OF EMPLOYED MALES IN HOTELS AND LODGING PLACES AND IN ENTER-
TAINMENT AND RECREATION SERVICES IN SELECTED STANDARD METROPOLITAN AREAS AND
URBAN PLACES, BY METROPOLITAN STATUS AND LEVEL OF SPECIALIZATION IN MANUFACTURING:
1950

[Base line: All urban employed males in the United States]

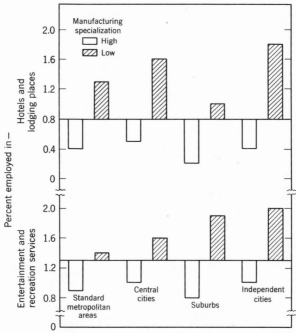

Note: See table 119.

Communities not specialized in manufacturing are more often sites of
large military installations than are manufacturing communities.   Of the
34 SMA's ranked high in manufacturing specialization, only 2 have large
military installations, as defined in Chapter 19, as compared with 15 of
the 34 nonmanufacturing SMA's.   Similarly, none of the 38 manufacturing
central cities has 2,000 or more persons in the Armed Forces, but 12 of
the 38 nonmanufacturing central cities do.   Among suburbs and independent cities, respectively, 3.6 and 1.5 percent of the manufacturing centers
have substantial numbers of military personnel, as compared with 25.3
and 11.4 percent of the corresponding nonmanufacturing places.   These
differences may simply reflect the Federal Government's policy of locating
military installations disproportionately in the South and West, where few
of the manufacturing centers are located.   Nevertheless, they are important
differences from the standpoint of the problem investigated in this chapter,
since a military installation exerts important economic and social influences on the community in which it is located.

Table 121 presents data on the percentage of persons aged 20 to 24
enrolled in school, as an indicator of specialization in higher education.
Independent cities and suburbs which rank low in manufacturing have a

significantly higher proportion of persons aged 20 to 24 enrolled in school than do comparable places which specialize in manufacturing. The direction of the differences is the same for central cities, but it is not statistically significant, while the reverse relationship appears for SMA's. There is, therefore, a tendency for specialization in manufacturing to exclude specialization in higher education unless the unit of functional specialization is a standard metropolitan area.

Per capita wholesale trade and retail sales data are affected by the income level and maintenance requirements of a local population as well as by the metropolitan status and size of a place. It is not surprising, therefore, that no consistent differences are found between manufacturing and nonmanufacturing centers in per capita wholesale and retail trade sales (table 121). Differences in income as well as in type and size of place were controlled in the index of wholesale-retail trade developed for this study. Table 122 presents the percentage distribution by wholesale-retail classification for each group of SMA's and urban places.

Manufacturing communities show relatively little tendency to specialize also in trade as compared with places which rank low in manufacturing. There are, in fact, at least one-third more of the nonmanufacturing than of the manufacturing places specialized in some form of trade, if large central cities and all suburban comparisons are excluded. Among SMA's, for example, only roughly one-fifth of all manufacturing SMA's as compared

TABLE 122.—PERCENT DISTRIBUTION BY WHOLESALE-RETAIL TRADE CLASSIFICATION, 1948, OF SELECTED STANDARD METROPOLITAN AREAS AND URBAN PLACES, BY METROPOLITAN STATUS, SIZE, AND LEVEL OF SPECIALIZATION IN MANUFACTURING: 1950

Metropolitan status and size of place	Specialization level	Number of places	Percent of all classes, by wholesale-retail trade classification[1]						
			All classes	Wholesale trade	Retail trade	Trade center	Maintenance trade center	Non-trade center	Not classified[2]
Standard metropolitan areas:									
50,000 to 250,000	High	18	100	...	17	6	22	50	5
	Low	18	100	17	11	28	33	11	...
250,000 or more	High	16	100	6	6	6	38	44	...
	Low	16	100	12	19	19	31	19	...
Central cities:									
Under 100,000	High	20	100	5	10	15	20	50	...
	Low	19	100	11	10	37	16	16	10
100,000 or more	High	18	100	6	28	11	11	44	...
	Low	19	100	11	21	5	32	21	10
Suburbs:									
10,000 to 25,000	High	55	100	9	9	6	20	27	29
	Low	56	100	9	5	22	21	13	30
25,000 or more	High	27	100	15	4	18	41	22	...
	Low	27	100	4	11	41	15	29	...
Independent cities:									
10,000 to 25,000	High	97	100	4	5	2	25	45	19
	Low	100	100	11	12	30	14	17	16
25,000 to 50,000	High	31	100	...	7	3	32	55	3
	Low	31	100	6	16	23	23	22	10

[1] See Chapter 16 for explanation of classification.
[2] Data for wholesale and/or retail trade not available in the 1948 Census of Business.

Source: Appendix tables B–17 to B–20.

with over one-half of all nonmanufacturing SMA's are specialized in some form of trade. The relative absence of trade in manufacturing places likewise is clearly seen in the comparisons for nontrade centers. More than twice as many of the manufacturing as of the nonmanufacturing places are nontrade centers, if large suburbs are excluded. The lower incidence of trade specialization in manufacturing than in nonmanufacturing places is more marked for wholesale trade and trade centers than for retail trade centers. At least one-tenth of all nonmanufacturing centers also are wholesale trade centers, regardless of type and size of place. For SMA's, central cities, and independent cities, more than twice as many of the nonmanufacturing as of the manufacturing places also specialize in wholesale trade. Suburbs, as expected, are as likely, or more so, to specialize in both manufacturing and wholesale trade as to specialize in wholesale trade only. These are the "industrial" as compared with the "residential" suburbs of large cities. There is very little difference in the proportion of manufacturing as compared with nonmanufacturing places which are specialized also in retail trade. Somewhat more of the nonmanufacturing than of the manufacturing places also are retail trade centers for large SMA, large suburban, and independent city comparisons, but the reverse holds for small SMA and suburban and large central city comparisons. Nonmanufacturing communities are more likely to be trade centers, specializing in both wholesale and retail trade, however, than are manufacturing communities. Except for large central cities, the percentage of nonmanufacturing communities which also are trade centers is considerably larger than the percentage for manufacturing communities. For example, while but 2 percent of all small independent cities specializing in manufacturing also are trade centers, 30 percent of all small independent cities ranking low in manufacturing employment are trade centers, specializing in both wholesale and retail trade. The index of wholesale-retail trade classified places as maintenance trade centers when there is no pattern of over- or underspecialization in either wholesale or retail trade. The data show that independent cities, regardless of size, small central cities, and large suburbs which are manufacturing centers also more often are maintenance trade centers than are nonmanufacturing centers in the comparable groups of places. The reverse pattern seems to hold for large central cities.

Socio-economic status

Pronounced differences in occupational structure are expected in comparing cities and SMA's which are highly specialized in manufacturing with those having very little manufacturing. There are two reasons for this: First, in a specialized manufacturing center a half or more of the employed labor force may be working in manufacturing; hence, the occupational composition of the entire labor force is heavily weighted by the occupational composition of manufacturing workers. Second, in

general, manufacturing industries employ a substantially smaller proportion of white-collar workers than most other major industry groups.   In
the United States as a whole, only 22 percent of the males employed in
manufacturing are in white-collar occupations.   A lower percentage is
observed for only 2 of the other 10 major urban industry groups: 11 percent for mining and 14 percent for construction.   Of all the females
employed in manufacturing, 28 percent work in white-collar occupations.
The only major urban industry group with a lower figure is personal
services with 9 percent.[3]

Figure 31 shows the comparisons between places rated "high" and
"low" on manufacturing specialization with respect to the percentage of
males employed in white-collar occupations.   These data clearly confirm
the expectation that specialized manufacturing centers should have smaller
proportions of white-collar workers than communities lacking such specialization.   The difference is especially large for suburbs, but it is substantial
for SMA's, central cities, and independent cities as well.

The foregoing conclusion can be refined by investigating whether the
low proportion of white-collar workers in specialized manufacturing centers
can be accounted for solely by their concentration of employment in manufacturing.   A negative answer to this question is indicated by the analysis
summarized in table 123.   The problem was approached as follows: In
the entire United States the proportion of white-collar workers among males

FIGURE **31.**—PERCENT OF EMPLOYED MALES IN WHITE-COLLAR OCCUPATIONS IN SELECTED
STANDARD METROPOLITAN AREAS AND URBAN PLACES, BY METROPOLITAN STATUS AND LEVEL
OF SPECIALIZATION IN MANUFACTURING: 1950

[Base line: All urban employed males in the United States]

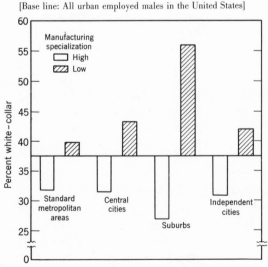

Note: See table 124.

---

[3] Based on data in *1950 Census of Population, op. cit.,* table 134, p. 291.

TABLE **123.**—PERCENT OF EMPLOYED MALES IN WHITE-COLLAR OCCUPATIONS, COMPARED WITH
PERCENT EXPECTED ON THE BASIS OF PERCENT EMPLOYED IN MANUFACTURING, FOR SELECTED
STANDARD METROPOLITAN AREAS AND URBAN PLACES, BY METROPOLITAN STATUS, SIZE, AND
LEVEL OF SPECIALIZATION IN MANUFACTURING: 1950

Metropolitan status and size of place	Special- ization level	Percent in manufac- turing	Percent white-collar workers		
			Expected	Actual	Actual minus expected
Standard metropolitan areas:					
50,000 to 250,000..............	High..........	51.6	32.3	28.1	-4.2
	Low..........	11.8	40.8	36.2	-4.6
250,000 or more................	High..........	49.7	32.7	32.4	-0.3
	Low..........	13.6	40.5	40.6	0.1
Central cities:					
Under 100,000..................	High..........	55.6	31.5	31.3	-0.2
	Low..........	10.9	41.0	41.6	0.6
100,000 or more................	High..........	51.0	32.4	31.4	-1.0
	Low..........	13.2	40.5	43.5	3.0
Suburbs:					
10,000 to 25,000..............	High..........	63.2	29.8	24.5	-5.3
	Low..........	16.6	39.8	57.4	17.6
25,000 or more................	High..........	60.9	30.3	28.1	-2.2
	Low..........	22.6	38.5	55.4	16.9
Independent cities:					
10,000 to 25,000..............	High..........	53.8	31.8	30.6	-1.2
	Low..........	7.9	41.7	41.0	-0.7
25,000 to 50,000..............	High..........	51.3	32.4	31.1	-1.3
	Low..........	8.4	41.6	43.4	1.8

Source:'*1950 Census of Population*, Vol. II, *Characteristics of the Population*, Parts 2 to 50, table 35; see text for source of expected percentages.

employed in manufacturing is 0.2194, and the proportion of white-collar
workers in all other industries, except agriculture, forestry, and fishing, is
0.4337. Hence, for SMA's with 50,000 to 250,000 inhabitants ranking
"high" in manufacturing and having 51.6 percent of all males employed in
manufacturing and 48.4 percent in all other industries, it would be expected that the percentage of white-collar workers would be (0.2194)
(51.6) + (0.4337) (48.4) = 32.3 percent. In fact, only 28.1 percent of
the employed males in this group of SMA's are in white-collar occupations;
hence, the actual proportion of white-collar workers falls short of the
"expected" proportion by 4.2 percentage points.

In the last column of table 123 it may be seen that each of the eight
groups of manufacturing communities has a smaller percentage of white-
collar workers than expected. For six of the eight groups of communities
at a low level of manufacturing specialization, the actual percentage of
white-collar workers exceeds the expected percentage. In the case of independent cities with 10,000 to 25,000 inhabitants, both the high and low
specialization groups have actual percentages of white-collar workers
smaller than the expected, but the figure for the low group is closer to its
expected size than is the one for the group of cities specialized to a high
degree in manufacturing. Only in the case of the smaller SMA's does the
allowance for industrial composition change the comparison of the manufacturing centers with the nonmanufacturing places in regard to the proportion of white-collar workers. These results are based on a somewhat
rough standardization procedure. Nevertheless, they appear to justify the

conclusion that manufacturing centers have low proportions of white-collar workers, not only because the manufacturing industries themselves employ relatively small numbers in white-collar jobs, but also because the concentration in manufacturing exerts an indirect or selective influence on the remainder of the community's occupational structure.

Tables 124 and 125 provide additional details of the comparison between manufacturing centers and nonmanufacturing places with respect to occupational composition. The comparatively large proportion of white-collar male workers in nonmanufacturing communities is accounted for by their significantly greater proportions of men employed as managers, officials, and proprietors, and as sales workers, among the white-collar occupations, and their smaller proportions of operatives and kindred workers in the group of manual occupations, regardless of type and size of place. The differences are not quite as great for the professional, technical and kindred, and the clerical and kindred worker white-collar occupations and the craftsmen, foremen, and kindred worker manual occupations, although many of these differences also are significant for type and size-of-place groups. The larger proportion of male laborers in nonmanufacturing communities (except for suburbs) is somewhat surprising, given the fact that manufacturing industries employ relatively large numbers of laborers. The high proportion of female workers in manual occupations in manufacturing communities is largely due to the marked differences in

TABLE 124.—PERCENT DISTRIBUTION OF EMPLOYED MALES BY MAJOR OCCUPATION GROUP, FOR SELECTED STANDARD METROPOLITAN AREAS AND URBAN PLACES, BY METROPOLITAN STATUS, SIZE, AND LEVEL OF SPECIALIZATION IN MANUFACTURING: 1950

[Asterisk (*) denotes difference between high and low groups significant at 0.05 level of probability. Farm occupations and occupation not reported are omitted]

Metropolitan status and size of place	Specialization level	Professional, techn'l, and kindred workers	Managers, off'ls, and propr's, except farm	Clerical and kindred workers	Sales workers	Craftsmen, foremen, and kindred workers	Operatives and kindred workers	Private household and service workers	Laborers, except farm
Standard metropolitan areas:									
50,000 to 250,000...	High.....	*6.4	*9.5	6.4	*5.8	*22.7	*30.5	*5.8	*7.5
	Low......	8.4	12.4	7.2	8.2	18.0	15.7	7.7	9.4
250,000 or more.....	High.....	8.1	*10.1	*7.7	*6.5	*23.6	*27.8	*6.1	7.4
	Low......	10.2	12.9	9.5	8.0	20.5	15.0	8.1	9.1
Central cities:									
Under 100,000.......	High.....	7.7	*10.0	7.3	*6.3	*22.9	*29.9	*6.5	8.1
	Low......	8.8	15.6	7.5	9.7	20.4	15.3	9.5	9.7
100,000 or more.....	High.....	*7.4	*9.3	*8.2	*6.5	*22.9	*29.9	*7.1	*7.6
	Low......	10.3	13.8	10.5	8.9	19.6	15.2	10.1	10.0
Suburbs:									
10,000 to 25,000....	High.....	*5.9	*7.5	6.9	*4.2	*24.7	*32.1	*5.4	*12.0
	Low......	16.7	21.3	7.8	11.6	17.5	10.3	6.2	5.2
25,000 or more......	High.....	*7.2	*8.8	7.4	*4.7	*25.0	*30.3	*5.9	*9.7
	Low......	15.8	19.6	8.5	11.5	20.0	13.5	7.7	6.2
Independent cities:									
10,000 to 25,000....	High.....	*7.1	*10.8	6.4	*6.3	*21.7	*31.4	*6.2	7.8
	Low......	11.2	14.8	6.0	9.0	19.6	16.6	8.5	8.1
25,000 to 50,000....	High.....	*6.6	*10.8	6.8	*6.9	*22.0	*31.3	*6.8	*7.1
	Low......	11.6	15.5	7.1	9.2	19.1	15.1	10.4	8.6

Source: *1950 Census of Population*, Vol. II, *Characteristics of the Population*, Parts 2 to 50, table 35.

TABLE **125.**—PERCENT OF EMPLOYED FEMALES IN SPECIFIED MAJOR OCCUPATION GROUPS, FOR SELECTED STANDARD METROPOLITAN AREAS AND URBAN PLACES, BY METROPOLITAN STATUS, SIZE, AND LEVEL OF SPECIALIZATION IN MANUFACTURING: 1950

[Asterisk (*) denotes difference between high and low groups significant at 0.05 level of probability]

Metropolitan status and size of place	Special- ization level	Sales, clerical, and kindred workers	Operatives and kindred workers	Private household and service workers
Standard metropolitan areas:				
50,000 to 250,000...............	High..........	31.4	*36.7	*13.2
	Low...........	36.3	9.3	30.1
250,000 or more..................	High..........	39.4	*24.0	*16.9
	Low...........	43.5	9.6	24.3
Central cities:				
Under 100,000...................	High..........	34.2	*34.1	*13.6
	Low...........	38.2	9.4	27.6
100,000 or more..................	High..........	39.5	*24.9	*17.5
	Low...........	43.0	9.1	27.3
Suburbs:				
10,000 to 25,000................	High..........	35.8	*32.5	*14.1
	Low...........	42.1	7.1	23.6
25,000 or more..................	High..........	37.7	*31.0	*13.7
	Low...........	42.0	9.2	22.0
Independent cities:				
10,000 to 25,000................	High..........	*30.3	*34.7	*15.7
	Low...........	38.5	7.6	28.0
25,000 to 50,000................	High..........	32.3	*34.2	*15.8
	Low...........	37.5	6.8	29.5

Source: See table 124.

the percentage of women employed as operatives, as between the manufacturing and the nonmanufacturing communities. The proportion of women working as operatives is from 3 to 5 times greater in manufacturing than in nonmanufacturing communities.

The proportions of men and women employed in private household and service work are higher in nonmanufacturing than in manufacturing communities. For all groups of nonmanufacturing communities, except the smaller suburbs, the percentage of males employed in private household and service work is equal to or above 7.8, which is the figure for all urban males in the United States. All groups of manufacturing communities have less than 7.8 percent employed in these occupations. Similarly, the percentage of females employed in private household and service work in each of the groups of nonmanufacturing communities considerably exceeds the United States figure of 20.6 percent, and it falls well below this mark in each group of manufacturing communities. Without attempting to explain this finding completely, it may be pointed out that manufacturing industries employ relatively small numbers of service workers, and also that a disproportionate number of the nonmanufacturing communities are located in the South, which has a comparatively large proportion of its labor force engaged in private household and other kinds of service work.

Table 126 presents data on three other aspects of socio-economic status: income, educational attainment, and home ownership. The median income of families and unrelated individuals is significantly higher in manufacturing than in nonmanufacturing SMA's, central cities, and independent cities,

TABLE **126.**—MEDIAN INCOME IN 1949 OF FAMILIES AND UNRELATED INDIVIDUALS, EDUCA-
TIONAL ATTAINMENT, AND PERCENT OF OCCUPIED DWELLING UNITS OWNER-OCCUPIED, FOR
SELECTED STANDARD METROPOLITAN AREAS AND URBAN PLACES, BY METROPOLITAN STATUS,
SIZE, AND LEVEL OF SPECIALIZATION IN MANUFACTURING: 1950

[Asterisk (*) denotes difference between high and low groups significant at 0.05 level of probability]

Metropolitan status and size of place	Special- ization level	Median income of families and unrelated individuals[1] (dollars)	Median school years completed[1] — Persons 25 years old and over	Percent of occupied dwelling units owner- occupied
Standard metropolitan areas:				
50,000 to 250,000...............	High...........	*3,140	9.2	55.9
	Low............	2,310	10.2	52.2
250,000 or more.................	High...........	*3,217	9.9	57.6
	Low............	2,694	11.0	52.6
Central cities:				
Under 100,000...................	High...........	*3,287	*9.5	48.8
	Low............	2,568	11.1	53.8
100,000 or more.................	High...........	*3,188	*9.5	50.2
	Low............	2,506	11.2	45.3
Suburbs:				
10,000 to 25,000................	High...........	3,290	*9.0	56.6
	Low............	3,239	12.4	63.3
25,000 or more..................	High...........	3,412	*9.3	53.5
	Low............	3,433	12.2	51.2
Independent cities:				
10,000 to 25,000................	High...........	*2,927	*9.7	56.1
	Low............	2,750	10.8	55.4
25,000 to 50,000................	High...........	*3,012	*9.6	54.9
	Low............	2,568	11.5	52.4

[1] The figure shown is the one for the median place in each group. Excludes from comparisons all places with 25 percent or more of the population 20 to 24 years old enrolled in school.

Source: *1950 Census of Population*, Vol. II, *Characteristics of the Population*, Parts 2 to 50, tables 10 and 37; *1950 Census of Housing*, Vol. I, *General Characteristics*, Part 1, U. S. Summary, table 22, and Parts 2 to 6, table 1.

regardless of size of place. (There are no significant differences for suburbs.) The differences remain even when all places with 25 percent or
more of persons aged 20 to 24 enrolled in school are removed from the
comparisons. It may be that even after removing these communities from
the comparisons, some of the remaining differences in median income are
due to the fact that, on the average, nonmanufacturing communities have
more unrelated individuals in school or in military establishments than
do manufacturing communities. The income of these unrelated individuals
reporting incomes usually is quite small, and it probably reduces the
median income somewhat for families and unrelated individuals.

The differences observed for income run counter to the finding that
manufacturing centers have much smaller proportions of white-collar
workers than do communities with little manufacturing. Probably the
major explanation of this result lies in the concentration of nonmanufacturing communities in the South. The median income in 1949 of all urban
and rural-nonfarm families in the South was about $2,200, whereas the
median was approximately $3,000 in each of the other three regions.[4]

---

[4] *1950 Census of Population, op. cit.*, table 84.

The figure for the South is, of course, lowered by the inclusion of a large proportion of nonwhite families and unrelated individuals. However, it is possible that the income differential in favor of manufacturing centers would not disappear entirely, even if the comparison were standardized for region and color. Although the nonmanufacturing communities have higher proportions of white-collar workers than do manufacturing centers, they also tend to have higher proportions in the lowest paid occupations, laborers and private household and service workers.

The educational level of persons 25 years of age and over is higher in nonmanufacturing than in manufacturing communities, although the differences are not statistically significant for SMA's. For nonmanufacturing suburbs, regardless of size, the median level of educational attainment for the adult population is that of a high school graduate. The median year of school completed, by contrast, is only 9 years in manufacturing suburbs. This difference clearly cannot be attributed to the fact that more of the nonmanufacturing communities are college communities. Excluding college communities from the nonmanufacturing group, the level of educational attainment remains significantly higher than that for manufacturing communities. In any case, undergraduate enrollment does not affect the statistic on educational attainment much, since the number of school years completed is reported only for persons 25 years old and over. Although the enrollment figures for undergraduates in college do not materially affect the educational attainment figures, those of graduate enrollment may affect the statistics slightly. However, the elimination of all communities with a high percentage of persons aged 25 to 29 enrolled in school likewise does not materially alter the fact that the level of educational attainment is considerably lower in manufacturing than in nonmanufacturing communities. The data on educational attainment are consistent with those for occupational composition, suggesting a somewhat lower average socio-economic status level for manufacturing communities.

There are no significant differences in the proportion of home owners between communities which rank high and low in specialization in manufacturing. In no group of SMA's or urban places is the percentage of dwelling units owner-occupied significantly greater for the manufacturing than for the nonmanufacturing communities. There, of course, is no reason to expect that it should be greater.

Summary and conclusions

This chapter examines the relationship between degree of specialization in manufacturing and the demographic, economic, and socio-economic characteristics of communities. The relationship was measured by comparing groups of SMA's and urban places in the upper and lower quintiles on the percentage of employed persons at work in manufacturing. Places in the upper quintile are called manufacturing communities while those in the lower quintile are called nonmanufacturing communities.

Manufacturing communities differ markedly from nonmanufacturing communities in regional location: 88.7 percent of all urban places specializing in manufacturing are in the Northeast and North Central Regions, while 76.7 percent of those ranking low on manufacturing employment are in the South and West. There are proportionately more persons 21 years of age and over in SMA's, central cities, and independent cities with a high than with a low percentage of persons employed in manufacturing. The somewhat lower average age of persons in nonmanufacturing communities can be traced, in part, to such factors as the larger proportion of persons enrolled in college, more military personnel, and a greater rate of in-movement. The stability of residence is much greater in manufacturing than in nonmanufacturing communities, regardless of type and size of place.

The nature of employment and form of economic opportunity differs between communities ranking high and low on manufacturing specialization. The rate of labor force participation, for males, is greater in central cities, suburbs, and independent cities which specialize in manufacturing than in those which do not, regardless of size of place. These differences are not observed for women. The differences in form of economic opportunity between the two types of communities, however, is quite marked. Somewhat more of the employed persons in nonmanufacturing communities than in manufacturing communities are found in industries unrelated to manufacturing. These industries include higher education, public administration, entertainment and recreation, hotels and lodging places, and mining. That specialization in these industries should occur more often in nonmanufacturing than in manufacturing communities is not surprising, since a community with very little manufacturing must find sustenance through other economic activities. It is also true, however, that places which specialize in manufacturing have a lower proportion employed in transportation than those which do not.

The relationship between specialization in wholesale and retail trade and specialization in manufacturing was examined. Specialization in trade occurs with much greater frequency in nonmanufacturing than in manufacturing communities. The differences are particularly marked for the wholesale trade center, trade center, and nontrade center comparisons. This suggests that wholesale trade, like the other minor forms of functional specialization, is not especially linked with manufacturing in location.

An examination of the differences in socio-economic status levels between manufacturing and nonmanufacturing communities leads to the conclusion that manufacturing communities have a somewhat lower general socio-economic level, but a somewhat higher average income level. This is probably due to greater homogeneity in occupation and educational attainment in manufacturing, as compared with nonmanufacturing places. The specific comparisons for educational attainment show that the educational level of persons 25 years old and over is far lower for residents of manufacturing communities than for residents of nonmanufacturing communities.   Nonmanufacturing centers likewise have a much higher proportion of white-collar workers than do the manufacturing centers.   In particular, nonmanufacturing centers show much larger proportions of persons employed as managers, officials, and proprietors, and as sales workers, while manufacturing centers show much larger proportions in the operative and kindred worker occupations.   The median income of families and unrelated individuals nevertheless is greater for manufacturing than for nonmanufacturing communities.   This difference may reflect in part the difference in military and school populations, as well as the regional differential in the location of manufacturing and nonmanufacturing communities.   Some of the difference, however, may be related to the fact that nonmanufacturing centers have proportionately more unskilled workers, while manufacturing communities have fewer workers at either end of the socio-economic status continuum.

CHAPTER 18

CHARACTERISTICS OF TRADE CENTERS

Chapter 16 considered at some length the characteristics of wholesale and retail trade and the nature of specialization in trade in cities with 10,000 inhabitants or more and in standard metropolitan areas. A scheme was developed there for classifying urban communities into nine classes on the basis of their per capita wholesale and retail trade, considered jointly, with allowance for the effects of metropolitan status, community size, and income level. The purpose of this chapter is to determine whether there are demographic, economic, and socio-economic characteristics which distinguish one type of trade center from another, or trade centers from places lacking specialization in trade.

For purposes of a comparative study the ninefold classification was considered unwieldy. Hence, this chapter is based on a condensation of that classification into five classes of communities:

Wholesale trade centers (Ww)
Retail trade centers (Rr)
Trade centers (TC)—combining types TC, TCw, and TCr
Maintenance trade centers (MTC)
Nontrade centers (NT)—combining types NT, NTw, and NTr

Scope and technique of analysis

Wholesale trade, retail trade, trade, maintenance trade, and nontrade centers are compared on some 30 population characteristics. The differences observed were not subjected to tests of statistical significance because of the large amount of clerical work involved. The analysis includes, however, all SMA's and urban places in the United States which had 10,000 inhabitants or more in 1950, except those few for which trade data are lacking. Conclusions are based only on those differences apparently large and consistent enough in subgroup comparisons to be considered significant.

There are some differences in the regional location of types of trade center which may need to be taken into account for the interpretation of specific comparisons. The regional location of urban places in each of the five classes in table 127, of course, differs according to the income level of the population. For all classes of trade center, other than maintenance trade centers, more of the low than of the high income urban places are in

274

TABLE **127.**—PERCENT DISTRIBUTION OF CENTRAL CITIES, SUBURBS, AND INDEPENDENT CITIES, BY REGIONS, BY 1948 WHOLESALE-RETAIL TRADE CLASSIFICATION AND 1949 INCOME LEVEL

Wholesale-retail classification	1949 income level	Number of urban places[1]	Percent of all places, by region				
			United States	North-east	North Central	South	West
Total, five classes.......	High.......	555	100.0	26.1	44.3	9.4	20.2
	Low.........	547	100.0	28.1	21.4	40.6	9.9
Wholesale trade centers.........	High.......	54	100.0	31.5	42.6	9.3	16.6
	Low.........	68	100.0	30.9	10.3	50.0	8.8
Retail trade centers............	High.......	41	100.0	26.8	41.5	2.4	29.3
	Low.........	63	100.0	30.2	20.6	30.2	19.0
Trade centers...................	High.......	153	100.0	18.3	41.8	7.2	32.7
	Low.........	142	100.0	27.5	21.1	40.1	11.3
Maintenance trade centers.......	High.......	164	100.0	22.5	48.8	18.3	10.4
	Low.........	146	100.0	22.6	26.7	7.5	43.2
Nontrade centers...............	High.......	143	100.0	36.4	43.3	12.6	7.7
	Low.........	128	100.0	32.8	21.9	38.3	7.0

[1] Excludes 160 places for which data on trade are not available.

Source: Appendix tables B–18, B–19, and B–20.

the South. Correlatively, fewer of the low income urban places are in the North Central and West, except that more of the low than of the high income maintenance trade centers are located in the West. If comparable income groups are considered, differences in regional location among the types of trade center are not very large. Roughly three-fourths of the high income wholesale trade, retail trade, maintenance trade, and nontrade centers are in the Northeast and North Central States. Only three-fifths of the high income trade centers are in these States, however. About one-half of all low income centers, except wholesale trade centers, are in the Northeast and North Central States, while only two-fifths of the wholesale trade centers are located there. (Compare with the distribution of all urban places, figure 2, p. 31.)

Other differences in regional location among the wholesale-retail classes of urban places may be observed in table 127. Most of the differences are small, however. It is important to note that the association between regional location and income level is such that using income level as a control factor gives a measure of control over the regional location factor as well. Differences by income level, of course, are apt to be as important as regional differences, and income is controlled, roughly, in all comparisons in this chapter.

Standard metropolitan areas show a much greater regional bias in a comparison of the location of types of wholesale-retail trade centers than do urban places, except suburbs. (See figure 18, p. 153, for location of all SMA's.) Among high income SMA's, wholesale trade centers are largely concentrated in the Northeast (71 percent); retail trade centers are largely in the Northeast (50 percent) and North Central (25 percent); maintenance trade centers are mainly in the North Central (60 percent) and Northeast (20 percent); trade centers are predominantly in the North Central (67 percent); and nontrade centers are in the Northeast (30 percent) and North Central (50 percent). Low income SMA's show a quite different pattern. All low income SMA's which are wholesale trade centers are found in the South, as are 55 percent of all maintenance trade centers and 54 percent of all trade and nontrade centers. Only 22 per cent of all SMA's which are retail trade centers are located in the South, however. One-third of all retail trade and nontrade SMA's are in the Northeast. Suburbs show little concentration in the South. Two-thirds or more of all suburbs, except low income suburbs specializing in retail trade, are in standard metropolitan areas of the Northeast or North Central States. Among all low income suburbs, there is relatively greater concentration in the Northeast than in the North Central States, regardless of type of trade specialization, while the reverse is true for high income cities, except wholesale trade centers.

Population composition

Table 128 shows the percentage of the population 21 years old and over and the sex ratio of the population, for the five classes of communities considered in this chapter. In general, retail trade centers (Rr) and trade centers (TC) have somewhat older populations (i.e., a larger proportion of adults) than do wholesale trade centers (Ww), maintenance trade centers (MTC), or nontrade centers (NT). In 11 of the 16 comparisons (4 metropolitan status groups times 2 size-of-place groups times 2 income groups) of the five types of centers, both the Rr and TC places have higher proportions 21 years old and over than the Ww, MTC, or NT places. Eleven groups of Rr places and 10 groups of TC places have a percentage of

TABLE **128.**—AGE AND SEX COMPOSITION OF THE POPULATION BY TYPE OF WHOLESALE-RETAIL TRADE CENTER, 1948, FOR STANDARD METROPOLITAN AREAS AND URBAN PLACES, BY METROPOLITAN STATUS, SIZE, AND 1949 INCOME LEVEL, 1950

Metropolitan status and size of place	1949 income level	Percent of population 21 years old and over					Sex ratio				
		Ww	Rr	TC	MTC	NT	Ww	Rr	TC	MTC	NT
Standard metropolitan areas:											
50,000 to 250,000...	High..	60.4	67.4	65.8	66.3	65.6	100.0	94.2	96.5	98.0	98.2
	Low...	62.1	67.0	64.7	61.3	61.3	95.0	99.1	94.0	97.6	96.7
250,000 or more.....	High..	69.7	70.0	69.0	66.9	66.5	95.0	94.7	97.7	98.8	100.1
	Low...	64.5	68.8	67.2	66.8	64.5	92.2	102.4	94.2	95.8	100.2
Central cities:											
Under 100,000.......	High..	64.9	67.6	68.8	67.0	67.1	99.0	95.3	93.2	94.5	96.8
	Low...	66.3	71.7	68.4	67.0	67.6	88.8	91.0	90.2	94.6	94.4
100,000 or more.....	High..	70.8	71.2	71.2	70.1	68.4	95.3	95.6	94.4	95.3	95.6
	Low...	69.3	69.7	69.5	70.3	65.1	91.9	96.6	91.6	92.2	92.8
Suburbs:											
10,000 to 25,000....	High..	67.1	69.1	69.2	67.7	65.4	95.6	91.0	92.5	94.7	96.4
	Low...	65.2	68.7	68.2	66.0	66.4	97.1	95.0	94.2	96.6	97.4
25,000 or more......	High..	66.9	72.9	71.5	69.4	68.5	100.1	86.6	92.2	94.6	92.5
	Low...	67.9	72.1	71.1	68.2	72.0	96.0	93.6	93.2	94.5	95.0
Independent cities:											
10,000 to 25,000....	High..	64.8	66.9	67.2	65.4	66.0	96.6	93.0	95.3	94.3	95.0
	Low...	62.5	68.1	65.5	65.0	64.1	92.0	91.0	89.9	92.0	96.8
25,000 to 50,000....	High..	63.7	67.9	68.2	67.4	68.4	95.8	92.2	94.8	92.4	95.1
	Low...	64.9	69.6	66.8	66.3	63.5	86.9	96.6	94.0	91.0	102.9

Source: *1950 Census of Population*, Vol. II, *Characteristics of the Population*, Parts 2 to 50, table 33.

adults exceeding that of the entire urban population of the United States (67.9 percent); but only 4 groups of MTC and NT places, and 3 groups of Ww places, have in excess of 67.9 percent aged 21 and over. The factor which TC and Rr places have in common, as contrasted to Ww, MTC, and NT places, is specialization in retailing. Hence, it appears that retail specialization is associated with comparatively high proportions of adults. The contrast is particularly marked between retail trade centers and wholesale trade centers, with the former having the higher proportion of adults in each of the 16 comparisons, and with the difference amounting to at least 4 percentage points in 9 of the comparisons.

The sex ratio comparisons do not fall into any very consistent pattern, and, for the most part, the differences among wholesale-retail classes are small. The safest generalizations appear to be that nontrade centers (NT) tend to have slightly higher sex ratios than the other classes, and that trade centers (TC) have somewhat lower sex ratios than the other classes. The sex ratio is higher for NT places than for TC places in 14 of the 16 group comparisons. But this simply means that TC places have a somewhat greater excess of females than do NT places, because females outnumber males in the United States as a whole. For all but 6 of the 80 groups of places covered in table 128, there is an excess of females.

The variation among types of wholesale-retail centers in the percentage of the population nonwhite is not very systematic in table 129, and seems largely to reflect differences in regional location. Except among suburbs, where there is relatively little variation in the percentage nonwhite, wholesale trade centers tend to have larger proportions of nonwhite persons than do the other types. Suburbs, of course, are not as concentrated in the South as central and independent cities.

The data in table 129 on residential stability indicate that, by and large, nontrade centers are more stable in that they have higher proportions of persons living in the same house in 1949 and 1950 than do centers with any type of trade specialization (TC, Ww, and Rr places). Retail trade centers present the greatest contrast with nontrade centers, having higher percentages of movers in 13 of the 16 comparisons. Maintenance trade centers, as well, seem to have greater residential stability than do places with some retail (Rr and TC), but not wholesale, specialization. These findings are consistent with the opinion that communities where trade is thriving should have more in-migration than places with less trade activity. However, the several exceptions to the finding mean that other factors are also involved.

The proportion of males 14 years old and over who are married (table 130) tends to be slightly lower in nontrade centers than in any of the kinds of centers with trade specialization, except in the cases of large central cities and high income suburbs of both size groups. However, there is little consistent variation among the other four types of centers (Ww, Rr,

TABLE **129.**—COLOR AND MOBILITY OF THE POPULATION BY TYPE OF WHOLESALE-RETAIL TRADE CENTER, 1948, FOR STANDARD METROPOLITAN AREAS AND URBAN PLACES, BY METROPOLITAN STATUS, SIZE, AND 1949 INCOME LEVEL, 1950

Metropolitan status and size of place	1949 in- come level	Percent nonwhite					Percent living in same house, 1949 and 1950[1]				
		Ww	Rr	TC	MTC	NT	Ww	Rr	TC	MTC	NT
Standard metropolitan areas:											
50,000 to 250,000...	High..	4.7	3.5	2.6	6.2	2.9	83.2	82.7	77.6	82.0	83.0
	Low...	24.0	6.7	16.6	19.9	22.1	78.6	79.1	75.4	72.9	79.4
250,000 or more.....	High..	8.0	5.7	9.7	8.2	4.0	87.8	76.5	79.9	82.5	83.0
	Low...	31.7	8.5	13.4	13.9	6.3	78.1	65.4	78.4	79.6	81.8
Central cities:											
Under 100,000.......	High..	2.2	6.6	4.8	7.7	4.4	80.2	79.6	79.6	80.3	84.3
	Low...	26.4	13.3	14.6	13.9	10.2	78.0	87.2	78.2	78.6	82.1
100,000 or more.....	High..	12.3	9.4	10.0	7.2	6.6	86.4	82.4	79.7	81.0	83.4
	Low...	22.7	9.4	14.5	16.3	9.5	84.9	70.7	81.0	77.0	80.7
Suburbs:											
10,000 to 25,000....	High..	2.7	3.4	2.9	2.5	14.5	79.9	84.8	81.9	81.7	82.0
	Low...	4.6	6.7	6.2	7.2	5.4	84.4	82.2	84.9	79.3	86.5
25,000 or more......	High..	6.9	5.8	5.9	2.6	1.2	84.0	83.1	83.4	84.3	84.4
	Low...	5.3	6.0	7.1	12.0	6.0	87.2	74.2	81.1	85.1	80.8
Independent cities:											
10,000 to 25,000....	High..	1.3	3.3	3.3	2.3	4.1	81.5	79.9	75.4	79.4	82.2
	Low...	19.9	7.6	17.1	13.8	11.0	75.3	78.4	76.6	77.7	75.5
25,000 to 50,000....	High..	8.7	1.3	2.4	3.1	2.1	72.5	72.3	77.6	81.2	84.7
	Low...	29.6	14.1	13.5	16.0	11.6	77.2	71.3	75.5	76.0	72.4

[1] Persons 1 year old and over.

Source: *1950 Census of Population*, Vol. II, *Characteristics of the Population*, Parts 2 to 50, tables 33 and 34.

TABLE **130.**—MARITAL STATUS OF THE POPULATION AND PERSONS PER HOUSEHOLD BY TYPE OF WHOLESALE-RETAIL TRADE CENTER, 1948, FOR STANDARD METROPOLITAN AREAS AND URBAN PLACES, BY METROPOLITAN STATUS, SIZE, AND 1949 INCOME LEVEL, 1950

Metropolitan status and size of place	1949 income level	Percent married, males 14 years old and over					Persons per household[1]				
		Ww	Rr	TC	MTC	NT	Ww	Rr	TC	MTC	NT
Standard metropolitan areas:											
50,000 to 250,000...	High...	70.5	70.7	70.4	69.3	68.4	3.49	3.37	3.15	3.30	3.40
	Low....	68.5	64.2	69.0	68.2	67.7	3.56	3.23	3.28	3.56	3.59
250,000 or more.....	High...	66.6	70.0	70.0	68.9	67.5	3.45	3.23	3.19	3.34	3.38
	Low....	71.2	68.0	70.5	67.9	65.8	3.38	3.03	3.25	3.34	3.47
Central cities:											
Under 100,000.......	High...	69.3	71.1	69.8	70.0	68.6	3.22	3.31	3.10	3.28	3.43
	Low....	70.5	62.1	67.0	64.8	66.7	3.41	3.10	3.16	3.22	3.38
100,000 or more.....	High...	66.9	68.2	67.4	67.1	68.5	3.23	3.27	3.11	3.17	3.32
	Low....	66.9	67.2	66.3	68.4	67.6	3.36	2.97	3.29	3.27	3.40
Suburbs:											
10,000 to 25,000....	High...	74.7	71.0	73.5	74.2	76.8	3.37	3.53	3.26	3.33	3.43
	Low....	70.0	68.6	68.3	70.4	66.0	3.56	3.45	3.32	3.29	3.48
25,000 or more......	High...	69.9	71.7	69.4	71.9	73.0	3.46	3.03	3.28	3.25	3.40
	Low....	64.0	68.9	68.6	68.4	66.8	3.35	3.17	3.25	3.36	3.26
Independent cities:											
10,000 to 25,000....	High...	67.4	70.2	70.5	70.6	69.9	3.29	3.11	3.07	3.15	3.25
	Low....	69.3	69.0	69.5	69.1	62.8	3.35	3.05	3.21	3.19	3.20
25,000 to 50,000....	High...	73.3	66.0	68.8	70.3	68.7	3.27	2.99	3.09	3.15	3.23
	Low....	73.1	60.9	65.8	71.2	58.5	3.37	2.98	3.24	3.17	3.28

[1] The figure shown is the one for the median place in each group.

Source: *1950 Census of Population*, Vol. II, *Characteristics of the Population*, Parts 2 to 50, table 34.

TC, and MTC). Some of the differences which appear are due to factors unrelated to the present problem. For example, there is a large difference in the percentage married between Ww and Rr places among the larger, low income independent cities, which is attributable to the fact that none of these wholesale trade centers is a college community, while over half of these retail trade centers are college communities, as defined in Chapter 16.

Table 130 provides data on household size. There is a clear difference between the centers specializing in retail trade (TC and Rr places), on the one hand, and centers lacking such specialization (Ww and NT), on the other. Maintenance trade centers occupy the rank between these two types of centers. Communities with retail specialization have smaller households on the average, as measured by the number of persons per household. This contrast between places specializing in retail trade and those lacking such specialization holds rather consistently among groups of places differing in metropolitan status, size, and income. Despite the consistency of the difference, however, its magnitude is small—around 0.2 or 0.3 persons per household, as a rule.

Economic characteristics

Together, wholesale and retail trade employ a larger proportion (21.9 percent) of the urban working force than any other major industry group except manufacturing (29.4 percent).[1] But workers in retail trade are more than 4 times as numerous as those in wholesale trade: The two industries employ, respectively, 17.6 percent and 4.3 percent of all urban employed persons. A somewhat higher proportion (23.5 percent) of the urban employed women than of the men (21.2 percent) are in trade. Proportionately more of the men than of the women are in wholesale trade, however. While 5.0 percent of all urban employed males are in wholesale trade, only 2.7 percent of all urban employed females are in wholesale trade. The corresponding figures for retail trade are 16.2 percent (males) and 20.8 percent (females). Specialization in wholesale trade may be expected, therefore, to have less effect on female than on male employment, while the opposite relationship might be expected for retail trade. Further, since wholesale employment is so much smaller than retail, the effect of wholesale specialization on total employment may be less pronounced than that of retail specialization.

Trade, historically, was one of the major forces toward urbanization. Prior to the Industrial Revolution most of the major cities of the world were primarily specialized in trade. Even today in the United States, there are many urban places where trade is the major industry group employer. For the most part, places which are defined as specialized in trade in this chapter are places where trade is the major employer. But this is not always the case, particularly for suburbs. Since the types of trade center are here defined by per capita expenditures in trade, there is no necessary lower limit for the percentage employed in trade for an urban place to be considered a trade center, as is true of other systems of functional classification of trade centers. This section examines the way in which economic

---

[1] These and similar statistics below are from *1950 Census of Population*, Vol. II, *Characteristics of the Population*, Part 1, table 55, p. 103.

characteristics vary among the five major classes of the wholesale-retail classification.

The male and female labor force participation rates are presented in table 131 for wholesale trade, retail trade, trade, maintenance trade, and nontrade centers. Labor force participation rates are affected by the size of college enrollment, and there are some differences in the percentage of persons aged 20 to 24 enrolled in school in the several classes of communities. Retail trade and trade centers have somewhat higher percentages of school enrollment than do wholesale trade, maintenance trade and nontrade centers. The same order of difference is not observed, however, for specialization in higher education. That is, retail trade and trade centers are no more often college communities than are wholesale trade, maintenance trade, and nontrade centers. This makes it difficult to control, statistically, college enrollment differences affecting labor force participation rates. Differences in college enrollment, therefore, are introduced only as a factor of interpretation. The ratio of the military to the civilian population also affects labor force participation rates. However, the elimination of all urban places with large military establishments does not alter the pattern of differences observed, even though the size of the differences may be affected somewhat.

The percentage of males in the labor force is greater for trade centers than for retail trade centers in 13 out of 16 comparisons. In the majority of cases, about 2 to 4 percent more of the males 14 years old and over are in the labor force in trade centers than in retail trade centers. The 3 differences in the opposite direction are quite small. These differences cannot be attributed to differences in military population, since retail trade

TABLE **131**.—PERCENT OF PERSONS IN THE LABOR FORCE BY SEX AND TYPE OF WHOLESALE-RETAIL TRADE CENTER, 1948, FOR STANDARD METROPOLITAN AREAS AND URBAN PLACES, BY METROPOLITAN STATUS, SIZE, AND 1949 INCOME LEVEL, 1950

Metropolitan status and size of place	1949 income level	Male					Female				
		Ww	Rr	TC	MTC	NT	Ww	Rr	TC	MTC	NT
Standard metropolitan areas:											
50,000 to 250,000...	High...	81.7	82.8	80.5	80.0	80.5	26.6	33.7	31.7	31.6	30.9
	Low....	75.4	75.0	78.0	79.5	79.6	31.7	34.9	34.1	33.4	32.2
250,000 or more.....	High...	79.1	78.7	82.9	81.5	80.8	31.9	32.5	34.2	30.9	29.2
	Low....	79.8	79.2	80.1	78.7	78.7	30.8	30.5	32.8	34.1	27.6
Central cities:											
Under 100,000.......	High...	80.5	80.0	80.3	81.0	81.2	29.9	28.0	34.3	33.4	31.6
	Low....	78.0	72.4	75.5	78.0	76.5	38.8	34.9	36.5	35.6	32.3
100,000 or more.....	High...	80.5	81.2	80.8	79.5	82.1	34.7	35.8	38.0	35.7	32.7
	Low....	78.3	77.9	78.7	78.7	77.4	34.1	33.9	36.1	35.5	33.3
Suburbs:											
10,000 to 25,000...	High...	84.5	80.5	83.0	82.8	82.7	29.9	28.7	30.5	28.4	25.2
	Low....	79.0	79.0	79.6	78.8	76.8	29.7	29.4	30.8	28.9	29.8
25,000 or more......	High...	84.2	80.1	82.0	83.8	83.1	32.2	33.1	34.4	32.2	30.1
	Low....	76.6	78.9	79.2	80.6	78.8	33.9	32.4	33.1	32.6	32.6
Independent cities:											
10,000 to 25,000....	High...	77.8	80.0	79.9	80.9	80.1	31.3	32.2	33.6	32.0	32.4
	Low....	75.8	72.5	76.5	74.0	68.5	32.7	32.3	35.0	32.5	30.9
25,000 to 50,000....	High...	83.1	75.9	80.2	80.7	79.4	31.2	34.7	34.0	33.0	33.1
	Low....	79.6	65.3	73.2	69.8	70.7	37.3	36.9	34.5	34.9	32.6

Source: *1950 Census of Population*, Vol. II, *Characteristics of the Population*, Parts 2 to 50, table 35.

centers are actually less likely than trade centers to have sizable military populations. Furthermore, the elimination of places with sizable proportions of college enrollment does not change the relationship, because both retail trade and trade centers have sizable college enrolled populations. In general wholesale trade and maintenance trade centers also have higher male labor force participation rates than do retail trade centers, but there are several exceptions. Nonetheless, the pattern of differences in labor force participation rates among types of communities suggests that it is wholesale trade rather than retail trade which increases male employment, a conclusion generally borne out by the data presented in figure 32.

The percentages of women in the labor force are greater in trade centers than in nontrade centers, for each of the 16 comparisons, of which 5 show a difference between trade and nontrade centers of 5 percent or more. Trade centers, also, have somewhat greater female labor force participation rates than do maintenance trade centers for 14 of the 16 comparisons, although the differences are smaller than for the trade and nontrade center comparisons. Table 131 likewise shows somewhat greater female labor force participation rates in trade centers than in wholesale trade centers, except for small, low income central cities; large, low income suburbs; and large, low income independent cities. Finally, trade centers show somewhat greater female labor force participation rates than do retail trade centers for 12 of 16 comparisons. The exceptions are small, low and high income SMA's and large, low and high income independent cities. But, retail trade centers, in turn, seem more favorable to the labor force participation of women than do nontrade centers for 12 of 16 comparisons, with no systematic pattern of exceptions, since the differences are very small. Maintenance trade centers, likewise, seem more favorable to the employment of women than do nontrade centers for 12 of 16 comparisons, although the size of the differences is very small. These comparisons support the observation that trade specialization, particularly in retail trade, is conducive to the employment of women. This is not surprising in view of the heavy demand of retail trade for female employment.

Manufacturing and trade are the largest industry groups in terms of employment. Therefore, it seems unlikely that places which specialize in manufacturing will often specialize in trade, or vice versa. Table 132 presents data for employment in manufacturing for the five types of community. The data show that employment in manufacturing is generally greater in nontrade communities than it is in any type of trade center, except for high income suburbs. Since maintenance trade centers also lack specialization in trade, it is not surprising that employment in manufacturing in most cases is greater in maintenance trade centers than in wholesale, retail, or trade centers.

Nontrade centers uniformly have a greater percentage of persons employed in manufacturing than do retail trade centers. They, likewise, have a greater percentage in manufacturing than do trade centers, in 14 of 16

Figure 32.—Percent of Males 14 Years Old and Over in the Labor Force in Standard Metropolitan Areas and Urban Places Classified as Wholesale Trade Centers (Ww), Trade Centers (TC), and Retail Trade Centers (Rr), by Metropolitan Status and 1949 Income Level: 1950

[Base line: All males 14 years old and over in the United States]

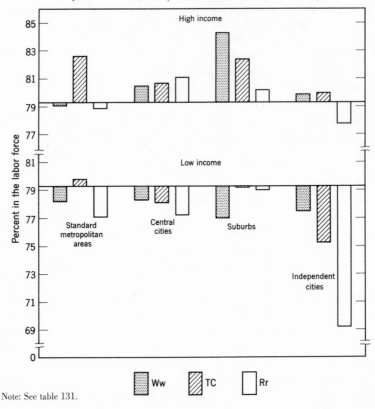

Note: See table 131.

comparisons. The only exceptions are large, high and low income suburbs. Similarly, nontrade centers have higher proportions of employed in manufacturing than do maintenance trade centers in 12 of 16 comparisons, with large, high income suburbs, small suburbs, and large, low income independent cities as exceptions. Finally, nontrade centers show higher proportions of employment in manufacturing than do wholesale trade centers in 12 of 16 comparisons. The exceptions are large, low income central cities; small, high income suburbs; and large suburbs at both income levels. The fact that suburbs provide most of the exceptions for the several comparisons is understandable. Suburban wholesale trade centers have the highest percentage employed in manufacturing in high income suburbs, while nontrade centers have the highest percentage in small, low income suburbs, and maintenance trade centers have the highest percentage in large, low income suburbs. Given the fact that the manufacturing employment data are for place of residence rather than for place of employment, suburbs are expected to show the least consistent pattern. Maintenance trade centers are more likely to have specialization in manufacturing than are retail trade or trade centers, as 13 of the 16 comparisons show maintenance trade centers have the higher proportion of workers employed in manufacturing. In 10 of 16 comparisons, maintenance trade centers, also, show somewhat greater proportions of workers in manufacturing than do wholesale trade centers, with suburbs providing the major exception. It seems relatively clear, then, that specialization in manufacturing, generally, is not associated with specialization in trade. A similar conclusion was reached in Chapter 17.

Yet, when high employment in manufacturing occurs with specialization in trade, it more often occurs with specialization in wholesale trade. Wholesale trade centers have a somewhat greater percentage of employment in manufacturing than do trade centers in 12 of 16 comparisons, and a greater percentage than do retail trade centers in 10 of 16 comparisons. There are no consistent differences in manufacturing employment between retail trade centers and trade centers. The comparisons suggest, therefore, that wholesale trade is more likely to locate with manufacturing than is retail trade, a fact which human ecologists often have noted.[2]

Employment opportunities in manufacturing generally differ among types of trade centers more for high than for low income communities.

TABLE 132.—MANUFACTURING EMPLOYMENT IN 1950 AND VALUE ADDED BY MANUFACTURE IN 1947, BY TYPE OF WHOLESALE-RETAIL TRADE CENTER, 1948, FOR STANDARD METROPOLITAN AREAS AND URBAN PLACES, BY METROPOLITAN STATUS, SIZE, AND 1949 INCOME LEVEL

Metropolitan status and size of place	1949 income level	Workers in manufacturing as percent of all employed persons, 1950					Per capita value added by manufacture, 1947 (dollars)				
		Ww	Rr	TC	MTC	NT	Ww	Rr	TC	MTC	NT
Standard metropolitan areas:											
50,000 to 250,000...	High....	31.0	36.4	25.0	38.0	45.0	544	643	561	871	866
	Low.....	23.0	21.7	19.7	20.5	28.2	507	234	327	339	487
250,000 or more...	High....	32.5	27.4	30.5	41.4	43.9	730	561	767	921	891
	Low.....	18.8	10.7	25.1	23.5	27.2	365	140	521	421	378
Central cities:											
Under 100,000.......	High....	23.4	35.9	42.4	36.0	48.0	615	997	783	809	1,313
	Low.....	28.4	21.4	17.5	25.5	33.3	918	369	431	641	651
100,000 or more.....	High....	31.8	36.3	27.6	33.8	40.8	800	1,105	852	939	985
	Low.....	30.8	15.6	24.3	21.6	26.9	756	313	650	555	528
Suburbs:											
10,000 to 25,000....	High....	34.7	28.5	29.6	34.0	31.3	153	262	188	512	42
	Low.....	37.8	36.2	30.0	34.7	43.7	1,099	643	650	1,009	622
25,000 or more......	High....	47.2	25.7	34.9	37.9	34.7	2,007	111	761	783	540
	Low.....	34.7	32.0	35.6	43.1	32.5	1,046	707	817	851	576
Independent cities:											
10,000 to 25,000....	High....	29.5	29.5	17.9	32.4	42.6	516	387	321	893	805
	Low.....	16.2	20.6	19.4	21.6	21.7	187	297	316	464	366
25,000 to 50,000....	High....	22.4	23.1	19.3	33.4	43.7	555	508	588	1,061	1,215
	Low.....	20.6	9.6	18.3	23.3	22.4	366	221	432	445	367

Source: *1950 Census of Population*, Vol. II, *Characteristics of the Population*, Parts 2 to 50, table 35; *1947 Census of Manufactures*, Vol. III, *Statistics by States*, table 2 for each State.

[2] See, for example, E. W. Burgess, "The Growth of the City: An Introduction to a Research Project," in *The City*, by R. E. Park, E. W. Burgess, and R. D. McKenzie, University of Chicago Press, Chicago, 1926.

This is probably related to the fact that manufacturing occurs with much greater frequency in high than in low income communities.[3] In some cases, e.g., in high income independent cities, the percentage employed in manufacturing is roughly 25 points higher in nontrade than in trade centers. By comparison there is a difference of only 5 percentage points for small, low income independent cities and a 14-point difference for large, low income independent cities.

The data for per capita value added by manufacture are not entirely consistent with those for employment in manufacturing. Nontrade and maintenance trade centers generally have a somewhat greater per capita value added by manufacturing than do trade centers (Ww, Rr, and TC), particularly when the suburban comparisons are excluded. There are, nevertheless, numerous exceptions. Since dollar volume in manufacturing is affected to a large degree by the nature of the manufactured product, the observed differences between employment and per capita findings may be due to differences in kinds of manufacture in the several classes of trade community. The statistics on per capita value added by manufacture, for suburbs in particular, suggest this may be true. This problem is not explored here.

Trade not infrequently occurs with other nonmanufacturing industries.[4] The question naturally arises, whether a particular type of trade center is more selective of a particular kind of nonmanufacturing industry than are the other types. Tables 133 and 134 present data for employment in certain nonmanufacturing industries: government, mining, transportation, public administration, hotels and lodging, and entertainment and recreation. Table 135 presents data on the percentage of persons aged 20 to 24 enrolled in school, as an indicator of specialization in higher education.

Specialization in trade is not particularly associated with employment in public administration or work for a government employer. It is somewhat surprising that the percentage of government employees does not vary more for the types of trade community, given the facts that employment in higher education is greater in retail trade and, particularly, trade centers than in wholesale trade and nontrade centers, and that government often is a major employer of persons who operate educational institutions. It does seem that retail trade centers may tend to have somewhat more persons with a government employer than wholesale trade centers, and a similar difference appears for male employment in public administration; but the exceptions are so numerous as to make the conclusion doubtful. If suburbs are excluded, it seems that nontrade centers generally have fewer employed males in public administration than do retail trade, wholesale trade, maintenance trade, or trade centers. The differences are quite

---

[3] See Chapter 22.

[4] See, for example, the relationship of trade to nonmanufacturing in the classification of Victor M. Jones (Chapter 16, footnote 7).

small in some cases and a number of exceptions occur. The finding is not unreasonable, in that places with low employment in manufacturing are much more likely to be centers of public administration than are places with high employment in manufacturing, and nontrade centers rank high in manufacturing employment. Suburbs also tend to be the only major exception to the higher employment in manufacturing in nontrade centers than in other types of trade community.

There is substantial linkage between specialization in public administration and military specialization. Since there is very little association between specialization in trade and employment in public administration,

TABLE 133.—PERCENT OF EMPLOYED PERSONS IN SELECTED NONMANUFACTURING INDUSTRIES BY TYPE OF WHOLESALE-RETAIL TRADE CENTER, 1948, FOR STANDARD METROPOLITAN AREAS AND URBAN PLACES, BY METROPOLITAN STATUS, SIZE, AND 1949 INCOME LEVEL, 1950

Metropolitan status and size of place	1949 income level	Government workers as percent of all employed persons[1]				
		Ww	Rr	TC	MTC	NT
Standard metropolitan areas:						
50,000 to 250,000.............	High........	13.3	6.2	9.6	8.3	8.4
	Low........	11.6	15.1	9.6	10.4	11.8
250,000 or more................	High........	9.0	10.6	9.4	8.6	7.6
	Low........	10.3	12.8	9.5	17.8	11.9
Central cities:						
Under 100,000.................	High........	16.3	10.6	10.9	8.8	7.9
	Low........	11.0	11.6	12.9	13.6	11.0
100,000 or more................	High........	8.8	11.7	9.6	8.6	8.1
	Low........	9.3	13.4	10.5	10.5	13.7
Suburbs:						
10,000 to 25,000.............	High........	7.3	8.1	8.6	9.1	8.7
	Low........	9.1	9.1	10.6	10.7	9.6
25,000 or more................	High........	8.0	10.1	8.2	9.5	8.8
	Low........	9.5	10.4	9.0	8.0	10.1
Independent cities:						
10,000 to 25,000.............	High........	13.6	11.2	11.0	9.0	8.3
	Low........	13.3	11.5	11.3	12.1	17.8
25,000 to 50,000.............	High........	8.3	19.1	10.6	9.1	7.4
	Low........	9.3	16.5	12.4	11.1	20.4

Metropolitan status and size of place	1949 income level	Percent of all employed persons in--									
		Mining					Transportation				
		Ww	Rr	TC	MTC	NT	Ww	Rr	TC	MTC	NT
Standard metropolitan areas:											
50,000 to 250,000.	High...	0.1	0.1	0.5	0.3	0.2	7.2	3.5	5.7	5.8	3.6
	Low....	0.8	0.1	1.3	1.3	0.5	7.3	4.1	6.5	4.9	7.3
250,000 or more...	High...	0.4	0.4	0.3	0.3	0.3	5.9	4.6	7.2	4.4	4.3
	Low....	3.2	0.1	0.6	1.4	6.9	9.6	5.8	7.3	5.8	5.9
Central cities:											
Under 100,000.....	High...	0.1	0.4	0.3	0.3	0.1	14.7	6.5	5.2	5.6	3.8
	Low....	0.4	...	1.3	0.8	0.2	6.1	4.8	6.8	6.1	8.9
100,000 or more...	High...	0.1	0.1	0.2	0.4	0.2	6.8	5.5	6.7	6.1	6.1
	Low....	0.3	0.1	0.2	0.6	1.1	7.4	5.8	7.2	5.5	5.2
Suburbs:											
10,000 to 25,000..	High...	0.6	0.1	0.6	0.1	0.5	5.3	3.5	5.3	5.3	3.8
	Low....	0.2	0.2	3.8	1.1	3.6	6.7	3.7	5.3	4.6	5.5
25,000 or more....	High...	0.1	0.2	0.1	0.1	0.1	5.4	4.0	4.6	4.9	4.6
	Low....	0.1	0.5	0.8	0.6	0.1	8.7	3.1	3.9	5.0	5.5
Independent cities:											
10,000 to 25,000..	High...	1.5	1.8	1.7	2.2	1.5	5.7	5.5	7.0	5.2	5.2
	Low....	2.2	2.9	0.7	1.4	3.1	5.8	5.1	5.3	5.9	4.7
25,000 to 50,000..	High...	5.5	0.4	2.6	0.6	0.1	6.0	4.0	6.4	6.8	4.9
	Low....	0.2	0.2	0.3	1.1	1.0	8.7	3.7	7.7	5.3	3.9

[1] Based on class-of-worker statistics; includes persons who worked for any governmental unit (Federal, State, or local), regardless of the activity which the particular agency carried on.

Source: *1950 Census of Population,* Vol. II, *Characteristics of the Population,* Parts 2 to 50, table 35.

it is not surprising, then, that a separate tabulation of the association between specialization in trade and the location of large military establishments shows very little association. There is somewhat less likelihood that
a large military installation will locate in a retail trade or a wholesale
trade center than in a trade center, maintenance trade center, or a nontrade center.

Employment in transportation is associated with specialization in wholesale trade more than with specialization in retail trade (figure 33) or a
relative absence of trade. Employment in transportation is greater for
wholesale trade than retail trade centers for all groups of places but small,
low income SMA's. These differences for employment in transportation
generally are rather substantial, in view of the relatively small percentage
of persons employed in transportation in all urban areas. In the case of
small, high income central cities, the difference is as much as 8 percent.

FIGURE 33.—PERCENT OF EMPLOYED PERSONS IN TRANSPORTATION IN STANDARD METROPOLITAN
AREAS AND URBAN PLACES CLASSIFIED AS WHOLESALE TRADE CENTERS (Ww), TRADE CENTERS
(TC), AND RETAIL TRADE CENTERS (Rr), BY METROPOLITAN STATUS AND 1949 INCOME
LEVEL: 1950

[Base line: All urban employed persons in the United States]

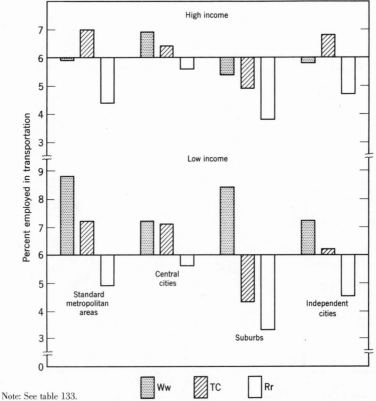

Note: See table 133.

TABLE **134.**—PERCENT OF EMPLOYED MALES IN SELECTED NONMANUFACTURING INDUSTRIES BY TYPE OF WHOLESALE-RETAIL TRADE CENTER, 1948, FOR STANDARD METROPOLITAN AREAS AND URBAN PLACES, BY METROPOLITAN STATUS, SIZE, AND 1949 INCOME LEVEL, 1950

Metropolitan status and size of place	1949 income level	Public administration				
		Ww	Rr	TC	MTC	NT
Standard metropolitan areas:						
50,000 to 250,000	High	9.9	3.0	4.6	3.6	4.3
	Low	4.8	6.7	4.5	5.5	6.1
250,000 or more	High	5.1	5.8	5.1	4.3	3.5
	Low	5.9	8.8	5.6	10.8	3.3
Central cities:						
Under 100,000	High	11.0	5.4	5.1	4.6	4.1
	Low	5.1	8.3	6.5	6.0	5.6
100,000 or more	High	5.1	7.4	5.4	5.4	4.3
	Low	5.9	8.6	6.5	5.8	8.9
Suburbs:						
10,000 to 25,000	High	3.5	3.5	4.3	4.7	4.6
	Low	4.5	4.0	4.9	6.0	4.4
25,000 or more	High	4.8	4.9	4.2	5.4	4.5
	Low	5.7	4.6	4.9	4.2	7.4
Independent cities:						
10,000 to 25,000	High	6.4	4.2	4.9	4.0	3.6
	Low	5.4	5.0	4.7	5.0	4.7
25,000 to 50,000	High	3.8	6.9	5.2	4.5	4.0
	Low	4.4	4.9	8.0	5.4	5.6

Metropolitan status and size of place	1949 income level	Hotels and lodging places					Entertainment and recreation services				
		Ww	Rr	TC	MTC	NT	Ww	Rr	TC	MTC	NT
Standard metropolitan areas:											
50,000 to 250,000	High	0.4	0.4	0.7	0.5	0.4	0.9	1.2	1.1	0.9	0.8
	Low	0.7	2.1	0.8	0.8	0.6	0.9	1.3	1.3	1.0	1.0
250,000 or more	High	0.8	0.7	0.8	0.5	0.4	1.2	2.5	1.2	1.0	0.9
	Low	0.8	2.8	1.0	0.8	0.7	1.4	2.3	1.1	1.1	0.9
Central cities:											
Under 100,000	High	0.5	0.5	0.8	0.8	0.4	1.1	1.0	1.1	1.1	0.9
	Low	0.8	8.6	1.2	1.0	0.8	1.2	1.6	1.5	1.2	1.1
100,000 or more	High	1.1	0.6	1.1	0.7	0.4	1.3	1.0	1.2	1.0	0.9
	Low	0.8	2.3	1.1	0.9	0.9	1.1	2.0	1.3	2.8	1.3
Suburbs:											
10,000 to 25,000	High	0.2	0.3	0.3	0.3	0.2	1.4	1.2	1.6	1.4	1.1
	Low	0.5	0.4	0.6	0.5	0.4	0.7	1.4	1.1	1.4	1.1
25,000 or more	High	0.2	0.3	0.4	0.3	0.3	0.8	1.4	1.6	1.5	1.1
	Low	0.6	2.6	0.5	0.3	0.8	1.0	2.2	1.1	1.0	1.0
Independent cities:											
10,000 to 25,000	High	0.6	0.6	1.4	0.6	0.6	1.2	1.1	1.8	1.2	1.1
	Low	0.8	1.1	1.0	0.9	1.3	1.6	1.7	1.6	1.4	1.5
25,000 to 50,000	High	0.6	1.2	1.0	0.6	0.4	1.5	1.1	1.7	1.1	1.0
	Low	0.8	2.8	1.2	1.2	1.1	1.3	2.2	1.8	1.6	1.4

Source: See table 133.

More often, it is 3 or 4 percent. Employment in transportation, likewise, is greater for wholesale trade than nontrade centers in all comparisons except those for small, low income SMA's and central cities. These differences also are quite large. The percentage employed in transportation in wholesale trade centers appears, generally, to be somewhat greater than in trade and maintenance trade centers, but the exceptions are more numerous. There seems, in fact, to be a rough rank order of types of trade centers by percentage employed in transportation: Wholesale trade centers have the highest proportion employed in transportation, followed by trade centers, maintenance trade centers, nontrade centers, and retail trade centers. Among the 16 comparisons, however, there are a rather large number of shifts in rank. Nevertheless, the comparisons closely support the hypothesis that wholesale trade centers and trade centers have a higher percentage employed in transportation than do retail trade, maintenance trade, or nontrade centers, since wholesale trade requires more transport facilities and access to a large geographical network of transportation than does retail trade.

A sizable proportion of employment in mining is infrequent in large communities. The occurrence of mining also is dependent on natural conditions which give rise to extractive communities. Hence, there is no particular reason to assume that a particular class of trade community would be more selective of mining than others. This does not gainsay the possibility that communities which specialize in mining may attract certain kinds of trade more often than others. The problem is not examined here. The data in this chapter show no consistent relationship between employment in mining and type of trade center. Even for independent cities, where mining contributes a greater proportion of total employment than elsewhere, no consistent differences are observed in mining employment by type of trade center.

Employment in hotels and lodging places, or in entertainment and recreation services, is only a small proportion of the total employment in an urban place. Only 0.8 percent of all urban males are employed in hotels and lodging places and 1.3 percent in entertainment and recreation services.[5] The differences among trade communities with respect to employment in these industries, therefore, will be small. Employment in hotels and lodging places and in entertainment and recreation is greater in retail trade and trade centers than in wholesale trade or nontrade centers, regardless of metropolitan status, size, and income level of the population. Maintenance trade centers usually occupy the intermediate rank. These findings are partly explained by the frequent occurrence of entertainment and recreation in conjunction with retail eating and drinking places and undoubtedly with other retail as well. Entertainment and recreation is an export commodity somewhat like retail trade. It may also be conjectured that the comparatively high proportion employed in hotels and lodging places in places with retail specialization (Rr and TC) results from a stimulation of transiency by retail trade. If a city exports retail trade, it probably does so in large part through sales to visitors and temporary residents.

The percentage of persons aged 20 to 24 enrolled in school may be taken as a rough indicator of the degree to which a place offers employment in higher education and opportunities for study in college and/or professional schools. Summary figures on school enrollment of college-age persons in table 135 show that the centers with retail specialization (Rr and TC) generally outrank the communities without retail specialization (Ww, MTC, and NT), though there are several exceptions to this

---

[5] *1950 Census of Population, op. cit.*

generalization. The proportion of "college communities" (25 percent or more of persons 20 to 24 years old enrolled in school) is not consistently high in any of the trade community groups, however.

TABLE 135.—SCHOOL ENROLLMENT OF PERSONS 20 TO 24 YEARS OLD BY TYPE OF WHOLESALE-RETAIL TRADE CENTER, 1948, FOR STANDARD METROPOLITAN AREAS AND URBAN PLACES, BY METROPOLITAN STATUS, SIZE, AND 1949 INCOME LEVEL, 1950

Metropolitan status and size of place	1949 income level	Percent of persons 20 to 24 years old enrolled in school[1]				
		Ww	Rr	TC	MTC	NT
Standard metropolitan areas:						
50,000 to 250,000............	High........	10.3	13.3	12.2	10.3	12.2
	Low........	10.9	13.0	12.4	12.8	8.5
250,000 or more..............	High........	13.4	14.5	13.9	14.0	10.7
	Low........	10.1	10.8	13.2	14.0	9.9
Central cities:						
Under 100,000................	High........	16.9	7.0	12.5	8.6	7.1
	Low........	11.2	21.6	21.4	14.5	9.3
100,000 or more..............	High........	14.1	14.6	14.5	14.8	12.8
	Low........	11.8	13.2	18.0	12.4	10.6
Suburbs:						
10,000 to 25,000.............	High........	11.7	21.4	13.7	13.8	16.6
	Low........	9.7	14.0	9.3	9.7	8.8
25,000 or more..............	High........	11.4	23.7	13.3	12.4	15.5
	Low........	12.9	7.9	12.5	7.7	9.7
Independent cities:						
10,000 to 25,000.............	High........	7.5	5.3	6.9	5.9	4.8
	Low........	8.9	8.4	10.0	9.8	9.6
25,000 to 50,000.............	High........	5.3	13.4	10.5	10.2	7.6
	Low........	7.6	24.5	16.2	11.8	18.0

[1] The figure shown is the one for the median place in each group.

Source: *1950 Census of Population*, Vol. II, *Characteristics of the Population*, Parts 2 to 50, table 34.

Socio-economic status

The comparison of cities varying in kind and degree of specialization in trade is expected to reveal rather marked differences in occupational structure, for three reasons. First, a city which is specialized in trade will have a fairly large proportion of the employed labor force in wholesale and/or retail trade. Its occupational structure, therefore, is rather heavily weighted by the occupational composition of workers in wholesale and retail trade. Second, wholesale and retail trade employ substantially larger proportions of white-collar workers than most other industry groups. In the United States as a whole, 61.8 percent of all males employed in wholesale and retail trade are in white-collar occupations. The figures are 62.6 and 61.6 percent for wholesale and retail trade, respectively. A higher percentage of male white-collar workers is observed for only 2 of the other 10 major urban industry groups: 81.9 percent for finance, insurance, and real estate; and 71.3 percent for professional and related services. Almost the reverse relationship is true for employed women. Of all employed women in wholesale and retail trade, 69.3 percent are in white-collar occupations. The only major urban industry groups with a lower percentage of white-collar workers for women are personal services with 9 percent, and manufacturing with 28 percent. Nonetheless, since 64.3 percent of all female employment in wholesale and retail trade is in white-collar occupations, the white-collar effect is large. Third, the specific occupation group composition of wholesale trade differs from that of retail trade. Somewhat more of the men in retail trade (31.4 percent) than in wholesale trade (24.4 percent) are managers, officials, and proprietors; and more of the men in wholesale (10.7 percent) than in retail (3.7 percent) are clerical and kindred workers. More of the men in wholesale trade (20.8 percent) than in retail trade (14.2 percent) are operatives and kindred workers, and the proportion of laborers also is somewhat greater (8.0 and 3.6 percent, respectively). But the proportion of male service workers is greater in retail trade (11.3 percent) than in wholesale trade (1.2 percent). Among women, there is a higher proportion of white-collar workers in wholesale trade (75.2 percent) than in retail trade (68.5 percent). Among female workers there are large differences in the percentage of clerical and kindred workers and in sales workers; 63.8 percent of all women in wholesale trade as compared with only 18.0 percent in retail trade are clerical and kindred workers, while 38.0 percent of all women in retail trade are sales workers, compared with only 4.2 percent in wholesale trade. There are more managers, officials, and proprietors among women in retail trade (11.5 percent) than in wholesale trade (5.3 percent). The manual worker differences for women are similar to those for men. More of the women in wholesale trade are operatives (20.8 percent) than in retail trade (4.2 percent) while female service workers comprise a much greater proportion in retail trade (25.4 percent) than in wholesale trade (1.1 percent).[6] In brief, the differences in occupation composition between wholesale and retail trade are the same for women as for men, except for sales workers. The differences between wholesale and retail trade are greater for women than for men, however.

Table 136 shows the comparisons between the five classes of trade centers with respect to the percentage of males in white-collar occupations. The percentage of male white-collar workers, generally, is greater in retail trade and trade centers than in wholesale trade, maintenance trade, and nontrade centers. The low percentage of white-collar workers for nontrade and maintenance trade centers is consistent with the above data on occupation composition of industry groups, but the low percentage for wholesale trade centers does not follow from the occupation composition of wholesale trade. Some other factors must be considered. First, wholesale trade generally has less effect on total employment than does retail trade. Second, certain industries with a low proportion of white-collar workers tend to locate with wholesale trade. This is true of transportation, for example. Third, the difference between wholesale trade centers and places specializing in retail trade varies by metropolitan status. Whole-

---

[6] The foregoing statements are based on data in *1950 Census of Population*, Vol. II, *Characteristics of the Population*, Part 1, table 134, pp. 290, 291.

TABLE **136.**—Percent of Employed Males in White-Collar Occupations by Type of Wholesale-Retail Trade Center, 1948, for Standard Metropolitan Areas and Urban Places, by Metropolitan Status, Size, and 1949 Income Level, 1950

Metropolitan status and size of place	1949 income level	Wholesale-retail classification				
		Ww	Rr	TC	MTC	NT
Standard metropolitan areas:						
50,000 to 250,000............	High........	29.8	38.3	37.1	31.6	28.6
	Low.........	33.4	34.4	37.0	33.5	28.9
250,000 or more..............	High........	40.8	41.4	39.5	33.9	29.8
	Low.........	35.4	40.9	38.9	37.8	32.9
Central cities:						
Under 100,000...............	High........	36.2	34.3	40.7	36.4	31.7
	Low.........	37.7	37.0	41.7	38.6	30.3
100,000 or more..............	High........	40.8	35.9	40.3	38.2	33.8
	Low.........	36.2	42.0	39.8	41.3	36.5
Suburbs:						
10,000 to 25,000.............	High........	50.0	63.8	51.3	49.6	59.0
	Low.........	28.8	36.1	34.0	33.3	29.7
25,000 or more..............	High........	32.2	60.7	43.6	42.2	51.2
	Low.........	32.9	41.2	35.6	31.0	37.2
Independent cities:						
10,000 to 25,000.............	High........	33.6	35.1	40.3	35.0	31.7
	Low.........	36.9	38.1	39.8	38.4	37.5
25,000 to 50,000.............	High........	37.5	40.5	42.0	36.7	31.1
	Low.........	40.2	44.2	41.6	38.8	38.1

Source: *1950 Census of Population*, Vol. II, *Characteristics of the Population*, Parts 2 to 50, table 35.

sale trade centers are more likely to rank low in white-collar employment if they are suburbs or independent cities than if they are central cities.

While white-collar employment is generally greater for retail trade and trade centers than it is for wholesale trade, maintenance trade, and non-trade centers, there is some variation by metropolitan status. Among SMA's and suburbs, Rr places tend to have slightly higher proportions of white-collar workers than do TC places, while the reverse holds for three groups of central cities and three groups of independent cities. Among central cities there are only small and inconsistent differences among the Ww, Rr, TC and MTC classes, but all four do tend to have higher proportions of white-collar workers than NT centers. But among suburbs, Ww and MTC places have consistently the lowest proportion of white-collar workers.

The relationship between the percentage of males in all white-collar occupations and type of center tends to hold for three of the four major occupation groups in the white-collar category, i.e., professional, technical, and kindred workers; managers, officials, and proprietors; and sales workers. Table 137 reveals a general tendency for the highest proportion in each of these occupations to be found in the Rr or TC places and lower proportions in the Ww, MTC, and NT places. NT places, generally, have the lowest proportion in each occupation group, except among suburbs. There are, of course, several exceptions to these tendencies. The pattern is different for clerical and kindred workers. In 12 of 16 comparisons Ww places have a higher proportion of male clerical workers than do Rr places. This is no doubt related to the fact that a larger proportion of workers in wholesale trade are clerical workers than is true of retail trade.

TABLE **137.**—PERCENT OF EMPLOYED MALES IN MAJOR WHITE-COLLAR OCCUPATION GROUPS BY TYPE OF WHOLESALE-RETAIL TRADE CENTER, 1948, FOR STANDARD METROPOLITAN AREAS AND URBAN PLACES, BY METROPOLITAN STATUS, SIZE, AND 1949 INCOME LEVEL, 1950

Metropolitan status and size of place	1949 income level	Professional, technical, and kindred workers					Managers, officials, and proprietors, except farm				
		Ww	Rr	TC	MTC	NT	Ww	Rr	TC	MTC	NT
Standard metropolitan areas:											
50,000 to 250,000	High..	6.0	10.4	8.2	7.6	6.8	10.1	14.3	12.4	10.5	8.8
	Low...	7.3	8.8	7.4	7.1	6.0	11.6	11.8	13.1	12.2	10.3
250,000 or more	High..	10.0	11.0	9.7	8.8	7.2	13.4	13.8	12.6	10.3	9.7
	Low...	7.4	9.3	8.7	10.0	6.2	12.6	15.7	12.4	11.0	13.8
Central cities:											
Under 100,000	High..	7.4	7.7	8.8	9.0	8.0	12.7	12.5	14.0	11.8	10.4
	Low...	7.8	7.9	9.0	9.4	5.6	13.4	13.0	14.0	12.6	11.3
100,000 or more	High..	9.1	8.3	8.9	9.2	7.5	13.1	11.6	12.5	11.7	10.4
	Low...	7.6	9.3	9.0	10.1	8.2	10.8	15.0	12.1	13.7	12.2
Suburbs:											
10,000 to 25,000	High..	14.2	19.9	14.6	14.2	17.0	17.1	25.5	18.5	16.8	21.5
	Low...	6.2	9.5	8.3	8.1	7.4	9.6	11.9	12.1	11.2	9.1
25,000 or more	High..	8.2	19.2	12.4	11.8	14.0	10.2	20.1	14.5	12.8	17.7
	Low...	7.5	9.9	8.5	7.4	10.4	9.6	15.9	12.3	10.0	11.0
Independent cities:											
10,000 to 25,000	High..	7.6	8.0	8.4	7.7	7.7	12.2	12.6	15.6	13.2	11.2
	Low...	7.9	8.8	8.2	8.7	11.7	14.1	14.3	15.2	14.4	12.4
25,000 to 50,000	High..	8.2	10.3	9.0	7.9	6.7	13.9	14.2	15.4	12.9	10.9
	Low...	6.8	13.6	9.6	8.4	10.7	15.5	15.3	15.0	14.3	13.3

Metropolitan status and size of place	1949 income level	Clerical and kindred workers					Sales workers				
		Ww	Rr	TC	MTC	NT	Ww	Rr	TC	MTC	NT
Standard metropolitan areas:											
50,000 to 250,000	High..	7.5	6.4	7.6	7.1	7.2	6.2	7.2	8.9	6.4	5.8
	Low...	6.8	6.2	7.2	6.2	6.0	7.7	7.6	9.3	8.0	6.6
250,000 or more	High..	9.6	7.7	9.2	7.9	6.7	7.8	8.9	8.0	6.9	6.2
	Low...	7.7	6.7	9.3	9.8	6.4	7.7	9.2	8.5	7.0	6.5
Central cities:											
Under 100,000	High..	9.5	7.3	8.2	7.8	7.5	6.6	6.8	9.7	7.8	5.8
	Low...	7.5	8.3	8.2	8.0	6.5	9.0	7.8	10.5	8.6	6.9
100,000 or more	High..	10.6	8.4	9.8	9.2	8.6	8.0	7.6	9.1	8.1	7.3
	Low...	10.1	7.7	9.8	8.4	7.9	7.7	10.0	8.9	9.1	8.2
Suburbs:											
10,000 to 25,000	High..	8.8	7.5	8.6	9.1	8.0	9.9	10.9	9.6	9.5	12.5
	Low...	7.6	7.2	6.9	7.5	7.6	5.4	7.5	6.7	6.5	5.6
25,000 or more	High..	8.4	9.3	8.2	9.6	8.8	5.4	12.1	8.5	8.0	10.7
	Low...	9.4	7.2	7.1	7.6	8.7	6.4	8.2	7.7	6.0	7.1
Independent cities:											
10,000 to 25,000	High..	6.7	6.8	6.6	6.4	6.6	7.1	7.7	9.7	7.7	6.2
	Low...	5.9	5.9	6.0	6.0	5.8	9.0	9.1	10.4	9.3	7.6
25,000 to 50,000	High..	7.0	6.9	7.8	7.6	7.0	8.4	9.1	9.8	8.3	6.5
	Low...	7.7	6.2	7.1	6.9	6.4	10.2	9.1	9.9	9.2	7.7

Source: See table 136.

It follows from the foregoing that wholesale trade, maintenance trade, and nontrade centers generally have larger proportions of manual workers than do retail trade and trade centers. Table 138 compares the five types of trade community with respect to the percentage in each of four major occupation groups in the manual category. Although the proportion of male craftsmen, foremen, and kindred workers is large, its variation by type of trade center is slight and does not explain the pattern for all manual occupations. The major variation is for operatives and kindred workers, but a similar pattern holds for laborers; i.e., higher proportions among NT, Ww, and MTC places than among Rr and TC places. This pattern is perhaps related to the fact that NT and MTC places employ comparatively large numbers of workers in manufacturing, while for the Ww places it may be the fact that larger proportions of wholesale workers are operatives and laborers than is true of retail. The pattern for male private household and service workers is the reverse. Retail trade centers and trade centers tend, generally, to have higher proportions of service workers than do wholesale trade centers, maintenance trade centers, and nontrade centers. This means that the pattern for service workers resembles that of the white-collar occupations more than it does that of the remaining manual occupations.

Table 139 shows the comparisons among the type of trade centers with respect to the percentage of women employed in three important occupation groups. Disregarding suburbs, there is a clear pattern for trade centers to have the highest proportion of female sales, clerical, and kindred

TABLE **138.**—PERCENT OF EMPLOYED MALES IN MAJOR MANUAL OCCUPATION GROUPS BY TYPE OF WHOLESALE-RETAIL TRADE CENTER, 1948, FOR STANDARD METROPOLITAN AREAS AND URBAN PLACES, BY METROPOLITAN STATUS, SIZE, AND 1949 INCOME LEVEL, 1950

Metropolitan status and size of place	1949 income level	Craftsmen, foremen, and kindred workers					Operatives and kindred workers				
		Ww	Rr	TC	MTC	NT	Ww	Rr	TC	MTC	NT
Standard metropolitan areas:											
50,000 to 250,000.........	High..	23.1	21.2	21.2	21.7	22.7	24.5	22.1	20.0	25.9	28.8
	Low...	19.2	18.4	19.1	19.3	21.6	20.2	18.5	19.1	20.1	23.3
250,000 or more...........	High..	20.3	22.4	22.1	23.3	23.1	20.6	19.1	19.8	27.1	27.3
	Low...	20.1	22.8	20.7	20.7	21.4	20.6	13.0	19.5	20.3	26.9
Central cities:											
Under 100,000.............	High..	23.7	24.4	21.7	22.2	23.8	22.5	22.3	20.9	24.6	27.0
	Low...	18.6	19.2	18.6	19.8	23.0	22.7	18.2	19.5	21.6	26.4
100,000 or more...........	High..	19.4	22.0	21.3	22.1	22.6	21.8	24.7	20.5	22.9	27.1
	Low...	20.5	21.2	19.8	20.2	21.4	22.6	15.8	19.6	19.2	23.3
Suburbs:											
10,000 to 25,000..........	High..	21.8	13.8	20.2	22.1	19.8	17.0	11.8	15.7	16.7	13.4
	Low...	24.6	23.4	22.5	23.8	22.4	26.6	21.0	22.8	23.2	30.0
25,000 or more...........	High..	25.1	17.2	20.8	24.2	21.5	23.5	11.2	20.7	21.2	17.4
	Low...	22.2	21.0	22.0	22.9	24.1	25.5	19.9	23.8	27.2	22.0
Independent cities:											
10,000 to 25,000..........	High..	21.2	22.8	20.7	21.7	22.3	25.9	23.2	19.2	25.8	27.9
	Low...	19.1	19.9	19.5	19.9	19.0	20.4	21.2	19.7	21.5	22.3
25,000 to 50,000..........	High..	21.7	23.2	20.0	22.1	22.5	24.4	18.3	19.8	25.5	29.2
	Low...	19.0	18.6	20.1	19.5	18.8	21.0	12.8	18.4	20.8	21.3

Metropolitan status and size of place	1949 income level	Private household and service workers					Laborers, except farm				
		Ww	Rr	TC	MTC	NT	Ww	Rr	TC	MTC	NT
Standard metropolitan areas:											
50,000 to 250,000.........	High..	5.2	6.0	6.0	6.2	6.2	7.9	7.0	6.9	7.9	7.5
	Low...	6.8	8.9	7.2	7.0	6.6	9.9	6.9	8.8	9.7	11.5
250,000 or more...........	High..	8.7	7.1	7.7	6.2	5.7	7.4	6.6	8.1	6.6	9.1
	Low...	7.8	9.5	7.3	10.6	6.3	13.2	8.1	8.6	8.6	9.7
Central cities:											
Under 100,000.............	High..	6.7	6.5	7.2	7.0	6.6	9.6	10.3	7.3	8.2	9.4
	Low...	8.8	17.2	9.4	8.8	7.5	10.4	6.9	9.0	9.5	10.7
100,000 or more...........	High..	9.9	7.8	8.9	7.7	7.1	6.9	8.4	7.8	7.7	8.5
	Low...	9.2	10.6	10.0	8.8	8.7	9.9	8.5	9.4	8.8	8.8
Suburbs:											
10,000 to 25,000..........	High..	4.3	4.8	5.3	4.6	3.6	5.1	4.3	6.2	5.5	3.3
	Low...	6.3	6.8	7.2	6.4	6.1	10.3	10.7	10.8	10.3	10.4
25,000 or more...........	High..	6.3	6.0	7.0	5.8	4.8	10.9	3.6	6.7	5.7	4.0
	Low...	8.4	8.7	7.4	7.1	7.1	9.8	8.0	8.9	10.7	8.0
Independent cities:											
10,000 to 25,000..........	High..	6.8	7.4	7.6	6.5	6.6	7.6	7.6	8.4	8.2	9.0
	Low...	8.7	7.7	7.9	7.7	8.7	10.3	9.0	9.6	9.3	9.0
25,000 to 50,000..........	High..	6.5	8.1	8.0	7.0	6.9	8.0	8.4	7.7	6.4	8.4
	Low...	8.2	12.0	9.4	9.0	10.2	9.5	9.4	8.5	9.6	9.3

Source: See table 136.

TABLE **139.**—PERCENT OF EMPLOYED FEMALES IN SELECTED MAJOR OCCUPATION GROUPS BY TYPE OF WHOLESALE-RETAIL TRADE CENTER, 1948, FOR STANDARD METROPOLITAN AREAS AND URBAN PLACES, BY METROPOLITAN STATUS, SIZE, AND 1949 INCOME LEVEL: 1950

Metropolitan status and size of place	1949 income level	Sales, clerical, and kindred workers					Operatives and kindred workers				
		Ww	Rr	TC	MTC	NT	Ww	Rr	TC	MTC	NT
Standard metropolitan areas:											
50,000 to 250,000	High...	39.9	34.3	43.6	36.7	35.5	15.8	23.2	12.1	22.2	28.5
	Low....	31.5	33.5	33.7	31.1	27.8	19.2	24.1	18.7	19.1	22.7
250,000 or more..	High...	40.5	41.9	44.5	42.5	36.1	23.1	17.2	16.9	19.1	24.9
	Low....	36.7	37.1	41.4	41.8	29.9	12.0	9.8	15.8	16.9	26.5
Central cities:											
Under 100,000....	High...	43.6	41.7	45.1	38.4	37.4	12.6	14.3	14.6	19.4	25.1
	Low....	29.6	33.6	36.5	35.5	30.8	24.0	20.4	16.2	20.4	29.1
100,000 or more..	High...	42.2	40.6	45.0	42.5	41.5	22.0	23.5	16.1	19.7	26.4
	Low....	37.0	37.7	41.6	38.8	35.2	22.5	14.2	16.4	17.4	24.0
Suburbs:											
10,000 to 25,000.	High...	47.5	39.5	45.7	47.4	47.9	15.0	9.2	11.1	13.6	10.9
	Low....	37.3	37.2	36.6	38.6	37.2	25.9	17.8	21.2	18.3	31.5
25,000 or more...	High...	43.6	45.4	42.1	47.6	46.8	26.3	8.7	17.3	17.9	16.3
	Low....	39.5	38.5	36.0	36.0	41.5	28.1	14.0	22.9	26.0	18.6
Independent cities:											
10,000 to 25,000.	High...	37.7	34.8	40.0	36.3	33.0	19.8	19.0	13.2	21.5	27.3
	Low....	30.7	31.8	30.7	31.7	31.7	14.4	20.8	17.9	19.7	18.7
25,000 to 50,000.	High...	38.6	38.4	40.2	38.5	35.2	12.5	12.4	14.0	19.9	29.8
	Low....	29.1	34.0	34.2	31.6	31.5	19.5	8.2	14.6	20.0	19.6

Metropolitan status and size of place	1949 income level	Private household and service workers				
		Ww	Rr	TC	MTC	NT
Standard metropolitan areas:						
50,000 to 250,000..............	High........	20.3	20.5	20.5	19.7	15.5
	Low.........	27.7	20.3	26.5	28.6	27.9
250,000 or more................	High........	16.6	17.8	18.0	18.3	17.8
	Low.........	31.5	28.5	22.3	22.0	19.7
Central cities:						
Under 100,000..................	High........	19.8	21.0	20.4	20.8	17.9
	Low.........	27.6	27.4	24.7	23.7	21.1
100,000 or more...............	High........	16.8	16.7	19.1	18.8	17.4
	Low.........	22.5	25.8	22.7	22.9	21.1
Suburbs:						
10,000 to 25,000..............	High........	14.4	26.0	19.1	14.6	17.1
	Low.........	15.4	21.0	19.4	19.8	13.7
25,000 or more................	High........	11.9	18.3	17.8	13.5	13.8
	Low.........	14.0	23.4	18.4	18.7	16.3
Independent cities:						
10,000 to 25,000..............	High........	20.1	20.5	23.0	20.6	18.6
	Low.........	33.7	24.5	28.7	26.2	25.9
25,000 to 50,000..............	High........	26.9	22.7	21.4	19.7	15.8
	Low.........	32.5	31.2	27.0	27.7	26.4

Source: See table 136.

workers, and for nontrade centers to have the lowest proportion. There is no consistent difference between wholesale trade and retail trade centers, but maintenance trade centers usually have a higher percentage of female sales, clerical, and kindred workers than either type of place. The generally high standing of TC places is readily explained as due to the large proportion of sales and clerical workers employed in trade, and the relative absence of trade in NT places doubtless accounts for their low proportion of sales and clerical workers. Although no difference between Ww and Rr centers appears from the data shown here, there would doubtless be a difference if sales workers were separated from clerical workers. Wholesaling employs clerical workers in greater numbers than sales workers, while the reverse is true of retailing. Among suburbs the relative positions of TC and NT places are virtually reversed, although MTC places also rank high. This reversal noted for suburbs is not readily explained, but is probably related to suburban patterns of residential specialization.

The proportion of females employed as operatives and kindred workers is generally highest in NT and MTC places, no doubt because these places generally have more manufacturing than do places specializing in trade. The percentage of operatives tends to be higher in Ww than in Rr or TC places, but the differences are not as large or as consistent as might be suggested by the fact that 20.8 percent of all females employed in whole-saling are operatives and kindred workers, as compared with only 4.2 percent of females in retail trade.[7] Women, however, comprise only a relatively small proportion of the total employed in wholesale as compared with retail trade, and this fact may obscure the comparisons somewhat.

The only clear-cut finding with respect to the percentage of females employed as private household and service workers is that nontrade centers generally rank below the other four types of centers. A partial explanation may be made again by reference to the greater volume of manufacturing employment in NT places, but it must be remembered that MTC places likewise have a high percentage employed in manufacturing. It is somewhat surprising that Ww places do not more consistently rank below Rr and TC places in the percentage of private household and service workers, since 25.4 percent of females in retail are service workers, as compared with only 1.1 percent of those in wholesale.[7] The relationship may be obscured by the regional factor. It appears as expected for 6 of the 8 comparisons for high income groups, but not for the low income groups. Low income places often are in the South, where the proportion of private household workers is high.

Table 140 presents data on two other aspects of socio-economic status: educational attainment and home ownership. The data on educational attainment, like those for occupational composition, present a contrast between places with retail specialization (Rr and TC) and those without retail specialization (Ww, MTC, and NT). The former generally have somewhat higher levels of educational attainment. The most pronounced contrast, however, is between retail trade centers and wholesale trade centers, with the Rr places outranking the Ww places in 14 out of 16 comparisons. These differences seem easily related to differences in the occupational composition of the classes of trade centers discussed above. They are not due, primarily, to differences in the occupational composition of wholesale as compared with retail trade, however, since the percentage of white-collar workers in the two types of places is very similar. The differences may also be affected by the fact that the retail trade centers generally have a somewhat larger proportion of persons 20 to 24 years old enrolled in

[7] *Ibid.*, p. 291.

TABLE **140.**—EDUCATIONAL ATTAINMENT AND PERCENT OF OCCUPIED DWELLING UNITS OWNER-OCCUPIED BY TYPE OF WHOLESALE-RETAIL TRADE CENTER, 1948, FOR STANDARD METROPOLITAN AREAS AND URBAN PLACES, BY METROPOLITAN STATUS, SIZE, AND 1949 INCOME LEVEL, 1950

Metropolitan status and size of place	1949 in-come level	Median school years completed[1]					Percent of occupied dwelling units owner-occupied				
		Ww	Rr	TC	MTC	NT	Ww	Rr	TC	MTC	NT
Standard metropolitan areas:											
50,000 to 250,000...	High..	10.6	11.2	10.9	10.0	9.2	67.5	59.1	63.5	63.2	58.5
	Low...	8.8	9.1	10.2	9.4	8.7	50.6	52.6	54.0	50.0	51.9
250,000 or more.....	High..	9.5	10.3	11.2	10.2	10.3	41.2	54.4	50.4	59.9	64.4
	Low...	8.5	11.6	10.7	9.5	8.8	46.2	53.3	54.4	51.5	55.9
Central cities:											
Under 100,000.......	High..	10.5	10.4	10.6	9.9	9.5	58.7	58.4	58.4	57.4	54.6
	Low...	9.1	9.2	10.5	9.1	9.4	47.0	36.1	48.1	45.5	49.2
100,000 or more.....	High..	9.9	9.5	11.0	10.6	10.4	29.9	53.3	47.8	49.5	51.8
	Low...	8.7	11.0	9.9	9.3	9.3	46.5	47.9	41.8	47.4	47.6
Suburbs:											
10,000 to 25,000....	High..	11.7	12.6	12.1	11.9	12.3	67.0	72.4	63.8	69.8	80.6
	Low...	10.1	10.8	10.2	9.5	9.1	58.1	61.3	52.8	57.4	54.4
25,000 or more......	High..	9.1	12.4	10.8	11.4	12.0	45.2	57.2	50.0	53.3	67.2
	Low...	10.0	10.6	9.2	9.5	10.8	42.5	44.8	47.7	48.2	52.6
Independent cities:											
10,000 to 25,000....	High..	10.1	10.2	9.7	10.3	11.0	57.2	56.1	56.1	59.7	58.5
	Low...	9.0	10.2	9.8	9.8	9.7	52.6	57.2	51.0	54.5	57.0
25,000 to 50,000....	High..	10.8	12.1	11.1	10.4	9.6	53.3	55.5	53.9	59.0	56.5
	Low...	9.0	11.3	9.9	9.9	10.1	50.4	53.6	49.6	52.8	49.6

[1] Persons 25 years old and over. The figure shown is the one for the median place in each group.

Source: *1950 Census of Population*, Vol. II, *Characteristics of the Population*, Parts 2 to 50, table 34; *1950 Census of Housing*, Vol. I, *General Characteristics*, Part 1, U. S. Summary, table 22, and Parts 2 to 6, table 1.

school than do wholesale trade centers, as this holds in 12 of the 16 comparisons in table 135. The data for home ownership are not consistent with those for the two major socio-economic status variables of occupation composition and level of educational attainment. A general tendency may be noted for NT, Rr, and MTC places to rank higher on home ownership than TC or Ww places. Thus, home ownership appears to be related to a relative absence of wholesaling. An explanation for this finding is not easy to suggest, since it does not conform entirely with the other findings on socio-economic status. The fact that the comparisons for trade centers are controlled for income may mean that the element of socio-economic status involved in home ownership is largely eliminated.

Summary and conclusions

This chapter compares the demographic, economic, and socio-economic characteristics of five major classes of trade community: wholesale trade centers, retail trade centers, trade centers, maintenance trade centers, and nontrade centers. The regional location of the types of trade center differs according to the income level of the population. More of the low than of the high income places are in the South, except for maintenance trade centers. If comparable income groups are considered, however, differences in regional location among the types of trade center are not very large.

Comparisons among the types of trade center and of each with those lacking specialization in trade show that the degree of specialization in retail trade determines a large number of the observed differences between types of trade and nontrade communities. The major contrast is between communities which specialize in retail trade, either as retail trade or trade centers, and those which do not, i.e., wholesale trade, maintenance trade, and nontrade centers. This is not surprising, given the fact that retail trade employs substantially greater proportions of persons than does wholesale trade, and is, therefore, expected to exert a more discernible impact on an urban community.

The contrast between specialization in retail trade and the absence of it is observed for the following comparisons: Rr and TC have (1) somewhat older populations; (2) somewhat smaller households, on the average; (3) somewhat greater labor force participation rates for women, but not for men; (4) a somewhat higher percentage enrolled in college; (5) higher proportions of employed males in hotels and lodging places; (6) higher proportions of employed males in entertainment and recreation services; (7) greater proportions of white-collar workers (and correlatively, smaller proportions of manual workers); (8) higher proportions of male professional, technical, and kindred workers; managers, officials, and proprietors; sales workers; and private household and service workers; and (9) somewhat higher levels of educational attainment than do Ww, MTC, or NT places.

Despite its generally small effect on total employment, specialization in wholesale trade appears to have a discernible impact on the social morphology of communities which specialize in wholesale trade. This is apparent in the following conclusions: (1) Wholesale trade specialization increases the proportion of males in the labor force over that produced by retail specialization; (2) transportation accounts for more of the total employment in Ww and TC than in Rr, MTC, or NT centers; and (3) the percentage of employed males who are clerical and kindred workers is greater in Ww than in Rr communities.

The absence of trade specialization likewise conditions the social morphology of communities. This can be inferred from the following statement of relationships: (1) nontrade centers have higher proportions of persons living in the same house in 1949 and 1950 than do centers with trade specialization, and maintenance trade centers have higher proportions than do retail trade or trade centers, but not wholesale trade centers; (2) the proportion of males 14 years old and over who are married tends to be slightly lower in nontrade centers than in centers with trade specialization; (3) nontrade and maintenance trade centers have a greater percentage of persons employed in manufacturing than do Rr, Ww, or TC communities, except for Ww and TC suburban comparisons noted above; (4) there are higher proportions of male operatives and kindred workers among NT, MTC, and Ww places than among Rr and TC places; (5) the proportion of females employed as operatives and kindred workers is generally highest in nontrade and maintenance trade centers. The differences between non-trade and maintenance trade communities and centers of trade specialization probably arise in large part from the higher percentages employed in manufacturing in the former, although some minor types of functional specialization also are associated with a relative absence of trade.

CHAPTER 19

MINOR TYPES OF FUNCTIONAL SPECIALIZATION

Urban communities are basically similar in that there is some employment in each of the major industry groups in almost every community. This is because every urban community not only has the productive function of exporting goods, services, and capital to a hinterland, but it must also maintain itself. The labor force producing for export has to be housed, fed, entertained, educated, moved between residence and workplace, protected and governed, and provided with a variety of additional services. Estimates indicate that more than one-half of the employed persons in an urban place are employed in the maintenance of the local population. Hildebrand and Mace estimated that roughly 64 percent of the employed persons in Los Angeles in September 1947 were engaged in production for the local market, and Hoyt estimated that about 68 percent in the New York metropolitan region in 1940 were engaged in producing for or servicing residents of the region.[1] A rather large proportion of the output in any relatively large urban place then goes to maintain the local population. This seems particularly the case for the output in trade and the minor forms of industrial activity. At the same time, however, some urban places become specialized in one or more of these maintenance activities, so that it becomes an export function. A city, thus, may specialize in offering economic functions, such as transportation and wholesale trade, governmental services, professional services, such as health and education facilities, and leisure activities, such as amusements, entertainment, or recreation. To specialize in any of these functions, however, does not exclude the possibility that there are sizable proportions of employed persons in other productive or maintenance industries.

Manufacturing and retail trade provide the major sources of employment in most standard metropolitan areas and urban places in the United States, if residential suburbs are excluded. These industries, in fact, accounted, respectively, for 29.4 percent and 17.6 percent of the total urban employ-

---

[1] George H. Hildebrand and Arthur Mace, Jr., "The Employment Multiplier in an Expanding Industrial Market: Los Angeles County, 1940–47," *Review of Economics and Statistics*, August 1950; and *The Economic Status of the New York Metropolitan Region in 1944*, The Regional Plan Association, Inc., New York, 1944, table 4, p. 6.

ment in 1950.[2] They are, therefore, considered major forms of economic specialization in this study, although a far greater volume of trade than of manufacturing, relatively, is consumed locally.   All other types of specialization are considered minor forms of economic specialization, because they seldom account for a majority of the employed in an urban place.   This chapter examines the effect of five such minor forms of industrial specialization on the social morphology of the community in which the specialization occurs: a professional service, higher education; a commercial service, transportation; leisure services, as in entertainment and recreation; and two governmental services, public administration and military national defense.

Minor types of functional specialization defined

Urban communities differ in the extent to which they offer opportunities for higher education, if by higher education is meant that beyond the secondary school level in a college, university, or professional school. Some urban communities are entirely lacking in these educational facilities beyond the secondary school level, while others become known as centers of higher education.   This study employs an operational definition of functional specialization in higher education which is based on the distributions of SMA's and urban places by the percentage of all persons in the age interval 20 to 24 enrolled in school.   Specialization in higher education is defined in terms of enrollment in institutions of higher education, but it is assumed that differences in percentage enrolled reflect differences in industrial specialization of employment.   An urban place or SMA is said to be specialized in higher education if it falls in the upper quintile of the distribution, or if about 19 to 20 percent or more of its population 20 to 24 years old is enrolled in school.   For convenience of expression, places in the upper quintile on the percentage of persons aged 20 to 24 in school are called "college communities."

Many of the cities founded before the Industrial Revolution were centers of administration.   Throughout much of the civilized world both ecclesiastical and state administration were a major basis for founding cities and perpetuating them.   In the modern world, these cities more often have been built around the uniquely governmental functions of the nation-state and its governing units.   These governmental functions are commonly referred to as public administration.   They include legislative, judicial, and most executive agency activities allied with the definition, execution, and administration of public law.   An SMA or urban place is considered to be functionally specialized in public administration, if it falls in the upper decile on the distribution of places by the percentage of employed males working in public administration.   The upper decile for each group

---

[2] *1950 Census of Population*, Vol. II, *Characteristics of the Population*, Part 1, table 55, p. 103.

of urban places is defined by roughly 8 to 10 percent of the employed males in public administration.

Transportation, like communication, is a major prerequisite for extensive urbanization. Much of modern industrial specialization in urban places would not be possible without a highly developed transportation system to facilitate the exchange of goods and services between specialized places. Transportation also links a city with its hinterland, and it makes possible the rapid movement of people and goods within urban agglomerations. Almost all large urban places, therefore, require some employment in transportation. Not all places, however, develop specialization in transportation, itself. Generally, the transportation of people and goods by auto, rail, air, or water transport becomes a specialized function of a place, (1) when the place is a collection point for distribution to a large number of places, (2) when it is located at the points of change from one transportation form to another, or (3) when the form of transportation is necessarily or conveniently serviced at that point. Specialization in transportation may be said to occur when the industrial effort in transportation is largely given over to the movement of people and goods created by extralocal, rather than local demand. From an operational point of view it is difficult to separate the proportion of the work force required for the local movement of people and goods from that required for extralocal movement, as data are not enumerated in such a way as to permit their separation. The crude indicator of the export function of transportation used in this chapter defines specialized transportation centers as those in the upper decile of the distribution of places by the percentage of all employed persons working in transportation in 1950.

The typical military center in the contemporary United States is an SMA or urban place which serves as a host community to a military installation. The location of these military establishments is determined by Federal executive and legislative authority. It, therefore, is less likely that an ecologically competitive relationship with other places in an area leads to military specialization in a particular place. The number and size of military installations fluctuate with national defense policies. The effect of the installation on the host community, therefore, also will vary with these policies. The effect which the military establishment has on the economic base of the host community is twofold: it provides some civilian employment at the military establishment, and it creates a demand for goods and services which the host community may be said to export to the establishment and its personnel. In this study a community is designated a military center if there is evidence of a sizable military establishment near it or within its boundaries. The employment status statistics were used to determine the size of the Armed Forces population in the community. Chapter 16 sets forth the specific criteria of military specialization, based on these statistics.

Community specialization in one or more leisure time activities classified as amusements, entertainment or recreation, is based on the local and
extralocal demand for the activity, together with certain local advantages
for some forms of leisure.   The local demand is a product of a number of
factors, but in large part it is conditioned by two factors: a reduction of
time spent at work in American society and the existence of large numbers
of nonfamily persons who rely upon public and private leisure activities
for much of their nonworking activity.   The extralocal demand depends
upon the kind of leisure specialization and the existence of hinterland populations with specific types of leisure demands, e.g., the demand of military
persons at a nonlocal installation for certain kinds of amusements.   The
operational definition of specialization in leisure employed in this study is
based on the statistics for male employment in entertainment and recreation.   The upper decile of the distribution of places by the percentage of
all employed males in entertainment and recreation operationally defines
entertainment and recreation centers.

Scope, techniques, and problems of analysis

Some 30 characteristics of the population of urban places and SMA's
were selected to examine demographic, economic, and socio-economic differences between the specialized places and the average for all places in
the United States of comparable size and metropolitan status.   The differences observed were not subjected to tests of statistical significance because of the large amount of clerical work involved.   Conclusions are
based primarily on those differences which appear large and consistent
enough in the eight metropolitan status-size comparisons to be considered
significant.

There is marked variation in the regional location of specialized types
of places, and significant differences in the location of all places (figure 2,
p. 31, and figure 18, p. 153) and those of any functionally specialized type
of place.   Table 141 shows that the five minor types of functionally specialized urban places have proportionally fewer places in the Northeast and
more in the South than do all urban places.   More of the entertainment
and recreation, and of the military, centers than of the other minor types
are located in the South, while fewer of these places are located in the
Northeast.   There are somewhat more urban places specialized in higher
education and in transportation in the North Central Region than is true
of all places, while there are substantially fewer public administration,
military, and entertainment and recreation centers in the North Central
States.   The West has high proportions of public administration and military centers, as compared with the proportion of all places located in the
West, while there are relatively fewer centers of higher education and of
transportation in the West.   It would seem reasonably safe to ignore
regional differences only in the comparisons where centers of higher education and of transportation are compared with all places in this chapter.

TABLE **141.**—Percent Distribution of All Urban Places and of Selected Urban Places by Minor Type of Functional Specialization, by Regions: 1950

Region	All urban places	Type of specialization for selected places[1]				
		Ed	PA	Tr	My	ER
United States, number of places..	1,262	249	131	126	108	132
Percent......................	100	100	100	100	100	100
Northeast.........................	27	20	17	19	14	14
North Central.....................	31	36	11	37	8	14
South.............................	15	24	30	26	33	46
West..............................	27	20	42	18	45	26
Index of dissimilarity[2].............	...	14	30	17	36	31

[1] Ed—higher education, PA—public administration, Tr—transportation, My—military, ER—entertainment and recreation.

[2] Percentage of places in the specialized group that would have to be in another region to make its regional distribution the same as the one for all urban places.

Source: Appendix tables B–18, B–19, and B–20.

There are some other special problems of analysis in connection with the minor types of specialization. The fact that each of them provides only a relatively small proportion of the total employment in a specialized place makes it difficult to attribute direct effects to the minor form of specialization. The effects generally should be more apparent for small than large places, however, since the industry of specialization provides a larger proportion of their total employment. The mode of gathering the employment statistics also presents special problems of analysis. The 1950 Census data are for places of residence rather than places of work, and, hence, the indicators of specialization do not necessarily pertain to the place in which the actual employment occurs. Of course, in the case of transportation, the actual place of employment is indefinite in many instances, anyway. The operators of transport carriers in extralocal transport live at the origin or destination point only. Airline, steamship, and railroad crews and truck drivers travel between cities. Generally, a relatively high proportion of the resident labor force employed in a minor form of functional specialization may be assumed to indicate specialization in that place, if it is not a suburb. The suburban classifications, however, may not be as valid as those for other groups of places. The procedure of enumerating college students in the places where they were attending college in 1950 also creates difficulties of interpretation for statistics affected by disproportionate numbers in the college age groups. Since the proportion of college communities in some specialized types of places was greater than that among all places, college communities were eliminated from the specialized places in the comparisons for proportions in the labor force and married, and the median income of families and unrelated individuals. There, finally, are special problems of interpretation related to variation in the types of activity subsumed under a particular kind of functional specialization. For example, variation in public administration may be expected from the fact that the specialization in places like Norfolk, Va., arises from military installations, while in places like Oak Ridge, Tenn., it is related to Federal resource development, and in Leavenworth, Kans., to Federal penal, as well as military, administration. Similarly, the types of leisure activity included under entertainment and recreation services may range from those of an ocean resort, as in Miami Beach, Fla., to that of gambling, as in Las Vegas, Nev. These differences cannot be explored here, for lack of detailed industry data for the smaller SMA's and urban places. They suggest, however, that future research might investigate whether such variation induces significant morphological differences in communities.

Population composition

Table 142 presents summary age and sex comparisons for the five minor types of functionally specialized communities considered in the chapter, together with data for all SMA's and urban places of the corresponding size and metropolitan status. Entertainment and recreation centers regularly have higher proportions of persons 21 years old and over than do all the communities of the United States in comparable size and metropolitan status categories. They also rank either first or second in comparison with the other four types of specialized centers. At the other extreme, with comparatively young populations, are the public administration, military, and transportation centers. The results for centers of higher education are not sufficiently consistent to warrant a conclusion. The higher average age in entertainment and recreation centers is doubtless due to the attraction some of the centers have as health resorts or places of retirement. The comparatively low average age in military centers is perhaps partly ex-

TABLE 142.—AGE AND SEX COMPOSITION OF THE POPULATION, FOR ALL STANDARD METROPOLITAN AREAS AND URBAN PLACES OF 10,000 INHABITANTS OR MORE, AND FOR SELECTED PLACES BY MINOR TYPE OF FUNCTIONAL SPECIALIZATION, BY METROPOLITAN STATUS AND SIZE: 1950

| Metropolitan status and size of place | Percent of population 21 years old and over | | | | | | Sex ratio | | | | | |
| | All places | Type of specialization for selected places | | | | | All places | Type of specialization for selected places | | | | |
		Ed	PA	Tr	My	ER		Ed	PA	Tr	My	ER
Standard metropolitan areas:												
50,000 to 250,000...	64.5	64.6	62.2	63.2	61.2	66.5	96.9	98.0	96.4	97.1	101.0	93.7
250,000 or more.....	68.3	68.8	66.0	66.4	69.4	68.9	96.3	95.6	99.7	98.2	96.1	94.7
Central cities:												
Under 100,000.......	67.6	67.5	66.2	67.2	63.9	70.5	93.4	94.0	91.6	93.4	98.3	88.1
100,000 or more.....	70.1	70.6	68.5	67.3	71.0	[1]70.6	94.1	92.7	94.9	91.9	94.2	[1]94.2
Suburbs:												
10,000 to 25,000....	66.9	68.8	65.1	65.9	63.5	67.9	95.8	92.2	96.1	97.2	96.7	97.0
25,000 or more......	66.4	72.1	68.0	67.4	68.7	72.4	94.1	88.3	96.1	94.8	96.7	88.1
Independent cities:												
10,000 to 25,000....	65.6	64.8	66.0	65.0	64.4	65.6	93.8	96.8	94.1	93.6	95.6	95.2
25,000 to 50,000....	66.6	66.0	64.2	66.2	64.8	67.9	94.1	98.7	101.2	93.0	99.5	98.9

[1] Excludes New York City.

Source: *1950 Census of Population*, Vol. II, *Characteristics of the Population*, Parts 2 to 50, table 33.

plained by the low average age of the military population. This factor may also be involved in the result for centers of public administration, many of which are also military centers.

The sex ratio is greater in public administration and military centers than in centers with other minor types of specialization, or in all urban places of comparable size and metropolitan status. The differences are small, however, and not wholly consistent. Military centers, of course, are expected to show fairly high sex ratios, but public administration centers might be expected to show low sex ratios. A separate tabulation shows that places which specialize only in public administration have lower sex ratios than places where public administration is linked with some other form of functional specialization, particularly military specialization. The elimination of these places, therefore, yields the expected low sex ratio.

There are somewhat smaller proportions of nonwhite persons in college communities than in communities with other minor types of functional specialization. Table 143 shows that there are generally larger proportions of nonwhite persons in places with minor types of specialization, except for college communities, than in all urban places of comparable size and metropolitan status. The differences are not large, nor are they entirely consistent, suggesting that the type of specialization itself is not selective of nonwhite persons. Differences in the regional location of centers may account for some of the difference, since somewhat more of the urban places with minor forms of specialization than of all urban places are located in the South, where the nonwhite percentages in cities are relatively high. College communities, however, are located in the South almost as frequently as places with other minor forms of specialization.

TABLE 143.—COLOR AND MOBILITY OF THE POPULATION, FOR ALL STANDARD METROPOLITAN AREAS AND URBAN PLACES OF 10,000 INHABITANTS OR MORE, AND FOR SELECTED PLACES BY MINOR TYPE OF FUNCTIONAL SPECIALIZATION, BY METROPOLITAN STATUS AND SIZE: 1950

Metropolitan status and size of place	Percent nonwhite						Percent living in same house, 1949 and 1950[1]					
	All places	Type of specialization for selected places					All places	Type of specialization for selected places				
		Ed	PA	Tr	My	ER		Ed	PA	Tr	My	ER
Standard metropolitan areas:												
50,000 to 250,000....	11.3	13.4	17.2	9.9	18.0	14.8	79.2	77.0	74.6	78.1	72.9	77.4
250,000 or more.....	9.5	7.3	15.4	16.5	10.0	9.6	82.4	77.5	76.6	77.1	82.1	72.5
Central cities:												
Under 100,000.......	10.6	11.7	17.0	10.0	21.4	17.2	79.9	75.6	77.2	78.5	71.1	81.4
100,000 or more.....	13.3	11.7	19.5	17.7	13.3	[2]14.2	82.5	78.2	74.2	81.7	83.5	[2]73.6
Suburbs:												
10,000 to 25,000....	4.5	3.5	9.4	5.8	6.8	4.9	81.7	80.7	75.4	80.7	72.1	76.5
25,000 or more......	5.8	5.2	8.1	9.7	5.7	5.0	83.2	82.0	77.5	83.1	77.7	77.7
Independent cities:												
10,000 to 25,000....	9.0	7.4	11.8	7.7	16.1	12.8	77.7	73.9	75.5	78.6	71.7	72.4
25,000 to 50,000....	10.1	7.9	12.5	15.3	14.6	13.2	77.3	73.1	70.0	79.4	70.7	68.4

[1] Persons 1 year old and over.
[2] Excludes New York City.

Source: *1950 Census of Population*, Vol. II, *Characteristics of the Population*, Parts 2 to 50, tables 33 and 34.

The somewhat lower percentage of nonwhite persons in college communities cannot, therefore, be attributed to differences in regional location.

The stability of residence is substantially lower for the five minor types of specialized places than it is for all places, regardless of metropolitan status and size of place (table 143). The differences are particularly large for places specializing in entertainment and recreation, public administration, and national defense. For 3 of the 8 comparisons for entertainment and recreation centers, the difference is as much as 9 percent. The somewhat higher percentage of residential mobility for centers of public administration as compared with military centers in 4 of the 8 comparisons suggests that all forms of public administration, including administration of military posts, create somewhat greater mobility than do most types of specialization. Places with these forms of specialization should have substantially higher percentages of residentially mobile persons than do other specialized places. The patronage practices of state and local governments, and the personnel transfer practices in federal civilian and military agencies probably induce comparatively high residential mobility. The substantially higher percentages of residential mobility in entertainment and recreation centers than in all urban places are probably largely due to the high rate of residential mobility in those centers which attract migrants seeking resort, retirement, leisure, and "health" services. A comparison of residential mobility in places with minor types of functional specialization with the mobility in places specialized in manufacturing shows that residential stability is substantially greater in manufacturing centers. For all 40 comparisons of minor types of specialized places with the manufacturing places, manufacturing centers have a higher percentage of persons who are residentially stable.[3] The somewhat greater incidence of residential mobility in college communities than in all places of comparable metropolitan status and size may be almost entirely due to the enumeration of college students at the place of college attendance in 1950. The 1950 freshman class in colleges, for the most part, was reported as residing elsewhere in 1949. All college communities, therefore, should show some population movement from this source.

Family composition

The marriage rate of men enrolled in college is low as compared with that of men of the same age who are not in college. The data in table 144 bear out the supposition that men in college communities have a lower proportion married than men in noncollege communities. The percentage of married males 14 years of age and over is lower in college communities than in all communities of comparable size and metropolitan status. The

---

[3] The 8 metropolitan status–size-of-place groups of table 117 are compared with comparable groups for each of the 5 minor types of specialization, making a total of 40 comparisons.

difference between the percentage of married males in college communities and in all urban communities is as much as 8 percent for large suburbs and large and small independent cities. College communities have a lower percentage of males married than do places with other minor types of functional specialization, except for military centers. The percentage of married males in military centers is as low as that in college communities among SMA's and central cities, but not among suburbs and independent cities. Military establishments undoubtedly affect the statistics more for small than large places. It seems unlikely, therefore, that the presence of military establishments, as such, explains the low percentages of married males in SMA's and central cities classified as military centers. The percentage of married males in centers of entertainment and recreation is somewhat above that for all comparable places, except for large suburbs and independent cities. The reason for this pattern of marriage is not known.

There is not much variation in the average size of households among SMA's or urban places with different minor types of functional specialization. The number of persons per household for places specialized in higher education and in entertainment and recreation seems somewhat smaller than that for all places of comparable size and metropolitan status on the basis of the data in table 144. The differences are quite small, particularly for centers of higher education. One expects entertainment and recreation centers to have somewhat smaller households, assuming the majority of these places have an attraction for older retired persons. The

TABLE 144.—MARITAL STATUS OF THE POPULATION AND PERSONS PER HOUSEHOLD, FOR ALL STANDARD METROPOLITAN AREAS AND URBAN PLACES OF 10,000 INHABITANTS OR MORE, AND FOR SELECTED PLACES BY MINOR TYPE OF FUNCTIONAL SPECIALIZATION, BY METROPOLITAN STATUS AND SIZE: 1950

Metropolitan status and size of place	Percent married, male						Persons per household[2]					
	All places	Type of specialization for selected places[1]					All places	Type of specialization for selected places				
		Ed	PA	Tr	My	ER		Ed	PA	Tr	My	ER
Standard metropolitan areas:												
50,000 to 250,000....	69.2	66.7	70.2	69.0	66.4	70.9	3.37	3.34	3.46	3.46	3.44	3.27
250,000 or more.....	68.1	67.6	67.3	68.7	67.4	70.8	3.33	3.34	3.33	3.26	3.27	3.07
Central cities:												
Under 100,000.......	68.2	66.0	68.9	70.9	65.0	69.6	3.21	3.14	3.31	3.22	3.27	3.10
100,000 or more.....	67.1	65.5	66.7	67.8	65.7	[3]68.9	3.26	3.23	3.19	3.32	3.19	[3]3.12
Suburbs:												
10,000 to 25,000....	72.5	69.0	73.4	75.3	76.2	74.3	3.40	3.30	3.35	3.42	3.32	3.30
25,000 or more......	72.9	65.1	72.3	69.7	69.8	72.3	3.33	3.25	3.25	3.23	3.28	3.14
Independent cities:												
10,000 to 25,000....	69.2	61.9	74.3	70.4	72.0	71.6	3.19	3.12	3.25	3.11	3.28	3.11
25,000 to 50,000....	67.6	59.4	64.9	71.1	67.7	67.0	3.20	3.16	3.20	3.23	3.17	3.01

[1] All places with 25 percent or more of the population 20 to 24 years old enrolled in school are excluded from the PA, Tr, My, and ER comparisons.

[2] The figure shown is the one for the median place in each group.

[3] Excludes New York City.

Source: *1950 Census of Population*, Vol. II, *Characteristics of the Population*, Parts 2 to 50, table 34.

pattern of living arrangements for college students suggests, however, that college communities should have a somewhat larger average household than noncollege communities. Many persons enrolled in college reside either in institutional dormitories or in lodging houses with 5 or more lodgers. These quasi-households are excluded from the data on population per household. The enumeration of this segment of the college population at the place of college enrollment, therefore, does not affect materially the number of persons per household. The pattern of living arrangements for college students not in quasi-households nevertheless may affect the ratio somewhat. It seems reasonable to assume that, ordinarily, the unmarried college student who does not reside in a quasi-household lives in a dwelling unit with a group of unrelated individuals, or as an unrelated individual in some household. Correlatively, the proportion of college students living in one-person households probably is below that of the general population, and perhaps even below the proportion for this age group. This reasoning suggests that college communities should have a somewhat larger average household than do all urban communities. The contrary fact in table 144 is not readily explained.

Economic characteristics

None of the minor types of functional specialization considered in this research generally accounts for a very large proportion of the economic activity in an urban community, either in large or small communities. Since this study considers functional specialization only for places with 10,000 inhabitants or more, the direct effects of any single minor type of specialization on the community's economic structure are not likely to be great. Both the direct and indirect effects vary with the type of specialization. The following discussion sets forth some hypotheses about these effects.

Specialization in higher education is expected to have at least two effects on the economic structure of college communities. One is that the college student population directly affects the character of certain industries in the community, since the export of education means students are imported as consumers not only of education but of other goods and services associated with their temporary residence in the community. College students, for example, are expected to increase the volume in certain types of retail trade, such as clothing and eating and drinking establishments, and in certain types of services, such as laundry and dry cleaning establishments. The other and more important way in which specialization in higher education may affect the economic base of a community is that it creates an environment favorable to the white-collar occupations and industries. The data below suggest that college communities are more likely to favor industries in which employment in white-collar occupations comprises a relatively large proportion of total employment.

Public administration generally does not account for a very large proportion of the economic activity in a community. The 3 highest proportions of males employed in public administration for all of the central or independent cities in the United States with 10,000 inhabitants or more are 40.9 percent in Warrington and 30.5 percent in Key West, military centers in Florida, and 27.0 percent in Washington, D. C. Only 2 suburbs had proportions employed in public administration in excess of that for Washington, D. C. These were Midwest City, Okla., with 50.6 percent, and Coronado, Calif., with 31.2 percent. If one adds to these places the Washington, D. C., suburbs of Mt. Rainier, Md. (26.0 percent), and Alexandria, Va. (26.9 percent), and the naval center of Newport, R. I. (25.5 percent), only 8 urban places have more than one-fourth of all employed males in public administration. On the other hand, every urban place with 10,000 inhabitants or more has some resident workers in public administration. The average for all urban places with 10,000 inhabitants or more is 5.7. There are a number of specific forms of specialization in public administration, stemming from legislative, judicial, and executive activities of government. Specialization in public administration, however, arises primarily from executive rather than legislative or judical activities. Most frequently specialization in public administration arises from locating either a Federal military establishment or a State capital in a city. Specialization in public administration can arise, however, from a large variety of executive agency functions, such as the administration of penal institutions, Indian affairs, and resource development. The Federal Government is more likely to create such centers outside the capital city than are State governments in the United States. In this study, the major source of employment in public administration was not clearly identified for all of the 128 urban places and 19 SMA's defined as specializing in public administration. All but 2 of the SMA's were military centers (14 SMA's) and/or State capitals (8 SMA's). Of the 128 urban places, 51 percent were defined as military centers; 16 percent were capitals of Federal or State governments; 2 percent were resource development centers. About two-fifths, 42 percent, were not specialized in any of these forms of public administration, however. The exact nature of the effect of the different forms of specialization in public administration on the economic structure of a community is not clearly perceived. It seems likely that specialization in military administration affects the economy quite differently from specialization in state administration, but only the military centers are separately considered in this research.

Specialization in transportation generally requires that only a small proportion of the total employed persons work in transportation. Only 7 percent of the 1,262 urban places with 10,000 inhabitants or more have 12 percent or more of all employed persons in transportation. By way of contrast, 45 percent of the 1,262 urban places with 10,000 inhabitants or more have fewer than 4 percent of all employed persons in transportation. The average for all urban places with 10,000 inhabitants or more is 6.1 percent.[4] Transport facilities exist to transport people and goods, although specialized employment occurs for the latter more than the former. One, therefore, expects places specialized in transportation also to specialize in some other major type of economic activity, e.g., wholesale trade. This problem is examined below.

Military establishments frequently are placed in the rural areas adjacent to urban places. Fort Campbell, Ky., for example, is located between Clarksville, Tenn., and Hopkinsville, Ky. Clarksville and Hopkinsville are 26 miles apart, but both are sufficiently influenced by Fort Campbell to be classified as military centers in this study. This arises from the fact that personnel attached to the military center reside in considerable numbers in both of these independent cities of 10,000 to 25,000 inhabitants. The effect of the military establishment on a community, therefore, is in part dependent on the actual location of the establishment with respect to a community and in part on the census definition of the geographical boundaries of the community. The effect may be more clearly discerned for SMA's than for urban places, for this reason. Generally, the effect of a military establishment stems from two sources. The resident military population is highly selected in terms of age, sex, and marital status; this, in turn, influences certain types of economic demand, e.g., for entertainment and recreation, and certain types of retail trade. The existence of the military establishment within the area of dominance of a community in turn creates certain demands for civilian employment, e.g., in public administration, and it thereby further conditions the economic base of a community. It is not possible to separate empirically these several effects in the following analysis.

Specialization in entertainment and recreation generally does not require very large proportions of employed persons in these activities. Among SMA's, for example, Los Angeles had the largest percentage of employed males in entertainment and recreation in 1950, with 3.3 percent. The movie industry, in fact, provided the largest proportion of employed persons in entertainment and recreation in any urban place, with 11.6 percent in the motion picture center of Culver City, Calif., and 11.3 percent in Beverly Hills, Calif., a "home of the stars." These examples serve to illustrate the fact that certain of the employment in entertainment and recreation occurs in the mass communication entertainment industries of motion pictures, television, and radio broadcasting. The derivative effects of this kind of specialization in entertainment and recreation on the economic structure of a community are perhaps somewhat less pronounced

---

[4] The percentages in this paragraph are based on data in table 113, Chapter 16.

than in the cases where entertainment and recreation is participated in directly by the clientele. This latter kind of specialization usually leads to a demand for hotels and lodging places and retail services, to mention only two of the possible derivative effects on the economic base of these communities.

Table 145 presents male and female labor force participation rates for the five types of communities. Differences between college communities and all comparable groups of communities are expected, because of the low rates of labor force participation of college students. Of the urban males aged 20 to 24 in the United States in 1950, only 37.8 percent of those enrolled in school, as compared with 91.3 percent of those not enrolled in school, were in the labor force.[5] The corresponding percentages for females were 39.2 and 50.6, respectively. The differences in labor force participation rates between urban females enrolled in school and those not enrolled in school are not as large as the differences for males. A large percentage of the women 20 to 24 years old not enrolled in school are married women with children under 5 years of age. Their rate of participation in the labor force is expected to be low just as that of the college females is expected to be low. On the basis of these observations, it would be expected that SMA's and urban places with a high percentage of persons aged 20 to 24 enrolled in school would show lower rates of participation in the labor force than do all comparable groups of communities, and that the difference would be especially marked for males.

TABLE 145.—LABOR FORCE PARTICIPATION BY SEX, FOR ALL STANDARD METROPOLITAN AREAS AND URBAN PLACES OF 10,000 INHABITANTS OR MORE, AND FOR SELECTED PLACES BY MINOR TYPE OF FUNCTIONAL SPECIALIZATION, BY METROPOLITAN STATUS AND SIZE: 1950

Metropolitan status and size of place	Male						Female					
	All places	Type of specialization for selected places[1]					All places	Type of specialization for selected places[1]				
		Ed	PA	Tr	My	ER		Ed	PA	Tr	My	ER
Standard metropolitan areas:												
50,000 to 250,000...	79.7	74.9	80.0	78.2	80.7	79.9	32.4	33.1	31.8	28.4	31.9	34.9
250,000 or more.....	79.8	78.1	81.5	80.5	79.7	78.6	32.4	33.7	34.8	31.1	33.1	32.1
Central cities:												
Under 100,000.......	79.8	74.1	77.9	78.1	81.9	74.7	34.1	36.3	34.7	31.5	35.5	34.0
100,000 or more.....	78.9	77.1	80.9	79.7	78.6	[2]78.9	37.6	37.5	37.9	34.3	35.7	[2]34.1
Suburbs:												
10,000 to 25,000....	80.5	75.6	80.2	81.1	82.9	81.8	29.2	29.1	31.6	29.6	29.1	29.4
25,000 or more......	80.9	77.0	82.9	81.6	81.4	79.6	32.6	33.2	32.4	33.0	31.3	32.2
Independent cities:												
10,000 to 25,000....	77.1	67.3	77.0	77.8	79.5	77.8	32.7	32.4	33.0	29.3	32.8	33.4
25,000 to 50,000....	76.5	65.9	75.0	80.0	81.8	76.3	34.1	34.1	32.0	32.2	32.5	34.3

[1] All places with 25 percent or more of the population 20 to 24 years old enrolled in school are excluded from the PA, Tr, My, and ER comparisons.

[2] Excludes New York City.

Source: *1950 Census of Population*, Vol. II, *Characteristics of the Population*, Parts 2 to 50, table 35.

[5] Data on labor force participation for the entire urban population of the United States are taken from *1950 Census of Population, op. cit.*, table 122, p. 258.

The rates of participation in the labor force for males 14 years of age and over are lower in SMA's and urban places with a high percentage of the population aged 20 to 24 enrolled in school than in all places of comparable size and metropolitan status. The difference in rate of participation in the labor force is particularly marked for independent cities, where college communities have on the average roughly 10 percent fewer males in the labor force than do all independent cities. Among SMA's and central cities the difference in labor force participation rates between college communities and all communities is greater for small than large places, reflecting the fact that the effect of the college population is greater in small than large places. The rate of participation in the labor force for females 14 years of age and over in college communities is very nearly that of all communities of comparable size and metropolitan status. The difference in labor force participation rates, in fact, is less than 1 percent for 6 of the 8 metropolitan status-size comparisons. The data for female labor force participation in college communities, then, are contrary to expectations. The finding suggests there is some tendency for college communities to offer more employment opportunities for females not enrolled in school than does the average community of comparable size and metropolitan status.

The fact that specialization in higher education reduces labor force participation rates considerably for males led to the exclusion of all SMA's and urban places with 25 percent or more of the persons aged 20 to 24 enrolled in school from the other minor types of functional specialization in table 145. Inasmuch as there is known to be variation in the extent to which specialization in higher education occurs with specialization in the four other minor types, their inclusion would substantially affect certain of the comparisons for labor force participation rates of males.[6] Labor force participation rates are also affected by the ratio of the military to the civilian population. The degree to which military specialization occurs with the other minor forms of specialization is not large, except for specialization in public administration. Almost necessarily, a city which is the site of a large military establishment also employs a fairly large number of persons in public administration, though perhaps not always in sufficient proportions to make for specialization in public administration as defined in this study. The elimination of military centers from places specialized in public administration, however, would mean excluding 40 percent of all centers of public administration. Hence, they were retained in computing the labor force participation rates for places specialized in public administration. Their inclusion, however, affects the size of the

[6] The following percentages of urban places were excluded from the total specialized places when places with 25 percent or more of the persons aged 20 to 24 enrolled in school were eliminated: 18 percent of the 131 public administration centers; 7 percent of the 126 transportation centers; 11 percent of the 108 military centers; and 17 percent of the 132 entertainment and recreation centers.

proportions and obscures the actual relationship for the civilian population. The effect of excluding military centers would be to decrease the labor force participation rate in public administration centers, as can be seen by comparing the rates for the two types of centers in table 145. The reason for this is that members of the Armed Forces are counted in the labor force.

Among males, it appears that there generally is not much variation between the labor force participation rates of public administration, transportation, military, and entertainment and recreation centers, and the rate for all places of comparable size and metropolitan status. In 31 of 32 comparisons with manufacturing places, however, the rates for places with minor types of functional specialization are below that for manufacturing places.[7] These differences in labor force participation rates usually are small, and the differences in rates between the four minor types of specialization and manufacturing centers usually are less than that between any of the four minor types and places specialized in higher education. The pattern is particularly marked for independent cities. This would suggest that labor force participation rates are affected less by major versus minor forms of economic specialization than by the particular type of specialization.

Despite the relatively small variation in male labor force participation rates among the minor types of functionally specialized places, excluding those specialized in higher education, one pattern of difference is worth noting. If military centers were excluded from public administration centers it appears that public administration centers and places of entertainment and recreation would have relatively smaller labor forces than do transportation and military centers. Support of this assumption for public administration centers is found in the fact that the lower rates occur for the smaller urban places and the independent cities where the effect of specialization in public administration should be most marked.

The labor force participation rates for women do not differ much from the rates for all places of comparable size and metropolitan status, except for centers of transportation. The female labor force participation rates in places with the five minor types of specialization actually are above those for places specialized in manufacturing for large SMA's and central cities. On the other hand, they are somewhat below those for small SMA's and central cities, and independent cities. The differences are small, however, suggesting that manufacturing specialization is not necessarily more favorable to the employment of women than any of the minor types of functional specialization. These findings also confirm those of Chapter 17, where it was observed that there were no significant differences in the labor force participation rates of women in manufacturing and nonmanu-

[7] Eight metropolitan status-size groups for the four minor types of specialization, excluding higher education centers.

facturing places, other than for independent cities with 10,000 to 25,000 inhabitants.[8] The fact that places specialized in transportation, except for suburbs, have a somewhat smaller female labor force than do places with other minor types of functional specialization is not surprising. Transportation offers relatively fewer opportunities for female employment than do the other minor types of functional specialization. Only 7 percent of all employed persons in transportation are women. The 170,245 urban employed women in transportation in the United States in 1950 represent only 1.4 percent of all urban employed women in 1950.[9]

The data of table 105 in Chapter 16 show that the percentage of all employed persons in manufacturing in 1950 is roughly 2 to 4 times as great in manufacturing (the upper quintile) as in nonmanufacturing places (the lower quintile on the percentage of all employed persons in manufac-

TABLE 146.—PERCENT OF EMPLOYED PERSONS IN MANUFACTURING, FOR ALL STANDARD METROPOLITAN AREAS AND URBAN PLACES OF 10,000 INHABITANTS OR MORE, AND FOR SELECTED PLACES BY MINOR TYPE OF FUNCTIONAL SPECIALIZATION, BY METROPOLITAN STATUS AND SIZE: 1950

Metropolitan status and size of place	All places	Type of specialization for selected places				
		Ed	PA	Tr	My	ER
Standard metropolitan areas:						
50,000 to 250,000	29.8	24.5	14.6	18.0	18.4	19.7
250,000 or more	30.6	22.5	15.8	18.2	29.0	20.3
Central cities:						
Under 100,000	29.0	21.2	18.9	18.4	15.3	17.5
100,000 or more	29.1	21.7	11.8	19.9	25.6	[1]18.5
Suburbs:						
10,000 to 25,000	35.0	13.4	22.3	29.1	23.8	25.0
25,000 or more	38.1	24.5	23.7	35.4	26.6	21.3
Independent cities:						
10,000 to 25,000	26.0	19.1	14.8	14.8	15.5	15.5
25,000 to 50,000	26.2	15.9	11.5	21.7	16.9	10.1

[1] Excludes New York City.

Source: See table 145.

turing). These data suggest that the percentage of employed persons in manufacturing will be fairly low in all minor types of functionally specialized places. The data in table 146 support this deduction, since the percentage of all employed persons in manufacturing among minor types of places is almost always considerably below the average percentage for all places of comparable size and metropolitan status.

There is some variation, however, among minor types of specialized places in the percentage employed in manufacturing. College communities generally have somewhat higher percentages of all employed persons in manufacturing (one-sixth to one-fourth of all employed) than do other minor functional types. Correlatively, centers of public adminstration have somewhat lower percentages (one-tenth to one-fifth) of all employed

[8] See table 119, Chapter 17, for these comparisons.

[9] Based on data in *1950 Census of Population, op. cit.,* table 55, p. 102.

persons in manufacturing. There are several exceptions. For example, among suburbs with minor types of functional specialization, the highest percentages of persons employed in manufacturing occur for places specialized in transportation. It is somewhat surprising to find that the average rank on manufacturing employment of the metropolitan status-size groups of places specialized in higher education is above that for the public administration, transportation, military, and entertainment and recreation centers. The result is not readily explained. It is clear that a high degree of specialization in manufacturing seldom is associated with specialization in transportation, however. Among the urban places specialized in manufacturing, there are only 4 which are in the upper decile of the percentage employed in transportation, but 67 in the lower decile.

Per capita sales in wholesale and retail trade are affected by the export demand of hinterland populations as well as by the income level and maintenance requirements of the resident population. This export demand should increase the need for transportation facilities much more in the case of wholesale than in the case of retail trade. The export of wholesale trade means the movement of goods, while the export of retail trade means mainly to import customers and to furnish goods locally. One then would expect more linkage between wholesale trade and transportation than between retail trade and transportation specialization. Table 147 shows that, except for small SMA's and large central cities, the per capita expenditures for wholesale trade in transportation centers are above the average for all comparable places. Per capita expenditures for retail trade in transpor-

TABLE 147.—PER CAPITA SALES IN WHOLESALE AND RETAIL TRADE, 1948, FOR ALL STANDARD METROPOLITAN AREAS AND URBAN PLACES OF 10,000 INHABITANTS OR MORE, AND FOR SELECTED PLACES BY MINOR TYPE OF FUNCTIONAL SPECIALIZATION, BY METROPOLITAN STATUS AND SIZE, 1950

[Per capita sales in dollars]

Metropolitan status and size of place	Wholesale trade						Retail trade					
	All places	Type of specialization for selected places					All places	Type of specialization for selected places				
		Ed	PA	Tr	My	ER		Ed	PA	Tr	My	ER
Standard metropolitan areas:												
50,000 to 250,000...	1,074	976	877	992	946	1,832	929	948	846	858	835	1,016
250,000 or more.....	2,040	1,761	1,044	2,507	2,308	1,530	989	1,029	937	962	1,006	1,037
Central cities:												
Under 100,000.......	1,364	1,630	1,200	1,382	1,445	1,786	1,299	1,416	1,149	1,200	1,194	1,491
100,000 or more.....	3,165	2,725	1,062	2,545	3,457	[1]2,491	1,164	1,164	867	1,065	1,049	[1]1,215
Suburbs:												
10,000 to 25,000....	391	235	213	514	512	270	900	904	911	803	1,096	933
25,000 or more......	585	534	638	637	576	559	1,081	1,169	1,031	976	997	1,532
Independent cities:												
10,000 to 25,000....	726	652	703	818	809	821	1,309	1,290	1,270	1,314	1,385	1,423
25,000 to 50,000....	1,023	915	679	1,088	819	797	1,340	1,392	1,194	1,340	1,265	1,393

[1] Excludes New York City.

Source: *1950 Census of Population*, Vol. II, *Characteristics of the Population*, Parts 2 to 50, table 10; *1948 Census of Business*, Vol. III, *Retail Trade—Area Statistics*, tables 102 and 103 for each State; Vol. V, *Wholesale Trade—Area Statistics*, tables 102 and 103 for each State.

FIGURE 34.—PER CAPITA RETAIL SALES IN 1948, FOR SELECTED STANDARD METROPOLITAN AREAS AND URBAN PLACES, BY METROPOLITAN STATUS AND MINOR TYPE OF FUNCTIONAL SPECIALIZATION: 1950

[Education (Ed); Public Administration (PA); Transportation (Tr); Military (My); Entertainment and Recreation (ER). Base line: Per capita sales for all places in the metropolitan status group]

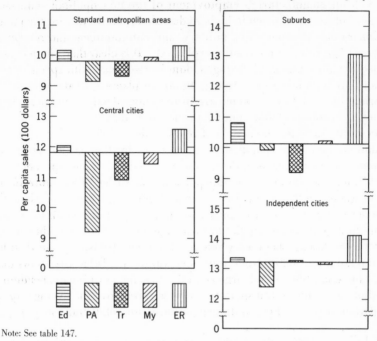

Note: See table 147.

tation centers are below those for all comparable places, except for independent cities where they are about equal to the per capita expenditures for comparable places.   (See figure 34.)   The relationship of per capita expenditures in wholesale and retail trade with military specialization is similar to that for transportation.   Table 147 shows that per capita retail sales for military centers are below the United States average for 5 of the 8 comparisons, while per capita wholesale sales are above the average for 5 of the 8 comparisons.

Public administration centers generally have the lowest per capita expenditures for both wholesale and retail trade of all the minor types of functionally specialized places considered in this chapter.   The lowest per capita expenditures for wholesale trade occur for public administration centers in 6 of 8 comparisons, and except for large suburbs, the average per capita expenditures for wholesale sales in public adminstration centers are below those for all places.   Per capita wholesale expenditures in public administration centers are about $1,000 lower than the United States average for large SMA's and about $2,000 lower for large central cities. The lowest per capita retail expenditures among the five minor types of places occur for public administration centers in 5 of 8 metropolitan status-size comparisons, and, except for small suburbs, the per capita retail expenditures in public administration centers are less than those of all places combined.   Evidently specialization in public administration does not greatly stimulate the export function of trade.   The lower per capita retail sales in public administration centers may be due, in part, to the comparatively low income levels in places specialized in public administration.

Places specializing in higher education and entertainment and recreation in table 147 generally have somewhat higher per capita retail sales than all places, but somewhat lower wholesale expenditures.   The comparatively high retail expenditure in centers of entertainment and recreation is not surprising.   Many types of recreation stimulate retail trade, particularly in eating and drinking places, gasoline service stations, liquor stores, sporting goods stores, gift, novelty, and souvenir stores, and camera and photographic supply stores.   This effect counteracts that of the relatively low median income of persons in entertainment and recreation centers.   The fact that per capita retail sales in college communities are above those of all communities in 6 of 8 comparisons, while anticipated, also runs counter to the fact that the median incomes of SMA's, central and independent cities specialized in higher education are below the corresponding United States averages.   The lower medians of college communities are due, in part, to the "artificially" low incomes of college students, and the effect of low income on trade therefore may be less than that for entertainment and recreation places.

The general relationship observed between wholesale and retail trade and specialization in minor types of economic functions in table 147 is as follows: Transportation and military centers have low retail and high wholesale per capita sales.   Higher education and entertainment and recreation centers have high retail and low wholesale per capita sales.   Public administration centers have low per capita sales in both retail and wholesale trade.   None of the minor types of specialization has high per capita expenditures in both wholesale and retail sales.   If the per capita expenditures for wholesale and retail sales of the manufacturing places in Chapter 17 are compared with the figures for all places in table 147, manufacturing places are most like public administration centers with respect to trade in that they have relatively low per capita expenditures in both retail and wholesale trade.   The differences are not as large as for public administration, however.

Table 148 shows that with a very few exceptions places with any type of minor functional specialization have higher average percentages of persons at work for a government employer, and of employed males in public administration than do all places of comparable size and metropolitan status.   They also have much higher percentages than do the specialized

TABLE **148.**—PERCENT OF EMPLOYED PERSONS IN GOVERNMENT AND OF EMPLOYED MALES IN PUBLIC ADMINISTRATION, FOR ALL STANDARD METROPOLITAN AREAS AND URBAN PLACES OF 10,000 INHABITANTS OR MORE, AND FOR SELECTED PLACES BY MINOR TYPE OF FUNCTIONAL SPECIALIZATION, BY METROPOLITAN STATUS AND SIZE: 1950

Metropolitan status and size of place	Government workers as percent of all employed persons[1]						Percent of employed males in public administration					
	All places	Type of specialization for selected places					All places	Type of specialization for selected places				
		Ed	PA	Tr	My	ER		Ed	PA	Tr	My	ER
Standard metropolitan areas:												
50,000 to 250,000...	10.0	13.8	17.8	11.9	13.3	11.1	4.8	5.0	10.8	6.0	6.4	5.9
250,000 or more.....	10.1	14.4	28.5	12.2	11.0	10.6	5.9	8.1	18.4	7.5	6.5	6.2
Central cities:												
Under 100,000.......	11.1	14.0	17.1	14.0	15.3	11.0	5.5	5.9	8.6	7.3	7.5	6.2
100,000 or more.....	10.4	14.7	25.4	11.9	10.8	[2]11.1	6.2	8.3	17.4	7.4	7.6	[2]6.3
Suburbs:												
10,000 to 25,000....	9.5	7.6	20.4	9.7	15.4	9.0	4.9	5.7	14.3	5.6	10.0	4.9
25,000 or more......	8.8	10.9	18.7	11.7	18.0	9.4	5.0	5.7	10.7	6.7	9.0	4.9
Independent cities:												
10,000 to 25,000....	11.5	17.6	19.5	9.9	18.2	14.1	4.8	4.8	13.1	4.3	11.3	4.9
25,000 to 50,000....	11.7	17.9	22.2	10.1	17.9	14.6	5.2	5.0	13.9	5.2	10.8	5.5

[1] Based on class-of-worker statistics; includes persons who worked for any governmental unit (Federal, State, or local), regardless of the activity which the particular agency carried on.

[2] Excludes New York City.

Source: *1950 Census of Population*, Vol. II, *Characteristics of the Population*, Parts 2 to 50, table 35.

manufacturing places in Chapter 17. There nonetheless is considerable variation among the several minor types. The percentage of all employed persons at work for a government employer, as of employed males in public administration, is greatest in public administration centers (by definition) and lowest in entertainment and recreation centers. There also is sizable government employment in places specialized in higher education and in military centers, but the percentage of employed males in public administration is fairly high only for military centers. Transportation centers, like entertainment and recreation centers, rank low on both government employment and employment in public administration. These results are easy to explain. All persons employed in public administration work for a government employer, as do the majority of those employed in educational institutions and the civilians employed to maintain the military establishment. Since public administration is far more necessary to the military establishment than to the public educational institution, military specialization increases public administration employment, while specialization in higher education generally does not.

Among the five types of communities under discussion, only transportation centers have considerable employment in transportation (table 149). In fact, specialization in higher education, or in entertainment and recreation, decreases the percentage of employed males in transportation below the United States average. It is somewhat surprising that military centers do not show sizable proportions of employed males in transportation. Apparently the movement of persons and goods associated with military establishments generally is insufficient, by itself, to create much specialization in transportation, or to induce location at transport centers. When military and transport specialization occur together, they almost always occur for naval centers at ocean ports such as Jacksonville, Fla.; Savannah, Ga.; New Orleans, La.; and Alexandria, Va.; or at western transport centers such as Cheyenne, Wyo.; Aurora, Colo.; and Great Falls, Mont.

The percentage of persons aged 20 to 24 years enrolled in school was used as the operational definition of centers of higher education. The very large percentage of persons in these ages enrolled in school in college communities, as compared with all other specialized and nonspecialized types of community, occurs, therefore, by definition (table 149). Entertainment and recreation centers have enrollment percentages equal to or slightly greater than those for all comparable places, except among large suburbs and independent cities, where their enrollment percentages are, respectively, 4 and 10 points higher than the United States percentages. It is somewhat surprising that the effect is greater for large than small places, however.

The differences in the percentage of persons aged 20 to 24 enrolled in school among public administration, transportation, and military centers are quite small, as are the differences between places of any of these types and all places of comparable size and metropolitan status. The enrollment percentages are on the whole roughly equal to or less than those for places of comparable size and metropolitan status, but the differences generally are slightly higher for large than for small places. For 9 of the 12 large

TABLE **149.**—PERCENT OF EMPLOYED PERSONS IN TRANSPORTATION AND PERCENT OF PERSONS ENROLLED IN SCHOOL, FOR ALL STANDARD METROPOLITAN AREAS AND URBAN PLACES OF 10,000 INHABITANTS OR MORE, AND FOR SELECTED PLACES BY MINOR TYPE OF FUNCTIONAL SPECIALIZATION, BY METROPOLITAN STATUS AND SIZE: 1950

Metropolitan status and size of place	Percent of employed persons in transportation						Percent of persons 20 to 24 years old enrolled in school[1]					
	All places	Type of specialization for selected places					All places	Type of specialization for selected places				
		Ed	PA	Tr	My	ER		Ed	PA	Tr	My	ER
Standard metropolitan areas:												
50,000 to 250,000...	5.5	4.2	7.1	14.4	5.7	4.6	10.9	22.8	12.4	10.9	10.5	11.6
250,000 or more.....	6.0	5.7	5.9	10.5	6.0	5.2	13.2	20.4	9.7	12.8	13.4	12.5
Central cities:												
Under 100,000.......	6.2	5.2	7.0	18.4	5.6	5.5	11.5	28.2	15.2	9.8	11.5	12.8
100,000 or more.....	6.5	5.7	6.2	11.5	6.5	[2]5.1	13.5	22.3	11.2	13.1	13.8	[2]13.5
Suburbs:												
10,000 to 25,000....	5.0	2.5	5.3	12.1	5.1	5.3	10.9	30.6	10.0	8.7	7.8	10.9
25,000 or more......	5.1	3.9	5.8	12.1	4.9	3.6	12.4	23.4	11.4	10.7	10.5	16.3
Independent cities:												
10,000 to 25,000....	5.6	5.4	5.4	18.4	5.0	5.2	7.1	38.6	7.3	5.8	7.0	8.9
25,000 to 50,000....	5.8	5.3	5.2	14.2	6.4	4.1	9.9	37.8	10.2	8.6	8.5	20.0

[1] The figure shown is the one for the median place in each group.
[2] Excludes New York City.

Source: *1950 Census of Population*, Vol. II, *Characteristics of the Population*, Parts 2 to 50, tables 34 and 35.

SMA or urban place comparisons, the percentage of persons aged 20 to 24 enrolled in school is somewhat below that for all places. The percentages of persons aged 20 to 24 enrolled in school in public administration, transportation, and military centers are not greatly different from those for manufacturing centers (Chapter 17), although by comparison manufacturing places generally have somewhat smaller percentages of persons in these ages enrolled in school.

Persons employed in entertainment and recreation services comprise only a small proportion of the labor force in any urban center. Only 1.3 percent of the employed urban males in the United States in 1950 were employed in entertainment and recreational services.[10] Places specialized in entertainment and recreation, by definition, have comparatively high percentages of employed males in entertainment and recreation. Yet, their deviation from the average for all comparable places is very small, from roughly 1 to 2 percent. Centers of higher education and military centers have somewhat greater percentages of males employed in entertainment and recreation than do comparable groups of all places, while transportation and public administration centers have somewhat smaller percentages. Both higher education and military specialization should increase the demand for entertainment and recreation services somewhat, since young single persons living in a residential setting of generally high sex ratios make relatively greater demands for entertainment and recreation services than do other segments of the population.

The demand for hotel and lodging space is in part determined by the availability of recreation in an urban place. It also is determined somewhat by other functions, particularly those which attract other transient or temporary residential populations, as do higher education, military, and trade functions. Table 150 shows that all the minor forms of functional specialization, except possibly transportation, increase the demand for employment in hotels and lodging places. This effect is most pronounced for entertainment and recreation centers. The percentages of employed males at work in hotels and lodging places are above the averages for all places, also, for public administration and military centers. Suburbs and independent cities specialized in higher education have somewhat higher male employment in hotels and lodging places than does the average place of comparable size and metropolitan status. The percentage of males employed in hotels and lodging places in transportation centers is roughly equal to that in all comparable places.

Socio-economic status

The occupational composition of the five minor types of functionally specialized places is expected to vary considerably, since the relative demand for specific white-collar and manual jobs is known to vary con-

---

[10] *Ibid.*, p. 103.

TABLE **150.**—PERCENT OF EMPLOYED MALES IN ENTERTAINMENT AND RECREATION SERVICES AND IN HOTELS AND LODGING PLACES, FOR ALL STANDARD METROPOLITAN AREAS AND URBAN PLACES OF 10,000 INHABITANTS OR MORE, AND FOR SELECTED PLACES BY MINOR TYPE OF FUNCTIONAL SPECIALIZATION, BY METROPOLITAN STATUS AND SIZE: 1950

Metropolitan status and size of place	Entertainment and recreation services						Hotels and lodging places					
	All places	Type of specialization for selected places					All places	Type of specialization for selected places				
		Ed	PA	Tr	My	ER		Ed	PA	Tr	My	ER
Standard metropolitan areas:												
50,000 to 250,000...	1.0	1.1	1.1	1.0	1.1	1.6	0.7	0.7	0.8	0.8	0.9	1.8
250,000 or more.....	1.3	1.8	1.2	1.3	1.4	2.7	0.8	0.8	1.1	0.9	0.9	1.2
Central cities:												
Under 100,000......	1.2	1.3	1.2	1.2	1.3	2.0	1.0	1.0	0.9	0.9	1.0	2.7
100,000 or more.....	1.4	2.1	1.3	1.2	1.8	[1]3.2	1.0	1.1	1.2	1.0	1.2	[1]1.3
Suburbs:												
10,000 to 25,000....	1.3	1.4	1.1	1.4	1.4	3.3	0.4	0.8	0.7	0.5	1.1	0.8
25,000 or more......	1.2	1.7	1.1	1.0	1.1	3.3	0.5	0.7	0.7	0.5	0.5	1.3
Independent cities:												
10,000 to 25,000....	1.4	1.5	1.5	1.3	2.4	3.3	0.9	1.2	1.0	0.8	1.4	2.0
25,000 to 50,000....	1.4	1.7	1.4	1.2	1.7	3.2	1.0	1.5	1.2	0.8	1.1	2.7

[1] Excludes New York City.

Source: *1950 Census of Population*, Vol. II, *Characteristics of the Population*, Parts 2 to 50, table 35.

siderably by type of export activity. One expects places specialized in higher education, entertainment and recreation, and public administration to have substantially higher proportions of white-collar workers than transportation or military centers. The major reason for this is that the former industries employ substantially higher proportions of white-collar workers than do most industry groups. In the United States as a whole, 69.5 percent of the males in educational services, 54.9 percent of the males employed in public administration, and 53.5 percent of those in entertainment and recreation services are in white-collar occupations. As high a percentage is observed for only 2 of the other 8 major industry groups: 81.9 percent for finance, insurance, and real estate; and 61.8 percent for wholesale and retail trade. Of the employed women in public administration, 92.9 percent work in white-collar occupations. No major industry group has as high a proportion of white-collar employment for women. Educational services, likewise, have a high percentage (88.2 percent) of women in white-collar occupations, but the percentage of women in white-collar jobs in entertainment and recreation services is fairly low when compared with that in the other 10 major industry groups, being 74.1 percent. By way of contrast, only 23.9 percent of all males employed in transportation are white-collar workers, although 77.7 percent of all women in transportation are white-collar workers.[11] The over-all effect for male and female employment, however, is for transportation to rank low in white-collar employment as compared with higher education, public administration,

---

[11] All figures on occupational composition of industry groups cited in this chapter are based on data in *1950 Census of Population, op. cit.*, table 134, pp. 290, 291.

and entertainment and recreation. There are no comparable data for military centers, and it is difficult to assess the effect of military specialization
on civilian employment. The demand for civilian clerical help should be
high, but so should the demand for construction and maintenance workers,
and the like.

The fact that employment in the industries giving rise to minor types of
specialization is a relatively small proportion of the total employment in a
city, compared with that in manufacturing or trade, means that the effect
of specialization in a minor economic function on the occupational composition of a place may be obscured somewhat by the effect of the occupational composition of other major industry groups. Table 151 presents the
percentages of males in white-collar occupations in the eight metropolitan
status and size classes for each of the five minor types of specialized
places. The occupational composition of the minor types of specialized
places is very much like that of the nonmanufacturing places in Chapter 17.
They all have substantially larger percentages of male white-collar workers
than do manufacturing centers. There is, of course, some variation among
the minor types of specialized places. (See figure 35.) The percentage of
male white-collar workers is, on the average, greatest in centers of higher
education, followed in rank order by entertainment and recreation, public
administration, military, and transportation centers. The centers of higher
education, public administration, and entertainment and recreation have
substantially larger percentages of male white-collar workers than do all
places of comparable size and metropolitan status, while transportation and
military centers have percentages roughly equal to, or below, those for all
comparable places.

Centers of higher education have larger percentages of male white-collar
workers than any of the other minor types of places. A relative absence

TABLE **151**.—PERCENT OF EMPLOYED MALES IN WHITE-COLLAR OCCUPATIONS, FOR ALL
STANDARD METROPOLITAN AREAS AND URBAN PLACES OF 10,000 INHABITANTS OR MORE, AND
FOR SELECTED PLACES BY MINOR TYPE OF FUNCTIONAL SPECIALIZATION, BY METROPOLITAN
STATUS AND SIZE: 1950

Metropolitan status and size of place	All places	Type of specialization for selected places				
		Ed	PA	Tr	My	ER
Standard metropolitan areas:						
50,000 to 250,000..............	32.6	35.9	35.9	33.6	34.3	39.4
250,000 or more................	38.5	42.5	41.1	37.1	41.1	43.7
Central cities:						
Under 100,000..................	37.4	42.3	40.3	38.2	40.3	40.1
100,000 or more................	39.7	43.3	43.0	40.2	42.9	[1]44.9
Suburbs:						
10,000 to 25,000..............	42.3	67.3	40.0	36.4	38.6	46.7
25,000 or more................	39.6	55.4	43.5	34.5	39.4	52.3
Independent cities:						
10,000 to 25,000..............	36.7	41.4	40.0	36.7	38.1	39.7
25,000 to 50,000..............	38.1	43.5	42.3	36.9	37.6	41.8

[1] Excludes New York City.

Source: See table 150.

FIGURE **35.**—PERCENT OF EMPLOYED MALES IN WHITE-COLLAR OCCUPATIONS, IN SELECTED
STANDARD METROPOLITAN AREAS AND URBAN PLACES, BY METROPOLITAN STATUS AND MINOR
TYPE OF FUNCTIONAL SPECIALIZATION: 1950

[Education (Ed); Public Administration (PA); Transportation (Tr); Military (My); Entertainment and Recreation (ER). Base line: All employed males in the metropolitan status group]

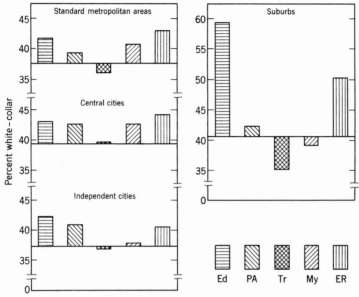

Note: See table 150.

of manufacturing employment cannot account for this, however, because
these centers also have the largest proportion of manufacturing workers
among the minor types of specialized places. Evidently, then, college
communities are more likely to attract industries with a relatively marked
male white-collar composition than are the other minor types of specialized
places, since educational specialization, by itself, cannot account for all of
the difference. Transportation centers, by way of contrast, clearly have
the lowest percentage of male white-collar workers among the minor types
of specialized places. This cannot be largely due to differences in manufacturing employment among the minor types of places, since higher
education and military centers have relatively as great employment in
manufacturing. Part of the relatively low incidence of male white-collar
employment in transportation centers may be attributed to a low ratio of
male white-collar to manual employment in transportation compared with
that in the other industries leading to minor types of specialization. It
probably indicates, also, that transportation centers do not usually attract
industries with a relatively high proportion of male white-collar workers.

    The specific occupation group composition of the minor types of special-
ized places is presented in appendix table B–21. The most important
single fact about the occupational composition of the minor types of

functionally specialized places is that they all show fewer male operative and kindred workers than does the average place.   In 38 of the 40 comparisons for minor types of specialized places, the percentage of male operative and kindred workers is below that of all places.   They have primarily, therefore, the occupational composition of a nonmanufacturing place.   Several differences in the specific occupation group composition of minor types of specialized places are worth noting, since they appear to account for the white-collar or manual worker concentrations.   The relatively high concentration of male white-collar workers in college communities is in large part due to their relatively higher percentage of male professional, technical, and kindred workers.   College professors and the technicians associated with their specialties undoubtedly account for much of this concentration in professional, technical, and kindred workers.   The relatively large concentration of male managers, officials, and proprietors in entertainment and recreation services accounts for much of the concentration of male white-collar workers in this type of specialized center. This is expected, since about one-fifth of all males employed in entertainment and recreation services are managers or proprietors.   Only wholesale and retail trade, and finance, insurance, and real estate, of the major urban industry groups, have higher proportions of male managers, officials, and proprietors.   The concentration of male white-collar workers in centers of public administration is largely accounted for by an excess of male clerical and kindred workers and of male professional, technical, and kindred workers as compared with all places.   The excess of male clerical and kindred workers is understandable, since they comprise 32.4 percent of all employed males in public administration; no other industry group has as large a concentration of male clerical and kindred workers.   The male clerical and kindred employment in public administration accounted, in fact, for 22.9 percent of all male clerical and kindred employment in the United States in 1950.

The relatively greater concentration of male manual workers in transportation centers than in other minor types of specialized places is due to somewhat greater than average employment of male craftsmen, foremen, and kindred workers, and of male laborers in these places than in all comparable places.   This is in keeping with the fact that transportation requires relatively larger numbers of males in these occupation groups than do most industries.   Skilled craftsmen, foremen, and kindred workers comprise 19.1 percent of all males employed in transportation in the United States.   Only construction with 57.9 percent, business and repair services with 53.1 percent, and manufacturing with 24.8 percent had as large a percentage of males in the craft occupations in 1950.   The 15.4 percent of all males in transportation employed as laborers is exceeded only by the percentage in construction among the 11 major urban industry groups.

The nature of employment of women in the minor types of functionally specialized centers is somewhat similar to that for men, although the relationships are obscured somewhat by two factors. One is that the proportion of women in some industry groups, such as in transportation, is very small, and the other is that the analysis of occupational composition was undertaken in less detail for women than for men. Table 152 presents data on the percentage of women employed in the major occupation groups accounting for the major proportion of all female nonagricultural employment.

In 1950, 76 percent of all women in public administration were clerical and kindred workers. It is not surprising, therefore, that centers of public administration have larger proportions of female sales, clerical, and kin-

TABLE 152.—PERCENT OF EMPLOYED FEMALES IN SELECTED MAJOR OCCUPATION GROUPS, FOR ALL STANDARD METROPOLITAN AREAS AND URBAN PLACES OF 10,000 INHABITANTS OR MORE, AND FOR SELECTED PLACES BY MINOR TYPE OF FUNCTIONAL SPECIALIZATION, BY METROPOLITAN STATUS AND SIZE: 1950

Major occupation group, metropolitan status, and size of place	All places	Type of specialization for selected places				
		Ed	PA	Tr	My	ER
SALES, CLERICAL, AND KINDRED WORKERS						
Standard metropolitan areas:						
50,000 to 250,000....................	34.5	36.5	37.4	37.2	32.7	35.9
250,000 or more.....................	41.3	44.6	46.7	40.6	41.5	40.6
Central cities:						
Under 100,000........................	36.9	37.4	38.4	40.4	33.6	33.9
100,000 or more......................	41.4	43.7	46.1	41.2	41.7	[1]40.9
Suburbs:						
10,000 to 25,000.....................	41.8	44.6	43.3	44.7	42.5	41.1
25,000 or more.......................	41.6	43.6	45.0	42.6	44.2	41.0
Independent cities:						
10,000 to 25,000.....................	33.9	35.3	37.6	36.9	34.3	32.8
25,000 to 50,000.....................	34.8	36.7	39.2	36.2	35.9	33.5
OPERATIVES AND KINDRED WORKERS						
Standard metropolitan areas:						
50,000 to 250,000....................	21.0	17.1	9.6	14.2	15.7	16.2
250,000 or more.....................	19.9	14.3	10.0	12.8	20.2	14.4
Central cities:						
Under 100,000........................	19.7	16.4	14.9	13.2	14.4	14.0
100,000 or more......................	19.5	14.8	8.7	14.5	19.5	[1]14.4
Suburbs:						
10,000 to 25,000.....................	18.0	6.0	15.8	19.1	14.2	14.5
25,000 or more.......................	20.6	11.1	12.0	22.0	15.6	10.6
Independent cities:						
10,000 to 25,000.....................	19.5	14.4	14.8	14.3	14.6	14.3
25,000 to 50,000.....................	18.8	10.9	10.4	15.9	13.0	10.4
PRIVATE HOUSEHOLD AND SERVICE WORKERS						
Standard metropolitan areas:						
50,000 to 250,000....................	22.6	23.8	28.7	25.5	29.3	26.5
250,000 or more.....................	18.9	18.8	22.7	24.6	18.1	12.4
Central cities:						
Under 100,000........................	22.6	23.4	28.2	23.7	30.4	29.8
100,000 or more......................	19.7	20.6	24.5	24.1	19.1	[1]23.1
Suburbs:						
10,000 to 25,000.....................	17.5	20.7	19.6	16.6	21.9	20.6
25,000 or more.......................	16.2	18.8	17.7	16.4	16.9	22.6
Independent cities:						
10,000 to 25,000.....................	24.3	26.1	26.0	25.2	29.0	29.6
25,000 to 50,000.....................	24.5	26.3	27.1	26.6	28.2	31.9

[1] Excludes New York City.

Source: See table 150.

dred workers than do the other minor types of specialized places, or that they show an excess of these workers as compared with that for all places of comparable size and metropolitan status. All minor types of specialized places have substantially smaller percentages of female operatives and kindred workers, again reflecting the essentially nonmanufacturing character of places specializing in minor types of export activity. Correlatively, there are substantially larger proportions of female private household and service workers in all minor types of specialized places, a characteristic of nonmanufacturing places which, however, is markedly affected by the regional location of these places.

Income was chosen as a second indicator of socio-economic status. The income data are reported for families and unrelated individuals. The median figures for families and unrelated individuals are somewhat above those for persons in the experienced civilian labor force. The medians in table 153, therefore, are computed on a somewhat different basis from those in table 154.

Community specialization in an industry can affect its income distribution in two major ways. One is that the income provided by the industry will modify the average income in the community, if it is markedly different from that of other industries in the community. The second is that the specialization may attract related industries which are markedly different in average income. The actual statistics reported for an urban place, however, also may be affected somewhat by the method of reporting and tabulating census items. In the 1950 Census, college students were enumerated at the place of college attendance. Although data on the family status of college students are not available, it seems likely that many are unrelated individuals with a very low average income. This would tend to depress the average income in college communities somewhat artificially. The data for median family income, alone, probably would show somewhat different results.

Table 153 presents data on the median income of men and women in the experienced civilian labor force in 1950 in selected industry groups. The education data are for all educational services, including higher education, and no data were available for military persons residing in urban places. The data for other industry groups, however, are for the industry groups used in classifying places by functional type, except that sales data rather than employment data were used for the trade classification. Among both men and women, the median income of the experienced civilian labor force in manufacturing, wholesale trade, transportation, education, and public administration is above the median income of the experienced civilian labor force in the United States, while the medians for retail trade and entertainment and recreation are below the United States median. The direct effect of specialization in one of the former industries then should be to raise the median income of a place specializing in that industry,

TABLE **153**.—MEDIAN INCOME IN 1949 OF THE EXPERIENCED CIVILIAN LABOR FORCE FOR SELECTED INDUSTRIES, BY SEX: 1950

[In dollars]

Industry	Male	Female	Industry	Male	Female
Experienced civilian labor force............	2,668	1,575	Transportation[3]...............	3,067	2,313
			Entertainment and recreation services....................	2,338	1,279
Manufacturing...............	[1]2,966	1,784	Education[4]...................	2,976	2,114
Wholesale trade..............	3,143	1,927	Public administration.........	3,221	2,425
Retail trade[2]................	2,626	1,314			

[1] The figure for manufacturing is a correction of the published figure.
[2] Computed for the combined 10 classes of retail trade.
[3] Computed for the combined 6 classes of transportation.
[4] Computed for the combined private and government educational services.

Source: *1950 Census of Population*, Vol. II, *Characteristics of the Population*, Part 1, U. S. Summary, table 136.

while the effect of specializing in one of the latter should be to lower the median, assuming that the remaining industry group composition in each place yields a median income similar to that for all places. Actually, if the employment in a specialized industry group is small, as it generally is for all but specialization in manufacturing and retail trade, the general effect of the minor specialization on the income distribution of a place may not be apparent.

Table 154 shows that, in general, the median income of places with minor forms of specialization is below that of all places of comparable size and metropolitan status. The principal exceptions are that suburban places specialized in higher education or entertainment and recreation have median incomes above that of all suburbs of comparable size. This

TABLE **154**.—MEDIAN INCOME IN 1949 OF FAMILIES AND UNRELATED INDIVIDUALS, FOR ALL STANDARD METROPOLITAN AREAS AND URBAN PLACES OF 10,000 INHABITANTS OR MORE, AND FOR SELECTED PLACES BY MINOR TYPE OF FUNCTIONAL SPECIALIZATION, BY METROPOLITAN STATUS AND SIZE: 1950

[In dollars]

Metropolitan status and size of place	All places[1]	Type of specialization for selected places[1]				
		Ed	PA	Tr	My	ER
Standard metropolitan areas:						
50,000 to 250,000...........	2,751	2,644	2,756	2,491	2,197	2,458
250,000 or more..............	2,985	3,140	2,808	2,700	2,945	2,748
Central cities:						
Under 100,000..................	2,895	2,585	2,403	2,863	2,126	2,380
100,000 or more..............	2,961	2,851	2,791	2,712	2,838	[2]2,731
Suburbs:						
10,000 to 25,000..............	3,458	4,430	3,049	3,296	3,229	3,514
25,000 or more................	3,412	3,573	3,573	3,279	3,309	3,438
Independent cities:						
10,000 to 25,000..............	2,593	2,116	2,569	2,647	2,750	2,336
25,000 to 50,000..............	2,682	2,162	2,469	2,597	2,390	2,261

[1] The figure shown is the one for the median place in each group. All places with 25 percent or more of the population 20 to 24 years old enrolled in school are excluded from the PA and ER figures.
[2] Excludes New York City.

Source: *1950 Census of Population*, Vol. II, *Characteristics of the Population*, Parts 2 to 50, table 37.

contradicts the expectation from table 153 that only entertainment and recreation places (and possibly military places) should have a median income below the median for all comparable places, since the median income of the average person in educational services, public administration, and transportation is above that of the average person. The median income for males in educational services, in fact, is exceeded only by that for males in transportation, public administration, the major professional services, and finance, insurance, and real estate among the major industry groups, while the median income of males in public administration is exceeded only by that for males in finance, insurance, and real estate. The data also run somewhat counter to the fact that there generally is an excess of the higher paid professional, technical, and kindred workers, and managers, officials, and proprietors in all but the transportation places.

There is not even a clear-cut pattern of differentiation among the five minor types of places in table 154, although there is some evidence that centers of higher education, public administration, and transportation have a somewhat higher median income than do military and entertainment and recreation centers. Although there are exceptions to this general pattern, it is in keeping with the expectations based on the median income distribution of the several industry groups in table 153. When comparisons are made among the medians of places specialized in manufacturing (table 126) with those in the five minor types of places (table 154), it is clear that manufacturing places uniformly have a higher median income, except for the suburban centers of higher education and entertainment and recreation, the large suburbs specialized in public administration, and the small suburbs specialized in transportation. This holds despite the fact that the median income in transportation and public administration industry groups in table 153 is above that in manufacturing.

There are a number of reasons why the minor types of specialized places show so little variation in median income and why the average income is below that for all comparable places, despite expectations that only transportation and military specialization should depress the median income of a place below that of all comparable places. There is first of all the fact that despite the excess of the high income white-collar workers in these centers, there also is an excess of the very low income service workers and laborers with deficiencies of the higher income manual workers. The over-all effect of these differences may be to depress the median income of these specialized places below that of all comparable places. It should be pointed out, however, that this depression of income in higher education, public administration, and transportation centers cannot be traced to the occupational composition of the specialization itself, since the average income in these industry groups is above the United States average. It, furthermore, is equal to or greater than that in manufacturing, and it usually is above that of other major industry groups, except for finance, insurance, and real estate and professional services. Apparently the effect of specialization in a minor form of economic activity is to attract other industries which depress the average income of a place as compared with the United States average income. A related fact is that places specialized in manufacturing account for a large proportion of all employment in a place, and therefore for much of the income level in a place, while minor types of specialization generally do not determine the pattern to as large an extent. A second likelihood is that differences in the geographical location of the specialized places depress the income somewhat. Proportionally, more of all minor types of specialized places than of all places are located in the South, where the median income of families and unrelated individuals is on the average lower than that of families and unrelated individuals in other major regions of the United States. The median income of families and unrelated individuals in 1949 of all urban and rural-nonfarm families in the South was about $2,200, whereas the median was approximately $3,000 in each of the other three regions.[12] The differences in regional composition of specialized places, however, seem too small to account wholly for the observed differences in median income. There is, finally, the possibility that a set of factors unique to each specialization explains the general depression of income in minor types of specialized places. For example, the manner of enumerating the college population in 1950 may depress the average income in college communities considerably. The problem of explaining these differences in median income in different types of specialized places should be of special interest to students of social morphology and invite further investigation. Only some of the possible bases of explanation are suggested above.

Two other indicators of socio-economic status are presented in table 155 as a means of differentiating the social morphology of the minor types of specialized places. They are educational attainment and home ownership. The median educational attainment, in general, is highest among centers of higher education and of entertainment and recreation, and lowest among centers of transportation. Among the five specialized types of places, college communities have the highest average rank on median education, followed in order by entertainment and recreation centers, military centers, public administration centers, and transportation centers. The median number of years of school completed by the population 25 years of age and over in college communities exceeds by at least a year the median for all comparable places, except small SMA's and central cities. Communities specialized in entertainment and recreation likewise have higher levels of educational attainment than do all places of comparable size and metropolitan status, except for small independent cities. Small independent

---

[12] *1950 Census of Population, op. cit.*, table 84.

TABLE **155.**—EDUCATIONAL ATTAINMENT AND PERCENT OF OCCUPIED DWELLING UNITS OWNER-OCCUPIED, FOR ALL STANDARD METROPOLITAN AREAS AND URBAN PLACES OF 10,000 INHABITANTS OR MORE, AND FOR SELECTED PLACES BY MINOR TYPE OF FUNCTIONAL SPECIALIZATION, BY METROPOLITAN STATUS AND SIZE: 1950

Metropolitan status and size of place	Median school years completed[1]						Percent of occupied dwelling units owner-occupied					
	All places	Type of specialization for selected places[2]					All places	Type of specialization for selected places[2]				
		Ed	PA	Tr	My	ER		Ed	PA	Tr	My	ER
Standard metropolitan areas:												
50,000 to 250,000...	9.6	9.8	9.8	9.2	9.3	10.3	56.8	57.9	54.1	55.7	50.8	55.4
250,000 or more.....	10.1	11.4	10.6	9.8	10.0	11.4	50.0	52.1	51.5	53.5	44.9	53.8
Central cities:												
Under 100,000.......	9.8	10.3	9.7	10.1	9.8	10.0	52.1	52.8	49.7	57.9	45.4	50.1
100,000 or more.....	9.9	10.8	10.3	9.6	10.9	[3]11.6	40.7	44.8	44.6	42.6	34.8	[3]46.1
Suburbs:												
10,000 to 25,000....	10.9	12.5	10.7	9.9	11.6	11.5	63.5	69.7	54.6	59.9	57.5	63.4
25,000 or more......	10.7	12.3	12.0	9.9	11.2	12.0	51.1	52.4	44.5	47.3	46.5	52.2
Independent cities:												
10,000 to 25,000....	10.0	10.9	10.1	10.1	10.2	9.7	55.7	54.9	51.8	60.2	52.1	53.7
25,000 to 50,000....	10.1	11.4	10.6	9.3	10.8	11.0	53.8	55.1	51.5	51.1	49.8	53.4

[1] Persons 25 years old and over. The figure shown is the one for the median place in each group.

[2] All places with 25 percent or more of the population 20 to 24 years old enrolled in school are excluded from the PA, Tr, My, and ER figures.

[3] Excludes New York City.

Source: *1950 Census of Population*, Vol. II, *Characteristics of the Population*, Parts 2 to 50, table 34; *1950 Census of Housing*, Vol. I, *General Characteristics*, Part 1, U. S. Summary, table 22, and Parts 2 to 6, table 1.

cities specialized in entertainment and recreation, in fact, are somewhat below the United States median educational level. An examination of these places suggests that the group includes a disproportionate number of recreational centers for servicemen and similar transient groups. Neither the clientele and employees of these services, nor the related economic activities in these communities, seem likely to require sizable proportions of persons whose educational level is above the United States median. The median level of educational attainment in transportation centers is below that of all comparable places in 6 of 8 comparisons, but in all cases the median for transportation centers is within one year of the United States median.

The high levels of educational attainment in college communities and in centers of entertainment and recreation, and correlatively the rather low levels in centers of transportation, as compared with the level for all places of comparable size and metropolitan status, seem largely due to the fact that the proportion of white-collar workers is greater in college communities and centers of entertainment and recreation than in transportation centers. Other factors operate in favor of college communities, however. The data for median school years completed are only for persons 25 years of age and over. The observed differences cannot be due, therefore, to differences in the percentage of persons 20 to 24 years enrolled in school. They can be due, however, to differences in the percentages 25 years old and over enrolled in school. Many colleges and universities offer graduate and professional school programs of study. At least four-fifths of the SMA's and cities in the upper quintile on the percentage of persons 20 to 24 years old enrolled in school also were in the upper quintile on the percentage of persons aged 25 to 29 enrolled in school. Many of the latter persons are graduate or professional students, and their enumeration in the college community increases the median level of educational attainment somewhat. These persons, of course, are not usually included in the white-collar worker statistics. The high level of education associated with professional persons in college teaching and administration, therefore, seems to be responsible for a sizable part of the higher median level of education in college communities.

Home ownership [13] is somewhat less frequent in public administration, military, and entertainment and recreation centers than in the average place of comparable size and metropolitan status. There are a number of exceptions in that large SMA's and central cities specialized in public administration, and large SMA's, central cities, and suburbs specialized in entertainment and recreation show a small excess of home owners. Since these are large places, it is doubtful whether the excess is in any way related to the type of specialization. By way of contrast, centers of higher education usually show a small excess of home owners as compared with the average place, although small central and independent college cities show some deficiency. The pattern is not at all clear for transportation centers, with small SMA's, suburbs, and large independent cities showing proportions somewhat below that of the average place of comparable size and metropolitan status. The lower percentage of home owners in public administration, military, and entertainment and recreation centers seems related to the fact that the percentage of unrelated individuals is relatively high in places with these types of specialization. It is true, of course, that the proportion of unrelated individuals also is somewhat greater in college communities, but it is more likely that college students are living in quasi-households, which are excluded from the above comparisons. The proportion of home ownership, of course, is lower for unrelated individuals than for families. It also seems reasonable to assume that owner occupancy will be relatively low for the families of military personnel, government officials, and retired persons at recreational centers, since their rate of transiency presumably is comparatively high. The somewhat higher proportion of home owners in college communities than in all communities is consistent with the fact that college communities had the highest proportions of the high income white-collar workers.

---

[13] A dwelling unit is considered "owner-occupied" if the owner lives in the unit, even if the dwelling unit is not fully paid for or has a mortgage on it. If the owner was a member of the household but was temporarily away from home in 1950, as in the case of temporary employment away from home or for absence in military service, the dwelling unit still was considered owner-occupied. All dwelling units that are not owner-occupied were classified as renter-occupied whether or not any money was paid for the living quarters. Institutions and quasi-households (such as college dormitories and military barracks) are excluded from the dwelling unit data.

Relationship among types of functional specialization

There is specialization in more than one form of economic activity in a substantial number of communities, given the operational definitions of specialization employed in this research. The occurrence of several types of specialization in a community is referred to as "linkage" among these types. Table 156 presents data on the extent of linkage of manufacturing with minor types of functional specialization and the extent of linkage among the minor types.

There is some variation in the percentage of places with some type of functional specialization, other than trade, among the SMA and urban place groups, but this variation is on the whole small. Roughly two-thirds of the places in each group of SMA's and central cities are functionally specialized places, while the proportion is slightly less for suburbs and independent cities. To some extent the absence of specialization simply reflects the fact that the criteria of specialization in the research set an upper limit on the number of specialized places. If there were no linkage among the several types of functional specialization (i.e., no place with more than one type of specialization), then each metropolitan status–size-of-place group would be composed of the following:

	Percent
Manufacturing centers	20
Higher education centers	20
Public administration centers	10
Transportation centers	10
Entertainment-recreation centers	10

To the total of 70 percent represented by these five types of specialization would be added a percentage of military centers, varying in proportion by metropolitan status and size of place. The third line from the bottom in table 156 gives the upper limit to the total percentage of specialized places on the assumption of no linkage among the six types of places. This upper limit varies from 75.3 percent of the small independent cities to 93.7 percent of the large central cities. There is, nonetheless, some actual linkage among the types of specialization. The last line of table 156 shows the proportion of places which are not specialized because of the actual linkage among the six types. Among independent cities, suburbs, and the smaller central cities and SMA's, from 15 to 18 percent of the places are not specialized which could be if there were no linkage. About one-fourth of the large SMA's and central cities similarly are not specialized, although they would be if there were no linkage among the six types of specialization.

These results from table 156 clearly suggest that while most places are functionally specialized, they develop only a single functional specialization. There are, nonetheless, some differences in the extent of linkage related to the nature of the specialization. The amount of linkage among

TABLE **156.**—PERCENT DISTRIBUTION OF PLACES BY TYPE OF FUNCTIONAL SPECIALIZATION AND DEGREE OF LINKAGE AMONG TYPES OF SPECIALIZATION, BY METROPOLITAN STATUS AND SIZE: 1950

Functional specialization and degree of linkage	Standard metropolitan areas		Urban places						
			Total	Central cities		Suburbs		Independent cities	
	50,000 to 250,000	250,000 or more		Under 100,000	100,000 or more	10,000 to 25,000	25,000 or more	10,000 to 25,000	25,000 to 50,000
Total places..............	91	77	1,262	98	95	276	134	502	157
Percent..................	100.0	100.0	100.0	100.0	100.0	100.0	100.0	100.0	100.0
Manufacturing specialization....	19.8	20.8	19.6	20.4	18.9	20.0	20.2	19.1	19.8
Manufacturing, only...........	17.6	16.9	17.7	18.4	17.8	18.2	19.4	17.5	17.2
With minor specialization[1]....	2.2	3.9	1.9	2.0	1.1	1.8	0.8	1.6	2.6
Minor forms of specialization, only[1]...........................	48.3	48.1	43.3	45.9	50.5	43.1	45.5	40.7	43.9
Single specialization.........	34.0	29.9	30.3	30.6	31.6	30.8	29.8	28.1	29.9
Double specialization.........	13.2	11.7	11.1	14.3	14.7	9.8	12.7	11.4	12.1
Triple specialization.........	1.1	6.5	1.9	1.0	4.2	2.5	3.0	1.2	1.9
No specialization..............	31.9	31.1	37.1	33.7	30.6	36.9	34.3	40.2	36.3
Expected percent of specialized places[2].....................	83.5	93.5	79.9	82.6	93.7	80.1	82.8	75.3	81.5
Actual percent of specialized places......................	68.1	68.9	62.9	66.3	69.4	63.1	65.7	59.8	63.7
Expected minus actual percent...	15.4	24.6	17.0	16.3	24.3	17.0	17.1	15.5	17.8

[1] Minor forms of specialization are education, transportation, public administration, entertainment and recreation, and military.

[2] Assuming no linkage among the types of specialization.

Source: Appendix tables B–17 to B–20.

the types of specialization, for example, is related somewhat to the percentage employed in the specialization. Table 156 shows that no more than 4 percent of any group of places has manufacturing linked with some form of specialization, other than trade. There is considerably more linkage among the minor types of specialization. Among large SMA's, central cities, and suburbs, there are only twice as many places with a single minor form of functional specialization as there are places with linkage among the minor types of specialization. There are roughly three times as many places with a single minor type of functional specialization as with linkage among the minor types for the small SMA's, central cities, and suburbs. Most of the linkage occurs when a place has two types of functional specialization. There are relatively few instances where a place has three types of minor specialization.

Places classified as specialized in manufacturing show a relatively low degree of linkage with the minor types of functional specialization. Only one-tenth of the manufacturing places show linkage with one of the five minor types of functional specialization, whereas 27 percent of all places with a minor form of functional specialization are linked with at least one other minor form of specialization. The linkage of manufacturing with a minor type of specialization is mainly with military or educational specialization. Two-thirds of the linkages are of this nature. The number of places involved, however, is small.

Table 157 provides information on the linkage of specialization in wholesale and retail trade with manufacturing and the minor types of functional specialization. The patterns are shown for places with a relative absence of trade, the nontrade centers, as well as for the maintenance trade centers, and the three specialized types of trading centers, wholesale trade, retail trade, and trade centers. It is clear that places highly specialized in trade are not very likely to specialize also in manufacturing. The percent-

TABLE **157.**—PERCENT DISTRIBUTION OF ALL STANDARD METROPOLITAN AREAS AND URBAN PLACES OF 10,000 INHABITANTS OR MORE, AND FOR SELECTED PLACES BY TYPE OF FUNCTIONAL SPECIALIZATION, BY 1948 WHOLESALE-RETAIL TRADE CLASSIFICATION, BY METROPOLITAN STATUS: 1950

Metropolitan status and trade classification	All places	Type of specialization for selected places						
		Mfg.	Ed	PA	Tr	My	ER	All other
STANDARD METROPOLITAN AREAS								
Number[1]......................	207	34	33	19	16	35	17	53
Percent...................	100	100	100	100	100	100	100	100
Wholesale trade center...........	11	3	10	10	31	17	6	8
Retail trade center..............	11	12	12	16	...	9	29	9
Trade center.....................	26	6	36	10	19	28	35	34
Maintenance trade center.........	28	29	30	32	31	23	18	30
Nontrade center..................	24	50	12	32	19	23	12	19
CENTRAL CITIES								
Number[2]......................	223	38	39	19	19	25	22	61
Percent...................	100	100	100	100	100	100	100	100
Wholesale trade center...........	12	5	3	5	32	16	18	16
Retail trade center..............	11	21	5	21	5	8	18	5
Trade center.....................	31	11	56	16	16	28	41	34
Maintenance trade center.........	26	16	28	26	26	36	14	30
Nontrade center..................	20	47	8	32	21	12	9	15
SUBURBS								
Number[3]......................	394	66	64	31	38	34	38	125
Percent...................	100	100	100	100	100	100	100	100
Wholesale trade center...........	12	15	8	6	25	15	8	12
Retail trade center..............	8	9	14	6	...	6	16	5
Trade center.....................	24	12	19	20	22	23	24	34
Maintenance trade center.........	31	32	22	42	31	35	37	31
Nontrade center..................	25	32	37	26	22	21	15	18
INDEPENDENT CITIES								
Number[4]......................	665	109	121	52	59	42	56	226
Percent...................	100	100	100	100	100	100	100	100
Wholesale trade center...........	10	4	7	15	14	19	9	13
Retail trade center..............	8	6	11	8	5	7	14	8
Trade center.....................	27	3	27	27	29	21	30	37
Maintenance trade center.........	28	31	27	23	30	29	16	29
Nontrade center..................	27	56	28	27	22	24	31	13

[1] Trade classification is unknown for 1 manufacturing place.

[2] Trade classification is unknown for 1 education, 2 public administration, 4 military, and 1 place without any form of specialization.

[3] Trade classification is unknown for 16 manufacturing, 15 education, 11 public administration, 5 transportation, 11 military, 6 entertainment and recreation, and 23 places without any form of specialization.

[4] Trade classification is unknown for 19 manufacturing, 8 education, 14 public administration, 7 transportation, 10 military, 9 entertainment and recreation, and 33 places without any form of specialization.

Source: Appendix tables B–17 to B–20.

age of manufacturing places which are nontrade centers is much greater than the percentage of all places which are nontrade centers. This is not surprising since manufacturing and trade are the two largest employers among the 11 major industry groups. The minor types of specialized places are more likely to occur with some form of trade specialization, however. They are found less often among the nontrade centers than are all places, except for SMA's and central cities specialized in public administration, and suburban places specialized in higher education. The absence of specialization in manufacturing and/or one of the minor types of specialization in a place occurs more often in trade centers and maintenance trade centers than one would expect on the basis of the relative frequency of trade and maintenance trade centers among all places. The absence of specialization in a place, then, occurs either with specialization in both wholesale and retail trade, or with "average trade" for a particular metropolitan status–size-of-place group.

There are some differences in the linkage of the minor types of specialization with specialization in trade. Except for suburbs, specialization in higher education more often is linked with specialization in both wholesale and retail trade than one would expect, given the percentage trade centers are of all places. Among suburbs specialized in higher education, nontrade centers are proportionally more frequent than among all places. Specialization in public administration is not associated with specialization in, or an absence of, trade in independent cities; but among SMA's, central cities, and suburbs specialized in public administration, centers specialized in wholesale trade (Ww and TC places) are proportionately less frequent than among all places. Military establishments show no marked preference for host communities specialized in a particular type of trade, although proportionally fewer are nontrade centers than one would expect on the basis of the proportion of nontrade centers among all places. Specialization in transportation is associated with the presence of wholesale and an absence of exclusively retail specialization. Among places specialized in transportation, wholesale trade and trade centers are proportionally more frequent than among all places. This contrast is least pronounced, however, for independent cities specialized in transportation. The linkage of retail trade specialization with that of entertainment and recreation is readily apparent in the retail trade and trade center comparisons. A disproportionate number of the entertainment and recreation centers, as compared with all places, also are retail trade and trade centers. The examination of the linkage of trade with other forms of specialization in table 157 on the whole lends support to the findings of previous sections. Trade specialization generally is not associated with specialization in manufacturing, military, or public administration. Retail trade is linked with specialization in entertainment and recreation, while wholesale trade and transportation are frequently linked in location.

Most urban places and SMA's have no more than one minor type of

functional specialization. It is not infrequent, however, that a community
will support two minor forms of functional specialization. It was noted
earlier that there is some linkage among the five minor types of economic
specialization for 13 percent of all urban places. The actual pattern of
this linkage for places where two types of specialization occur in a single
place is presented in table 158. There are an additional 5 SMA's and 25
urban places where three minor types of functional specialization are
linked in location, and 1 SMA with four minor types.[14] The following
patterns in table 158 predominate in the approximately 11 percent of
places where two minor functions are linked. A place specializing in higher
education is most likely to link this specialization with specialization in

TABLE **158.**—NUMBER OF PLACES WITH SPECIFIC PATTERNS OF LINKAGE AMONG MINOR TYPES OF
FUNCTIONAL SPECIALIZATION, FOR STANDARD METROPOLITAN AREAS AND URBAN PLACES OF
10,000 INHABITANTS OR MORE WITH TWO MINOR TYPES OF FUNCTIONAL SPECIALIZATION, BY
METROPOLITAN STATUS: 1950

Linkage pattern	Standard metro- politan areas, total	Urban places			
		Total	Central cities	Suburbs	Inde- pendent cities
Total places...................................	22	142	27	40	75
Education--Public administration.....................	...	19	3	7	9
Education--Transportation............................	1	12	1	1	10
Education--Military..................................	6	11	6	1	4
Education--Entertainment and recreation.............	2	29	6	8	15
Public administration--Transportation...............	2	7	3	2	2
Public administration--Military.....................	4	41	5	13	23
Public administration--Entertainment and recreation.	2	5	1	1	3
Transportation--Military............................	2	6	1	2	3
Transportation--Entertainment and recreation........	1	6	...	3	3
Military--Entertainment and recreation..............	2	6	1	2	3

Source: Appendix tables B–17 to B–20.

entertainment and recreation, and the reverse also is true. If there is specialization in public administration, it most often is linked with military
specialization, and vice versa. Transportation is infrequently linked with
other minor forms of specialization, but is most likely to be linked with
specialization in higher education. Examples of places where specialization in higher education is linked with that in entertainment and recreation
include the central cities of Los Angeles, Calif., and Salt Lake City, Utah,
and the independent cities of Santa Barbara, Calif., and Saratoga Springs,
N. Y. The linkage of military specialization with that of public administration is illustrated by the central cities of Washington, D. C., and Mont-
gomery, Ala., and the suburban centers of Annapolis, Md., and Midwest
City, Okla. The linkage of transportation with higher education occurs

---

[14] The specific linkage patterns for SMA's are: Ed-PA-My-ER; PA-Tr-My (2); Ed-PA-My; Ed-My-ER;
PA-My-ER. For urban places, the linkage patterns are: Ed-My-ER; Ed-PA-ER; Tr-My-ER (2);
Ed-Tr-ER (2); Ed-PA-My (8); PA-My-ER (5); PA-Tr-My (6).

most frequently in such western independent cities as Emporia, Kans., Jamestown, N. D., Laramie, Wyo., and Nampa, Idaho.

Profiles of the minor types of specialization

This chapter examines the relationship between specialization in five minor types of functions and the demographic, economic, and socio-economic characteristics of communities. The relationship was determined by comparing the incidence of a characteristic in groups of SMA's and urban places with the incidence in comparable groups of all places in the United States. The five minor types of specialization are in higher education, public administration, transportation, military installations, and entertainment and recreation. Table 159 presents a summary of the comparisons of each characteristic for the eight metropolitan status and size

TABLE **159.**—SUMMARY OF COMPARISONS WITH ALL STANDARD METROPOLITAN AREAS AND URBAN PLACES OF 10,000 INHABITANTS OR MORE, FOR MANUFACTURING CENTERS AND MINOR TYPES OF SPECIALIZATION

Characteristic	Number of comparisons in which specialized places have a higher figure than all places[1]					
	Mfg.	Ed	PA	Tr	My	ER
Percent of population 21 years old and over	5	5	2	1	3	7
Sex ratio	7	4	6	4	7	4
Percent nonwhite	2[2]	2	8	5	6	7
Percent living in same house, 1949 and 1950	8	...	...	3[2]	1	1
Percent married, male	5	...	4	6	3	6
Persons per household	8	1	3	5	3	...
Percent in labor force:						
Male	8	...	4	6	6	3
Female	5	4	5	2[2]	3	4
Percent employed in manufacturing	8	...	...	...	...	...
Per capita wholesale trade	1	...	1	6	5	3
Per capita retail trade	1	6	1	1	3	8
Percent government workers	...	7	8	6	8	6
Percent employed in transportation	...	...	4	8	3	1
Percent of males employed in--						
Public administration	...	6	8	6	8	6
Hotels and lodging places	...	5	7	3	6	8
Entertainment and recreation	...	8	2	1	7	8
Percent of males employed as white-collar workers	...	8	7	3	5	8
Percent of males employed as--						
Professional, technical, and kindred workers	...	8	7	...	5	7
Managers, officials, and proprietors, exc. farm	...	8	4	6	5	8
Clerical and kindred workers	1	3	8	8	4	1
Sales workers	...	8	4	...	6	8
Craftsmen, foremen, and kindred workers	8	4[2]	5	6	5	2
Operatives and kindred workers	8	...	...	2[2]	...	...
Private household and service workers	...[2]	6	7	4	8	7
Laborers, except farm and mining	2[2]	...	7	8	6	4
Percent of females employed as--						
Sales, clerical, and kindred workers	...	8	8	6	6	1
Operatives and kindred workers	...	...	...	2[2]	1	...
Private household and service workers	...	7	8	7	6	7
Median school years completed	8	8	6	2	5	8
Percent enrolled in school, persons 20 to 24 yrs. old	1	8	4	1	2	5
Median income of families and unrelated individuals	6	3	2	1	1	2[2]
Percent of occupied dwelling units owner-occupied	5	6	2	4	...	3

[1] Eight comparisons are involved: Two size groups each of standard metropolitan areas, central cities, suburbs, and independent cities.

[2] Suburbs only.

[3] Independent cities only.

[4] Standard metropolitan areas only.

Source: Tables in Chapters 17 and 19.

groups, showing the number of comparisons in which the incidence of each characteristic exceeds the figure for all places. Since there are eight comparisons, two each for SMA's, central cities, independent cities, and suburbs, the number may vary from zero to eight. In most cases where the incidence of the characteristic does not exceed the figure for all places, it is below the figure rather than equal to it. The comparisons also are presented for the places specialized in manufacturing, since it is generally true that minor specialization increases as manufacturing specialization decreases.

The causal explanation of observed differences between places with minor forms of specialization and the average place is made complex by several facts. First, specialization in a minor type of function may exercise less influence on the social morphology of an urban place than specialization in the major forms of manufacturing or trade, since it involves a relatively smaller segment of the employed population. The case of military specialization is even more complex than that of the other types of minor specialization, for the effect of military specialization on civilian employment generally is slight. Second, the regional location of places with minor forms of specialization differs from that of all places of comparable size and metropolitan status. The differences in regional location are most likely to affect income and occupation comparisons, although the effect on other comparisons may not be negligible. Third, variation in the nature and source of employment in some of the minor industries probably produces significant morphological differences. This is particularly true of the public administration and entertainment and recreation industries which are not very homogeneous in the nature and source of employment. Fourth, comparisons between minor types of specialized places and all places actually involve, to a considerable extent, comparisons between manufacturing and the minor types of specialization, owing to the fact that manufacturing communities affect the average figures to a large degree. These factors render causal interpretations of the effects of minor forms of economic specialization on a community somewhat questionable, and give rise to the need for more detailed investigation. The following profiles of minor types of specialized places are based on the summary comparisons in table 159. Detailed causal explanations for the profile characteristics are not offered.

College communities, when compared with places of comparable size and metropolitan status, have a higher socio-economic level, and the character of their economic base is more favorable to employment in the white-collar occupations. This can be seen in the higher percentage of men and women in all specific white-collar occupations, except that of male clerical and kindred workers, the higher median level of school completed, and the greater proportion of workers in government and entertainment and recreation. Correlatively, college communities have a lower percentage of manual workers (other than private household and service workers) than does the average place and a smaller volume of manufacturing employment. The data for median income are not consistent with the high levels of white-collar employment in centers of higher education, particularly since the lower paid sales and clerical jobs for males are a smaller proportion of the total white-collar employment than are the higher paid professional and managerial ones. It also is known that educational services have a higher average income than do most major industry groups. The depression of income in centers of higher education seems, therefore, to be due to other factors, perhaps to an excess of the low paid private household and service workers, or by reason of attracting some low income industries to the community.

The population of college communities is somewhat more residentially mobile than that in all places of comparable size and metropolitan status. Some of this mobility may be due to their comparatively high rates of population growth during the 1940–50 decade, and to the fact that the 1950 freshman class in college, for the most part, was reported as residing elsewhere in 1949. If the enumeration of the college population were primarily responsible for the somewhat higher incidence of residential mobility in college communities, it would be expected that this would be reflected more in the independent cities than in other places. This is not the case, suggesting the mobility is primarily due to other causes. The proportion married for men 14 years of age and over is somewhat lower in college communities than in all comparable places. This finding is not entirely consistent with findings for the sex ratio. College communities have somewhat larger proportions of persons 21 years old and over than do all urban places of a similar size, a fact which is hardly explained by the age composition of college students alone.

Public administration centers do not differ markedly from all places in the percentage of persons 21 years old and over, but they do have somewhat greater sex ratios and percentages of nonwhite persons. The somewhat higher sex ratios seem primarily due to the fact that a large number of the places specialized in public administration are host communities to large military installations. Differences in the regional location of centers of public administration, as compared with that of all places, undoubtedly account for some of the difference in the percentage of nonwhite persons, for there is no evidence that employment in public administration generally is selective of nonwhite persons. The stability of residence is lower in public administration centers than in all places, presumably, in part, because public administration is an industry which induces considerable residential mobility through personnel transfer policies, patronage systems of employment, bureau changes, and so on. No particular differences are observed between public administration centers and all places in household size. The somewhat greater sex ratios in public administration centers as compared with all places seem too small to affect the male marriage rate, although there is a slightly greater percentage of married males 14 years old and over in small public administration centers, regardless of metropolitan status, than in all comparable places.

The nature of employment opportunities in public administration centers is not very different from that in the average place of comparable size and metropolitan status. The labor force participation rates in centers of public administration are affected somewhat by the ratio of military to the civilian population. If military centers are excluded, it appears that places specialized in public administration probably have a relatively smaller labor force than do all comparable places. There are no substantial differences between places specialized in public administration and all places in the labor force participation rates of women.

There is a smaller proportion of employed persons in manufacturing in public administration centers than in all places, or in any of the minor types of specialized places. Evidently, there is little tendency for places specialized in public administration to attract manufacturing industries. Centers of public administration are also below the average place with respect to the nonmanufacturing industries of wholesale and retail trade, transportation, and entertainment and recreation. Per capita expenditures in wholesale and retail trade generally are lowest in public administration centers of all minor types of places. The somewhat lower income of persons in public administration places compared with that in all places probably accounts for some, but not all, of the lower per capita expenditures in trade. Centers of public administration have only about the same proportions employed in transportation and in entertainment and recreation as do all places of comparable size and metropolitan status. On the other hand, specialization in public administration is often linked with military and educational specialization, and it increases employment in hotels and lodging places. The demand for hotel and lodging space, of course, is stimulated by institutions of higher education and military establishments.

The socio-economic level of SMA's and urban places specialized in public administration is above that of the average place. There is a substantial excess of white-collar workers in public administration centers as compared with all places of comparable size and metropolitan status. This is no doubt related to the occupational composition of public administration. More specifically, public administration centers have disproportionately high numbers of males employed in the professional, technical, and kindred, and clerical and kindred positions. There also is a substantial excess of female sales, clerical, and kindred workers in public administration centers as compared with all places, and the percentages of women in sales, clerical, and kindred jobs are greater than those for any of the other minor types of specialized places. The correlatively smaller proportions in manual jobs are not explained by deficiencies in all specific manual occupations. The substantial deficiency of both male and female operatives and kindred workers in public administration centers, as compared with the average for all places, reflects their low employment in manufacturing. There are no substantial differences in the employment of male craftsmen, foremen, and kindred workers in public administration centers, and there are slight excesses of male laborers, and of male and female private household and service workers in these comparisons.

The educational level of persons 25 years of age and over is higher in centers of public administration than in all comparable places, except for small central cities and suburbs. Both income and home ownership are generally lower in centers of public administration than in the average place of comparable size and metropolitan status. Thus, specialization in public administration enhances the status level of a community only as measured by occupational composition and educational attainment. The fact that public administration centers tend to have an excess of employment at both ends of the socio-economic continuum probably accounts for the somewhat lower median income in public administration centers as compared with the average place, while the high residential mobility in public administration may discourage home ownership.

Transportation centers are very little different from the average place of comparable size and metropolitan status in the proportions of persons 21 years old and over and of nonwhite persons, or in the sex ratio. The stability of residence is somewhat lower in transportation centers than in all comparable places, except for independent cities. There is no great difference in the proportion of males 14 years old and over who are married, or in the average size of households, but transportation centers perhaps are somewhat more favorable to the marriage of males and have larger households than the average place.

Specialization in transportation seems to enhance opportunities for male, but not female, employment. The labor force participation rate of women in transportation centers is low compared with that in all comparable places, or in the other minor types of functionally specialized places, while that for men is generally higher. Transportation centers have comparatively little employment in manufacturing, with very little linkage between the two specializations, and specialization in transportation leads to low retail per capita sales. The percentage of persons aged 20 to 24 enrolled in school is slightly below that of the average place. There are somewhat greater proportions working for a government employer and in public administration, but the percentage difference is very small, suggesting relatively little actual difference. There seem to be few male employment opportunities in entertainment and recreation or in hotels and lodging places, relative to those in other minor types of functionally specialized places or in all comparable places.

There are somewhat smaller proportions of male white-collar workers in transportation centers than in all comparable places, except for central cities. This results from deficiencies of professional, technical, and kindred workers, since transportation centers have an excess of male managers, officials, and proprietors and of clerical and kindred workers. Transportation centers clearly reflect the fact that transportation is a relatively large employer of unskilled male labor, for there are substantially larger proportions of male laborers in transportation centers than in all places, regardless of size and metropolitan status. Except for suburbs, transportation centers are not generally favorable to the employment of male operatives and kindred workers, but they do have somewhat higher proportions of male craftsmen, foremen, and kindred workers, if the large SMA and central city comparisons are excluded. Specialization in transportation cannot directly affect the employment of women in specific occupations to any great extent, for relatively few women work in transportation. The fact that transportation centers generally have higher proportions of women employed in sales, clerical, and kindred and in private household and service jobs, and relatively lower proportions in operative and kindred jobs than do all places must be due to other selective factors.

Generally speaking, transportation centers are of rather low socioeconomic status. The median school year completed for persons 25 years old and over is somewhat below that in all places, as is the median income. The substantially lower median income in transportation centers cannot be attributed directly to specialization in transportation, however, since the median income of males in transportation is substantially higher than that in most major industry groups, including manufacturing. The occupational composition of transportation, however, would indicate lower median levels of educational attainment. Home ownership probably is not substantially different in transportation centers from that in all comparable places.

Military centers do not differ consistently from all comparable places in the proportion of persons 21 years old and over. The sex ratio is greater in military centers than in all comparable places, or other minor types of specialized places, except for public administration, but the differences are small. The fact that a high proportion of military centers are located in the South probably explains the fact that military centers show some excess of nonwhite persons. The relatively high percentage of residentially mobile persons in military centers reflects the high residential mobility of military personnel. The family composition of military centers differs from that of the average place, in that SMA's and central cities which are hosts to large military installations have lower percentages of males 14 years old and over who are married. Since military specialization should have a greater impact on small than on large places, it seems that military specialization itself is not primarily responsible for the lower incidence of marriage among males in these host communities. There are no substantial differences in the average size of household.

Places with military specialization have somewhat larger proportions of males employed in entertainment and recreation and in hotels and lodging places than does the average place. No doubt the military population stimulates the demand for extrafamily services. Per capita expenditures for wholesale sales probably are somewhat higher, while those in retail trade are somewhat lower, in communities which are host to military installations than in the average place. Communities with military installations have substantially larger proportions of employed persons in government and of employed males in public administration, suggesting that military specialization provides increased opportunities for employment with a government employer. There are relatively fewer males employed in manufacturing and transportation in military centers than in the average place, and there is a relatively smaller enrollment of persons aged 20 to 24 in school.

Despite their industrial composition, military centers do not consistently have an excess of white-collar workers. The most striking aspect of their occupational structure is the low percentage of male operatives and kindred workers. Employment of males in private household and service work is the only case where military centers are consistently above all places, and this difference probably is due to their relative concentration in the South. The occupational composition of military communities probably is mainly influenced by the fact that they have somewhat less employment in manufacturing and in retail trade than does the average place and more employment in the industries oriented to a transient population.

The socio-economic level of military centers probably is somewhat above that of all places of comparable size and metropolitan status, if occupational composition and median level of educational attainment are taken as indicators of socio-economic level, although there are a number of exceptions to this relationship. But other indicators of socio-economic level (income and home ownership) give a contrary result. The high transiency of the military population and the geographical concentration of military centers in the South and West probably influence, respectively, the home ownership and income indicators.

Entertainment and recreation centers differ in many respects from the average place. The demographic data for these specialized places show that they have, comparatively, old populations, small households, and a high incidence of residential mobility. These are characteristics expected of resort and retirement centers, if not of all types of entertainment and recreation centers. Entertainment and recreational centers have substantially larger nonwhite populations than do all comparable places, but this probably is largely due to their concentration in the South.

The opportunities for male and female employment in entertainment and recreation centers are probably not quite as good as those in the average place of comparable size and metropolitan status, but the differences are very small and there are numerous exceptions. The pattern of economic activity in entertainment and recreation places includes high per capita retail, but low per capita wholesale expenditures, and relatively sizable male employment in hotels and lodging places. These activities, of course, are closely related to specialization in entertainment and recreation. There probably is a somewhat higher level of school enrollment for persons aged 20 to 24 in entertainment and recreation centers than in the average place. Manufacturing and transportation make relatively little contribution to male employment in these centers, however. The percentage of persons at work for a government employer or of employed males in public administration in centers of entertainment and recreation is not substantially different from that in all places.

There are considerably larger proportions of male white-collar workers in entertainment and recreation centers than in all places of comparable size and metropolitan status. This is largely accounted for by an excess of male managers, proprietors, and officials, and of male sales workers, since there is some deficiency of male clerical and kindred workers in entertainment and recreation centers. The corollary deficiency of male manual workers is made up of deficiencies in all manual occupations, other than private household and service workers. Entertainment and recreation establishments, of course, employ substantial numbers of male and female service workers. The relatively low demand for female clerical and kindred workers, and operative and kindred workers in these specialized places also is apparent.

The median level of educational attainment in centers of entertainment and recreation is above that in comparable groups of all places. This is consistent with their white-collar excess. Both the median income and home ownership levels in these communities are relatively low, however. The higher incidence of transiency in entertainment and recreation centers and their relatively greater concentration in the South again may account for their somewhat lower socio-economic levels on these two indicators.

The several types of minor specialization may be contrasted with manufacturing specialization. The effect of manufacturing activity on an urban community is considerable, since, with the exception of residential suburbs, the percentage of employment in manufacturing in a place is on the average larger than that in any other form of industry, except perhaps retail trade. It generally is assumed that manufacturing has a marked effect on all forms of industry specialization, in that, as employment in manufacturing increases, employment in all other industries decreases, and vice versa. There is considerable support for that proposition in this study, so far as the minor forms of functional specialization and retail trade specialization are concerned. The data in table 159 show that the percentage employed in transportation, public administration, hotels and lodging places, and entertainment and recreation, and the per capita wholesale and retail sales are lower in manufacturing centers than in all places of comparable size and metropolitan status.   There is, furthermore, very little linkage between specialization in manufacturing and the minor forms of specialization.   Finally, the proportion of males in the labor force is substantially larger in manufacturing communities than in all places.

The demographic composition of manufacturing places is not greatly different from that of some of the minor types of functionally specialized places, except that the populations in manufacturing centers are residentially more stable and the average household is larger.   But there are very substantial differences in socio-economic level.   Manufacturing places have substantially smaller proportions of all white-collar and manual workers, other than the craftsman, foreman, and kindred, and operative and kindred workers (which comprise a substantial proportion of all manufacturing jobs).   The effect of this mode of occupational specialization is to decrease the proportion of workers in both the highest and lowest paid occupational categories, and to provide a fairly high median income for persons employed in manufacturing.   The median income level of manufacturing places is above that of all places of comparable size and metropolitan status, except for suburbs.

C H A P T E R 2 0

HIGH AND LOW INCOME COMMUNITIES

Income differences produce rather large differences in what individuals can do in a community. The amount of income an individual receives is related to such facts as whether he owns or rents a house, how his leisure is spent, what kinds of services he purchases, his educational and other opportunities, and how much he saves. Differences among communities in the average income of persons or families can be analyzed from two standpoints of social morphology. One can investigate how such differences affect community structure. For example, how do differences in income affect the volume of wholesale or retail trade? Or, one can investigate how differences in community structure produce differences in income of persons living in these communities. For example, how do various local industry and employment conditions affect income levels of local residents?

Data available from the 1947 Census of Manufactures, the 1948 Census of Business, and the 1950 Censuses of Population and Housing do not permit an analytical separation of hypotheses regarding the effect of income differences on the social morphology of communities from those regarding the effect of social morphology of communities on income differences. This chapter compares standard metropolitan areas and urban places which differ considerably in average income of families and unrelated individuals. The object is to describe how high income communities differ from low income communities with respect to selected characteristics of places and their resident populations.

Scope and technique of analysis

All urban places with 10,000 inhabitants or more in 1950 were classified in one of three groups—central cities, independent cities, and suburbs. This is necessary, since these political units vary rather markedly in type and degree of residential specialization. Suburbs, in particular, tend to specialize very markedly by socio-economic level as defined by various indexes of occupation, income, or type of housing. Then, too, suburbs frequently specialize only in providing residence, while central cities and independent cities frequently are highly specialized in some form of basic economic activity. Standard metropolitan areas were employed as a fourth group. Following the procedure of earlier chapters, each class of urban

346

place or SMA was further divided into large and small places, since income is known to vary somewhat with size of place.

The income data used here are based on the reports of 1949 income for
families and unrelated individuals. Data also are available for the 1949
income of persons. The data on income for families and unrelated individuals, rather than for persons, were used to define high and low income
places. It is thought that community differences in family or unrelated
individual income more realistically represent differences related to expenditures and savings in the community. Actually, the two distributions
provide roughly similar groups of high and low income places.

The 1950 Census reports income for a 20-percent sample of persons
14 years of age and over. Income was defined as the amount of wages
or salary received in 1949, plus the amount of net income received from
self-employment in 1949, and the amount of other 1949 income from
sources such as interest, pensions, dividends, rents, or veterans' allowances.
The income tabulated for families is the combined income of all members
of the family. The composition of families is as found at the time of the
census interview, although the income statistics refer to 1949. The income tabulated for persons who are not members of families is, of course,
the amount of their own income. The income figures on family income
may understate the amount of family income somewhat in that the Bureau
of the Census assumed, in the editing process, that there was no other
income in the family when only the family head's income was reported.
This procedure was followed for about 5 percent of all families in the
United States.

The frequency distribution of each metropolitan status and size group
of places by 1949 median income of families and unrelated individuals
is presented in table 160. The income distributions for SMA's and central
cities are very similar. Only one SMA and one central city have a median
income of less than $1,500, and none has a median income in excess of
$4,000. Three-fifths or more of all SMA's and central cities have median
incomes between $2,500 and $3,500. The distribution of medians for
independent cities is quite similar to that of SMA's and central cities,
except that more of the places have median incomes of less than $1,500
and from $1,500 to $1,999. Only one independent city has a median
income in excess of $4,000. The distributions for SMA's, central cities,
and independent cities are very leptokurtic in form and somewhat negatively skewed. By contrast, the distributions of medians for suburbs in
both size groups are somewhat positively skewed. Almost 30 percent of
all small suburbs and 16 percent of all large suburbs have median incomes
in excess of $4,000. Only three suburbs have a median income of less
than $2,000. Clearly, suburbs are more often residential places for upper
income groups than are central cities or independent cities. The suburban
population is usually a relatively small proportion of the total SMA pop-

TABLE **160.**—PERCENT DISTRIBUTION OF STANDARD METROPOLITAN AREAS AND URBAN PLACES BY 1949 MEDIAN INCOME OF FAMILIES AND UNRELATED INDIVIDUALS, BY METROPOLITAN STATUS AND SIZE: 1950

Metropolitan status and size of place	Number of places	Percent of all places, by median income							
		Total	Under $1,500	$1,500 to $1,999	$2,000 to $2,499	$2,500 to $2,999	$3,000 to $3,499	$3,500 to $3,999	$4,000 and over
Standard metropolitan areas:									
50,000 to 250,000......	90	100.0	1.1	6.7	26.7	30.0	32.2	3.3	...
250,000 or more........	78	100.0	...	...	15.4	35.9	44.9	3.8	...
Central cities:									
Under 100,000..........	95	100.0	...	1.1	19.0	38.9	38.9	2.1	...
100,000 or more........	97	100.0	1.0	9.3	16.5	35.1	35.1	3.0	...
Suburbs:									
10,000 to 25,000.......	276	100.0	1.1	...	5.5	12.7	33.3	18.1	29.3
25,000 or more.........	135	100.0	...	...	3.0	17.8	40.0	23.0	16.2
Independent cities:									
10,000 to 25,000.......	502	100.0	4.8	14.1	24.3	34.9	18.5	3.2	0.2
25,000 to 50,000.......	157	100.0	7.0	10.8	22.3	33.1	24.2	2.6	...

Source: *1950 Census of Population*, Vol. II, *Characteristics of the Population*, Parts 2 to 50, table 37.

ulation.   Standard metropolitan areas also contain rural-farm and rural-nonfarm inhabitants, and residents of places with fewer than 10,000 inhabitants, whose median incomes are generally below those of suburbs with over 10,000 inhabitants.   Hence, the SMA figure approximates that for central cities, which contain the greater proportion of the SMA population.

Places with a high income are defined as those where the median income of the place is in the upper quintile of median income for all places of a particular metropolitan status and size.   Correlatively, places with a low income are defined as those where the median income of the place is in the lower quintile of the distribution.   Table 161 presents the upper and lower quintiles of the distributions for the eight classes of cities and SMA's.

TABLE **161.**—QUINTILE LIMITS USED TO SELECT STANDARD METROPOLITAN AREAS AND URBAN PLACES WITH HIGH AND LOW 1949 INCOME, BY METROPOLITAN STATUS AND SIZE

Metropolitan status and size of place	High income		Low income		Difference between upper and lower quintile (dollars)
	Number of places	Upper quintile[1] (dollars)	Number of places	Lower quintile[1] (dollars)	
Standard metropolitan areas:					
50,000 to 250,000..................	18	3,185	19	2,228	957
250,000 or more...................	19	3,219	18	2,776	343
Central cities:					
Under 100,000.....................	19	3,248	19	2,287	961
100,000 or more...................	19	3,182	19	2,434	748
Suburbs:					
10,000 to 25,000..................	55	4,253	55	3,011	1,224
25,000 or more....................	27	3,903	26	2,995	908
Independent cities:					
10,000 to 25,000..................	101	3,027	100	2,033	994
25,000 to 50,000..................	31	3,069	31	2,025	1,044

[1] 1949 income for families and unrelated individuals; the figure reported is the median income for the place which is the quintile limit.

Source: See table 160.

The 1949 median income for urban families and unrelated individuals in the entire United States was $2,970.[1] The median income for families is greater than that for individuals. The 1949 median income for all urban families was $3,431, while that for all urban unrelated individuals was only $1,150.[2] The median income of families and unrelated individuals for urban places, therefore, varies somewhat with the ratio of unrelated individuals to families. The upper quintile of the distribution of median incomes of families and unrelated individuals is above the United States urban median of $2,970 for each of the eight groups of cities and SMA's. The lower quintile is below the United States urban median for all groups except suburbs. Suburbs have median incomes well above those of other urban places. This accounts for the fact that the lower quintile for suburbs is above the United States urban median. No doubt the residential specialization of suburbs and their higher average socio-economic level account for this somewhat higher average income when compared with other metropolitan status groups.

The difference between the medians defining the upper and lower quintiles is quite large for each size and type of place. Except for large SMA's and large central cities, the difference between medians for high and low income places is at least $900. This means there are sizable income differences between the groups of SMA's and urban places which are compared below.

There are very marked differences in regional location between high income and low income places. (See figure 2, p. 31, and figure, 18, p. 153, for location of all places.) Table 162 shows that 59 percent of all low income cities are in the South, while 46 percent of the high income cities are in the North Central Region. This pattern of regional location of the selected high and low income urban places is characteristic of SMA's, central cities, and large independent cities. The pattern is quite different for suburbs, and it also differs somewhat for small independent cities. While the North Central Region ranks first in the number of high income suburbs, low income suburbs are found most often in the Northeast. Somewhat more of the high income small independent cities are located in the West (40 percent) than in the North Central Region (33 percent). The fact that low income suburbs are most often found in the Northeast is understandable. Low income suburbs more often are employing suburbs rather than residential (or dormitory) suburbs,[3] and employing suburbs more often are found in the Northeast Region.[4] Suburbs of southern

---

[1] *1950 Census of Population*, Vol. II, *Characteristics of the Population*, Part 1, table 57.

[2] *Idem.*

[3] See Sanford M. Dornbusch, "A Typology of Suburban Communities: Chicago Metropolitan District, 1940," Chicago Community Inventory, University of Chicago, Urban Analysis Report, Number 10, May 1952.

[4] Victor M. Jones, "Economic Classification of Cities and Metropolitan Areas," *The Municipal Yearbook*, 1953, pp. 49–57.

TABLE **162.**—PERCENT DISTRIBUTION OF SELECTED STANDARD METROPOLITAN AREAS AND URBAN PLACES, BY REGIONS, BY METROPOLITAN STATUS, SIZE, AND 1949 INCOME LEVEL: 1950

Metropolitan status and size of place	1949 income level	Number of places	Percent of all places, by region				
			United States	North-east	North Central	West	South
Standard metropolitan areas:							
50,000 to 250,000...........	High.......	18	100	33	61	...	6
	Low........	19	100	5	5	...	90
250,000 or more.............	High.......	19	100	16	58	21	5
	Low........	18	100	22	...	17	61
Urban places of 10,000 or more[1].	High.......	252	100	21	46	23	10
	Low........	251	100	16	16	9	59
Central cities:							
Under 100,000...............	High.......	19	100	32	58	...	10
	Low........	19	100	5	...	...	95
100,000 or more.............	High.......	19	100	21	63	16	...
	Low........	19	100	5	...	...	95
Suburbs:							
10,000 to 25,000............	High.......	55	100	33	49	7	11
	Low........	55	100	40	16	20	24
25,000 or more..............	High.......	27	100	19	63	11	7
	Low........	26	100	46	15	24	15
Independent cities:							
10,000 to 25,000............	High.......	101	100	15	33	40	12
	Low........	100	100	2	22	5	71
25,000 to 50,000............	High.......	31	100	19	52	23	6
	Low........	31	100	7	16	...	77

[1] Excludes standard metropolitan areas.

Source: Appendix tables B–17 to B–20.

cities seldom are employing suburbs.   The generally low income of the South, as compared with other regions, is reflected in the fact that 95 percent of the low income central cities are in the South.   Except for suburbs, differences between high and low income places may reflect regional differences as well.   But such an interpretation, at best, is ambiguous, because it can well be argued that regional differences are partly produced by income differences.   For example, when it is observed that high income urban places have fewer private household and service workers than do low income urban places, it can be shown that this difference is due to regional differences, as more of the private household and servant labor is found in the southern cities.   But, of course, this regional characteristic is related to the low income of the region.

Population composition

There are proportionately more persons 21 years of age and older in SMA's, central cities, and independent cities in high than in low income communities (table 163).   This difference cannot be accounted for by the fact that more of the low income than of the high income communities are also college communities, since the elimination of places with substantial college populations does not greatly alter the percentage point differences between high and low income places.   Some of the differences can be attributed to the fact that low income cities are more likely to have a resident military population, but the effect of this factor is slight.   It seems likely that the lower average age of low income places reflects, at least in part, a higher level of fertility.

There is a somewhat higher sex ratio in high than in low income communities, regardless of size, except for large SMA's and small suburbs. The difference in sex ratios, however, is substantial only for small independent cities (table 163). Apparently low income independent cities with 10,000 to 25,000 inhabitants attract disproportionate numbers of women or lose disproportionate numbers of men by out-migration. The sex ratio of high income small suburbs is below that for low income small suburbs. This exception to the general finding perhaps can be explained by the fact that the labor force participation rates of women are significantly lower in high than in low income urban places only among the small suburbs. The small high income suburbs may be places where nonworking women with independent incomes are more likely to reside.

The percentages of nonwhite persons in high and low income places are shown in table 163. Substantially larger proportions of nonwhite persons are found in low than in high income places, regardless of size. The difference between high and low income places, however, is much greater for SMA's, central, and independent cities than it is for suburbs. More than one-fifth of the population is nonwhite in low income SMA's (excluding large SMA's), central cities, and independent cities. Fewer than 5 percent of the residents in low income places (except large SMA's) are nonwhite. Roughly 2 percent of persons in high income suburbs as compared with 9 percent in low income suburbs are nonwhite. These differences

TABLE 163.—AGE AND SEX COMPOSITION, PERCENT NONWHITE, MARITAL STATUS, AND PERSONS PER HOUSEHOLD, FOR SELECTED STANDARD METROPOLITAN AREAS AND URBAN PLACES, BY METROPOLITAN STATUS, SIZE, AND 1949 INCOME LEVEL: 1950

[Asterisk (*) denotes difference between high and low groups significant at 0.05 level of probability]

Metropolitan status and size of place	1949 income level	Percent 21 years old and over[1]	Sex ratio	Percent non-white	Percent married, male[1]	Persons per household[2]
Standard metropolitan areas:						
50,000 to 250,000	High	*66.4	*98.2	*4.6	69.4	3.37
	Low	64.6	95.9	29.4	68.2	3.50
250,000 or more	High	*69.4	96.6	*9.1	68.0	3.28
	Low	65.3	96.8	15.8	68.1	3.42
Central cities:						
Under 100,000	High	*68.2	*96.2	*4.7	70.2	3.30
	Low	67.0	92.7	29.8	67.5	3.29
100,000 or more	High	*69.9	*96.8	*11.7	67.4	3.27
	Low	66.9	91.2	27.2	69.3	3.33
Suburbs:						
10,000 to 25,000	High	69.4	*92.9	*2.1	*74.6	3.44
	Low	66.0	94.9	9.1	68.7	3.34
25,000 or more	High	68.4	*95.7	*1.6	*73.7	*3.35
	Low	69.3	93.3	9.5	69.0	3.27
Independent cities:						
10,000 to 25,000	High	*65.4	*97.6	*2.6	71.7	3.16
	Low	64.1	89.9	21.6	70.9	3.21
25,000 to 50,000	High	*67.7	96.7	*3.0	*70.8	3.16
	Low	63.7	95.6	23.3	65.8	3.23

[1] Excludes from comparisons all places with 25 percent or more of the population 20 to 24 years old enrolled in school.

[2] The figure shown is the one for the median place in each group.

Source: *1950 Census of Population*, Vol. II, *Characteristics of the Population*, Parts 2 to 50, tables 33 and 34.

reflect both regional and income differences. Clearly, the comparatively high proportion of nonwhites in low income SMA's, central cities, and independent cities is related to the fact that they are largely concentrated in the South. The regional factor does not wholly explain the findings for suburbs. The large nonwhite populations in the large low income suburbs are found primarily in places outside the South. For small low income suburbs, more than half of the places with large nonwhite populations are outside the South.

Table 163 shows the percentage married for males 14 years old and over for high and low income places. The percentage married is significantly greater in high than in low income suburbs and large independent cities only. The direction of the difference for small SMA's, central cities, and independent cities is consistent with this finding. The exclusion of college communities, where the proportion of married males is somewhat lower, decreases the size but not the significance of the difference. Whether high income communities are more conducive to the marriage of men cannot be determined from these data, though that conclusion seems a reasonable inference, particularly for the data for suburbs and independent cities. It is possible that there are migration differences not due to income, which attract more single individuals to low income places.

Table 163 provides data on the number of persons per household. The size of households is somewhat greater in high than in low income places among large suburbs. The differences are not significant for the other type and size of place comparisons, most of them being in the opposite direction.

The stability of residence is greater in SMA's, central cities, and large independent cities with high incomes than in those with low incomes (table 164), but high income suburbs show no greater residential stability than do low income suburbs. This probably is due to the fact that high income suburbs experienced somewhat greater average growth during the 1940–50 decade. Since there is greater in-movement due to the construction of new housing in growing communities, the over-all rate of residential stability for high income suburbs is somewhat lower.

The 1940–50 rates of growth of high and low income places are presented in table 164. High income SMA's, central cities, and independent cities grew at a much slower rate during the decade than did comparable low income places. Suburbs show the reverse pattern of growth in relation to income. High income suburbs grew at a greater rate during the decade than did low income suburbs. The differences between the rates of growth of high and low income places are significant for all groups except the small SMA's and the small suburbs. Part of the explanation for the reversal in the case of suburbs is based on differences in regional location. While the low income SMA's, central, and independent cities are concentrated in the South and West—regions with high urban growth rates—the

TABLE **164.**—MOBILITY STATUS OF THE POPULATION AND 1940–1950 GROWTH RATE, FOR
SELECTED STANDARD METROPOLITAN AREAS AND URBAN PLACES, BY METROPOLITAN STATUS,
SIZE, AND 1949 INCOME LEVEL: 1950

[Asterisk (*) denotes difference between high and low groups significant at 0.05 level of probability]

Metropolitan status and size of place	1949 income level	Percent living in same house, 1949 and 1950[1]	Growth rate, 1940 to 1950[2]	Metropolitan status and size of place	1949 income level	Percent living in same house, 1949 and 1950[1]	Growth rate, 1940 to 1950[2]
Standard metropolitan areas:				Suburbs:			
50,000 to 250,000..	High....	*83.1	18.5	10,000 to 25,000....	High....	80.8	30.0
	Low.....	75.0	28.4		Low.....	81.2	17.2
250,000 or more....	High....	*84.0	*19.7	25,000 or more......	High....	83.7	*26.0
	Low.....	76.5	35.9		Low.....	85.2	13.1
Central cities:				Independent cities:			
Under 100,000......	High....	*82.3	*13.9	10,000 to 25,000....	High....	75.8	*18.2
	Low.....	75.3	40.0		Low.....	73.4	29.5
100,000 or more....	High....	*83.8	*8.5	25,000 to 50,000....	High....	*80.6	*14.4
	Low.....	75.8	21.5		Low.....	72.0	43.3

[1] Persons 1 year old and over.

[2] The figure shown is the one for the median place in each group.

Source: *1950 Census of Population,* Vol. II, *Characteristics of the Population,* Parts 2 to 50, tables 10 and 34.

same is not true of suburbs. Whatever the explanation, the classification by income levels produces differences of the order of 2 to 1 in growth rates.

Economic characteristics

Income is both a cause and a result of economic opportunity. High income levels may attract certain kinds of services, such as the professional and related services, or the personal services. Clearly, however, certain economic activities provide higher income opportunities than do others. Manufacturing, for example, pays higher average wages than do wholesale and retail trade. The median 1949 income for male workers (experienced labor force) in manufacturing was $2,966, while that for men in wholesale and retail trade was only $2,752.[5] Accordingly one would expect the industrial structure and measures of economic opportunity to vary as between high and low income communities. The materials in this section of the chapter generally confirm the validity of this hypothesis.

Table 165 presents male and female labor force participation rates. More of the men in high than in low income SMA's and urban places are in the labor force. The percentages of males in the labor force are lower for college than for noncollege communities. The elimination of all college communities from the comparisons for high and low income places raises the labor force participation rates in low income central and inde-

---

[5] *1950 Census of Population,* op. cit., table 136, p. 294. Note that these data are for income of persons, rather than families and unrelated individuals. The figure for manufacturing workers was recomputed from the income distribution and does not agree with the published median, which appears to be in error.

TABLE **165.**—PERCENT OF PERSONS IN THE LABOR FORCE BY SEX, FOR SELECTED STANDARD METROPOLITAN AREAS AND URBAN PLACES, BY METROPOLITAN STATUS, SIZE, AND 1949 INCOME LEVEL: 1950

[Asterisk (*) denotes difference between high and low groups significant at 0.05 level of probability. All places with 25 percent or more of the population 20 to 24 years old enrolled in school are excluded from comparisons]

Metropolitan status and size of place	1949 income level	Male	Female	Metropolitan status and size of place	1949 income level	Male	Female
Standard metropolitan areas:				Suburbs:			
50,000 to 250,000...	High.....	*81.9	31.9	10,000 to 25,000.....	High.....	*79.8	*26.9
	Low......	79.0	33.5		Low......	77.7	30.6
250,000 or more.....	High.....	*80.8	33.6	25,000 or more.......	High.....	*83.1	32.2
	Low......	78.1	30.9		Low......	79.4	31.2
Central cities:				Independent cities:			
Under 100,000.......	High.....	*83.5	33.7	10,000 to 25,000.....	High.....	*82.5	32.9
	Low......	77.9	36.8		Low......	74.9	33.0
100,000 or more.....	High.....	*82.0	35.0	25,000 to 50,000.....	High.....	*82.3	34.2
	Low......	79.7	36.1		Low......	78.6	33.6

Source: *1950 Census of Population*, Vol. II, *Characteristics of the Population*, Parts 2 to 50, table 35.

pendent cities and reduces somewhat these rates in high income suburbs. Labor force participation also is affected by the size of the military population. Somewhat more of the low than of the high income urban places have large military populations. The differences are significant only for small SMA's, central cities, and large independent cities. The elimination of the Armed Forces from the population 14 years old and over reduces the proportion of persons in the labor force. Neither the elimination of the military population nor the elimination of places specializing in higher education is sufficient, however, to eliminate the difference in labor force participation rates between high and low income places. Their elimination affects the size of the difference, however.

Women fail to show higher labor force participation rates in high than in low income places. The elimination of urban places with a high percentage enrolled in school reduces the female labor force participation rates in low income central and independent cities, since more of these low income places are college communities, and central cities which are college communities generally show a higher proportion of females in the labor force than do central cities which are not college communities. The only significant difference between high and low income places in female labor force participation occurs for small suburbs, among which the high income suburbs have a noticeably smaller proportion of economically active women than do the low income suburbs.

Manufacturing provides relatively high income as compared with the income from other major industries. Data are not available for the income of families and unrelated individuals in relation to industry of employment. The data for income of persons in the 11 major urban industry groups of the 1950 Census show that the 1949 median income of $2,966 for males in manufacturing was exceeded only by the medians for males in finance, insurance, and real estate; transportation, communication, and other public utilities; and public administration. The pattern is quite different for women, however, since the median income of $1,784 for women employed in manufacturing is exceeded by the median income for employed women in all urban-based industries other than wholesale and retail trade; personal services; and entertainment and recreation services. Since urban men comprised 73.9 percent of all urban persons employed in manufacturing in 1950,[6] a high proportion of employment in manufacturing will mean a fairly high income level for a city, however.

The data for specialization in manufacturing in Chapter 17 show that the median income of families and unrelated individuals is significantly greater in manufacturing than in nonmanufacturing SMA's, central cities, and independent cities, regardless of size of place.

High income places are more likely to have a large proportion employed in manufacturing than are low income places. Table 166 and figure 36

TABLE **166.**—EMPLOYMENT IN MANUFACTURING, PER CAPITA VALUE ADDED BY MANUFACTURE, PER CAPITA WHOLESALE AND RETAIL TRADE, SCHOOL ENROLLMENT, AND HOTEL ROOMS PER 1,000 INHABITANTS, FOR SELECTED STANDARD METROPOLITAN AREAS AND URBAN PLACES, BY METROPOLITAN STATUS, SIZE, AND 1949 INCOME LEVEL

[Asterisk (*) denotes difference between high and low groups significant at 0.05 level of probability]

Metropolitan status and size of place	1949 income level	Workers in manufacturing as percent of all employed persons, 1950[1]	Per capita value added by manufacture, 1947[2] (dollars)	Per capita sales, 1948[3] (dollars)		Percent enrolled in school	Number of hotel rooms, 1948, per 1,000 inhabitants
				Wholesale trade	Retail trade	Persons 20 to 24 years old, 1950	
Standard metropolitan areas:							
50,000 to 250,000..	High...	*42.1	*888	695	*1,007	10.5	...
	Low....	15.4	255	1,002	860	11.8	...
250,000 or more....	High...	*32.6	*784	2,514	*1,036	13.6	...
	Low....	20.9	243	1,418	881	11.1	...
Central cities:							
Under 100,000......	High...	*46.0	*1,198	*723	1,252	*7.5	*8.1
	Low....	17.2	350	1,288	1,210	12.6	32.3
100,000 or more....	High...	*38.7	*1,027	2,680	1,214	12.8	17.2
	Low....	17.7	386	2,570	1,167	11.6	37.7
Suburbs:							
10,000 to 25,000...	High...	26.7	*34	*224	878	*20.5	*0.1
	Low....	31.4	308	337	971	9.8	4.9
25,000 or more.....	High...	39.6	613	*355	*922	12.5	*3.2
	Low....	30.3	700	806	1,207	11.7	21.4
Independent cities:							
10,000 to 25,000...	High...	*30.7	*550	675	*1,420	*5.3	14.5
	Low....	14.7	118	709	1,175	13.9	9.7
25,000 to 50,000...	High...	*33.9	*1,053	982	*1,444	*8.0	15.6
	Low....	12.8	209	701	1,105	20.0	13.4

[1] Resident employed labor force.

[2] Value added by establishments located in the standard metropolitan area or urban place.

[3] Sales by establishments located in the standard metropolitan area or urban place.

Source: *1950 Census of Population,* Vol. II, *Characteristics of the Population,* Parts 2 to 50, tables 34 and 35; *1948 Census of Business,* Vol. III, *Retail Trade—Area Statistics,* tables 102 and 103 for each State; Vol. V, *Wholesale Trade—Area Statistics,* tables 102 and 103 for each State; Vol. VII, *Service Trade—Area Statistics,* table 103C for each State; *Census of Manufactures,* Vol. III, *Statistics by States,* table 2 for each State.

[6] Based on data in table 55, *ibid.,* p. 102.

FIGURE **36.**—PERCENT OF EMPLOYED MALES IN MANUFACTURING AND IN WHITE-COLLAR OCCU-
PATIONS, IN SELECTED STANDARD METROPOLITAN AREAS AND URBAN PLACES, BY METROPOLITAN
STATUS AND 1949 INCOME LEVEL: 1950

[Base line: All urban employed males in the United States]

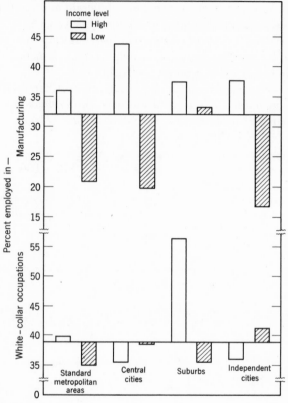

Note: See table 166.

present data on employment in manufacturing and per capita value added
by manufacture in high and low income communities. The proportion of
employed persons working in manufacturing is considerably greater in
high than in low income SMA's, central cities, and independent cities,
regardless of size. These differences are very large. For example, only
about 17 or 18 percent of all employed persons in low income central
cities are at work in manufacturing, but 46 percent of all employed persons in small, and 39 percent of all employed persons in large, high income central cities are at work in manufacturing. The differences are not
significant for the same comparisons between high and low income suburbs.

The data for per capita value added by manufacture are consistent with
these findings for SMA's, central cities, and independent cities. The per
capita value added by manufacture is greater in high than in low income
SMA's, central, and independent cities. Small suburbs, however, show a

significantly lower per capita value added by manufacture in high than in low income suburbs. The difference is in the same direction, but it is not significant for large suburbs. Especially in the case of suburbs, it must be remembered that the employment data pertain to workers residing in the community (but not necessarily working there), while the data on value added pertain to establishments located in the community (but perhaps drawing part of their work force from areas outside the community).

Expenditures for wholesale and retail trade in an urban place are affected by the export demand of hinterland populations as well as by the income level and maintenance requirements of a local population. One therefore does not expect the difference in per capita expenditures for wholesale and retail trade to be entirely consistent, when urban place groups differing in income are compared. Table 166 presents data on the per capita sales in wholesale and retail trade for SMA's and urban place groups.

Per capita wholesale trade expenditures are significantly lower in high than in low income small central cities and suburbs, regardless of size. The direction of the difference is consistent with this finding in small SMA's and independent cities. While the differences are not significant, large SMA's, central cities, and independent cities show the opposite pattern; here per capita wholesale trade expenditures are greater in high than in low income places. The generally low figures for suburbs may be explained by the fact that suburbs typically are more residence oriented and therefore less likely to specialize in any form of industrial activity.

Per capita retail sales are directly related to the income level of a population. Urban place statistics on per capita retail sales may not reflect this correlation, however, since a high income person probably is more likely to shop outside his area of residence than is a low income person. The data on per capita retail sales for high and low income places of different metropolitan status are consistent with this observation. High income SMA's and independent cities have significantly greater per capita retail sales than do comparable low income places, regardless of size. The finding for high and low income central cities is consistent with this, but the differences are not significant. High income suburbs show a lower per capita dollar expenditure for retail sales than do low income ones, though the differences are not significant for small suburbs. Perhaps both the opportunity for retail purchase and the actual purchases of specialized retail goods are smaller in high than in low income suburbs. Data for this study on specialization of suburbs in wholesale and retail trade show that more of the large low income than high income suburbs are trade centers (specializing in wholesale or retail trade), indicating rather large differences in opportunity between high and low income suburbs.

Places with high income are less likely to specialize in nonmanufacturing industries, other than wholesale and retail trade, regardless of size of place. Table 167 presents comparisons of high and low income places for employment in selected nonmanufacturing industries: public administration; mining; transportation; hotels and lodging places; and entertainment and recreation services. In addition, table 166 presents data for specialization in higher education and hotels. With few exceptions, employment in these nonmanufacturing industries is greater in low income than in high income places. None of the differences is very large, but these nonmanufacturing industries do not employ a large proportion of the working force in the United States as a whole.

Attendance at college is a function of opportunities to attend college, including income and the availability of a college campus in the local urban area. The 1950 Census practice of enumerating college students at the place of college attendance does not permit one to determine whether more persons from high income places enroll in college and professional or graduate schools than do persons from low income places. The data in table 166 indicate, however, whether high income places are more likely to provide places of higher education than are low income places, or vice versa. The data on the percentage of persons 20 to 24 years old enrolled in school show no consistent pattern of relationship between income level and school enrollment. Large central cities and independent cities with a low income level, regardless of size, have significantly more places with

TABLE 167.—EMPLOYMENT IN SELECTED NONMANUFACTURING INDUSTRIES, FOR SELECTED STANDARD METROPOLITAN AREAS AND URBAN PLACES, BY METROPOLITAN STATUS, SIZE, AND 1949 INCOME LEVEL: 1950

[Asterisk (*) denotes difference between high and low groups significant at 0.05 level of probability]

Metropolitan status and size of place	1949 income level	Government workers as percent of all employed persons[1]	Percent of all employed persons in--		Percent of all employed males in--			
			Mining	Transportation	Public administration	Hotels and lodging places	Entertainment and recreation services
Standard metropolitan areas:								
50,000 to 250,000	High	*8.1	0.2	3.8	*3.8	*0.4	*0.9	
	Low	13.7	1.0	5.6	6.8	1.4	1.3	
250,000 or more	High	10.6	*0.1	6.0	6.0	0.8	1.2	
	Low	11.5	3.1	6.5	6.9	1.2	1.3	
Central cities:								
Under 100,000	High	*7.5	0.1	*3.6	*3.6	*0.4	*1.0	
	Low	13.7	0.6	5.2	6.7	2.0	1.5	
100,000 or more	High	8.6	0.1	6.5	4.7	*0.7	*1.0	
	Low	12.6	0.5	7.8	7.5	1.3	1.4	
Suburbs:								
10,000 to 25,000	High	*8.4	*0.6	4.3	*4.0	*0.3	1.4	
	Low	12.1	3.4	4.9	5.8	0.7	1.2	
25,000 or more	High	9.9	*0.1	5.2	5.0	*0.3	1.3	
	Low	10.9	0.9	6.2	5.5	1.0	1.2	
Independent cities:								
10,000 to 25,000	High	*10.0	3.1	5.7	5.0	*0.8	*1.4	
	Low	16.5	0.8	4.4	5.1	1.4	1.7	
25,000 to 50,000	High	*9.3	1.0	6.0	4.4	*0.7	*1.4	
	Low	19.8	0.8	5.4	6.7	1.7	1.6	

[1] Based on class-of-worker statistics; includes persons who worked for any governmental unit (Federal, State, or local) regardless of the activity which the particular agency carried on.

Source: *1950 Census of Population*, Vol. II, *Characteristics of the Population*, Parts 2 to 50, table 35.

a high percentage of college enrollment than do comparable places with a high income level. But small suburbs with a low income level have significantly fewer places with a high percentage of enrollment than do comparable high income suburbs. The differences are not significant for the other four groups. Since the percentage of persons aged 20 to 24 enrolled in school does differ for high and low income places which are small central cities or suburbs and independent cities, school enrollment is controlled in all comparisons where the statistics are affected by the inclusion of places with a high proportion of college enrollment.

Places with low income generally are more likely to be centers of public administration, as well as centers where government is a major employer, than are places with high income. Government employment is significantly larger in low than in high income places which are small in size, regardless of metropolitan status. The difference is significant only for large independent cities. In the urban United States as a whole, governments employ 10.6 percent of all workers.[7] The proportion of government workers is equal to, or below, the United States figure in all high income places, and above it in all low income places, for each size and metropolitan status group. The fact that government more often is an employer in low income places is not readily understood, since the income of persons in government educational services and public administration is considerably above the United States median for men and women in the experienced civilian labor force. The relatively larger proportion of government workers in low as compared with high income places, therefore, must be attributed to other characteristics of these places, e.g., their regional location, or to relatively low income industries with private employers.

Class-of-worker data provide information on the percentage of persons at work for a government employer. They do not provide a clear statement of what percentage of men are engaged in the uniquely governmental functions, such as legislative and judicial activities and most of the activities in the executive agencies. This is indicated by the data on employment in public administration. Somewhat fewer of the employed men in high than in low income places are at work in public administration. The differences are significant, however, only for the large SMA's, central cities, and suburbs. The median income of men at work in public administration is relatively high when compared with the median for men in other industry groups. The fact that public administration is a comparatively small industry in most places may mean that it is possible for the general income level to be low despite somewhat larger proportions of workers in public administration.

The proportion employed in mining varies by community size. Mining occurs with much greater frequency in small than in large places. Given

---

[7] *Ibid.*, table 53, p. 101.

the small number of places with substantial numbers employed in mining, it is surprising to find that large SMA's and both size groups of suburbs with low income levels have higher proportions of persons in mining than do comparable places with high income levels. The findings for high and low income independent cities are not significant, but the direction of the difference is opposite to those just noted.

There appears to be somewhat greater employment in transportation in low than in high income places, except for independent cities. However, the difference is significant only for the group of smaller central cities.

Male residents of high income places are less often employed in hotels and lodging places than are males in low income places, regardless of size of place. This is not an unexpected finding in that the median income of men in hotels and lodging places is low. The median 1949 income of $1,942 for men at work in hotels and lodging places is below that for men in any of the other major industry groups.[8] Yet the existence of sizable male employment in hotels and lodging places in independent cities probably means that the hotels and lodging places also are located there. If this is correct, then not only are the men at work in hotels and lodging places more likely to reside in low than in high income places, but low income places have disproportionate numbers of hotels and lodging places. The data in table 166 support this expectation, except for the findings for independent cities.

The male residents of high income SMA's, central, and independent cities are less often employed in entertainment and recreation services than are the male residents of low income places, regardless of size of place. Again, this is not an unexpected finding in the sense that the median income of men in entertainment and recreation is comparatively low among major industry groups.[8] The existence of sizable male employment in entertainment and recreation in low income independent cities also suggests that low income places have disproportionate numbers of places of entertainment and recreation as compared with high income places.

Socio-economic status

There is a substantial correlation between the rank order of major occupation groups according to status criteria and the average income for persons in these major occupation groups. The white-collar occupations generally have a higher median income than the manual occupations for both men and women. Male craftsmen, foremen, and kindred workers, however, have a higher median income than male clerical or sales workers, and the median income of female sales workers is below that of women at work in the craft, operative, and manual laboring occupations.[9]

---

[8] The data are for persons rather than for families and unrelated individuals. See *1950 Census of Population, op. cit.*, table 136, pp. 294–296.

[9] See *1950 Census of Population, op. cit.*, table 129, pp. 279–282.

Given the fairly substantial correlation between occupation and personal income, one would expect that cities with a high ratio of white-collar to manual workers also would be high income cities, while those with a low ratio would be low income cities. Table 168 presents the percentage distributions of employed males by major occupation groups for large and small, high and low income, SMA's and urban places. Only for suburbs and for large SMA's is there a greater percentage of white-collar workers in high than in low income places. The ratio of white-collar to manual workers is particularly large for the high income suburbs, especially the

TABLE **168.**—PERCENT DISTRIBUTION OF EMPLOYED MALES BY MAJOR OCCUPATION GROUP, FOR SELECTED STANDARD METROPOLITAN AREAS AND URBAN PLACES, BY METROPOLITAN STATUS, SIZE, AND 1949 INCOME LEVEL: 1950

[Asterisk (*) denotes difference between high and low groups significant at 0.05 level of probability]

Metropolitan status and size of place	1949 income level	White-collar occupations					Manual occupations				
		Total[1]	Profess'l, techn'l, and kindred workers	Managers, officials, & propr's, exc. farm	Clerical and kindred workers	Sales workers	Total[1]	Craftsmen, foremen, and kindred workers	Operatives and kindred workers	Private household and service workers	Laborers, except farm
Standard metropolitan areas:											
50,000 to 250,000...	High....	*31.5	8.0	*10.4	6.9	*6.2	*62.9	*22.6	*27.3	*6.0	*7.0
	Low.....	34.6	7.4	12.6	6.5	8.1	54.8	19.0	17.3	8.1	10.4
250,000 or more.....	High....	*40.4	*10.1	12.9	9.7	7.7	*57.3	*21.0	21.3	8.2	*6.8
	Low.....	35.2	7.4	12.1	7.8	7.9	59.1	20.5	21.4	7.6	9.6
Central cities:											
Under 100,000.......	High....	*34.0	8.7	*11.0	7.5	*6.8	*64.5	*23.7	*27.0	*6.3	*7.5
	Low.....	39.1	8.4	14.2	7.0	9.5	58.4	18.6	18.5	10.7	10.6
100,000 or more.....	High....	*35.9	8.3	*10.7	9.7	*7.2	*61.8	*21.7	*25.7	*8.0	*6.4
	Low.....	38.7	8.0	13.0	8.8	8.9	59.7	19.4	19.0	10.1	11.2
Suburbs:											
10,000 to 25,000....	High....	*67.4	*20.4	*25.6	8.5	*12.9	*31.4	*15.7	*9.1	*3.8	*2.8
	Low.....	33.0	8.5	10.7	7.1	6.7	63.8	21.5	24.5	7.2	10.6
25,000 or more......	High....	*48.8	*14.4	*15.7	*9.5	*9.2	*50.2	*22.7	*18.3	*4.9	*4.3
	Low.....	36.8	9.4	11.8	8.1	7.5	61.2	21.1	21.8	8.4	10.0
Independent cities:											
10,000 to 25,000....	High....	*35.8	9.0	*13.0	*6.6	*7.2	*61.5	*22.0	*24.3	*6.9	*8.3
	Low.....	40.5	11.2	14.2	5.7	9.4	54.8	17.7	17.5	9.0	10.6
25,000 to 50,000....	High....	*36.2	*8.0	*12.9	*7.5	*7.8	*65.4	*23.2	*27.6	*7.5	*7.1
	Low.....	41.8	12.4	14.2	6.6	8.6	55.7	17.9	16.4	10.5	10.9

[1] Sum of white-collar and manual occupations does not equal 100 percent, because farm occupations and persons whose occupations were not reported are omitted.

Source: See table 167.

smaller ones. For the other five groups, high income places show somewhat smaller proportions of white-collar workers than do low income places (figure 36, p. 356). These results should be interpreted with the regional distributions of high and low income places in mind. More of the low than of the high income places are in the South, and more of the non-manufacturing communities than of the manufacturing communities are in the South. These facts, together with the observation that manufacturing centers have relatively low percentages of white-collar workers, may help to explain the failure to find the expected correlation between average income and occupational composition for the independent and central cities and the smaller SMA's.

Further details of the occupational comparison are given in tables 168 and 169. Male professional, technical, and kindred workers and male clerical and kindred workers are somewhat more frequent in high than in low income places, except that low income independent cities have somewhat more professional, technical, and kindred workers than do high income independent cities. The differences between high and low income places are significant only for large SMA's and independent cities and suburbs for professional, technical, and kindred workers, and for large suburbs and independent cities for clerical and kindred workers. To some extent these differences between high and low income places may be a happenstance of census enumeration procedures, rather than a real difference. Some places may be classified as low income places, particularly the independent cities, because of a relatively large number of college students with low incomes who were enumerated at the place of college attendance rather than at their parental home. As college communities generally have a higher ratio of white-collar to manual workers than do noncollege communities, the low income independent cities, in particular, will tend to show more professional, technical, and kindred workers than the high income ones. It does not seem that the differences are largely due to this artifact of data collection, however, for the differences are significant for large independent cities, and not for the small ones. Large places should show less of the effect of enumerating college students at the place of college attendance than small ones.

High and low income places show the same pattern of differences for male managers, officials, and proprietors, and sales workers, as for all white-collar workers. High income suburbs, regardless of size, have significantly higher percentages of males employed as managers, officials, and proprietors, while for small SMA's, central cities, and independent cities, the high income places have the higher percentages of managers, officials, and proprietors. The same pattern of differences between high and low income places holds for male sales workers.

High income places have a greater proportion of males employed as manual workers than do low income places, except for suburbs and large SMA's, where the reverse pattern holds. The pattern of differences for manual occupations between high and low income places is not consistent for the four major manual occupation groups given in table 168. The high status manual occupations generally predominate in high income places while the low status manual occupations predominate in low income places.

The proportion of craftsmen, foremen, and kindred workers is greater in high than in low income places, regardless of size. Only small suburbs are an exception to this pattern. This relationship between income level and the proportion in skilled worker occupations is clearly consistent with

TABLE **169.**—PERCENT OF EMPLOYED FEMALES IN SPECIFIED MAJOR OCCUPATION GROUPS, FOR SELECTED STANDARD METROPOLITAN AREAS AND URBAN PLACES, BY METROPOLITAN STATUS, SIZE, AND 1949 INCOME LEVEL: 1950

[Asterisk (*) denotes difference between high and low groups significant at 0.05 level of probability]

Metropolitan status and size of place	1949 income level	Sales, clerical, and kindred workers	Operatives and kindred workers	Private household and service workers
Standard metropolitan areas:				
50,000 to 250,000................	High..........	*38.0	*23.0	*17.7
	Low..........	30.7	13.1	33.3
250,000 or more..................	High..........	*43.2	*20.1	16.9
	Low..........	35.2	19.0	24.8
Central cities:				
Under 100,000....................	High..........	*41.0	,*21.4	*17.3
	Low..........	30.4	15.8	33.5
100,000 or more..................	High..........	*43.7	*21.1	*16.4
	Low..........	35.6	14.7	31.0
Suburbs:				
10,000 to 25,000................	High..........	*46.2	*7.4	19.3
	Low.......,.......	33.5	23.9	20.8
25,000 or more..................	High..........	*50.1	*14.5	*13.9
	Low..........	37.9	19.4	19.6
Independent cities:				
10,000 to 25,000................	High..........	*38.5	*18.5	*20.4
	Low..........	30.9	12.7	32.9
25,000 to 50,000................	High..........	*37.6	*23.7	*18.7
	Low..........	32.0	10.1	34.4

Source: See table 167.

the data for median incomes of persons in major occupation groups. The median income of male craftsmen, foremen, and kindred workers is exceeded only by those of male professional, technical, and kindred workers and male managers, officials, and proprietors, except farm. This finding also seems consistent with that above showing employment in manufacturing is much greater in high than in low income places, except for small suburbs. The pattern of employment for operatives and kindred workers in high and low income places is similar to that for employment of all manual workers. The percentage of male operatives and kindred workers is significantly higher for high income places among the small SMA's and both size groups of central and independent cities. Among suburbs, regardless of size, the high income places have fewer operatives and kindred workers than do the low income places.

The low status manual occupations occur with greater frequency in low than in high income places, regardless of size of place. Low income places have a significantly greater proportion of men in the low status and low income manual occupations of private household and service workers, and of nonfarm laborers. The large SMA's show this significant difference only in the case of laborers.

Women in white-collar occupations are found more often in high than in low income places regardless of size of place. Table 169 and figure 37 show that the percentage of female sales, clerical, and kindred workers is greater in all high income SMA's and urban places than in low income ones. The employment of women as operatives and kindred workers is

FIGURE 37.—PERCENT OF EMPLOYED FEMALES IN SELECTED MAJOR OCCUPATION GROUPS, IN SELECTED STANDARD METROPOLITAN AREAS AND URBAN PLACES, BY METROPOLITAN STATUS AND 1949 INCOME LEVEL: 1950

[Base line: All urban employed females in the United States]

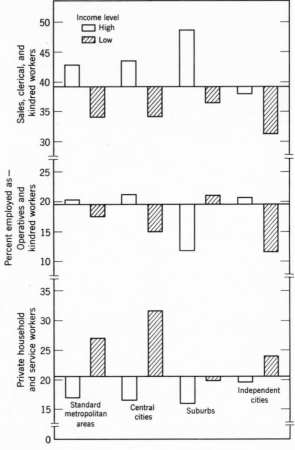

Note: See table 167.

also significantly greater in high than in low income SMA's, central cities, and independent cities, regardless of size.   As in the case of the employment of male operatives and kindred workers, female operatives and kindred workers are found less often in high than in low income suburbs. But female private household and service workers are far more numerous in low than in high income places regardless of size. This difference holds even when regional location is controlled.

Table 170 presents data on two other aspects of socio-economic status: educational attainment and home ownership.   Educational attainment is measured by the median year of school completed by persons 25 years old and over.   The median year of school completed is somewhat greater

in high than in low income places, for both size groups.   The differences
are not significant, however, for small SMA's and central cities, and large
independent cities.   Residents of high income suburbs, on the average,
show much higher levels of educational attainment than do residents of
low income suburbs.   Half of the residents of high income suburbs who
are 25 years old and over have completed at least a high school education,
while a similar group of residents of low income suburbs have only a ninth
grade education, or less.   Since income and level of educational attainment are known to be positively correlated, it is to be expected that urban
places, particularly suburbs, will show a similar correlation.

The percentage of occupied dwelling units which are owner-occupied
is shown in table 170 for each type and size of place.   It is to be expected
that tenure of occupied dwelling units will vary with the income level of
a population.   Given the prevailing standards for urban housing in the
United States, upper income persons are in a better position to own their
own home than are low income persons.   The correlation is by no means
high, however, since many factors other than income determine tenure.
More of the residents in high than in low income places own their own
homes, unless the place is very large.   Significantly more of the residents in
high income places among the small SMA's and central cities, and among
the suburbs and independent cities, regardless of size, own their own
homes.   The differences in tenure between high and low income places
are not statistically significant for large SMA's and large central cities.
The greatest differences in tenure status occur for suburbs.   In small high
income suburbs, over three-fourths of all residents are home owners,

TABLE 170.—EDUCATIONAL ATTAINMENT AND PERCENT OF OCCUPIED DWELLING UNITS
OWNER-OCCUPIED, FOR SELECTED STANDARD METROPOLITAN AREAS AND URBAN PLACES, BY
METROPOLITAN STATUS, SIZE, AND 1949 INCOME LEVEL: 1950

[Asterisk (*) denotes difference between high and low groups significant at 0.05 level of probability]

Metropolitan status and size of place	1949 income level		Median school years com- pleted[1]	Percent of occupied dwelling units owner- occupied	Metropolitan status and size of place	1949 income level		Median school years com- pleted[1]	Percent of occupied dwelling units owner- occupied
Standard metropolitan areas:					Suburbs:				
50,000 to 250,000	High...		10.0	*61.9	10,000 to 25,000.	High...		*12.5	*77.1
	Low....		9.4	48.8		Low....		9.3	53.3
250,000 or more..	High...		*10.5	44.3	25,000 or more...	High...		*12.0	*63.9
	Low....		9.4	51.6		Low....		9.3	46.3
Central cities:					Independent cities:				
Under 100,000....	High...		10.3	*56.9	10,000 to 25,000.	High...		*10.8	*57.9
	Low....		9.3	44.0		Low....		9.6	51.5
100,000 or more..	High...		*10.1	44.2	25,000 to 50,000.	High...		10.4	*55.9
	Low....		9.5	44.0		Low....		10.1	49.2

[1] Persons 25 years old and over. The figure shown is the one for the median place in each group.

Source: *1950 Census of Population*, Vol. II, *Characteristics of the Population*, Parts 2 to 50, table 34;
1950 Census of Housing, Vol. I, *General Characteristics*, Part 1, U. S. Summary, table 22, and Parts 2 to 6,
table 1.

while in small low income suburbs only slightly more than one-half are home owners. The difference is substantial even for large suburbs; 64 percent of the dwelling units of high income suburbs as compared with 46 percent of the dwelling units of low income suburbs were owner-occupied in 1950.

Summary and conclusions

This chapter examines the relationship between the average income level of communities and their demographic, economic, and socio-economic characteristics. The relationship was measured by comparing SMA and urban place groups which were in the upper and lower quintiles of the distributions of places by 1949 median income of families and unrelated individuals. There are very marked differences in regional location between the high and low income places, which affect comparisons between them. Except for suburbs, most of the low income places are located in the South and most of the high income places in the North Central or Northeast Regions. Low income suburbs are most often found in the Northeast.

High income communities seem more selective of older persons, of nonwhite persons, of men who are married, and of males, generally, than are low income places. There are proportionately more persons 21 years of age and older in SMA's, central cities, and independent cities with high income levels than in comparable places with low income levels, regardless of size. The ratio of males to females is greater in high than in low income places, except for small suburbs. Substantially larger proportions of nonwhite persons are found in low than in high income places regardless of size. The proportion of males married is significantly greater in high than in low income suburbs and large independent cities, though small SMA's, central, and independent cities show only small differences between high and low income places.

The stability of residence is greater in SMA's, central cities, and large independent cities with high incomes than in those with low incomes, but high income suburbs show no greater residential stability than do low income suburbs. This probably is due to the fact that high income suburbs experienced somewhat greater average growth during the 1940–50 decade than did low income ones. High income SMA's, central cities, and independent cities, by contrast, grew at a much slower rate during the decade than did comparable low income places.

Income is both a cause and a result of economic opportunity. Data on economic conditions in high and low income areas show that manufacturing generally is greater in high than in low income places, regardless of size, except for suburbs. Conversely, high employment in nonmanufacturing industries is more characteristic of low than of high income places. Places with low income have high proportions of persons in the nonmanufacturing industries of public administration, mining, wholesale trade, transportation, hotels and lodging places, and entertainment and recreation services. The differences· are not significant for all metropolitan status and size groups, and a few exceptions occur for independent cities. Places which specialize in higher education also seem to locate more often in low than in high income places, since low income places generally have a higher percentage of persons aged 20 to 24 enrolled in school than do high income places. Small suburbs show the reverse pattern, however. The only nonmanufacturing industry which shows greater evidence of being in high than in low income places is retail trade. Retail sales per capita are significantly greater in high than in low income SMA's and independent cities, regardless of size, and the data for central cities are consistent with this finding. In general, employment opportunities seem greater in high than in low income places. More of the men in high than in low income places are in the labor force, regardless of size of place. Although low income places have more college students and military personnel who are 14 years of age and over, but not in the civilian labor force, the elimination of these groups from the comparisons shows that labor force participation rates remain greater for high than for low income places.

Urban places with high and low income are roughly grouped according to high and low socio-economic status, since income is rather directly correlated with other variables of socio-economic status. One therefore expects high and low income places to be differentiated in terms of these other variables of socio-economic status. Three such variables were examined in this chapter: tenure of dwelling units, educational attainment, and occupation of employed male and female residents of high and low income places. In general, the high positive correlation among socio-economic status variables, including income, holds for similar comparisons between high and low income urban places. More of the residents of high than of low income places own their own home, unless the community of residence is very large. The median year of school completed by persons 25 years old and over is somewhat greater in high than in low income places, regardless of size. An examination of the relationship between the income level of a place and the predominance of occupations of varying socio-economic status does not always yield results consistent with the correlation between the status rank of occupations and income of persons, but some positive correlation exists for certain subgroups.

Employment in the low status, low income manual occupations, such as private household and service workers and manual laborers, is significantly greater in low than in high income places, regardless of size, for both men and women. Employment in the high status, high income, manual occupation group, craftsmen, foremen, and kindred workers, is greater in high than in low income places, regardless of size, except for small suburbs. Employment of male and female operatives and kindred workers, male proprietors, managers, and officials, and male sales workers generally follows the pattern that these occupations occur with greater frequency in low than in high income places, except that in suburbs, more are found in high than in low income places.   The high status, high income professional, technical, and kindred workers are found more often in high than in low income places, regardless of size, except for independent cities, where the reverse pattern prevails.   Male clerical and kindred workers and female sales, clerical, and kindred workers, which are low status, low income white-collar occupations, nonetheless occur with somewhat greater frequency for residents of high than of low income places.

Historical note

Ogburn in his study of the social characteristics of American cities compared what he called wealthy and industrial suburbs.[10]   Industrial suburbs were places with 45 to 50 percent of the population engaged in manufacturing and no more than the average proportion in trade and transportation.   Twenty-nine such places were selected and their average population in 1930 was 48,300.   Suburbs were classified as wealthy if the median value of homes was over $10,000 and the median monthly rent was over $50.   Ten wealthy suburbs were chosen; their average 1930 population was 53,300.   The actual median value of homes in industrial suburbs was $6,800 while that in wealthy suburbs was $15,000.   The median monthly rent was $32 in industrial and $69 in wealthy suburbs. The industrial suburbs had 57 percent of the gainful workers employed in manufacturing, while the wealthy suburbs had but 21 percent in manufacturing.[11]

High and low income suburbs in this study were defined by the upper and lower quintiles of median income of families and unrelated individuals. Given the indicators of value of homes and rent for wealthy and industrial suburbs in Ogburn's study, his categories seem roughly comparable with those used here.   They differ, however, in that Ogburn's industrial suburbs were chosen to have a high percentage of persons employed in manufacturing, and his wealthy ones ranked low in manufacturing; while the larger low income suburbs in the present study had a low percentage of employment in manufacturing and high income suburbs a high percentage in manufacturing.   Only rough comparisons of the findings in the two studies, therefore, are possible.   The comparisons of Ogburn's suburbs with those in the present study perhaps are also more accurate if they are limited to large suburbs, since the average size of the suburbs Ogburn selected is quite large.

The findings for which comparable data exist for the two studies are compared below.   High (wealthy) as compared with low (industrial) in-

---

[10] W. F. Ogburn, *Social Characteristics of Cities*, International City Managers' Association, Chicago, 1937, Chapter III.

[11] *Ibid.*, pp. 56–57.

come suburbs have a higher proportion of (*a*) persons 21 years old and over, (*b*) employment in professional occupations, (*c*) employment in clerical occupations, (*d*) employment in trade (Ogburn) and retail trade (present study), and (*e*) home ownership. High income suburbs in both places had a somewhat smaller percentage of employed persons in (*f*) mining, (*g*) transportation, and (*h*) public service (Ogburn) and in public administration and in government (present study). Ogburn found a higher proportion of personal and domestic service workers in the wealthy than in the industrial suburbs, but in this study private household and service workers (combining the two occupation groups) were relatively more numerous in low than in high income suburbs.

Ogburn and Coombs made a study of the variation in selected social characteristics with the economic level of two groups of cities in the United States in 1930.[12] The first group of 57 cities varied in population from 30,000 to 50,000, and the second group of 131 cities varied in population from 20,000 to 75,000. Ogburn and Coombs excluded what they termed extraordinary types of cities—places with a high degree of functional specialization in entertainment and recreation, government, etc., and cities in the South, because of the biracial factor in their population statistics. Correlations were calculated for each group of cities between the economic index and selected social characteristics. The factors comprising the economic index in the study were thought to give the best available indication of per capita income in the cities.[13]

The Ogburn and Coombs study, therefore, examined the relationship between economic level (largely, income level) and selected social characteristics, as does this study. Ogburn and Coombs employed correlation analysis, whereas the present study analyzed differences between extreme groups. Metropolitan status and size of place were controlled in their study, in that they excluded suburbs from their analysis and studied only places of 20,000 to 75,000 inhabitants. These cities, therefore, are treated as roughly comparable with the large independent and small central cities of this study. Where similar social characteristics were related to differences in income level, a comparison of results from the two studies can be made.

The comparison shows that high income levels of cities are associated, in both studies, with a large proportion of (*a*) males, (*b*) older persons, and (*c*) gainful workers (Ogburn and Coombs) and persons in the labor force (present study). The (*d*) educational level of persons is greater for high income places in both studies. The measures employed were library and magazine circulation, radio ownership, and teachers' salaries in the Ogburn and Coombs study, and median school years completed in the

---

[12] W. F. Ogburn and Lolagene C. Coombs, "An Economic Interpretation of the Social Characteristics of Cities," *American Journal of Sociology* 46, November 1940, pp. 305–315.

[13] *Ibid.*, pp. 307–309.

present study.   The two studies show divergent findings for rate of growth, home ownership, and professional worker statistics.   Ogburn and Coombs found that high income was associated with high growth rates, low proportions of home ownership, and a high proportion of professional workers. The opposite relationships hold for small central cities and large independent cities in the present study.   Some of this difference may reflect differences in the composition of the samples in the two studies.   Ogburn and Coombs excluded most cities in the South, while the present study included them.   More of the low income places in the present study are in the South, where the 1940–50 growth rates are high.   The findings of Chapter 15 suggest, too, that a high rate of growth of an urban place increases the proportion of owner occupancy somewhat.

A P P E N D I X   A

DEFINITIONS OF AREA UNITS

The following definitions have been extracted from the Introduction to Volume I of the *1950 Census of Population.*

Urban and rural areas. According to the new definition that was adopted for use in the 1950 Census, the urban population comprises all persons living in (*a*) places of 2,500 inhabitants or more incorporated as cities, boroughs, and villages, (*b*) incorporated towns of 2,500 inhabitants or more except in New England, New York, and Wisconsin, where "towns" are simply minor civil divisions of counties, (*c*) the densely settled urban fringe, including both incorporated and unincorporated areas, around cities of 50,000 or more, and (*d*) unincorporated places of 2,500 inhabitants or more outside any urban fringe. The remaining population is classified as rural. According to the old definition, the urban population had been limited to all persons living in incorporated places of 2,500 inhabitants or more and in areas (usually minor civil divisions) classified as urban under special rules relating to population size and density.

In both definitions, the most important component of the urban territory is the group of incorporated places having 2,500 inhabitants or more. A definition of urban territory restricted to such places would exclude a number of equally large and densely settled places, merely because they were not incorporated places. Under the old definition, an effort was made to avoid some of the more obvious omissions by the inclusion of the places classified as urban under special rules. Even with these rules, however, many large and closely built-up places were excluded from the urban territory. To improve the situation in the 1950 Census, the Bureau of the Census set up, in advance of enumeration, boundaries for urban-fringe areas around cities of 50,000 or more and for unincorporated places outside urban fringes. All the population residing in urban-fringe areas and in unincorporated places of 2,500 or more is classified as urban according to the 1950 definition. (Of course, the incorporated places of 2,500 or more in these fringes are urban in their own right.) Consequently, the special rules of the old definition are no longer necessary.

Urbanized areas. An urbanized area is an area that includes at least one city with 50,000 inhabitants or more in 1940 or later according to a special census taken prior to 1950 and also the surrounding closely settled incorporated places and unincorporated areas that meet the criteria

371

listed below. Since the urbanized area outside of incorporated places was defined on the basis of housing or population density, its boundaries for the most part are not political but follow such features as roads, streets, railroads, streams, and other clearly defined lines which may be easily identified by census enumerators in the field. The urbanized area boundaries were selected after careful examination of all available maps, aerial photographs, and other sources of information, and then were checked in detail in the field by trained investigators to insure that the criteria were followed and that the boundaries were identifiable.

The delineation of the boundaries of the urbanized areas had to be completed prior to the beginning of enumeration; consequently, it was not possible to establish urbanized areas in connection with those cities which attained a population of 50,000 or more according to the 1950 Census. Urbanized areas were established for Fort Smith, Ark., and Muskegon, Mich., both of which had in excess of 50,000 inhabitants according to special censuses conducted prior to 1950. The population of both of these cities fell below 50,000 in 1950. The urbanized areas defined for these two cities, however, were retained in the tabulations.

The urban fringe of an urbanized area is that part which is outside the central city or cities. The following types of areas are embraced if they are contiguous to the central city or cities or if they are contiguous to any area already included in the urban fringe:

1. Incorporated places with 2,500 inhabitants or more in 1940 or at a subsequent special census conducted prior to 1950.

2. Incorporated places with fewer than 2,500 inhabitants containing an area with a concentration of 100 dwelling units or more with a density in this concentration of 500 units or more per square mile. This density represents approximately 2,000 persons per square mile and normally is the minimum found associated with a closely spaced street pattern.

3. Unincorporated territory with at least 500 dwelling units per square mile.

4. Territory devoted to commercial, industrial, transportation, recreational, and other purposes functionally related to the central city.

Also included are outlying noncontiguous areas with the required dwelling unit density located within 1½ miles of the main contiguous urbanized part, measured along the shortest connecting highway, and other outlying areas within one-half mile of such noncontiguous areas which meet the minimum residential density rule.

Although an urbanized area may contain more than one city of 50,000 or more, not all cities of this size are necessarily central cities. The largest city of an area is always a central city. In addition, the second and third most populous cities in the area may qualify as central cities provided they have a population of at least one third of that of the largest city in the area and a minimum of 25,000 inhabitants. The names of the individual urbanized areas indicate the central cities of the areas.

Standard metropolitan areas. Except in New England, a standard metropolitan area is a county or group of contiguous counties which contains at least one city of 50,000 inhabitants or more. In addition to the county, or counties, containing such a city, or cities, contiguous counties are included in a standard metropolitan area if according to certain criteria they are essentially metropolitan in character and socially and economically integrated with the central city.

The criteria of metropolitan character relate primarily to the character of the county as a place of work or as a home for concentrations of nonagricultural workers and their dependents. Specifically, these criteria are:

1. The county must (*a*) contain 10,000 nonagricultural workers, or (*b*) contain 10 percent of the nonagricultural workers working in the standard metropolitan area, or (*c*) have at least one-half of its population residing in minor civil divisions with a population density of 150 or more per square mile and contiguous to the central city.

2. Nonagricultural workers must constitute at least two-thirds of the total number of employed persons of the county.

The criteria of integration relate primarily to the extent of economic and social communication between the outlying counties and the central county as indicated by such items as the following:

1. Fifteen percent or more of the workers residing in the contiguous county work in the county containing the largest city in the standard metropolitan area, or

2. Twenty-five percent or more of the persons working in the contiguous county reside in the county containing the largest city in the standard metropolitan area, or

3. The number of telephone calls per month to the county containing the largest city of the standard metropolitan area from the contiguous county is four or more times the number of subscribers in the contiguous county.

In New England, the city and town are administratively more important than the county, and data are compiled locally for such minor civil divisions. Here towns and cities were the units used in defining standard metropolitan areas, and criteria relating to the number and proportion of nonagricultural workers set forth above could not be applied. In their place, a population density criterion of 150 or more persons per square mile, or 100 or more persons per square mile where strong integration was evident, has been used.

Although there may be several cities of 50,000 or more in a standard metropolitan area, not all are necessarily central cities. The largest city in a standard metropolitan area is the principal central city. Any other city of 25,000 or more within a standard metropolitan area, and having a population amounting to one-third or more of the population of the principal city, is also a central city. However, no more than three cities have been defined as central cities of any standard metropolitan area.

Metropolitan districts. Metropolitan districts were defined for every city of 50,000 inhabitants or more in 1940, two or more such cities sometimes being in one district. In general, metropolitan districts included in addition to the central city or cities, all adjacent and contiguous minor civil divisions or incorporated places having a population density of 150 or more per square mile. Since the metropolitan districts are being replaced by the standard metropolitan areas, no attempt was made to redefine the 1940 metropolitan districts or to define metropolitan districts for those cities which attained a population of 50,000 or more in 1950.

Incorporated and unincorporated places. Political units recognized as incorporated places in the 1950 Census are those which are incorporated as cities, boroughs, towns, and villages with the exception that towns are not recognized as incorporated places in the New England States, New York, and Wisconsin. The towns in these States are minor civil divisions similar to the townships found in other States and are not necessarily thickly settled centers of population such as the cities, villages, and towns elsewhere.

In the 1950 Census the larger unincorporated places outside the urbanized areas were delineated, and those with a population of 1,000 or more are presented in the same manner as incorporated places of equal size. Each unincorporated place possesses a definite nucleus of residences and has its boundaries drawn so as to include, if feasible, all the surrounding closely settled area. Although there are unincorporated places in the urban-fringe areas, it was not considered feasible to establish boundaries for such places and therefore they were not identified as separate places.

The term "place" as used by the Bureau of the Census refers to a compact agglomeration, or a population center. Thus some minor civil divisions that are "incorporated" in one legal sense of the word are not regarded by the Census Bureau as "incorporated places." Without this restriction all of the towns in New England, New York, and Wisconsin and the townships in New Jersey would have to be counted as incorporated places without any consideration of the nature of population settlement. On the other hand, unincorporated agglomerations without any kind of legal boundaries are recognized here as "places" and are listed as unincorporated places.

A P P E N D I X   B

SUPPLEMENTARY TABLES

Table B–1 provides base populations for Chapters 2 to 11.

Table B–2 provides base populations for Chapter 13.

Tables B–3 to B–12 provide supplementary data for Chapter 13.

Tables B–13 to B–16 provide lists of individual places included in the analysis of Chapter 15.

Tables B–17 to B–20 provide lists and classifications of individual places included in the analyses of Chapters 14 and 16 to 20.

Table B–21 provides supplementary data for Chapter 19.

TABLE **B-1.**—POPULATION BY SIZE OF PLACE, BY REGIONS: 1950

Size of place	United States	North-east	North Central	South	West
URBANIZED AREAS					
3,000,000 or more..................	21,184,020	12,287,910	4,907,550	...	3,988,560
Central cities..................	14,208,750	8,630,730	3,613,290	...	1,964,730
Outside central cities.........	6,975,270	3,657,180	1,294,260	...	2,023,830
1,000,000 to 3,000,000.............	16,608,450	6,674,040	5,428,740	2,441,730	2,063,940
Central cities..................	10,106,460	3,544,350	3,613,080	1,746,330	1,202,700
Outside central cities.........	6,501,990	3,129,690	1,815,660	695,400	861,240
250,000 to 1,000,000...............	17,380,080	3,280,890	5,827,290	6,208,530	2,063,370
Central cities..................	12,991,920	2,064,450	4,450,440	4,887,900	1,589,130
Outside central cities.........	4,388,160	1,216,440	1,376,850	1,320,630	474,240
Under 250,000......................	13,942,050	3,918,870	3,778,890	4,621,050	1,623,240
Central cities..................	10,996,590	2,913,810	3,098,700	3,871,260	1,112,820
Outside central cities.........	2,945,460	1,005,060	680,190	749,790	510,420
OUTSIDE URBANIZED AREAS					
25,000 or more.....................	7,108,050	1,272,870	2,469,360	2,346,060	1,019,760
10,000 to 25,000...................	8,204,070	1,685,100	2,517,870	2,768,550	1,232,550
2,500 to 10,000....................	11,822,340	2,196,570	3,446,130	4,499,130	1,680,510
1,000 to 2,500.....................	6,440,550	1,234,380	2,122,350	2,290,140	793,680
Nonfarm.........................	6,311,310	1,214,910	2,090,850	2,242,290	763,260
Farm............................	129,240	19,470	31,500	47,850	30,420
Incorporated places under 1,000....	4,010,580	356,160	2,069,550	1,212,900	371,970
Nonfarm.........................	3,795,630	340,920	1,987,050	1,125,960	341,700
Farm............................	214,950	15,240	82,500	86,940	30,270
Other rural........................	43,588,440	6,444,870	11,711,760	20,715,360	4,716,450
Nonfarm.........................	20,929,410	4,704,390	4,414,680	8,955,150	2,855,190
Farm............................	22,659,030	1,740,480	7,297,080	11,760,210	1,861,260

Source: *1950 Census of Population*, Vol. IV, *Special Reports*, Part 5, Chapter A, Characteristics by Size of Place, tables 1 and 6.

TABLE **B-2.**—RURAL-NONFARM AND RURAL-FARM POPULATION BY TYPE OF COUNTY, BY DIVISIONS: 1950

Division and residence	All counties	Metropolitan, by size of largest place in standard metropolitan area		Nonmetropolitan, by size of largest place in county	
		250,000 or more	Under 250,000	25,000 or more	Under 25,000
RURAL NONFARM					
United States...............	31,181,325	5,210,413	3,903,814	2,991,028	19,076,070
New England......................	1,809,842	745,551	276,348	161,142	626,801
Middle Atlantic..................	4,503,683	1,633,709	721,176	388,749	1,760,049
East North Central..............	5,510,241	979,386	817,156	618,014	3,095,685
West North Central..............	3,027,024	244,573	158,425	164,219	2,459,807
South Atlantic..................	6,158,176	510,678	882,231	680,979	4,084,288
East South Central..............	2,944,336	260,587	250,116	161,449	2,272,184
West South Central..............	3,243,129	240,990	267,979	265,125	2,469,035
Mountain........................	1,430,508	36,020	146,964	167,057	1,080,467
Pacific.........................	2,554,386	558,919	383,419	384,294	1,227,754
RURAL FARM					
United States...............	23,048,350	1,127,505	1,534,942	1,598,732	18,787,171
New England......................	403,100	88,942	43,807	43,006	227,345
Middle Atlantic..................	1,388,161	293,867	248,480	136,008	709,806
East North Central..............	3,703,414	233,169	351,760	381,085	2,737,400
West North Central..............	3,729,151	93,365	125,408	186,757	3,323,621
South Atlantic..................	4,632,996	104,071	287,903	305,229	3,935,793
East South Central..............	4,048,074	76,544	141,000	163,729	3,666,801
West South Central..............	3,214,615	55,368	114,806	162,930	2,881,511
Mountain........................	858,602	16,655	52,202	60,704	729,041
Pacific.........................	1,070,237	165,524	169,576	159,284	575,853

Source: *1950 Census of Population*, Vol. II, *Characteristics of the Population*, Parts 2 to 50, tables 48 and 49.

TABLE **B-3.**—SEX RATIO OF THE RURAL-NONFARM AND RURAL-FARM POPULATION BY TYPE OF COUNTY, BY DIVISIONS: 1950

Division and residence	All counties	Metropolitan, by size of largest place in standard metropolitan area		Nonmetropolitan, by size of largest place in county	
		250,000 or more	Under 250,000	25,000 or more	Under 25,000
RURAL NONFARM[1]					
United States...............	100.7	102.0	101.9	101.1	100.0
New England......................	98.7	98.9	96.7	98.1	99.7
Middle Atlantic..................	101.2	102.0	100.8	99.8	101.0
East North Central..............	102.1	104.6	104.2	104.1	100.5
West North Central..............	99.0	104.2	106.0	101.1	98.0
South Atlantic..................	98.7	100.8	99.6	98.9	98.2
East South Central..............	97.5	100.0	102.6	98.6	96.5
West South Central..............	99.4	102.4	98.8	99.3	99.2
Mountain........................	105.8	104.5	101.7	100.1	107.3
Pacific.........................	107.6	103.4	109.6	105.1	109.8
RURAL FARM					
United States...............	110.1	111.7	110.9	110.8	109.9
New England......................	113.9	113.4	112.3	113.2	114.6
Middle Atlantic..................	111.8	111.0	110.6	111.0	112.8
East North Central..............	112.5	111.8	112.3	112.8	112.5
West North Central..............	115.6	112.8	114.9	116.0	115.6
South Atlantic..................	105.5	108.6	106.4	106.0	105.3
East South Central..............	105.0	105.2	104.0	105.4	105.1
West South Central..............	109.1	110.7	110.5	109.7	109.0
Mountain........................	117.5	114.3	111.9	113.9	118.3
Pacific.........................	117.4	116.2	118.9	114.8	118.1

[1] Civilian population only.

Source: See table B-2.

TABLE **B-4.**—MEDIAN AGE OF THE RURAL-NONFARM AND RURAL-FARM POPULATION BY TYPE OF COUNTY, BY DIVISIONS: 1950

Division and residence	All counties	Metropolitan, by size of largest place in standard metropolitan area		Nonmetropolitan, by size of largest place in county	
		250,000 or more	Under 250,000	25,000 or more	Under 25,000
RURAL NONFARM					
United States................	27.9	29.1	27.3	27.4	27.8
New England......................	30.7	30.9	32.0	29.0	30.3
Middle Atlantic..................	30.4	30.9	29.5	31.9	30.0
East North Central..............	29.4	28.6	28.0	28.5	30.3
West North Central..............	32.3	28.7	30.3	29.6	33.2
South Atlantic..................	25.0	26.6	25.1	25.4	24.7
East South Central..............	24.9	26.2	25.3	24.8	24.8
West South Central..............	26.7	26.7	25.0	25.0	27.1
Mountain........................	25.6	26.5	24.0	25.6	25.9
Pacific.........................	28.5	28.3	27.5	28.0	29.1
RURAL FARM					
United States................	26.3	31.9	28.0	27.0	25.7
New England......................	31.4	33.6	34.5	30.8	30.0
Middle Atlantic..................	29.7	32.0	27.8	30.5	29.3
East North Central..............	30.1	32.3	30.2	29.4	30.0
West North Central..............	28.4	31.7	30.7	27.6	28.3
South Atlantic..................	22.6	28.4	24.7	23.6	22.2
East South Central..............	23.0	27.6	23.8	23.6	22.8
West South Central..............	25.5	31.7	25.2	24.7	25.5
Mountain........................	25.0	29.5	24.3	25.1	24.9
Pacific.........................	31.3	34.7	30.9	29.6	30.9

Source: See table B-2.

TABLE **B-5.**—FERTILITY RATIO OF THE RURAL-NONFARM AND RURAL-FARM POPULATION BY TYPE OF COUNTY, BY DIVISIONS: 1950

Division and residence	All counties	Metropolitan, by size of largest place in standard metropolitan area		Nonmetropolitan, by size of largest place in county	
		250,000 or more	Under 250,000	25,000 or more	Under 25,000
RURAL NONFARM					
United States................	681	618	670	671	704
New England......................	621	594	574	658	670
Middle Atlantic..................	592	559	602	575	626
East North Central..............	671	642	682	673	679
West North Central..............	669	691	694	721	661
South Atlantic..................	710	648	687	661	731
East South Central..............	743	666	708	737	757
West South Central..............	720	677	729	736	722
Mountain........................	771	747	788	695	782
Pacific.........................	676	664	686	690	675
RURAL FARM					
United States................	762	613	700	741	778
New England......................	670	553	571	684	739
Middle Atlantic..................	671	583	681	688	703
East North Central..............	699	609	684	705	709
West North Central..............	742	671	697	780	744
South Atlantic..................	815	673	716	764	830
East South Central..............	824	701	768	799	830
West South Central..............	777	609	768	779	781
Mountain........................	811	621	789	775	820
Pacific.........................	651	596	645	690	658

Source: See table B-2.

TABLE **B-6.**—PERCENT OF THE RURAL-NONFARM AND RURAL-FARM POPULATION AGED 65 AND OVER BY TYPE OF COUNTY, BY DIVISIONS: 1950

Division and residence	All counties	Metropolitan, by size of largest place in standard metropolitan area		Nonmetropolitan, by size of largest place in county	
		250,000 or more	Under 250,000	25,000 or more	Under 25,000
RURAL NONFARM					
United States	8.6	7.3	7.0	7.8	9.5
New England	9.9	9.1	9.3	9.6	11.1
Middle Atlantic	9.2	8.2	8.8	10.5	10.1
East North Central	10.0	6.8	7.6	9.0	11.8
West North Central	13.5	7.5	10.4	11.2	14.5
South Atlantic	6.0	5.2	5.2	5.8	6.4
East South Central	7.2	5.9	5.5	6.1	7.7
West South Central	8.3	5.4	5.6	6.6	9.1
Mountain	6.7	5.6	4.5	5.1	7.3
Pacific	7.5	6.9	6.8	7.2	8.0
RURAL FARM					
United States	7.6	9.2	7.9	7.6	7.5
New England	10.9	11.4	12.2	10.9	10.5
Middle Atlantic	9.4	10.0	8.1	9.7	9.6
East North Central	9.0	9.1	8.9	8.3	9.1
West North Central	7.2	8.7	8.3	7.0	7.1
South Atlantic	6.9	8.3	7.4	7.1	6.8
East South Central	7.3	8.3	7.4	7.4	7.2
West South Central	7.1	7.9	6.3	6.7	7.2
Mountain	5.7	6.6	5.5	5.8	5.7
Pacific	7.5	8.8	7.3	7.0	7.4

Source: See table B–2.

TABLE **B–7.**—PERCENT DISTRIBUTION OF THE RURAL-NONFARM POPULATION BY RACE AND NATIVITY, BY TYPE OF COUNTY AND DIVISION: 1950

Division, race, and nativity	All counties	Metropolitan, by size of largest place in standard metropolitan area		Nonmetropolitan, by size of largest place in county	
		250,000 or more	Under 250,000	25,000 or more	Under 25,000
New England...................	100.0	100.0	100.0	100.0	100.0
Native white.......................	90.4	88.4	89.6	91.9	92.5
Foreign-born white..................	8.9	10.7	9.5	7.3	6.9
Negro..............................	0.6	0.8	0.8	0.5	0.4
Other races........................	0.1	0.1	0.1	0.3	0.2
Middle Atlantic...............	100.0	100.0	100.0	100.0	100.0
Native white.......................	91.4	87.7	94.7	91.5	93.4
Foreign-born white..................	6.3	8.8	4.1	7.0	4.8
Negro..............................	2.1	3.3	1.2	1.5	1.6
Other races........................	0.2	0.2	(1)	(1)	0.2
East North Central...........	100.0	100.0	100.0	100.0	100.0
Native white.......................	94.7	91.9	94.7	95.0	95.4
Foreign-born white..................	3.7	5.6	3.9	3.2	3.2
Negro..............................	1.3	2.4	1.3	1.6	1.0
Other races........................	0.3	0.1	0.1	0.2	0.4
West North Central...........	100.0	100.0	100.0	100.0	100.0
Native white.......................	93.8	94.8	93.3	96.3	93.6
Foreign-born white..................	4.2	3.4	5.6	3.2	4.3
Negro..............................	0.9	1.7	0.7	0.4	0.8
Other races........................	1.1	0.1	0.4	0.1	1.3
South Atlantic...............	100.0	100.0	100.0	100.0	100.0
Native white.......................	78.5	80.6	83.8	82.4	76.4
Foreign-born white..................	0.9	1.8	1.3	1.5	0.6
Negro..............................	20.5	17.5	14.9	16.0	22.8
Other races........................	0.1	0.1	(1)	0.1	0.2
East South Central...........	100.0	100.0	100.0	100.0	100.0
Native white.......................	83.1	82.4	85.6	83.4	82.9
Foreign-born white..................	0.3	0.7	0.4	0.3	0.3
Negro..............................	16.5	16.9	13.9	16.2	16.7
Other races........................	0.1	(1)	0.1	0.1	0.1
West South Central...........	100.0	100.0	100.0	100.0	100.0
Native white.......................	82.3	88.1	84.8	81.0	81.6
Foreign-born white..................	1.8	1.6	2.5	3.0	1.6
Negro..............................	15.2	10.1	12.5	15.3	16.0
Other races........................	0.7	0.2	0.2	0.7	0.8
Mountain......................	100.0	100.0	100.0	100.0	100.0
Native white.......................	89.1	95.9	91.5	91.4	88.2
Foreign-born white..................	4.3	3.2	3.9	4.7	4.3
Negro..............................	0.8	0.5	2.1	1.7	0.5
Other races........................	5.8	0.4	2.5	2.2	7.0
Pacific.......................	100.0	100.0	100.0	100.0	100.0
Native white.......................	90.9	90.9	88.5	91.6	91.5
Foreign-born white..................	6.1	6.7	6.9	5.7	5.7
Negro..............................	1.3	1.3	2.4	1.3	1.0
Other races........................	1.7	1.1	2.2	1.4	1.8

[1] Less than 0.05 percent.

Source: See table B–2.

TABLE **B-8.**—PERCENT DISTRIBUTION OF THE RURAL-FARM POPULATION BY RACE AND NATIVITY, BY TYPE OF COUNTY AND DIVISION: 1950

Division, race, and nativity	All counties	Metropolitan, by size of largest place in standard metropolitan area		Nonmetropolitan, by size of largest place in county	
		250,000 or more	Under 250,000	25,000 or more	Under 25,000
New England...................	100.0	100.0	100.0	100.0	100.0
Native white......................	89.5	83.9	87.8	90.6	91.8
Foreign-born white.................	10.1	15.5	11.7	9.2	7.9
Negro..............................	0.3	0.5	0.4	0.2	0.2
Other races........................	0.1	0.1	0.1	(1)	0.1
Middle Atlantic..............	100.0	100.0	100.0	100.0	100.0
Native white......................	93.1	89.1	94.8	92.1	94.5
Foreign-born white.................	5.9	8.9	4.4	7.1	4.9
Negro..............................	0.9	1.8	0.8	0.7	0.5
Other races........................	0.1	0.2	(1)	0.1	0.1
East North Central............	100.0	100.0	100.0	100.0	100.0
Native white......................	96.3	92.9	95.6	96.8	96.5
Foreign-born white.................	3.2	6.3	4.0	2.8	3.0
Negro..............................	0.4	0.8	0.3	0.3	0.4
Other races........................	0.1	(1)	0.1	0.1	0.1
West North Central............	100.0	100.0	100.0	100.0	100.0
Native white......................	96.1	95.9	94.7	97.6	96.1
Foreign-born white.................	2.9	3.3	5.1	2.2	2.8
Negro..............................	0.6	0.8	0.1	0.2	0.6
Other races........................	0.4	(1)	0.1	(1)	0.5
South Atlantic................	100.0	100.0	100.0	100.0	100.0
Native white......................	69.0	81.2	77.7	68.5	68.2
Foreign-born white.................	0.4	2.0	0.7	0.6	0.3
Negro..............................	30.0	16.7	21.6	30.8	30.9
Other races........................	0.6	0.1	(1)	0.1	0.6
East South Central............	100.0	100.0	100.0	100.0	100.0
Native white......................	73.5	72.9	70.6	67.9	73.9
Foreign-born white.................	0.2	0.7	0.2	0.3	0.2
Negro..............................	26.2	26.4	29.2	31.8	25.8
Other races........................	0.1	(1)	(1)	(1)	0.1
West South Central............	100.0	100.0	100.0	100.0	100.0
Native white......................	77.4	91.1	73.7	71.5	77.6
Foreign-born white.................	1.7	2.2	5.1	4.5	1.4
Negro..............................	20.1	6.3	20.9	23.3	20.2
Other races........................	0.8	0.4	0.3	0.7	0.8
Mountain......................	100.0	100.0	100.0	100.0	100.0
Native white......................	89.0	90.5	87.9	87.7	89.1
Foreign-born white.................	3.9	5.0	4.8	3.9	3.8
Negro..............................	0.4	0.5	1.8	0.5	0.3
Other races........................	6.7	4.0	5.5	7.9	6.8
Pacific.......................	100.0	100.0	100.0	100.0	100.0
Native white......................	86.9	85.6	78.5	88.8	89.2
Foreign-born white.................	8.6	9.9	11.9	7.2	7.7
Negro..............................	0.6	0.3	1.0	1.2	0.4
Other races........................	3.9	4.2	8.6	2.8	2.7

[1] Less than 0.05 percent.

Source: See table B-2.

TABLE **B–9.**—MEDIAN YEARS OF SCHOOL COMPLETED BY PERSONS 25 YEARS OLD AND OVER OF THE RURAL-NONFARM AND RURAL-FARM POPULATION, BY TYPE OF COUNTY AND DIVISION: 1950

Division and residence	All counties	Metropolitan, by size of largest place in standard metropolitan area		Nonmetropolitan, by size of largest place in county	
		250,000 or more	Under 250,000	25,000 or more	Under 25,000
RURAL NONFARM					
United States................	8.8	10.0	9.0	8.9	8.7
New England..........................	10.6	10.9	11.2	10.3	10.1
Middle Atlantic......................	9.0	9.6	8.8	9.3	8.9
East North Central..................	9.0	10.0	9.4	9.0	8.9
West North Central..................	8.9	10.1	9.3	8.9	8.8
South Atlantic......................	8.1	9.0	8.6	8.4	7.7
East South Central..................	8.2	8.8	8.4	8.4	8.1
West South Central..................	8.3	9.0	8.9	8.2	8.2
Mountain............................	9.8	11.1	10.6	11.1	9.7
Pacific.............................	10.2	11.4	10.0	10.1	10.1
RURAL FARM					
United States................	8.4	8.8	8.6	8.5	8.3
New England..........................	9.3	9.9	9.9	9.0	9.0
Middle Atlantic......................	8.7	8.8	8.6	8.9	8.7
East North Central..................	8.7	8.8	8.8	8.7	8.7
West North Central..................	8.7	8.8	8.8	8.7	8.7
South Atlantic......................	7.1	8.1	7.7	7.3	7.0
East South Central..................	7.3	8.3	7.5	7.5	7.2
West South Central..................	7.8	8.6	8.0	7.5	7.7
Mountain............................	9.0	9.5	9.2	9.1	8.9
Pacific.............................	9.2	9.9	8.9	9.0	9.2

Source: See table B–2.

TABLE **B–10.**—PERCENT OF RURAL-NONFARM AND RURAL-FARM MALES IN THE LABOR FORCE, BY TYPE OF COUNTY AND DIVISION: 1950

Division and residence	All counties	Metropolitan, by size of largest place in standard metropolitan area		Nonmetropolitan, by size of largest place in county	
		250,000 or more	Under 250,000	25,000 or more	Under 25,000
RURAL NONFARM[1]					
United States................	73.0	74.2	74.1	72.3	72.6
New England..........................	74.3	73.8	76.6	73.8	74.0
Middle Atlantic......................	72.8	72.8	75.7	71.4	72.0
East North Central..................	73.0	75.4	75.6	70.0	72.2
West North Central..................	71.4	77.1	72.7	70.7	70.9
South Atlantic......................	74.8	75.5	74.6	73.9	74.9
East South Central..................	70.8	73.1	67.6	73.9	70.7
West South Central..................	71.7	75.7	74.3	69.2	71.3
Mountain............................	74.8	76.9	76.8	74.6	74.5
Pacific.............................	73.4	74.2	67.9	75.1	74.2
RURAL FARM					
United States................	82.7	82.1	82.1	82.9	82.8
New England..........................	80.7	80.9	81.5	80.5	80.4
Middle Atlantic......................	82.0	81.7	83.6	83.2	81.4
East North Central..................	83.7	83.4	83.1	85.0	83.6
West North Central..................	86.9	85.8	85.6	86.9	86.9
South Atlantic......................	81.7	80.9	79.3	81.1	82.0
East South Central..................	80.7	79.7	78.8	80.3	80.9
West South Central..................	80.0	81.2	81.5	79.7	79.9
Mountain............................	84.5	84.8	80.6	83.0	84.9
Pacific.............................	83.0	81.1	83.0	82.7	83.7

[1] Based on civilian population only.

Source: See table B–2.

TABLE **B-11.**—PERCENT OF RURAL-NONFARM AND RURAL-FARM FEMALES IN THE LABOR FORCE, BY TYPE OF COUNTY AND DIVISION: 1950

Division and residence	All counties	Metropolitan, by size of largest place in standard metropolitan area		Nonmetropolitan, by size of largest place in county	
		250,000 or more	Under 250,000	25,000 or more	Under 25,000
RURAL NONFARM					
United States................	22.7	23.5	23.3	23.9	22.2
New England.......................	26.7	27.9	26.9	26.6	25.0
Middle Atlantic...................	23.3	22.5	25.5	25.5	22.6
East North Central................	21.9	22.3	21.9	23.3	21.5
West North Central................	22.3	23.3	21.7	22.8	22.3
South Atlantic....................	25.5	26.6	24.8	26.6	25.4
East South Central...............	20.5	20.4	20.9	21.5	20.4
West South Central...............	19.1	20.9	19.9	18.6	18.9
Mountain..........................	21.8	23.4	21.1	23.7	21.5
Pacific...........................	22.0	22.5	21.2	22.0	22.0
RURAL FARM					
United States................	15.7	20.0	18.8	17.6	15.0
New England.......................	20.7	25.1	23.6	22.3	18.0
Middle Atlantic...................	19.3	20.7	21.0	20.7	17.9
East North Central................	16.3	18.4	16.6	17.9	15.8
West North Central................	14.3	16.7	16.7	15.1	14.0
South Atlantic....................	18.5	21.7	19.9	19.4	18.3
East South Central...............	13.3	17.0	19.6	15.3	12.9
West South Central...............	12.4	16.9	16.4	13.4	12.1
Mountain..........................	15.3	21.9	17.3	15.8	14.9
Pacific...........................	19.4	20.9	20.2	19.5	18.6

Source: See table B-2.

TABLE **B-12.**—PERCENT OF THE RURAL-NONFARM AND RURAL-FARM CIVILIAN LABOR FORCE UNEMPLOYED, BY TYPE OF COUNTY AND DIVISION: 1950

Division and residence	All counties	Metropolitan, by size of largest place in standard metropolitan area		Nonmetropolitan, by size of largest place in county	
		250,000 or more	Under 250,000	25,000 or more	Under 25,000
RURAL NONFARM					
United States................	5.1	4.3	4.7	5.6	5.3
New England.......................	6.0	4.9	4.4	7.3	7.7
Middle Atlantic...................	5.5	4.7	4.2	5.2	6.9
East North Central................	4.3	3.5	3.6	4.0	4.7
West North Central................	3.8	2.5	3.5	3.7	4.0
South Atlantic....................	4.2	2.8	4.2	5.3	4.1
East South Central...............	4.8	4.2	5.3	5.3	4.8
West South Central...............	5.1	3.4	4.7	5.5	5.2
Mountain..........................	6.8	3.3	7.0	6.3	6.9
Pacific...........................	8.4	6.3	9.2	8.9	8.9
RURAL FARM					
United States................	1.7	2.4	2.4	2.2	1.6
New England.......................	4.0	3.2	3.1	4.9	4.4
Middle Atlantic...................	3.0	2.8	2.2	2.7	3.4
East North Central................	1.7	2.0	1.8	1.5	1.6
West North Central................	0.9	1.1	1.7	0.9	0.8
South Atlantic....................	1.5	1.9	2.2	1.8	1.4
East South Central...............	1.4	2.3	2.2	2.0	1.3
West South Central...............	1.8	1.7	2.1	2.1	1.8
Mountain..........................	2.5	1.5	4.7	3.5	2.3
Pacific...........................	3.8	3.3	4.2	4.3	3.7

Source: See table B-2.

TABLE **B-13.**—PERCENT INCREASE IN POPULATION, 1940 TO 1950 AND 1930 TO 1940, FOR STANDARD METROPOLITAN AREAS SELECTED FOR HIGH AND LOW GROWTH RATES, BY SIZE, 1950

[Minus sign (−) denotes decrease]

High growth rate standard metropolitan areas, by size	Percent increase		Low growth rate standard metropolitan areas, by size	Percent increase	
	1940 to 1950	1930 to 1940		1940 to 1950	1930 to 1940[1]
50,000 TO 250,000			**50,000 TO 250,000**		
Albuquerque, N. Mex............	109.9	52.7	Altoona, Pa....................	-0.6	0.4
Amarillo, Texas................	41.8	15.6	Atlantic City, N. J............	6.7	-0.6
Austin, Texas[2]...............	45.0	42.8	Brockton, Mass.................	8.5	-0.5
Baton Rouge, La.[2]............	79.0	29.6	Fall River, Mass...............	1.6	1.1
Corpus Christi, Texas..........	78.6	79.0	Huntington, W. Va.--Ashland, Ky.	8.9	7.3
Galveston, Texas...............	39.3	26.0	Lawrence, Mass.................	0.9	1.4
Lubbock, Texas.................	95.1	32.4	Lowell, Mass...................	2.2	4.3
Macon, Ga......................	42.0	7.7	Manchester, N. H...............	7.9	15.6
Mobile, Ala....................	62.8	19.9	New Bedford, Mass..............	2.3	-1.4
Ogden, Utah....................	46.9	8.7	Pittsfield, Mass...............	9.1	0.4
Orlando, Fla...................	64.0	40.9	St. Joseph, Mo.................	2.9	-4.6
San Angelo, Texas..............	49.9	9.1	Sioux City, Iowa...............	0.3	1.9
Stockton, Calif................	49.6	30.4	Terre Haute, Ind...............	5.5	0.9
Wichita, Kans..................	55.1	5.1			
			250,000 OR MORE		
250,000 OR MORE			Boston, Mass...................	8.8	1.7
			Duluth, Minn.--Superior, Wis....	-0.5	1.1
Dallas, Texas..................	54.3	22.4	Johnstown, Pa..................	-2.4	5.1
Fort Worth, Texas..............	60.2	14.2	New Haven, Conn................	9.9	5.0
Fresno, Calif..................	54.9	23.7	Pittsburgh, Pa.................	6.3	2.9
Miami, Fla.....................	84.9	87.3			
Norfolk-Portsmouth, Va.........	72.3	12.8	Providence, R. I...............	8.9	2.5
			Reading, Pa....................	5.7	4.4
Phoenix, Ariz..................	78.2	23.3	Scranton, Pa...................	-14.6	-2.9
Sacramento, Calif..............	62.7	20.0	Utica-Rome, N. Y...............	8.0	0.1
San Bernardino, Calif..........	74.8	20.3	Wheeling, W. Va.--Steubenville,		
San Diego, Calif...............	92.4	38.0	Ohio.......................	-2.8	4.6
San Francisco-Oakland, Calif...	53.3	8.5	Wilkes-Barre--Hazleton, Pa......	-11.2	-0.8
San Jose, Calif................	66.1	20.6	Worcester, Mass................	9.3	0.6

[1] The 1930–1940 growth rates for the New England standard metropolitan areas were calculated by totaling the 1930 population of the constituent towns and/or counties which make up the standard metropolitan area.

[2] 25 percent or more of the population 20 to 24 years old enrolled in school in 1950.

Source: Donald J. Bogue, *Population Growth in Standard Metropolitan Areas, 1900–1950*, Housing and Home Finance Agency, Washington, 1953, appendix table 1; *1950 Census of Population*, Vol. I, *Number of Inhabitants*, U. S. Summary, table 26; *1940 Census, Population*, Vol. I, *Number of Inhabitants*, table 4 for each State.

TABLE **B-14.**—PERCENT INCREASE IN POPULATION, 1940 TO 1950 AND 1930 TO 1940, FOR CENTRAL CITIES SELECTED FOR HIGH AND LOW GROWTH RATES, BY SIZE: 1950

[Minus sign (−) denotes decrease]

High growth rate central cities, by size	Percent increase		Low growth rate central cities, by size	Percent increase	
	1940 to 1950	1930 to 1940		1940 to 1950	1930 to 1940
UNDER 100,000			**UNDER 100,000**		
Albuquerque, N. Mex.........	173.1	33.4	Altoona, Pa....................	-3.8	-2.2
Amarillo, Texas..............	43.6	19.8	Asheville, N. C...............	3.3	2.2
Columbia, S. C.[1]...........	39.3	21.0	Atlantic City, N. J...........	-3.8	-3.2
Columbus, Ga................	49.4	23.5	Binghamton, N. Y..............	3.0	2.1
Fresno, Calif................	51.1	15.6	Brockton, Mass................	0.8	-2.3
Gadsden, Ala................	50.7	53.8	Holyoke, Mass.................	1.6	-4.9
Greenville, S. C.[1].........	67.4	19.1	Jackson, Mich.................	2.9	-10.0
Jackson, Miss................	58.2	28.6	Johnstown, Pa.................	-5.2	-0.5
Lubbock, Texas[1]............	125.2	55.2	Lancaster, Pa.................	4.0	2.3
Madison, Wis.[1].............	42.4	16.5	Lawrence, Mass................	-4.5	-0.9
Ogden, Utah.................	30.7	8.5	Lowell, Mass..................	-4.1	1.2
Orlando, Fla.................	42.5	34.4	St. Joseph, Mo................	3.8	-6.5
Portsmouth, Va...............	57.7	11.0	Schenectady, N. Y.............	4.8	-8.5
St. Petersburg, Fla..........	59.1	50.4	Sioux City, Iowa..............	2.0	4.0
San Bernardino, Calif........	44.5	16.4	Terre Haute, Ind..............	2.4	-0.2
San Jose, Calif.[1]..........	39.2	18.7	Troy, N. Y....................	2.9	-3.4
Stockton, Calif.[1]..........	29.5	14.1	Wheeling, W. Va...............	-3.6	-0.9
Waco, Texas[1]...............	51.3	5.9	Wilkes-Barre, Pa..............	-10.9	-0.5
100,000 OR MORE			**100,000 OR MORE**		
Austin, Texas[1].............	50.6	65.5	Albany, N. Y..................	3.4	2.5
Baton Rouge, La..............	261.8	13.0	Boston, Mass..................	4.0	-1.3
Charlotte, N. C..............	32.8	22.0	Buffalo, N. Y.................	0.7	0.5
Corpus Christi, Texas........	89.0	106.6	Cleveland, Ohio...............	4.2	-2.5
Dallas, Texas................	47.4	11.3	Duluth, Minn..................	3.4	-0.4
Denver, Colo.................	29.0	12.0	Fall River, Mass.............	-3.0	0.1
Fort Worth, Texas............	56.9	8.7	Jersey City, N. J.............	-0.7	-4.9
Houston, Texas...............	55.0	31.5	Newark, N. J..................	2.1	-2.8
Los Angeles, Calif...........	31.0	21.5	New Bedford, Mass.............	1.0	-2.0
Memphis, Tenn................	35.2	15.7	New Haven, Conn...............	2.4	-1.3
Miami, Fla...................	44.8	55.6	Pittsburgh, Pa................	0.8	0.3
Mobile, Ala..................	63.9	15.4	Providence, R. I..............	-1.9	0.2
Montgomery, Ala..............	36.4	18.2	Reading, Pa...................	-1.1	-0.5
Norfolk, Va..................	47.9	11.3	Rochester, N. Y...............	2.3	-1.0
Phoenix, Ariz................	63.3	35.9	Scranton, Pa..................	-10.6	-2.1
Sacramento, Calif............	29.8	13.0	Trenton, N. J.................	2.7	1.1
San Diego, Calif.............	64.4	37.4	Utica, N. Y...................	1.0	-1.2
Shreveport, La...............	29.5	28.1	Wilmington, Del...............	-1.9	5.5
Spokane, Wash................	32.6	5.6	Youngstown, Ohio..............	0.4	-1.3

[1] 25 percent or more of the population aged 20 to 24 enrolled in school in 1950.

Source: *1950 Census of Population*, Vol. I, *Number of Inhabitants*, table 4 for each State; *1940 Census, Population*, Vol. I, *Number of Inhabitants*, tables 2 and 5 for each State.

TABLE **B-15.**—PERCENT INCREASE IN POPULATION, 1940 TO 1950 AND 1930 TO 1940, FOR
SUBURBS SELECTED FOR HIGH AND LOW GROWTH RATES, BY SIZE: 1950

[Minus sign (−) denotes decrease]

High growth rate suburbs, by size	Percent increase		Low growth rate suburbs, by size	Percent increase	
	1940 to 1950	1930 to 1940		1940 to 1950	1930 to 1940
10,000 TO 25,000			10,000 TO 25,000		
Allen Park, Mich..............	253.6	269.4	Ambridge, Pa...................	−13.4	−6.2
Arcadia, Calif................	152.9	74.9	Braddock, Pa...................	−10.0	−5.2
Aurora, Colo..................	232.3	49.8	Campbell, Ohio.................	−6.6	−6.1
Bellaire, Texas...............	805.1	188.2	Carbondale, Pa.................	−15.9	−3.4
El Cerrito, Calif.............	193.5	58.6	Central Falls, R. I...........	−6.7	−2.5
Evergreen Park, Ill..........	217.9	107.8	Coatesville, Pa...............	−1.3	−3.5
Fair Lawn, N. J...............	164.9	50.5	Cohoes, N. Y...................	−3.1	−5.5
Grosse Pointe Woods, Mich....	270.1	91.9	Donora, Pa.....................	−7.5	−5.2
Hialeah, Fla..................	397.1	52.2	Harrison, N. J.................	−4.8	−4.7
La Mesa, Calif.[1].............	178.9	56.2	Homestead, Pa..................	−47.2	−5.5
Manhattan Beach, Calif.......	170.9	238.3	McKees Rocks, Pa..............	−4.6	−6.0
Montebello, Calif............	171.1	45.8	Monessen, Pa..................	−11.7	−0.1
Newport Beach, Calif.........	173.1	101.5	Nanticoke, Pa.................	−17.3	−6.4
Pasadena, Texas..............	554.3	108.6	No. Braddock, Pa..............	−6.1	−6.6
Richfield, Minn..............	363.3	190.4	Pittston, Pa..................	−15.8	−2.3
St. Louis Park, Minn.........	192.7	64.3	Plymouth, Pa..................	−16.0	−6.3
San Carlos, Calif............	308.3	210.9	Steelton, Pa..................	−4.1	−1.3
Texas City, Texas............	189.1	62.6	Watervliet, N. Y..............	−5.7	−0.2
25,000 OR MORE			25,000 OR MORE		
Alexandria, Va................	84.3	38.8	Aliquippa, Pa..................	−3.3	−0.3
Burbank, Calif................	128.8	106.1	Bayonne, N. J..................	−2.5	−11.0
Compton, Calif................	196.3	29.4	Chelsea, Mass..................	−5.7	−9.9
Euclid, Ohio..................	131.7	40.1	East Chicago, Ind.............	−0.7	−0.3
Independence, Mo.............	130.1	5.0	East Cleveland, Ohio..........	1.4	−0.4
Inglewood, Calif.............	53.4	54.6	Everett, Mass.................	−1.7	−3.4
Lincoln Park, Mich...........	92.4	23.5	Garfield, N. J................	−1.8	−5.7
Long Beach, Calif............	52.7	15.7	Hamtramck, Mich...............	−13.0	−11.4
Lynwood, Calif...............	135.1	50.0	Highland Park, Mich...........	−8.7	−4.1
Miami Beach, Fla.............	65.2	331.4	Hoboken, N. J.................	1.1	−15.4
Palo Alto, Calif.[1]...........	51.9	22.6	Kearny, N. J..................	1.2	−3.1
Parma, Ohio..................	76.6	17.7	Lakewood, Ohio................	−1.6	−1.9
Redondo Beach, Calif.........	92.7	40.1	McKeesport, Pa................	−7.0	1.3
Redwood City, Calif..........	105.1	38.9	Passaic, N. J.................	−6.0	−2.5
Richmond, Calif..............	321.1	15.0	Paterson, N. J................	−0.2	1.9
Royal Oak, Mich..............	86.9	9.5	Perth Amboy, N. J.............	0.2	−5.2
San Leandro, Calif...........	88.6	27.5	Salem, Mass...................	1.6	−4.9
San Mateo, Calif.............	115.3	44.3	Sommerville, Mass.............	0.2	−1.7
South Gate, Calif............	89.7	37.3	Union City, N. J..............	−1.1	−4.2
Valley Stream, N. Y..........	61.0	41.5	Woonsocket, R. I..............	1.8	−0.1
Vancouver, Wash..............	121.8	19.2	Lynn, Mass....................	1.6	−4.1

[1] 25 percent or more of the population aged 20 to 24 enrolled in school in 1950.

Source: See table B-14.

TABLE **B-16.**—PERCENT INCREASE IN POPULATION, 1940 TO 1950 AND 1930 TO 1940, FOR INDEPENDENT CITIES SELECTED FOR HIGH AND LOW GROWTH RATES, BY SIZE, 1950

[Minus sign (−) denotes decrease]

High growth rate independent cities, by size	Percent increase		Low growth rate independent cities, by size	Percent increase	
	1940 to 1950	1930 to 1940		1940 to 1950	1930 to 1940
10,000 TO 25,000			**10,000 TO 25,000**		
Alice, Texas.................	111.1	83.8	Ansonia, Conn.................	-2.6	-3.5
Auburn, Ala.[1]...............	178.1	66.1	Berlin, N. H.................	-12.9	-4.7
Bastrop, La..................	92.7	29.4	Bradford, Pa.................	-1.9	-8.4
Borger, Texas................	80.3	53.4	Cambridge, Ohio..............	-2.0	-6.7
Bossier City, La.............	167.4	44.5	Clinton, Mass................	-1.2	-3.0
Burlington, N. C.............	101.3	25.3	Farrell, Pa..................	-1.8	-3.2
Carlsbad, N. Mex.............	152.6	91.9	Fort Scott, Kans.............	-2.1	-1.9
Clovis, N. Mex...............	72.1	25.4	Hannibal, Mo.................	-2.0	-8.3
Hollywood, Fla...............	130.0	117.5	Harrisburg, Ill..............	-4.0	-1.5
Lamesa, Texas................	77.3	71.1	Hornell, N. Y................	-3.8	-3.7
Las Vegas, Nev...............	199.4	63.1	Independence, Kans...........	-2.0	-9.5
Longview, Texas..............	78.1	173.2	Ironwood, Mich...............	-14.2	-6.5
Midland, Texas...............	132.2	70.5	La Salle, Ill................	-5.7	-2.6
Moscow, Idaho[1]..............	76.1	34.4	Mahonoy City, Pa.............	-18.7	-9.1
Oxnard, Calif................	153.2	35.5	Mt. Carmel, Pa...............	-20.0	-1.1
Pascagoula, Miss.............	83.1	36.0	Ogdensburg, N. Y.............	-1.1	-3.4
Pullman, Wash.[1].............	172.2	33.0	Oil City, Pa.................	-3.9	-7.7
Snyder, Texas................	214.8	26.8	Shamokin, Pa.................	-10.3	-7.2
Springfield, Oreg............	184.0	60.9	Shenandoah, Pa...............	-20.6	-9.2
State College, Pa.[1].........	176.7	39.9	Tamaqua, Pa..................	-7.8	-3.5
Stillwater, Okla.[1]..........	100.4	43.9	West Frankfort, Ill..........	-8.1	-15.7
25,000 to 50,000			**25,000 to 50,000**		
Abilene, Texas...............	71.2	14.8	Amsterdam, N. Y..............	-3.3	-4.3
Biloxi, Miss.................	114.2	17.7	Auburn, N. Y.................	2.7	-2.5
Bremerton, Wash..............	82.9	48.8	Butte, Mont..................	-10.3	-6.2
Champaign, Ill.[1]............	69.8	14.5	Cumberland, Md...............	-4.6	4.6
Columbia, Mo.[1]..............	73.8	22.9	Danville, Ill................	2.6	0.4
Eugene, Oreg.[1]..............	72.2	10.2	Fitchburg, Mass..............	2.1	2.8
Fayetteville, N. C...........	99.2	33.5	Haverhill, Mass..............	1.1	-4.0
Fort Lauderdale, Fla.........	101.9	107.7	Jamestown, N. Y..............	1.7	-5.6
Gainesville, Fla.[1]..........	95.3	31.4	Kingston, N. Y...............	0.8	1.8
Lafayette, La................	74.6	31.3	Newburgh, N. Y...............	0.2	1.9
Lake Charles, La.............	94.6	34.2	Newcastle, Pa................	2.5	-2.1
Lawton, Okla.................	92.5	48.9	New London, Conn.............	0.3	2.8
Norman, Okla.[1]..............	136.3	19.0	Paducah, Ky..................	-2.8	0.7
Odessa, Texas................	208.1	297.7	Parkersburg, W. Va...........	-1.4	1.6
Panama City, Fla.............	122.3	114.9	Portsmouth, Ohio.............	-9.1	-4.9
Rapid City, S. D.[1]..........	82.8	33.1	Poughkeepsie, N. Y...........	1.3	0.5
Roswell, N. M................	90.9	20.7	Quincy, Ill..................	2.4	3.1
Talahassee, Fla.[1]...........	67.7	51.8	Watertown, N. Y..............	2.9	3.7
Tuscaloosa, Ala.[1]...........	68.8	33.1	Williamsport, Pa.............	1.6	-3.0

[1] 25 percent or more of the population aged 20 to 24 enrolled in school in 1950.

Source: See table B-14.

Explanatory Note for Tables B–17 to B–20

These tables give a list including each standard metropolitan area (table B–17), each central city (B–18), each suburb of 10,000 inhabitants or more (B–19), and each independent city of 10,000 inhabitants or more (B–20), together with its population in 1950, the functional classification(s) into which it falls according to the criteria described in Chapter 16, and its income level. The symbols used to designate functional classes are as follows (see Chapter 16 for more complete definitions):

Manufacturing: "High"—in upper quintile of places on percentage of the employed labor force in manufacturing; "Low"—in lower quintile of places on percentage in manufacturing.

Trade: "Ww"—Wholesale trade centers; "Rr"—Retail trade centers; "TC"—Trade centers; "TCw"—Trade centers, wholesale; "TCr"—Trade centers, retail; "MTC"—Maintenance trade centers; "NT"—Nontrade centers; "NTw"—Nontrade centers, wholesale; "NTr"—Nontrade centers, retail. Places marked ". . ." are those for which trade data are not available.

Education (Ed): Places in the upper quintile of places on the percentage of persons 20 to 24 years old enrolled in school.

Public administration (PA): Places in the upper decile of places on the percentage of employed males in public administration.

Transportation (Tr): Places in the upper decile of places on the percentage of employed persons in transportation.

Military (My): Central cities and SMA's with more than 100,000 inhabitants were classified as military centers if they contained 2,000 or more members of the Armed Forces in 1950. All other SMA's and all urban places of 50,000 to 100,000 inhabitants were required to have at least 500 military persons, and all urban places with less than 50,000 were required to have 200 or more military persons residing within their boundaries to be classified as military centers.

Entertainment and recreation (ER): Places in the upper decile of places on the percentage of employed males in entertainment and recreation.

Income level: Four income levels are identified for the distribution of places on the median income of families and unrelated individuals in 1949: (1) Upper quintile; (2) between median and upper quintiles; (3) between median and lower quintiles; (4) lower quintile. Chapter 18 on "Characteristics of Trade Centers" classifies all places at income levels (1) and (2) as "high" income places, and all places at levels (3) and (4) as "low" income places. This differs from the procedure in Chapter 20 on "High and Low Income Communities" where comparisons between "high" and "low" income communities are between income levels (1) and (4), respectively.

Unincorporated places: All unincorporated places are designated with a single asterisk (*).

APPENDIX B

TABLE B–17.—FUNCTIONAL CLASSIFICATIONS AND 1950 POPULATION OF STANDARD METROPOLITAN AREAS

[See explanatory note for tables B–17 to B–20 above]

Standard metropolitan area	1950 population (thousands)	Functional classification			
		Manufacturing	Trade	Type of minor specialization	Income level
1,000,000 or more (14):					
Baltimore, Md........................	1,337	....	MTC	My	3
Boston, Mass.........................	2,370	....	Ww	Ed, My	2
Buffalo, N. Y........................	1,089	High.......	Ww	...	2
Chicago, Ill.........................	5,495	....	TC	My	1
Cleveland, Ohio......................	1,466	High.......	TCw	...	1
Detroit, Mich........................	3,016	High.......	MTC	...	1
Los Angeles, Calif...................	4,368	....	Rr	Ed, ER, My	2
Minneapolis–St. Paul, Minn...........	1,117	....	TC	Ed	2
New York–Northeastern New Jersey......	12,912	....	Ww	My	1
Philadelphia, Pa.....................	3,671	....	Ww	My	2
Pittsburgh, Pa.......................	2,213	....	Ww	...	2
St. Louis, Mo........................	1,681	....	TCw	My	3
San Francisco–Oakland, Calif.........	2,241	....	TCw	Ed, My	1
Washington, D. C.....................	1,464	Low.......	MTC	Ed, PA, My	1
500,000 to 1,000,000 (19):					
Albany–Schenectady–Troy, N. Y........	514	....	Rr	...	2
Atlanta, Ga..........................	672	....	TCw	...	4
Birmingham, Ala......................	559	....	Ww	...	4
Cincinnati, Ohio.....................	904	....	TCw	...	3
Columbus, Ohio.......................	503	....	MTC	Ed	2
Dallas, Texas........................	615	....	TC	ER	2
Denver, Colo.........................	564	Low.......	TC	Ed, My	3
Houston, Texas.......................	807	....	TCw	My	2
Indianapolis, Ind....................	552	....	TC	...	1
Kansas City, Mo......................	814	....	TC	Tr	3
Louisville, Ky.......................	577	....	MTC	...	3
Milwaukee, Wis.......................	871	High.......	MTC	...	1
New Orleans, La......................	685	Low.......	Ww	Tr, Er	4
Portland, Oreg.......................	705	....	TCr	...	2
Providence, R. I.....................	737	High.......	MTC	My	4
San Antonio, Texas...................	500	Low.......	NTw	PA, My	4
San Diego, Calif.....................	557	Low.......	Rr	PA, My, ER	4
Seattle, Wash........................	733	....	TCw	Ed, My	1
Youngstown, Ohio.....................	528	High.......	NT	...	2
250,000 to 500,000 (44):					
Akron, Ohio..........................	410	High.......	NTr	...	1
Allentown–Bethlehem–Easton, Pa.......	438	High.......	NT	...	2
Bridgeport, Conn.....................	258	High.......	Rr	...	2
Canton, Ohio.........................	283	High.......	NT	...	2
Charleston, W. Va....................	322	....	MTC	...	3
Dayton, Ohio.........................	457	High.......	MTC	PA	1
Duluth, Minn.—Superior, Wis.........	253	Low.......	MTC	Tr	3
Flint, Mich..........................	271	High.......	NT	...	1
Fort Worth, Texas....................	361	....	TCr	My	3
Fresno, Calif........................	277	Low.......	TCr	...	3
Grand Rapids, Mich...................	288	....	MTC	...	1
Harrisburg, Pa.......................	292	....	MTC	PA	3
Hartford, Conn.......................	358	....	Rr	...	1
Jacksonville, Fla....................	304	Low.......	Ww	PA, Tr, My	4
Johnstown, Pa........................	291	....	NT	...	4
Knoxville, Tenn......................	337	....	NTw	Ed	4
Memphis, Tenn........................	482	....	TC	My	4
Miami, Fla...........................	495	Low.......	Rr	ER	4
Nashville, Tenn......................	322	....	MTC	Ed	4
New Haven, Conn......................	265	....	MTC	Ed	2
Norfolk–Portsmouth, Va...............	446	Low.......	NTw	PA, Tr, My	4
Oklahoma City, Okla..................	325	Low.......	TCw	PA, ER	3
Omaha, Nebr..........................	366	....	TC	Tr	3
Peoria, Ill..........................	251	....	MTC	...	2
Phoenix, Ariz........................	332	Low.......	MTC	...	4
Reading, Pa..........................	256	High.......	NTr	...	3
Richmond, Va.........................	328	....	TCr	...	3
Rochester, N. Y......................	488	High.......	MTC	...	1
Sacramento, Calif....................	277	Low.......	Rr	PA	1
Salt Lake City, Utah.................	275	Low.......	MTC	Ed, ER	1
San Bernardino, Calif................	282	Low.......	NTr	Tr	4
San Jose, Calif......................	291	....	NTr	Ed	2

TABLE **B-17.**—FUNCTIONAL CLASSIFICATIONS AND 1950 POPULATION OF STANDARD METRO-
POLITAN AREAS—Cont.

[See explanatory note for tables B-17 to B-20 above]

Standard metropolitan area	1950 population (thousands)	Functional classification			
		Manufac-turing	Trade	Type of minor specialization	Income level
250,000 to 500,000--Cont.					
Scranton, Pa.	257	....	NT	...	4
Springfield-Holyoke, Mass.	407	High.......	NTr	...	2
Syracuse, N. Y.	342	....	TCr	Ed	3
Tacoma, Wash.	276	....	NT	My	2
Tampa-St. Petersburg, Fla.	409	Low........	MTC	ER, My	4
Toledo, Ohio.	396	....	Rr	...	1
Tulsa, Okla.	252	....	TCr	...	3
Utica-Rome, N. Y.	284	....	NTr	...	3
Wheeling, W. Va.--Steubenville, Ohio.	354	....	NT	...	3
Wilkes-Barre--Hazleton, Pa.	392	....	NT	...	4
Wilmington, Del.	268	....	MTC	...	3
Worcester, Mass.	276	High.......	MTC	Ed	3
100,000 to 250,000 (74):					
Albuquerque, N. Mex.	146	Low........	NTw	PA, My	2
Altoona, Pa.	140	....	NTr	Tr	3
Asheville, N. C.	124	....	NTw	...	3
Atlantic City, N. J.	132	....	Rr	ER	4
Augusta, Ga.	162	....	NT	My	4
Austin, Texas.	161	Low........	Rr	Ed, PA, My, ER	4
Baton Rouge, La.	158	....	NTr	Ed	3
Beaumont-Port Arthur, Texas.	195	....	MTC	...	1
Binghamton, N. Y.	185	High.......	MTC	...	1
Brockton, Mass.	129	....	NT	...	2
Cedar Rapids, Iowa.	104	....	TC	...	2
Charleston, S. C.	165	....	NTw	My	4
Charlotte, N. C.	197	....	TCw	ER	3
Chattanooga, Tenn.	246	....	MTC	...	3
Columbia, S. C.	143	Low........	Ww	Ed, My	4
Columbus, Ga.	171	....	NT	My	4
Corpus Christi, Texas.	165	Low........	MTC	PA, My	3
Davenport, Iowa--Rock Island--Moline, Ill.	234	....	MTC	...	1
Des Moines, Iowa.	226	....	TC	ER	2
Durham, N. C.	102	....	MTC	Ed	3
El Paso, Texas.	195	Low........	MTC	Tr, My	3
Erie, Pa.	219	High.......	MTC	...	2
Evansville, Ind.	160	....	MTC	...	2
Fall River, Mass.	137	High.......	Rr	...	3
Fort Wayne, Ind.	184	....	MTC	...	1
Galveston, Texas.	113	....	MTC	Tr	2
Greensboro-High Point, N. C.	191	....	TCw	Ed	3
Greenville, S. C.	168	....	MTC	...	3
Hamilton-Middletown, Ohio.	147	High.......	NT	Ed	2
Huntington, W. Va.--Ashland, Ky.	246	....	Ww	Tr	3
Jackson, Mich.	108	....	MTC	...	2
Jackson, Miss.	142	Low........	MTC	...	4
Kalamazoo, Mich.	127	....	MTC	Ed	2
Lancaster, Pa.	235	....	MTC	...	2
Lansing, Mich.	173	....	TCr	Ed	1
Lawrence, Mass.	126	High.......	NTr	...	2
Lexington, Ky.	101	Low........	TC	Ed, ER	4
Lincoln, Nebr.	120	....	Rr	Ed	3
Little Rock-North Little Rock, Ark.	197	....	TCw	...	3
Lorain-Elyria, Ohio.	148	High.......	NT	...	1
Lowell, Mass.	134	High.......	NT	...	3
Lubbock, Texas.	101	Low........	TC	Ed, My	3
Macon, Ga.	135	....	NTw	PA, ER	4
Madison, Wis.	169	....	Rr	Ed	3
Mobile, Ala.	231	....	NT	PA	4
Montgomery, Ala.	139	Low........	MTC	PA, My	4
New Bedford, Mass.	137	High.......	Rr	...	3
New Britain-Bristol, Conn.	147	High.......	NT	...	1
Orlando, Fla.	115	Low........	MTC	ER	4
Portland, Maine.	120	....	TC	...	3
Racine, Wis.	110	High.......	MTC	...	1
Raleigh, N. C.	136	Low........	Ww	Ed	4
Roanoke, Va.	133	....	MTC	Tr	2

TABLE **B-17.**—FUNCTIONAL CLASSIFICATIONS AND 1950 POPULATION OF STANDARD METRO-
POLITAN AREAS—Cont.

[See explanatory note for tables B–17 to B–20 above]

Standard metropolitan area	1950 population (thousands)	Functional classification			
		Manufac- turing	Trade	Type of minor specialization	Income level
100,000 to 250,000--Cont.					
Rockford, Ill..........................	152	High.......	TCr	...	1
Saginaw, Mich..........................	154	....	Ww	...	1
Savannah, Ga..........................	151	....	Ww	Tr, My	4
Shreveport, La.........................	177	Low........	TCr	...	4
Sioux City, Iowa......................	104	....	TC	...	2
South Bend, Ind.......................	205	High......	MTC	...	1
Spokane, Wash.........................	222	....	TCw	My	2
Springfield, Ill......................	131	....	TC	PA	2
Springfield, Mo.......................	105	....	TCw	Ed, Tr	4
Springfield, Ohio.....................	112	....	NTr	...	2
Stamford-Norwalk, Conn................	196	....	Rr	ER	1
Stockton, Calif.......................	201	Low.......	Rr	...	3
Terre Haute, Ind......................	105	....	TCr	Ed	3
Topeka, Kans..........................	105	....	MTC	PA, Tr	2
Trenton, N. J.........................	230	....	MTC	Ed	1
Waco, Texas...........................	130	....	MTC	Ed	4
Waterbury, Conn.......................	155	High......	NT	...	1
Waterloo, Iowa........................	100	....	Rr	...	1
Wichita, Kans.........................	222	....	TCw	...	2
Winston-Salem, N. C...................	146	....	Ww	...	3
York, Pa..............................	203	High......	NTr	My	3
Under 100,000 (17):					
Amarillo, Texas.......................	87	Low.......	TC	...	2
Bay City, Mich........................	88	....	NTw	...	2
Decatur, Ill..........................	99	....	TC	...	2
Gadsden, Ala..........................	94	High......	NT	...	3
Green Bay, Wis........................	98	....	TCw	...	2
Kenosha, Wis..........................	75	High......	NTr	...	1
Laredo, Texas.........................	56	Low.......	NT	...	4
Lima, Ohio............................	88	....	MTC	...	2
Manchester, N. H......................	88	High......	Rr	...	3
Muncie, Ind...........................	90	....	NT	Ed	2
Ogden, Utah...........................	83	Low.......	Ww	PA, Tr	1
Pittsfield, Mass......................	67	High......	...	...	1
Pueblo, Colo..........................	90	....	NT	PA	2
St. Joseph, Mo........................	97	....	TCw	ER	3
San Angelo, Texas.....................	59	Low.......	TCr	My	3
Sioux Falls, S. Dak...................	71	....	TC	...	2
Wichita Falls, Texas..................	98	Low.......	MTC	My	4

TABLE **B-18.**—FUNCTIONAL CLASSIFICATIONS AND 1950 POPULATION OF CENTRAL CITIES

[See explanatory note for tables B–17 to B–20 above]

City	1950 population (thousands)	Functional classification			
		Manufac- turing	Trade	Type of minor specialization	Income level
1,000,000 or more (5):					
Chicago, Ill..........................	3,621	....	Ww	...	1
Detroit, Mich.........................	1,850	High..........	Ww	...	1
Los Angeles, Calif....................	1,970	....	MTC	Ed, ER, My	3
New York City, N. Y...................	7,892	....	Ww	My, ER	2
Philadelphia, Pa......................	2,072	....	Ww	My	3
500,000 to 1,000,000 (13):					
Baltimore, Md.........................	950	....	MTC	My	3
Boston, Mass..........................	801	....	TC	Ed, My	3
Buffalo, N. Y.........................	580	....	Ww	...	2
Cincinnati, Ohio......................	504	....	TCw	...	3
Cleveland, Ohio.......................	915	High..........	TCw	...	2

TABLE **B-18.**—FUNCTIONAL CLASSIFICATIONS AND 1950 POPULATION OF CENTRAL CITIES—Cont.

[See explanatory note for tables B-17 to B-20 above]

City	1950 population (thousands)	Functional classification			
		Manufac-turing	Trade	Type of minor specialization	Income level
500,000 to 1,000,000--Cont.					
Houston, Texas..................	596	....	Ww	...	2
Milwaukee, Wis..................	637	High..........	MTC	...	1
Minneapolis, Minn...............	522	....	TC	Ed	2
New Orleans, La.................	570	Low...........	Ww	Tr, My, ER	4
Pittsburgh, Pa..................	677	....	TCw	...	3
St. Louis, Mo...................	857	....	Ww	...	3
San Francisco, Calif............	775	....	TCw	My	2
Washington, D. C................	802	Low...........	...	Ed, PA, My	2
250,000 to 500,000 (22):					
Akron, Ohio.....................	275	High..........	NT	...	1
Atlanta, Ga.....................	331	....	TC	Ed	4
Birmingham, Ala.................	326	....	Ww	...	4
Columbus, Ohio..................	376	....	MTC	Ed	2
Dallas, Texas...................	434	....	TC	ER	2
Denver, Colo....................	416	....	TCw	Ed, My	3
Fort Worth, Texas...............	279	....	TCr	My	3
Indianapolis, Ind...............	427	....	TC	My	2
Jersey City, N. J...............	299	....	NTw	Tr	1
Kansas City, Mo.................	457	....	TC	...	3
Louisville, Ky..................	369	....	MTC	...	3
Memphis, Tenn...................	396	....	Ww	...	4
Newark, N. J....................	439	....	MTC	...	2
Oakland, Calif..................	385	....	Rr	PA, My	1
Omaha, Nebr.....................	251	....	Ww	Tr	2
Portland, Oreg..................	374	....	TC	Ed	2
Rochester, N. Y.................	332	High..........	MTC	...	2
St. Paul, Minn..................	311	....	MTC	Ed, Tr	1
San Antonio, Texas..............	408	Low...........	NT	PA, My	4
San Diego, Calif................	334	Low...........	Rr	PA, My, ER	3
Seattle, Wash...................	468	....	MTC	Ed, My	2
Toledo, Ohio....................	304	....	MTC	...	1
100,000 to 250,000 (55):					
Albany, N. Y....................	135	....	TC	PA, Tr	3
Allentown, Pa...................	107	High..........	Rr	...	2
Austin, Texas...................	132	Low...........	NT	Ed, ER	4
Baton Rouge, La.................	126	....	NT	Ed	3
Bridgeport, Conn................	159	High..........	Rr	...	2
Canton, Ohio....................	117	High..........	Rr	...	2
Charlotte, N. C.................	134	....	TCw	ER	3
Chattanooga, Tenn...............	131	....	MTC	...	4
Corpus Christi, Texas...........	108	Low...........	NTr	PA	3
Dayton, Ohio....................	244	High..........	Rr	...	1
Des Moines, Iowa................	178	....	TC	...	2
Duluth, Minn....................	105	....	Ww	Tr	2
El Paso, Texas..................	130	Low...........	MTC	Tr, My	3
Erie, Pa........................	131	High..........	NTr	...	1
Evansville, Ind.................	129	High..........	NTw	...	3
Fall River, Mass................	112	High..........	NT	...	3
Flint, Mich.....................	163	High..........	NTr	...	1
Fort Wayne, Ind.................	134	....	MTC	...	1
Grand Rapids, Mich..............	177	....	TCr	...	1
Hartford, Conn..................	177	....	TCr	...	2
Jacksonville, Fla...............	205	Low...........	TCw	Tr	4
Knoxville, Tenn.................	125	....	Rr	Ed	4
Little Rock, Ark................	102	Low...........	MTC	...	4
Miami, Fla......................	249	Low...........	Rr	ER	4
Mobile, Ala.....................	129	Low...........	NT	PA, Tr	4
Montgomery, Ala.................	107	Low...........	...	PA, My	4
Nashville, Tenn.................	174	....	TCr	Ed	4
New Bedford, Mass...............	109	High..........	NT	...	3
New Haven, Conn.................	164	....	MTC	Ed	3
Norfolk, Va.....................	214	Low...........	MTC	PA, My	4
Oklahoma City, Okla.............	244	Low...........	MTC	PA	3
Peoria, Ill.....................	112	....	TCr	Ed	2
Phoenix, Ariz...................	107	Low...........	Rr	ER	3
Providence, R. I................	249	....	TCr	Ed	4

TABLE **B-18.**—FUNCTIONAL CLASSIFICATIONS AND 1950 POPULATION OF CENTRAL CITIES—Cont.

[See explanatory note for tables B–17 to B–20 above]

City	1950 population (thousands)	Functional classification			
		Manufac- turing	Trade	Type of minor specialization	Income level
100,000 to 250,000--Cont.					
Reading, Pa.	109	High	Rr	...	2
Richmond, Va.	230	...	TC	...	3
Sacramento, Calif.	138	Low	Rr	PA	1
Salt Lake City, Utah.	182	Low	Ww	Ed, ER	1
Savannah, Ga.	120	...	Ww	Ed, ER	4
Scranton, Pa.	126	...	NTr	Tr	3
Shreveport, La.	127	Low	MTC	...	4
South Bend, Ind.	116	High	Rr	...	1
Spokane, Wash.	162	Low	MTC	...	2
Springfield, Mass.	162	...	NTr	...	2
Syracuse, N. Y.	221	...	TCr	Ed	3
Tacoma, Wash.	144	...	NTw	My	2
Tampa, Fla.	125	...	MTC	ER	4
Trenton, N. J.	128	...	Rr	...	1
Tulsa, Okla.	183	...	MTC	...	2
Utica, N. Y.	102	...	Rr	...	3
Waterbury, Conn.	104	High	NT	...	1
Wichita, Kans.	168	...	NTw	...	2
Wilmington, Del.	110	...	TC	...	3
Worcester, Mass.	203	High	NTr	Ed	3
Youngstown, Ohio.	168	High	NTr	...	1
50,000 to 100,000 (84):					
Albuquerque, N. Mex.	97	Low	MTC	Ed, My	2
Altoona, Pa.	77	Low	NT	Tr	3
Amarillo, Texas.	74	Low	...	...	1
Asheville, N. C.	53	...	TCr	ER	3
Atlantic City, N. J.	62	Low	Rr	ER	4
Augusta, Ga.	72	...	Ww	PA, My	4
Bay City, Mich.	53	...	MTC	...	2
Beaumont, Texas.	94	...	MTC	...	2
Bethlehem, Pa.	66	High	NT	Ed	2
Binghamton, N. Y.	81	...	MTC	...	2
Brockton, Mass.	63	...	NTr	...	3
Cedar Rapids, Iowa.	72	...	TCw	...	2
Charleston, S. C.	70	...	MTC	My	4
Charleston, W. Va.	74	...	TC	...	2
Columbia, S. C.	87	Low	TCw	Ed, PA, My	4
Columbus, Ga.	80	...	...	My	4
Davenport, Iowa.	75	...	TCw	...	2
Decatur, Ill.	66	...	TCw	...	2
Durham, N. C.	71	...	MTC	Ed	4
Fresno, Calif.	92	Low	TC	Ed	2
Gadsden, Ala.	56	High	NT	...	3
Galveston, Texas.	67	Low	MTC	Tr	3
Green Bay, Wis.	53	...	TCw	...	2
Greensboro, N. C.	74	...	TC	Ed, ER	3
Greenville, S. C.	58	...	TC	Ed	4
Hamilton, Ohio.	58	High	NTr	...	2
Harrisburg, Pa.	90	...	TC	...	3
Holyoke, Mass.	55	High	MTC	...	3
Huntington, W. Va.	86	...	Ww	...	3
Jackson, Mich.	51	...	TCr	...	2
Jackson, Miss.	98	...	Ww	...	4
Johnstown, Pa.	63	...	MTC	...	3
Kalamazoo, Mich.	58	...	TCr	Ed	3
Kenosha, Wis.	54	High	NTr	...	1
Lancaster, Pa.	64	...	MTC	...	2
Lansing, Mich.	92	...	TCr	...	1
Laredo, Texas.	52	Low	NT	PA	4
Lawrence, Mass.	81	High	NTr	...	3
Lexington, Ky.	56	Low	TC	Ed, ER	4
Lima, Ohio.	50	...	TCr	...	2
Lincoln, Nebr.	99	...	MTC	Ed, PA	3
Lorain, Ohio.	51	High	NTr	...	1
Lowell, Mass.	97	High	NT	...	3
Lubbock, Texas.	72	Low	TC	Ed, My	3
Macon, Ga.	70	...	MTC	PA, ER	4

TABLE **B–18.**—FUNCTIONAL CLASSIFICATIONS AND 1950 POPULATION OF CENTRAL CITIES—Cont.

[See explanatory note for tables B–17 to B–20 above]

City	1950 population (thousands)	Functional classification			
		Manufac- turing	Trade	Type of minor specialization	Income level
50,000 to 100,000—Cont.					
Madison, Wis......................	96	....	MTC	Ed	3
Manchester, N. H..................	83	High...........	MTC	...	3
Muncie, Ind......................	58	High...........	MTC	Ed	2
New Britain, Conn................	74	High...........	NT	...	1
Ogden, Utah......................	57	Low...........	Ww	Tr	2
Orlando, Fla.....................	52	Low...........	TCr	ER	4
Pittsfield, Mass.................	53	High...........	NTr	...	1
Port Arthur, Texas...............	58	....	NT	...	1
Portland, Maine..................	78	....	TC	My	3
Portsmouth, Va...................	80	....	NT	My	4
Pueblo, Colo.....................	64	....	NTw	PA	2
Racine, Wis......................	71	High...........	MTC	...	1
Raleigh, N. C....................	66	Low...........	TCw	Ed, PA	4
Roanoke, Va......................	92	....	MTC	Tr	2
Rockford, Ill....................	93	High...........	TCr	...	1
Saginaw, Mich....................	93	....	MTC	...	1
St. Joseph, Mo...................	79	....	Ww	ER	3
St. Petersburg, Fla..............	97	Low...........	NTr	ER	4
San Angelo, Texas................	52	Low...........	...	My	3
San Bernardino, Calif............	63	Low...........	Rr	Tr	2
San Jose, Calif..................	95	....	TCr	Ed	2
Schenectady, N. Y................	92	High...........	MTC	...	1
Sioux City, Iowa.................	84	....	TCw	...	2
Sioux Falls, S. Dak..............	53	....	TC	ER	2
Springfield, Ill.................	82	....	TC	...	2
Springfield, Mo..................	67	....	TCw	Ed, Tr	3
Springfield, Ohio................	79	....	TCr	...	2
Stamford, Conn...................	74	....	NTw	...	1
Stockton, Calif..................	71	Low...........	TCr	Ed, ER	2
Terre Haute, Ind.................	64	....	TCr	Ed, ER	3
Topeka, Kans.....................	79	....	MTC	PA, Tr	3
Troy, N. Y.......................	73	....	Rr	Ed, PA	3
Waco, Texas......................	85	....	MTC	Ed, My	4
Waterloo, Iowa...................	65	....	MTC	...	1
Wheeling, W. Va..................	59	....	TC	ER	3
Wichita Falls, Texas.............	68	Low...........	MTC	My	4
Wilkes-Barre, Pa.................	77	....	TCw	...	3
Winston-Salem, N. C..............	88	....	Ww	...	4
York, Pa.........................	60	....	MTC	...	3
Under 50,000 (14):					
Ashland, Ky......................	31	....	NTw	...	2
Bristol, Conn....................	36	High...........	NT	...	1
Easton, Pa.......................	36	High...........	TCr	Ed	3
Elyria, Ohio.....................	30	High...........	Rr	...	1
Hazleton, Pa.....................	35	....	MTC	...	3
High Point, N. C.................	40	High...........	Ww	...	3
Middletown, Ohio.................	34	High...........	Rr	...	1
Moline, Ill......................	37	High...........	TCw	...	1
North Little Rock, Ark...........	44	....	NT	Tr	4
Norwalk, Conn....................	49	....	NT	...	1
Rock Island, Ill.................	49	....	Ww	...	1
Rome, N. Y.......................	42	....	NT	PA	2
Steubenville, Ohio...............	36	....	Rr	...	2
Superior, Wis....................	35	Low...........	Ww	Tr	2

TABLE **B-19.**—FUNCTIONAL CLASSIFICATIONS AND 1950 POPULATION OF SUBURBS WITH 10,000 INHABITANTS OR MORE

[See explanatory note for tables B–17 to B–20 above. Asterisk (*) designates an unincorporated place]

Suburb	1950 population (thousands)	Functional classification			Income level
		Manufacturing	Trade	Type of minor specialization	
50,000 or more (53):					
Alameda, Calif....................	64	Low..........	NT	PA, My	3
Alexandria, Va...................	62	Low..........	MTC	PA, Tr, My	1
Alhambra, Calif..................	51	Low..........	TCr	Ed	2
Aurora, Ill......................	51	....	TC	Tr	2
Bayonne, N. J....................	77	....	Ww	My	2
Berkeley, Calif..................	114	Low..........	NTw	Ed, PA, My	4
Berwyn, Ill......................	51	....	MTC	...	1
Burbank, Calif...................	79	....	MTC	ER	2
Cambridge, Mass..................	121	....	Ww	Ed, Pa	4
Camden, N. J.....................	125	....	TCw	...	4
Chester, Pa......................	66	....	TC	...	3
Cicero, Ill......................	68	High.........	MTC	...	1
Cleveland Heights, Ohio..........	59	....	NTr	Ed	1
Clifton, N. J....................	65	High.........	Ww	...	1
Covington, Ky....................	64	....	NTr	Tr	4
Cranston, R. I...................	55	....	Ww	...	3
Dearborn, Mich...................	95	High.........	MTC	...	1
East Chicago, Ind................	54	High.........	Ww	...	2
East Orange, N. J................	79	....	MTC	Ed	2
East St. Louis, Ill..............	82	....	MTC	Tr	4
Elizabeth, N. J..................	113	High.........	TCw	...	2
Evanston, Ill....................	74	Low..........	TC	Ed	2
Gary, Ind........................	134	High.........	MTC	...	3
Glendale, Calif..................	96	Low..........	TC	Ed, ER	2
Hammond, Ind.....................	88	High.........	TC	...	1
Hoboken, N. J....................	51	....	Ww	Tr	4
Irvington, N. J..................	59	....	MTC	...	2
Joliet, Ill......................	52	....	TC	Tr	2
Kansas City, Kans................	130	....	Ww	Tr	4
Lakewood, Ohio...................	68	....	MTC	...	1
Long Beach, Calif................	251	Low..........	TCw	My	4
Lynn, Mass.......................	100	....	MTC	...	3
Malden, Mass.....................	60	....	NT	...	3
McKeesport, Pa...................	52	....	TCr	...	4
Medford, Mass....................	66	....	NTw	Ed, PA	2
Mount Vernon, N. Y...............	72	Low..........	TCw	ER	2
New Rochelle, N. Y...............	60	Low..........	MTC	Ed, ER	3
Newton, Mass.....................	82	Low..........	NT	Ed	2
Niagara Falls, N. Y..............	91	High.........	MTC	...	2
Oak Park, Ill....................	64	....	Rr	Ed	1
Pasadena, Calif..................	105	Low..........	TCr	Ed, ER	4
Passaic, N. J....................	58	High.........	TC	...	3
Paterson, N. J...................	139	....	TCw	...	3
Pawtucket, R. I..................	81	High.........	MTC	...	3
Pontiac, Mich....................	74	High.........	MTC	...	3
Quincy, Mass.....................	84	....	MTC	Ed, My	2
Richmond, Calif..................	100	....	Ww	PA, Tr, My	2
Santa Monica, Calif..............	72	Low..........	Rr	Ed, ER	3
Somerville, Mass.................	102	....	Ww	Tr	3
South Gate, Calif................	51	....	NTw	...	2
Union City, N. J.................	56	....	MTC	Tr	3
Woonsocket, R. I.................	50	High.........	Ww	...	4
Yonkers, N. Y....................	153	....	MTC	...	2
25,000 to 50,000 (81):					
Aliquippa, Pa....................	26	High.........	NTr	...	3
Alliance, Ohio...................	26	....	TCw	...	4
Alton, Ill.......................	33	....	Rr	...	3
Barberton, Ohio..................	28	High.........	MTC	...	3
Belleville, Ill..................	33	....	MTC	PA	3
Belleville, N. J.................	32	....	NTw	...	2
Bessemer, Ala....................	28	....	MTC	...	4
Beverly, Mass....................	29	....	NT	...	4
Beverly Hills, Calif.............	29	Low..........	TC	Ed, ER	1
Bloomfield, N. J.................	49	....	Ww	Ed	2
Chelsea, Mass....................	39	....	Ww	My	4
Chicopee, Mass...................	49	High.........	NT	My	3
Compton, Calif...................	48	....	MTC	...	2
Council Bluffs, Iowa.............	45	Low..........	Ww	Tr	3

TABLE **B–19.**—FUNCTIONAL CLASSIFICATIONS AND 1950 POPULATION OF SUBURBS WITH 10,000 INHABITANTS OR MORE—Cont.

[See explanatory note for tables B–17 to B–20 above. Asterisk (*) designates an unincorporated place]

Suburb	1950 population (thousands)	Functional classification			
		Manufacturing	Trade	Type of minor specialization	Income level
25,000 to 50,000--Cont.					
Cuyahoga Falls, Ohio.............	29	....	NTr	...	1
East Cleveland, Ohio.............	40	....	NTr	...	2
Elgin, Ill.......................	44	....	...	...	2
Euclid, Ohio.....................	41	High..........	NT	...	1
Everett, Mass....................	46	....	Ww	...	3
Ferndale, Mich...................	30	....	MTC	...	1
Garfield, N. J...................	28	High..........	NT	...	2
Granite City, Ill................	29	....	NT	My	3
Hackensack, N. J.................	29	....	TC	...	3
Hamtramck, Mich..................	43	High..........	TC	...	2
Hempstead, N. Y..................	29	Low..........	TCr	PA, ER	2
Highland Park, Mich..............	46	....	TC	...	2
Huntington Park, Calif...........	29	....	TCr	...	2
Independence, Mo.................	37	....	NT	...	3
Inglewood, Calif.................	46	....	Rr	Ed, ER	2
Kearney, N. J....................	40	....	Ww	...	2
Lackawanna, N. Y.................	28	High..........	Ww	...	3
Lincoln Park, Mich...............	29	High..........	NTr	...	1
Linden, N. J.....................	31	High..........	Ww	...	1
Lockport, N. Y...................	25	....	MTC	...	3
Lynwood, Calif...................	26	....	NTw	...	2
Massillon, Ohio..................	30	High..........	MTC	...	3
Maywood, Ill.....................	27	....	NTr	...	1
Melrose, Mass....................	27	Low..........	NT	Ed	2
Miami Beach, Fla.................	46	Low..........	Rr	ER	4
Mishawaka, Ind...................	33	High..........	MTC	...	2
Montclair, N. J..................	44	Low..........	Rr	Ed	2
New Albany, Ind..................	29	....	MTC	...	4
New Brunswick, N. J..............	39	....	TC	Ed	2
New Kensington, Pa...............	25	....	Rr	...	4
Newport, Ky......................	31	....	Rr	...	4
Norristown, Pa...................	38	....	MTC	...	4
Northampton, Mass................	29	....	NTr	Ed	4
Norwood, Ohio....................	35	....	Ww	...	3
Nutley, N. J.....................	27	....	NT	...	2
Oak Ridge, Tenn.*................	30	....	...	PA	1
Orange, N. J.....................	38	....	MTC	...	3
Palo Alto, Calif.................	25	Low..........	Rr	Ed, PA	2
Parma, Ohio......................	29	....	...	...	1
Perth Amboy, N. J................	41	High..........	TC	...	3
Plainfield, N. J.................	42	....	TCr	...	2
Pomona, Calif....................	35	Low..........	TCr	...	4
Redondo Beach, Calif.............	25	....	NT	ER	3
Redwood City, Calif..............	26	Low..........	MTC	Tr	2
Revere, Mass.....................	37	....	Ww	ER	3
Royal Oak, Mich..................	47	....	MTC	...	1
Salem, Mass......................	42	....	MTC	...	3
San Leandro, Calif...............	28	....	NTr	PA	2
San Mateo, Calif.................	42	Low..........	NTr	Ed, Tr, ER	1
Santa Ana, Calif.................	46	Low..........	TCr	PA, My	4
Shaker Heights, Ohio.............	28	....	NTr	Ed	1
University City, Mo..............	40	Low..........	NTw	Ed	1
Vallejo, Calif...................	26	....	Rr	PA, My	4
Valley Stream, N. Y..............	27	Low..........	NTr	ER	1
Vancouver, Wash..................	42	Low..........	MTC	...	3
Waltham, Mass....................	47	....	MTC	My	3
Warren, Ohio.....................	50	High..........	Rr	...	3
Warwick, R. I....................	43	....	NT	My	3
Washington, Pa...................	26	....	TCr	...	4
Waukegan, Ill....................	39	....	TC	PA, My	2
Wauwatosa, Wis...................	33	....	NTw	Ed	1
West Allis, Wis..................	43	High..........	NTr	...	2
West New York, N. J..............	38	....	MTC	Tr	2
West Orange, N. J................	29	....	...	...	1
White Plains, N. Y...............	43	Low..........	TCr	ER	2
Wilkinsburg, Pa..................	31	....	MTC	Ed	2
Wyandotte, Mich..................	37	High..........	MTC	...	2

TABLE **B-19.**—FUNCTIONAL CLASSIFICATIONS AND 1950 POPULATION OF SUBURBS WITH 10,000 INHABITANTS OR MORE—Cont.

[See explanatory note for tables B-17 to B-20 above. Asterisk (*) designates an unincorporated place]

Suburb	1950 population (thousands)	Functional classification			
		Manufac-turing	Trade	Type of minor specialization	Income level
10,000 to 25,000 (276):					
Albany, Calif................	18	....	MTC	Ed, PA	2
Allen Park, Mich.............	12	....	NT	...	1
Ambridge, Pa.................	16	High.........	Rr	...	3
Anaheim, Calif...............	15	....	TC	...	4
Annapolis, Md................	10	Low.........	TCr	PA, My	4
Antioch, Calif...............	11	High.........	MTC	...	2
Arcadia, Calif...............	23	Low.........	MTC	ER	2
Arnold, Pa...................	10	High.........	NTw	...	4
Attleboro, Mass..............	24	High.........	...	...	2
Aurora, Colo.................	11	Low.........	...	PA, Tr, My	2
Azusa, Calif.................	11	....	Ww	...	3
Baytown, Texas...............	23	....	TC	...	2
Beaver Falls, Pa.............	17	....	TC	...	4
Bell, Calif..................	15	....	TCr	...	2
Bellaire, Ohio...............	13	....	MTC	...	4
Bellaire, Texas..............	10	Low.........	...	...	1
Bellevue, Pa.................	12	....	MTC	...	2
Berea, Ohio..................	12	....	...	Ed, PA	3
Bergenfield, N. J............	18	....	MTC	...	1
Berkley, Mich................	18	....	Ww	...	1
Bethel, Pa...................	11	....	...	...	2
Bexley, Ohio.................	12	Low.........	NTW	Ed	1
Birmingham, Mich.............	15	....	TCr	...	1
Blue Island, Ill.............	18	High.........	TC	Tr	2
Braddock, Pa.................	16	High.........	TC	...	4
Brandon-Judson, S. C.*.......	11	High.........	...	...	4
Brentwood, Pa................	13	....	NTw	...	2
Bristol, Pa..................	13	High.........	Rr	...	3
Brookfield, Ill..............	15	....	Ww	...	1
Burlingame, Calif............	20	Low.........	TCr	Ed, Tr	1
Burlington, N. J.............	12	....	...	...	4
Calumet City, Ill............	16	....	Ww	...	2
Campbell, Ohio...............	13	High.........	NT	...	3
Canonsburg, Pa...............	12	....	MTC	...	4
Carbondale, Pa...............	16	....	NTr	Tr	4
Carlisle, Pa.................	17	....	...	Ed, PA, My	4
Carnegie, Pa.................	12	....	TCw	Tr	3
Carteret, N. J...............	13	High.........	Ww	...	3
Cedar Falls, Iowa............	14	....	MTC	Ed	4
Central Falls, R. I..........	24	High.........	NTw	...	4
Chicago Heights, Ill.........	25	....	MTC	...	3
Chula Vista, Calif...........	16	....	MTC	PA, My	2
Clairton, Pa.................	20	High.........	NTr	...	3
Clayton, Mo..................	16	Low.........	TC	Ed	1
Clearwater, Fla..............	16	Low.........	TCr	ER	4
Cliffside Park, N. J.........	17	....	MTC	ER	2
Coatesville, Pa..............	14	....	TC	...	3
Cohoes, N. Y.................	21	....	NTw	PA	3
College Park, Ga.............	15	....	...	PA, Tr	4
College Park, Md.............	11	Low.........	...	Ed, PA	4
Collingswood, N. J...........	16	....	TCr	...	2
Collinsville, Ill............	12	....	MTC	...	3
Colton, Calif................	14	Low.........	Ww	Tr	3
Columbia, Pa.................	12	High.........	NTr	PA	4
Conshohocken, Pa.............	11	High.........	...	...	3
Coral Gables, Fla............	20	Low.........	MTC	Ed, ER	4
Coraopolis, Pa...............	10	....	MTC	...	3
Coronado, Calif..............	13	Low.........	...	PA, My	3
Costa Mesa, Calif.*..........	12	Low.........	...	My, ER	4
Cudahy, Wis..................	12	High.........	Rr	...	2
Culver City, Calif...........	20	....	TC	ER	2
Daly City, Calif.............	15	....	MTC	ER	2
Darby, Pa....................	13	....	Rr	...	3
Decatur, Ga..................	22	Low.........	MTC	Ed	2
Des Plaines, Ill.............	15	....	TCw	...	1
Donora, Pa...................	12	High.........	...	...	3
Dormont, Pa..................	13	....	TCr	...	2
Dover, N. J..................	11	....	TC	...	3
Downers Grove, Ill...........	12	....	TCr	...	1
Dumont, N. J.................	13	....	...	Tr	2

TABLE **B–19.**—FUNCTIONAL CLASSIFICATIONS AND 1950 POPULATION OF SUBURBS WITH 10,000 INHABITANTS OR MORE—Cont.

[See explanatory note for tables B–17 to B–20 above. Asterisk (*) designates an unincorporated place]

Suburb	1950 population (thousands)	Functional classification			
		Manufacturing	Trade	Type of minor specialization	Income level
10,000 to 25,000--Cont.					
Dunmore, Pa...............	20	....	NTw	Tr	4
Duquesne, Pa...............	18	High...........	NT	...	4
East Detroit, Mich.........	21	High...........	NT	...	2
East Lansing, Mich.........	20	Low...........	NT	Ed	4
East Moline, Ill..........	14	High...........	MTC	...	2
East Patterson, N. J......	15	High...........	Ww	...	2
East Point, Ga...........	21	....	MTC	PA, Tr, My	3
Ecorse, Mich.............	18	High...........	NT	Tr	3
El Cerrito, Calif........	18	....	MTC	...	2
Ellwood City, Pa.........	13	High...........	...	...	3
Elmhurst, Ill...........	21	....	MTC	Ed	1
Elmwood Park, Ill........	19	....	NTr	...	1
Endicott, N. Y..........	20	High...........	...	...	3
Englewood, Colo.........	17	....	...	...	3
Englewood, N. J.........	23	....	TC	...	2
Evergreen Park, Ill.....	11	....	...	...	1
Fairfield, Ala.........	13	....	...	...	4
Fairlawn, N. J.........	24	....	MTC	...	1
Ferguson, Mo...........	12	....	NTw	...	2
Floral Park, N. Y......	15	....	MTC	Ed	1
Forest Park, Ill.......	15	....	TCw	...	2
Fort Lee, N. J.........	12	....	...	ER	2
Fort Thomas, Ky........	11	....	NT	Ed	3
Freeport, N. Y.........	25	....	Rr	...	3
Fullerton, Calif.......	14	....	MTC	ER	3
Gardena, Calif.........	14	....	Rr	ER	3
Garden City, N. Y......	14	....	TC	Ed	1
Garfield Heights, Ohio..	22	....	...	...	2
Garland, Texas.........	11	....	...	...	3
Girard, Ohio..........	10	High...........	...	...	3
Glen Cove, N. Y........	15	....	MTC	ER	3
Gloucester City, N. J..	14	....	Ww	My	3
Grand Prairie, Texas...	15	....	...	My	3
Greensburg, Pa........	17	....	TC	...	3
Gretna, La...........	14	....	NTr	Tr, ER	4
Grosse Pointe Park, Mich..	13	....	...	Ed	1
Grosse Pointe Woods, Mich..	10	....	NT	ER	1
Haddonfield, N. J......	10	....	NTr	Ed	1
Hanover, Pa...........	14	High...........	...	...	4
Harrison, N. J........	13	High...........	Ww	...	3
Harvey, Ill...........	21	....	MTC	Tr	2
Hawthorne, Calif......	16	....	MTC	...	3
Hawthorne, N. J.......	15	....	Ww	...	2
Hayward, Calif........	14	....	TC	...	3
Hazel Park, Mich......	18	High...........	MTC	...	2
Hermosa Beach, Calif...	12	....	...	ER	3
Hialeah, Fla..........	20	Low...........	...	Tr, ER	3
Hibbing, Minn.........	16	Low...........	TCw	...	2
Highland Park, Ill....	17	Low...........	Rr	ER	1
Highland Park, Texas..	11	Low...........	TCw	Ed	1
Hobart, Ind..........	10	....	MTC	...	2
Homestead, Pa........	10	High...........	Rr	...	4
Homewood, Ala........	13	Low...........	NTw	Ed	1
Hyattsville, Md......	12	Low...........	...	Ed, PA	1
Inkster, Mich........	17	High...........	NT	...	3
Jeanette, Pa.........	16	High...........	MTC	...	3
Jeffersonville, Ind...	15	....	MTC	PA	4
Jennings, Mo........	15	....	...	...	2
Johnson City, N. Y...	19	High...........	...	Ed	3
Kenmore, N. Y........	20	....	...	...	1
Kings Park, N. Y.*...	11	Low...........	...	...	3
Kingston, Pa........	21	....	TCr	...	2
Kirkwood, Mo........	19	....	MTC	...	1
La Grange, Ill......	12	....	Rr	Ed	1
La Mesa, Calif......	11	Low...........	...	Ed, PA, My	3
Lansdowne, Pa.......	12	....	Ww	...	1
Latrobe, Pa.........	12	....	TCr	...	4
Livonia, Mich.......	18	....	...	...	2
Lodi, Calif.........	14	Low...........	TC	...	4
Lodi, N. J..........	15	High...........	NTw	...	3

TABLE **B–19.**—FUNCTIONAL CLASSIFICATIONS AND 1950 POPULATION OF SUBURBS WITH 10,000 INHABITANTS OR MORE—Cont.

[See explanatory note for tables B–17 to B–20 above. Asterisk (*) designates an unincorporated place]

Suburb	1950 population (thousands)	Functional classification			
		Manufacturing	Trade	Type of minor specialization	Income level
10,000 to 25,000--Cont.					
Long Beach, N. Y.	16	Low	...	...	3
Lynbrook, N. Y.	17	...	TC	...	1
Madison, N. J.	10	...	NTr	Ed	1
Mamaroneck, N. Y.	15	...	Ww	ER	2
Manhattan Beach, Calif.	17	...	...	ER	2
Maple Heights, Ohio	16	...	...	...	2
Maplewood, Mo.	13	...	TCr	...	2
Marietta, Ga.	21	Low	MTC	PA, My, ER	4
Martins Ferry, Ohio	13	...	MTC	...	4
Maywood, Calif.	13	...	MTC	...	2
McKees Rocks, Pa.	16	...	TCw	Tr	4
Melrose Park, Ill	13	...	TCw	Tr	2
Menlo Park, Calif.	14	Low	...	Ed	2
Mesa, Ariz.	17	Low	...	Ed	3
Midwest City, Okla	10	Low	MTC	PA, My	4
Mineola, N. Y.	15	Low	NT	PA, My	2
Monessen, Pa.	18	...	TC	...	2
Montebello, Calif.	22	High	MTC	...	3
Monterey Park, Calif.	20	...	NTw	...	2
Monrovia, Calif.	20	Low	Rr	...	3
Morristown, N. J.	17	Low	TCr	...	3
Moundsville, W. Va.	15	...	NTw	...	4
Mount Clemens, Mich.	17	...	TC	My	3
Mount Rainier, Md.	11	Low	...	PA, My	2
Munhall, Pa.	16	High	MTC	...	2
Nanticoke, Pa.	20	...	NTr	...	4
National City, Calif.	21	Low	MTC	PA, My	3
Naugatuck, Conn.	17	High	...	...	2
Newport Beach, Calif.	12	Low	Rr	My, ER	3
Niles, Ohio	17	High	NTr	...	3
North Arlington, N. J.	16	...	NTw	...	2
North Braddock, Pa.	15	High	...	...	3
North Miami, Fla.	11	Low	...	Tr, ER	2
North Plainfield, N. J.	13	...	...	...	2
North Tonawanda, N. Y.	25	High	MTC	...	3
Oceanside, Calif.	13	Low	MTC	PA, My	4
Ontario, Calif.	23	...	MTC	...	4
Orange, Calif.	10	Low	Ww	...	4
Ossining, N. Y.	16	...	MTC	PA, Tr	3
Overland, Mo.	12	...	MTC	...	2
Painesville, Ohio	14	...	TCr	...	3
Park Ridge, Ill	17	...	NTr	Ed	1
Pasadena, Texas	22	...	...	My	2
Peabody, Mass.	23	High	Ww	...	3
Peekskill, N. Y.	18	...	TC	Tr	3
Pekin, Ill.	22	...	TCw	...	2
Phenix City, Ala.	23	...	...	My	4
Phillipsburg, N. J.	19	High	NTw	...	3
Phoenixville, Pa.	13	High	Rr	...	3
Piedmont, Calif.	10	Low	NT	Ed	1
Pittsburg, Calif.	13	...	TCr	My	3
Pittston, Pa.	15	...	TCw	...	4
Pleasantville, N. J.	12	Low	MTC	ER, My	4
Plymouth, Pa.	13	...	NT	...	4
Port Chester, N. Y.	24	...	TCw	ER	3
Pottstown, Pa.	23	High	TC	...	3
Prichard, Ala.	19	...	MTC	PA	4
Princeton, N. J.	12	Low	...	Ed	4
Puyallup, Wash.	10	...	...	...	4
Rahway, N. J.	21	...	MTC	ER	2
Redlands, Calif.	18	Low	Ww	Ed	4
Rensselaer, N. Y.	11	...	Ww	Tr	3
Renton, Wash.	16	...	MTC	...	3
Richfield, Minn.	18	...	NT	My	2
Richmond Heights, Mo.	15	...	Ww	Ed	2
Ridgefield Park, N. J.	12	...	Ww	...	2
Ridgewood, N. J.	17	...	Rr	Ed	1
River Forest, Ill.	11	...	...	Ed	1
River Rouge, Mich.	21	High	Ww	...	3
Robbinsdale, Minn.	11	...	...	...	2

TABLE **B-19.**—FUNCTIONAL CLASSIFICATIONS AND 1950 POPULATION OF SUBURBS WITH 10,000 INHABITANTS OR MORE—Cont.

[See explanatory note for tables B–17 to B–20 above. Asterisk (*) designates an unincorporated place]

Suburb	1950 population (thousands)	Functional classification			
		Manufacturing	Trade	Type of minor specialization	Income level
10,000 to 25,000—Cont.					
Rockville Centre, N. Y............	22	Low............	TCr	Ed	1
Rocky River, Ohio................	11	....	MTC	Ed	1
Roselle, N. J....................	18	....	Ww	...	1
Roselle Park, N. J...............	12	High...........	MTC	...	1
Roseville, Mich..................	16	....	...	...	2
Rutherford, N. J.................	17	....	MTC	...	1
Rye, N. Y........................	12	Low............	MTC	ER	1
St. Charles, Mo..................	14	....	MTC	...	4
St. Clair Shores, Mich..........	20	....	NT	...	2
St. Louis Park, Minn............	23	....	NTw	...	1
San Bruno, Calif.................	12	....	MTC	Tr, My, ER	2
San Carlos, Calif...............	14	Low............	MTC	Tr	1
San Fernando, Calif.............	13	Low............	TCr	...	4
San Gabriel, Calif..............	20	....	MTC	...	2
San Marino, Calif...............	11	Low...........	NTr	...	1
San Pablo, Calif................	14	....	...	...	3
San Rafael, Calif...............	14	Low...........	TC	PA, My	2
Santa Clara, Calif..............	12	....	NT	Ed	4
Sayreville, N. J................	10	High...........	...	...	2
Scarsdale, N. Y.................	13	Low...........	...	Ed	1
Shorewood, Wis..................	16	....	NTr	Ed	1
Skokie, Ill....................	15	....	Ww	ER	1
Somerville, N. J...............	12	....	TC	...	2
South Charleston, W. Va........	17	....	MTC	...	2
South Euclid, Ohio.............	15	....	NTw	Ed	1
South Milwaukee, Wis...........	13	High...........	MTC	...	2
South Norfolk, Va..............	10	....	MTC	PA, Tr, My	4
South Orange, N. J.............	15	....	Rr	Ed	1
South Pasadena, Calif..........	17	Low...........	MTC	Ed	2
South Portland, Maine..........	22	Low...........	Ww	Tr, My	3
South River, N. J..............	11	High...........	MTC	...	2
South St. Paul, Minn...........	16	....	TCw	...	2
South San Francisco, Calif.....	19	....	Ww	Tr, My	2
Steelton, Pa...................	13	....	NT	PA	4
Struthers, Ohio................	12	High...........	NT	ER	3
Summit, N. J...................	18	....	TCr	...	2
Swissvale, Pa..................	16	High...........	...	...	3
Takoma Park, Md................	13	Low...........	...	Ed, PA, My	2
Texas City, Texas..............	17	....	TCr	My	2
Tonawanda, N. Y................	15	High...........	MTC	...	3
Torrance, Calif................	22	....	Ww	...	2
Turtle Creek, Pa...............	12	High...........	NTr	Tr	3
University Heights, Ohio.......	12	....	NTw	Ed	1
University Park, Texas.........	24	Low...........	Ww	Ed	1
Verona, N. J...................	11	....	...	...	1
Virginia, Minn.................	12	Low...........	TCr	...	4
Watervliet, N. Y...............	15	....	NT	Tr	3
Webster Groves, Mo.............	23	....	MTC	Ed	1
Weirton, W. Va.................	24	High...........	...	...	2
Westbrook, Maine...............	12	High...........	NTr	...	3
West Chester, Pa...............	15	....	Rr	Ed	4
Westfield, Mass................	21	....	MTC	...	3
Westfield, N. J................	21	....	MTC	...	1
West Mifflin, Pa...............	18	High...........	...	...	3
West University Place, Texas...	17	Low...........	...	Ed	1
Wheaton, Ill...................	12	Low...........	NTr	Ed	4
Whitefish Bay, Wis.............	15	....	NTw	Ed	1
White Settlement, Texas........	11	High...........	...	My	3
Whittier, Calif................	24	....	TCr	Ed	2
Wilmette, Ill..................	18	....	MTC	Ed, ER	1
Winnetka, Ill..................	12	Low...........	...	Ed	1
Woburn, Mass...................	20	....	NTr	...	3
Woodbury, N. J.................	11	....	...	...	2
Wood River, Ill................	10	High...........	TC	...	2
Xenia, Ohio....................	13	....	TC	PA	4
Yeadon, Pa.....................	11	....	...	Ed	2

TABLE **B-20.**—FUNCTIONAL CLASSIFICATIONS AND 1950 POPULATION OF INDEPENDENT CITIES WITH 10,000 INHABITANTS OR MORE

[See explanatory note for tables B-17 to B-20 above. Asterisk (*) designates an unincorporated place]

City	1950 population (thousands)	Functional classification			
		Manufacturing	Trade	Type of minor specialization	Income level
25,000 to 50,000 (157):					
Abilene, Texas	46	....	MTC	Ed	3
Albany, Ga.	31	....	Ww	...	3
Alexandria, La.	35	....	MTC	...	4
Amsterdam, N. Y.	32	....	NT	...	4
Anderson, Ind.	47	High	NTr	...	1
Ann Arbor, Mich.	48	....	Rr	Ed	4
Anniston, Ala.	31	....	NTw	PA	3
Appleton, Wis.	34	....	MTC	...	1
Athens, Ga.	28	....	...	Ed, ER	4
Auburn, N. Y.	37	High	NT	...	2
Bakersfield, Calif.	35	Low	TC	...	1
Bangor, Maine	32	....	TC	...	3
Battle Creek, Mich.	49	....	MTC	My	1
Bellingham, Wash.	34	....	MTC	Ed	3
Beloit, Wis.	30	High	NTr	Ed	1
Billings, Mont.	32	....	TC	...	1
Biloxi, Miss.	37	....	NT	PA, My, ER	4
Bloomington, Ill.	34	....	TCr	Ed	2
Bloomington, Ind.	28	....	NT	Ed, ER	4
Boise City, Idaho	34	Low	TC	PA	2
Bremerton, Wash.	28	High	Rr	My	1
Brownsville, Texas	36	....	NTw	...	4
Burlington, Iowa	31	....	MTC	...	2
Burlington, Vt.	33	....	TC	Ed	3
Butte, Mont.	33	....	TCw	...	2
Champaign, Ill.	40	Low	TC	Ed	4
Charlottesville, Va.	26	....	Rr	Ed, ER	3
Cheyenne, Wyo.	32	Low	MTC	PA, Tr, My	1
Clarksburg, W. Va.	32	....	TC	...	2
Clinton, Iowa	30	....	NT	...	1
Colorado Springs, Colo.	45	....	MTC	My, ER	3
Columbia, Mo.	32	Low	NT	Ed	4
Concord, N. H.	28	....	NTw	...	2
Cumberland, Md.	38	....	TCr	Tr	2
Danville, Ill.	38	....	MTC	...	3
Danville, Va.	35	....	TC	...	2
Daytona Beach, Fla.	30	Low	Rr	ER	3
Dubuque, Iowa	50	....	MTC	Ed	2
East Bakersfield, Calif.*	38	Low	...	ER	2
Eau Claire, Wis.	36	....	Ww	...	1
Elkhart, Ind.	36	High	MTC	...	1
Elmira, N. Y.	50	....	MTC	...	2
Enid, Okla.	36	....	TCw	My, Er	3
Eugene, Oreg.	36	....	TC	Ed	3
Everett, Wash.	34	....	Rr	...	2
Fairmont, W. Va.	29	....	MTC	...	2
Fargo, N. Dak.	38	Low	TC	Ed	2
Fayetteville, N. C.	35	....	MTC	My	3
Fitchburg, Mass.	43	High	NTw	...	2
Fond du Lac, Wis.	30	....	MTC	...	1
Fort Dodge, Iowa	25	....	TC	...	2
Fort Lauderdale, Fla.	36	Low	Rr	ER	3
Fort Smith, Ark.	48	....	Ww	...	3
Gainesville, Fla.	27	Low	MTC	...	4
Galesburg, Ill.	31	....	MTC	Ed	2
Gloucester, Mass.	25	....	NTw	Tr	2
Grand Forks, N. Dak.	27	....	TC	Ed, Tr	2
Great Falls, Mont.	39	....	TCw	Tr, My	1
Greenville, Miss.	30	....	Ww	...	4
Hagerstown, Md.	36	....	Ww	Tr	2
Hattiesburg, Miss.	29	....	MTC	Ed	4
Haverhill, Mass.	47	High	NT	...	3
Hot Springs, Ark.	29	Low	MTC	ER	4
Hutchinson, Kans.	34	....	TCw	...	2
Iowa City, Iowa	27	Low	NTr	Ed	4
Ithaca, N. Y.	29	....	Rr	Ed	4
Jackson, Tenn.	30	....	MTC	Tr	4

TABLE **B-20.**—FUNCTIONAL CLASSIFICATIONS AND 1950 POPULATION OF INDEPENDENT CITIES WITH 10,000 INHABITANTS OR MORE—Cont.

[See explanatory note for tables B-17 to B-20 above. Asterisk (*) designates an unincorporated place]

City	1950 population (thousands)	Manufac- turing	Trade	Type of minor specialization	Income level
25,000 to 50,000--Cont.					
Jamestown, N. Y.	43	High	MTC	...	1
Jefferson City, Mo.	25	...	NTr	PA	3
Johnson City, Tenn.	28	...	TCw	ER	3
Joplin, Mo.	39	...	TCw	...	3
Kankakee, Ill.	26	...	TCr	...	1
Kannapolis, N. C.*	28	High	...	...	1
Key West, Fla.	26	Low	NT	PA, My	4
Kingston, N. Y.	29	...	TCw	...	2
Kokomo, Ind.	39	High	NT	...	2
La Crosse, Wis.	48	...	MTC	...	2
Lafayette, Ind.	36	...	MTC	...	2
Lafayette, La.	34	Low	NTw	Ed	4
La Grange, Ga.	25	High	NT	...	3
Lake Charles, La.	41	...	Ww	...	2
Lakeland, Fla.	31	...	MTC	Ed	4
Laurel, Miss.	25	...	...	...	4
Lawton, Okla.	35	Low	NT	PA, My	3
Lebanon, Pa.	28	High	Rr	...	2
Lewiston, Maine	41	High	MTC	...	3
Lynchburg, Va.	48	...	Ww	...	3
Manitowoc, Wis.	28	High	NTw	...	1
Mansfield, Ohio	44	High	MTC	...	1
Marion, Ind.	30	High	MTC	...	3
Marion, Ohio	34	...	NTr	Tr	2
Mason City, Iowa	28	...	TC	...	1
Meriden, Conn.	44	High	NT	...	1
Meridian, Miss.	42	...	Ww	...	4
Michigan City, Ind.	28	High	NT	...	1
Middletown, Conn.	30	High	NT	Ed	2
Monroe, La.	39	...	TC	...	4
Morgantown, W. Va.	26	...	NTr	Ed	4
Muskegon, Mich.	48	High	MTC	...	2
Muskogee, Okla.	37	...	Ww	...	3
Nashua, N. H.	35	High	NT	...	2
Newark, Ohio	34	...	NT	...	2
Newburgh, N. Y.	32	...	TCr	...	2
New Castle, Pa.	49	High	NTr	Tr	2
New London, Conn.	31	...	TCr	Ed, PA, My	3
Newport, R. I.	38	Low	NT	PA, My	2
Newport News, Va.	42	...	TCr	Tr, My	3
Norman, Okla.	27	Low	...	Ed, ER	4
Odessa, Texas	29	Low	Ww	...	1
Oshkosh, Wis.	41	High	MTC	...	2
Ottumwa, Iowa	34	...	NTw	...	2
Owensboro, Ky.	34	...	MTC	...	3
Paducah, Ky.	33	...	Ww	Tr	3
Panama City, Fla.	26	...	...	PA, My	3
Parkersburg, W. Va.	30	...	MTC	...	2
Pensacola, Fla.	43	Low	MTC	PA, My	4
Petersburg, Va.	35	...	MTC	My	3
Pine Bluff, Ark.	37	...	...	Tr	4
Pocatello, Idaho	26	Low	MTC	Ed, Tr	1
Port Huron, Mich.	36	...	...	...	1
Portsmouth, Ohio	37	...	MTC	Tr	3
Poughkeepsie, N. Y.	41	...	TCr	...	3
Provo, Utah	29	...	NT	Ed	2
Quincy, Ill.	41	...	MTC	...	3
Rapid City, S. Dak.	25	...	Rr	My	3
Reno, Nev.	32	Low	TC	Ed, ER	2
Richmond, Ind.	40	High	MTC	...	2
Riverside, Calif.	47	Low	MTC	PA, My	2
Rochester, Minn.	30	Low	Rr	...	2
Rocky Mount, N. C.	28	...	Ww	Tr	3
Rome, Ga.	30	...	...	...	3
Roswell, N. Mex.	26	Low	Ww	...	2
St. Cloud, Minn.	28	...	Rr	Ed	2
Salem, Oreg.	43	...	Rr	PA	2

TABLE **B-20.**—FUNCTIONAL CLASSIFICATIONS AND 1950 POPULATION OF INDEPENDENT CITIES WITH 10,000 INHABITANTS OR MORE—Cont.

[See explanatory note for tables B-17 to B-20 above. Asterisk (*) designates an unincorporated place]

City	1950 population (thousands)	Functional classification			
		Manufacturing	Trade	Type of minor specialization	Income level
25,000 to 50,000--Cont.					
Salina, Kans......................	26	....	TC	...	2
Sandusky, Ohio....................	29	High..........	NTr	...	1
Santa Barbara, Calif..............	45	Low...........	Rr	Ed, ER	3
Santa Fe, N. Mex..................	28	Low...........	...	PA	3
Sharon, Pa........................	26	High..........	TCr	...	1
Sheboygan, Wis....................	42	High..........	NTw	...	1
Spartanburg, S. C.................	37	....	TC	...	3
Tallahassee, Fla..................	27	Low...........	NTr	Ed, PA	4
Taunton, Mass.....................	40	High..........	NT	...	3
Temple, Texas.....................	25	Low...........	MTC	...	3
Torrington, Conn..................	28	High..........	NT	...	1
Tuscaloosa, Ala...................	46	....	NTw	Ed	4
Tucson, Ariz......................	45	Low...........	TCr	Ed	3
Tyler, Texas......................	39	....	MTC	...	3
Vicksburg, Miss...................	28	....	...	...	4
Watertown, N. Y...................	34	....	TCr	...	3
Wausau, Wis.......................	30	....	MTC	...	2
West Palm Beach, Fla..............	43	Low...........	Rr	ER	3
Williamsport, Pa..................	45	High..........	MTC	...	3
Wilmington, N. C..................	45	....	Ww	Tr	4
Winona, Minn......................	25	....	MTC	Ed	3
Yakima, Wash......................	38	....	TC	...	2
Zanesville, Ohio..................	41	High..........	MTC	...	3
10,000 to 25,000 (502):					
Aberdeen, S. Dak..................	21	Low...........	TC	...	2
Aberdeen, Wash....................	20	....	TCw	...	1
Ada, Okla.........................	16	....	MTC	Ed, ER	3
Adams-Renfrew, Mass.*.............	12	High..........	...	...	1
Adrian, Mich......................	18	High..........	MTC	...	2
Albany, Oreg......................	10	....	TC	...	1
Albemarle, N. C...................	12	High..........	Rr	...	3
Albert Lea, Minn..................	14	....	TCr	...	2
Albion, Mich......................	10	High..........	NT	Ed	4
Alice, Texas......................	16	Low...........	Ww	...	3
Alisal, Calif.*...................	17	....	...	My	1
Alpena, Mich......................	13	....	...	...	2
Americus, Ga......................	12	....	...	...	4
Ames, Iowa........................	23	Low...........	NT	Ed, ER	4
Amphitheater, Ariz................	13	Low...........	...	...	2
Anaconda, Mont....................	11	High..........	NT	...	1
Anderson, S. C....................	20	....	TCr	...	3
Ansonia, Conn.....................	19	High..........	NT	...	2
Ardmore, Okla.....................	18	Low...........	MTC	...	3
Arkansas City, Kans...............	13	....	NTr	Tr	3
Asbury Park, N. J.................	17	....	TCr	PA, ER	3
Ashland, Ohio.....................	14	High..........	MTC	...	2
Ashland, Wis......................	11	....	MTC	Ed, Tr	3
Ashtabula, Ohio...................	24	....	NTr	Tr	1
Astoria, Oreg.....................	12	....	TCr	PA, My	1
Atchison, Kans....................	13	....	Ww	...	3
Athens, Ohio......................	12	....	TCr	Ed	4
Auburn, Ala.......................	13	Low...........	...	Ed	4
Auburn, Maine.....................	23	High..........	NTw	...	3
Augusta, Maine....................	21	....	Ww	PA	2
Austin, Minn......................	23	High..........	NTr	...	1
Barre, Vt.........................	11	....	MTC	...	2
Bartlesville, Okla................	19	....	NTw	...	1
Bastrop, La.......................	13	High..........	NT	...	3
Batavia, N. Y.....................	18	....	TCw	...	1
Bath, Maine.......................	11	....	NT	...	3
Beacon, N. Y......................	14	....	NT	...	1
Beatrice, Nebr....................	12	....	Rr	...	3
Beaver Dam, Wis...................	12	High..........	MTC	...	2
Beckley, W. Va....................	19	Low...........	TCr	...	2
Bedford, Ind......................	13	....	MTC	PA	2
Bellefontaine, Ohio...............	10	....	TCr	Tr	2
Bemidji, Minn.....................	10	....	...	Ed	2

TABLE **B–20.**—FUNCTIONAL CLASSIFICATIONS AND 1950 POPULATION OF INDEPENDENT CITIES WITH 10,000 INHABITANTS OR MORE—Cont.

[See explanatory note for tables B–17 to B–20 above. Asterisk (*) designates an unincorporated place]

City	1950 population (thousands)	Functional classification			
		Manufacturing	Trade	Type of minor specialization	Income level
10,000 to 25,000--Cont.					
Bend, Oreg..........................	11	....	MTC	...	1
Benton Harbor, Mich................	19	High............	TC	...	2
Berlin, N. H.......................	17	High............	NT	...	2
Berwick, Pa........................	14	High............	NT	...	2
Biddeford, Maine...................	21	High............	NT	...	2
Big Spring, Texas..................	17	Low.............	MTC	...	1
Bismarck, N. Dak...................	19	Low.............	TC	PA	2
Bloomsburg, Pa.....................	11	....	Rr	Ed	3
Bluefield, W. Va...................	22	Low.............	...	Tr	2
Blytheville, Ark...................	16	....	TC	ER	4
Bogalusa, La.......................	18	....	NT	...	3
Boone, Iowa........................	12	Low.............	NTr	Tr	1
Borger, Texas......................	18	....	MTC	...	1
Bossier City, La...................	15	....	...	PA, My	1
Boulder, Colo......................	20	Low.............	NT	Ed	4
Bowling Green, Ky..................	18	....	TCr	Ed	4
Bowling Green, Ohio................	12	....	NTr	Ed	4
Bozeman, Mont......................	11	Low.............	TCr	Ed, PA	3
Bradenton, Fla.....................	14	....	Rr	ER	4
Bradford, Pa.......................	17	....	TCw	...	2
Brainerd, Minn.....................	13	....	TCr	Tr	2
Brawley, Calif.....................	12	Low.............	MTC	...	2
Bridgeton, N. J....................	18	High............	Rr	...	2
Bristol, R. I.*....................	10	High............	...	...	2
Bristol, Tenn......................	17	....	...	ER	3
Bristol, Va........................	16	....	...	...	3
Brownsville-Brent-Goulding, Fla.*	20	....	...	PA, My	2
Brownwood, Texas...................	20	....	NTw	Ed	4
Brunswick, Ga......................	18	....	NTw	...	4
Bryan, Texas.......................	18	Low.............	MTC	...	3
Bucyrus, Ohio......................	10	....	Rr	...	3
Burlington, N. C..................	25	High............	MTC	...	1
Butler, Pa.........................	23	....	TCr	...	2
Cadillac, Mich.....................	10	....	Ww	...	2
Cairo, Ill.........................	12	....	...	...	4
Caldwell, Idaho....................	10	....	TC	Ed	2
Cambridge, Md......................	10	....	MTC	...	4
Cambridge, Ohio....................	15	....	...	...	3
Camden, Ark........................	11	....	MTC	...	4
Canton, Ill........................	12	....	Rr	...	1
Cape Girardeau, Mo.................	22	....	MTC	Ed	3
Carbondale, Ill....................	11	Low.............	MTC	Tr	4
Carlsbad, N. Mex...................	18	Low.............	...	...	1
Carthage, Mo.......................	11	....	TCw	...	4
Casper, Wyo........................	24	....	TCw	...	1
Centralia, Ill.....................	14	....	TCw	Tr	2
Chambersburg, Pa...................	17	....	Rr	PA	3
Chanute, Kans......................	10	....	MTC	...	3
Charles City, Iowa.................	10	....	Ww	...	1
Chico, Calif.......................	12	....	TCr	Ed	2
Chickasha, Okla....................	16	....	MTC	...	4
Chillicothe, Ohio..................	20	....	MTC	...	2
Chippewa Falls, Wis................	11	....	Rr	...	2
Claremont, N. H....................	13	High............	NTr	...	2
Clarksdale, Miss...................	17	Low.............	TCw	...	4
Clarksville, Tenn..................	16	....	Ww	PA, My, ER	3
Cleburne, Texas....................	13	....	NT	Tr	2
Cleveland, Tenn....................	13	....	...	...	4
Clinton, Mass.*....................	12	High............	NT	...	2
Clovis, N. Mex.....................	17	Low.............	Ww	Tr, ER	2
Coeur d'Alene, Idaho...............	12	....	MTC	...	2
Coffeyville, Kans..................	17	....	MTC	...	3
Columbia, Tenn.....................	11	....	Rr	...	3
Columbus, Ind......................	18	High............	MTC	...	2
Columbus, Miss.....................	17	....	Ww	Ed	4
Concord, N. C......................	16	High............	MTC	...	3
Conneaut, Ohio.....................	10	....	...	Tr	1

TABLE **B-20.**—FUNCTIONAL CLASSIFICATIONS AND 1950 POPULATION OF INDEPENDENT CITIES WITH 10,000 INHABITANTS OR MORE—Cont.

[See explanatory note for tables B–17 to B–20 above. Asterisk (*) designates an unincorporated place]

City	1950 population (thousands)	Functional classification			
		Manufac- turing	Trade	Type of minor specialization	Income level
10,000 to 25,000--Cont.					
Connellsville, Pa................	13	....	Rr	Tr	2
Connersville, Ind................	16	High..........	...	...	2
Corning, N. Y....................	18	High..........	NT	...	1
Corona, Calif....................	10	....	Ww	...	3
Corsicana, Texas.................	19	....	MTC	...	3
Cortland, N. Y...................	18	High..........	NTr	Ed	3
Corvallis, Oreg..................	16	Low...........	Rr	Ed	4
Coshocton, Ohio..................	12	....	...	...	2
Crawfordsville, Ind..............	13	....	TCw	Ed	3
Crowley, La......................	13	....	NTw	...	4
Dalton, Ga.......................	16	High..........	NTr	...	3
Danbury, Conn....................	22	High..........	MTC	...	2
Decatur, Ala.....................	20	....	MTC	...	3
Defiance, Ohio...................	11	....	MTC	...	2
De Kalb, Ill.....................	12	....	TC	Ed	3
Delaware, Ohio...................	12	....	MTC	Ed	4
Del Rio, Texas...................	14	Low...........	NTw	ER	4
Denison, Texas...................	18	....	Ww	Tr, My	3
Denton, Texas....................	21	....	NT	Ed	4
Derby Conn.......................	10	High..........	NTr	...	1
Dixon, Ill.......................	12	....	MTC	...	1
Dodge City, Kans.................	11	Low...........	TC	...	2
Dothan, Ala......................	22	....	TCw	...	4
Dover, N. H......................	16	High..........	MTC	...	3
Dublin, Ga.......................	10	....	...	ER	4
Du Bois, Pa......................	11	....	TCr	Tr	2
Duncan, Okla.....................	15	Low...........	MTC	...	2
Dunkirk, N. Y....................	18	High..........	NT	...	2
Durant, Okla.....................	11	Low...........	MTC	Ed	4
Dyersburg, Tenn..................	11	....	TCr	...	4
East Liverpool, Ohio.............	24	High..........	MTC	...	2
Edinburg, Texas..................	12	Low...........	Ww	...	4
El Centro, Calif.................	13	Low...........	TC	ER	1
El Dorado, Ark...................	23	....	MTC	...	3
El Dorado, Kans..................	11	....	MTC	...	2
El Reno, Okla....................	11	Low...........	NT	PA, Tr	2
Elizabeth City, N. C.............	13	....	MTC	PA, My	4
Elizabethton, Tenn...............	11	....	...	...	2
Elwood, Ind......................	11	High..........	NT	...	2
Emporia, Kans....................	16	Low...........	Rr	Ed, Tr	3
Escanaba, Mich...................	15	....	MTC	Tr	3
Eureka, Calif....................	23	....	TCr	...	1
Faribault, Minn..................	16	....	NT	ER	2
Farrell, Pa......................	14	High..........	NT	...	2
Fayetteville, Ark................	17	....	Ww	Ed, ER	4
Fergus Falls, Minn...............	13	....	MTC	...	2
Findlay, Ohio....................	24	....	...	...	2
Florence, Ala....................	24	....	NTw	Ed	3
Florence, S. C...................	23	....	TCw	Tr	4
Fort Collins, Colo...............	15	Low...........	Rr	Ed	4
Fort Madison, Iowa...............	15	....	NT	Tr	1
Fort Myers, Fla..................	13	Low...........	Rr	...	4
Fort Pierce, Fla.................	14	Low...........	TCw	...	3
Fort Scott, Kans.................	10	....	...	Tr	4
Fostoria, Ohio...................	14	High..........	...	...	1
Frankfort, Ind...................	15	....	NTr	...	2
Frankfort, Ky....................	12	....	...	PA	2
Franklin, Pa.....................	10	High..........	...	...	2
Frederick, Md....................	18	....	TCr	PA	3
Fredericksburg, Va...............	12	....	TC	Ed, PA	3
Freeport, Ill....................	22	....	TCw	...	2
Fremont, Ohio....................	17	....	...	...	1
Fremont, Nebr....................	15	....	TCw	...	2
Fulton, Mo.......................	10	....	NT	Ed	4
Fulton, N. Y.....................	14	High..........	NT	...	2
Gainesville, Ga..................	12	....	TC	ER	4
Gainesville, Texas...............	11	....	Rr	...	3

TABLE **B-20.**—FUNCTIONAL CLASSIFICATIONS AND 1950 POPULATION OF INDEPENDENT CITIES WITH 10,000 INHABITANTS OR MORE—Cont.

[See explanatory note for tables B-17 to B-20 above. Asterisk (*) designates an unincorporated place]

City	1950 population (thousands)	Functional classification			Income level
		Manufacturing	Trade	Type of minor specialization	
10,000 to 25,000--Cont.					
Garden City, Kans	11	Low	TCr	ER	2
Gardner, Mass	20	High	Ww	...	2
Gastonia, N. C	23	High	TCw	...	2
Geneva, N. Y	17	...	MTC	Ed	2
Glens Falls, N. Y	20	...	TCr	...	2
Gloversville, N. Y	24	High	MTC	...	3
Goldsboro, N. C	21	...	TCw	...	4
Goshen, Ind	13	High	MTC	Ed	2
Grand Island, Nebr	23	...	TCw	...	2
Grand Junction, Colo	15	Low	TC	Tr	2
Great Bend, Kans	13	Low	TC	...	1
Greeley, Colo	20	Low	TCr	Ed, ER	3
Greenfield, Mass.*	15	...	...	...	2
Greenville, N. C	17	...	Ww	Ed	4
Greenville, Texas	15	...	TC	...	4
Greenwood, Miss	18	Low	...	...	4
Greenwood, S. C	14	...	Rr	...	3
Griffin, Ga	14	...	TCw	...	3
Gulfport, Miss	23	...	Ww	PA, My	3
Guthrie, Okla	10	...	NTw	PA, ER	4
Hanford, Calif	10	Low	...	...	2
Hannibal, Mo	20	...	NTw	ER	3
Harlingen, Texas	23	...	TCw	...	3
Harrisburg, Ill	11	Low	Rr	...	2
Harrisonburg, Va	11	...	TC	Ed, ER	4
Hastings, Nebr	20	...	MTC	...	2
Helena, Ark	11	...	TCw	ER	4
Helena, Mont	18	Low	...	PA	1
Henderson, Ky	17	...	Ww	...	3
Henderson, N. C	11	...	TC	...	3
Hickory, N. C	15	...	TCr	ER	3
Hobbs, N. Mex	14	Low	MTC	...	1
Holland, Mich	16	...	MTC	Ed	2
Hollywood, Fla	14	Low	NTr	ER	2
Hopewell, Va	10	High	NT	My	2
Hopkinsville, Ky	13	...	TC	My	4
Hoquiam, Wash	11	High	NT	...	1
Hornell, N. Y	15	...	MTC	Tr	2
Houma, La	12	...	MTC	...	2
Hudson, N. Y	12	...	MTC	...	2
Huntington, Ind	15	...	MTC	ER	2
Huntsville, Ala	16	...	TC	PA	4
Huron, S. Dak	13	...	MTC	...	2
Idaho Falls, Idaho	19	Low	TC	...	1
Independence, Kans	11	...	NTr	...	3
Indiana, Pa	12	...	Rr	...	2
Ironton, Ohio	16	...	...	Tr	2
Ironwood, Mich	11	...	Ww	...	2
Jacksonville, Ill	20	...	MTC	Ed	3
Jamestown, N. Dak	11	Low	TCr	Ed, Tr	2
Janesville, Wis	25	High	Ww	...	1
Johnstown, N. Y	11	High	...	...	2
Jonesboro, Ark	16	...	TCw	Ed	3
Junction City, Kans	13	Low	NTw	PA, My, ER	2
Kearney, Nebr	12	Low	TC	Ed, ER	3
Keene, N. H	16	...	...	Ed	2
Kennewick, Wash	10	...	MTC	...	1
Kent, Ohio	12	...	NT	Ed	4
Keokuk, Iowa	16	...	NTw	...	2
Kewanee, Ill	17	High	MTC	...	2
Kingsport, Tenn	20	High	...	...	1
Kingsville, Texas	17	...	NT	Ed, Tr	3
Kinston, N. C	18	...	TCw	...	4
Kirksville, Mo	11	...	Rr	Ed	4
Klamath Falls, Oreg	16	...	TC	...	1
Laconia, N. H	15	...	MTC	...	2
Lake Worth, Fla	12	Low	NT	ER	4

TABLE **B-20.**—FUNCTIONAL CLASSIFICATIONS AND 1950 POPULATION OF INDEPENDENT CITIES WITH 10,000 INHABITANTS OR MORE—Cont.

[See explanatory note for tables B-17 to B-20 above. Asterisk (*) designates an unincorporated place]

City	1950 population (thousands)	Functional classification			
		Manufac- turing	Trade	Type of minor specialization	Income level
10,000 to 25,000--Cont.					
Lamesa, Texas.................	11	....	MTC	ER	2
Lancaster, Ohio.................	24	High.........	NTw	...	2
La Porte, Ind.................	18	High.........	MTC	...	1
Laramie, Wyo.................	16	Low.........	NT	Ed, Tr	2
La Salle, Ill.................	12	High.........	MTC	...	1
Las Cruces, N. Mex.............	12	Low.........	Ww	PA, My	3
Las Vegas, Nev.................	25	Low.........	TCr	My, ER	1
Lawrence, Kans.................	23	....	NT	Ed	4
Leavenworth, Kans.............	21	....	NT	PA, My	3
Leominster, Mass.............	24	High.........	NT	...	1
Lexington, N. C.................	14	High.........	MTC	...	3
Lewiston, Idaho.................	13	....	TC	...	1
Lewistown, Pa.................	14	....	TCw	...	2
Lincoln, Ill.................	14	....	NTw	...	2
Lock Haven, Pa.................	11	High.........	MTC	Ed	3
Logan, Utah.................	17	Low.........	Rr	Ed, PA	4
Logansport, Ind.................	21	....	MTC	Tr	2
Long Branch, N. J.................	23	....	MTC	PA, My	1
Longview, Texas.................	25	....	TC	...	3
Longview, Wash.................	20	High.........	MTC	...	1
Lufkin, Texas.................	15	....	TCw	...	3
Macomb, Ill.................	11	....	TCr	Ed	4
Madera, Calif.................	10	Low.........	Rr	...	2
Madisonville, Ky.................	11	Low.........	Rr	...	3
Mahanoy City, Pa.................	11	....	NT	...	3
Manhattan, Kans.................	19	Low.........	MTC	Ed, PA, My	4
Mankato, Minn.................	19	....	TC	Ed	3
Marietta, Ohio.................	16	....	TCw	Ed	3
Marinette, Wis.................	14	....	MTC	...	2
Marion, Ill.................	10	....	MTC	...	3
Marlborough, Mass.................	16	High.........	NT	...	2
Marquette, Mich.................	17	....	Ww	Ed, PA, Tr	2
Marshall, Texas.................	22	....	...	Ed	4
Marshalltown, Iowa.................	20	....	TCw	...	1
Marshfield, Wis.................	12	....	TCw	...	2
Martinsburg, W. Va.................	16	....	MTC	...	3
Martinsville, Va.................	17	High.........	NTr	...	3
Massena, N. Y.................	13	High.........	NT	...	1
Mattoon, Ill.................	18	....	TCw	Tr	2
McAlester, Okla.................	18	Low.........	MTC	PA	4
McAllen, Texas.................	20	....	MTC	...	3
McComb, Miss.................	10	....	MTC	Tr	3
McKinney, Texas.................	11	....	MTC	...	3
Meadville, Pa.................	19	....	Rr	Ed	2
Medford, Oreg.................	17	....	TC	...	1
Menasha, Wis.................	12	High.........	NT	...	1
Menominee, Mich.................	11	High.........	Ww	...	2
Merced, Calif.................	15	Low.........	Rr	PA, My	2
Mercedes, Texas.................	10	Low.........	Ww	...	4
Mexico, Mo.................	12	....	MTC	...	2
Miami, Okla.................	12	....	NTr	ER	2
Middlesborough, Ky.................	14	....	NTw	ER	4
Middletown, N. Y.................	23	....	MTC	...	2
Midland, Mich.................	14	High.........	NTr	...	1
Midland, Texas.................	22	Low.........	...	...	1
Midway-Hardwick, Ga.*...........	15	Low.........	...	...	4
Milford, Mass.*.................	14	High.........	...	...	1
Millville, N. J.................	16	High.........	NT	...	2
Minot, N. Dak.................	22	Low.........	TCw	Tr	2
Mission, Texas.................	11	Low.........	Ww	...	4
Missoula, Mont.................	22	....	TCr	Ed	3
Mitchell, S. Dak.................	12	Low.........	TC	...	3
Moberly, Mo.................	13	....	...	Tr	2
Modesto, Calif.................	17	....	TC	...	2
Monmouth, Ill.................	10	....	Rr	Ed	4
Monroe, Mich.................	21	High.........	MTC	...	1
Monroe, N. C.................	10	....	TCr	...	3

TABLE **B-20.**—FUNCTIONAL CLASSIFICATIONS AND 1950 POPULATION OF INDEPENDENT CITIES WITH 10,000 INHABITANTS OR MORE—Cont.

[See explanatory note for tables B–17 to B–20 above. Asterisk (*) designates an unincorporated place]

| City | 1950 population (thousands) | Functional classification | | | |
		Manufac-turing	Trade	Type of minor specialization	Income level
10,000 to 25,000--Cont.					
Monterey, Calif...................	16	....	...	My, ER	2
Moorhead, Minn...................	15	....	TCw	Ed	2
Morristown, Tenn.................	13	....	...	...	4
Moscow, Idaho...................	11	Low..........	NTr	Ed	4
Moultrie, Ga....................	12	....	TCw	ER	4
Mount Carmel, Pa...............	14	....	NT	...	3
Mount Pleasant, Mich...........	11	....	TCw	Ed	4
Mount Vernon, Ill...............	16	....	...	...	2
Mount Vernon, Ohio.............	12	....	Rr	...	2
Murfreesboro, Tenn.............	13	....	MTC	Ed, My	4
Muscatine, Iowa.................	19	....	MTC	...	2
Muskegon Heights, Mich..........	19	High..........	NT	...	2
Nacogdoches, Texas.............	12	....	MTC	Ed, ER	4
Nampa, Idaho...................	16	....	TCr	Ed, Tr	3
Napa, Calif...................	14	....	Rr	...	1
Natchez, Miss..................	23	....	...	...	4
Neenah, Wis....................	12	High..........	NTw	...	1
Newark, N. Y..................	10	....	NTr	...	2
New Bern, N. C................	16	....	MTC	PA, My	4
New Braunfels, Texas...........	12	....	NTr	My	3
Newburyport, Mass.............	14	High..........	NTr	...	3
New Castle, Ind...............	18	High..........	NTr	...	1
New Iberia, La................	16	Low..........	Ww	...	3
New Philadelphia, Ohio.........	13	....	NTr	...	2
Newsome Park-Hilton Park, Va.*...	15	....	...	PA, My	2
Newton, Iowa..................	12	High..........	NTr	...	1
Newton, Kans..................	12	Low..........	MTC	Tr	2
Niles, Mich...................	13	High..........	NTr	...	1
Norfolk, Nebr.................	11	Low..........	TC	...	3
Norwich, Conn.................	23	....	TCw	...	2
North Adams, Mass.............	22	High..........	NTw	...	2
North Platte, Nebr............	15	Low..........	TCr	Tr	1
Ocala, Fla....................	12	....	TCr	...	4
Ogdensburg, N. Y..............	16	....	Ww	...	3
Oil City, Pa..................	20	....	MTC	...	2
Oildale, Calif.*..............	17	Low..........	...	...	1
Okmulgee, Okla................	18	....	NT	Ed	4
Olean, N. Y...................	23	....	MTC	...	2
Olympia, Wash.................	16	....	TCr	PA, My	1
Oneida, N. Y..................	11	High..........	MTC	...	1
Oneonta, N. Y.................	14	....	TCr	Ed, Tr	3
Opelika, Ala..................	12	....	...	...	4
Opelousas, La.................	12	....	MTC	...	4
Orange, Texas.................	21	....	NT	My, ER	2
Orangeburg, S. C..............	15	....	MTC	Ed	4
Oskaloosa, Iowa...............	11	....	TCr	...	2
Oswego, N. Y..................	23	....	NT	Ed	3
Ottawa, Ill...................	17	....	MTC	...	2
Ottawa, Kans..................	10	....	MTC	Ed	4
Owatonna, Minn................	10	....	MTC	...	2
Owosso, Mich..................	16	High..........	MTC	...	2
Oxnard, Calif.................	22	Low..........	Ww	PA, My	2
Palestine, Texas..............	13	....	NTr	Tr, ER	3
Pampa, Texas..................	17	....	MTC	ER	1
Paris, Texas..................	22	....	MTC	ER	4
Pascagoula, Miss..............	11	....	NT	PA	3
Pasco, Wash...................	10	Low..........	TCr	Tr	1
Parsons, Kans.................	15	Low..........	NT	PA, Tr	3
Pendleton, Oreg...............	12	....	TC	...	1
Peru, Ind.....................	13	....	MTC	Tr	2
Petaluma, Calif...............	10	....	TC	My	1
Piqua, Ohio...................	17	High..........	NTw	...	2
Pittsburg, Kans...............	19	....	Ww	Ed, Tr, ER	3
Plainview, Texas..............	14	....	TC	...	2
Plattsburgh, N. Y.............	18	....	MTC	Ed	4
Plymouth, Mass.*..............	11	....	...	...	2
Ponca City, Okla..............	20	....	NT	...	1

TABLE **B-20.**—FUNCTIONAL CLASSIFICATIONS AND 1950 POPULATION OF INDEPENDENT CITIES
WITH 10,000 INHABITANTS OR MORE—Cont.

[See explanatory note for tables B-17 to B-20 above. Asterisk (*) designates an unincorporated place]

City	1950 population (thousands)	Functional classification			
		Manufac-turing	Trade	Type of minor specialization	Income level
10,000 to 25,000--Cont.					
Poplar Bluff, Mo..................	15	....	MTC	Tr	4
Port Angeles, Wash..............	11	....	MTC	...	1
Portsmouth, N. H.................	19	....	Ww	...	2
Pottsville, Pa...................	24	....	TC	...	3
Pullman, Wash....................	12	Low...........	NTw	Ed	4
Red Bank, N. J...................	13	....	...	PA, My	1
Redding, Calif...................	10	....	TC	...	1
Red Wing, Minn...................	11	....	MTC	...	2
Reidsville, N. C.................	12	High..........	NTw	ER	3
Richland, Wash.*.................	22	High..........	...	...	1
Richmond, Ky.....................	10	Low...........	Ww	Ed, PA	4
Riverview, Va.*..................	14	....	...	PA, My	1
Rochester, N. H..................	14	High..........	NT	...	2
Rock Hill, S. C..................	25	High..........	NTw	Ed	2
Rock Springs, Wyo................	11	Low...........	MTC	Tr	1
Ruston, La.......................	10	Low...........	...	Ed	4
Rutland, Vt......................	18	....	TC	...	3
Saco, Maine......................	10	High..........	NT	...	2
St. Augustine, Fla...............	14	Low...........	...	Tr, ER	4
St. Joseph, Mich.................	10	High..........	MTC	...	1
Salem, Ohio......................	13	High..........	MTC	...	1
Salinas, Calif...................	14	....	TC	...	1
Salisbury, Md....................	15	....	TC	...	2
Salisbury, N. C..................	20	....	TCr	Ed, Tr	3
San Benito, Texas................	13	....	NTr	...	4
San Buenaventura, Calif..........	17	Low...........	TCr	PA	1
Sanford, Fla.....................	12	Low...........	...	ER	4
Sanford, Maine*..................	11	High..........	...	...	1
Sanford, N. C....................	10	....	Ww	...	3
San Luis Obispo, Calif...........	14	Low...........	MTC	Ed, PA	1
Santa Cruz, Calif................	22	....	Rr	ER	3
Santa Maria, Calif...............	10	Low...........	TC	...	1
Santa Paula, Calif...............	11	Low...........	Ww	PA	2
Santa Rosa, Calif................	18	Low...........	TC	...	2
Sapulpa, Okla....................	13	....	NT	...	3
Sarasota, Fla....................	19	Low...........	Rr	ER	3
Saratoga Springs, N. Y...........	15	....	MTC	Ed, PA, ER	3
Sault Ste. Marie, Mich...........	18	....	Ww	...	2
Scottsbluff, Nebr................	13	....	TC	...	2
Seaside, Calif.*.................	10	Low...........	...	PA, My	2
Sedalia, Mo......................	20	....	MTC	Tr	3
Selma, Ala.......................	23	....	Ww	My	4
Seminole, Okla...................	12	Low...........	Ww	...	3
Shamokin, Pa.....................	17	....	Rr	...	3
Shawnee, Okla....................	23	Low...........	MTC	Ed, PA	3
Sheffield, Ala...................	11	....	MTC	...	3
Shelby, N. C.....................	16	....	TCw	...	3
Shelbyville, Ind.................	12	....	MTC	...	2
Shelton, Conn....................	13	High..........	...	...	2
Shenandoah, Pa...................	16	....	NTw	...	3
Sheridan, Wyo....................	12	Low...........	Rr	...	1
Sherman, Texas...................	20	....	Ww	My	3
Sidney, Ohio.....................	11	High..........	Ww	...	2
Sikeston, Mo.....................	12	....	MTC	...	3
Snyder, Texas....................	12	Low...........	...	...	1
South Bakersfield, Calif.........	12	....	...	...	1
Southbridge, Mass.*..............	17	High..........	...	...	1
South Parkersburg, W. Va.*.......	11	High..........	...	...	2
Springfield, Oreg................	11	High..........	...	...	1
Springfield Place-Lakeview, Mich.	13	High..........	...	...	1
State College, Pa................	17	Low...........	NT	Ed, ER	4
Statesville, N. C................	17	....	MTC	...	3
Staunton, Va.....................	20	....	MTC	...	3
Sterling, Ill....................	13	High..........	MTC	...	1
Stevens Point, Wis...............	17	....	Ww	Ed	2
Stillwater, Okla.................	20	Low...........	NT	Ed, ER	4
Streator, Ill....................	16	High..........	Rr	...	1

TABLE **B-20.**—FUNCTIONAL CLASSIFICATIONS AND 1950 POPULATION OF INDEPENDENT CITIES WITH 10,000 INHABITANTS OR MORE—Cont.

[See explanatory note for tables B-17 to B-20 above. Asterisk (*) designates an unincorporated place]

City	1950 population (thousands)	Functional classification			
		Manufac- turing	Trade	Type of minor specialization	Income level
10,000 to 25,000--Cont.					
Suffolk, Va.....................	12	....	TC	PA	3
Sumter, S. C.....................	20	....	Ww	My	3
Sunbury, Pa......................	16	....	Rr	...	3
Sweetwater, Texas...............	14	....	...	...	2
Talladega, Ala..................	13	....	NTw	Ed, PA	4
Tamaqua, Pa......................	12	....	NT	Tr	4
Terrell, Texas..................	12	....	NT	...	4
Texarkana, Ark..................	16	....	...	PA	4
Texarkana, Texas...............	25	....	...	PA	3
Thomasville, Ga.................	14	....	Ww	...	4
Thomasville, N. C...............	11	High..........	NT	...	2
Tiffin, Ohio....................	19	....	Ww	Ed	2
Traverse City, Mich.............	17	....	TCr	...	3
Trinidad, Colo..................	12	Low...........	...	...	4
Troy, Ohio......................	11	High..........	Rr	...	1
Tulare, Calif...................	12	Low...........	TCr	ER	2
Tupelo, Miss....................	12	....	...	...	4
Twin Falls, Idaho...............	18	Low...........	TC	...	1
Two Rivers, Wis.................	10	High..........	...	ER	1
Uniontown, Pa...................	20	....	TC	...	2
Urbana, Ill.....................	23	Low...........	NT	Ed, My	4
Valdosta, Ga....................	20	....	NTw	...	4
Valparaiso, Ind.................	12	....	MTC	Ed	3
Van Wert, Ohio..................	10	....	MTC	...	2
Vernon, Texas...................	13	....	MTC	...	3
Victoria, Texas.................	16	Low...........	Rr	...	2
Vincennes, Ind..................	19	....	Rr	...	3
Visalia, Calif..................	12	Low...........	TC	PA, ER	1
Wabash, Ind.....................	11	High..........	NTw	...	2
Walla Walla, Wash...............	24	Low...........	TCw	Ed, PA	1
Wallingford, Conn...............	12	High..........	...	...	1
Warren, Pa......................	15	....	TC	...	2
Warrington, Fla.................	14	Low...........	...	PA, My	1
Washington, Ind.................	11	....	Rr	Tr	3
Washington, Ohio...............	11	....	TC	...	3
Watertown, S. Dak..............	13	....	TC	...	2
Watertown, Wis..................	12	....	MTC	...	2
Waterville, Maine..............	18	....	MTC	Ed	3
Watsonville, Calif.............	12	....	TC	...	2
Waukesha, Wis...................	21	....	MTC	Ed	1
Waxahachie, Texas...............	11	....	NTr	Ed	4
Waycross, Ga....................	19	....	MTC	Tr	3
Waynesboro, Pa..................	10	High..........	...	PA	2
Waynesboro, Va..................	12	High..........	NT	...	2
Webster, Mass.*................	12	High..........	...	...	2
Wenatchee, Wash.................	13	Low...........	TC	...	1
West Frankfort, Ill.............	11	Low...........	NTr	...	3
West Lafayette, Ind.............	12	Low...........	NT	Ed	4
West Monroe, La.................	10	....	NTw	...	2
Willimantic, Conn...............	14	High..........	Rr	...	1
Willow Run, Mich................	11	....	...	Ed	2
Wilson, N. C....................	23	....	Ww	ER	4
Winchester, Va..................	14	....	TC	...	3
Winfield, Kans..................	10	....	MTC	Ed	4
Wisconsin Rapids, Wis...........	13	High..........	MTC	...	1
Wooster, Ohio...................	14	....	TC	Ed	3
Ypsilanti, Mich.................	18	....	MTC	Ed	3

TABLE **B-21.**—Percent of Employed Males in Specified Major Occupation Groups, for All Standard Metropolitan Areas and Urban Places of 10,000 Inhabitants or More, and for Selected Places by Minor Type of Functional Specialization, by Metropolitan Status and Size: 1950

Metropolitan status and size of place	All places	Type of specialization for selected places					All places	Type of specialization for selected places				
		Ed	PA	Tr	My	ER		Ed	PA	Tr	My	ER
	Professional, technical, and kindred workers						Managers, officials, and proprietors					
Standard metropolitan areas:												
50,000 to 250,000...	7.1	9.3	8.2	6.9	7.5	9.0	11.2	11.3	12.4	11.8	11.8	14.0
250,000 or more.....	9.4	11.5	11.3	7.5	10.2	10.8	12.4	13.3	12.0	12.7	13.4	15.3
Central cities:												
Under 100,000.......	8.4	10.4	9.7	7.7	8.3	7.9	12.7	14.1	13.1	13.2	14.8	14.8
100,000 or more.....	9.0	11.2	10.5	8.3	9.9	[1]11.1	12.5	13.0	13.1	13.0	13.9	[1]15.1
Suburbs:												
10,000 to 25,000....	11.6	21.1	10.7	8.2	9.6	12.5	14.5	24.6	11.8	11.9	12.5	17.5
25,000 or more......	10.5	17.0	14.4	7.6	10.8	14.7	12.8	18.2	12.1	10.3	12.3	19.1
Independent cities:												
10,000 to 25,000....	8.6	12.5	10.3	7.3	10.2	9.9	13.5	13.6	14.1	14.2	13.5	15.0
25,000 to 50,000....	8.7	12.9	10.4	7.2	8.4	10.7	13.7	14.2	15.4	13.8	13.9	15.8
	Clerical and kindred workers						Sales workers					
Standard metropolitan areas:												
50,000 to 250,000...	6.9	6.9	7.8	7.8	7.0	7.2	7.4	7.8	7.5	7.1	8.0	9.2
250,000 or more.....	8.9	8.8	10.3	9.1	9.4	7.9	7.8	8.9	7.5	7.8	8.1	9.7
Central cities:												
Under 100,000.......	7.8	7.8	8.5	9.1	7.3	7.4	8.5	10.0	9.0	8.2	9.9	10.0
100,000 or more.....	9.9	9.9	11.0	10.9	10.5	[1]8.6	8.3	9.2	8.4	8.0	8.6	[1]10.1
Suburbs:												
10,000 to 25,000....	8.0	8.4	9.7	9.3	8.2	7.3	8.2	13.2	7.8	7.0	8.3	9.4
25,000 or more......	8.4	8.7	9.2	10.0	8.2	7.6	7.8	11.5	7.8	6.6	8.1	10.9
Independent cities:												
10,000 to 25,000....	6.3	6.3	7.2	7.0	6.3	5.8	8.3	9.0	8.4	8.2	8.1	9.0
25,000 to 50,000....	7.1	7.2	7.7	7.6	6.9	6.0	8.6	9.2	8.8	8.3	8.4	9.3
	Craftsmen, foremen, and kindred workers						Operatives and kindred workers					
Standard metropolitan areas:												
50,000 to 250,000...	18.5	19.5	21.0	22.0	19.4	19.7	22.8	20.3	17.4	19.4	19.1	17.3
250,000 or more.....	21.4	21.5	22.0	20.9	20.8	22.4	21.3	17.5	15.8	18.2	19.5	17.5
Central cities:												
Under 100,000.......	21.2	19.5	19.4	23.2	20.4	18.2	22.7	18.0	18.6	18.1	17.9	18.1
100,000 or more.....	20.3	19.8	20.4	19.4	19.0	[1]19.6	21.4	18.0	15.4	18.4	18.6	[1]16.1
Suburbs:												
10,000 to 25,000....	22.3	14.0	24.3	25.2	25.9	22.3	20.3	8.3	17.9	20.4	19.0	14.8
25,000 or more......	22.5	18.0	22.0	22.8	24.1	20.0	22.2	12.7	17.0	22.8	19.7	12.6
Independent cities:												
10,000 to 25,000....	20.8	19.9	21.2	23.2	21.5	19.0	22.9	18.6	16.8	21.0	17.0	18.0
25,000 to 50,000....	20.6	19.0	20.5	22.7	23.0	19.0	22.3	16.9	14.9	20.8	17.4	14.3
	Private household and service workers						Laborers, except farm					
Standard metropolitan areas:												
50,000 to 250,000...	6.7	7.5	7.4	6.8	7.6	8.2	8.5	7.6	10.4	11.2	10.2	8.2
250,000 or more.....	7.9	7.9	7.9	7.6	8.9	7.9	7.9	7.1	8.5	11.2	7.5	7.9
Central cities:												
Under 100,000.......	8.0	9.3	9.2	8.3	8.9	11.1	8.9	8.8	10.0	9.6	10.5	9.7
100,000 or more.....	9.3	9.7	9.9	9.1	10.6	[1]9.5	8.0	7.6	9.6	11.6	7.5	[1]8.1
Suburbs:												
10,000 to 25,000....	5.5	5.0	7.1	6.1	6.4	6.2	7.6	4.8	8.2	9.0	7.7	6.9
25,000 or more......	6.2	7.0	8.2	7.8	7.2	7.6	7.6	4.9	7.5	10.9	8.0	5.2
Independent cities:												
10,000 to 25,000....	7.4	8.9	8.8	6.7	9.9	9.8	8.8	8.1	9.5	9.5	10.3	9.1
25,000 to 50,000....	8.3	10.1	8.9	7.2	9.0	11.7	8.5	7.7	9.8	10.4	10.0	9.9

[1] Excludes New York City.

INDEX

Adult population, *see* Age composition

Age, control of, 24, 69–70, 92–94

Age and sex composition, by type of county, 155–159

for Chicago rural-urban fringe, 139–142

for central cities and suburbs, 119–121

(*see also* Population pyramids, Sex ratio by age)

Age at entry into and departure from labor force, 94–95

Age at leaving school, 91

Age at marriage, measurement of, 67–68

rural-urban comparison, 67–68

Age composition, by size of place, 33–34, 41–43, 45–46

by type of county, 155–157

by type of minor specialization, 304–305

for growing and declining places, 190–192

for high and low income places, 350–351

for manufacturing centers, 255–256

for race and nativity groups, 62–64

for suburbs and independent cities, 172

for trade centers, 276–277

(*see also* Age and sex composition, Dependency ratio, Fertility ratio, Median age, Population pyramid)

Age-standardized comparisons, for labor force participation, 92–94, 145–147

for marital status, 69–72, 123–124, 142–143

Aged persons, *see* Age composition

Albuquerque, New Mexico, growth by annexation, 7, 184

Alexandria, Virginia, employment in public administration, 309

military and transport center, 319

Altoona, Pennsylvania, transportation center, 245

Anderson, William F., II, 134

Andrews, Richard B., 216, 238

Annapolis, Maryland, dual specialization, 336

Annexation, in relation to growth of urban places, 184–185

Area, metropolitan, *see* Metropolitan district, Standard metropolitan area

Areas, rural, definition of, 371

Areas, urban, definition of, xi (preface), 371

Armed Forces population, as basis for functional classification, 246–247

effect on size-of-place comparisons, 44, 74

elimination from fringe comparisons, 139

(*see also* Military population)

Atlantic City, New Jersey, low growth rate, 188

Aurora, Colorado, military and transport center, 319

Baton Rouge, Louisiana, growth by annexation, 7, 184

Beverly Hills, California, entertainment and recreation center, 249, 310

Biloxi, Mississippi, effect of military population on income, 209

Blizzard, Samuel W., 134

Bogue, Donald J., xiii (preface), 8, 21, 151

Break in transportation, 215–216, 243

Brunner, Edmund de S., 151

Buffalo, New York, low growth rate, 199

Burgess, E. W., 283

California, rapid growth of cities in, 186

Carpenter, David B., 19, 150

Causal inferences, difficulties of, 186–188, 250–251

Census tract, xii (preface)

Central city, definition of, 372, 373

Central-place cities, 215–216

Cheyenne, Wyoming, military and transport center, 319

Chicago, Illinois, characteristics of fringe and suburbs, 136–150

Chicago Standard Metropolitan Area, components, 137–139

Clarksville, Tennessee, military center, 310

Class-of-worker statistics, *see* Government employment

Clerical and kindred workers, *see* Occupational composition

Code for size-of-place groups, 32–33